MW01202056

Shōbōgenzō

Shōbōgenzō

The Treasure House of the
Eye of the True Teaching

A Trainee's translation of
Great Master Dōgen's
Spiritual Masterpiece

Rev. Hubert Nearman, O.B.C.
Translator

Shasta Abbey Press,
Mount Shasta,
California

First Edition—2007
© 2007 Shasta Abbey

This edition reformatted—2022

ISBN: 978-0-930066-35-2
Imprint: Shasta Abbey Press

Shasta Abbey
3724 Summit Drive
Mt. Shasta, California 96067-9102
(530) 926-4208

Volume I of III

This Volume contains Chapters 1 to 29

Offered in memory of
Reverend Master Jiyu-Kennett

Acknowledgments

Considering the scope and length of this work and the demands, both monastic and scholarly, that it puts on any translator, a reader may well wonder what could possibly motivate anyone to take on such an enormous task. Whatever may be the motives for other translators, mine has been quite simple. I had finished translating the various texts that were included in *Buddhist Writings on Meditation and Daily Practice* (Shasta Abbey Press, 1994) and asked Rev. Daizui MacPhillamy, my editorial consultant at the time, whether Rev. Master Jiyu-Kennett had anything else she wanted me to translate for her. He took my question to her, and, he said, he was dumbfounded when, without a moment's pause, she replied "*The Shōbōgenzō,*" for such a monumental undertaking would obviously take me many years to complete, not only because of its length but also because of its reputed obscurity and even incomprehensibility. Simply because she was my Master, I agreed to her request, knowing that I would never have taken on such a task for any other reason. It has been my monastic offering to the Sangha over some fourteen years. During that time I have had the great good fortune to live at Shasta Abbey, a traditional Buddhist monastery where the life that Dōgen extolled is practiced. I wish to express my deep gratitude for all the assistance my fellow monks have given me, and in particular:

—Rev. Master Jiyu-Kennett, Abbess of Shasta Abbey when the initial volume of the first eleven of Dōgen's discourses was published. (This has been reworked in light of the whole of the present book and is not simply a reprint.) She can never be thanked enough for opening the Way of the Buddha, and of Dōgen, to an immeasurable number of people;

—Rev. Daizui MacPhillamy, whose sharp intellect and broad experience in the Dharma provided me with critical editing and consultation, but who sadly died unexpectedly before he could work with me on the last half of the discourses;

—Rev. Ekō Little, successor to Rev. Master Jiyu-Kennett as Abbot of Shasta Abbey, who has given me the unflagging support, encouragement, and assistance needed to complete the work;

—Rev. Oswin Hollenbeck of the Eugene Buddhist Priory for help with the introduction and who, together with Rev. Meikō Jones of Portland Buddhist Priory and Rev. Chōsei Swann of Shasta Abbey, read and commented on a number of the discourses;

—Rev. Fidelia Dolan who not only transformed electronic information into formats that could be made available to all, but also worked tirelessly as my editorial consultant after Rev. Daizui passed on, and helped me find ways to convey Dōgen's medieval Japanese and Chinese into hopefully comprehensible English;

—Rev. Meian Elbert, Rev. Shikō Rom, and Rev. Veronica Snedaker, who brought the book to completion;

—and to all the monastics, known and unknown, who have kept the Buddha's Transmission of the living Dharma vibrant down the centuries.

May the merit of this work benefit all beings.

Acknowledgments for the reformatted edition

The reformatting of this edition into three volumes to enable the use of print-on-demand services was undertaken by Rev. Lambert Tuffrey of Throssel Hole Buddhist Abbey, UK.

Contents

Title Page   i

Copyright   ii

Dedication   iv

Acknowledgements   v

Contents   vii

Translator's General Introduction   xvii

Volume I of III

1. **Bendōwa**
   A Discourse on Doing One's Utmost in Practicing the Way
   of the Buddhas   1

2. **Makahannya-haramitsu**
   On the Great Wisdom That Is Beyond Discriminatory Thought   30

3. **Genjō Kōan**
   On the Spiritual Question as It Manifests Before Your Very Eyes   37

4. **Ikka Myōju**
   On 'The One Bright Pearl'   44

5. **Jūundō-shiki**
   On Conduct Appropriate for the Auxiliary Cloud Hall   52

6. **Soku Shin Ze Butsu**
   On 'Your Very Mind Is Buddha'   57

7. **Senjō**
   On Washing Yourself Clean   65

8. **Keisei Sanshoku**
   On 'The Rippling of a Valley Stream, The Contour of a Mountain'   79

9. *Shoaku Makusa*
   On 'Refrain from All Evil Whatsoever' 95

10. *Raihai Tokuzui*
    On 'Respectful Bowing Will Secure for You the Very
    Marrow of the Way' 108

11. *Uji*
    On 'Just for the Time Being, Just for a While, For the Whole
    of Time is the Whole of Existence' 128

12. *Den'e*
    On the Transmission of the Kesa 144

13. *Sansuikyō*
    On the Spiritual Discourses of the Mountains and the Water 171

14. *Busso*
    On the Buddhas and the Ancestors 189

15. *Shisho*
    On the Record of Transmission 193

16. *Hokke Ten Hokke*
    On 'The Flowering of the Dharma Sets the Dharma's
    Flowering in Motion' 209

17. *Shin Fukatoku*
    On 'The Mind Cannot Be Held Onto' *Oral version* 228

18. *Shin Fukatoku*
    On 'The Mind Cannot Be Grasped' *Written version* 236

19. *Kokyō*
    On the Ancient Mirror 253

20. *Kankin*
    On Reading Scriptures 278

21. **Busshō**
On Buddha Nature 295

22. **Gyōbutsu Iigi**
On the Everyday Behavior of a Buddha Doing His Practice 338

23. **Bukkyō**
On What the Buddha Taught 362

24. **Jinzū**
On the Marvelous Spiritual Abilities 379

25. **Daigo**
On the Great Realization 394

26. **Zazen Shin**
On Wanshi's 'Kindly Advice for Doing Seated Meditation' 404

27. **Butsu Kōjō Ji**
On Experiencing That Which Is Above and Beyond Buddhahood 424

28. **Immo**
On That Which Comes Like This 438

29. **Gyōji**
On Ceaseless Practice 450

Volume II of III

30. **Kaiin Zammai**
On 'The Meditative State That Bears the Seal of the Ocean' 524

31. **Juki**
On Predicting Buddhahood 536

32. **Kannon**
On Kannon, the Bodhisattva of Compassion 551

33. *Arakan*
    On Arhats 561

34. *Hakujushi*
    On the Cypress Tree 569

35. *Kōmyō*
    On the Brightness of the Light 579

36. *Shinjin Gakudō*
    On Learning the Way Through Body and Mind 590

37. *Muchū Setsumu*
    On a Vision Within a Vision and a Dream Within a Dream 602

38. *Dōtoku*
    On Expressing What One Has Realized 613

39. *Gabyō*
    On 'A Picture of a Rice Cake' 621

40. *Zenki*
    On Functioning Fully 630

41. *Sesshin Sesshō*
    On Expressing One's True Nature by Expressing One's Intent 634

42. *Darani*
    On Invocations: What We Offer to the Buddhas and Ancestors 646

43. *Tsuki*
    On the Moon as One's Excellent Nature 654

44. *Kūge*
    On the Flowering of the Unbounded 662

45. *Kobusshin*
    On What the Mind of an Old Buddha Is 677

46. **Bodaisatta Shishōbō**
    On the Four Exemplary Acts of a Bodhisattva   684

47. **Kattō**
    On the Vines That Entangle: the Vines That Embrace   691

48. **Sangai Yuishin**
    On 'The Threefold World Is Simply Your Mind'   701

49. **Shohō Jissō**
    On the Real Form of All Thoughts and Things   711

50. **Bukkyō**
    On Buddhist Scriptures   729

51. **Butsudō**
    On the Buddha's Way   745

52. **Mitsugo**
    On the Heart-to-Heart Language of Intimacy   768

53. **Hosshō**
    On the True Nature of All Things   776

54. **Mujō Seppō**
    On the Dharma That Nonsentient Beings Express   782

55. **Semmen**
    On Washing Your Face   798

56. **Zazengi**
    On the Model for Doing Meditation   816

57. **Baika**
    On the Plum Blossom   818

58. **Jippō**
    On the Whole Universe in All Ten Directions   834

59. *Kembutsu*
On Encountering Buddha 842

60. *Henzan*
On Seeking One's Master Far and Wide 860

61. *Ganzei*
On the Eye of a Buddha 870

62. *Kajō*
On Everyday Life 879

63. *Ryūgin*
On the Roar of the Dragon 887

64. *Shunjū*
On Spring and Autumn: Warming Up and Cooling Down 892

65. *Soshi Seirai I*
On Why Our Ancestral Master Came from the West 903

66. *Udonge*
On the Udumbara Blossom 909

67. *Hotsu Mujō Shin*
On Giving Rise to the Unsurpassed Mind 915

68. *Nyorai Zenshin*
On the Universal Body of the Tathagata 926

69. *Zammai-ō Zammai*
On the Meditative State That Is the Lord of Meditative States 931

70. *Sanjūshichihon Bodai Bumpō*
On the Thirty-Seven Methods of Training for Realizing
Enlightenment 937

Volume III of III

71. **Tembōrin**
On Turning the Wheel of the Dharma 965

72. **Jishō Zammai**
On the Meditative State of One's True Nature 969

73. **Daishugyō**
On the Great Practice 985

74. **Menju**
On Conferring the Face-to-Face Transmission 999

75. **Kokū**
On The Unbounded 1013

76. **Hatsu'u**
On a Monk's Bowl 1019

77. **Ango**
On the Summer Retreat 1024

78. **Tashintsū**
On Reading the Minds and Hearts of Others 1051

79. **Ō Saku Sendaba**
On 'The King Requests Something from Sindh' 1065

80. **Jikuin Mon**
On Instructions for Monks in the Kitchen Hall 1072

81. **Shukke**
On Leaving Home Life Behind 1076

82. **Shukke Kudoku**
On the Spiritual Merits of Leaving Home Life Behind 1083

83. *Jukai*
On Receiving the Precepts 1115

84. *Kesa Kudoku*
On the Spiritual Merits of the Kesa 1123

85. *Hotsu Bodai Shin*
On Giving Rise to the Enlightened Mind 1161

86. *Kuyō Shobutsu*
On Making Venerative Offerings to Buddhas 1174

87. *Kie Buppōsō Hō*
On Taking Refuge in the Treasures of Buddha, Dharma,
and Sangha 1205

88. *Jinshin Inga*
On the Absolute Certainty of Cause and Effect 1223

89. *Sanji Gō*
On Karmic Retribution in the Three Temporal Periods 1233

90. *Shime*
On 'The Four Horses' 1252

91. *Shizen Biku*
On the Monk in the Fourth Meditative State 1259

92. *Ippyakuhachi Hōmyōmon*
On the One Hundred and Eight Gates to What the Dharma
Illumines 1286

93. *Shōji*
On Life and Death 1303

94. *Dōshin*
On the Mind's Search for Truth 1305

95. *Yui Butsu Yo Butsu*
On 'Each Buddha on His Own, Together with All Buddhas' 1309

96. *Hachi Dainingaku*
   On the Eight Realizations of a Great One 1320

Glossary xxxi

Appendix of Names xxxvii

About the Translator xlv

The *Shōbōgenzō*

A Trainee's Translation
of Great Master Dōgen's Spiritual Masterpiece

Translator's General Introduction

The *Shōbōgenzō* is the recognized spiritual masterpiece by the thirteenth-century Japanese Sōtō Zen Master Eihei Dōgen. It is comprised of discourses that he gave to his disciples, in person or in writing, at various times between 1231 and his death twenty-two years later at age fifty-three.[†] These discourses cover a wide range of topics pertinent to those in monastic life though often also relevant to those training in lay life. He discusses matters of daily behavior and religious ceremonial as well as issues involving the Master-disciple relationship. He also explores the deeper meaning that informs the so-called Zen kōan stories, which often puzzle readers by their seeming illogicality and contrary nature.

I have translated the title as *The Treasure House of the Eye of the True Teaching*, though a fuller, more comprehensive rendering would be *The Treasure House for What the Spiritual Eye of Wise Discernment Perceives from the Vantage Point of the True Teachings of Shakyamuni Buddha and His Heirs*. The term 'Teaching' in the title is synonymous with the Buddhist use of the term 'Dharma', which refers not only to what the historical Buddha taught to His disciples but also to the Truth that flows from the Unborn and which all things give expression to when they are functioning directly from their innate True Self. However, it does not address what may be a scholar's particular interest in producing a translation, though it is

---

† The present translation is based primarily on Kawamura Kōdō's edition of Dōgen's complete works Dōgen Zenji Zenshū (Tokyo: Shunjūsha, 1993), in consultation with the editions by Tamaki Kōshirō, Dōgen Shū (Tokyo: Chikuma Shobō, 1969), by Ōkubo Dōshū, Kohon Kōtei Shōbōgenzō (Tokyo: Chikuma Shobō, 1971), by Terada Tōru and Mizunoya Oko, Dōgen (Tokyo: Iwanami Shoten, 1972), and by Masutani Fumio, Gendaigoshaku Shōbōgenzō (Tokyo: Kadokawa Shoten, 1975).

obvious that translating anything from medieval Japanese and Chinese requires special academic training: hence the subtitle "A Trainee's Translation of Great Master Dōgen's Spiritual Masterpiece". That is, it is intended primarily for those who practice Zen Buddhism rather than those whose interest is purely academic.

There are various ways in which Dogen's discourses can be presented, each having its particular advantages. The way I have chosen is simply to divide the discourses into those that were completed before his death and those that were still in draft form when he died, ordered where possible chronologically by the date when the discourse was given.

The discourses were originally written out by hand, primarily by his chief disciple and amanuensis, the Second Japanese Sōtō Zen Ancestor, Kōun Ejō. Most of the discourses have a two-part postscript (printed in italics, usually at the end of a discourse). The first half indicates who the recipients of the discourse were, along with when and where it was presented. If this is signed, it will customarily be by Dōgen. The second half supplies a short account of when and where the copy was made. These copies are most often signed by Ejō, though three were signed by Giun, one of Ejō's Dharma-heirs who later became the fifth abbot of Dōgen's Eihei-ji Monastery.

The majority of the discourses focus on exploring the spiritual significance of some topic drawn from Buddhist Scriptures or Chinese Chan (Zen) texts. Dōgen's commentaries on these texts are not lectures as would be understood in academic circles, but are talks that arise from a Zen Master's deepest understanding of the spiritual meaning and relevance of his topic to Buddhist training and practice. They come out of Dōgen's mind of meditation and are being presented to his monastic and lay disciples, who are presumably listening from their mind of meditation.□

The discourses carry a strong flavor of the conversational and the personal, and he enriches them with colorful Chinese and Zen phrases, as well as with medieval Chinese and Japanese colloquialisms. When translated literally, many of these metaphors and figures of speech may well have little meaning for English-speaking readers. However, by the thirteenth century they would have been a common way for a Buddhist Meditation Master to refer to That which is the True Nature of all beings. The function of these metaphors is, to some extent, to 'ground' a Master's disciples by providing them with a colorful and more easily remembered image instead of some more abstract, 'intellectual' definition. They point to the Great Matter for which one trains in Serene Reflection Meditation, which is to awaken to one's True Nature.□

Dōgen sometimes uses a manner of speaking that closely resembles a dialogue. One specific instance occurs in 'A Discourse on Doing One's Utmost in Practicing the Way of the Buddhas' (*Bendōwa*), his earliest dated text in the *Shōbōgenzō*. The major part of this particular discourse consists of an imaginary dialogue between Dōgen and a potential disciple. While it takes the form of someone asking questions and Dōgen giving answers, it is not a catechism. That is, it is not a series of formal questions and answers. Rather, the questions arise from an attitude of mind which has misgivings about the efficacy and worth of the type of seated meditation that Dōgen advocates. Dōgen's responses, by contrast, arise from a place that lies beyond the intellective, duality-based mind and are aimed at helping the questioner to recognize that duality and to let go of it. Hence, the attitude of mind of both the questioner and the Master is as important as the specific question being asked. For the translator, one challenge in rendering Dōgen's text is to convey to the reader the attitudes implied in the exchanges between the two.

These interchanges between a Master and a potential or real disciple are not speculative in nature, but invariably have the purpose of helping disciples find that spiritual certainty which is the hallmark of a genuine kenshō, 'the seeing of one's Original Face', that is, the direct experiencing of one's innate Buddha Nature. This is not the same as having an intellectual understanding or intuition, since the experience takes one beyond those functions associated with the so-called rational mind, which are the foundation and authority for those who are not dedicated to spiritual pursuits. Furthermore, the certainty arising from a kenshō is not speculative in nature or the product of rational persuasion or a form of blind faith.

Dōgen's teaching in the *Shōbōgenzō* is neither confined to nor limited by conventional mental categories, which is why practitioners of Dōgen's type of meditation are admonished to be willing to be disturbed by the Truth, that is, to have not only their intellectual preconceptions questioned but also to have their reliance on solely what makes conventional, worldly sense called into question. Despite the view of some that Dōgen is therefore 'anti-intellect', once the spiritual certainty arises in those who are doing the training, the previous need to depend solely on the 'boxes' fabricated by their intellect disappears. Or as several Meditation Masters describe it, once we give up 'the walls and fences' that our intellect constructs from the bits and pieces of experience, this dependency disappears, and we metaphorically 'drop off our body and mind' but without rejecting the intellect itself or denying its natural and useful functions.

Conventions

In the present work, when a common word is used having spiritual significance, I have employed initial capitals to signal to the reader that word *X* is not intended literally but is part of a code which Zen Masters have used to convey spiritual meaning. Indeed, when people spiritually awaken, this is customarily signaled by their expressing their understanding in some unique and personal way. When the use of this code is ignored or overlooked by a translator, a kōan story may well become totally unintelligible and give rise to the erroneous notion that Zen promotes the indescribable. To avoid this, I have added some footnotes intended to point out places where the code may not have been spotted by readers.

An example of this may occur in a dialogue in which a Master and his disciple use the same words but with a totally different meaning. For example, a Master and his disciple are having a discussion, and the Master tests his disciple's understanding of what his True Nature is by asking, "Do you get It?" with the disciple answering, "No, I don't get it." The Master's question is a spiritual one: "Have you got to the heart of your spiritual question?" to which the disciple's reply reveals that he is still attached to conventional, worldly ways of thinking.

Elements of Style

In the present translations, four stylistic elements are used whose purpose may not be immediately apparent:

First is the capitalizing of words that would not usually be proper nouns, such as 'Original Nature', 'the Self', 'the Truth', 'It', 'One's Original Face'. Such words refer either to one's own Buddha Nature or to That which is the spiritual source of one's Buddha Nature. For instance, there is a difference between the term 'good friend' which refers to a Buddhist who has the ability to teach and train others in Buddhism (usually synonymous with a Zen Master), and the term 'Good Friend', which is another name for one's Buddha Nature.

Second, a word that is underlined is to be understood as emphatic within the context of the particular sentence in which it occurs. Were the text to be read aloud, the underlined word would be given emphasis.

Third, Dōgen sometimes abruptly changes his topic within his talks. Whereas many of these shifts are signaled by some introductory word, such as 'further' and 'also', which appears at the beginning of a new paragraph, in some instances this is not the case. Thus it has seemed advisable to aid the reader by inserting a plum blossom asterisk (`) between paragraphs where a sudden shift might otherwise prove disconcerting.

Fourth, single quotation marks are often used in the sense of 'so-called', 'what I (or someone else) would call', or 'the term' or 'the phrase', in addition to their customary use for marking a quote within a quote.

Special Terms

Dōgen often alludes to 'training and practice'. This consistently refers specifically to doing seated meditation, applying 'the mind of meditation' to all one's daily activities, and attempting to live in accord with the Precepts of Mahayana Buddhism, that is, the Precepts as spelled out in Dōgen's *Text for a Precepts Master's Giving the Mahayana Precepts* (*Kyōjukaimon*) and *The Scripture of Brahma's Net* (*Bommō Kyō*). Similarly, references to 'studying' denote training under a Zen Master, and do not signify the undertaking of a scholastic regimen.

To render the Japanese word *tennin* (or *ninden)* I have used the phrase 'ordinary people and those in lofty places'. Some translators render it as 'gods and men'. There is the danger that some readers may therefore assume that it means 'immortals and mortals'. However, in a Buddhist context it refers to those who are in the celestial and human realms among the six Realms of Existence, the four others being those of beasts, those in a hellish state, those who are hungry ghosts, and those who are asuras (heaven stormers). Those in the celestial and human realms are potentially able to hear the name of Buddha and absorb the Dharma, whereas those in the other four are so preoccupied with their suffering that it is exceedingly difficult for them to believe that they can transcend their suffering long enough to hear the Teaching and thereby free themselves from their spiritual obsessions.

Dōgen often uses the terms Mahayana and Hinayana (translated as 'the Greater Course' and 'the Lesser Course'). A widely voiced view is that references in Mahayana writings to those who follow a Lesser Course denote practitioners of the Theravadan Buddhist tradition. The Theravadan tradition, however, was not active in medieval Japan during Dōgen's lifetime. Also, the Pali Canon upon which the Theravadan tradition is grounded was known to Dōgen through Chinese translations and was held in great esteem by him. Allusions in Dōgen's writings to 'those who follow the Lesser Course' are clearly to persons whom trainees may well encounter in their daily life. Thus it is likely that he is referring to shravakas (those who merely seek to gain an intellectual understanding of Buddhism) or to pratyekabuddhas (those who undertake some aspects of Buddhist practice but only for their own personal benefit).

The Issue of Gender and Sex

This issue is sometimes raised in regard to translating medieval Chinese and Japanese texts into English. It involves the attitude of Buddhism in general, and Dōgen in particular, toward women in spiritual life. While it is true that in some cultures during some periods negative social attitudes toward women have unfortunately colored the practice of Buddhism, Dōgen's view is unequivocal: males and females are spiritual and monastic equals, for enlightenment knows no such distinction as sex. The English language, however, has not yet developed a universally accepted way to express what is gender neutral. When Dōgen refers to monks or laity in general or as 'someone who', it should be understood that he is including both males and females, even though the English pronominal reference is, for brevity's sake, 'he', 'him', or 'his': I have used 'she', 'her', and 'hers' only where the sex of the person is known to be female.

Appendices

Two appendices have been added to the book. The first is a listing of the Japanese names of the major figures in the various kōan stories along with their Chinese equivalents. The second is a glossary of words and idiomatic phrases, such as hossu and kōan, which need some explanation because they do not have an easy equivalent in English.

On Kōan Stories

Dōgen makes wide use of stories from Zen kōan collections. Since these stories may strike some readers as strange or incomprehensible, the following observations may prove helpful.

Originally, the term 'kōan' meant 'a public case', and in Chinese Zen referred to a notable, authenticated instance when a disciple came to realize his or her True Nature. By Dōgen's time, the term 'kōan' had become synonymous with the spiritual question which epitomizes that which keeps disciples, as well as anyone else, from directly experiencing what their Original Nature is. It is the spiritual doubt that keeps someone 'looking down'. The kōan stories, then, are usually accounts of how a particular trainee's doubt was resolved.

In these stories, the spiritual problem of a trainee often involves a habitual acting counter to at least one of the ten major Mahayana Buddhist Precepts on either a literal or a figurative level. That is, in some way the disciple will have persisted in taking the life from someone or something, in taking things that are not given, in giving in to covetous feelings, in saying that which is not so, in trafficking in something that intoxicates or deludes, in putting oneself up and others down, in insulting others, in giving in to anger or resentfulness, in being stingy, or in acting in a disrespectful manner toward Buddha, Dharma, or Sangha.

When reading such dialogues, it is prudent to consider what the mental attitude of the questioner is and not just what is being asked. This is important because the question asked arises from a particular frame of mind. Determining who is asking the question (and sometimes where and when) will help clarify what this frame of mind is and, therefore, what is really being asked, since the answer given will not be an absolute one, independent of the questioner, but one that speaks to the questioner's mental attitude and perspective. This is sometimes referred to in Zen writings as 'two arrows meeting in mid-air', one meaning of which is that the questioner thinks he knows what the target, or goal, is and has 'shot his arrow' of discriminatory thought at that target only to have his 'arrow' deflected by the Master's response so that, to mix metaphors, the disciple's 'train of discriminatory thought' is derailed. At the same time, the Master's 'arrow' points to a way for the disciple to go in his Buddhist training.

However, in some cases the roles are reversed: the Master asks the disciple a question or 'invites' him to respond from a perspective beyond the discriminatory mind. If the disciple has truly awakened, he will respond appropriately from the mind of meditation and not from the discriminatory mind of duality. In such an instance, the 'two arrows meeting in mid-air' is an expression for their oneness of mind.

The stories may follow any of several different patterns or their combination. Almost all will involve at least one of the following three patterns:

In the first, a disciple will ask the Master a question which arises from a reliance on dualistic thinking to comprehend his own spiritual doubt. This encounter with the Master will often occur in the context of a formal spiritual examination ceremony, but this will not always be made explicit in the text. The Master will then do or say something which cuts through the disciple's confusion and points him directly toward 'seeing' his Original Nature. What the Master does or says arises from a source that transcends the dualistic, intellective mind: it is not a philosophical, doctrinal, or 'rational' answer to the question. If the disciple is 'ripe'—that is, spiritually ready to shift his perspective away from reliance on what his intellect is doing so that he can realize That which transcends intellect—he has an experience referred to by some such phrase as 'realizing the Truth' or 'awakening to his True Nature'. In some kōan stories, the trigger for this experience may not be directly supplied by the Master but by some other external condition, such as seeing peach blossoms or hearing a piece of tile strike bamboo.

In the second, a Meditation Master initiates an exchange with a disciple who is still in doubt, and tries through his conversation with the disciple to steer him toward facing up to what his spiritual problem is. In such dialogues, the Master's questions may seem upon first reading to be casual ones. In kōan stories, when a Master asks a question, he is not trying to engage the disciple in some social interchange: his question will have a deeper purpose or meaning, which the disciple may or may not pick up on. If the disciple fails to 'get it', the Master will usually persist in his questioning until either the disciple has an awakening or until the Master decides that the disciple is still not yet 'ripe' enough.

In the third pattern, a Master-disciple interchange occurs, but with a disciple who has already awakened to the Truth. In such an instance, since what the disciple is saying or doing no longer arises from the mind of duality, there will be some clear indication of the Master's approval.

In those cases where the disciple is still in doubt, one useful clue as to what his spiritual problem is can be found in how the Master addresses the disciple. For instance, in one story, a monk who is given to striving too hard is addressed as 'Shibi the Austere Monk'. In another, a monk who has become entangled in erudition through his academic pursuit of studying Scriptures is addressed by his Master as 'you who are a learned scholar of considerable intelligence'.

In identifying the disciple's spiritual problem, it is helpful to determine what the disciple's attitude of mind is, and not to treat his questions or responses on a purely informational level. Once the disciple's spiritual problem has been identified, how he responds to his Master will reflect that problem until he has an awakening, at which time he may compose a poem which expresses the change in perspective that has emerged.

Another aspect which may be difficult for the reader to fathom immediately is the relevance of the Master's actions in word or deed to what the disciple's problem is. Since such actions are not 'pre-planned' but reflect the on-the-spot skillful means of the Master, it can only be said that whatever is done will arise from the mind of meditation, will be free of any dualistic tendency, will not break any of the Precepts, and will arise out of his compassion for the suffering of the disciple. In one famous kōan story (Nansen's cat), the roles are reversed: Meditation Master Nansen puts himself in a spiritually unsupportable position by trying to teach his monks to keep to the Precepts by seriously breaking one himself, and it is his chief disciple who points this out to him.

Another topic that arises from the kōan stories deals with who the participants are. The Master is easily identified. On the other hand, the one who asks a question is often referred to simply as a monk. In such cases the person is most likely a junior monk, one who has not yet been Transmitted and who is asking his question at a ceremony called shōsan. This is the formal spiritual examination ceremony which is customarily held twice a month in Zen monasteries during which junior trainees ask a question that reflects their present spiritual state.

When the monk asking a question is specifically identified, this refers to a senior monk, one who is already Transmitted or who will be Transmitted. These are monks who will ultimately function as a Master, and often as the founder of a temple or a lineage. Whether in the kōan story they have already been Transmitted or are still juniors can only be determined by the nature of their question.

Applying the Principles

To see how the preceding principles apply to an actual kōan story, the following one, taken from Dōgen's *Bendōwa*, is given with my exegetical remarks in square brackets. The kōan story itself is given in indented text:

> Long ago, there was a monk in Meditation Master Hōgen's
> monastic community named Gensoku, who was a subordinate under
> the Temple's administrative director. Master Hōgen asked him,
> "Director Gensoku, how long have you been in our community?"

[Although Gensoku is not the director, he is apparently acting as though he thought he was, thus breaking a Precept by 'putting himself up'. Hōgen's question is not a casual but a leading one, arising from his compassionate sensitivity to Gensoku's spiritual suffering from pride.]

Gensoku replied, "Why, I've been in the community for
three years now."
[Gensoku tacitly acknowledges recognition of his importance as self-evident and responds in a casual manner. Had he not been absorbed in his pride, he might have responded, as would be expected not only from a novice but also from any Chinese, by some such statement as "You flatter me by addressing me by too exalted a title, considering that I have been training here for only three years now." Had he already had a kenshō, his response, though not predictable, would not be impolite or disrespectful in tone but, on the other hand, would probably not be a conventional, 'socially correct' one either.]

The Master asked, "As you are still a junior monk, why
have you never asked me about the Buddha Dharma?"
[Hōgen gently corrects Gensoku by now pointing out his actual position as a junior monk. He then asks another leading question, which implies that Gensoku thinks that he is above all other novices and does not need instruction.]

Gensoku replied, "I will not lie to Your Reverence. Previously, when I was with Meditation Master Seihō, I fully reached the place of joyful ease in the Buddha Dharma."
[The delusion underlying Gensoku's pride begins to emerge more clearly, for he claims to have attained a spiritual state which he has not yet reached. This is what Hōgen had probably surmised and which had led him to engage Gensoku in this dialogue. Gensoku is now breaking the Precepts by saying that which is not so and by having sold himself the wine of delusion.]

The Master said, "And what was said that gained you entry
to that place?"
[Hōgen now probes directly into the heart of Gensoku's problem.]

Gensoku said, "I once asked Seihō what the True Self of a
novice is, and Seihō replied, 'Here comes the Hearth God looking
for fire.' "
[The nature of the question and the response suggest that this interchange had occurred as part of a shōsan ceremony (referred to above) held before the assembled monks,

during which novices ask a Meditation Master a question which presumably reflects their current spiritual understanding. Because at this point Gensoku is still operating from the mind of duality, it is likely that the question was asked from the intellect rather than from the heart. The significance of Seihō's response will be discussed later.]

> Hōgen responded, "Nicely put by Seihō. But I'm afraid you may not have understood it."

[Gensoku had heard Master Seihō's words but had not grasped their import. Hōgen makes a complimentary remark about Seihō's comment. Had Hōgen suspected that Gensoku had already had a kenshō, it is unlikely that he would have done this, but instead might have made some remark that on the surface looked as though he were disparaging Seihō, such as "That old rascal! Is he still going around saying such things?" but which Gensoku would see as being the way a Master may acknowledge another Master whilst avoiding judgmentalism.]

> Gensoku said, "A Hearth God is associated with fire, so I understand it to mean that, just as fire is being used to seek for fire, so the True Self is what is used to seek for the True Self."

[Gensoku has worked out an intellectual interpretation of Seihō's remark, and therefore thinks that this type of understanding is what constitutes awakening to one's True Self. Gensoku's error is in thinking that there are two True Selves: the one that seeks and the one that is sought.]

> The Master said, "Just as I suspected! You have not understood. Were the Buddha Dharma like that, it is unlikely that It would have continued on, being Transmitted down to the present day."

[The Master now sets Gensoku straight as to where he is spiritually, in order to shake up his proud complacency and break through his deluded view.]

> Gensoku was so distressed at this that he left the monastery. While on the road, he thought to himself, "In this country the Master is known as a fine and learned monastic teacher and as a great spiritual leader and guide for five hundred monks.

Since he has chided me for having gone wrong, he must undoubtedly have a point." So, he returned to his Master, respectfully bowed in apology, and said, "What is the True Self of a novice?"

[Leaving the monastery when asked to confront one's spiritual problem 'head on' is not an uncommon occurrence in kōan stories. Similarly, the turning about in one's heart by recognizing that it is oneself who may be wrong is a crucial moment in the life of a trainee. Here it marks Gensoku's letting go of his pride, so that he now returns with the appropriate attitude of mind for asking his spiritual question, which now arises from his heart-felt need to know the truth, and without any preconceptions.]

The Master replied, "Here comes the Hearth God looking for The Fire." Upon hearing these words, Gensoku awoke fully to the Buddha Dharma.

[What a Meditation Master says or does at a formal spiritual examination ceremony in response to a spiritual question is often multilayered in meaning and application. Since it is not intellectually contrived but arises from the Master's spiritual depths, it may in some way speak not only to the questioner but also to others who are present.]

[In Master Seihō's original remark to Gensoku several layers of meaning were occurring simultaneously. On one level, he was inviting Gensoku to give up his attitude of self-importance and 'play' with him; hence, the form in which the response was given: it forms a first line for a couplet and would have been spoken in the equivalent of English doggerel, the translated version read to the rhythmic pattern of *dum-dum-di-dum-dum dum-di-dum-di-dum*. If Gensoku were open enough, he would have come up with a second line, such as 'Burning up his false self upon the funeral pyre'.]

[On another level, Master Seihō was pointing Gensoku toward his spiritual problem. A 'Hearth God' is the title given to the temple boy whose task it is to light the monastery lamps. Thus, Seihō was saying in effect, "You are acting like a temple boy, not like a monk, and are seeking for that which you already have—in your case, the spiritual flame of your training."]

[Hōgen uses the same words and intonation as Seihō did, but context brings out a third level of meaning, which Gensoku now hears, "Here comes the one most innocent of heart whose practice lights the way for all of us, truly seeking That which is the True Light (The Fire)." Gensoku, upon hearing this, realized that this is what he has been truly seeking—not social position or erudition—and awoke to the Truth where the distinction of self and other completely drops away.]

[In the original Chinese text, as given by Dōgen, the words used by Seihō and Hōgen are the same, but the context indicates that there has been a shift in meaning from how Gensoku interpreted these words when spoken by Seihō and what they implied to him when reiterated by Hōgen. To convey that difference in meaning in English, the two quotes are translated in a slightly, but significantly, different way. In other kōan stories where the same phrase is used in two different contexts, the translation will also attempt to convey the shift in meaning, rather than leave it to the reader to puzzle out from a mere repetition what that shift may be. While footnotes have occasionally been supplied to help readers over such difficult points in a kōan story, the translator has not attempted to supply full explanations of these stories, trusting that the preceding guidelines, plus the footnotes, will be sufficient.]

A Discourse on Doing One's Utmost
in Practicing the Way of the Buddhas

(*Bendōwa*)

Translator's Introduction: *Bendōwa*, the earliest dated work in the *Shōbōgenzō*, begins with a long introductory section which places seated meditation *(zazen)* within the context of what has been transmitted through the ages as the practice of Buddhism, as well as giving Dōgen's reasons for writing the present discourse. This is followed by an imaginary dialogue between a disciple and Dōgen as Master, which forms the core of the discourse. While this discourse superficially resembles a catechism in that the disciple asks questions to which Dōgen supplies answers, the nature of the questions and the attitude of the questioner imply that more is transpiring. Essentially, the imaginary disciple, filled with mistrust, raises various objections to the method of serene reflection meditation which Dōgen was engaged in introducing into Japan, and presents concerns that Dōgen's actual disciples were probably encountering from others or might even be holding in their own minds. The obvious expressions of doubt which the questions voice are bypassed by Dōgen, who replies from the mind of meditation, and thereby keeps to the task of clarifying the misunderstanding that lies at the heart of the questioner's doubt. Although Dōgen's writing style in this work, particularly in his introductory section, is clearly literary, he often intersperses this more formal manner of communication with conversational expressions and colorful figures of speech, which lend a compassionate warmth and gentle humor to his discussion.

All Buddhas, without exception, confirm Their having realized the state of enlightenment by demonstrating Their ability to directly Transmit the wondrous Dharma.[1] As embodiments of the Truth, They have employed an unsurpassed, inconceivably marvelous method which functions effortlessly. It is simply this method that Buddhas impart to Buddhas, without deviation or distortion, and Their meditative

---

1. A reference to the direct, Face-to-Face Transmission between Master and disciple, in contrast to the transmission of Dharma through lectures or Scriptural writings.

state of delight in the Truth is its standard and measure. As They take pleasure wherever They go to spiritually aid others while in such a state, They treat this method of Theirs—namely, the practice of seated meditation—as the proper and most straightforward Gate for entering the Way.

People are already abundantly endowed with the Dharma in every part of their being, but until they do the training, It will not emerge. And unless they personally confirm It for themselves, there is no way for them to realize what It is. But when they give It out to others, It keeps filling their hands to overflowing for, indeed, It makes no distinction between 'for the one' and 'for the many'. When they give voice to It, It flows forth from their mouths like a tide, limitless in Its breadth and depth. All Buddhas continually dwell within this state, with None holding onto any of Their thoughts or perceptions, regardless of whatever may arise, whereas the great mass of sentient beings perpetually make use of what is within this state, but without their being fully awake to any situation.

As I would now explain it, diligently practicing the Way means letting all things be what they are in their Self-nature, as you put your essential oneness into operation by following the road away from discriminatory and dualistic thinking. When you have abandoned that type of thinking and have thus passed beyond its barriers, you will cease to be affected by its explanations, which, like the nodes in bamboo, block free passage, or by its theories, which are as convoluted as the knots in a piece of pine wood.

In my own case, shortly after I gave rise to the intention to seek for the Dharma, I went searching everywhere throughout our country for a knowledgeable spiritual teacher until I chanced to meet Master Myōzen of Kennin-ji Temple. The autumn frosts and the spring blossoms quickly passed each other for nine cycles, as I absorbed from him a bit about the Rinzai tradition. As chief disciple of the Ancestral Master Eisai, Master Myōzen alone was correctly Transmitting the unsurpassed Dharma of the Buddha: among his Japanese contemporaries there was definitely no one who was his equal. I next turned towards the land of the great Sung dynasty to seek out spiritual teachers on both sides of the Ts'ien-t'an River in Chekiang Province and to learn about our tradition as propounded through its Five Gates.[2] Ultimately I encountered Meditation Master Nyojō on Mount Tendō, and the Great Matter[*] which I had spent my life seeking to understand was resolved with him.

After that, at the beginning of the Chinese Sho-ting era (1228), I returned to my native land with the intention of spreading the Dharma and rescuing sentient beings. It seemed as if I were shouldering a heavy load, so I decided to bide my time until I could vigorously promote the spread of 'letting go of the discriminatory mind'. As a result, I drifted the while like a cloud, finding lodging as a floating reed does, ready to learn from the customs and habits of those Clear-minded Ones of the past.

However, it occurred to me that there might be some who, by their very nature, were genuinely seeking to study the Way with no regard for fame and gain, as they tried to treat mindfulness as their prime goal, but perhaps they were unfortunately being led astray by some false teacher so that the correct understanding of the Truth was needlessly being kept from them. As a result, they may have fruitlessly let themselves become stupefied with self-satisfaction, having been too long immersed in the realms of self-delusion. And so, I wondered how the true seed of spiritual wisdom could sprout and grow in them so that they would have the chance to realize the Truth. Though I was still such a poor monk in the Way, since I was now devoted to letting myself drift like a cloud and float like a reed, on what mountain or by what river could they seek me out? Because of my feelings of pity for these persons, I have undertaken here to write down what I saw and learned of the customs and practices in Chinese Zen monasteries, as well as to preserve the Transmission of what my spiritual teacher understood to be the most profound Purpose, and thereby to propagate the true Dharma of Buddhism. I trust that what follows is the genuine inner meaning of this.

As my Master put it, the honored Great Master Shakyamuni, whilst with His assembly on India's Divine Vulture Peak, imparted to Makakashō this Dharma, which Ancestor after Ancestor then correctly Transmitted down to the Venerable Bodhidharma. This Venerable One proceeded on his own to China where he imparted

---

2.   An allusion to the five Chinese Zen Buddhist traditions in existence at the time. Dōgen will identify them later in this discourse.

*   See Glossary.

the Dharma to Great Master Eka. This was the first time that the Transmission of the Buddha Dharma had come to the Eastern lands. It ultimately reached the Sixth Chinese Ancestor, Meditation Master Daikan Enō, by being directly Transmitted in this manner. The genuine Dharma of the Buddha then flowed out through the land of the Han, Its main purpose being revealed without entanglement in sectarian or scholastic concerns. In time, the Sixth Ancestor had two spiritual followers: Nangaku Ejō and Seigen Gyōshi. Since they both had the Buddha seal* Transmitted to them, they were, alike, spiritual leaders for human and celestial beings. With the spreading out of those two branches, the Five Instructional Gates opened up. These are, namely, the Hōgen, Igyō, Sōtō, Ummon, and Rinzai traditions. In present-day Sung China, only the Rinzai tradition is widespread throughout the country. Even though these five monastic families differ, they are still the One Seal of the Buddha Mind.

Also, ever since the latter part of the Han dynasty (ca. 3rd century C.E.), all sorts of instructional books were leaving their mark in China; although they pervaded the whole country, which ones were preferable had not yet been established. After the Ancestral Master Bodhidharma came from the West, he immediately cut off at their roots those tangled vines of verbalized confusion and let the genuine, pure Buddha Dharma spread abroad. I earnestly pray that the same may happen in our country.

As my Master also said, all the Buddhas, as well as all the Ancestors, have kept to the Buddha Dharma as Their dwelling place. One and All have not only sat upright in Their meditative state of delight in the Truth, but They have also put the Precepts into practice, and thus They have taken this combination as the precise and certain way for awakening to the Truth. Those in India and China who have experienced an awakening have likewise conformed to this approach. This is based on Master directly passing on to disciple, in private, this wondrous method, and the latter preserving its genuine inner meaning.

When we speak of the correct Transmission in our tradition, the straightforward Buddha Teaching of direct Transmission is 'the best of the best'. From the very moment when a disciple comes to meet face-to-face with the one who is to be his spiritual friend and knowing teacher, there is no need to have the disciple offer incense, make prostrations, chant the names of the Buddhas, do ascetic practices and penances, or recite Scriptures: the Master just has the disciple do pure meditation until he lets his body and mind drop off.

Even though it may be merely for a moment, when someone, whilst sitting upright in meditation, puts the mark of the Buddha seal upon his three types of volitional actions—namely, those of body, speech and thought—the whole physical universe and everything in it becomes and is the Buddha seal; all of space, throughout, becomes and is enlightenment. As a result, all Buddhas, as embodiments of Truth, experience a compounding of Their delight in the Dharma of Their own Original Nature, and the awesome splendor of Their realization of the Way is refreshed for Them. In addition, all sentient beings everywhere throughout the physical universe— and in whichever of the six worlds* of existence they may be, including the three lower ones—are, in that instant, bright and pure in body and mind, as they confirm the Foundation of their great liberation and reveal their Original Face. At that moment, all things realize what confirmation of the Truth really is. Everything, all together, employs its body as a Buddha does, quickly leaping in one bound beyond the limits of any 'correct' understanding to sit erect like the Lord Buddha beneath His Bodhi tree. In an instant, everything turns the unparalleled Great Wheel of the Dharma as It opens up and gives expression to the profound Wisdom that is of the Ultimate, of the Uncreated.

Moreover, these equally fully-enlightened Ones turn back to the six worlds of existence in order to personally travel the path of giving help in unseen ways. Consequently, those who sit in meditation will, beyond doubt, drop off body and mind, and cut themselves free from their previous confused and defiling thoughts and opinions in order to personally realize what the innate Dharma of the Buddha is. That is, in each training ground of every Buddha as the embodiment of Truth, the work of Buddhas finds expression and is put into practice down to the smallest detail, as They create for others far and wide the circumstances that help them go beyond the notion of 'being a Buddha', through Their vigorous promotion of the Teaching that one goes on, always becoming Buddha. At this very moment, the lands of the earth with their trees and grasses, as well as the walls and fences with their tiles and stones, are all seen to be performing the work of Buddhas. As a consequence, all who make profitable spiritual use of whatever storms and floods may arise will be receiving guidance and assistance in unseen ways from the profound and inscrutable instructions of Buddhas, and they will give expression to their innate Understanding, which is ever intimate with the Truth.[3] Because persons who accept and make profitable spiritual use of such floods and firestorms all gladly receive from the Buddhas instruction and guidance on their innate Understanding, those who reside with such persons and are spiritually conversant with them, in turn, mutually provide each other with the unbounded, endless virtues of Buddhas and cause the unceasing, wondrous, immeasurable Dharma of Buddhas to roll forth far and wide until It spreads throughout the whole universe, both within and without. However, these persons of whom I speak are not kept in the dark by being wedded to their senses, for they straightaway realize the Truth by not fabricating anything within the hush of their meditation. If, as ordinary people believe, spiritual practice and personal realization are two different sorts of things, then each could be seen and recognized separately from the other. Should someone become all involved with his sensory perceptions and intellectual understanding, he will not be in 'the realm of enlightenment' because the realm of enlightenment is beyond the reach of delusory, discriminatory thinking.

Furthermore, even though, amidst the stillness of meditation, someone experiences—not only subjectively within heart and mind, but also objectively within outer conditions—an 'entering into realization' and a 'going beyond awakening to Truth', because he is in the realm of delight in the Truth, he does not disturb a single dust mote or shatter the aspect of 'oneness with all things'. Simultaneously, the far-reaching works of a Buddha create a Buddha's profound and wondrous instructions and guidance. At no time does the vegetation or the earth from which it springs—which are the very places that this instructional path reaches—cease to send forth great luminosity as they give expression to the profoundly subtle Dharma. Both 'vegetation' and 'walls' clearly and effectively let the Dharma be known in the world for the sake

---

3.   'Storms and floods' refer to whatever befalls us physically, psychologically, or spiritually which threatens to 'blow us over' or overwhelm us. Yet, as Dōgen comments, even these seemingly negative and destructive occurrences can have spiritual benefits when examined from the mind of meditation.

of all forms of sentient beings, be they of ordinary minds or of awakened ones.[4] All forms of sentient beings, awakened or not, are ever giving expression to It for the sake of 'vegetation' and 'walls'. In the realm where one's own awakening awakens others, from the very moment that you are provided with personal certainty, there is no hanging onto it, <u>and</u>, once your personal certainty begins to function, you must see to it that it never ceases.[5]

This is why even the meditating of just one person at one time harmonizes with, and is at one with, all forms of being, as it tranquilly permeates all times. Thus, within the inexhaustible phenomenal world, across past, present, and future, the meditator does the unending work of instructing and guiding others in the Way of Buddhas. It is the same practice, in no way different for all, just as it is the same realization and personal certifying by all. Not only is it the practice of simply sitting: it is 'striking unbounded space and hearing It reverberate', which is Its continuous, wonderful voice before <u>and</u> after the mallet has struck the bell. But do not limit the matter to this! Everyone has his own Original Face, as well as his own training and practice to do, all of which are beyond the fathoming of human speculations. You must realize that even if all the Buddhas, who are as immeasurable as the sands of the Ganges, were to exercise Their spiritual strengths and attempt to gauge the meditation of a single person by means of Their awakened Buddha Wisdom, They would be unable to reach its boundaries, try as They might to fathom them.

You have now heard just how great and vast the virtues and spiritual merits of this seated meditation are. However, someone who is befuddled by doubts may ask,

---

4.　Here, 'vegetation' refers to all things (physical or non-physical) that are organic or growing, and 'walls' to all things that are inorganic or fabricated.

5.　The 'personal certainty' of which Dōgen speaks should not be confused with any rigid and intractable 'certitude' that may arise from intellectual speculation, insistence on 'logical necessity', religious dogma, personal delusion, etc. Unlike Dōgen's personal certainty, which arises from direct, honest, and self-less spiritual experience, such rigid 'certitude' is the hallmark of the realm where one's deluded thinking attempts to coerce others into accepting that which is deluded.

"Since there are many gates into the Buddha's Teachings, why bother to do just seated meditation?"

I would point out in response, "Because it is the proper and most straightforward entryway into what the Buddha taught."

He may then ask, "Why is this the one and only proper and straightforward entryway?"

I would then point out, "Undoubtedly, the Venerable Great Master Shakyamuni Transmitted it directly as the most excellent method for realizing the Way, and Those who embody the Truth in the three temporal worlds, alike, have realized, do realize, and will realize the Way by doing seated meditation. Therefore, They pass it on generation after generation as the proper and most straightforward gate to the Dharma. Not only that, the Indian and Chinese Ancestors all realized the Way by doing seated meditation, which is why I have now indicated it to be the proper gate for those in both human and celestial worlds."

He may then ask, "Since this depends on someone's receiving the correct Transmission, or on his inquiring into the evidence left by the Ancestors, truly these are beyond the reach of ordinary people like me. However, reading Scriptures and reciting the names of the Buddhas, by themselves, can certainly be the cause for one's spiritually awakening. I fail to see the point in merely sitting idly and doing nothing, so how can such a method be relied on for achieving a spiritual awakening?"

I would point out, "That you should now regard the deep meditative state of all the Buddhas and the peerless Great Dharma to be a pointless 'sitting idly and doing nothing' makes you one who is slandering the Greater Course.* Your delusion is as profound as one who says, 'There is no water,' whilst he is sinking down in a vast sea. Thankfully, all the Buddhas are already sitting sedately in the meditative state that is the consummate delight in the Truth. Is this not creating vast spiritual merits? Alas, your Eye is not yet open and your mind is still in a stupor, as though you were drunk.

"True, the realm of Buddhas is marvelous and beyond the power of the intellect to comprehend, to say nothing of what one who is lacking in faith and scant in spiritual understanding can grasp! Only the one whose readiness for genuine faith is great is able to easily enter the Way. He whose faith is nil, even though he is given teaching, finds it hard to accept. On the Divine Vulture Peak, there were those whom

Shakyamuni said might depart if they so wished whilst He was giving voice to the Dharma. Broadly speaking, if genuine faith arises in your heart, you will need to train and practice, as well as seek out a Master to study with. Otherwise, this faith of yours will fade away before long and, sad to say, the Dharma from the past will cease to enrich you.

"Furthermore, I am not certain whether you really know what the virtue is in performing such services as reciting Scriptures and chanting the names of the Buddhas. Merely to move your tongue about and let your voice roll forth, thinking that this will have the merit and virtue of the work of a Buddha, is utterly pitiful. Compared to a Buddha's Dharma, it is far afield and will take you ever farther in the wrong direction.

"In addition, 'to open a Scriptural text' means that you clarify for yourself what the Buddha taught as the principles for training and practice in both the 'sudden approach' and the 'gradual approach'.[6] When you do your training and practice as He taught, without doubt it will help you realize spiritual certainty. Compared with the merit of actually realizing enlightenment now, expending mental effort in pondering upon matters is nothing. Foolishly using your mouth to repeatedly chant something thousands upon thousands of times in an attempt to arrive at the Way of Buddhas is like believing you can reach the south by driving your cart northward. It is also like someone trying to put a square peg in a round hole. Someone who reads passages in religious works while remaining in the dark about the path of spiritual training is someone who would pay a visit to a doctor and leave behind what the doctor has prescribed. What is to be gained from that? Keeping sound flowing incessantly from the mouth is like the springtime day-and-night croaking of a frog in a rice paddy: ultimately, this too produces no benefit. How much more does this apply to those who are deeply committed to their delusions and go wandering off after fame and gain.

---

6. The sudden and gradual 'approaches' are not the same as sudden versus gradual enlightenment. The 'sudden approach' is the awakening to Truth through the practice of serene reflection meditation, which is the letting go of everything and sitting in pure faith and trust in the Eternal. With the 'gradual approach', the trainee works to cleanse his karma and clarify matters by application of the Precepts to all his actions.

Such things are difficult to abandon since the inclination of such persons towards success and greed goes deep indeed! Since people of this sort existed in the past, it is certainly likely that they exist in the world today, so very sad to say!

"What you must grasp is that when a trainee who has committed both heart and mind to personally confirming the Truth is in accord with a Master in our tradition—that is, with one who has realized the Way and is clear-minded—on how to practice, and has received Transmission of the wonderful Dharma of the Seven Buddhas,* the true meaning and purpose of this Dharma comes forth and will be preserved. This is beyond what Scriptural scholars who study only the words know about. So, quit your doubts and delusions, and do your utmost to practice the Way by doing seated meditation in accordance with a genuine Master's instructions, so that you may realize for yourself the meditative state of all the Buddhas, which is Their delight in the Truth."

He may then ask, "Both the Tendai tradition, which is based on the *Lotus Scripture*, and the Kegon tradition, which is based on the *Avatamsaka Scripture*, as they have been transmitted to our country, are considered to be the fundamental traditions in Mahayana* Buddhism, to say nothing of traditions such as that of Shingon, which was personally transmitted to Kongosatta by the Tathagata Vairochana* and has been passed generation after generation from Master to disciple in an orderly manner. The main thrust of what these traditions talk about is that 'Our very mind is Buddha' and that 'This mind of ours creates Buddhahood', and they set forth the correct perception of the Five Dhyāni Buddhas,[7] which is realized in a single sitting without spending many eons in training. Surely, these should be considered the most sublime of the Buddha's Teachings. So, what is so superior about the training and practice which you are going on about, that you disregard those Teachings in pursuit of your own method alone?"

---

7. The 'Five Dhyāni Buddhas' are the five Great Buddhas of Wisdom, each of whom represents a particular aspect of the Cosmic Buddha. These Buddhas are: Vairochana, the Eternal Buddha; Akshobya, the Immovable Buddha; Ratnasambhava, the Jewel-Born Buddha; Amitabha, the Buddha of Immeasurable Light; and Amoghasiddhi, the Fearless Buddha.

I would point out, "You should understand that within the Buddha's family there is no arguing over 'superior' or 'inferior' Teachings, and no singling out of some Dharma as being more shallow or profound. You should simply try to recognize the genuine from the false in training and practice. Some, attracted by a natural setting of mountains and water with its plants and flowers, have flowed from there into the Way of Buddhas. Others, whilst gathering up in their hands the soil with its sand and pebbles, have preserved the Buddha seal. How much more are the myriad images which fill the universe surpassed by the far-reaching words of a Buddha—which are all the more rich!—and the turning of the Great Wheel of the Dharma is contained within each single dust mote. This is why a phrase like 'Your very mind is Buddha Itself' is as the moon within water, and why the import of 'Sitting in meditation is itself becoming Buddha' is as a reflection in a mirror. Do not get tangled up or taken in by a clever use of words. In order that you may now push on in your training to realize enlightenment in an instant, I show you the marvelous path which the Buddhas and Ancestors have directly Transmitted, and I do this that you may become a genuine follower of the Way.

"Furthermore, the Transmitting of the Buddha Dharma must be done by a Master of our tradition whose personal awakening has been certified. Scholars who go about counting up words are not adequate to serve as teachers and guides: they would be like the blind trying to lead the blind. All who are now within our tradition's Gate, where the proper Transmission of the Buddhas and Ancestors is done, esteem and revere the expert guide whose realization of the Way has been attested to, and place their trust in him as an upholder of the Buddha Dharma. Because of this, when non-human beings—both visible and invisible—come to him to take refuge, or when arhats,* though already enjoying the fruits of realizing enlightenment, come to ask him about the Dharma, this Master never fails to give them a helping hand in clarifying what lies at the bottom of their hearts. As this is something unheard of in the gateways offered by other religions, disciples of the Buddha should just study the Buddha Dharma.

"Also, you should keep in mind that even though, from the first, we are in no way lacking in unsurpassed enlightenment and ever have it available to us for our delight and use, we cannot believe this, and so we become habituated to needlessly giving rise to discriminatory thoughts and personal opinions, chasing after these as if they were something real and, stumbling, we sadly fall off the Great Path. By our relying on these thoughts and opinions, many and varied are the illusory 'flowers in the sky' that we create. Do not immerse yourself in or get stuck on pondering over the twelvefold stages of Dependent Origination or the twenty-five types of existence within the worlds of desire, form, and beyond form, or speculating on the Three Vehicles or the Five Vehicles, or on whether Buddha has existence or not. By following thoughts and opinions like these, you will be unable to consider the correct pathway for training in and practicing the Buddha Dharma. Even so, when, at this very moment, in compliance with the Buddha seal, you let go of everything and earnestly sit in meditation, you will go beyond the boundaries set by any concern that you may have had over being deluded or enlightened. Uninvolved with whether the path is mundane or sanctified, you will at once be strolling about in realms beyond ordinary thinking, as you delight in the Great Enlightenment. How can those who are caught in the nets and snares of words possibly be equal to such a one as this?"

He may then ask, "Among the three traditional ways of spiritual learning, there is the study of meditative concentration, and among the six bodhisattvic practices, there is the perfecting of meditation. Because both of these have been studied by all bodhisattvas* from the moment their hearts first opened to a desire to realize enlightenment, they have been part of training and practice for everyone, bright or dull, without exception. This seated meditation that you are now talking about can possibly be included as one form of them, but what leads you to contend that all the genuine Teachings of the Tathagata are brought together within it?"

I would point out, "This question of yours has come about because this peerless Great Teaching of the Tathagata, which is the Treasure House of the Eye of the True Teaching on the One Great Matter for which we train, has been given the name of 'the Zen School'.[8] However, you must realize that this name first arose in

---

8.   *Zenshū*, rendered here as 'the Zen School', has a significance in Dōgen's text that is not apparent in translation. Rendering *shū* as 'school' may be somewhat misleading if it suggests to the reader something academic or philosophical. On the other hand, to use the term 'sect' might invite associations with Christian sectarianism. In some other places, I have used the word 'tradition' in order to avoid either misunderstanding. However, Dōgen

China and then spread eastwards; it was unknown in India. It began while Great Master Bodhidharma was spending nine years 'facing the wall' at Shōrin-ji Temple on Mount Sūzan. Neither monks nor laity had yet learned of the Buddha's True Dharma, so they called him the Brahman who makes seated meditation *(zazen)* his main focus. Later, all his descendants over the generations continually devoted themselves to seated meditation. Lay people, baffled when they saw this, did not understand what was actually going on, and spoke of it in general as 'the Zazen (Seated Meditation) School'. Nowadays, the *za* is dropped, and it is referred to simply as 'the Zen School'. But its heart and spirit is made clear through the vast sayings of the Ancestors. It is not something to be compared or grouped with the contemplative concentration or the meditation alluded to in the Six Bodhisattva Practices or the Three Ways of Learning.

"That this Buddha Dharma has been authentically Transmitted from Master to disciple has not been a secret to any generation. Long ago, at the assembly on the Divine Vulture Peak, it was only to the Venerable Makakashō that the Tathagata entrusted this Dharma—which is the Treasure House of the Eye of the True Teaching and the Wondrous Heart of Nirvana—as His peerless Great Teaching. As this ceremony was personally witnessed by the host of celestial beings who are at present residing in heavenly worlds, it is not something that one need mistrust. Since Buddha Dharma, in general, is something that the host of celestial beings ever and ever looks after and protects, the merit of their actions has still not died away. Beyond doubt, you should recognize that this practice is the complete and whole Way of the Buddha Dharma: there is nothing to compare it to."

He may then ask, "Of the four manners of bodily carriage in the Buddha's family—namely, standing, walking, sitting, and reclining—why is it that you lay the full burden of practice merely on sitting, and talk of attaining certainty and entering Buddhahood by promoting meditative contemplation?"

---

specifically reveals a few sentences further along that he understands the word to be synonymous with mune, 'the main point or focus'; that is, *zenshū* refers to those who make zen (meditation) the focus of their training, just as those of the *Kegonshū* make the *Kegon Sutra (Avatamsaka Scripture)* the focus of their training.

I would point out, "The ways in which all the Buddhas from the ages past, one after the other, trained and practiced, and by which They arrived at certainty and entered Buddhahood, are impossible to know in full detail. If you are asking what the authority for this is, you should understand that what Those in the family of Buddhas made use of is the authority. You need not seek for an authority beyond this. To put it simply, in praise of the practice, Ancestors and Masters have said that seated meditation is the gateway to ease and joy. From this we can surmise that, among the four manners of bodily carriage, it is the easiest and most joyful. And even further, it has not been the way of practice for just one or two Buddhas: this has been the way for all Buddhas and all Ancestors."

He may then ask, "Granted that someone who has not yet clearly understood what Buddha Dharma is may possibly secure certainty by diligently doing seated meditation. But what about those who are already clear as to what the Buddha's True Teaching is? What could they possibly expect from doing seated meditation?"

I would point out, "Since it is said that we should not discuss our dreams in front of those who are befuddled, or uselessly put oars into the hands of a woodcutter,[9] I am disinclined to answer your question directly. Still there is some teaching that I can give you.

"Now then, to think that practice and realization are separate from each other is a non-Buddhist view, or a misunderstanding of the Way. In Buddhism, practice and realization are completely one and the same. Because it is a practice based on being spiritually awake at this very moment, the diligent training which springs forth from our initial resolve to seek the Way is, in itself, the whole of one's innate certainty. For

---

9. Dōgen's first analogy derives from the Chinese saying, "Do not share your dreams with a fool," but has been modified to refer here to discussing experiences which are as yet beyond the questioner's present level of direct understanding. The second analogy makes this more explicit: one does not discuss such matters because it is like giving tools to someone who cannot make use of them. Further, a 'woodcutter' is a Zen term applied to a monk who has not yet had a kenshō (that is, the experiencing of his own Buddha Nature) and is still working on cutting his karmic tendencies off at the roots, whereas 'oars' is an allusion to the tools needed by one who has awakened to his True Nature to help him ferry others to the Other Shore.

this reason, we teach that you should not hold in mind any expectation of being enlightened as something outside of, or apart from, practice, since this practice directly points you towards your own original, innate certainty.

"Since this certainty is a spiritually awakened one that already exists within the practice, your certainty will know no limits: since the practice already exists within spiritually awakened certainty, your practice will know no beginning. This is why the Tathagata Shakyamuni and the Venerable Makakashō were both governed by Their practice, which was based on being spiritually awake. Great Master Bodhidharma and the exalted Ancestor Daikan Enō, likewise, were 'hauled and tumbled about' by their practice based on being spiritually awake. Such are the signs of one who resides in, and keeps to, the Buddha Dharma.

"A practice that is not separate from being spiritually awake already exists. It is our good fortune to have had this wondrous practice Transmitted to us individually, and to diligently pursue it with the attitude of mind which first awakened in us the desire to seek the Truth is, in itself, to arrive at that original, spiritually awakened state which is our innate, 'uncreated' Foundation. Be aware that the Buddhas and Ancestors repeatedly taught that we must not be slack in our training and practice, so that we do not stain or tarnish our innate enlightenment, which is inseparable from our practice. If you let go of any thought of 'I am doing a marvelous practice,' your innate enlightenment will fill your hands to overflowing. If you purge yourself of any thought of 'being enlightened', this wondrous practice will operate throughout your whole being.

"Further, when I was in the land of the great Sung dynasty, what I saw with my own eyes, in all the Zen monasteries everywhere, was a Meditation Hall with anywhere from five or six hundred to one or two thousand monks peacefully continuing to do seated meditation day and night. When I asked those Masters of our tradition—namely, those who had had the Buddha Mind seal Transmitted to them and were serving as Abbots of these monasteries—what Buddhism is in sum and substance, I was instructed that it was the principle that 'Training and being spiritually awake are not two separate things.' Therefore, not only for the sake of those trainees within the gates of our temple, but also for those who, distinguished by their seeking for the Dharma, yearn for the Truth within the Buddha's Teachings, I have followed the path of the skillful teachers of our tradition. And in accordance with what these Buddhas and Ancestors have taught, I have put forth that one must diligently practice the Way by doing seated meditation. I have done so without distinguishing between those with the attitudes of a novice or of a senior, and without concerning myself with whether those being instructed are ordinary people or saintly ones.

"Surely you have heard what Masters have said: 'It is not that practice and enlightenment do not exist. It is just that they cannot be taken hold of and defiled,' and 'The one who clearly sees what the Way is, is the one who practices the Way.' Understand that you must do your training and practice amidst the realizing of the Way."

He may then ask, "What about those Japanese teachers of earlier generations who spread Scriptural teachings throughout our country? At the time when they crossed over to China during the T'ang dynasty and brought the Dharma back with them, why did they ignore this principle of seated meditation and just pass on Scriptural teachings?"

I would point out, "The reason why those human teachers of the past did not pass on this Teaching was that the time was not yet ripe for It."

He may then ask, "Did the teachers of those earlier times understand this Dharma?"

I would point out, "Had they understood It, they would have communicated It."

He may then respond, "There are some who say:

> Do not grieve over birth and death, since there is an extremely quick method for freeing yourself from them, namely, by understanding the principle that it is the innate nature of one's mind to be ever-abiding, to persist without change. This means that, because this physical body has been born, it will inevitably come to perish, but even so, this innate nature of the mind will never perish. When someone fully comprehends that the innate nature of his mind—which is never swept away by birth and death—is in his body, he sees it to be his true and genuine nature. Thus, his body is

but a temporary form, being born here and dying there, ever subject to change, whilst his mind is ever-abiding, so there is no reason to expect it to vary over past, present, and future. To understand the matter in this way is what is meant by being free from birth and death. For the one who understands this principle, his future births and deaths will come to an end, so that when his body expires, he will enter the ocean of real existence. When he flows into this ocean of being, he will undoubtedly possess wonderful virtues, just as all the Buddhas and Tathagatas have done. Even though he may realize this in his present life, he will not be exactly the same as those Holy Ones, since he has a bodily existence which was brought about through deluded actions in past lives. The person who does not yet understand this principle will be ever spun about through successive births and deaths. Therefore, we should just make haste and fully comprehend the principle of the innate nature of the mind being ever-abiding and persisting without change. To pass one's life just sitting around idly, what can be gained by that?

Such a statement as this truly corresponds to the Way of all the Buddhas and all the Ancestors, don't you think?"

I would point out, "The view that you have just expressed is in no way Buddhism, but rather the non-Buddhist view of the Shrenikans.[10] This erroneous view of theirs may be stated as follows:

In our bodies there is a soul-like intelligence. When this intelligence, or intellect, encounters conditions, it makes distinctions between good and bad as well as discriminating right from wrong. It is conscious of what is painful or itches from desire, and is awake to what is hard to bear or easy. All such responses are

---

10. The Shrenikans were a group of non-Buddhists who are thought to have followed the teachings of Shrenika, a contemporary of Shakyamuni Buddha. On occasion, they used terms similar to those in Buddhism, but with different meanings.

within the capacity of this intelligence. However, when this body of ours perishes, this soul-like nature sloughs it off and is reborn somewhere else. As a result, even though it appears to perish in the here and now, it will have its rebirth in another place, never perishing, but always abiding unchanged.

"So this erroneous view goes. Be that as it may, your modeling yourself upon this view and regarding it as the Buddha's Teaching is more foolish than clutching onto a roof tile or a pebble in the belief that it is gold or some precious jewel. The shamefulness of such befuddled ignorance and delusion beggars comparison. National Teacher Echū in Great Sung China has strongly warned us about such a view. For you to now equate the wondrous Dharma of all the Buddhas with the mistaken notion that your mind will abide whilst your physical features perish, and to imagine that the very thing which gives rise to the cause of birth and death has freed you from birth and death—is this not being foolish? And how deeply pitiable! Be aware that this is the mistaken view of one who is outside the Way, and do not lend an ear to it.

"Because I now feel even greater pity for you, I cannot leave the matter here, but will try to rescue you from your erroneous view. You should understand that, in Buddhism, we have always spoken not only of body and mind as being inseparable, but also of the nature of something and the form it takes as not being two different things. As this Teaching was likewise well known in both India and China, we dare not deviate from It. Even more, in Buddhist instruction that speaks of what is persistent, all things are said to have persistence without their ever being separated into categories of 'body' and 'mind'.[11] In instruction that talks about cessation, all things are said to be subject to cessation without differentiating whether they are of some particular nature or have some particular form. So why do you risk contradicting the correct principle by saying that the body ceases whilst the mind permanently

---

11. Dōgen makes a distinction between the Buddhist concept of persistence and the Shrenikan concept of abiding. With the former, all phenomena, physical and non-physical, arise and continue on ('persist') for an unspecified period before disintegrating and disappearing, whereas with the latter, the mind is thought to remain ('abide') unchanged and unchanging forever.

abides? Not only that, you must fully understand that 'birth and death' is nirvana: there has never been any talk of a nirvana outside of birth and death. Moreover, even though you may erroneously reckon that there is a Buddha Wisdom that is separate from birth and death because you have worked it out that the mind permanently abides apart from the body, this 'mind' of yours—which understands, and works matters out, and perceives things, and knows what they are—is still something that arises and disappears, and is in no way 'ever-abiding'. Surely, this 'mind' of yours is something completely transitory!

"You will see, if you give it a taste, that the principle of the oneness of body and mind is something constantly being talked about in Buddhism. So, how does the mind, on its own, apart from the body, keep from arising and disappearing as this body of yours arises and perishes? Furthermore, were they inseparable at one time and not inseparable at another, then what the Buddha said would, naturally, be false and deceiving.

"In addition, should you suddenly get the notion that eradicating birth and death is what the Dharma is really about, it would lead you to sullying the Precept against despising the Buddha Dharma. Do watch out for this!

"You must also understand that what is spoken of in the Buddha's Teachings as 'the Gate to the Teaching on the vast characteristics common to the nature of all minds' takes in the whole universe, without dividing it into innate natures and their forms or ever referring to things as 'coming into existence' or 'perishing'. Nothing, up to and including realizing enlightenment and nirvana, is excluded from the innate nature of your mind. Each and every thing throughout the whole of the universe is simply 'the One Mind' from which nothing whatsoever is excluded. All Gates to the Teaching are equally of this One Mind. To assert that there are no differences whatsoever is the way the Buddhist family understands the nature of Mind. So, within this one all-inclusive Dharma, how can you separate body from mind or split 'birth and death' off from 'nirvana'? You are already a disciple of the Buddha, so do not give ear to the clatter of a lunatic's tongue as he utters views that are off the True Track."

He may then ask, "Do those who devotedly do seated meditation have to stringently observe the Precepts and monastic rules?"

I would point out, "Keeping to the Precepts and leading a pure life are standard customs in the Zen tradition and are the habitual conduct of the Buddhas and Ancestors. However, for those who have not yet formally taken the Precepts, or who have broken them, we cannot say that their seated meditation is without value or merit."

He may then ask, "Surely, someone who is endeavoring to do seated meditation can also do practices like the Shingon mantra chanting or like the Tendai form of introspection, wherein you try to stop thinking evil thoughts and contemplate what Truth is. Right?"

I would point out, "When I was in China, I asked Masters of our tradition about the genuine keys to successful training. None of them said that they had heard of any of our Ancestors to whom the Buddha seal had been properly Transmitted— either in India and China, now or in the past—ever having done practices such as those two. Truly, if you do not make the One Matter for which you train the thing that you focus on, you will never make it to the Unique Wisdom."

He may then ask, "Can this practice be done by men and women in lay life, or is it only suitable for monks?"

I would point out, "The Ancestors have said in their Teaching, 'When it comes to realizing the Buddha Dharma, make no distinction between male and female, or between the exalted and the lowly.'"

He may then ask, "By leaving home life behind, monks are quickly separated from all their various ties so that they have no impediments to diligently practicing seated meditation. But how can those of us involved in the daily pressures of lay life turn to doing training and practice so that we may realize the Way of the Buddhas, which is unconcerned with worldly affairs?"

I would point out, "The Buddhas and Ancestors, out of Their overflowing sympathy, have opened the great, wide Gates of Their compassion. They have done this so that They might help all sentient beings realize the Truth and enter the Way. Who amongst those in the worlds of either the mundane or the saintly could possibly be excluded from entering? Because of this, should you seek examples from the past up to the present, authenticated instances of it are many indeed.

"For instance, the T'ang Chinese emperors T'ai-tsung and Shun-tsung were deeply involved with myriad matters of state, yet by diligently practicing seated meditation, they succeeded in traversing the Great Way of the Buddhas and Ancestors. The ministers Li and Fang, while councilors, served as right-hand men to their emperor, yet by diligently doing their seated meditation, they also realized the Truth and entered the Great Way of the Buddhas and Ancestors. It simply depends on whether you have the determination or not: it has nothing to do with being a householder or a monk. In addition, those who can deeply discern the difference between what is excellent and what is mediocre will naturally give rise to faith and trust. How much more evident it is that those who regard worldly affairs as an impediment to the Buddha Dharma are only inferring that Buddha Dharma does not exist within the mundane world, and they do so because they have not yet recognized that, within Buddha Dharma, there are no 'worldly ways'.

"More recently, there was a minister in Great Sung China named Councilor Feng. He was a high official who was extremely mature in the Way of the Ancestors. Later, he composed a poem about himself:

> *When free from official duties,*
> > *I am fond of doing my meditation.*
> *Rarely do I ever lie down*
> > *or go sleep in my bed.*
> *Though I bear the semblance*
> > *of a minister of state,*
> *'The old Buddhist monk' is what they call me*
> > *from sea to sea.*

This poem is saying that, even though he had a position that left him little free time from his duties, his determination towards the path of the Buddhas was so deep that he realized the Way. With him in mind, we should reflect upon ourselves and see how our present condition looks in the mirror of his former times. In Great Sung China, I never heard it said that present-day rulers and their ministers, gentry and commoners, men and women, had not fixed their hearts on the Way of the Ancestors. Both those in the military and those in civil service were intent on seeking training in meditation and studying the Way. Among those who were intent, many undoubtedly illumined That which is the Foundation of their hearts and minds. This should let you know that worldly duties do not, in and of themselves, impede the Buddha Dharma.

"If the authentic Buddha Dharma spreads throughout a country, all the Buddhas and all the celestial beings will continually offer Their protection and, as a result, the ruler will transform his nation into a peaceful one. Since it is the wise and saintly who bring about peacefulness, the Buddha Dharma becomes ever stronger.

"Furthermore, when the Venerable Shakyamuni was in the world, even those who were perverse in their actions or twisted in their views found the Way. In the assemblies of Ancestors and Masters, both the 'young hunters' and the 'old woodcutters' alike experienced a spiritual awakening.[12] So it is certainly possible for people other than these! Simply seek out the instructive path of a genuine Master."

He may then ask, "If I decide to do this practice, can I realize the Truth even in this present-day world, which is in the final, degenerate stage of the Buddha's Teachings?"

I would point out, "Although those who devote themselves to the study of Scriptures make a big thing out of various terms and aspects, in the genuine Teachings of the Greater Course no distinction is made about a true, a superficial, or a final period of the Dharma, and it is said that everyone will realize the Way if they do the training. Not only that, with this Genuine Dharma that is directly Transmitted, once you have entered the practice and left your 'self' behind, you will likewise enjoy making use of the wondrous treasures within yourself. Whether or not someone has personally realized the Truth is something that those who have done the training will naturally know, just as those who drink water discern whether it is cool or warm."

---

12. The 'young hunters' is an allusion to those new to training who, having given rise to the intention of realizing Buddhahood, are eagerly seeking it. The 'old woodcutters' are those who have been long in training, but who remain preoccupied with cutting the roots of their past karmic tendencies. These two types are hindering themselves from awakening, the former by overzealousness, and the latter by clinging to a notion of "I still have so very far to go in training."

He may then ask, "There are some who say that, according to the Buddha Dharma, if I fully comprehend the import of 'Our very mind is Buddha,' then, even though I do not chant the Scriptures or physically put the Buddha's Way into practice, I do not lack for Buddha Dharma. Simply knowing that the Buddha Dharma has always existed within me is what the whole of realizing the Way comes down to. Apart from this, there is no need to turn to others to seek anything. So why should I become all involved in diligently practicing seated meditation?"

I would point out, "This statement of yours is hopelessly unreliable. If the matter were as you have put it, then anyone with a conscious mind could explain the principle of the Buddha Dharma without having to realize anything.

"You must understand that Buddha Dharma is to be investigated without holding onto any notion of 'self' or 'other'. If knowing that 'You yourself are Buddha' were what realization of the Way is, the Venerable Shakyamuni, in the long past, would not have gone to all the trouble He did to try and help others realize the Way.

"Let me take a moment to substantiate this with a wonderful case concerning an ancient one of great virtue:

Long ago, there was a monk in Meditation Master Hōgen's monastic community named Gensoku who was a subordinate under the Temple's administrative director. Master Hōgen asked him, "Director Gensoku, how long have you been in our community?"

Gensoku replied, "Why, I've been in the community for three years now."

The Master asked, "As you are still a junior monk, why have you never asked me about the Buddha Dharma?"

Gensoku replied, "I will not lie to Your Reverence. Previously, when I was with Meditation Master Seihō, I fully reached the place of joyful ease in the Buddha Dharma."

The Master said, "And what was said that gained you entry to this place?"

Gensoku said, "I once asked Seihō what the True Self of a novice is, and Seihō replied, 'Here comes the Hearth God looking for fire.'" [13]

Hōgen responded, "Nicely put. But I'm afraid you may not have understood it."

Gensoku said, "A Hearth God is associated with fire, so I understand it to mean that, just as fire is being used to seek for fire, so the True Self is what is used to seek for the True Self."

The Master said, "Just as I suspected! You have not understood. If this is what the Buddha Dharma was like, it is unlikely that It would have continued on, being Transmitted down to the present day."

Gensoku was so distressed at this that he left the monastery. While on the road, he thought to himself, "In this country, the Master is known as a fine and learned monastic teacher and as a great spiritual leader and guide for five hundred monks. Since he has chided me for having gone wrong, he must undoubtedly have a point." So, he returned to his Master, respectfully bowed in apology, and said, "What is the True Self of a novice?"

The Master replied, "Here comes the Hearth God looking for The Fire." Upon hearing these words, Gensoku awoke fully to the Buddha Dharma.

"It is quite clear from this that an intellectual understanding of 'One's very Self is Buddha' is insufficient grounds for saying that you have understood the Buddha Dharma. If an intellectual understanding of 'One's very Self is Buddha' were what Buddha Dharma is, the Master, based on what had previously been said, would not

---

13. The Hearth God was a nickname for the temple boy who attended to lighting the lamps. Temple boys, who ranged in age from seven to fifteen, had not yet taken the Precepts and were not monks. The relevance of this reference is discussed in the Translator's General Introduction.

have had to offer guidance or admonish his disciple in the manner that he did. From the moment you meet a good spiritual friend, undoubtedly you should straightaway inquire into the procedures and principles of training and practice, as well as unswervingly do your utmost to practice seated meditation and keep to the Way, without ever letting your mind be content with any partial understanding. The wonderful technique of the Buddha Dharma will then not prove fruitless."

He may then ask, "I have heard that in India and China in the present day, as well as in the past, there have been those who have awakened to the Way by hearing the sound of bamboo being struck, and others who, upon seeing the color of a flower, have clarified what their mind is, to say nothing of Great Master Shakyamuni who realized the Way upon seeing the morning star, or the Venerable Ananda who, upon the occasion of the debater's flagpole toppling, became clear as to what Dharma is. In addition, from the time of the Sixth Chinese Ancestor on, there have been many within the five families of our tradition who have clarified what the foundation of mind is through encountering a single word or half a verse of Scripture. Surely, not <u>all</u> these were people who were always diligently practicing the Way by just doing seated meditation, were they?"

I would point out, "What you need to know is that neither of those particular persons—the one who, upon seeing a color, clarified what Mind is and the one who was awakened to the Way by a resonating sound—spent time in speculation and critical assessment whilst diligently practicing the Way, nor did they create a second 'person'—be it a 'self' or an 'other'—while they were directly engaged in that practice."

He may then ask, "People in India and China have always been basically honest and straightforward. Because both countries have been centers of culture, their people, once instructed in the Buddha Dharma, have succeeded in entering the Way ever so quickly. Our country, from ancient times, has been extremely short on benevolence and wise discernment, so that it has been hard for us to accumulate genuine spiritual seeds. Because we have been a land of savage barbarians, such seeds are, alas, not to be seen. Furthermore, the monks in our country are inferior even to the householders in those great nations. Our people are foolish, narrow-minded, and petty. They cling tightly to transitory successes and delight in surface virtues. Will such a people, even if they do sit in meditation, succeed in quickly realizing the Buddha Dharma?"

I would point out, "As you say, people in our country are not yet universally benevolent and wise in their discernings, and are also given to laziness and prejudice. Were they given the Dharma straight on, Its Sweet Dew would turn sour and become a poison to them. A taste for fame and gain comes easily, whilst delusion and grasping are hard to let go of. Even so, it does not necessarily require the worldly wisdom of either the mundane or the saintly for people to recognize and enter the Buddha Dharma so that they may serve as a ferry to carry others beyond the mundane. While the Buddha was in the world, a certain man came to experience all four fruits leading to arhathood when he was hit in the head with a handball. And a certain woman came to understand what the Great Way is due to her playfully dressing up in a monk's kesa* in a previous life. These frivolous and dense persons were both like foolish and confused animals. Nevertheless, when their genuine faith and trust rescued them, they were provided with a path which led them out of their delusions. Also, upon seeing an ignorant old monk dumbly sitting, a faithful lay woman who had brought him food opened up and was awakened. Her experience did not depend on 'enlightened wisdom' or on Scripture, nor did she rely on words or explanations: she was rescued simply by her genuine faith and trust.

"Also, Shakyamuni's instructions have been spreading through the three thousand worlds for something like two thousand years. The countries within these worlds are of all kinds and are not necessarily lands of benevolence and wisdom, nor are their people necessarily always astute or intellectually brilliant! Even so, the true Dharma of the Tathagata has always possessed a marvelous, unimaginably great, meritorious strength so that, when the time is ripe, It spreads throughout those lands. When people duly train and practice with genuine faith and trust—be they bright or dull—all alike will realize the Way. Do not give way to thoughts that our country is not a land of benevolence and wise discernment, and that its people are too foolish or stupid to be able to understand what Buddha Dharma is. Moreover, the people are all well endowed with the genuine seed of spiritual Wisdom. Simply, it is rare for them to be in exact harmony with It, and, as a result, they do not yet completely accept and enjoy It."

The preceding exchange of questions and responses may prove confusing due to my shifting back and forth between the perspectives of guest and host.[14] To some extent, I may have made illusory flowers appear in an empty sky. Be that as it may, since our tradition's principle of diligent practice of the Way by doing seated meditation has not yet been brought into this country, how sad for those with spiritual intentions! It is for this reason that I have brought together a bit of what I saw and heard whilst in China, contenting myself with setting down the genuine keys of clear-eyed Masters, so that those desirous of training in the practice can learn about them. Apart from this, I do not have sufficient time, at present, to set down the rules and regulations of Zen monasteries, or the rankings, standards, and ceremonies for temples. Besides, such a task must not be done in haste.

Even though our country lies east of the Dragon Sea separating it from China, which lies far beyond the clouds and mist, around the time of the Japanese emperors Kimmei and Yōmei in the sixth century, the Buddha's Teachings from the western lands gradually moved eastwards, to the good fortune of our people. However, Their terms and subtleties, as well as the ritual formalities associated with Them, have often become entangled, so that doubts of how to do the practice have weighed heavily. But now, if you make your tattered robe and your patched-up alms bowl your lifetime career, setting up a thatched hut near to where the white rock protrudes from the moss-covered cliffs, whilst sitting upright and polishing your training, in a twinkling you will be one who 'goes beyond being Buddha', and you will quickly bring to a conclusion the Great Matter for which you have trained and studied your whole life.[15]

---

14. That is, between the attitude of a questioning disciple and of a responding Master.

15. In this sentence, the description of a trainee is not simply an idyllic portrait of a hermit-monk but also gives a concise metaphoric description of how someone is to train, employing traditional Chinese Zen Buddhist imagery. The robe, or kesa, is associated here with the Precepts; its tatters arise from one's breakage of those Precepts, and its repair results from one's true resolve to do better. The alms bowl suggests one's willingness to train by being all-accepting; its patches are the signs of one's attempt to repair 'leaks' in that willingness. Despite the less than 'perfect' condition of these two

These are precisely the friendly admonitions of Master Kodon of Dragon's Fang Mountain and the legacy in how to train bequeathed by Makakashō on Cock's Foot Mountain. As to the procedures for doing seated meditation, you should follow what is in my *Rules for Meditation*,[16] which I compiled during the recent Kanroku period (1225-1227).

Although one should have a ruler's permission before spreading Buddhism throughout a country, if we think once again of the legacy from the Divine Vulture Peak, then all the rulers, lords, ministers, and generals who have appeared in the hundreds of thousands of millions of lands are persons who had graciously accepted the Buddha's decrees, and now, due to their past lives, live on without losing sight of their cherished desire to protect the Buddha Dharma. Those regions in which spiritual help is spread, wherever they may be, need not be strictly Buddhist countries. Therefore, in letting the Way of the Buddhas and Ancestors flow forth, you need not necessarily wait for all conditions to be perfect. Just think of today as the day to begin!

Thus, I leave what I have assembled here for those who are concentrating upon their desire for the Buddha's Teachings, as well as for any within the genuine stream of students who, in search of the Way, drift as a cloud and lodge as a floating reed.

---

aspects of training, the trainee is still willing to continue on, while recognizing that there are still things he needs to do and that he need not be 'perfect' in order to keep going onwards. The hut often refers to one's 'place of training'—namely, one's body and mind—which is kept 'thatched' so that the trainee protects himself from the karmic and emotional storms that may assail him either physically 'outside himself' or mentally 'within himself'. While his seat is within the mundane world with all its surrounding growth, he chooses to sit before the white rock, Bodhidharma's 'wall', which is not only a physical place of meditation, but a mental one as well. If he then sits upright—doing his meditation, acknowledging the tatters he has made of the Precepts and the leaks from his lapses in being all-accepting, and attempting to repair them—he will quickly be able to let go of any thoughts of arriving at Buddhahood and will resolve his spiritual question.

16.   *Fukan Zazengi*. A translation of this work by Rev. Master P.T.N.H. Jiyu-Kennett appears in *Serene Reflection Meditation*, 6th ed. revised (Mount Shasta, California: Shasta Abbey Press, 1996), pp. 1-3.

Written down on the mid-autumn day in the third year of the Kanki era (September 12, 1231) by me, the mendicant monk Dōgen, who went to Sung China that I might receive and bring back the Transmission of the Dharma.

2

On the Great Wisdom
That Is Beyond Discriminatory Thought

(Makahannya-haramitsu)

Translator's Introduction: *Makahannya-haramitsu*, the earliest dated Dharma talk in the *Shōbōgenzō*, was given by Dōgen to his monks in his renovated monastery, which he had renamed Kannondōri. The discourse consists largely of paraphrases from the *Scripture Which Is the Heart of the Prajñāpāramitā*, also called the *Heart Scripture* (J. *Hannya Shin Gyō*), and lengthy quotations from the *Larger Scripture on Spiritual Wisdom* (J. *Dai Hannya Gyō*), plus a poem by his Chinese Master Tendō Nyojō, to all of which he has added comments.

There is an allusion in the discourse that may not be as obvious in the translation as it is in the original. In passages from the *Larger Scripture on Spiritual Wisdom*, the questioner is identified as Tentaishaku, 'the Lord of the Heavens', a common epithet for Indra. Thus, at first glance, the ensuing dialogue would appear to be between a divine personage from the Hindu pantheon and Subhuti, one of the Buddha's chief disciples who was known for his understanding of the Buddha's Teachings on the Immaculacy of Emptiness. However, in the original text the reader is given a subtle hint as to the questioner's real identity when Subhuti addresses him as Kaushika ('He Whose Eyes Look Askance at Things'), an epithet applied to Indra when taking human form. In other words, the questioner is a human who, from haughtiness, considers himself the equal of the Lord of the Heavens, as he looks askance at the Buddha's Teachings.

When Avalokiteshvara Bodhisattva[*] was at one with the deepest Wisdom of the Heart which is beyond discriminatory thought, He saw with utmost clarity that the five skandhas which comprise one's whole being were as space.

The five skandhas are our physical form, our sensory perceptions, our mental conceptions and ideas, our volition, and our consciousness: they are a fivefold manifestation of Wisdom. 'To see with utmost clarity' is what is meant by Wisdom. To clarify what the meaning and import of this is, He said, "Our physical form is as

---

[*]   See Glossary.

30

pure and unbounded as space," and "The Unbounded is what our physical form is." Our physical forms are forms: the Unbounded is what is unbounded. The former are 'the hundreds of individual sproutings':[1] the Latter is the multiplicity of form.

When the Wisdom Beyond Discriminatory Thought manifests in twelvefold form, It is the twelve sensory fields—that is, the six sensory faculties along with what they perceive to be the properties of all thoughts and things. And this Wisdom has an eighteenfold manifestation, comprised of the six sensory faculties of eyes, ears, nose, tongue, tactile body, and mind plus their six perceived properties, respectively, color, sound, odor, taste, feel, and mental contents, along with the six forms of consciousness associated with eyes, ears, nose, tongue, tactile body, and mind. And this Wisdom has a fourfold manifestation: the arising of suffering, its cause, its ultimate extinguishing, and the method whereby it is extinguished. And this Wisdom has a sixfold manifestation, consisting of almsgiving, keeping to the Pure Precepts, practicing patience, making diligent effort, doing serene reflection meditation, and applying wise discernment. And the Wisdom Beyond Discriminatory Thought has a singular expression, which is constantly manifesting before our very eyes here and now: It is total and absolute enlightenment. And the Wisdom Beyond Discriminatory Thought has a threefold manifestation as past, present, and future. And this Wisdom has a sixfold manifestation as earth, water, fire, wind, space, and consciousness. And this Wisdom has a fourfold manifestation which occurs in daily life as moving, standing, sitting, and reclining.

There was once a mendicant monk in the assembly of the Tathagata Shakyamuni who was thinking to himself, "I bow in deepest respect to the profound Wisdom Beyond Discriminatory Thought. And well I should, for even though within this Wisdom there is nothing that gets born or becomes extinct, nevertheless You have been able to establish that by following the Precepts, our

---

1.   'The hundreds of individual sproutings', an expression often used by Dōgen, refers to the manifold forms that arise or 'sprout up' because of a set of conditions, persist for a while, then disappear when the conditions that brought them about change.

physical skandha will be beyond dualistic morality; that by meditative contemplation, our sensory skandha will be tranquil and freed from all false ideas; that by practicing wise discernment, our consciousness skandha will be wise in what it sees; that by practicing non-attachment, our volitional skandha will be fully liberated from defiling passions; and that by practicing all-acceptance, our thought skandha will have complete comprehension of this liberated state. You have also been able to establish that the fruits of entering the stream of training, the fruits of returning but once more to the world of desire, the fruits of not returning to that world, and the fruits of arhathood* truly exist. You have been able to establish that there is the enlightenment solely realized by oneself, as well as the supreme awakening wherein all things are viewed alike as enlightened.[2] You have been able to establish that there are the Treasures of Buddha, Dharma, and Sangha, as well as to establish that there is a turning of the Wheel of the Dharma and a ferrying of all manner of sentient beings to the Other Shore."

The Buddha, aware of these thoughts, addressed the monk, saying, "It is just as you have been thinking, just as you have thought: the profound Wisdom Beyond Discriminatory Thought is subtle and difficult for the intellect to fathom."

In regard to the private thoughts of this monk, whenever someone bows down in respect to all things, the wisdom that prompted this monk to say, "even though there is no being born or becoming extinct, nevertheless…," expresses a 'bowing down in respect'. When there is this moment of 'being duly respectful', the wisdom of what the Buddha was able to establish in this connection is right before your very eyes and

---

2.   A reference to Shakyamuni's awakening on His own, without the aid of a master, and His realizing as part of that enlightenment experience that all things are simultaneously enlightened just as they are.

encompasses everything the monk had in mind, from the practicing of Precepts, meditation, and wise discernment up through the ferrying of sentient beings to the Other Shore. It is this that we mean when we speak of *'Mu'*.[3] What this expedient term *'Mu'* refers to can be realized through the practices just outlined, for this *'Mu'* is the profound, subtle, and inscrutable Wisdom Beyond Discriminatory Thought.

Someone present, a veritable Indra, Lord of the Heavens, asked the Buddha's long-standing senior disciple Subhuti, "O great virtuous one, if some bodhisattva or mahasattva[*] were desirous of studying this 'Profound Wisdom That is Beyond Discriminatory Thought', just how, precisely, should he go about studying such a thing?"

Subhuti replied, "O you who look with doubting eyes, if a bodhisattva or mahasattva is desirous of learning about the Profound Wisdom Beyond Discriminatory Thought, he should study It with a mind as completely open as open space, with no preconceptions to hamper him."

Thus, 'learning what Wisdom is' means 'to be free of preconceptions': 'being free of preconceptions' is what 'studying Wisdom' is.

This Indra Lord of the Heavens then addressed the Buddha, saying, "World-honored One, if virtuous men and women were to receive this teaching on Your purported 'Wisdom That is Beyond Discriminatory Thought', hold to it, and recite it to others chapter and verse, were they to explore its implications and then lecture upon it to others, what could they possibly do to defend it from critical attack? All I am really asking, O World-honored One, is that You, out of Your compassion, give us instruction."

---

3.   *'Mu'* is the Japanese reading of the Chinese character that is sometimes used in Zen texts to represent That which 'is beyond' the ability of any words or descriptions to encompass.

This time, the Buddha's senior monk Subhuti responded to this lordly Indra by saying, "O you with the doubting eyes, do you see any way in which this Teaching can be defended?"

The lordly one replied, "No, O great virtuous one, I do not see any way in which this teaching can be defended."

Subhuti then said, "O you with the doubting eyes, if virtuous men and women explain the matter as the Buddha has, the profound Wisdom Beyond Discriminatory Thought will, in fact, be Its own defense. If virtuous men and women put forth the matter in this way, they will never be far from the profound Wisdom Beyond Discriminatory Thought. You need to understand that, as long as any being—human or non-human—seeks to be told what It means while acting from a desire to do harm or mischief, that being will ultimately not be able to realize It. O you with the doubting eyes, if your motive is to defend and protect It, you should act in accordance with what has been said here. All bodhisattvas and the Deepest Wisdom That is Beyond Discriminatory Thought are in no way different from the desire to defend and protect That which is like the clear and empty sky."

Understand that to receive this Teaching, keep to It, accurately recite It to others, and explore Its implications is precisely what 'defending and protecting Wisdom' means. To desire to defend and protect It means that you receive the Teaching, keep to It, accurately recite It to others, and so forth.

My former Master, a Buddha of old, once said in verse:

> *My whole being is like the mouth of a bell*
> *suspended in empty space:*
> *It does not ask whether the wind blows east or*
> *west, north or south.*
> *Impartial to all, it sounds the Wisdom for the sake*
> *of others:*

> *"Bong bong bong," says the wind bell, "bong*
> *bong bong."*

This is the sounding of Wisdom, which is the right Transmission of Buddhas and Ancestors. His whole being is this Wisdom, the whole of others is this Wisdom, the whole of oneself is this Wisdom, the whole of east and west, north and south is this Wisdom.

Shakyamuni Buddha then said, "Shariputra,[4] when it comes to the matter of the Wisdom Beyond Discriminatory Thought, all sentient beings, of whatever sort they may be, are to be offered spiritual provisions and respectfully bowed to, each treated as a place where a Buddha dwells. Your exploration of the Wisdom Beyond Discriminatory Thought should be done as though you were making spiritual offerings and respectfully bowing to the Buddha as the Awakened and Revered One.

"And why so? Because the Wisdom Beyond Discriminatory Thought is not something different from the Buddha as the Awakened and Revered One, nor is the Buddha as the Awakened and Revered One something different from what the Wisdom Beyond Discriminatory Thought is. The Wisdom Beyond Discriminatory Thought is, in fact, the Buddha as the Awakened and Revered One, just as the Buddha as the Awakened and Revered One is, in fact, the Wisdom Beyond Discriminatory Thought.

"And how so? Because, Shariputra, all Tathagatas as arhats and Fully Awakened Ones have, without exception, been able to appear in the world by virtue of the Wisdom Beyond Discriminatory Thought. And because, Shariputra, all bodhisattvas, mahasattvas, pratyekabuddhas*, arhats, non-returners, once-returners, and stream-enterers have, without exception, been able to appear in the

---

4.   Shariputra was one of the chief disciples of the Buddha. He was renowned for his spiritual Wisdom.

world by virtue of the Wisdom Beyond Discriminatory Thought.[5] And because, Shariputra, in all the worlds, the ten ways of doing good, the four meditations leading to heavenly states, the four meditative states beyond the world of form, and the five wondrous faculties have, without exception, been able to appear in the world by virtue of the Wisdom Beyond Discriminatory Thought."

Thus it is that the Buddha as the Awakened and Revered One <u>is</u> the Wisdom Beyond Discriminatory Thought: the Wisdom Beyond Discriminatory Thought <u>is</u> all the various thoughts and things. All these various things are as empty space: they are neither born nor do they wholly die, they are not stained nor yet immaculate, increasing not, decreasing not. When this Wisdom Beyond Discriminatory Thought is manifesting before our very eyes, It is the Buddha as the Awakened and Revered One manifesting before our very eyes. Inquire into this; keep it in mind. To make offerings and bow respectfully is, indeed, to look with reverence to, trust in, and faithfully follow the Buddha as the Awakened and Revered One: to look with reverence to, trust in, and faithfully follow Him is to <u>be</u> the Buddha as the Awakened and Revered One.

This was delivered to the monastic assembly at Kannondōri during the summer retreat in the first year of the Tempuku era (1233).

On the twenty-first day of the third lunar month in the second year of the Kangen era (April 29, 1244), this was copied out by Ejō, while in the chief disciple's quarters at Kippō-ji Temple in Echizen Province.

---

5.   These four terms, from arhat through stream-enterers, are the 'four stages of arhathood' and are explained briefly in the Glossary.

3

On the Spiritual Question
as It Manifests Before Your Very Eyes

(Genjō Kōan)

Translator's Introduction: *Genjō Kōan,* composed by Dōgen for a lay disciple, resembles in form and style a type of essay popular in medieval Japan. Highly evocative, often seemingly ambiguous, rich with imagery, resonant in tone, heavily endowed with phrases and sentences based on Chinese syntax, this discourse is akin to a prose poem. In content, however, it is clearly Buddhist in intent. That is, the focus is not on intellectual constructs and logical progressions of thought, but on lived experiences and what our relationship is to them. For instance, his remarks about time are not intended to be studied as if they were part of some philosophical or scientific discourse, but to be viewed as a way of talking about how we experience time while we train upon the path to Buddhahood. This can be seen, for instance, in the opening paragraph of Dōgen's discourse, where the first sentence refers to the span of time which a trainee perceives as a period of 'undergoing training', and the second to the span during which this trainee experiences his 'being enlightened'.

In that period of time when Buddhas give voice to the Teachings on existence in all its variety, there is talk of 'delusion and enlightenment', of 'practice and training', of 'birth', of 'death', of 'Buddhas', of 'ordinary beings'. In that period of time when it is no longer relevant to speak of an 'I' along with its 'whole universe', there is no delusion or enlightenment, no Buddhas or ordinary beings, no being born, no extinction.[1]

Because the path to Buddhahood naturally springs forth from a feeling that there is 'too much' of one thing or 'not enough' of another, there is 'birth and extinction', there is 'delusion and enlightenment', there are 'ordinary beings and Buddhas'. Yet, even though this is the way things are, still, we feel regret at a blossom's falling and we loathe seeing the weeds envelop everything.

To undertake enlightening the whole universe through one's training while carrying the burden of a self is a delusion: to enlighten oneself through training while urging all things onward is an awakening from delusion. To have a great awakening to one's delusion is to be as all Buddhas are: to be greatly deluded within one's enlightenment is to be as ordinary people are. Moreover, there are those folks who realize enlightenment on top of their enlightenment: there are those folks who are deluded within their delusion.

When Buddhas are truly Buddhas, They need not perceive that They Themselves are Buddha. Even so, having awakened to Their Buddha Nature, They will carry along with Themselves Their confirmation of Their Buddha Nature.

Since we are provided with both a body and a mind, we grasp onto the physical forms we see: since we are provided with both a body and a mind, we cling to the sounds we hear. As a consequence, we make ourselves inseparable from all things, yet we are not like some shadowy figure 'lodging' in a mirror or like the moon

---

1.   The opening paragraph of the chapter is an allusion to the two 'states' of 'being engaged with doing one's training' and 'experiencing the realization of Truth'. While someone is consciously engaged in the former, talk employing terms which the intellect can grasp is common and helpful, but when someone is living in the direct experience of one's True Nature, all such terms lose their relevance. Dōgen's statement here and in later, similar passages may suggest that when someone realizes enlightenment, training stops. He clarifies the error of such an interpretation in Discourse 11: On 'Just for the Time Being, Just for a While, for the Whole of Time is the Whole of Existence' *(Uji)*. Prior to delivering the present talk, he had already taken up the question of the relationship between training and enlightenment with his monks in his work, "Rules for Meditation" *(Fukan Zazengi)*, written in 1233.

in water.[2] Whenever we witness what is on the one side, its opposite side will be in darkness.[3]

To learn what the path to Buddhahood is, is to learn what the True Self is. To learn what the True Self is, is to forget about the self. To forget about the self is to become one with the whole universe. To become one with the whole universe is to be shed of 'my body and mind' and 'their bodies and minds'. The traces from this experience of awakening to one's enlightenment will quiet down and cease to show themselves, but it takes quite some time for all outer signs of being awake to disappear.

When someone first begins to search for the Dharma, he is very far from the realm of the Dharma: once he has had the Dharma passed on to him, he will quickly become one who abides in his Original State.[4]

When someone riding in a boat turns his gaze towards the shore, he misjudges the shore to be moving: when he fixes his eye firmly upon the boat, he will recognize that the boat is plowing on. Likewise, should you let your mind and body run riot, going along with what you perceive the world to be, you will make the mistake of thinking that you have a permanently abiding self-nature within your body and mind. If you commit yourself fully to traveling the Way and you then return to that Place within, the reason why there is no personal 'self' within the whole universe will become clear.

A stick of firewood, once reduced to ashes, cannot once again revert to being a stick of firewood. Nevertheless, you should not hold onto the opinion that the ashes are the future of that which the stick was the past. What you need to understand is that, when firewood is persisting in the physical state of being firewood, there will be

---

2. Here, Dōgen uses the image of 'the moon in water' to refer to something that is only a reflection of the actual object; the phrase is not used in the sense of the common Buddhist metaphor for the Buddha Nature reflected in all things.

3. That is, when we are still clinging to things, we do not see the duality inherent within our own thinking and thus we perceive only one side of the duality.

4. Dōgen's point is that not knowing the Dharma impedes one's arriving at Truth. That is, the passing on of the Dharma helps the trainee to realize his Original State, but it does not necessarily cause him to realize It simply upon hearing the Teachings.

a before and there <u>will</u> be an after. Although there is a before and an after, there is a now which is cut off from 'before' and 'after'. While ashes persist in the physical state of being ashes, they will have their 'after' and their 'before'.

After a stick of firewood has turned to ashes, just as it does not once again become firewood, so after someone dies, he does not come back to life again. Even so, as was the customary way the Buddha taught, we do not speak of life <u>becoming</u> death, which is why He spoke of things 'not arising'. The Buddha also passed on through His turning of the Wheel of the Dharma that death does not <u>become</u> life, which is why He spoke of things 'not perishing'. Life is the situation at one time, and death is the situation at another. For example, it is like winter and spring: do not imagine that winter 'becomes' spring, or speak of spring 'becoming' summer.

When someone has spiritually awakened, he resembles the moon's 'residing' in water: the moon does not get wet nor is the water shattered. Although the moon is a great, broad light, it lodges in the tiniest bit of water. The moon at its fullest, as well as the whole of the heavens, lodges within the dewdrop poised on a blade of grass, just as it lodges in any single bit of water. Spiritual awakening does not tear a person asunder; thus, it is like the moon's not making a dent in the water. A person no more impedes his spiritual awakening than a dewdrop impedes the moon in the heavens. The deeper the reflection, the higher the light: how long the period of your spiritual awakening will last depends on how large your drop of water is and how full your moon is seen to be.

When the Truth has not yet completely filled someone's body and mind, he is apt to think that his knowledge of the Dharma is already sufficient. When the Truth sufficiently fills his body and mind, he feels sure that some aspect is still lacking. By way of analogy, when you go out in a boat to the middle of the ocean, beyond the sight of any land or mountain, and look around you, all you see is the vast encircling water. Or, as another might put it, there is nothing to be seen. Be that as it may, this great Ocean is not a vast circle, and how we perceive It does not depend on what direction we look in. It is simply that we cannot exhaust what the rest of this Ocean's nature is, though some have likened it to a dragon's splendid palace or its jeweled necklace. Although this Ocean extends as far as our eye can see, after a while It will seem to be simply 'a vast encircling'—indeed, even the whole universe will seem to be just the same.

Whether we are caught up in the dust of the world or have removed ourselves from it, we are involved with many doings, yet we only realize what our eyes can see through practicing meditation and studying the Way, for we are limited by what we can see and comprehend at the present moment. Taking our spiritual tradition's viewpoint of the universe as your model, you will realize that, apart from appearing angular or round, the remaining attributes of the ocean and the mountains are vast and limitless, and that the world exists on all sides of us. But it is not only as if It were just on all sides. You must realize that It is what is beneath your very feet and within every drop of water.

A fish in the ocean, wherever it swims, finds the water limitless; a bird in the sky, wherever it flies, finds the air unbounded. Nevertheless, fish and birds, from the very beginning, have always been one, respectively, with the water and the sky. To put it simply, when their need is great, their use is great; when their need is small, their use is small. Acting in this manner, they never fail to make the fullest use of their environs at all times, nor do they ever reject what they may find there. Even so, if a bird is pulled out of the air, in short order it will perish; if a fish is pulled out of the water, it will quickly die. You must have realized by now that 'the water' signifies 'life', just as 'the sky' signifies 'life'. 'A bird' refers to 'a life', just as 'a fish' refers to 'a life'. 'Being alive' should be taken to mean 'the bird', as well as 'the fish'. Moreover, this should be taken one step further, since the situation is no different for spiritual practice and realization, or with the flow of life and the life in that flow. Nevertheless, after someone has thoroughly explored what 'water' is and what 'sky' is, if 'the bird' or 'the fish' should remain so that they stand in contrast to 'water' or 'sky', then he will not find his way in either Ocean or in Space: he will not arrive at the Place.

When you arrive at this Place, you will have been spiritually questioning what is before your very eyes by traveling the Way of the Buddhas and Ancestors. When you locate the path you have been following, you will discover that it is the spiritual question that has been before your very eyes as you have traveled the Way. This path and this Place are neither large nor small, neither 'self' nor 'other', nor something from the past, nor something revealed in the now: It is just as It is. Thus, when someone spiritually practices and realizes the Way of the Buddhas, it is a matter of his having received some Teaching and penetrated into that Teaching, a matter of his having received some sentence of instruction and put into practice what that sentence says. Here is where the Place is. Accordingly, as we penetrate deeper and deeper into the Way, our spiritual surroundings, which we should have known, we clearly do not know, but because we are living together with our ever-deepening investigation of Buddha Dharma and training with It, we have what we need.

To be sure, having once realized the Place, you must not analyze It in order to understand It through discriminatory thought and, thereby, reduce It to fit your own opinions. When you have bored through to certainty, It all at once manifests before your very eyes, yet That which is the most intimate will not necessarily take some visible form. 'Manifesting before your very eyes' may or may not have a literal meaning.

Meditation Master Mayoku Hōtetsu, one summer day, sat fanning himself when a monk came up to him and said, "It is said that the nature of the wind always abides and that there is no place where it does not circulate, so why does my reverend monk fan himself?"

The Master replied, "You are merely aware that the Nature of the Wind always abides, but you have not yet grasped the principle that there is no place where It is not present and active."

When the monk then asked, "What is this underlying principle of Its being universally present?" the Master simply continued to fan himself. The monk respectfully bowed to the Master.

Unequivocal and genuine experiences of the Buddha's Dharma, which is the living Path of the genuine Transmission, are just like this. Since It always abides, the Master did not need to use a fan; yet, even when it is not used, the Sound of the Wind—that is, the voicing of the Dharma—can be heard. Not to know That which is ever-abiding is not to know the Nature of the Wind. Because the Nature of the Wind is always abiding, the winds of training for our Buddhist family bring about the manifesting before one's very eyes of That which is the True Gold of the Great Earth, and bring to maturity the nourishing waters of the Greatest River.

This was written around mid-autumn—that is, the fifteenth day of the eighth lunar month—in the first year of the Tempuku era (September 20, 1233), and given to my lay disciple Yanagi Kōshū of Kyūshū.

Included in 1252.

4

On 'The One Bright Pearl'

(Ikka Myōju)

Translator's Introduction: *Ikka Myōju* follows a form that Dōgen later uses in many of his discourses of the *Shōbōgenzō*. Namely, he relates, often in his own words, one of the classic kōan stories found in Chinese Zen literature. During the telling, he inserts his own commentary to clarify or underscore points which are relevant to monastic training and perspectives.

In this world of ours, there once was a Great Master named Sōitsu, who lived in the monastery on Gensha Mountain in Fukien Province, in the great kingdom of China. His religious name was Shibi and his family name was Sha. While still in lay life, he was fond of fishing and would sail his boat out on the Nant'ai River, as was the habit with all sorts of fishermen. However, he had not the slightest hint that the Golden Fish would, of Its own accord, leap up into his boat, without Its even being hooked.

Near the beginning of the Chinese Kan-t'ong era of the T'ang dynasty (ca. 865), he suddenly aspired to leave the dust of secular life behind him; so, in his thirtieth year, he abandoned his boat so as to dwell on a mountain.[1] Having awakened to the ceaseless fluctuations of the floating world, he had come to recognize the great worth of the Buddha's Way. In time, he went to Seppō Mountain to seek spiritual instruction under Great Master Seppō Shinkaku and to practice the Way day and night.

One day, with his travel bag upon his back, he set out from the mountain top, intending to deepen his practice by studying with other Masters elsewhere. Just as he was climbing down, he stubbed his toe on a rock, and it began to bleed and smart terribly. Suddenly he had a deep realization.

---

1. 'To dwell on a mountain' is a common Buddhist metaphor for entering monastic life and doing one's meditation as part of that life. 'Abandoning his boat' refers not only to Shibi's giving up his attachment to a beloved object in his lay life but also to his giving up his simply drifting along on the river of life.

44

Thereupon, he said, "This body has no independent existence, so where is the pain coming from?" He then returned to Seppō and told him what had happened.

Seppō asked him, "Is this Shibi the Austere Monk?"

Shibi responded, "I have never dared to deceive anyone about that!"

Delighted by this response, Seppō said, "Who could fail to cherish this response? Who could have expressed the Matter* more fully?"

On another occasion, Seppō called out to him, "O Shibi, my austere monk, why haven't you gone out on a pilgrimage to seek a Master to train with?"

When Shibi answered, "Bodhidharma did not come east to China for that, nor did the Second Ancestor go west to India for that!" Seppō highly praised what he had said.

Shibi had been devoted to fishing for so much of his life that he had never set eyes on the voluminous body of Buddhist Scriptures and spiritual writings, even in his dreams. Nevertheless, when he put the depth of his resolve to realize the Truth above all else, a spirit of determination emerged, which surpassed that of the other monks around him. Seppō realized that Shibi excelled all others within the assembly and praised him as towering above Seppō's other disciples.

For his robe, Shibi used a coarse hemp cloth, and, since he had no other change of clothing, it was filled with hundreds of patches. Against his skin, he wore an undergarment made from paper, and for a lining between the two, he used mugwort leaves kneaded until they were pliant. Apart from working under Seppō, he did not seek out any other Master to train with. Even though he kept to just one Master, he

---

* See Glossary.

certainly found within himself the spiritual strength to become the heir to his Master's Dharma.[2]

In time, he realized the Way and, afterwards, in pointing It out to people, he would say, "The whole universe throughout all its ten directions is the One Bright Pearl."

One time a monk inquired of him, "Reverend Monk, I have heard you say that the whole universe throughout all its ten directions is one bright pearl. How am I, as a trainee, to understand the meaning of this?"

Shibi answered, "Since the whole universe throughout all its ten directions is the One Bright Pearl, what use is there in trying to understand this with the intellect?"

However, the next day the Master asked this monk, "The whole universe throughout all its ten directions is the One Bright Pearl, so what do you think this means?"

The monk responded, "Since the whole universe throughout all its ten directions is the one bright pearl, what use is there in my trying to understand this with my intellect?"

Shibi replied, "It is indeed clear to me that, even though you are blindly looking into the demon's cave within the pitch black mountains of ignorance, you are doing your training."

Shibi was the first to voice the statement, "The whole universe throughout all its ten directions is the One Bright Pearl." Its basic idea is that the whole universe throughout all its ten directions is not to be thought of as vast and grand or minute and insignificant, nor as made up of angles and curves, nor as the center or core of

---

2.   Since making pilgrimages to spiritually call on other Zen Masters was still a widespread tradition among Chinese Zen trainees of his day, Dōgen is pointing out that this is not an essential practice, and that what is truly essential is for each trainee to find within himself the spiritual strength to be a Dharma heir of their Master.

something else, nor does it act like some lively fish darting about in a sea of space or like dewdrops brightly whirling in the wind. Moreover, because it is not something that was born and will die, not something that is coming or going, it is being born <u>and</u> dying, coming <u>and</u> going all the time. Because of its being just what it is, it is from <u>here</u> that the days of yore have forever departed and from <u>here</u> that the present arises. By thoroughly doing one's training, who will say, once he has looked deeply, that the universe is just something fluttering about. Or who will say, once he has fully investigated the matter, that the universe is merely a motionless thing?

In speaking of 'throughout all its ten directions', Shibi was referring to our ceaselessly creating a 'self' by chasing after things or creating 'things' through our pursuit of a self. In response to a disciple's statement, "When we give rise to delusory feelings, we alienate ourselves from Wisdom," Shibi affirmed that there was such a separation by a turn of his head or a change of expression on his face. This was his hitting the nail on the head through word or gesture; it was the trainee presenting his understanding and the Master agreeing with it. Because we create 'things' through the pursuit of a self, the universe is ever restless throughout all its ten directions, unceasing in its arising, but since this causal principle is one that exists prior to the arising of anything, its operation is beyond our intellect to control.

This 'One Pearl' is still not Its name, but It can be expressed so, and this has come to be regarded as Its name. The 'One Pearl' is what refers directly to That which is beyond the measurement of years, for in Its extending endlessly over the past, It also extends over the present and into the future. Even though we have a body and mind at this very moment, they are the Bright Pearl. They are not some vegetation sprouting up here or there, nor are they 'mountains and rivers that arise from a duality like that of Heaven and Earth'. They <u>are</u> the Bright Pearl.

By his question, "How am I, as a trainee, to understand the meaning of this?" the monk seems to be operating from his delusory karmic* consciousness, yet, as a manifestation of the functioning of That Which Is Reality, this consciousness <u>is</u> the Absolute Principle of Reality. Further, you need a foot of water to make a one-foot wave rise up, which is to say that a ten-foot high pearl will give off a ten-foot high light.

Shibi's way of stating this was to say, "Since the whole universe throughout all its ten directions is the One Bright Pearl, what use is there in trying to understand this with the intellect?" This saying is the way of speaking which Buddhas inherit from Buddhas, Ancestors inherit from Ancestors, and Shibi inherited from Shibi. Even if you were to try to evade being Their heir to this way of speaking, there is ultimately no place where you can go to completely evade It. Even were you able to evade the obvious for a while, sooner or later there will be some remark that will occasion Its manifesting before your very eyes.

However, the next day the Master asked this monk, "The whole universe throughout all its ten directions is the One Bright Pearl, so what do you think this means?"

On the previous day Shibi had given voice to the Dharma of Certainty; now he was giving voice to the Dharma of Uncertainty. By voicing the Dharma of Uncertainty on this day, he was saying just the reverse of what he had said the previous day, as he smiled and nodded his head approvingly.

The monk, parroting Shibi, responded, "Since the whole universe throughout all its ten directions is the one bright pearl, what use is there in my trying to understand this with my intellect?"

One could say that the monk was riding the robber's own horse in pursuit of the robber. Shibi has taken a completely different approach, whereby the Old Buddha explains the Matter for you. Just turn your light around and return to That which shines within, for how much use is there in trying to understand This through the intellect? When someone gives voice to It, it will be a matter of 'seven sweet dumplings and five savory dumplings';[3] even so, it will be instructive guidance that is 'south of the

---

3. Sweet dumplings are associated with Southern Chinese cuisine, and savory ones with the cuisine of the Northern Chinese. Like many other references to food in Zen texts, 'dumplings' serves as a metaphor for the Dharma, which spiritually nourishes the trainee. Dōgen's point is that even though the flavor and size of the servings of Dharma may differ among Buddhists because of such things as local customs and habits, the Dharma Itself is fundamentally the same in Its capacity to sustain those who ingest It.

Hsiang River and north of the Liu', that is, two different ways of designating the same area.

> Shibi said, "It is certainly clear to me that, even though you are blindly looking into the demon's cave within the pitch black mountains of ignorance, you <u>are</u> doing your training."

You must realize that the faces of the sun and the moon have never yet at any time changed places. The face of the sun always rises as the sun's face; the face of the moon always rises as the moon's face. Therefore, even if we say that the season right now is mid-summer, we should not say that it is our Original Nature that is sweltering. This is why this Bright Pearl exists not only without a beginning but also without an end. It is 'One Bright Pearl as the whole universe throughout all its ten directions': It is not said to be two or three. Your whole being <u>is</u> your pair of eyes of the True Dharma; your whole being <u>is</u> the embodiment of Truth; your whole being <u>is</u> a single line of Scripture; your whole being <u>is</u> luminosity; your whole being <u>is</u> your whole heart and mind. When your whole being exists, your whole being has no impediments: it is perfect in its completeness and is ever-turning, like the rumbling on of cart wheels. Because the merit of the One Bright Pearl takes some 'visible' form like those stated above, Avalokiteshvara[*] and Maitreya[*] exist right now, seeing Its forms and hearing Its sounds. And there are old Buddhas and there will be new Buddhas who manifest in bodily form in order to give voice to the Dharma.

When the time is right, you will find the Dharma enfolded in empty space or enfolded within the lining of that which clothes you; or you will find It stored in the folds of the dragon's chin or stored in the folds of the king's headdress, and all are the One Bright Pearl that is the universe throughout all the ten directions. Keeping It enfolded beneath your robes is proper deportment: do not talk about displaying It on the outside. Enfolding It in your headdress or underneath your chin is proper deportment: do not imitate those who would playfully display It upon their headdresses or around their necks. Whenever you are drunk on delusion, there will be a Close Friend who will present you with this Jewel, and you must, without fail, present this Jewel to your Close Friend. Come a time when you take to hanging the

Jewel around your own neck, you are, beyond doubt, drunk with delusion. Because this is the way things are, the world in its entirety is the One Bright Pearl.

This is why, even though it seems that, on the surface, things are either fluctuating or still, everything is the Bright Pearl. To know that this is precisely how the Jewel is, is what the Bright Pearl is. In this manner we can perceive the sounds and forms of the Bright Pearl. Because this is the way things can be, even though you may be uncertain about whether or not something is the Bright Pearl, you should have no doubt about whether or not there is the Jewel. Whether you actively pursue your doubts, cling to them, or let them go, they are simply momentary observations of little significance, fleeting images of small weight.

Do we not cherish the Bright Pearl with Its infinite variety of shades and hues like this? Its multifaceted, brilliantly hued sparkling is the merit of the universe throughout all its ten quarters; who can take this from you by force? After all, there is no one in any of the market places of this world who throws away a roof tile, so do not worry about which of the six worlds* of existence you will fall into due to causality.[4] Never hidden, It is, from the first, synonymous with always doing one's training, and doing it consistently as well as thoroughly. The Bright Pearl is your Original Face: the Bright Pearl is your very Eye in all Its brightness.

Nevertheless, neither you nor I know precisely what this Bright Pearl is and precisely what It is not, but hundreds of notions and opinions about this subject all too obviously have become associated with 'food for thought'. Now, through Shibi's voicing of the Dharma, we have learned and had clarified for us the point that what appears as our body and mind is, and always has been, the Bright Pearl. Hence, the conscious mind is not what we are, so who is it that arises and passes away? Why worry yourself over whether or not something is the Bright Pearl? Even if you are perplexed as you grope along, do not think that this is not the Bright Pearl. Since there is no action or thought that can be generated that is not of the Bright Pearl, even your going back and forth, in and out of the demon's cave within the black mountains is nothing other than the One Bright Pearl.

---

4.   That is, just as those in the marketplace can recognize the value of a mere roof tile, so even someone's being reborn in some hell, for instance, will have its spiritual value.

This was delivered to the monks at Kannondōri in Kōshōhōrin-ji Temple, Uji Prefecture, Yamashiro Province, on the eighteenth day of the fourth lunar month in the fourth year of the Katei era (June 2, 1238).

It was transcribed by me, while in my quarters in Kippō-ji Temple, Shibi Manor, Yoshida County, Echizen Province, on the twenty-third day of the seventh lunar month in the first year of the Kangen era (August 10, 1243).

The monk Ejō,
Abbot's Assistant

5

On Conduct Appropriate
for the Auxiliary Cloud Hall

(Jūundō-shiki)

Translator's Introduction: In this discourse, Dōgen presents an outline of how trainees should behave in the auxiliary Meditation Hall, which was annexed to the main Monks' Hall. This newly built hall would have been used primarily by novice monks. The tone of the original is somewhat informal, for the text was written not in Chinese, which was the customary language used for setting down monastic regulations, but in colloquial Japanese. In the discourse, Dōgen is not putting forth a series of impersonal, formalized rules and regulations so much as giving helpful instructions to those new to the etiquette of Buddhist monastic life, particularly as it would have been carried out in the Chinese monastery where Dōgen had trained. Some points which may strike a present-day reader as obvious were apparently not so obvious for Zen trainees in Dōgen's day.

Those who earnestly desire to seek the Way and to cast off fame and gain may enter: those who are aimless and lack sincerity should not. Should you have entered for the wrong reasons, once you have determined that you have made a mistake, you should depart. Understand that when the desire to seek the Way arises in your heart, you are someone who has, then and there, discarded fame and gain. In the billions of worlds that comprise the universe, it is quite rare to be affiliated with the rightful heirs of the Buddha. Even though our country, from ancient times until now, has treated this connection with Buddhism as something fundamental to it and has been keenly concerned for what the future may hold, what is right now before you should be what you focus on.

The community in the Hall should be in accord with one another, like milk mixing with water, and should encourage each other in practicing the Way. Though we are now, for a short while, as guest and host,[1] later we will forever be Ancestors of the Buddha. Because this is so, do not lose sight of your sincere belief that each and

---

1. 'Guest' refers to a Meditation Hall trainee and 'host' to the monk responsible for overseeing his or her training.

every one of you has encountered something which is hard to encounter, and practices something which is difficult to practice. This is called the true heart of the Buddha's Teachings: without doubt you <u>will</u> become a Buddha; you <u>will</u> become an Ancestor. You have already left your home and departed from your native village. You have asked to be as clouds: you have asked to be as water.[2] In aiding yourself, you aid the Way. And, as a consequence, the gratitude this community has for you surpasses even that which we have for our parents. Father and mother are your intimates for only a short while within the passage of birth and death: this community will be together with you on the Buddha's Path at all times.

You should not become fond of going outside the monastery. <u>Once</u> a month, for instance, is tolerable for something essential. Those of old lived on remote mountains and trained in isolated forests; not only was their involvement with worldly affairs rare, they also severed all their other worldly ties. You should train yourself in an attitude which conceals Its light and covers Its traces, for now is the time to train as though your hair were on fire. Were you to waste this time by surrounding yourself with worldly entanglements, how lamentable that would be! Alas, the impermanent cannot be relied on, for who knows on what blade of roadside grass our dew-like life will fall?

Whilst in the Hall, you should not read books, even though it may be a book on meditation, nor should you bring in personal correspondence. Since it is a Meditation Hall, you should pursue the Truth through diligently practicing the Way and relegate to the well-lit Monks' Common Room the illumining of your mind through study of the ancient writings on the Teachings. Do not waste even a moment, for you should devote yourself exclusively to your training.

You should keep the monk in charge of the Meditation Hall informed of what you are up to, day and night. Do not indulge in diversions as it pleases you to do, for this will take its toll on the monastic discipline of the community. Though we know

---

2.　A common Japanese term for one who has entered monastic life is *unsui*, 'clouds and water', a metaphor for one who asks for no fixed abode and desires to live free of preconceptions and entanglements.

not when this life will end, it <u>will</u> end. Doubtless, it <u>will</u> later be regretted, should you end your life amidst idle amusements.

You should not lend support to the misconduct of others, nor should you look upon the human errors of others with a hateful heart. There is an old saying, "Not to see the faults of others is what is natural for me." Also, you should not make comparisons of the faults of one trainee with those of another, but should just put into practice your own virtues. Even though the Buddha had brought His own faults under control, He had no feeling of loathing for those who had not.

You should, by all means, let the monk in charge of the Meditation Hall know what you are going to do <u>before</u> doing it, no matter whether it is an important or a small undertaking. Someone who is given to doing things without mentioning them to the Meditation Hall Monk should depart. When the courtesies between guest and host become confused, it is difficult for the trainee to distinguish what is true from what is merely superficial.

When in the Hall or in its vicinity, you should not speak in a loud voice or loiter about, conversing. And the monk in charge of the Meditation Hall will see to this.

You should not do kinhin[3] in the Hall to keep yourself awake.

You should not hold onto your rosary whilst in the Hall, nor should you recite the names of the Buddhas or chant Scriptures aloud in the Hall on your own. But it is all right to do so were a donor to request a Scriptural recitation for a ceremony.

You should not blow your nose noisily or loudly cough up phlegm whilst in the Hall. You should not laugh aloud. You should grieve that the proper ways have not yet fully permeated your training. You should regret that time, in unseen ways, is depriving you of your life of training in the Way. Thereby, you may naturally have a feeling of being a fish in a small puddle.[4]

---

3. A form of walking meditation which all monks do together between periods of seated meditation, but which is not to be done individually during general meditation periods or when other monks are sleeping.

4. That is, be aware of how limited one's life really is.

When together in the Hall with the community, you should not wear richly brocaded robes, but just a simple one made from waste cloth. From ancient times, those who awakened to the Way all dressed like this.

You should not enter the Hall in a drunken state. Should you make such a mistake out of a lack of mindfulness, you should bow down and do sange.[5] Also, you should not bring rice wine in with you, nor should you enter the Hall reeking of strong pickles.

If two monks start quarreling, both should retire to the Common Room because they are not only hindering their own practice, they are also disturbing the practice of others. Someone who sees a quarrel breaking out and does not stop it is just as much at fault.

All who refuse to involve themselves in keeping these instructions will be expelled from the Hall.[6] Those who are amused by, or are in sympathy with, such behavior by trainees are also at fault.

You should not invite visiting monks or laity into the Hall and thereby disturb those trainees already assembled there. When conversing with a privileged guest within even the vicinity of the Hall, you should not speak in a loud voice, to say nothing of bragging about yourself as a trainee out of greed for the patron's offerings.

Those with a long-standing determination to train and, obviously, those who are sincerely on a pilgrimage may enter, but even at such a time, you should not fail to let the monk in charge of the Meditation Hall know of their presence.

Seated meditation should be done as it is done in the Monks' Hall. Never neglect to attend morning meditation and services, or evening instruction periods.

---

5.   'To do sange' is to recognize that what one has done is counter to the Precepts and to ensure that it is accompanied by true remorse and repentance.

6.   Having been deprived of a place to sleep and eat within the monastery, the monk may then choose either to leave the monastery or to turn his heart around (that is, do 'sange') by giving up his intransigence and asking to be reinstated.

In accordance with monastic etiquette, someone who spills the contents of his alms bowl onto the floor during the morning or noon meal should 'see to the oil'.[7]

Beyond question, you should adhere to the Precepts as set down by the Buddhas and Ancestors. You should impress the monastery's regulations into your bones and engrave them onto your heart.

You should pray that you may live your life tranquilly and do your training in the Way free of attachment to any preconceptions.

The preceding items are the body and mind of former Buddhas: follow them with reverence.

The twenty-fifth day of the fourth lunar month in the first year of the En'ō era (May 29, 1239).

---

7.   A standard practice for someone committing a light breach of monastic etiquette through carelessness, in which the monk is personally and/or financially responsible for seeing that the oil lamp in front of the Hall's main statue is provided with sufficient fuel, so that it may keep burning over the next twenty-four hours.

6

On 'Your Very Mind Is Buddha'

(Soku Shin Ze Butsu)

Translator's Introduction: In this discourse, Dōgen makes clear that the saying "Your very mind is Buddha" is to be understood in a particular way: it is a remark addressed to one who has already given rise to the intention to train and realize Buddhahood. Those who have not yet done so are apt to think of 'mind' as referring to intellective, perceptual, and cognitive functions, which are viewed as constituting a personal 'self', a misconception akin to the Shrenikan view that such functions constitute an immortal soul. Because of this danger, Dōgen gives a detailed presentation of this Shrenikan view, which he immediately refutes through quoting the kōan story alluded to in Discourse 1: A Discourse on Doing One's Utmost in Practicing the Way of the Buddhas *(Bendōwa)*. He then goes on to show how the meaning of the saying "Your very mind is Buddha" can be explored more deeply and what some of its implications are.

What the Buddhas and Ancestors, without exception, have traditionally maintained and entrusted to us is, simply, that this very mind of ours is Buddha. Even so, the statement "Your very mind is Buddha" did not come from India, but was first heard in China. Many trainees have misunderstood what it means, but have failed to explore their misunderstanding to their advantage. Because many have not seen their misunderstanding through to its obviously erroneous conclusion, they have wandered off onto non-Buddhist paths.

Hearing talk of 'your very mind', those befuddled by doubts speculate that the intellective, cognitive, and perceptual functions of sentient beings are synonymous with 'the Mind of enlightenment before someone has awakened to It', and accordingly fancy themselves to be a Buddha. This is due to their never having encountered a genuine Teacher of Buddhism.[1]

---

1. That is, had they met such a Teacher, he would never have permitted such folly. The original text carries no implication that anyone who encounters a genuine Teacher of Buddhism will automatically and instantaneously be freed from all delusions, or that, if a

The sort of non-Buddhist view I am referring to existed in India under the name of the Shrenikan view. The following is in accord with that viewpoint:

A Great Principle resides in our present body whose presence can readily be discerned. Specifically, it discriminates between suffering and pleasure, knows what is cold or hot, and perceives the misery of pain and the itch of desire. It is not limited by any physical thing or affected by any surrounding conditions. Although physical things come and go, and conditions arise and disappear, this Spiritual Intelligence forever exists, unchanging.

This Spiritual Intelligence permeates all living beings far and wide. The mundane and the saintly alike harbor this spirit, without any difference between them. Even though the illusory flowerings of false teachings may exist in humans temporarily, once they become aware of this wise discernment through its accord with a particular thought, physical 'things' fall away and conditions disappear; thereupon, the Spiritual Intelligence alone remains in its original nature, ever clear and bright. Even though the bodily aspect ultimately breaks down, the Spiritual Intelligence comes out intact, just as when a house is being completely destroyed by a fire, the householder emerges and escapes.

This Intelligence, which is clear in its functions yet whose substance is mysterious and beyond our grasp, is referred to as the nature of those who are spiritually awakened and wise. We also call it 'Buddha', as well as 'enlightenment'. We ourselves, as well as all others, are equally endowed with it; the deluded and the enlightened are both permeated with it. Whatever myriad things and conditions may exist, this Spiritual Intelligence is neither linked to these conditions nor the same as these things, but abides forever throughout the eons. Since all conditions existing in the present are

---

disciple is deluded, it is inevitably because his or her teacher is inadequate. Even the Buddha could not help those who would not take His Teachings to heart.

dependent on the Spiritual Intelligence, they can be regarded as being real. Because they are innately conditioned to arise, they actually exist. Even so, they do not abide forever, as does the Spiritual Intelligence, since they only exist for a while before they disappear.

Because this Intelligence understands things in mysterious ways, without depending on light or darkness, it is called 'that which knows what the spirit is'. It is also referred to as 'the True Self', 'the Source of Enlightenment', 'One's Original Nature', and 'One's Fundamental Substance'. One who awakens to this Original Nature is said to return to the Ever-abiding and is called a Mahasattva, that is, 'a Great Being who has returned to the True'. After this, he does not transmigrate through the cycle of birth and death, but comes to realize the non-arising, non-perishing 'Ocean of his Original Nature', and enters therein.

Apart from this Intelligence, there is no reality or truth. To the extent that someone is unaware of this Nature of his, the three temporal worlds and the six worlds[*] of existence compete to arise.

Such is the view of the non-Buddhist Shrenikans.

The fully awakened Chinese National Teacher Echū of the great T'ang dynasty once asked a monk, "Where do you come from?"

The monk replied, "I come from the South."

The Master asked, "Do you have good spiritual friends in the South?"

The monk replied, "We have quite a few."

The Master asked, "What do they point out to people?"

---

[*]   See Glossary.

The monk said, "Spiritual friends there point out to trainees, right from the start, that their own minds are Buddha. 'Buddha' means 'enlightenment', and we are all, right now, fully equipped with a Nature that experiences and knows through what It sees and hears. This Nature is innately good, and has the capacity to raise the eyebrows and make the eyes twinkle. Since It exists throughout the whole body, when It rustles through the head, the head 'knows', and when It rustles through the foot, the foot 'knows'. This is why it is called samyak-sambuddha, 'the One Who Knows Everything Perfectly'. No other Buddha exists apart from this. This body of ours experiences birth and extinction, but the Nature of our mind, from time without beginning, has never yet arisen or perished. The body's arising and perishing is like a dragon's changing his bones for lighter ones,[2] a snake's shedding its skin, or someone moving from a former residence—that is, the physical aspect is transient, but this Nature is permanent. This is roughly what is taught in the South."

The Master said, "If this is so, then there is no difference between their teaching and the non-Buddhist view of the Shrenikans. The latter view states that there is a sort of 'Divine Nature' in this body of ours, which has the capacity to know pain and itch, and that, when the body disintegrates, this divine aspect departs from it, like a householder fleeing when his house is on fire—the dwelling is impermanent whilst its householder is forever. Were the matter like this, there would be no way, upon examination, to distinguish right from wrong, so how can we accept it as correct?

"When I used to go on pilgrimages, I would often encounter this sort of thing. In recent times it has flourished even more widely. These 'good friends' would gather together an

---

2.   A reference to the Chinese folk belief that fossil bones belonged to dragons who had left them behind in order to live and fly about in the sky.

assembly of some three to five hundred and, seeing stars in their listeners' eyes, would say that this is our Buddhist tradition's Teachings in the South. Taking up the Sixth Ancestor's *Platform Scripture*, they would alter what It says by garnishing It with vulgar and rude comments and stories, whilst adulterating or deleting the wise and saintly intentions of the Ancestor, thereby deluding and confusing their followers. How can this be considered the uttering of our Teachings? How painful! It will be the death of our tradition. Were we intended to take our perceptual and cognitive functions to be our Buddha Nature, Vimalakirti[*] would certainly not have said that the Dharma is apart from our perceptual and cognitive functions, and that, when we are occupied with these functions, then this is being engaged in perceiving and cognizing, and is not a seeking of the Dharma."

The National Teacher was a leading disciple of the former Buddha Daikan Enō and was the outstanding good spiritual friend of celestial and human beings. Grasping the spiritual import of what the National Teacher has pointed out, you should take it as the model for your training and study. When you detect the discriminatory view of the non-Buddhist Shrenikans, do not follow it.

In more recent times, of all our colleagues who are Abbots or Masters in the various monasteries of Great Sung China, none compares with the National Teacher. From ancient times, a spiritual friend who could equal the National Teacher has still not entered this world. And yet, ordinary, worldly people mistakenly hold the opinion that Zen Masters like Rinzai and Tokusan are the equals of the National Teacher. Fellows who hold such a view are all too many. These people, alas, are not clear-eyed teachers.

The saying "Your very mind <u>is</u> Buddha," which Buddhas and Ancestors have assured us is so, is something not even dreamed of by non-Buddhists or by followers of the two Lesser Courses.[*] Only Buddhas and Ancestors—and They alone—pass on that one's mind is Buddha, and only They experience its meaning to the fullest.

Having heard of it, They have put it into practice and have come to realize it for Themselves.

The term Buddha implies that the hundreds of karmic seedlings from defiling passions have been weeded out and discarded. However, I am not speaking of this term as it is applied to a sixteen-foot tall golden statue.

The term *soku* ('that which is immediate') refers to one's spiritual question before one deals with what is right before one's eyes, and before one learns to avoid the blunders that may arise from not dealing with that question.

The term *ze* ('is') refers to the three temporal worlds of 'was', 'is', and 'will be', from which there is no retreating or escaping, and which are not merely a figment of the mind.

The term *shin* ('mind') implies the walls and fences of discernment before they have been mudded fast with mortar, and before one has fabricated anything or added fixtures.

We may thoroughly examine these terms in the form, for instance, of "Your very mind is Buddha," or in the form of "Your mind, at this very moment, is Buddha," or "Buddha, right now, is your mind," or "Your very mind is what 'Buddha' is," or "This 'Buddha' is your mind right now." To thoroughly explore the meaning in this manner is precisely an instance of one's very mind being Buddha. In promoting the meaning, the Ancestors passed it on in a straightforward manner as "Your very mind is Buddha," and it has come down to us today, accurately transmitted in this form.

The so-called 'mind which has been correctly Transmitted' refers to the whole mind being synonymous with 'all thoughts and things', and all thoughts and things are what constitute 'the whole mind'. This is why someone in the past once said, "When a person fully realizes what his mind really is, not an inch of solid ground will exist upon the earth." You must understand that when you fully realize what your mind is, the whole canopy of the heavens is knocked down and the spinning earth is completely torn asunder. On the other hand, when you come to see what your mind really is, the earth becomes three inches thicker.

An ancient one of great virtue once said, "And just what is this wondrously pure, bright mind? It is the great earth with its mountains and rivers, along with the sun, the moon, and all the stars."

Now you know clearly: what is called 'mind' is the great earth with its mountains and rivers; it is the sun, the moon, and the stars. Even so, when you take what is being expressed here one step further, something is lacking; when you draw back from what it is saying, something has gone too far. The mind that is the great earth with its mountains and rivers is simply the great earth with its mountains and rivers: there are no surging waves nor is there any wind-driven spindrift to disturb or upset it. The mind that is sun, moon, and stars is simply sun, moon, and stars: there is no fog nor is there any mist to obscure its clarity. The mind that is the coming and going of birth and death is simply the coming and going of birth and death: there is no 'being deluded' nor is there any 'realizing enlightenment'. The mind that is the tiles* and stones for walls and fences is simply the tiles and stones for walls and fences: there is no mud nor is there any water to make a binding mortar. The mind that is the four elements* and the five skandhas* is simply the four elements and the five skandhas: there are no wild horses of unbridled willfulness nor any monkeys with insatiable desires. The mind that is the Master's Dharma seat and his ceremonial hossu* is simply the Master's seat and hossu: there is no bamboo whose joints block clear passage nor is there any wood twisted up with knots. Since this is the way things are, "Your very mind is Buddha" means, pure and simply, that your very mind is Buddha; all Buddhas are, pure and simply, all Buddhas.

Thus, "Your very mind is Buddha" refers to all Buddhas, that is, to Those who have given rise to the intention to realize Buddhahood by practicing and training until They awaken to Their enlightenment and realize nirvana. Those who have not given rise to the intention to realize Buddhahood by practicing and training until they awaken to their enlightenment and realize nirvana are not those whose very mind is Buddha. Even if, for a fraction of an instant, you give rise to the intention to train and realize the Truth for yourself, your very mind will be Buddha. Even if, for the tiniest, imperceptible moment, you give rise to the intention to train and realize the Truth for yourself, your very mind will be Buddha. Even if, for immeasurable eons, you give rise to the intention to train and realize the Truth for yourself, your very mind will be Buddha. Even if, for the length of only one single thought, you give rise to the intention to train and realize the Truth for yourself, your very mind will be Buddha. Even if, half-heartedly, you give rise to the intention to train and realize the Truth for yourself, your very mind will be Buddha. Nevertheless, were you to say of someone who is taking ever so long to train to become a Buddha that his mind is not Buddha, you have not yet seen your mind to be Buddha, nor do you yet know what the saying means, nor are you yet truly training in the Way. You have not met a genuine Teacher of Buddhism who knows how to open up your very mind to be Buddha.

The term 'all Buddhas' means Shakyamuni Buddha: Shakyamuni Buddha is synonymous with one's very mind being Buddha. At that very moment when all the Buddhas of past, present, and future have become, do become, and will become Buddha, without fail, They become Shakyamuni Buddha. This is what "Your very mind is Buddha" means.

This was delivered to the monastic assembly at Kannondōri in Kōshōhōrin-ji Temple, Uji County, Yamashiro Province, on the twenty-fifth day of the fifth lunar month in the first year of the En'o era (June 28, 1239).

It was written down by me on the twelfth day of the seventh lunar month in the third year of the Kangen era (August 5, 1245), while in the chaplain's quarters at Daibutsu-ji Temple, Yoshida Prefecture, Echizen Province.

Ejō

7

On Washing Yourself Clean

(Senjō)

Translator's Introduction: On the surface, *Senjō* contains Dōgen's instructions to his monks on the monastic procedures for dealing with the act of relieving nature. On a deeper level, it is a detailed analysis of how a monk is to practice mindfulness at every stage in the process of handling that most physical and mundane of activities, one that humans too often treat with disgust or think of as not having any spiritual relevance. On a deeper level still, it reveals how attending to the mundane can function as a spiritual cleansing.

The tone of the original is difficult to reproduce in English without misleading the reader. Much of it is written in what might be called Japanese cookbook style. That is, the instructions are often expressed as though addressed impersonally. For example, a rather literal rendering of a particular phrase would be "Next, one washes one's hands," which in English cookbook style would appear as "Next, wash your hands." The latter, however, may sound in the present context like an injunction or rigid command, a laying down of the rules. In this translation, I have tried to find a middle path between the rather stilted, impersonal 'one' and the raw command of the imperative, and have therefore chosen the simple instructional style, "Next, you wash your hands." Only on occasion does Dōgen use a form that is herein rendered as "You should," and even more rarely one that is a negative command, "Do not."

In historical terms, Dōgen's instructions represent the most advanced ideas of personal hygiene for his times, even though today some of them might be considered unsanitary. Had he lived in the present, undoubtedly his instructions would take into account the principles of modern-day hygiene. It is quite likely that his views were influenced by his Chinese Master Tendō Nyojō, who, as a novice, had requested to be appointed as Head of Purification (that is, the monk in charge of the lavatories) for his monastery, and he was later allowed to take on this responsibility.

The realization of enlightenment through practice, which the Buddhas and Ancestors have protected and preserved, has been described by Them as 'being freed from stain'.

The Sixth Ancestor Enō once asked his disciple Nangaku Ejō of Kannon-in Temple, "Looking back, do you think that what we do has always been based on realizing enlightenment through practice?"

Nangaku responded, "It is not that realizing enlightenment by means of practice has not existed in the past, but should someone act in a way that is stained, then he will not realize it."

Enō said, "It is this 'being freed from stain' that all Buddhas have preserved in Their hearts and kept in mind. You have done this, as have I, as have our Indian Ancestral Masters."

It says the following in the *Great Scripture on the Three Thousand Forms of Everyday Behavior for Monks,* "Purifying the body refers to cleansing yourself of its excretions and keeping your nails clipped." Therefore, even though our bodies and minds are unstained, there is a method for cleansing the body, which is also a method for cleansing the mind. Not only will it purify body and mind, it will also purify those in our nation and those who train 'under a tree'. Even though no one in our nation has ever yet been sullied by the dust of existence, purifying is what all Buddhas keep in mind. Upon reaching the fruits of Buddhahood, They do not neglect or discontinue Their cleansing. The meaning of this is impossible to fully fathom. Proper decorum is one thing that is meant by it, and realizing the Way through ordination is one form of proper decorum.

A verse in the "Pure Deeds" chapter of the *Avatamsaka Scripture* says:

> *Whilst relieving nature,*
> *By all means pray that all sentient beings*
> *Will eliminate their impurities*
> *By completely ridding themselves of lust, anger, and*
> *delusion.*

> *Whilst washing up afterwards,*
> *By all means pray that all sentient beings*
> *May turn towards the Peerless Way*
> *And leave worldly things behind them.*
>
> *Whilst cleaning off the soil with water,*
> *By all means pray that all sentient beings*
> *Will avail themselves of purifying patience,*
> *That they may, after all, be free from any defilement.*

Water is not necessarily 'fundamentally pure' nor is it 'fundamentally impure': the body is not necessarily 'fundamentally pure' nor is it 'fundamentally impure'—so it is with all things. This does not mean that water is or is not something sentient; it does not mean that the body is or is not something sentient—again, so it is with all things. This is what the World-honored Buddha gave voice to. Even so, it is not water that makes our bodies clean: relying on the Buddha's Dharma and keeping to the Buddha's Dharma is what 'washing yourself clean' really means. This Dharma is the very being and spirit of what the Buddhas and Ancestors have personally and correctly Transmitted; It is the very words and phrases used to describe That which the Buddhas and Ancestors directly experienced; It is the very Light in which the Buddhas and Ancestors clearly abide and to which They hold. In sum, It is an immeasurable, unbounded, meritorious virtue which They make manifest before our very eyes. When, at the right moment, They supply the forms for training body and mind, They fully provide the basic elements of conduct, which are timeless. As a result, what we call 'the mind and body of one who is training' naturally manifests.

You should keep the nails on your ten fingers clipped. Whereas 'ten fingers' is a reference to the fingernails of both your hands, right and left, you should likewise clip your toenails. It says in the Scriptures that we are doing wrong if we let our nails be longer than an eighth of an inch.[1] So, you should not let your nails grow long like non-Buddhist old-timers do, and you should take care to clip your nails. In present-day Sung China, there were those fellows within our monastic family who lacked an eye for the way to train and let their nails grow very long. On some, they were one or two inches long, and on some, even as long as three or four inches.[2] This is counter to the Teachings and is neither the flesh nor the spirit of the Buddha's Dharma. They acted like this because they did not maintain the customs or practice of the Buddha's family. Among the venerable Elders who have held to the Way, such behavior is not to be found.

Similarly, there were some of my fellow monks who let their hair grow. This is also counter to the Teachings. Do not make the mistake of thinking that this may be in accord with the True Teaching just because some say that monks in a great and powerful country do it.

My former Master, a venerable Buddha, had the following words of instruction for any monks in the Greater Sangha who sported long hair or nails,[3] "It is neither lay folk nor monks who do not understand the practice of our shaving our heads—it is animals. Who among the Buddhas and Ancestors of the past failed to shave Their heads? If any of you fail to grasp why you should shave your head, you are truly an animal through and through." After instructing his community in this way, many of my fellow monks who had not shaved their heads for years did so. Whether giving a Dharma talk in the Meditation Hall or speaking informally to his monks, he would snap his fingers loudly while pointing in rebuke, saying something to the effect of:

---

1. The inch referred to here is about forty percent longer than an English inch. Hence, the recommended length, in Western terms, would be just under three-sixteenths of an inch. Similar computations should be made for later references to lengths in inches or feet.

2. It was a long-established custom in China, particularly among the Confucianist public officials, to let their nails grow as long as possible as a sign that they did not engage in menial labor, which they considered demeaning.

3. 'The Greater Sangha' refers here not only to the monks in Tendō Nyojō's monastery but also to any other monks who might come to visit.

For what reason I know not, you have rashly let your hair and nails grow long. How pitiful that you have let the human body and mind which you have received fall into aimless ways. For the past two or three hundred years, the Way of the Ancestors has been in decline, so that fellows like you are many indeed. Such persons have sometimes become heads of temples, and have even received titles of respect from emperors, whilst making a pretense of spiritually leading others—what a misfortune for both human and celestial beings alike! Now, in all the mountain temples here in China, people with hearts intent on the Way are all disappearing, and those who would gain the Path have long been dying out. Only hooligans remain!

When my Master spoke in this manner, those from various places who had imprudently been given the title of Elder did not grumble about this, nor did they offer any defense either.[4]

You should realize that long hair on a monk is something that the Buddhas and Ancestors remonstrated against and that growing long nails was something that non-Buddhists practiced. The descendants of Buddhas and Ancestors should not take delight in these sorts of practices, which are contrary to the Dharma. You should keep yourself pure in body and mind, and keep yourself clean by seeing that you trim your nails and shave the hair off your head.

Do not neglect to wash after relieving nature. Shariputra once brought about the conversion of a non-Buddhist by means of this Teaching. Although it was not something that the non-Buddhist originally expected, nor was it something that Shariputra had consciously intended, even so, when the forms of dignified behavior

---

4.   The term 'Elder' generally refers to someone who has been a monk for ten years or more.

of the Buddhas and Ancestors are kept before one's eyes, false teachings are spontaneously humbled.[5]

When doing your training under a tree in the forest or out in the open, you will not find a privy already built. So, using water from some convenient valley stream or river, clean yourself off with sand. Since you do not have any ashes at this time to cleanse yourself with, simply use two sets of seven balls of sandy soil. The way to use these fourteen balls is as follows: after having removed your robe, folded it, and put it aside, you take soil that is sandy [rather than dark earth], shape it into balls about the size of a large soybean, and place these atop a stone or some other convenient place, with two rows of seven balls each. Then, provide yourself with some pebbles that can be used for scouring your hands. After that, you relieve yourself. After you have finished relieving yourself, use a wooden or bamboo toilet spatula, or some paper, to clean yourself off. You then go to the edge of the water to wash. Make sure to take three of the balls with you to clean yourself. Put one of the balls in the palm of your hand, add just a little water, mix the ingredients together until their consistency is thinner than mud and quite soupy, and begin by cleaning off your genitals. Then take another sand ball and, preparing it as before, clean off your buttocks. Again, prepare a sand ball as before and, in the same manner, clean off your hands.[6]

After monks began to reside in temple quarters, they constructed a building that they referred to as 'the Eastern Quarters'. Sometimes it was called a water closet

---

5. The reference to Shariputra and the non-Buddhist may be to an incident recorded in the *Code of Behavior for Members of the Greater Sangha*, where a non-Buddhist was converted to Buddhism out of admiration and respect for Shariputra's scrupulous observance of the code of monastic decorum, which the man had observed whilst the monk was on his alms rounds. Shariputra was one of the two chief disciples of Shakyamuni Buddha.

6. Dōgen does not specifically indicate how the remaining eleven balls are to be used, but considering how he uses numbers in other discourses, it is likely that he means, "If you need more than three, well, you have them right at hand."

and at other times a lavatory. It is absolutely essential to have a lavatory in a place where a family of monks resides.

When going to the Eastern Quarters, you should be sure to take a hand towel with you. The way to do this is to fold the hand towel in half and put it over your left shoulder, letting it hang down over the sleeve of your gown. When you have arrived at the Eastern Quarters, you should hang your towel over the clean-clothes pole. Hang it in the same way it was when it was hanging on your shoulder. If you come wearing a nine- or seven-striped kesa,* you should be sure to hang it next to your towel. You should hang it so that it will not fall off. Do not hastily toss it over the pole.

You should be sure to pay particular attention to the name marker. The name marker is for putting your name on the pole. Write your name on a piece of white paper in the shape of a full moon and then align this marker on the rack. We use a name marker so that we will not forget where we have put our robe. When our monks come in numbers, we must be sure not to confuse our place on the rack with that of others.

If a number of monks come and line up at this time, make shashu* and bow in greeting to the others. When bowing in greeting, you need not bow deeply: simply hold your hands in shashu before your chest and bow in recognition of the others. When in the Eastern Quarters, we acknowledge the monks assembled by bowing to them even when we are not in our robes. If your two hands are not occupied or you are not carrying something in them, you should keep them in shashu and bow.

If one of your hands is already occupied, or when you are carrying something in one hand, you should make your bow with a one-handed gasshō.* In bowing with a one-handed gasshō, the hand is raised, with the fingers slightly cupped as if you were going to use the hand to scoop up water; the head is lowered slightly, as in greeting. When another monk behaves in this way towards us, we should behave similarly: when we behave in this way, the other monk should do likewise.

The procedure for taking off your undershirt and outer robe is to remove your robe along with the undershirt by bringing the two sleeves together in back, putting the two arm holes together, and lifting up the sleeves. You then fold the two sleeves,

---

*   See Glossary.

one atop the other, over the garment. Next, with the left hand, grasp the back of the collars and, with the right hand, draw up the robe and fold it down the middle of the sleeve bags[7] and the two collars. Having folded over the two sleeves and collars, you again fold the robe in two, lengthwise, and drape it over the pole with the collars on the far side; the skirt of the robe and the sleeve cuffs hang on the near side of the pole. That is to say, the robe hangs at the waist over the pole.

Next, avoid mistaking whose towel is whose when there are two poles and two towels are hanging one in front of the other. So that your towel does not get separated from your robe or get taken by someone who has not hung up a towel, tie it down by wrapping it around your robe two or three times and tying it, without letting your robe fall onto the ground. Then, facing your robe, you make gasshō.

Next, you take a sash cord and hang it over your shoulders.[8] Then go to the wash stand and fill a clean bucket with water; carrying the bucket with your right hand, go into a toilet stall. In putting water in the bucket, do not fill it to the brim, but fill it up nine-tenths of the way.

When you reach the lavatory door, you should change your slippers. Put on a pair of rush slippers, leaving your own slippers by the front of the lavatory door. This is what is meant by 'changing slippers'.

It says in the *Procedures for Cleanliness in a Zen Temple,* "When you need to go to the Eastern Quarters, by all means anticipate this need. Deal with it in time, so that you do not hurry from urgency. Give yourself time to fold your kesa, and leave it on your table in the Monks' Quarters or on the clean pole in the lavatory."

Upon entering the toilet stall, close the door with your left hand. You next pour just a little water from your bucket into the toilet basin. Next, put the bucket in front of you in the place provided for it. Then, while standing, face the basin and snap your fingers three times. Whilst snapping your fingers, your left hand is held in a fist

---

7. On some monastic robes, the sleeves are quite full, forming a bag-like appendage.

8. A sash cord is used to tie clothes out of the way.

at your left side at waist level. Next, you lift and gather up your under-skirt by its corners, face the door and, straddling the basin between your feet, squat down and relieve yourself. Do not soil either side of your garments; do not let them get stained front or back. During this time, you should remain silent. Do not talk or joke with the person in the next stall, chant, sing, or recite anything aloud. Do not spit or blow mucus from your nose onto the area around you. Do not strain or make grunting sounds excessively. You should not write on the walls. Do not dig at or draw on the ground with your toilet spatula; it should be used for cleaning yourself after you have evacuated your bowels. Also, if you use paper, you should not use old paper or paper with characters written on it.

You should keep in mind the difference between a clean spatula and a soiled one. The spatula is eight inches long, triangular in shape. In thickness, it is the width of one's thumb. Some are lacquered, others are not. Put your soiled spatula in the used spatula box. Clean ones will already be in the spatula stand. The spatula stand is kept near the sign in front of the toilet basin.

After using a spatula or paper, the way you clean yourself is as follows: hold the bucket in your right hand and moisten your left hand well. Then, cupping some water in your left hand, you first clean off your genitals three times. Then, you wash your buttocks. This is the way you should clean yourself.

Do not tip the bucket roughly, spilling the water into your hand and quickly using it all up.

After you have finished cleaning yourself, put the bucket down in its proper place; then, take the used spatula and wipe it clean and dry with paper. You should wipe your genitals and buttocks dry. Next, adjust your under-skirt and robe with your right hand, and, also with your right hand, pick up the bucket. Then go out the door, take off the rush slippers, and put on your own. Next, you return to the wash stand and put the bucket in its original place.

Next, you should wash your hands. With your right hand you take a spoonful of ashes, place it atop some pebbles, drip some water on them, and wash your contacting hand with your right hand,[9] using the pebbles to scour it, just as though you were cleaning rust off a sword. You should wash with ashes in this manner three times. Then, you should take some sand, add some water, and wash three times. Next, take some cleansing powder made from ground orange seeds in your right hand, moisten it with water from the small bucket, and wash by rubbing your hands together. The washing should be done thoroughly, even up your forearms. You should wholeheartedly devote your attention to washing in a conscientious manner. Ashes thrice, sand thrice, and cleansing powder once—all together seven times, an appropriate number. Next, you wash in a large bucket. This time, you simply wash in cold or warm water, without using any cleanser, sand, or ashes. After washing once, transfer that water into the small bucket, put in fresh water, and rinse both hands. In the *Avatamsaka Scripture*, a verse says:

> *When washing your hands,*
> *By all means pray that all sentient beings*
> *May acquire the finest hands*
> *With which to receive the Buddha's Teachings.*

When you use a water ladle, you should, of course, hold it with your right hand. When using it, do so quietly, without making a great noise with bucket or ladle.

Do not splash water about, scatter the cleansing powder, or get the area around the water stand wet. That is to say, do not be hasty or careless: do not be disorderly with things or treat them roughly.

Next, you dry your hands with the towel for general use or dry them with your own towel. Once you have finished drying your hands, go to where your robe is hanging over the pole, undo the sash cord, and hang the cord over the pole. Next, hang your towel over your left shoulder and rub some incense on yourself. There is rubbing incense for general use. It is made of fragrant wood in the shape of small vials. The size of each is about the thickness of a thumb and four times that amount in length.

---

9. In India, China, and Japan, it was customary to use the left hand to clean oneself after relieving oneself. As this hand might well become soiled through this contact, it was called, literally, 'the contacting hand'.

You take a piece of string about a foot long and thread it through the holes that are bored in each end of the incense stick. This is hung over the pole. When you rub it between the palms of your hands, the fragrance of this incense will naturally impregnate your hands.

When you hang your sash cord over the pole, do not hang it over another one so that they become entangled, and do not leave it in a disorderly fashion.

When matters are handled in this way, everything will be a purified Buddha Land, a Buddha World well adorned. You should do everything with care, without a lapse: you should not act from haste, as though in a dither. Do not entertain the thought, "If I hurry, I can get back to what I was doing." You should keep in mind the principle that, when you go to the Eastern Quarters, the Buddha's Dharma is not something to be talked about, but lived.

Do not stare at the faces of monks coming and going.

In cleansing yourself whilst in the lavatory, it is fine to use cool water, since it is said that hot water may cause diarrhea. Using warm water to wash your hands will not prove disturbing to your health. A kettle has been provided for heating water to wash your hands with.

Concerning the duties of the monk in charge of the lavatory, it says in the *Procedures for Cleanliness in a Zen Temple,* "Later in the evening, see that water is heated and oil is put out for the night lamp. Always make sure that there is someone to take over the boiling of the water, and do not let the community do it with a discriminatory attitude." From this it is clear that both hot and cold water are used.

If the interior of the lavatory becomes dirty, you should screen off the entry door and hang the sign that says 'Dirty' on it. If a bucket is accidentally knocked over, you should screen off the entry door and hang up the 'Spilled Bucket' sign. Do not enter the building when such signs have been put up.

Even though you may have already entered a stall, if there is someone else who snaps his fingers to let you know of his presence, you should leave shortly.

In the *Procedures for Cleanliness in a Zen Temple* it says, "If you do not wash yourself clean, you cannot truly take a seat in the Meditation Hall or bow to the Triple Treasure. Also, you cannot accept bows from others." And in the *Great Scripture on the Three Thousand Forms of Everyday Behavior for Monks* it says, "If you do not clean yourself after relieving nature, you are committing an offensive act.[10] You cannot truly sit upon a monk's pure cushion, nor can you truly pay homage to the Triple Treasure. Although you may bow, you will have neither happiness nor merit from doing so."

On the basis of these quotations, you should put this matter foremost when you are training in the temple. How can we possibly not want to pay homage to the Triple Treasure, nor to accept the respectful bows of others, nor to bow to them in return? The training halls of the Buddhas and Ancestors undoubtedly had these forms for dignified behavior. Those in the training halls of the Buddhas and Ancestors undoubtedly implemented these forms for dignified behavior. These are not things we force ourselves to do, for they are the words and deeds that arise naturally from the forms of dignified behavior. They are the constant conduct of all Buddhas and the everyday behavior of all Ancestors. And such forms are not limited just to the Buddhas of this world: they are the conduct of Buddhas in all ten directions. They are the conduct of Buddhas in both the Pure Lands and in the besmirched realms of existence. Those folks who are poorly informed fancy that the Buddhas have no forms of dignified behavior for using the lavatory, or they imagine that the forms of dignified behavior for the Buddhas in this world of ordinary beings are not the same as those

---

10. An 'offensive act' is a technical term that refers to the category of least serious breaches of monastic conduct.

for the Buddhas in the Pure Lands, but this is not what 'learning the Way of the Buddhas' means. You should realize that 'purity and stain' is clotted blood that has trickled from a corpse: one minute warm, the next minute horribly cold.[11]

In the fourteenth section of the *Ten Procedures to Be Recited* it says:

> When Rahula, the Buddha's son, was a novice, he took to spending his nights in the Buddha's lavatory. The Buddha, fully aware of what His son was doing, patted Rahula on the head with His right hand and recited this verse:
>
> > *My son, it was not to be poor or in want,*
> > *Nor to rid yourself of fortune or position,*
> > *But simply to seek the Way that you left home,*
> > *Which will surely bring hardships enough to bear.*

So, you see, the Buddha's temple had its lavatory too. The form for dignified behavior in the Buddha's lavatory was to wash oneself clean, and the Ancestors, in turn, passed this on to us. The conduct of the Buddhas has still been preserved: to follow the ancient ways is a great joy and something indeed hard to come by. Further, thankfully, the Tathagata gave voice to the Dharma for Rahula whilst in the lavatory. The lavatory was a place fit for the Buddha to turn the Wheel of the Dharma. How to conduct oneself in that training place of the Way is what the Buddhas and Ancestors truly Transmitted.

In the thirty-fourth chapter of the *Code of Behavior for Members of the Greater Sangha* it says, "The lavatory is not to be placed in the east or the north; it should be situated in the south or the west. Urinals should also be located in this manner." We should go by the directions given here as the proper ones. This is the plan for all the training halls in both China and India, and was actually the way the

---

11. This is Dōgen's image for a distinction that once was considered the lifeblood of practice but which has become frozen and dead through viewing the matter from a discriminatory and judgmental perspective.

Tathagata erected them. You should realize that this was not just this one Buddha's way of doing things. It applied to the temples and training halls of the Seven Buddhas,[*] as well as to the temples and training halls of all the Buddhas. Shakyamuni was not the first to do this; it has been the dignified conduct of all Buddhas. Mistakes will be many, should someone set up a temple or monastery without first understanding this and then attempt to do the practice and training. Such a person will not have prepared for a Buddha's dignified conduct, and the enlightenment of Buddha will not yet have manifested before his very eyes. If you would construct a training hall and establish a temple or a monastery, you will have to do it in accordance with the methods and procedures directly passed on by the Buddhas and Ancestors. Because this is the true Transmission of true heirs, merit and virtues will more and more accumulate. If you are not an heir to the true Transmission of the Buddhas and Ancestors, you do not yet know the Body and Mind of the Buddha's Teachings. If you do not know the Body and Mind of the Buddha's Teachings, you will be unable to clarify what a monk's Buddhist activities are. Now, 'the Great Teacher Shakyamuni Buddha's Teachings being Transmitted throughout the ten quarters' means the Buddha's Body and Mind being made manifest before our very eyes. A proper time for manifesting the Buddha's Body and Mind is when we act in accordance with what has been said here.

This was delivered to the monks at Kannondōri in Kōshōhōrin-ji Temple, Uji Prefecture, Yamashiro Province, on the twenty-third day of the tenth lunar month in the first year of the En'o era (November 21, 1239).

8

On 'The Rippling of a Valley Stream, The Contour of a Mountain'

(Keisei Sanshoku)

Translator's Introduction: Dōgen's discourse on "The Rippling of a Valley Stream, the Contour of a Mountain" is centered on the nature of a kenshō, that is, the experiencing of one's Buddha Nature. In the first half of his discourse, he focuses on the topic of the external condition which serves as a trigger or catalyst for this experience when the disciple is spiritually open and ready for the kenshō to occur. This trigger may be something heard (a valley stream) or seen (springtime blossoms) or felt (the stubbing of a toe). It may be some event occurring in nature, or it may be some gesture or remark that a Master may make upon sensing the 'ripeness' of his disciple. Such a trigger is not the cause of the kenshō occurring, but it is an integral part of the kenshō process. This trigger is a requisite form of external conditions in which someone or something gives voice to the Dharma—that is, gives expression (as, in reality, all things are always doing) to That which is beyond duality—and the trainee, 'hearing' this, makes the connection between the Source of this voicing and his own Original Nature.

The second half of the talk examines various obstacles that may interfere with the kenshō occurring, with emphasis given to the pursuit of personal fame and gain.

The Buddhas and Ancestors have been many indeed. Their deeds are instructive for teaching others the Way to supreme enlightenment. Among those deeds are not a few examples of 'bone-crushing' diligence. For instance, you can draw instruction from the Second Ancestor Eka's 'severing of his arm'.[1] And do not miss the meaning behind the Buddha's action in a previous life when He covered the mud

---

1. 'Cutting off one's arm' is being used metaphorically to refer to giving up one's willfulness at all costs. Such a 'severing' is done by applying Manjushri's Sword of Wise Discernment. Dōgen is not recommending self-mutilation.

79

with His long hair.[2] Once each of you has succeeded in 'removing your husk',[3] and you are no longer attached to any prior intellectual understanding, the Matter[*] which had been unclear to you for ever so long will immediately emerge before you. The very 'nowness' of this is beyond anything I know of, beyond anyone's ability to comprehend intellectually, beyond all your expectations, even beyond a Buddha's Eye to catch a glimpse of. So how can it possibly be fathomed by any human speculations?

In Great Sung China there was a lay Buddhist called Tōba. His family name was So, his official name was Shoku, and his name as an adult was Shisen. He must have been a veritable dragon in the sea of letters, for he had trained under dragon elephants in the ocean of Buddhism.[4] Swimming in the fathomless waters of Buddhism, he would soar up through the cloud banks to plunge once again into the depths of that ocean. Then there came a time when, whilst on a visit to Mount Ro,[5] he was struck by the sound of the valley stream rippling through the night, and he awoke to the Way. He composed the following poem about the experience, which he presented to Meditation Master Jōsō:

---

2.   Shakyamuni Buddha was an ascetic monk then. He spread his long hair over a mud puddle so that the Buddha of that time could cross the mud without staining Himself. This serves as an allusion to the willingness to go to whatever lengths are necessary, however humbling, so that one's Buddha Nature may traverse the Path unsullied. As with the previous example, Dōgen is not encouraging blind imitation of a physical act, but pointing to an understanding of the intention behind the action.

3.   Or, in idiomatic English, 'taking your blinders off'.

*   See Glossary.

4.   As used here, the word 'dragon' by itself refers to someone markedly brilliant. The term 'dragon elephant' is explained in the Glossary.

5.   The home of many notable literary figures of his day.

> *The valley stream's rippling is indeed the eloquent*
> *tongue of Buddha:*
> *The mountain's contour is not other than that of the*
> *body of Buddha.*
> *With the coming of night, I heard the eighty-four*
> *thousand songs,[6]*
> *But with the rising of the sun, how am I ever to offer*
> *them to you?*

Upon his presenting this poem to Meditation Master Jōsō, the Master said in approval, "Just so!" Master Jōsō is Meditation Master Shōkaku Jōsō, who was the Dharma heir of Meditation Master Ōryū Enan, who, in turn, was the Dharma heir of Meditation Master Jimyō Soen.

There was also a time when layman Tōba had a spiritual interview with the Great Priest Ryōgen Butchin. The latter, investing Tōba with the Buddha seal,* gave him a monk's Dharma robe and the Buddhist Precepts, among other things. Layman Tōba, from then on, trained in the Way whilst wrapped in the kesa.* Out of respect and reverence, Tōba presented Butchin with a priceless jeweled sash. People at the time commented that this was not something that an ordinary, everyday person would possibly think of doing.

The situation was such that Tōba's awakening to the Way upon hearing the valley stream was, undoubtedly, due partly to the condition of its sound flowing through the night. How sad that so many countless times the voicing of the Dharma by the manifest body of Buddha has escaped our notice. What, moreover, do you see when you view the contour of a mountain, or hear when you listen to the sound of the valley stream? Is it a single phrase you hear, or half a phrase, or the whole eighty-four thousand songs?

6.　In Buddhism, 'eighty-four thousand' represents both the number of atoms in a human body and the number of forms of illumination assumed by Amitabha Buddha, the Buddha of Immeasurable Light.

What a pity that Its sound and form lie within the landscape, unseen. And how glad we will be for the occasion and conditions when It reveals Itself in the landscape! 'His giving tongue to' is never remiss, for how can the contours of His Body be subject to a temporal existence and dissolution? Nevertheless, when It comes into sight, we learn how very near It has always been: when It is lying unseen, how are we to learn how near It really is? Are Its sound and form the whole of It or are they but half of It? In past springs and autumns, Tōba had not seen or heard the Water. Then, on the occasion of a single night, he was just able to see the Mountain and hear the rippling of Its stream. Now you bodhisattvas* training in the Way, too, should open wide the gate to your training and enter by means of the verse, "That which flows is the Mountain: That which does not flow is the Water."

On the day preceding the night that this layman Tōba awoke to the Way, he had gone to Meditation Master Shōkaku Jōsō to ask him about the kōan* story concerning the non-sentient giving voice to the Dharma.[7] Although he had not yet directly understood what the Master meant when he spoke on that occasion of 'turning oneself around', nevertheless, upon his hearing the rippling of the valley stream, it was as though the swirling waters had struck the very heavens. Thus it was that the sound of the stream now startled Tōba. But was it the voice of the stream or was it what had poured forth from his Master Jōsō's lips? Perhaps Jōsō's comment that the Non-sentient gives voice to the Dharma had not yet ceased to reverberate in Tōba, and, unbeknownst to Tōba, had intermingled with the sound of the stream's rippling through the night. Who will say, upon discerning It, that It is 'a whole dipperful', or who will say, upon flowing into It, that It is 'a whole oceanful'? In short, was it layman Tōba who awakened to the Way or was it the landscape that awakened to the Way? What person is clear of eye and yet fails to quickly spot His eloquent tongue and His immaculate body?

---

7.   Here, 'non-sentient' carries a double meaning. On one level it refers to anything that is not a sentient being and, on another level, to That which transcends the duality of sentient and non-sentient.

As another example, at one time Meditation Master Kyōgen Chikan was training at Mount Daii in the community of Isan Reiyū. Isan said to him, "You are a learned scholar of considerable intelligence. So, without having to rely on what you have memorized from commentaries, surely you should be able to explain for me in your own words what the phrase 'before "father" and "mother" were born'* means."

However many times he tried, Kyōgen was unable to do so. Deeply ashamed of himself, he consulted all the Scripture books and their commentaries that he had amassed over the years, but he was still left at wit's end. Finally, he took a torch and burned the writings he had previously collected, saying, "A rice cake in a painting will never satisfy one's hunger! I swear that I will no longer crave after the Buddha's Teachings in this lifetime, but will just be a kitchen monk who serves up the rice and gruel."

And so he served up the rice and gruel as the months and years went by. 'The monk who serves up the rice and gruel' refers to one who serves meals to his fellow monks. It is like the person in our country who dishes out the food. After having worked in this way for many years, he remarked to Isan, "Dunce that I am, I am still in the dark, unable to find the words to speak. O Reverend Monk, please say something to help me." Isan responded, "It is not that I refuse to say anything for your sake, but I fear that later on you would come to resent me for it."

And so, several more years passed, and Kyōgen went to visit the site where the National Teacher Echū had lived. Arriving at Mount Butō, he collected up grass and built himself a hermit's hut on the spot where the National Teacher's hermitage had stood. He planted some bamboo, which served as his sole companion. One day, whilst intent on sweeping his walkway clean, he accidentally sent a piece of tile flying, which hit the bamboo. Upon hearing the knocking sound it made, he suddenly had a great awakening. He bathed himself and, abstaining from anything physical or mental that might be sullying, he turned in the direction of Mount Daii to offer incense and reverently bow. Then, as though facing Isan himself, he said, "O Great Monk Isan, if long ago you had said something to me for my sake, how would I now have had this experience? My indebtedness to you is so deep that it surpasses even that which I owe to my parents." He ended by composing the following poem:

> *At one blow, I have forgotten all that I had learned with*
> *my head.*
> *Truly, I myself am no longer the one in control.*
>
> *Breaking out in a smile, I make my way along the Old*
> *Path,*
> *Neither looking down in moments of despair*
> *Nor leaving behind, here and there, traces of where I have*
> *been.*
> *Only a dignified manner remains, which lies beyond*
> *anything heard or seen.*
>
> *Those everywhere who have realized the Way,*
> *All as one, say it is the moment supreme.*

When he presented this poem to Isan, the latter said, "This disciple has struck Home."

As still another example, Meditation Master Reiun Shigon had trained and practiced for thirty years. Then one day, whilst 'swimming about', visiting mountain monasteries,[8] he took a rest at the foot of a mountain, when in the distance he spied a village. It was spring at the time, and, glimpsing the peach blossoms in bloom there, he suddenly awoke to the Way. Composing a poem, he presented it to Isan:

> *Thirty years I sought for Him, the Good Friend with His Sword of*
> *Wisdom:*
> *For so many rounds have the leaves fallen and the branches burst*
> *anew with blooms!*

---

8. It was customary at the time for monks who had not yet had a kenshō to visit other monasteries for the summer retreat.

> But just one glance at those peach blossoms
> And straightaway—at that very moment—I arrived, never again to
>   be in doubt.

Isan said, "The person who enters the Truth by way of some external condition is not likely to ever retreat from It or lose It." Thereupon, he gave his approval to Reiun.

Is there anyone who has not entered by way of some external condition? Is there anyone who, once having entered, would retreat from this Place, or lose It? This is not something that applies to Reiun and Reiun alone. Ultimately he inherited the Dharma from Isan. Were it not that the contour of the mountain is the Pure Body of Buddha, how could a thing like this possibly happen?

Also, Meditation Master Chōsa Keishin was asked by a certain monk, "How is it possible to change the great earth with its mountains and rivers so that we make it return to the True Self?"

The Master responded, "No, the question is, 'How is it possible to change ourselves so that we make It return to the great earth with its mountains and rivers?'"

What is being said here is that the True Self is, in Its own right, the True Self. Even though we speak of the Self as being 'the great earth with its mountains and rivers', this is not something that should delude us as to what is returned to.

Similarly, the monk Egaku, who was a Dharma descendant of Nangaku, was once asked by Shison, a lecturer in the scholastic tradition, "How is it possible for one's Original Nature, which is immaculate, to all at once produce something as polluted as the great earth with its mountains and rivers?"

The monk pointed out in response, "Since our Original Nature is immaculate, how does It, all at once, produce the Great Earth with Its mountains and rivers?"

We must realize here that we are not to make the mistake of taking 'the Great Earth with Its mountains and rivers in their immaculate Original Nature' to be the great earth with its mountains and rivers. Yet, scholars who simply take Scriptures literally have never even dreamt of this, and consequently do not comprehend what 'the Great Earth with Its mountains and rivers' signifies.

We must understand that were Original Nature not the contour of a mountain and the rippling of a valley stream, then Shakyamuni would not have begun His voicing of the Dharma by holding a flower aloft, nor would Eka's reaching the Very Marrow of what Bodhidharma was teaching have come about. Because of the merit that comes to fruition in the rippling of a stream and the contour of a mountain, the great earth and its sentient beings simultaneously realize the Way, and there are Buddhas, such as Shakyamuni, who awaken to the Way upon seeing a morning star. Flesh-and-blood human beings like these are Masters of bygone days whose determination to seek the Dharma was profound indeed.

We humans today should, by all means, consider following in Their footsteps. And, likewise, we of today should give rise to a similar determination by pursuing genuine training, which is in no wise connected with personal fame or gain. In recent times, in far-flung places like Japan, people who are truly searching for the Buddha's Teachings are rare. It is not that such persons do not exist, but that it is difficult to encounter them.

Occasionally, there are some who appear to leave home to become monks, letting go of the mundane, but too many of them only use the Buddha's Way as a bridge to fame and gain, sad to say. It is such a pity for them to waste their days and nights without regret, vainly training in pursuit of such dark and wayward goals. When will come the time that they abandon such things and realize the Way? Even should they meet a genuine teacher, they probably would not be fond of this 'True Dragon'. Former Buddhas would say of such people that they are persons to be pitied, since such a response is due simply to their attitude of mind, which has arisen from bad karmic roots planted in some previous life of theirs. Although they have been born as a human being, they do not have the determination to seek the Dharma for Its own sake. As a result, when they encounter true Teaching, they are suspicious of the True Dragon. When they meet genuine Dharma, they are repelled by It. Since they have never lived—neither in body and mind, nor in bones and flesh—in accordance with the Dharma, they are not suited to It, nor do they accept and apply It.

For a long time now, Masters and disciples in our Ancestral Tradition have continued to pass on the Dharma as they had received It. But nowadays, to speak of 'the mind that seeks enlightenment' resembles talking about some dream dreamt long ago. How sad not to know of, or ever see, the precious ore that lies buried in a mountain of treasure, but how much more sad when it is the mother lode of the Dharma!

Once you have given rise to the intention to seek enlightenment, even though you are spinning about through the six worlds* of existence, being born through any of the four modes of birth, the very causes and conditions of your spinning will become your heartfelt practice of enlightenment. Accordingly, even though you have spent your past days and nights in vain pursuits, you should make the following vow while you are still in this present life:

> I pray that I and all sentient beings, from this life through
> all future lives, will ever be able to hear the True Teachings. Once
> I have heard the True Dharma, I will not harbor doubts about It or
> fail to trust in It. Right at the time when I encounter the True
> Dharma, I will let go of the whole world and embrace the Buddha's
> Teachings. Then, together with all sentient beings on the great earth,
> may we fulfill the Way.

If you make your vow in this manner, it will, of itself, be a cause for your enlightenment-seeking mind to arise. Never neglect the attitude of mind behind this vow.

Further, this land of Japan is a distant place separated from others by vast seas. The hearts of its people are befuddled in the extreme. From the distant past, it has not been common for saintly persons or those naturally gifted with good sense to be born here, to say nothing of the scarcity of true students of the Way. When the fellow who knows nothing of the heart that seeks the Way is told of this Way-seeking heart, he turns a deaf ear to this good instruction. As a result, he does not reflect upon himself and harbors resentment towards others.

In short, when you put into practice your intention to seek enlightenment, you should not concern yourself with letting worldly people know that you have given rise to the enlightenment-seeking mind and are practicing the Way. Rather, you should conduct yourself so that they may not know it; even more, you should not speak of it openly. People today who seek Truth are rare; as a result, the majority do not engage themselves in spiritual practice and have not awakened in their hearts. Desirous of praise from others, they seek for someone who will tell them how integrated their practice and understanding are. This is just what 'being deluded within delusion' means. You should immediately toss out such ridiculous notions.

When training in the Way, the most difficult thing to experience is the mental attitude of the True Dharma. That attitude of mind is something that Buddhas come to Transmit to each Other. We call this the mutual Transmission of a Buddha's Light and of a Buddha's Heart and Mind.

From the time when the Tathagata was in the world up to this very day, the number of fellows who appear to be paying heed to training in the Way with the sole purpose of seeking personal fame and gain have been many. But even in such cases, if they encounter the instructions of a genuine Master, turn themselves around, and seek the True Dharma, they will naturally realize the Way. You who are now training in the Way today need to know that a spiritual illness such as this seeking after fame and gain exists. It can occur, for instance, in those with a beginner's attitude of mind who have just begun to train, as well as in those, whether Transmitted or not, who have trained and practiced for a long time.

There will be those who dote on what has passed and try to mimic that, and there may even be demons who slander those above them and refuse to learn from them. Do not be attracted to either type or feel resentment towards either. Why do I say not to feel sorry for them or resent them? Because it is said that people who recognize the three poisons of greed, hatred, and delusion to be what they are, are rare enough, so there is no need to feel resentment towards those who do not. Even more importantly, you should not lose sight of the intention that arose when you first took delight in seeking the Way of the Buddhas. It is said that when we first give rise to this intention, we are not seeking the Dharma so that others will praise us, but are discarding thoughts of fame and gain. Without seeking fame or gain, we should simply be persons who hold to the true course of realizing the Way, never concerning ourselves with expectations of recognition or support from rulers or other officials.

Even though this is the ideal, there are some people today who, alas, are devoid of any fundamental spiritual aspirations, having no spiritual goal that they seek, and are not the least concerned over their delusive entanglements with both ordinary people and those in lofty positions. On the other hand, there are some befuddled people who once did have a heart intent on the Way, but have all too quickly forgotten about their original intention and have fallen into error, anticipating offerings from ordinary people and those in lofty positions, which offerings they joyfully consider to be merit accruing to them from the Buddha's Teachings. If they secure the confidence of some ruler or official, they fancy that they have succeeded in seeing what our Path is. This is one devil of an impediment to training in the Way. Even though you must not lose sight of the heart filled with pity for all beings, you must not delight in forming entangling relationships with them. Look! The Buddha once deigned to express it with His golden words, "Even in the present day, the Tathagata is greatly vilified and envied." Those who are foolish do not recognize what is bright and wise, which is why little brutes envy and resent great saints.

As a further example, our Ancestral Master from Western India, Bodhidharma, underwent great torments for the sake of non-Buddhists, shravakas,* pratyekabuddhas,* rulers, and the like. This was not because the paths of non-Buddhists were superior, nor because of some lack of deference to the Ancestral Master. After this First Ancestor came from the West, he hung up his traveling staff on Mount Sūzan at Shōrin-ji Temple when he discovered that neither Emperor Wu of Liang nor the king of Wei understood what the spirit of Buddhism is. About that time, there were two veritable dogs, Bodhiruchi and Vinaya Master Kōtō.[9] Fearing that

---

9. During that time, there were two Indian scholars named Bodhiruchi: one was an eminent translator of Scriptures and the other was a scholar who was envious of Bodhidharma. It is the latter Bodhiruci who is referred to here. The Chinese Vinaya Master Kōtō was a

Bodhidharma might hinder the spread of their false reputations and wicked influences among honest people, they conspired against him, just as if they had looked up at the sun and tried to put it into eclipse. They were even more excessive in their behavior than Devadatta was when the Buddha was alive.[10] The fame and gain that they, alas, so deeply doted on was even more repellent to Bodhidharma than excrement and filth. The reason for such things is not that the strength of the Buddha's Dharma is less than ideal: just be aware that there are dogs who bark at good people. Do not worry about barking dogs <u>and</u> do not resent them. Give rise to the wish to offer them guidance by providing them with the following Teaching, "Although you are, undoubtedly, beasts, you should still give rise to the intention to realize enlightenment." A former sage has called these two 'beasts with human faces'.

There is also that type of 'beast' who gives his confidence and support. As the former Buddha Shakyamuni said, "Do not seek to be an intimate of kings or princes, ministers or officials, brahmans or lay Buddhists." [11] Truly, this is a principle of practice which those who would train in the Buddha's Way should not forget. The meritorious fruits of a bodhisattva's first beginning to train will pile up as he continues on.

---

translator and writer of Scriptural commentaries. Both tried to discredit Bodhidharma's focus on meditation practice, and it is said that both attempted to poison him.

The *Vinaya* is the section of the Buddhist canon containing the rules of monastic discipline. Dōgen is not advocating that one should not follow the Teachings of this work, but rather that one should not become rule-bound simply for the sake of rules due to a lack of spiritual understanding of their purpose and aim.

10. Devadatta was Shakyamuni Buddha's cousin and His disciple. While a senior monk, he caused a schism in the assembly, with five hundred novices following him. Although maintaining that he was still Shakyamuni's disciple, he even attempted, unsuccessfully, to kill Shakyamuni.

11. Context implies that the confidence and support in this instance derive from a desire to gain control over or manipulate a monk. As a preventative, monks are instructed not to seek out or encourage close, emotionally binding personal relationships with lay people, which would be inviting entanglements.

Further, ever since ancient times, the skeptical Indra, Lord of Heaven, has come to test the intentions of practitioners, as has Mara the Tempter come to disturb and obstruct the practitioner's training in the Way. All instances of this have occurred when someone has not let go of hopes for fame and gain. When great compassion is deep within you, and your wish to spiritually aid sentient beings everywhere is well seasoned, there are no such obstructions. Then your training and practice will flower; they will be strong enough to win the citizenry over and will seem to permeate the course of events. At such periods in time, you should scrutinize yourself all the more for signs of attraction to fame and gain. Do not close your eyes to these and doze off. People who are confused by their follies rejoice in this flowering, like foolish dogs gnawing on dried-out bones. The wise and saintly treat this flowering with a repulsion such as that which the worldly have for excrement and filth. [12]

In general, the discriminatory disposition of the beginner's mind is incapable of measuring the Buddha's Way: though it may try to sound Its depths, it does not touch them. But this does not mean that, because one cannot fully fathom It with a beginner's mind, one is incapable of arriving at the farthest reaches of Its realm. That which penetrates to the deepest halls of this region is not the shallow cognitive functions of a beginner's mind. Simply, you should walk the Path that former saints have trod. At such a time as this, in order to visit a Master and inquire into the Way, you may have to scale mountains with a ladder and cross vast seas in a rowboat. [13] And, while you are seeking out a teacher to guide you or praying for a good friend to give you instruction, such a one may fall from the heavens or well up from the earth. When, with a beginner's mind, you encounter a teacher and let him guide you, he will let you hear him speak of things sentient and non-sentient, and you will hear of things pertaining to your body and to your mind. Even though hearing with one's ears is daily fare, to 'hear' sound with the eye is indeed something that seems impossible, but

---

12. That is, when Buddhism prospers and flourishes either within oneself or around oneself, one should not get caught up in or attached to either.

13. Allusions to the diligent effort one may be called on to make when training in the Way.

is not.[14] When you 'see Buddha', you will see Buddha in self and others: you will see great Buddhas and small Buddhas. Do not be startled or frightened by a great Buddha: do not be skeptical of, or troubled by, a small Buddha. What we call 'great Buddhas and small Buddhas' are Those whom, for the time being, we recognize as the contour of a mountain and the rippling of a valley stream. Here can be found the eloquent tongue and the eighty-four thousand songs. By offering these songs as our voicing of the Dharma, we free ourselves from the mundane. When we see through, piercing to the Truth, we root out the self. This is why the proverb says, "The higher, the harder." And, as my former teacher and Buddha put it, "Boundless as the heavens, pervasive as water." And there is the restrained demeanor of the pine tree in spring, and there is the radiant beauty of chrysanthemums in autumn: within themselves, just as they are, lies the Truth.

When a good friend reaches this region, he will be a great teacher to gods and men. If he has not yet reached this region and tries to give instruction to people indiscriminately, he will be a great thief of gods and men. Unaware of the springtime pine, blind to the autumnal chrysanthemums, what will he have as fodder for his teaching? How will he help others to sever their karmic roots?

Further, if you are lazy or negligent in mind or body, if you are lacking in faith and trust, you should, in all devotion and sincerity, admit this openly before the Buddhas and repent your actions. When we do this, the strength from the meritorious fruits of repenting before the Buddhas will rescue and cleanse us. These meritorious fruits are the result of our being unencumbered as we live in pure trust and foster an attitude of devotion. Once we have manifested pure trust, both we ourselves and others alike turn around. The benefits of this will spread far and wide, encompassing both the sentient and the non-sentient. The meaning of this repentance can be expressed as follows:

> Even though the wicked deeds that I have done in the past
> have piled up deep and cause obstructions to my training in the
> Way, I pray that all the Buddhas and Ancestors who have realized

---

14.   As, for example, when the 'eye' is the Eye of Wise Discernment.

the Truth in accordance with the Buddha's Way will have pity on me, help me let go of my karmic entanglements, and help me dissipate any impediments to training in the Way. May They help the Gateway to the inexhaustible Dharma ceaselessly pour forth Its meritorious fruits to permeate the whole universe, so that the compassionate pity of the Teachings will spread to all of us.

Keep in mind, we are as the Buddhas and Ancestors were in the ancient past: the Buddhas and Ancestors are what we will be in the future. When we look up to the Buddhas and Ancestors, we and They are but one single Buddha Ancestor. When we observe the arising of our resolve, it is but one and the same resolute Heart as Theirs. 'Making our compassionate pity permeate every nook and cranny' means knowing when to apply it and when to let go of it. This is why Zen Master Ryūge said, "If you have not yet realized your enlightenment in a past lifetime, by all means realize it now. In this life, ferry this body of yours, which is the product of successive past lives, to the Other Shore. Before the Buddhas of the past had awakened to the Truth, They were just like people today. Once they have completely awakened, people today will be as those Buddhas of the past." You should take time to study and investigate this principle, for this is what all Buddhas have guaranteed us will take place.

While being mindful in mind and decorous in body, own up to what you have done and openly admit it to Buddha. The power from owning up destroys the roots of what is defiling you. This is the whole body of true training and practice. It is the heart that truly trusts: it is the body of true faith. When you truly train and practice, the voice of valley streams and the appearance of valley streams, the appearance of mountains and the voice of mountains, along with their eighty-four thousand songs, will be unstinting. If you yourself do not prize fame or gain, body or mind, then the valley streams and mountains will, in turn, be unstinting in revealing to you That Which Is. Whether the voice of valley streams and the contour of mountains manifest for you the eighty-four thousand songs or not is, simply, what comes in the darkness of night. On the other hand, should you not yet possess the strength to proclaim valley stream and mountain as Valley Stream and Mountain, who will be able to hear you give forth the valley stream's True Voice or see you take the mountain's True Form?

Given to the assembly of monks at Kannondōri in Kōshōhōrin-ji Temple on the fifth day of the summer training period in the second year of the En'o era (May 12, 1240).

Recopied before the summer training period on the anniversary of the Buddha's birth in the first year of the Kangen era (April 28, 1243) in my room in the same temple.

Ejō

Recopied again on the eleventh day of the seventh lunar month in the first year of the Kenji era (August 2, 1275).

9

On 'Refrain from All Evil Whatsoever'

(Shoaku Makusa)

Translator's Introduction: In this discourse, Dōgen discusses the significance of a poem that appears in Chinese translations of the Pali *Āgama Scriptures,* the earliest known Buddhist Scriptures. Although they are part of the Theravadan tradition, they are nevertheless viewed as fundamental to Mahayana Buddhism. The poem is considered to encapsulate the Precepts, which form the moral basis for the actions of a Buddhist. Although there have been various interpretations of this poem over the centuries, this English translation reflects Dōgen's particular understanding of the Chinese version. After Dōgen has presented the significance of each of the four lines of the poem, he then explores the appropriate attitude of mind towards these Preceptual Teachings by means of a story concerning Haku Rakuten, whom the Japanese have traditionally regarded as the greatest of the Chinese poets.

The Buddha of long ago said in verse:

> *Refrain from all evil whatsoever,*
> *Uphold and practice all that is good,*
> *And thereby you purify your own intentions:*
> *This is what all Buddhas teach.*

These are the Precepts that the Seven Buddhas[*] and all the Ancestors of our Tradition have held in common. They are passed down from a previous Buddha directly to the next Buddha: They are what a Buddha inherits from a preceding Buddha. This refers not only to the Seven Buddhas, for these Precepts are what all Buddhas teach. You should examine Them with the mind of meditation and thoroughly investigate the principles They voice.

When mention is made of 'the Dharma voiced by the Seven Buddhas', it is doubtless a reference to this Teaching which the Seven Buddhas have given voice to. Moreover, what is passed on and what is inherited is precisely what is being communicated here through this Scriptural verse. It is 'what all Buddhas teach'. It is

---

[*]   See Glossary.

what the hundreds of thousands of millions of Buddhas have been instructed in, what They have practiced, and what They have personally come to realize.

The 'all evil' of which we are now speaking has the quality of 'being evil' among the three qualities of 'being good', 'being evil', and 'being neutral'.[1] This quality of 'being evil' is something that does not arise and perish, as thoughts and things do. Although the qualities of 'being good' and 'being neutral' are also beyond arising, as well as being without stain and bearing the characteristics of the Truth, these three qualities, in each instance, are quite diverse in form and character.

'All evil' is not exactly the same as what is considered wrong among us in the monastic community or among those in the mundane world, nor is it exactly the same as what was thought of as evil in the past or what is thought to be so in the present. And it is not exactly the same as what is considered evil among the lofty or among ordinary, everyday human beings. And vast indeed is the difference between the way that good, evil, and neutral are spoken of in Buddhism and the way they are spoken of in the world of ordinary, everyday people. What is seen as good and what is seen as evil depend on the times, but time itself is neither good nor evil. What is good and what is evil depend on what thoughts and things they give rise to, but whatever arises is likewise inherently neither good nor evil. To the extent that thoughts or things are alike, they partake of good alike, and to the extent that they are alike, they partake of evil alike.

Nevertheless, while we are pursuing our study of That which is 'absolute, supreme enlightenment', while we are listening to instruction on It, while we are training and practicing until we personally experience the fruits of realizing It, It seems something profound, something remote, something mysterious. We hear of this peerless enlightenment from our good spiritual friends and we learn of It from

---

1.   These three qualities refer to the nature of one's intentions and actions, as well as to the karmic consequences these intentions and actions set in motion. When the nature of one's intentions or actions is good, these intentions and actions produce good karmic effects; when evil, evil effects; when neutral, effects that are neither good nor evil.

Scriptures. And the first thing we hear is, "Refrain from all evil whatsoever." If you do not hear it said to refrain from all evil whatsoever, it is not the genuine Dharma of Buddha: it will be the preaching of demons. You must understand that to hear "Refrain from all evil whatsoever" is to hear what the genuine Dharma of Buddha is.

This "Refrain from all evil whatsoever" is not something that worldly people are apt to think of before concocting what they are going to do. Only by hearing enlightenment explained to them will they be able to learn of this phrase. When they hear of it in this way, it will merely be words related to supreme enlightenment. At this time, enlightenment will be for them only a word, and so the word 'enlightenment' is used. But when these people turn themselves around upon hearing supreme enlightenment being talked about, they will wish to refrain from all evil whatsoever, and they will act to refrain from all evil whatsoever. Once they have arrived at the point where they are no longer doing all manner of evil, the strength from their training and practice will immediately manifest itself before their very eyes. This blossoming of strength will extend beyond all places, all worlds, all times, all things. And the measuring of it will take 'refraining' as its yardstick.

Those who have arrived at this point in time may reside in some place where all manner of evil is going on, or they may be traveling back and forth there, or they may be confronted with conditions where all manner of evil actions may be going on, yet they do not perform such evil actions themselves because they are clearly manifesting the strength from their self-restraint. They do not speak of evil actions as, in and of themselves, evil actions, for there is no such thing as a predestined 'tool for evil'. At such a point in time, the principle that evil does not break a person will be understood: the principle that a person does not defeat evil will be crystal clear.

Rouse your heart and mind fully and do your training and practice, for when you rouse your heart and mind to do the training and practice, you will have already realized eight- or nine-tenths of the Way. Before you know it, you will have 'refraining' always in the back of your mind. Whether you pay heed to your own handling of mind and body whilst doing your training and practice, or pay heed to someone else's handling of mind and body whilst they are doing their training and practice, the strength from your practice and training with the four elements and the five skandhas* will instantly manifest before your very eyes. At such a time, the four elements and the five skandhas will not sully you; even with the four elements and the five skandhas being just as they are at the present time, your training and practice can go on. The strength from the four elements and the five skandhas, just as they are in our present training and practice, has been brought about through our previous training and practice with the four elements and the five skandhas.

Moreover, when we train and practice upon the great earth with its mountains and rivers, and beneath the sun, moon, and stars, then the great earth with its mountains and rivers, as well as the sun, moon, and stars, will help us to train ourselves and to do the practice. It is not a matter of being clear-eyed at one time: it is having your Eye open at all times. Because the Buddhas and Ancestors were clear-eyed, with Their Eye open at all times, It helped Them to do the training and practice, just as It helped Them to hear and heed what the Scriptures teach and to bring Their spiritual certainty to fruition. Because the Buddhas and Ancestors have never let the Scriptural teachings, Their practice, or Their certainty be sullied, these things have never stood in the way of any Buddha or Ancestor. This is why, in the training and practice of Buddhas and Ancestors, there are no Buddhas or Ancestors who have avoided or turned away from these three aspects or ever would, be it in the past, present, or future. At the time when a sentient being 'becomes' a Buddha or an Ancestor, the Buddhas and Ancestors that have existed previously do not hinder or act as obstacles to Him or Her. Even so, we must consider carefully the principle of 'becoming a Buddha' as we walk, stand, sit, or recline throughout the twenty-four hours of a day. Becoming a Buddha or Ancestor does not tear a sentient being to bits, or rob him of anything, or deprive him of something. It is simply his letting go.

The karmic[*] consequences of our good and bad actions are what we are training with. That is, we try not to set karmic consequences into motion or not to stir things up. There is a time when karmic consequences are what cause us to do the training and practice. Once the true face of our karma has been made clear to us, then we understand what 'refraining' really means, for this refraining is what Buddha Nature is: it is being impermanent, it is being subject to causality, and it is being free, because it is letting go. When we study the matter in this manner, we will bring about a state where we will completely refrain from all evil. To actualize this, we are helped by focusing on refraining from all evil until we succeed in penetrating to its heart, which is our sitting in meditation until we are able to sever ourselves from what is evil.

When we have actualized "Refrain from all evil whatsoever" from beginning to end, then, at such a point in time, there is just refraining, since evil is not something that arises from karmic causes and conditions. And since evil is not something that disappears along with karmic causes and conditions, there is just refraining, simply that. Were all evils alike, then all physical and mental things would be alike. If you suppose that evils arise due to some karmic cause or condition and do not see that such a cause or condition is, in itself, 'something not to be done', you are folks to be pitied. Just as the seed of Buddhahood comes along with the arising of co-existing conditions, so co-existing conditions will come along with the appearance of the seed of Buddhahood.

It is not that there are no evils: it is only that there are things that one should not do. It is not that there <u>are</u> evils: it is only that there are things that one should not do. It is not that evils are lacking in form: it is simply that they are things not to be done. It is not that evils have some particular form: simply they are things not to be done. Evils are not 'things that one should not do': they are simply things one does not do. For instance, it is not a matter of whether the springtime pine 'has existence' or 'does not have existence': the pine tree is simply a thing that we do not invent. It is not that the autumn chrysanthemum 'exists' or 'does not exist': this flower is something that we have not fabricated. Whether Buddhas exist or do not exist, there are things we do not do. Whether or not there is a round temple pillar, or a stone lantern, or a ceremonial hossu, or a traveling staff,[2] there are things we do not do. It is not a matter of whether we have existence or not: it is a matter of refraining from things not to be done.

---

2.   These four items are associated with a Meditation Master, one who serves as the fundamental support for his or her temple or monastery, who is a guiding light for his or her disciples, who pours forth the Water of the Spirit for their spiritual benefit, and who is willing to travel anywhere literally and figuratively to help sentient beings arrive at the Other Shore.

Our studying in this way will be our spiritual question manifesting right in front of us. Since it is a manifestation of our spiritual question, we should meditate on this from the perspectives of both the host and the guest. As regards what you have already done, to have done what you should not have done will create remorse in you. Even so, do not evade such feelings, since facing them will, in turn, prove to be a strength for you, a strength that arises from your training in refraining. Accordingly, should you head off in the direction of thinking, "If it is something I should not do, I ought to give it a try to see what it's like," you will be like someone going north to arrive at the south. To refrain from all evil whatsoever is not just the well looking at the donkey: it is the well looking at the well, the donkey looking at the donkey, the ordinary person looking at the ordinary person, the mountain looking at the mountain.[3] Because the cases spoken of here share a principle which, at bottom, is in accord with each of them, they all involve refraining from all evil.

> The true Dharma Body of the Buddha
> Is unbounded, like empty space.
> It reveals Its form in accordance with an object,
> Like the moon reflected in water.

Because this refraining is done in accordance with what an object is, it is a refraining that takes various forms. It resembles empty space, which is the same wherever you point, right or left. It is like the moon in water: the moon is not hampered by the water. Furthermore, these cases of refraining will, beyond doubt, manifest before your very eyes.

---

3. An allusion to a remark by Meditation Master Sōzan Honjaku that when a donkey looks into the well, the well looks at the donkey. The donkey here refers to the stubborn mind of the trainee (the guest position), and the well to That which he looks into in training. While he is looking into this Well, the Well (the host position) is 'looking at' the donkey. It is also the ordinary mind looking at the ordinary mind, and it is the mind in meditation looking at the mind of meditation.

"Uphold and practice all that is good." This 'all that is good' refers to the quality of 'being good' among the three qualities. Although 'all that is good' resides within the quality of 'being good', it does not mean that what is good already exists somewhere and is waiting for someone to put it into operation. At the very moment when someone does good, nothing but good comes forth. Although the myriad expressions of goodness are without an outer form, when good is done, it attracts goodness faster than a magnet attracts iron. Its strength surpasses that of the Great Storming Wind.[4] Even the strength amassed by the karma from the great earth with its mountains and rivers, as well as from the world with its nations and countries, will never hinder the accumulating of good.

Even so, what is good depends on what 'world' you are talking about, for it will not always be perceived as being the same thing, since people consider what 'good' is from their own perspective. It is also like this when Buddhas give voice to the Dharma in the three temporal worlds. What They give voice to is the same, but how It was voiced when Each was in the world has depended on the times. Even though Their length of life and the number of Buddhas may vary over time, what They all give voice to is the Teaching of non-discriminatory thinking.

This is why what is seen to be good from the perspective of practicing in faith and what is seen to be good from the perspective of practicing in accordance with the Dharma vary so widely, yet they are not separate Teachings.[5] For instance, it

---

4.   This wind, whose raging is capable of destroying all in its path, arises beyond the Iron Mountains which surround and protect Mount Sumeru. This is an allusion to the worst, most powerful form of karmic consequence which, like a storm, is capable of destroying ordinary human beings physically and mentally. However, the Iron Mountains (when understood as a metaphor for Buddhist practitioners sitting unmoved in their meditation) form a protective spiritual barrier against such a destructive force for the trainee who is meditating 'atop Mount Sumeru'.

5.   That is, what is good from the perspective of meditation (sitting in complete faith and trust) and the good which is derived from applying what the Buddha taught in the form

is like the situation of a shravaka's holding to the Precepts being a breaking of the Precepts in a bodhisattva.[6]

'All that is good' is independent of what karmically arises and what karmically undergoes dissolution. 'All that is good' is synonymous with 'all thoughts and things', yet all such things are not necessarily good. Since the cycles of karmic conditions, that which arises and ceases with them, and 'all good' are alike in having a beginning, so they will also have their ending. Although 'all good' is what we uphold and practice, since it is not of the self, it is not known via the self; since it is not of others, it is not known via others. When speaking of consciousness of self and other, there is a self and an other in what is known; there is a self and an other in what is seen. Hence, each and every Eye that has opened to the Truth, when activated, will have Its Sun and Its Moon: this is what is meant by 'upholding and putting into practice'.

At the very moment of our upholding and practicing, there will be the spiritual question arising before our eyes. Even so, it will not be the first time that it has manifested nor will the question remain indefinitely, continuing on, nor can we possibly say that it is the fundamental practice.

Although, as I have said, the doing of what is good is what we uphold and practice, it is not something to be speculated upon or intellectually analyzed. Even though the upholding and practicing of which I now speak are, indeed, the activities of the Eye That has opened to the Truth, it is not a subject for speculation. It is not something that has manifested for the purpose of our speculating on the Dharma. The

---

of the Precepts may sometimes superficially appear to be different, but when meditation and practice are properly undertaken, they are seen to be all one identical Dharma.

6. That is, someone who is new to training and has just begun to try to live in accordance with the Precepts (that is, a 'shravaka') may need to hold closely to the literal meaning of them. However, in someone whose training and practice have advanced to the point where he or she is naturally acting from the Precepts as their very blood and bones (that is, a 'bodhisattva'), this 'holding on tightly' is precisely what could work against the intent of the Precepts if the trainee were to apply them as a rigid yardstick, thereby opening the door to judgmentalism.

conclusions drawn by the opened Eye will not be the same as those drawn by other things.

'All that is good' does not depend on something having existence or not having existence, on something having form or being devoid of form, and so forth. It is simply what is upheld and practiced. No matter where it manifests, no matter when it manifests, it is what we uphold and practice, without fail. This adherence and practice <u>will</u> manifest what is good, without fail. Even though our adherence and practice are what manifest because of our spiritual question, 'all that is good' lies beyond birth, beyond annihilation, beyond any karmic conditions. The same holds true for our entering into adherence and practice, our persisting in them, our departing from them, and so forth. When, from among all of our acts, even a single good act is upheld and practiced, the goodness of every single thing in its totality—all of which together form the ground of reality—is upheld and put into practice.

The causes and effects of this goodness have, likewise, sprung from our spiritual question, which we have actualized by our adherence to and practice of what is good. Although it is not a matter of cause necessarily preceding effect, both cause and effect will be fully perfected. When the causes are alike, the thoughts and things they give rise to will be alike: when effects are alike, then it is because the thoughts and things have been alike. Although depending upon the cause we feel effects, it is not a matter of 'before and after', because 'before' and 'after' are merely ways of speaking.

In the statement, "You purify your own intentions," the 'you' is the 'you' that refrains, the 'purifying' is the purifying by refraining, the 'own' is the 'own' of yourself, the 'intention' is the intention that <u>you</u> have. The 'your own' is the 'your own' that refrains, the 'intention' is the intention to refrain. 'Intention' is 'the intention to uphold and practice', 'to purify' is 'to purify by upholding and practicing', 'your own' is 'your own adherence to practice', the 'you' is the 'you that upholds and practices'. This is why it is said, "This is what all Buddhas teach."

All Buddhas may resemble gods like Ishvara, the Indian creator of the world. Although They have some things in common with Ishvara, all such gods are not

Buddhas. They also resemble sovereign, Wheel-turning Lords.* However, it cannot be said that all those holy sovereign lords are Buddhas. We must carefully study the principle enunciated here. Although it seems that there are people who fail to examine what 'all Buddhas' means and thereby create suffering for themselves—and to no good purpose—nevertheless, this is simply suffering from being a sentient being; it has nothing to do with practicing the Way to Buddhahood. 'Refraining from' together with 'upholding and putting into practice' means "Before all the donkey matters have passed, horse matters have already arrived."[7]

The poet Haku Rakuten of the T'ang dynasty was a lay disciple of Meditation Master Bukkō Nyoman, who was a Dharma heir of Baso. When Rakuten was governor of Hangchow, he trained under Meditation Master Dōrin of Chōka.

Rakuten once asked Dōrin, "Just what is the major intention of the Buddha Dharma?"

Dōrin replied, "Refrain from all evil whatsoever; uphold and practice all that is good."

Rakuten remarked, "If that's all there is to it, even a child of three knows how to say that!"

Dōrin replied, "Though a three-year-old child can say it, there are old men in their eighties who still cannot put it into practice."

Upon hearing the matter put this way, Rakuten then bowed in gratitude.

Rakuten was actually a descendant of General Haku. Even so, he was a wizard of a poet, the likes of which is rare in any generation. People refer to him as 'the literary genius of twenty-four generations'. Some have called him a veritable Manjushri;* others, a Maitreya, the Buddha-next-to-come. There is no one who has

---

7.   That is, refraining from evil (which trains the stubborn 'donkey') is not something to be completed before beginning to practice good (putting the willing 'horse' to use.)

not heard of his personality; everyone in the world of letters pays court to him. Even so, when it comes to the Buddha's Way, he was a beginner, a youngster. Furthermore, it was as if he had never even dreamt of the meaning of "Refrain from all evil whatsoever; uphold and practice all that is good." Rakuten thought that in saying to refrain from all evil and practice all good, Dōrin was looking at the matter from the perspective of an ordinary, everyday person's way of thinking. Rakuten had failed to grasp the principle of refraining from evil and practicing good—a principle which has existed in Buddhism from ancient-most times and has extended even to the present— nor had he ever even heard of it; consequently he did not tread where the Buddha Dharma is. Lacking the strength of the Buddha Dharma, he said what he did. Even so, when we refrain from evil or practice good as understood by ordinary, everyday people, it will still be our actualizing of 'refraining'.

For the most part, what we first learn about Buddhism from a good spiritual friend and what we bring to fruition through our diligent practice are both one and the same. We describe this as 'learning, from start to finish'. It is also called 'the wondrous cause and the wondrous effect', as well as 'the cause of seeking Buddhahood and the effect of seeking Buddhahood'. Cause and effect in Buddhism should not be confused with such notions as 'effects are totally unrelated to their cause' and 'cause and effect are exactly the same thing', because these notions are not what is meant by 'seeking Buddhahood', and they will not achieve the effect of seeking Buddhahood. Because Dōrin enunciated this principle, he 'possessed' the Buddha Dharma.

Were evil to pile upon evil and spread throughout the whole world, absorbing everything into its mass, 'emancipation through refraining' would still hold true. Since all that is good is already good—beginning, middle, and end—the nature, characteristics, form, and strength of upholding and practicing it will likewise be good. Rakuten had never walked in such footsteps, which is why he said, "Even a child of three knows how to say that!" He said this because he was lacking in the strength to realize the Way. Poor, pitiful Rakuten, why did you say such a thing?

Since Rakuten had not yet got wind of what Buddhism is really about, it is unlikely that he was truly acquainted with any three-year-olds or with what such a child is naturally capable of. If someone can truly understand a three-year-old, he will surely know all the Buddhas of the three temporal worlds. If someone does not yet know all the Buddhas of the three temporal worlds, how will he be able to understand a three-year-old? Do not imagine that you understand such a child just because you have met one face-to-face. Do not think that you do not know such a child just because you have not met one face-to-face. He who knows but a single mote of dust knows the whole world: he who fully comprehends one thing comprehends all the myriad things that comprise the universe. He who fails to comprehend all the myriad things will not comprehend even one of them. When someone has fully trained himself in this principle of comprehending and has reached full comprehension, he will not only see the myriad things that comprise the universe but will also see each one of them. This is why the person who studies one mote of dust will undoubtedly be studying the whole universe. To think that a three-year-old child cannot give voice to the Buddha Dharma or to think that a three-year-old is 'cute' is the height of foolishness. This is because clarifying what birth is and clarifying what death is constitutes the most important matter for a Buddhist monk.

A virtuous elder once said, "When you were born, you were provided with the lion's roar." Being provided with the lion's roar is the meritorious fruit of a Tathagata's turning of the Wheel of the Dharma: it is the turning of the Wheel of the Dharma. And another virtuous elder said, "The coming and going of birth and death is the Real Body of man." Thus it is that clarifying what one's True Body is and possessing the merit from the lion's roar will indeed be the One Great Matter,* and I do not mean that the task is easy or simple. Hence, attempting to clarify what prompts the words and actions of a three-year-old is also the Great Cause for which we train, since it is the same—and yet not the same—as what prompts the words and actions of all the Buddhas in the three temporal worlds.

Befuddled Rakuten had never heard what a three-year-old child had to say, and so he had never questioned himself as to what the Great Matter was. Instead, he made the kind of remark that he did. He did not hear what Dōrin was voicing, though It resounded louder than thunder. In speaking of That which cannot be put into words, Rakuten said, "Even a child of three knows how to say that!" Not only did he not hear the child's lion roar, he also stumbled over the Master's turning of the Wheel of the Dharma.

The Master, out of pity, could not give up on Rakuten and went on to say, "Though a three-year-old child can say it, there are old men in their eighties who still cannot put it into practice." The heart of what he said exists in what a child of three can say, and this we must thoroughly investigate. Also, there is the practice which eighty-year-olds may not be doing, but which <u>we</u> must diligently engage in. What Dōrin has told us is that what the child is capable of saying has been entrusted to us, though it is not a task for a child, and what the old men were not able to practice has been entrusted to us, though it was not the task for old men such as these. In a similar way do we keep the Buddha's Dharma in mind and take It as our foundation, so that we may make It our reason for training.

Delivered to the monks on the evening of the full moon in autumn in the second year of the En'o era (September 2, 1240) at Kannondōri in Kōshōhōrin-ji Temple, Uji Prefecture, Yamashiro Province.

Transcribed by me on the twenty-seventh day of the third lunar month in the first year of the Kangen era (April 17, 1243) in the chief disciple's quarters.

Ejō

10

On 'Respectful Bowing Will Secure for You the Very Marrow of the Way'

(Raihai Tokuzui)

Translator's Introduction: Dōgen's title, *Raihai Tokuzui,* in addition to the translation given above, can also be rendered as 'Respectfully Bowing to Those Who Have Realized the Very Marrow of the Way'. The text is in two parts. The first, delivered to his monks in the spring of 1240, deals with being willing to learn from any who give voice to the Dharma, be they male or female, human or animal, living or dead, animate or inanimate. The second, given in the fall of the same year, specifically addresses various questions on learning from women. For unexplained reasons, the second part was not incorporated in the earlier versions of the *Shōbōgenzō,* but was kept under lock and key in Dōgen's temple, Eihei-ji. This may be due in part to the strong tone of this section, which might be misunderstood as being improperly critical of the practices and attitudes of other monks and other Buddhist traditions. When read in context, however, it is likely that Dōgen's initial talk on gratitude towards those who teach the Dharma, which includes female monks, garnered some negative reactions, and he found it necessary, to borrow his metaphor, to drive the wild foxes of delusion out from their lairs. Hence, his remarks are colored by strong rhetoric, along with his insistent use of the phrase 'and also' to punctuate his remarks, for he seems determined to rid his monks of any and all negative, conventional, non-Buddhist cultural attitudes towards women, including those arising from some long-standing practices within Buddhist communities.

At that time when a person undertakes spiritual training and practice in order to realize *anuttara-samyak-sambodhi*—that is, supreme, fully perfected enlightenment—it is extremely difficult to acquire a teacher and guide. Whether that guiding Master has the physical features of a male or a female, or whatever, is irrelevant, but it must be someone who is spiritually outstanding, one who is truly 'with It' here and now.[1] Whether he or she is someone of the past or a present-day

---

1. To be "'with It' here and now" is an attempt to render the term *immo* when used in its Chinese slang meaning for the condition of persons or things being just what they truly

person is of no matter; even one who has the nagging manner of a wild fox may prove a good spiritual friend,[2] for this is the countenance of one who has secured the very Marrow, one who will be a spiritual guide and of benefit to you. This is someone who does not deceive others about cause and effect, and who will treat you, me, and others as spiritual equals.

Once you have encountered a teacher and guide, from then on you should discard your myriad involvements, cease frittering away your time, and devote yourself to diligently practicing the Way. You should do your training and practice, even though you may still be attached to discriminatory thinking; you should do your training and practice, even if you have gone beyond discriminatory thinking; you should do your training and practice, even though you may be half-hearted in the attempt. Study with urgency, as though you were extinguishing a fire on your head: study with joy and hopefulness, as though you were standing on tiptoes.[3] Should you behave in this way, you will not be disturbed by bad-mouthing demons. Besides, the Second Chinese Ancestor's 'cutting off his arm to obtain the Marrow' of his Master's Teachings was a unique deed.[4] I myself had become 'the teacher who has cast off body and mind' before I was fully aware of it.

Securing the Marrow and communicating the Dharma inevitably depend on sincere devotion and a trusting heart. Sincerity and trust do not in the least come from outside ourselves, nor is there any place within from which they emerge. Simply,

---

are, without any sense of an existence separate from time and without any sense of a false self.

2. In Zen literature, the epithet 'wild fox (or jackal)' is usually applied to a person who is, as yet, unawakened to the Truth, one who tags after someone who is voicing the Dharma, and persists in asking nagging and vexatious questions. The term is sometimes applied in a positive sense to a Buddhist Master who keeps at his disciples, urging them in the direction of realizing the Truth through his probing questions.

3. A Buddhist metaphor similar to the English phrase 'walking on air'.

4. 'Cutting off one's arm' is being used metaphorically to refer to giving up one's willfulness at all costs. Such a 'severing' is done by applying Manjushri's Sword of Wise Discernment. Dōgen is not recommending self-mutilation.

beyond doubt, those who have done this emphasize the Dharma and play down themselves. These people flee society's world and make the Path their dwelling place. If they were then to pay heed to their false self, prizing that above the Dharma, then the Dharma would not be Transmitted to them and they would never realize the Way. This attitude of prizing the Dharma has not been limited to just a single case, so perhaps we can look at a few cases, without turning to any of the many other instructive examples.

It has been said, "Prizing the Dharma means that if our guide and teacher— be it one who is a supporting pillar[*] of the temple or a temple lantern,[*] a Buddha or a wild fox, a hungry ghost[*] or a divine being—is presenting the Great Dharma and has personally realized Its Marrow, we should respectfully serve him for immeasurable eons, with our bodies and minds as a resting place for the Teaching." Obtaining a body and mind comes easily enough—like the rice, hemp, bamboo, and reeds that sprout up throughout the world. What is rare is encountering the Dharma.

Shakyamuni Buddha once said:

> Should you meet teachers who expound supreme enlightenment, do not inquire into their family pedigree, do not look at their personal appearance, do not despise their shortcomings, do not be concerned with their behavior. Simply, out of respect and esteem for spiritual wisdom, feed such persons daily with hundreds of thousands of ounces of gold, bestow upon them food fit for the gods, make them offerings to meet their needs, and scatter celestial flowers upon them as a reverential offering.[5] Thrice every day— morning, noon, and evening—reverently bow to pay your respects, without letting any feelings of resentment arise in you. When you

---

[*]   See Glossary.

5.   What is being described here as 'gold', 'food', 'celestial flowers' and 'reverential offerings' are all metaphors for offerings of gratitude for the teacher's Dharma.

behave in this way, there will undoubtedly be a way to enlightenment for you. From the time when I first gave rise to the intention to realize Buddhahood, I have trained and practiced in this manner so that today I am realizing supreme enlightenment.

In accordance with this, we should pray that the trees and stones give voice to the Dharma for us: we should hold in our hearts the wish that the fields and the villages also give voice to It. We should ask It of the pillar of a temple: we should have the walls and fences explore It thoroughly with us.

In olden times, there was a celestial emperor, one Shakrendra, who respectfully bowed to a fox as his teacher and asked it about the Dharma, and, according to tradition, he gave it the title of Great Bodhisattva,* without concern whether, due to some deed in a previous life, it was a creature noble or humble.[6] Even so, those foolish and deluded ones who have not paid attention to the Buddha's Teachings express such views as: "I am a great monk, so I need not bow to some youngster's realization of what Dharma is." "I am one who has trained for a long time, so I need not bow to the realization of what Dharma is by someone who has come to training late in life." "I have had the office of Teacher of Buddhism bestowed upon me, so I need not bow to one who lacks such a title." "I am a business officer of the temple, so I need not bow to other monks." "I am the monastery's disciplinarian, so I need not bow to a lay person who has realized what Dharma is, be they male or female." "I am one 'thrice wise and ten times saintly',* so I need not bow to female monks or any other such, even though they have realized what Dharma is." "I am one of imperial descent, so I need not bow to ministers, their family members, or any in their retinue who have realized what Dharma is." Since befuddled persons like these have vainly separated themselves from the legitimate Realm of the Buddhas and wandered off onto the pathways of other realms, they neither see nor hear of the Buddha's Way.

---

6.   Dōgen will relate this story later in Discourse 87: On Taking Refuge in the Three Treasures of Buddha, Dharma, and Sangha *(Kie Buppōsō Hō).*

Long ago during the T'ang dynasty in China, Great Master Jōshū Shinsai, upon giving rise to the intention to seek the Way, set out on a pilgrimage of Zen monasteries, saying at the time, "Even though it be someone seven years old, if he or she is spiritually my superior, I will ask that person to instruct me. Even though it be someone a hundred years old, if he or she is spiritually less advanced than I, I will give him or her instruction." This old arhat* was bound to bow even when asking for teaching from a seven-year-old! Rare indeed is such an intention, <u>and</u> such was the aim of a Buddha of old.

When a female monk who has realized both the Way and the Dharma becomes head of a temple, male monks who, in seeking the Dharma, wish to train under a Master will join her community, respectfully bowing as they ask her about the Dharma, for she is a splendid model for their training and study. It will be for the trainee like receiving something to drink when he is thirsty.

In the land of China, Meditation Master Shikan was a highly venerated monk dwelling in Rinzai's temple. The first time Rinzai chanced to see Shikan coming his way, he suddenly grabbed hold of him, whereupon Shikan responded, "As you wish." Releasing him, Rinzai said, "I was just about to give you a thumping." Thereupon, Shikan became Rinzai's disciple.[7]

Later, Shikan left Rinzai's temple and paid a visit to the female Master Massan, whose name means 'the peak of the mountain'.

Massan asked him, "What place have you recently come from?"

Shikan replied, "From Luk'ou."

---

7. Shikan's lack of fear plus his respectful attitude of acceptance of Rinzai's method of teaching was the basis for his being immediately accepted by Rinzai as a disciple. A 'thumping' refers to any means Rinzai might employ to arouse a monk from his spiritual torpor.

Massan said, "Why haven't you put a lid on that mouth of yours?"[8]

Shikan was at a loss for words. Accordingly, he respectfully bowed, as one does when performing the ceremony of taking a Master.

Arising, Shikan asked Massan, "What could this mountain peak be?"[9]

Massan replied, "Its apex does not emerge."

Shikan asked, "What kind of person dwells in this mountain?"

Massan answered, "One whose characteristics are neither masculine nor feminine."

Shikan asked, "Why do you not transform yourself into a male?"[10]

Massan replied, "Not being a fox spirit, why should I transform myself into anything?"[11]

Shikan respectfully bowed. Then, giving rise to the intention to seek Buddhahood, he served her as the temple's head gardener for three years.

---

8. Luk'ou, the name of a village, means 'the mouth of—or entryway into—the path'. Since Massan was not asking a social question but a spiritual one, her response, which is based on 'path' being a reference to the spiritual Path, is asking Shikan why he is going about baldly claiming to have attained the Way, that is, to have realized Buddhahood.

9. A reference to her name, Massan, which means mountain peak.

10. A reference to a section of the *Lotus Scripture*, in which the Dragon King Sāgara's 8-year-old daughter, because she had already realized enlightenment, was capable of transforming herself into whatever it would take to quell the doubts of those who did not believe that a female could attain realization.

11. In China, fox spirits are believed to have the ability to transform themselves into manifestations of other beings. One example of this is contained in the kōan story of "Hyakujō's Fox", which Dōgen will explore later in his Discourse 73: On the Great Practice *(Daishugyō)*.

Later, when Shikan had become head monk of his own temple, he said as instruction to his community, "I received half a ladleful when I was with your grandfather Rinzai and the other half when I was with your grandmother Massan. Now that I have completely drunk a whole ladleful, it has been nourishment enough to satisfy me even to this very moment."

Now that you have heard of this way of his, you may hanker to know something about those former times. Massan was a model disciple of Master Daigu and had the strength and authority from the Transmission line to be a spiritual *jō* for Shikan. Rinzai was a Dharma heir of Ōbaku Unshi and had the strength and authority from his single-minded meditation to be a spiritual *ya* for Shikan. *Ya* is a respectful Chinese word for father, and *jō* is a respectful one for mother. Meditation Master Shikan's respectful bowing to the female monk Massan Ryōnen and his seeking the Dharma from her is a model of intent that we should follow. It is an example of constancy and integrity for those of us who study the Way in these latter days of the Dharma; it can be said to break down the barriers erected by discriminatory thinking.

The female monk Myōshin was a disciple of Kyōzan. At the time when Kyōzan was engaged in selecting a monk to serve as the temple's Head of Foreign Relations and Secular Affairs, he asked, among others, the monks who had long served in offices, as well as those seniors who had served as his personal attendants, which person would be ideal for the post. Since many opinions were voiced, Kyōzan finally said, "My disciple Myōshin is, indeed, a woman; even so, she has the strength of will associated with courageous men. Surely, she should be appointed Head of Foreign Relations and Secular Affairs." All the members of the community concurred with him, and Myōshin was then given this post. At that time, none of the other dragon elephants * in Kyōzan's community thought ill of him or of her. Although this post was not one of the truly lofty positions in a temple, as the person appointed, she would no doubt have been conscientious in her service.

One day while she was serving in this post, a group of seventeen monks from the independent state of Shu [which is now part of Szechwan Province] arrived on a

Zen-style pilgrimage to call on Masters and inquire of the Way. Intent on going up to seek an audience with Kyōzan, they were lodged in the temple for the night. While resting, they began an evening discussion, taking up the account of Great Ancestor Daikan Enō's 'wind and banner', but what each of the seventeen said was not on track.[12] At this time Myōshin, who was in the room next door, overheard what they had said and commented, "Seventeen blind donkeys have, to no avail, worn out who knows how many pairs of straw sandals without ever having caught sight of the Buddha Dharma even in their dreams!"

Also present at the time was a lay worker who overheard Myōshin's disapproving comment about the monks and told them what she had said. The seventeen, to a monk, felt no rancor at Myōshin's disapproval, but instead, felt embarrassed at not being able to say what Daikan Enō was talking about. Accordingly, they put on their formal robes and, making an offering of incense, respectfully bowed to her, requesting her to respond. Myōshin said to them, "Come right in front of me." The seventeen had barely taken a step towards her when she said, "This is not the wind moving, nor is This the flag moving, nor is This your mind moving." Upon her expressing the Matter* in this way, the seventeen, to a one, fully understood. They bowed, as disciples do when offering respect to their teacher. They immediately returned to the western state of Shu, without ever having gone up to visit Kyōzan.

Truly, her level of spiritual understanding is not surpassed even by those thrice wise and ten times saintly; her speech and actions are in direct descent from the Buddhas and Ancestors. For this reason, even today, when there is a vacant post for an Abbot or one who teaches in the Abbot's stead, we should invite a female monk who has realized what Dharma is to take the position. Even though a male monk be

---

12. Great Master Keizan's *Denkōroku* recounts the pertinent event: [Whilst still a layman,] Enō had taken up lodging on a temple verandah when a strong wind began to flap the temple banner, whereupon he heard two monks engaging in an argument with each other. One was saying that it was the banner that was moving, the other that it was the wind that was moving. The debate went back and forth without their being able to agree on the principle. Enō said to them, "Might a member of the laity be permitted to call a quick end to this lofty debate? Frankly, it is not the wind or the banner that is moving, kind sirs, it is your minds that are moving and nothing more."

one of greater age and longer residence, if he has not realized what Dharma is, why would you want him instead? The one who is the head monk for a community must undoubtedly be someone spiritually clear-eyed. A person who is as dissipated in body and mind as he is limited in outlook, however, will be so hard-headed that he will often be the laughing stock of ordinary people. When it comes to the Buddha's Dharma, such a one is not even worth mentioning as a candidate. Likewise, there have no doubt been lay women and female monks of long standing who have not gone along with making bows to the monastic teachers who have passed on the Dharma to them. Because such women have neither understood nor practiced the Dharma, they are close to being animals and far from being Buddhas or Ancestors.

Should people deeply commit their hearts to sincerely devoting body and mind to the Buddha Dharma, the Buddha Dharma will undoubtedly compassionately reveal Itself to such people. Among people of all stations, even the foolish and befuddled are sensitive to sincerity, so why would the genuine Teachings of all the Buddhas not respond compassionately to sincerity? Even the dirt, stones, sand, and pebbles are not impervious to feelings of sincerity.

In present-day Sung China, there are female monks who have hung up their bowl bag in a temple.[13] Should word get around that one of them has realized what Dharma is, an imperial decree will be issued by a government office that she should be appointed Abbess of her own temple, and as a result, she will begin to teach in the Monks' Hall of the temple in which she is presently residing. The community of monks from the Abbot on down will go to seek her Teaching, and stand there listening to her Teaching, with the male monks asking her to answer their spiritual questions as well. This has been, and still is, the standard procedure. Once such a woman has realized what Dharma is, then she is truly an Old Buddha, so we should not look upon her as we did in the past. When we are having an audience with her, our contact will be from a new and special standpoint. When we meet her, we should face her with an attitude of 'today is today', regardless of how things were in the past. For example, a female monk to whom the Treasure House of the Eye of the True Teaching has been Transmitted should respectfully be bowed to and asked for the Teaching by those in

---

13.   That is, they have entered a temple to train.

the four stages* of arhathood, those who are pratyekabuddhas,* and those thrice wise and ten times saintly, and she will acknowledge this bow. Why should only males be worthy of respect? Boundless space is simply boundless space; the four elements* are simply the four elements; the five skandhas* are simply the five skandhas. And they are no different for women. When it comes to realizing the Way, everyone may realize It. In any case, anyone who has realized what Dharma is should be deeply respected: do not concern yourself with whether it is a man or a woman. This is a most excellent rule of the Buddha's Way.

Also, in Sung China the term 'lay devotee' refers to a Buddhist gentleman who has not left home to become a monk. Some such gentlemen build a retreat for themselves and their wives, whereas others live alone in celibacy. It must be said, though, that they will still be troubled by various delusions and defiling passions as dense and entangling as a jungle. Nevertheless, once one of them has clarified the Matter, trainees will gather about him like clouds and mist, respectfully bowing and seeking spiritual benefits, behaving the same as they would towards a Master who had left home and become a monk. Be it a woman or be it an animal, you should do the same.

Someone who has not yet even dreamt of the Truth of Buddhism, even if he be an old monk of a hundred years, will not be the equal of a man or woman who has realized what Dharma is; he should not be reverenced, but simply paid common respect, as between guest and host. Even a seven-year-old—were he or she to train in and practice Buddhism, and then say something that is Buddha Dharma—can be a teacher and guide for monks and laity, male and female. This child will be a compassionate parent to all sentient beings, just as was, for instance, the dragon king's daughter who had become a Buddha. We should make offerings and pay respect to such a one the same as we would to all Buddhas and Tathagatas. This is an ancient custom of the Buddha's Way. Those who may still be in ignorance and who lack the direct Transmission are to be pitied.

Recorded on the Clear, Bright Day in the second year of the En'o era (April 28, 1240) at Kannondōri in Kōshōrin-ji Temple.

And also, in past and present China and Japan, there have been women who have occupied the Imperial Throne. As each of these countries comes under the dominion of their imperial person, the people serve as this person's subjects. These imperial persons are not revered as individuals, but are respected instead for their social position. In the very same manner, ever since ancient times, female monks have not been revered as individuals, but humbly respected for having realized what the Dharma is.

And also, whenever there are female monks who have become arhats, the spiritual merits from their complying with the four stages to arhathood will come forth. These spiritual merits will always accompany them, and who among ordinary people of any social station could possibly equal the spiritual merits of these four stages? All the heavenly ones in the three worlds of sensual desire, form, and beyond form are in no position to surpass them. Nevertheless, when someone renounces worldly views, this is something that all heavenly beings revere. So, who would possibly fail to revere a Tathagata who passes on to us the True Teaching, or a bodhisattva who has given rise to the greatest of intentions? Anyone who fails to respect such a person is a strange one indeed! Should any of you possibly fail to respect supreme enlightenment, you would be a foolish and befuddled being who slanders the Dharma.

And also, in our country, imperial daughters, as well as daughters of high ranking ministers, have, on occasion, followed the retiring imperial consort into a monastery and have been given the Empress's 'cloister name' as an honor. Some of these women have shaved their heads; others have not. Be that as it may, monks in name only who covet fame and crave gain are known to go in and out of the doors to the Empress's domicile, knocking their heads against the slippers of these women. Such people are even lower than the low. And worse still, how many of these male monks have grown old playing the role of slave to these women? [14] Alas, how pitiful that, for those born in a small, out-of-the-way country like ours, a form of wickedness like this has gone unrecognized. It does not exist in India or T'ang China. Only in our country, sorry to say, does this practice exist. These men have shaved their heads and then thoughtlessly transgressed the True Teachings of the Tathagata. Their defiling act, it must be said, is deep and heavy. How lamentable that, in losing sight of the fact that the worldly path is as the false flowers of fantasy and delusion, they have tied themselves down to the role of a slave. They have acted in this manner for the sake of some diverting and vain worldly way. In the name of that enlightenment which is unsurpassed, why have they passed over reverencing someone—be it male or female—who has truly realized that Teaching which is to be revered? It is simply because their resolve to esteem the Teaching is shallow and their determination to seek the Teaching is not broad in scope.

When someone is entangled with coveting jewels, he does not consider that he ought not to have them because they are a woman's jewels: when someone attempts to seek the Dharma, his determination should surely outdo this. When, indeed, it does, the sprouting grass and the trees, as well as the walls and the fences, dispense the True Dharma, and the myriad things that make up heaven and earth likewise bestow the True Dharma. This is a principle that, without fail, you need to be aware of. Even if you meet a genuine spiritual friend but have not yet given rise to this intention to seek the Dharma, you will be unable to take in the delightful, thirst-quenching waters of the Dharma. So, make a diligent effort.

And also, even today there are people, wretched from their folly, whose unconverted thinking has not gone beyond looking upon women simply as objects in the world of sensual desire. Disciples of Buddha should not be this way. Should you detest women because you think that they must be objects in the world of sensual desire, would you also detest all men? What causes staining and defilement to arise is treating men as comprising one world and women as another. In addition, looking

---

14.   In other words, even those ladies-in-waiting who 'shaved their heads'—that is, had formally entered monastic life—were not behaving as female monks should, but were manipulating these ambitious, worldly monks for their own personal purposes.

upon someone as being neither male nor female is also to treat that person as 'an object apart'; even looking at that person as though a phantasm or an illusory flower is likewise treating him or her as 'an object apart'. There have been those who have engaged in a sexual act in connection with some reflection in water, and there have been sexual acts committed in connection with the sun in the sky. Deities have been used as such objects, as have hungry ghosts. Connections such as these are surely beyond count. It is said that there are eighty-four thousand worlds of them. Shouldn't these all be things to be given up? Are they not things that should all be ignored?

It says in the *Vinaya:* [15] "The two orifices of a male and the three orifices of a female are alike when it comes to committing a grievous breakage of the Precepts; those doing so may not dwell within the monastic community." Thus, if you dislike women because you think that they must be objects in the world of sensual desire, then males and females will end up mutually disliking each other, and it is unlikely that there will be any opportunity for either to find a way to the Other Shore. You should explore this principle in detail.

And also, among non-Buddhists there are those who are unmarried. Although celibate, they have not comprehended the Buddha's Dharma, and, because of their false views, they are outside the Way. Also, among the Buddha's disciples there are lay men and women who are husband and wife. Even though living as husband and wife, they are disciples of the Buddha, and thus no one among ordinary people of any station is their equal.

And also, in T'ang China there have been foolish and befuddled monks who, having given rise to the intention to commit themselves to the Way, have said, "I will never look at a woman in this or any future lifetime, no matter how long such a life may be." [16] On what teaching is this vow founded? Is it founded on the rules of society? Or on the Buddha's Dharma? Or on the teachings of some non-Buddhist? Or on the doctrines of some distracting demon from the world of sensual desire? What

---

15. The *Vinaya* is a part of the Buddhist Canon which outlines and discusses the meaning and application of the Buddhist Precepts and various monastic rules and regulations.

16. This vow is probably based on a misunderstanding of one of ten vows listed in the *Avatamsaka Scripture*: "May my eye not look upon a woman (as a sexual object)."

fault is there in being female? What virtue in being male? When it comes to being wicked, there have been men who were wicked; when it comes to being virtuous, there have been women who were virtuous. To respectfully ask to hear the Teaching and to long to leave the world of delusion behind certainly do not depend on one's being male or female. When people have not yet cut themselves off from their delusions, they are equally attached to delusion whether they be male or female. When people cut themselves off from delusion and reach certainty as to what is Real, again, there is no dividing line between males and females. Further, should you vow never to look at a woman, ought you to forsake women even at the moment when you take the Bodhisattva Vow to save all sentient beings from suffering, howsoever innumerable they may be? Were you to forsake women, you would not be a bodhisattva, so how could you speak of Buddhist kindliness and compassion? This vow to never look at a woman is simply the raving words of one who has drunk too deeply of the wine that those who rigidly follow the Lesser Course* are wont to brew. No one of any station should believe this to be what Truth is.

And also, should you despise women because you think that in ancient times they have committed some offense, then you must despise all bodhisattvas as well. Or, should you despise women because you think that at some later date they will surely commit some offense, then you must despise all bodhisattvas who have given rise to the intention to realize Buddhahood. If you despise women in any such ways, you must despise every single person, so how will you make manifest the Buddha's Dharma? Words like the ones uttered by such monks are, sad to say, the wild remarks of foolish people who do not understand what the Buddha taught. If the matter were like this vow, did the Venerable Shakyamuni and the bodhisattvas who were alive during His lifetime all commit offenses? Have Their enlightened minds been shallower than yours? You would do well to quietly think about this. Since the Ancestors and Masters associated with the Treasure House of the Dharma, as well as the bodhisattvas who lived during the Buddha's lifetime, did not take this vow, as part of your training and study you should look to see whether there is any place in the Buddha's Teachings where this could possibly have been taught. Were the matter like this vow, not only would you fail to ferry women to the Other Shore, you would also be unable to come and hear a woman who, having realized what Dharma is, has come out among the people to give voice to the Dharma for the sake of people in all stations of life. To fail to come and hear her is to fail to be a bodhisattva and, consequently, to be outside the Path of Buddhism.

If we now take a look at present-day Sung China, among the monks who seem to have trained and practiced for a long time, there are those who are uselessly counting the grains of sand in the ocean [17] and are drifting on the waves that arise upon the sea of birth and death. But there are women who seek out a spiritual friend to train under, and diligently do their training until they become a teacher and guide for people of all stations. It is like the old woman who threw away her rice cakes rather than selling them. Sad to say, even though her customer was a male monk, he was so busy counting sand grains in the ocean of Scriptural writings that he had still not seen what the Buddha was teaching, even in his dreams. [18]

To speak in broader terms, upon seeing an object in the world of desire, it would be good for you to learn to clarify what it is that you are looking at. To learn only to flee when you are frightened by something is the teaching and practice of those in the Lesser Course who rigidly follow what they have learned by rote. Were someone to attempt to abandon the populous east to live in seclusion in the sparsely-settled west, it would not mean that there are no objects in the world of desire to be found in the west. Even though such persons may think that they have succeeded in fleeing, to the extent that they have not yet clarified the matter of sensual desire, whether they keep their distance or come up close, there <u>will</u> be a world of desire. But this is not intended to be a full explanation, for the long threads of sensual desires will prove to extend even deeper.

---

17. An allusion to those who waste their time, caught up in studying the words in Scriptures without comprehending their meaning in context.

18. A reference to a kōan story involving a famous scholar of Buddhist Scriptures who was unable to express Their meaning in his own words when asked to do so by an old woman selling rice cakes. When he failed, she refused to sell him a rice cake and he had to go hungry. Dōgen will discuss this in detail later in Discourse 17: On 'The Mind Cannot Be Held Onto' *(Shin Fukatoku)*.

And also, in Japan there is a situation which is truly ridiculous and worthy of laughter. It relates to what is called 'The Grounds of the Enclosed Realm' by some and 'The Training Ground of the Greater Course' by others, places that female monks and lay women are not permitted to enter.[19] This mistaken custom has been handed down for ever so long, and people have never questioned what it is all about. Those who have studied the ancient ways have never attempted to change this practice nor have scholars ever taken up the matter. Some refer to this practice as 'what an incarnation of a Buddha or a Bodhisattva does'; others speak of it as 'the tradition of our ancient predecessors'. Moreover, they have never called the matter into question. It is enough to make a person split a gut laughing. Just what is 'an incarnation of a Buddha or a Bodhisattva'? Is it a worldly-wise person or a saintly one? A god or a hungry ghost? One who is ten times saintly or one who is thrice wise? One who has realized what supreme enlightenment is or one who has realized the wondrous, full enlightenment of a Buddha? Furthermore, if we are not to alter anything from the past, are we not to abandon our drifting through the realms of birth and death?

And besides, the Venerable Shakyamuni, our Great Teacher, is *anuttara-samyak-sambodhi*, supreme, fully perfected enlightenment. What had to be clarified, He made completely clear; what had to be done, He did fully; what needed to be explained, He fully explained. Is there a single person today who surpasses Him? And yet, in the Buddha's community during His lifetime, there were all four groups—male monastics, female monastics, lay men, lay women—and there were the eight categories of heavenly and demonic beings, and there were the thirty-seven categories of Venerable Ones who reside in the Diamond Mandala, and there were the eighty-four thousand categories of thoughts and things. In that all of these form the enclosure of the Buddha Realm, they are patently the Buddha's community. So, what Buddhist community is without female monastics, or lay women, or lay men, or the eight

---

19. These terms are used in some Buddhist traditions for a monastery or the main training halls of a monastery. In Japan, it was a common practice to exclude women on the pretext of maintaining a strict adherence to the Precepts. However, as Dōgen will assert, this practice actually arises from a cultural bias and is both unsupported and unjustified by the Buddha Dharma.

categories? We should not pray for a more pure and immaculate Enclosed Realm than that of the Buddha's community when the Tathagata was in the world, because such would be the realm of the demons of greed and desire. The manner of organizing a Buddhist community is such that it never differs, be it in the Buddha's own realm or in any other realm, including the realms of all the ten thousand Buddhas in the three temporal worlds.

What are called 'the Four Fruitions of Arhathood' refer to ultimate stages.[20] Whether a person is following the Greater or the Lesser Course, there will be no difference in the spiritual merits accruing from realizing these ultimate stages. Indeed, female monks who have experienced the Four Fruitions are many indeed. Within the three worlds of desire, form, and beyond form, as well as in any of the Buddha lands throughout the ten directions of the universe, what world may they not reach? Who can ever possibly prevent anyone from doing his or her daily training in the Way?

And also, the wondrous, fully perfected enlightenment is the highest level. Since women are already acting as Buddhas, which of all the Teachings may they not thoroughly master?[21] Who could presume to hamper them or prevent them from realizing the goal? They already have spiritual merits that are said to illumine the whole universe in all ten directions, so who can put limits on them?

And also, would you hamper a celestial female who is in one of the heavens of the world of desire so as to prevent her from realizing the goal, or do the same to a daughter of some deity? Such celestial women have not as yet severed themselves from delusive views. They are still sentient beings who are drifting, and there are times when they commit acts that break the Precepts, and there has never been a time when this was not so, just as with female humans and animals who at times defile themselves, and there has never been a time when this was not so. Who is the one who would block these celestial women from the way of heaven or the way of the gods? They are already paying visits to the Buddhist communities in the three temporal worlds and have come to do spiritual training wherever a Buddha is. If you make a

---

20   These are the fruitions of the four stages of arhathood referred to previously in this discourse.

21.   'Acting as a Buddha' is synonymous with keeping the Precepts.

distinction between a place where a Buddha is and what a Buddhist community is, how will you accept either one in faith as a place of the Buddha Dharma? This is, simply, the height of folly of worldly people crazed by delusion: they are foolish when they fail to regret that someone has not wrested their wild fox of delusion from its dark and cavernous lair.

And also, the classification of disciples of the Buddha—be they bodhisattvas of the Greater Course* or shravakas* of the Lesser Course—is the same for both: first, male monastics; second, female monastics; third, lay men; fourth, lay women. This classification is known to those in the heavenly worlds as well as to those in the human worlds, and has been familiar since ancient times. Be that as it may, when it comes to the second group of Buddhist disciples, they surpass even a saintly ruler who makes the wheels of governance roll on, and they surpass even Shakrendra, Lord of the Thirty-three Heavens. There is no spiritual place that one of this group cannot realize, to say nothing of the ranks of rulers and high ministers in a small out-of-the-way nation like ours.

Now, when we look at a 'Training Ground' where they say female monks must not enter, male field hands, simple rustics, farmers, and woodcutters are given entrance with impunity, to say nothing of rulers, high ministers, officials of all types, and councilors: whoever is male may enter. Were we to discuss the understanding of the Way of a field hand, say, and a female monk, or the spiritual level they have realized, what quality would we ultimately come to ascribe to each? No matter whether we are discussing the matter in worldly terms or in Buddhist ones, the place that a female monk may realize cannot possibly be realized by a field hand or a simple rustic.[22] Small nations that are excessive in their turbulent and riotous behavior, first of all, have left the traces of their excess.[23] How lamentable that there is any place where a disciple of that Kindly Parent of the Three Temporal Worlds, upon arriving in a small country, is barred from and may not enter.

---

22. Not because such persons are spiritually deficient, but because it is improbable that they are devoting themselves to the spiritual training that a monk is undergoing.

23. Dōgen wrote this during the height of a series of clan wars that had already been devastating many areas of Japan for almost a century.

And also, some fellows who may dwell in a place they call 'the Enclosed Realm' show no dread of the ten evil acts and fully commit the ten most serious forms of them.[24] In a realm where defiling acts are cultivated, is it simply a matter of despising those who do not cultivate them?

Further, the five treacherous deeds* are considered even more serious, yet some who live within 'the Grounds of the Enclosed Realm' are apparently committing such acts. Devilish realms like these should, beyond question, be smashed.[25] Such monks would do well to study the edifying instructions given by the Buddha and thereby to enter into the Realm of Buddhas, which, of course, includes repaying one's indebtedness to the Buddha for His kindness. I wonder whether those of old who constructed such 'Enclosed Realms' really understood their purpose. From whom did they receive Transmission: from whom did they receive the seal* of Buddha Mind? As it has been described, the person who truly enters the Great Realm wherein all Buddhas are enclosed cuts himself free from any attachments, not only to 'all Buddhas' but also to 'sentient beings', not only to 'the physical world' but also to 'emptiness', and thus returns to the Source, Which lies within the wondrous Teachings of all the Buddhas. Accordingly, any sentient being who takes but one step into this Realm will nevertheless receive the spiritual merits of a Buddha. They will receive the merits from not having deviated from the Path, as well as the merits from realizing Immaculacy. When someone is attached to one place, then he is attached to the whole realm of thoughts and things: when someone is involved with one serious breakage of the Precepts, he is tied to the world of all thoughts and things.

There is a realm enclosed by Water, and there is an enclosing of this realm by Mind, and there is an enclosing of this realm by the Unbounded. You need to realize that, within this realm, beyond doubt, there is a Transmission and a passing on of the Buddha seal. Furthermore, once this realm has been enclosed, the Sweet Dew has

---

24. That is, the ten evil acts arising from breaking the Ten Precepts and the more serious forms of such breakage.

25. The term 'devilish' refers to those conditions wherein a trainee is faced with a delusive obstacle to his training which he allows to divert him from the Path.

flowed into it, the ceremony of Taking Refuge in the Triple Treasure has been performed, and the realm has been consecrated, then it is as the poem says:

> *This realm completely permeates*
> *the worlds of thoughts and things*
> *And, by its very nature,*
> *is bound to Boundless Immaculacy.*

I wonder whether those old men of former times who spoke of what is now habitually called 'the Enclosed Realm' understood the meaning of this poem. For, when you try to think about it, my dear monks, the mind cannot directly grasp that the whole universe of thoughts and things is enclosed within this Enclosure. Beyond doubt, should you drink of the wine of those who rigidly follow the Lesser Course, you will mistake the tiny world of self for the Great Matter.

I pray that you will quickly sober up from your habitual drunkenness on delusion and that you will not deviate from "The whole universe is the Great Realm of all Buddhas." In your trying to rescue all sentient beings from their suffering and ferry them across to the Other Shore, they will respectfully bow to you and venerate the merits from receiving your spiritual instructions. Who among them will not call this 'securing the very Marrow of the Way'?

Written at Kōshōhōrin-ji Temple on the day before the winter season in the first year of the Ninji era (October 16, 1240).

11

On 'Just for the Time Being,
Just for a While,
For the Whole of Time is the Whole of Existence'
(Uji)

Translator's Introduction: *"Uji"* is Dōgen's discourse on the significance of *anatta* and *anicca*—the Buddhist terms for 'no permanent, abiding self' and 'continual change'—and their application to treading the paths of Right Understanding and Right Thought. It is not, strictly speaking, a discourse, for Dōgen gave the text to his monks in written form, which suggests that he intended it to be read over and studied carefully, rather than to be absorbed by hearing it only once.

Because it is linguistically possible to translate the title as 'Being and Time', some modern scholars have been led to assume that Dōgen was engaging in a form of philosophical speculation akin to that of some Western existentialists. Such an approach, however, would seem counter to the purpose behind a discourse given by a Buddhist Master, since speculative thinking—philosophical or otherwise—is a type of mentation that trainees are working to disengage themselves from so that they may progress towards realizing spiritual Truth, which lies beyond the reaches of speculation.

The key term, which is presented as the title, has meanings which no single English rendering fully encompasses. To begin with, *uji* (the Japanese pronunciation of the Chinese *you-shih*) has long been a common, everyday phrase in China, as it has been for the Japanese when read as *aru toki*, encompassing in both languages such English equivalents as 'just for the time being', 'there is a time when', 'at some time', 'now and then', and the like. During his presentation, Dōgen also explores the two components from which the word *uji* is made, drawing examples of their usage from everyday Japanese. The first half (*u*) refers to 'existence' or 'being'; the second (*ji*) has a variety of close English equivalents, including 'time', 'a time', 'times', 'the time when', 'at the time when' (as well as 'hour' or 'hours' when used with a number) or as signifying what is temporal ('sometime', 'for a time', etc.). The phrase *aru toki* has already appeared with some frequency in several of Dōgen's earlier discourses, particularly as a phrase in an extended kōan story to signal that an important event is about to happen, such as a one-to-one exchange with a Master that will trigger the disciple's realization of what Truth is. In this context, it conveys the sense of 'and then, one day'.

Underlying the whole of Dōgen's presentation is his own experience of no longer being attached to any sense of a personal self that exists independent of time and of other beings, an experience which is part and parcel of his 'dropping off of body and mind'. From this perspective of his, anything having existence—which includes every thought and thing—is inextricably bound to time, indeed, can be said to '<u>be</u> time', for there is no thought or thing that exists independent of time. Time and being are but two aspects of the same thing, which is the interrelationship of *anicca*, 'the ever-changing flow of time' and *anatta*, 'the absence of any permanent self existing within or independent of this flow of time'. Dōgen has already voiced this perspective in Discourse 1: A Discourse on Doing One's Utmost in Practicing the Way of the Buddhas (*Bendōwa*), and in Discourse 3: On the Spiritual Question as It Manifests Before Your Very Eyes (*Genjō Kōan*), where he discussed the Shrenikan view of an 'eternal self' and the Buddhist perception of 'no permanent self'.

In the present discourse, Dōgen uses as his central text a poem by Great Master Yakusan Igen, the Ninth Chinese Ancestor in the Sōtō Zen lineage. In the Chinese version, each line of this poem begins with the word *uji*, which functions to introduce a set of couplets describing temporary conditions that appear to be contrastive, but which, in reality, do not stand against each other. These conditions comprise what might be referred to as 'an I at some moment of time'; this is a use of the word 'I' that does not refer to some 'permanent self', abiding unchanged over time (as the Shrenikans maintained) but to a particular set of transient conditions at a particular time. In other words, there is no permanent, unchanging 'Yakusan', only a series of ever-changing conditions, one segment of which is perceived as 'a sentient being', which is, for convenience, conventionally referred to as 'Yakusan'. Both Yakusan and Dōgen understand *uji* (in its sense of 'that which exists at some time') as a useful way of expressing the condition of *anatta*, and in this sense it is used to refer to a state of 'being' that is neither a 'permanent self' nor something separate from 'other'; it is the 'I' referred to in one description of a kenshō experience (that is, the experiencing of one's Buddha Nature) as 'the whole universe becoming I'. Hence, when the false notion of 'having a permanent self' is abandoned, then what remains is just *uji*, 'the time when some form of being persists'.

After presenting Yakusan's poem, Dōgen focuses on that aspect of the poem that does not deal with metaphors, images, symbols, etc., and which is the one element in the poem that readers are most likely to pay small heed to: the phrase *uji* itself. His opening statement encapsulates the whole of what he is talking about in this text, namely: "The phrase 'for the time being' implies that time in its totality is what existence is, and that existence in all its occurrences is what time is."

Dōgen then begins to 'unravel' this statement, describing not only its implications but also its applications to practice. The points that he takes up are dealt with as they come to him, as they 'flow forth'. Therefore, he talks about 'time' for the time being, and then talks about 'existence' for the time being, and then goes back to 'time' just for a while before moving on to some other aspect just for a while. In other words, his text is not only about *uji*, it is written from the perspective of one who lives *uji*, and who also writes *"Uji"* so that the very way in which he presents his discussion reflects what *uji* is about. That is to say, he holds onto nothing as absolute, for all that is phenomenal—that is, every thought and thing that ever arises—is just for the time being.

Within the original text, there are sudden, unexpected shifts, as though Dōgen were deliberately trying to help his readers bypass or short-circuit a purely intellectual comprehension of what he is saying in order to catch a glimpse of that state of being which Dōgen himself had already reached. To help the present-day reader keep from making unintentional links between sentences that appear in sequence but which take up different points, Dōgen's text has been divided accordingly.

Although the entire discourse contains a number of remarks that may require some reflection to penetrate, near the end of his discourse Dōgen has an extended discussion that may prove daunting to some readers because of its succinctness. To make what is being said there more accessible, paraphrases have been supplied in the footnotes, which make explicit in English what is implicit in the original.

Readers who find it helpful to refer to the Introduction and footnotes may find it rewarding to reread just the text of *"Uji"*, for there are aspects of this discourse, in particular, that may well open up for them through encountering the flow of Dōgen's presentation without interruptions.

A former Buddha once said in verse:

Standing atop a soaring mountain peak is for the time being
And plunging down to the floor of the Ocean's abyss is for the time
being;

Being triple-headed and eight-armed is for the time being
And being a figure of a Buddha standing sixteen feet tall or sitting
eight feet high is for the time being;

Being a monk's traveling staff or his ceremonial hossu is for the
time being
And being a pillar supporting the temple or a stone lantern before
the Meditation Hall is for the time being;

Being a next-door neighbor or a man in the street is for the time
being
And being the whole of the great earth and boundless space is for the
time being.[1]

The phrase 'for the time being' implies that time in its totality is what existence is, and that existence in all its occurrences is what time is. Thus, 'being a golden body sixteen feet tall' refers to a time. And because it is a time, its time will have a wondrous luminosity—a point that we will be studying and learning about during the present twenty-four hours. 'Being one with three heads and eight arms' also refers to a time. And because it is a time, it will be one and the same as the present twenty-four hours. Granted that we may not yet have measured the length of these twenty-four hours as to whether they are ever so long or as short as a sigh, still we speak of them as 'the twenty-four hours of our day'. The traces of this time having come and gone are clear, so people do not doubt that these hours have occurred. But, though people have no doubt about time having occurred, the past may be something that they have not known through their direct experience. And, just because sentient beings are always

---

1.   Dōgen appears to understand Yakusan's image of 'a figure of a Buddha standing sixteen feet tall or sitting eight feet high' as referring to one who has realized his or her Buddha Nature and lives accordingly at all times. It is likely that 'standing' and 'sitting' are references to the Four Bodily Postures: standing, walking, sitting, and reclining. The first two represent active modes, the latter two passive ones: that is, 'whether one is inwardly or outwardly active, whether one is awake or sleeping'.

'Being triple-headed and eight-armed' is an allusion descriptive of several guardian beings who protect Buddhist temples and their trainees. The most likely candidates in the Zen tradition would be Achalanātha, the Steadfast Bodhisattva, and Rāgarāja, the Passionate Bodhisattva. The former is sometimes associated with the firm commitment of trainees to train until they have overcome all hindrances to realizing enlightenment as they persist in helping others to realize Truth. The latter has associations with a passionate desire to help all sentient beings realize Buddhahood.

Please see the Glossary for the metaphorical meanings of a monk's traveling staff, a ceremonial hossu, a temple pillar, and a stone lantern.

having their doubts about anything and everything that they have not directly experienced, this does not mean that what they may have previously doubted is the same as what they may now have doubts about, for doubts themselves are merely 'just for the moment' kinds of time, and nothing more.

Since we human beings are continually arranging the bits and pieces of what we experience in order to fashion 'a whole universe', we must take care to look upon this welter of living beings and physical objects as 'sometime' things. Things do not go about hindering each other's existence any more than moments of time get in each other's way. As a consequence, the intention to train arises at the same time in different beings, and this same intention may also arise at different times. And the same applies to training and practice, as well as to realizing the Way. In a similar manner, we are continually arranging bits and pieces of what we experience in order to fashion them into what we call 'a self', which we treat as 'myself': this is the same as the principle of 'we ourselves are just for a time'.

Because of this very principle of the way things are, the earth in its entirety has myriad forms and hundreds of things sprouting up, each sprout and each form being a whole earth—a point which you should incorporate into your study of the Way, for the recognition of the coming and going of things in this manner is a first step in training and practice. When you reach such a fertile field of seeing the way things really are, then the earth in its entirety will be 'one whole sprouting, one whole form'; it will be comprised of forms that you recognize and forms that you do not, sproutings that you recognize and sproutings that you do not. It is the same as the times we refer to in 'from time to time', which contain all forms of existence and all worlds. So take a moment to look around and consider whether there is any form of being, that is, any 'world', that does or does not find expression at this very moment of time.

When ordinary, everyday people who do not take the Buddha's Teachings as their model hear the phrase 'just for the time being' in Yakusan's poem, they customarily hold a view like the following:

> There was once a time when Yakusan had become what he describes as 'someone with three heads and eight arms' and some other time when he had become 'someone eight or sixteen feet tall'. It is as though he were saying, "I have crossed the rivers and climbed over the mountains.[2] Even though those mountains and rivers may have existed in the past, I have completely gone beyond them and have now made a place for myself atop a vermilion pedestal in the Jeweled Palace.[3] I fancy that the mountains and rivers on the one hand and I on the other are now as far apart as heaven and earth."

But such a view is not all there is to the principle of the case.

At the time when, proverbially, a mountain was being climbed and a river was being crossed, an I existed, and it was the time for that particular I.[4] Since such an I existed, time could not abandon it. If time did not have the characteristic of

---

2.   An allusion to surpassing hindrances by training oneself to live by the Precepts and to surmounting obstacles by practicing meditation.

3.   A metaphor for being in the state of experiencing what 'being enlightened' is. The reference is to a lotus pedestal upon which an awakened being sits when residing in the Western Pure Land.

4.   Dōgen's point in using the word 'I' as a noun in this and the following paragraph is to indicate that there is no permanent, unchanging self that is being referred to, but rather a cluster of physical and mental characteristics that is flexible and fluid, undergoing change as the conditions and circumstances of what is existing change. Hence, this 'I' refers to a series of manifestations over time, which are perceived as related to 'a sentient being called Yakusan', but which have no unchanging, atemporal 'permanent self' passing through them.

'coming and going, being continually in flux', then the time when this I was 'climbing atop the mountain' would have remained forever, eternally comprised of that particular 'time when'. But, since time retains the characteristic of 'coming and going, being continually in flux', there is a flow of ever-present 'nows', each comprised of a time when an I exists. And this is what is meant by the phrase 'just for the time being'. Surely you don't think that the earlier time when the word 'I' referred to 'climbing the mountain' or 'crossing the river' gulped up the later time when the word 'I' referred to 'being on a vermilion pedestal within the Jeweled Palace', or think that the former has vomited out the latter, do you?!?[5]

Yakusan's 'being a triple-headed and eight-armed one' refers to a time that he would have called 'yesterday': his 'being someone eight or sixteen feet tall' refers to a time that he would have called 'today'. Be that as it may, this principle of a past and a present simply corresponds to the two periods of time when an I had headed straight into the mountains and when an I was now looking out from a vermilion pedestal over the thousands of peaks and the thousands beyond them. Nor have such periods passed away. The time of an I being 'triple-headed and eight-armed for the time being' had passed, but even though it seemed to be of another time and place, it was indeed a part of the ever-present now. The time of an I being 'eight or sixteen feet tall for the time being' has also passed, but even though it now seems to be something distant from us, it is indeed part of the ever-present now. Thus, we speak of the pine as an analogy for time, as we also do of the bamboo.[6]

---

5.   Most likely this sentence refers to common but erroneous views as to where the flowing moments of the ever-present now go to when they are no longer present, and where such moments come from. Dōgen is asserting that the past does not exist as an entity that 'swallows up' the instances of present time once they are over, nor is the present something thrown out from such a past, as fatalism might suppose.

6.   An allusion to the Zen saying, "The bamboo, all up and down its length, has joints (which mark the passage of the seasons); the pine (being ever-green) has no colors to differentiate past from present."

Do not look upon time as 'something that just flies away': do not teach yourself that 'flying away' is simply how time functions. Were we to endow time with the property of 'flying away', there would undoubtedly be a gap left by the time that has flown. Should anyone have not yet heard teaching upon the principle expressed by the phrase 'just for the time being', he may still think of time only as 'something which has gone away'.

In short, everything whatsoever that exists in the whole universe is a series of instances of time. Since everything is for the time being, we too are for the time being.

Time has the virtue of continuity: it continuously flows from the today that we are talking about to a tomorrow, from a today to a yesterday, from a yesterday to a today. It flows from a today to a today and from a tomorrow to a tomorrow. Because continual, continuous flow is a function of time, past and present times do not pile atop each other nor do they form an accumulative line. Yet, even so, Seigen, too, represents a time, as does Ōbaku, and likewise Baso and Sekitō represent times.[7] Because we ourselves and others, as previously stated, are already 'beings for a time',

---

7.   Seigen, Sekitō's Master, was already dead before Yakusan was born, and therefore represents a time that Yakusan did not know through direct experience. Ōbaku, whose Master was Baso Dōitsu, was a contemporary of Yakusan, and therefore 'a time' simultaneous with Yakusan's time. Baso was contemporary with Sekitō, both together representing a time that included a past that Yakusan did not know directly, a past that he did, a present that was also 'his time', and a future time that was not theirs. Although Yakusan was Sekitō's disciple and ultimately his Transmission heir, at one point Sekitō sent Yakusan to train under Baso, who triggered Yakusan's realization of the Truth. These relationships represent various ways in which the time of a particular sentient being (Yakusan) relates to the times of other sentient beings.

our training and practice are times, as is also our awakening to Truth. Our 'entering the mud or going into deep water'[8] is likewise a time.

The opinions of ordinary, everyday people today—as well as the source of those opinions—are based on what these people perceive. But this is not what ordinary people consider as being how things operate. For them, the way things operate is that they have 'simply come about for a while'. Because these people have convinced themselves that this time and this existence of theirs is not related to the way things really operate, they conclude that a golden body sixteen feet tall could not possibly be theirs.[9] Trying to free oneself from this opinion that "the golden body of a Buddha cannot be mine" is also a bit of what the phrase 'just for the time being' implies, and is something about which a trainee who has not yet reached spiritual certainty may say, "Oh, I see, I get it!"

In the world today, we structure time by segments which we name, for instance, the Hours of the Horse or the Hours of the Sheep.[10] Be that as it may, these segments are merely persistent fluctuations in the here and now of thoughts and things which arise and fall. It is the same with the Hours of the Rat and the Hours of the

---

8.　A traditional Zen saying alluding to the actions of a bodhisattva who is willing to go anywhere to help ferry sentient beings to the Other Shore.

9.　That is, they think, "I am no more than what I am right now, so I could not possibly be a Buddha, and being what I am now, I cannot see how I could possibly become a Buddha."

10.　In medieval Japan, a full day was divided into twelve two-hour segments, named after the twelve signs of the Chinese zodiac. The Time of the Horse was 12:00 noon, and the Hours of the Horse were the hours preceding and following noon. Similarly, the Time of the Sheep was equivalent to 2:00 p.m. Except in the imperial court, where a water-clock was used for assuring that a ceremony was performed at the most auspicious time, determining time throughout medieval Japan was approximated based on the position of the sun in relation to the zenith.

Tiger, which are also 'for a time'.[11] And being an ordinary creature is also 'for a time', as is being a Buddha. At such times as these, one will swear that being three-headed and eight-armed is the whole universe or that being a golden body sixteen feet tall is the whole universe. To universally penetrate the whole universe by means of the whole universe is called 'complete realization'. For us to give proof of a golden body sixteen feet tall by our attaining a golden body sixteen feet tall is to manifest our initial spiritual intention, our training and practice, our realizing of enlightenment, and our experiencing the freedom of nirvana—all of which comprises what existence is and what time is. It is a complete realization that the whole of time is what the whole of existence is, <u>and</u> that there is nothing more than this. Anything else would be a time when there was a partial 'complete realization', which would be a full realization of a part of what 'just for the time being' refers to.

Even at a stage where it would seem that you have taken a false step, this condition will be a state of 'being'. Further, should you leave the matter at this, your condition will still constitute a persistence of 'a time being', which will include both a before and an after to this 'having taken a false step'. Dealing with thoughts and things while they persist, like a fish darting about through the water,[12] is indeed what 'being just for the time being' is about. So, do not be upset over what is not, and do not be pressured by what is.

Should you reckon one-sidedly that time only goes by, you will not comprehend time as something that has not yet arrived. Although we can say that

---

11. The Time of the Rat was midnight, and that of the Tiger was 4:00 a.m., times which were still commonly referred to as 'segments of time', even though they could not be determined, since the sun was not visible. Dōgen's point is that all such divisions are cultural conventions and do not constitute what time really is.

12. A traditional Zen simile applied to a person who engages in the practice of all-acceptance and non-attachment.

comprehending something also constitutes a time, there is no connection that can link the one to the other.[13] No one with a human carcass who looks on time merely as 'something that rolls on by me' can have any insight into the 'time being' that persists just for a while, not to even mention the time when the barrier gate to realizing enlightenment is penetrated.

Even if we comprehend that It is what persists, who can express in words what This is that we have realized? Even if, over a long time, we have found ways to express It in words, there is no one yet who has not groped for ways to make It be manifest before your very eyes. Were we to leave the matter of what 'being for the time being' means to the way in which ordinary persons understand the phrase, it would be a 'being for the time being' in which enlightenment and nirvana were, at best, merely passing characteristics. The ever-present 'time being' of which I am speaking cannot be snared like some bird by net or cage: it is what is manifesting before us. It is a time when the heavenly lords and the other celestial inhabitants are now manifesting right and left of us, and are making every effort to do so, even at this very moment. In addition, it is a time when beings of water and land are making every effort to manifest. Beings of all sorts, who are visible or invisible for the time being, are all making every effort to manifest, making every effort to flow on. If they did not make every effort to flow on, not even a single thought or thing would ever manifest: nothing would continue on. You would do well to consider this point.

The transiting of time and being is not to be thought of as wind blowing the rain from east to west. And it would be inaccurate to say that the whole world is unchanging, or that it is motionless: it is in transition. The flow of time and being is like spring, for instance. The spring has an appearance of being abundant in its burgeoning, and we refer to this as its 'passage'. We should consider well that the spring 'passes' without excluding anything within it. In other words, the passing of spring is, to be sure, a passing of what we humans call 'spring'. 'Passing' is not what

---

13. That is, for instance, one cannot predict the precise moment when someone will comprehend something.

spring is, but refers to the passage of the springtime; hence, it is a transition that is now being actualized during the time of spring. You would do well to consider and reflect on this very carefully, for in speaking of 'transiting', some may think of it in reference to some place physically apart from themselves, which can be reached by turning eastward, say, or by traveling past myriad worlds over millions and millions of eons. But such people are not concentrating simply on the study of the Buddha's Way.

Yakusan, who by imperial decree was named 'The Great Teacher Whose Way Is Broad', one time, at the direction of Great Master Sekitō Kisen, made a spiritual call on Meditation Master Baso.

> Yakusan asked him, "The one standing before you has a fairly good idea of what all twelve divisions of the Scriptures as found among the followers of the Three Vehicles[*] of Buddhism are about, so just why did the Ancestral Teacher Bodhidharma come east to China???"
>
> Being queried in this manner, Meditation Master Baso responded, "There are times when we make That One's eyebrows rise and His eyes twinkle, and there are times when we do not make His eyebrows rise and His eyes twinkle. There are times when we who make That One's eyebrows rise and His eyes twinkle are right, and there are times when we who make His eyebrows rise and His eyes twinkle are not right."
>
> Upon hearing this, Yakusan had a great awakening and humbly said to Baso, "When I was with Sekitō, I was like a mosquito climbing over an iron ox, trying to find a place to bite."

Baso's way of putting things is unlike that of any other. 'Brows and eyeballs' would refer to the mountains and the oceans, because the mountains and the oceans

---

*   See Glossary.

are His brows and eyeballs.[14] Baso's 'making Him raise His eyebrows' would be comparable to Yakusan's focusing on the Mountain, and Baso's 'making His eyes twinkle' would be comparable to Yakusan's fixing his eyes on the Ocean. 'Being right' means attempting to learn from 'That One': 'That One' is That which is being invited to teach. 'Not being right' does not mean 'not causing Him to act as He did', nor does 'not causing Him to act as He did' mean 'not being right'.

Mountains are of time: oceans are of time. Were there no time, neither mountains nor oceans could be. Do not think that time does not exist for the mountains and oceans of the present moment. Were time to cease to exist, so would mountains and oceans cease to exist: if time does not become extinct, then mountains and oceans too will not become extinct. This is why the morning star arose, the Tathagata emerged, his clear Eye of Wise Discernment manifested, and the raising of the udumbara flower came about.[15] These are times: were they not times, there could not be any 'being with It' here and now.[16]

---

14. In this and the following paragraph, the images of 'mountain' and 'ocean' echo the opening couplet of Yakusan's poem. Context suggests that 'mountain' is an allusion to training and practice, and 'ocean' to the realization of one's innate state of 'being enlightened'.

15. Allusions to Prince Siddhārtha's awakening to the Truth upon seeing the morning star arise, and then, as the Tathagata, with eyes twinkling, holding aloft the udumbara flower, which set in motion the Transmission of the Truth, starting with his smiling disciple Makakashō.

16. To 'be with It' here and now is an attempt to render the term *immo* when used in its Chinese slang meaning for the condition of persons or things being just what they truly are, without any sense of an existence separate from time and without any sense of a false self.

Meditation Master Kisei of Sekken County was a Dharma descendant of Rinzai, as well as Shuzan's direct heir. One day, he addressed his monastic community in verse, saying:

> *There is a time when intending has arrived, but not expressing,*
> *There is a time when expressing has arrived, but not intending,*
> *There is a time when both intending and expressing have arrived,*
> *And there is a time when both intending and expressing have not*
> *arrived.*[17]

Both 'intending' and 'expressing' are 'for the time being': both 'having arrived' and 'having not arrived' are 'for the time being'. Even though one may say that "the time of arriving is not yet fully here," the time of 'having not arrived' is here. 'Intending' is the donkey; 'expressing' is the horse.[18] The role of the horse is assigned to expressing; the role of the donkey is assigned to intending. Just as 'arriving' is not synonymous with 'coming', 'having not arrived' does not mean 'still not having arrived', for this is what being 'just for the time' is like. Arriving is hindered by 'arrival', but is not hindered by not having arrived. Having not arrived is hindered by

---

17. To paraphrase these four conditions from the perspective of Dōgen's analysis of the poem: (1) there is a time when someone deliberately trains with the intention of realizing what the Truth is, but since he (or she) has not yet arrived at that state, he is unable to express what that Truth is, and (2) there is a time when the trainee realizes what this Truth is and spontaneously (that is, without intention) gives expression to It, but without being fully conscious that this is what he has done, and (3) there is a time after having realized the Truth when the trainee deliberately gives expression to It, and (4) there is a time after having realized the Truth when the trainee is simply going on with his training, without deliberately trying to 'make a point of it'. These four conditions correlate with Dōgen's terms 'intending', 'arriving', 'having arrived', and 'having not arrived', which he presents in the ensuing paragraph.

18. That is, trainees should not wait until they have completely finished all training ('doing the donkey work of training') before attempting to give voice to the Dharma ('doing the horse work of teaching').

'not having arrived', but is not hindered by arriving. So, when it comes to intending, we look at our intention as just an intention; when it comes to expressing, we look at our expression as just an expression; when it comes to hindrances, we look at what is hindering us as just a hindrance. It is a matter of 'obstructions' getting in the way of obstructions, all of which are 'just for a time'.[19] Although you may say that 'obstruction' is a word that we can apply to other situations, there is still nothing which I am calling 'an obstruction' that impedes those situations. It is ourselves encountering others; it is others encountering each other; it is ourselves encountering ourselves; it is one who is emerging encountering one who has emerged. If each of these did not have their specific time, being 'with It' here and now would be impossible. Furthermore, 'intending' refers to the time when the spiritual question manifests before our very eyes; 'expressing' refers to the time when one looks up and unbolts the barrier gate; 'arriving' refers to the time when body and mind are dropped off; and 'having not arrived' refers to the time when this 'dropping off' is left behind [as you go always onward, always 'becoming Buddha']. This is the way that you should diligently apply yourself, the way that you should treat whatever arises as 'just for a while'.

Although the venerable Masters up to the present time have spoken about the Matter[*] in such a way, might there not be something more that needs to be said? Well, I would add, "There are times when intending and expressing are halfway there, and there are times when intending and expressing are halfway not there." You would do well to investigate and clarify the Matter in such a way. And again, "Making That One's eyebrows rise and His eyes twinkle is half of what 'just for the time being' is

---

19. To help simplify this difficult and profound passage: One's arriving at realizing the Truth is hindered by any notion of 'having to arrive', but is not hindered by the fact that one has not yet arrived. One's state of having not arrived is hindered by a notion of 'not having arrived', but is not hindered by arriving. So, when it comes to intending to train, we look at our intention as just an intention; when it comes to expressing the Truth, we look at our expression as just an expression; when it comes to hindrances, we look at what is hindering us as just a hindrance. Similarly, it is a matter of our notions of 'obstructions' getting in the way of our seeing our obstructions (all of which, too, are just for the time being).

about, and making That One's eyebrows rise and His eyes twinkle may also be a counterfeit 'just for the time being', <u>and</u> making That One's eyebrows rise and His eyes twinkle may also be a completely false 'just for the time being.'"

In such a manner, coming to training, going on in training, training until you arrive, and training beyond arriving are, at all times, 'just for the time being, just for a while'.

Written at Kōshōhōrin-ji Temple on the first day of winter in the first year of the Ninji era
(October 17, 1240).

Copied by me during the summer training period in the first year of the Kangen era (1243).
Ejō

12

On the Transmission of the Kesa

(Den'e)

Translator's Introduction: This discourse and Discourse 84: On the Spiritual Merits of the Kesa *(Kesa Kudoku)* are both concerned with the kesa, the cloak-like robe which has traditionally been worn by most Buddhists, both monastic and lay, since the time of Shakyamuni Buddha. This discourse was based on a Dharma talk that Dōgen gave to his assembly and it appears in the earliest version of the *Shōbōgenzō*, whereas the *Kesa Kudoku* was apparently written to cover, in greater detail, certain points raised in *Den'e*, but it was not formally incorporated into the *Shōbōgenzō* until some time after Dōgen's death. While both discourses share common topics and even some similar or identical passages, each has much that is unique, and readers may well find the reading of both to be worthwhile, despite any repetitions.

Two technical Buddhist terms that are applied to the kesa in both texts need some explication. The first is *juji*, translated as 'to accept and keep to (the kesa)'. While, from a linguistic perspective, it might also be rendered as 'to receive and keep (the kesa)', Dōgen explicitly states in both texts that he does not intend this latter meaning with its passive implication of 'being given something which is then put away for safekeeping'. That is, it is not enough to receive a kesa, the recipient must also accept it and what it implies; likewise, the robe is not to be stored away, but is to be put to use. 'Putting it to use' implies keeping to it and what it stands for, just as one keeps to the Precepts and what they stand for, an analogy that Dōgen implies in both texts but does not explicitly make.

The second term is *butsue*, which has multiple meanings, including 'the Buddha robe', 'the Buddha's robe', 'a Buddha robe', and 'a robe for a Buddha', referring to both a physical garment and that which spiritually enrobes the trainee. In some contexts, it is clear which meaning Dōgen intends, whereas in other contexts more than one of these may be intended, so that the meaning of the passage becomes ambiguous, permitting a different understanding according to whether the reader is, say, a lay person, a novice monk, a transmitted monk, or one who has or has not had a kenshō, that is, the experience of one's Buddha Nature. And there are times when Dōgen is obviously talking about a physical robe, only to suddenly shift to talking about a spiritual robe, and then almost immediately to go back to his discussion of a physical robe. It is left to the reader to discover and enjoy this multidimensional, kaleidoscopic aspect in Dōgen's writing.

In these two texts, there is also an aspect of tone that needs comment, for it may seem to some readers that, in a number of passages, Dōgen is being singularly bombastic. This is not the case. Dōgen was faced with several problems in the training of his disciples. First, he was having difficulty with state and ecclesiastical authorities who did not want him (or anyone else) to teach pure meditation to the exclusion of other forms of meditation. Second, his reputation had already spread widely enough that he was beginning to attract disciples who had done training under other teachers, teachers who were given to mixing all manner of non-Buddhist teachings and methods in with their Buddhist training. Third, as a verse from the monastic ordination ceremony states, "All bodhisattvas, when converted to the Truth for the first time, search therefore, but their minds are hard and set and cannot be broken," but Dōgen attempts to help his bodhisattvas by hammering away at some of the hardness and rigidity of their thinking. Fourth, because trainees are apt to dismiss points of teaching which seem trivial to them, Dōgen, through his strong expression of feelings about these points, is helping his disciples to realize the vital importance of keeping true to the Dharma. Such an emotional appeal would have been more persuasive to his medieval Japanese compatriots (and more easily remembered) than a finely wrought, elegantly presented logical refutation of erroneous practices and teachings.

The robe and the Dharma which Buddhas correctly Transmit to Buddhas were, beyond doubt, properly Transmitted to China only by the Highest Ancestor Bodhidharma at Shōrin-ji Monastery. That is to say, the Highest Ancestor was the Ancestral Master of the twenty-eighth generation from Shakyamuni Buddha. The twenty-eight generations in India passed this robe and Dharma on in succession, and They were properly Transmitted through six generations in China. These comprised thirty-three generations altogether for India and China.[1]

The Thirty-third Generation Ancestor, Meditation Master Daikan Enō, received the Transmission of this robe and Dharma on Mount Ōbai in the middle of the night and safeguarded Them throughout his life. To this day, this robe is still safely enshrined at Hōrin-ji Temple on Mount Sōkei. Various generations of imperial rulers respectfully requested that it be brought to court, where they made venerative offerings to it. It is treated as an object protected by wondrous spiritual guardians. Three emperors of the T'ang dynasty—Chu-tsung, Su-tsung, and T'ai-tsung—repeatedly had it brought back to court, so that they might make venerative offerings

---

1. That is, Bodhidharma was considered both the twenty-eighth Indian Ancestor and the first Chinese Ancestor.

out of respect for it. Whenever it was sent for or returned, the emperors would have an imperial emissary accompany it, along with their edict on the matter. This is indicative of their great respect.

Emperor T'ai-tsung once sent the following edict when returning the Buddha's robe to Mount Sōkei, "I am now pleased to entrust to Commander General Liu Chung-ching, Pacifier of Our Nation, the return of this robe with all courtesies. We declare this robe to be a national treasure. Venerable Abbot, I pray that you will safely enshrine it in your temple, placing it under the rigorous care and protection of those monks of your community who have personally received from you the tenets of our religion, never letting it fall into neglect." Because of this attitude, emperors over a number of generations all regarded it as an important national treasure. Truly, the one who safeguards this robe of the Buddha in his country is also a great treasure who surpasses even those who may hold dominion over any of the three-thousand great-thousandfold worlds, which are as countless as the sands of the Ganges. It is an object that far outranks Pien-ho's jewel.[2] Even if such a gem were to serve as the imperial seal at an enthronement, how could it possibly compare with the wondrous treasure that Transmits Buddhahood?

From the time of the great T'ang dynasty on, the monks and laity who have looked upon this robe with reverence and bowed to it have undoubtedly had a great capacity for faith in the Dharma. Had they received no help from the good that they did in previous lives, how could they possibly have received that body of theirs which made possible their actually looking upon, and reverently bowing to, the Buddha's robe that Buddha after Buddha had directly passed on? The skin, flesh, bones, and marrow of those who accept it in faith will take delight in it; those who cannot accept it in faith, even though this is the result of their own doing, will regret the absence of this seed of Buddhahood.

Even common folk say, "To see someone's daily deeds is to see what that person really is." To look upon and respectfully bow to the robe of a Buddha is to see

---

2.　Pien-ho was a person in ancient China who offered to three rulers a huge, unpolished jewel that he had found, but none of these rulers were able to perceive its intrinsic value, and therefore summarily rejected the offering.

Buddha, in all humility, right now. We should erect hundreds of thousands upon thousands of stupas* in venerative offering to this Buddha robe. Any beings who possess a mind, be they in the heavens above or in the oceans below, will deeply respect it. Among humans too—from saintly ones who rule over vast empires on down—anyone who can discern what is true and recognize what is surpassing will prize it.

Sad to say, some of the kinsmen who became rulers of China in later generations did not realize the enormous treasure that they had in their country. Often misled and captivated by Taoist teaching, many indeed abandoned the Buddha Dharma. At those times, they did not don the kesa but put the cap of a Taoist upon their shaven domes, and, when they lectured, their talk was in the direction of how to extend the length of one's life. This occurred during both the T'ang and Sung dynasties. Even though such types were considered rulers of their nations, they must have been more base than any of their subjects.

You should calmly consider whether the Buddha robe has come to abide in our country and is present here now. And you would also do well to ponder whether ours could be a Buddha Land for the robe, for it is more valuable than any ash relic or such. As for ashes, we have them for rulers of vast lands, and for lions, and for ordinary folk, as well as for pratyekabuddhas* and the like, but mighty rulers do not have a kesa, nor do lions, nor do ordinary folk: accept in deepest faith that Buddhas alone have the kesa.

Nowadays, foolish people in great numbers highly prize ash relics whilst knowing nothing of the kesa, much less of how they should preserve and keep to one. This is due to the fact that those who have heard of the importance of a kesa are few, and even they may not yet have learned of the True Transmission of the Buddha's Dharma.

When we carefully take into consideration how much time has passed since the Venerable Shakyamuni was in the world, it has been scarcely some two thousand years. Many of our national treasures and ancient sacred utensils that have come down to us today are older by far: the Buddha's Dharma and the Buddha's robe are newer

---

*   See Glossary.

and nearer our times. As the *Lotus Scripture* observes, the spiritual benefits arising from the propagation of the Buddha's Teachings will be wondrous, no matter how widely this Teaching may spread—be it through farmlands or towns—even if one person passes It on to only fifty others. National treasures and sacred utensils do have their merits, and the merits of the Buddha robe can never be less than, or even merely equal to these, for this robe has been truly Transmitted by authentic Dharma descendants.

Be aware that we can realize the Way when we hear the four lines of the kesa verse, and we can realize the Way when we hear a single line of Scripture. Why can the four lines of the verse or a single line of Scripture produce such a profound spiritual experience of being 'with It' here and now?[3] Because, as it is said, they are part and parcel of the Buddha Dharma.

Now, each kind of robe, including the nine types of sanghati robe, has been correctly passed on from the Buddha's Teaching.[4] None can be inferior to the four lines of the kesa verse or less beneficial than a single line of Scripture. Because of this, for more than two thousand years, the various beings who have been exploring how to follow the Buddha—both those whose practice stems from faith and those whose practice stems from understanding the Dharma—have all protected and kept to the kesa, and treated it as their very Body and Mind. Those folks who are in the dark as to the True Teaching of Buddhas do not revere or prize the kesa. Now, both Shakrendra [ruling lord of the Trayastrimsha Heavens] and the dragon lord who dwells in Anavatapta Lake, for instance, have guarded and protected the kesa, even though the first is a celestial lay ruler and the second a dragon lord.

---

3.   To be 'with It' here and now is an attempt to render the term *immo* when used in its Chinese slang meaning for the condition of persons or things being just what they truly are, without any sense of an existence separate from time and without any sense of a false self.

4.   The sanghati robe is the largest of three basic types of kesa. Dōgen gives a detailed explanation of all three in Discourse 84: On the Spiritual Merits of the Kesa *(Kesa Kudoku)*.

Be this as it may, that type who shave their heads and then go around calling themselves 'disciples of Buddha' have not the slightest awareness of those who, having put on the kesa, accept and keep to it. This is to say nothing of their having any knowledge about its materials, colors, or dimensions, nor are they aware of the ways in which it is worn, nor, even less, have they ever seen, even in their dreams, the dignified manner in which it is treated.

From ancient times, when the kesa has been spoken of, it has been called 'the garment that protects us from overheating our brains' and 'the garment of liberation'. In short, its spiritual merits are beyond measure. By virtue of the kesa, a dragon's scales can be liberated from their three types of burning pain.[5] When any of the Buddhas fully realized the Way, it was undoubtedly due to Their having made use of this robe. Truly, even though we have been born in a remote region at the time of the final stages of the Teaching, if any of us have the opportunity to choose whether to be Transmitted or not, we must accept in faith—as well as guard and maintain—the true inheritance that is being passed on to us.

What other tradition has genuinely Transmitted the robe and the Dharma of our Venerable Shakyamuni as we have genuinely Transmitted Them? They exist only in the Buddha's Way. Who, upon encountering this robe and Dharma, would fail to be generous in respecting Them and in making venerative offerings to Them? Even if, in the space of a single day, we were to renounce our physical life for times as countless as the sands of the Ganges, we should make venerative offerings to Them. We should vow that we will humbly raise Them above our head whenever we encounter Them in life after life, for generation after generation. Even though we may have been born in a place separated from the Buddha's native land by more than a hundred thousand leagues of mountains and seas, and even though we may be muddle-headed, ignorant provincials, the fact that we have heard this True Teaching, and have accepted and are keeping to this kesa, even if it be only for a single day and night, and are exploring

---

5. Namely, suffering from fiery heat, from fierce desert winds, and from being devoured by a garuda bird.

how to put into practice a single line of Scripture or the whole of the kesa verse, this cannot be due simply to the blessings and merits from our having made venerative offerings to just one or two Buddhas; it must be due to the blessings and merits from our having made venerative offerings to, and having attended upon, countless hundreds of thousands of millions of Buddhas. Even if it were due to our own efforts, we should feel respect for the robe and Dharma, cherish Them, and prize Them.

We should show our gratitude to the Ancestral Masters for their great kindness in Transmitting the Dharma to us. Since even animals repay kindliness, how could humans fail to understand kindness? If people do not recognize kindness, they must be inferior to animals; they must be even denser than animals.

Those who are not Ancestral Masters who Transmit the Buddha's True Teaching do not even dream of the spiritual merits of this Buddha robe. How much less could they come up with anything that clarifies for others what its materials, colors, and measurements are? If you would follow in the footsteps of the Buddha, then you should, by all means, follow this robe and Dharma. Even after a hundred thousand myriad generations, people would still be able to correctly pass on the genuine Transmission for, undoubtedly, it will be the Buddha's Dharma. The proof of Its authenticity will indeed be evident.

Even the secular Confucian teaching admonishes its followers not to wear clothing which differs from that officially worn during the time of the previous ruler, nor to act in ways that go against the regulations of previous rulers. It is also the same for the Buddha's Way: if something is not in accord with the Dharma clothing of previous Buddhas, do not use it. If it is something other than the Dharma clothing of previous Buddhas, what are we to clothe ourselves with so that we may train in and practice the Buddha's Way and attend upon all the Buddhas? Were we not to clothe ourselves with this 'garment', it would be hard indeed for us to enter into the assembly of the Buddhas.

Since the middle of the Yung-p'ing era (67 C.E.) of Emperor Hsiao-ming of the Later Han dynasty, monks who came from India to eastern lands ceaselessly followed upon the heels of their predecessors, and we have often heard of monks heading to India from China, but none of these travelers said that they had ever encountered anyone who conferred the Buddha Dharma face-to-face. All they had to show were words and forms that they had vainly learned from disputatious teachers and pedantic scholars of the *Tripitaka.** They had not heard of the direct heirs of the Buddha's Dharma. Because of this, they could not go so far as to impart to anyone that the Buddha's robe was actually to be passed on, or to say that they had personally encountered anyone to whom the Buddha's robe had been passed on, or to tell of having seen or heard of anyone who had Transmitted the robe. Be very clear about this: they had not crossed the threshold and entered into the Buddha's family. Those fellows saw the kesa as just an item of clothing and nothing more, and did not realize that it was the most venerable and prized manifestation of the Buddha Dharma. Truly, what a pity!

Those who are genuine successors and have continued to Transmit the Treasure House of the Buddha's Dharma have also continued to pass on the robe of a Buddha, which they had received in turn. Among ordinary people, as well as among those in more lofty positions, it is widely known that the Ancestral Masters to whom the Treasure House of the Dharma has been genuinely Transmitted have never failed to see the Buddha robe or failed to pay attention to what it signifies. Hence, the Ancestors have come to accurately pass on what the materials, colors, and dimensions of a Buddha's kesa are. Since they have actually seen and paid attention to such a kesa, they have accurately Transmitted what its great spiritual merits are and have genuinely Transmitted the Body and Mind, Bones and Marrow of the kesa of a Buddha—all of which occurs only through the actions of those in the tradition of the authentic Transmission. It is unknown to the various traditions associated with the *Āgama Scriptures*. A robe that has been established according to some personal design of the moment is not a genuinely Transmitted one, nor is it the robe of any legitimate descendant.

When our Great Master, the Tathagata Shakyamuni, conferred on Makakashō the Dharma of Supreme Wisdom—which is the Treasure House of the Eye of the True Teaching—He passed on along with It the Buddha robe. After that, the robe was received by successor after successor down to Meditation Master Daikan Enō of Mount Sōkei, spanning thirty-three generations. Each generation had personally seen and passed on what the materials, colors, and dimensions of monastic robes were to be. Our Zen tradition has long passed this information on and, as is evident today, has accepted and kept to it. In other words, that kesa which the founding Ancestors of the five branches of Chinese Zen have each accepted and kept to is what they have correctly Transmitted. It is likewise evident that there has never been any confusion about this between any Master and his or her heir, not even in those traditions having forty, fifty, or even more generations. They have all worn and constructed the robe according to the methods of previous Buddhas, which each Buddha on His own has passed on, just as all the Buddhas have done, generation after generation, without the slightest interruption.

In the instructions of the Buddha which heir after heir has correctly passed on, the following are mentioned:

The robe of seven panels, each comprised of three long segments and one short segment.

The robe of nine panels, each comprised of four long segments and one short segment.

The robe of eleven panels, each comprised of three long segments and one short segment.

The robe of thirteen panels, each comprised of three long segments and one short segment.

The robe of fifteen panels, each comprised of four long segments and one short segment.

The robe of seventeen panels, each comprised of four long segments and one short segment.

The robe of nineteen panels, each comprised of four long segments and one short segment.

The robe of twenty-one panels, each comprised of four long segments and one short segment.

The robe of twenty-three panels, each comprised of four long segments and one short segment.

The robe of twenty-five panels, each comprised of four long segments and one short segment.

The robe of two hundred fifty panels, each comprised of four long segments and one short segment.

The robe of eighty-four thousand panels, each comprised of eight long segments and one short segment.

What I have now given you is an abbreviated list. There are, in addition, various other types of kesas which, all together, comprise the sanghati robes.

No matter whether a person is a householder or someone who has left home to be a monk, he or she accepts and keeps to the kesa. When I speak of accepting and keeping to it, I am referring to wearing it and putting it to use, not to uselessly keeping it all folded up and stored away somewhere.

Even if someone shaves their head and beard, should that person not accept and keep to the kesa, but instead hate and despise it, or be afraid of it, such a one is outside the path and will attempt to bedevil and obstruct others. As Meditation Master Hyakujō Daichi once said, "A person who has planted no good seeds in former lives will shun the kesa, despise the kesa, and both fear and despise the True Teaching."

The Buddha once said:

Let us suppose that some person enters into Our Teaching and then commits some heavy offense or falls into false views. If, within the space of a single thought, that person shows deep reverence for the sanghati robe out of a feeling of respect, then all the Buddhas, including Myself, will surely give this person a guarantee that he or she shall realize Buddhahood from within any one of the Three Courses.* If any—be they lofty beings, or dragons, or ordinary humans, or hungry ghosts*—are able to show even the slightest respect for the spiritual merits of this person's kesa, then, once having entered any of the Three Courses, they will neither regress nor turn away from them. Suppose that there is some hungry ghost or spirit, or even any other type of sentient being. Should such a one be able to obtain even a four-inch bit of a person's kesa, he or she will have what they hunger and thirst for completely satisfied. Suppose that there are sentient beings who are about to fall into false views through having antagonistic attitudes towards each other. If they hold in mind the spiritual potential of the kesa, then, due to the influence of the kesa, they will be able, before long, to give rise to a compassionate heart and return to a state of immaculacy. Suppose that there is some person who is in military service. Should he have in his possession the smallest bit of a kesa which he respects and reverently prizes, he will undoubtedly attain spiritual liberation.

So, obviously, these spiritual merits of the kesa are peerless and beyond anything that we can imagine or conceive of. Whenever anyone has faith in this kesa, accepts it, protects it, and keeps to it, he or she will, beyond question, attain future liberation as well as a state of non-regression. This was not proclaimed by Shakyamuni Buddha alone: it has likewise been proclaimed by all Buddhas.

We must recognize that the bodily aspect of all Buddhas is the kesa. This is why the Buddha said, "Anyone who has fallen into wicked ways will loathe the sanghati robe." Thus, whenever anyone sees a kesa and pays heed to it, should thoughts of loathing then arise, he or she should give rise to a compassionate heart, saying, "I am about to let myself fall into wicked ways," and, feeling remorse, admit to what he or she has done.

Moreover, Shakyamuni Buddha, right after He had left the royal palace on His way to entering the mountains, was forthwith presented with a sanghati robe by a tree spirit who said to Him, "If you respectfully place this robe above your head, you will avoid being disturbed by bedeviling obstructions." At that time, Shakyamuni Buddha accepted this robe and respectfully lifted it above His head, and then, it has been said, for the next twelve years until His awakening, He did not let it drop for even a moment. This is reported in the *Āgama Scriptures*.

Some say that the kesa is indeed an auspicious garment, and that anyone who makes use of it as raiment will surely arrive at an exalted spiritual rank. Speaking in more general terms, there has been no season when this sanghati robe has not existed right before us. Its manifestation at any particular time is an instance of its continual existence, and its continual existence reveals itself at some particular time within the long stretch of eons. To obtain a kesa is to obtain the banner that is the badge of Buddha. Because of this, there has not yet been any Buddha Tathagata who has not accepted and kept to the kesa. There has never been anyone who accepts and keeps to the kesa who will not realize Buddhahood.

The Methods for Wearing a Kesa

The usual method is to keep the right shoulder bare. There is also a method for wearing a kesa over both shoulders. [You begin with the unfolded kesa held behind your back by its upper corners.] When placing the upper right and left ends atop the left arm and shoulder, bring the right corner across in front [passing it under your right arm] and drape it back over the left shoulder. You then tuck the right vertical edge between your left arm and your torso. Next, bring the left corner to the front over the left shoulder and arm, and then tuck the left vertical edge in towards the back between your arm and your torso.[6] This reflects the Buddha's everyday behavior. It is not something that any of the shravakas* saw or heard about, nor did they pass it on, nor has a word of this leaked out from the teachings of any of the *Āgama Scriptures*. In general, the dignified procedure for wearing a kesa in the Buddha's Way is what was undoubtedly accepted and kept to by Ancestral Masters who passed on the True Teaching that was being manifested before them. Beyond question, what we accept and keep to should be what was accepted and kept to by these Ancestral Masters. Accordingly, the kesa that the Ancestors of the Buddha have correctly passed on is not something that Buddhas Transmitted to Buddhas in some haphazard manner. It is the kesa of former Buddhas and of present-day Buddhas: it is the kesa of old Buddhas and of new Buddhas. It transforms what 'the Way' means: it transforms what 'Buddha' means. It transforms the past, the present, and the future. In doing so, it makes a genuine Transmission from the past to the immediate present, from the immediate present to the future, from the immediate present to the past, from the past to the past, from present moment to present moment, from future to future, from the future to the immediate present, and from the future to the past—because it is the genuine Transmission of each Buddha on His own, just as it has been for all the Buddhas.

Because of this, starting with our Ancestral Master Bodhidharma's coming from the West and continuing through the hundreds of years of the great T'ang and Sung dynasties, there were many expert lecturers on the Scriptures who saw through what they were vainly doing. When these folks, who were involved with such things as philosophical schools and teachings on monastic rules and regulations, entered into the Buddha Dharma, they discarded their former kesa, which was a shabby old robe, and straightaway accepted the kesa that was authentically Transmitted in the Buddha's Way. The effects of their doing so are strung together, one after the other, in such works as the *Ching-te Era Record of the Transmission of the Lamp*, the *T'ien-sheng Era Record of the Widely Illumining Lamp*, the *Supplementary Record of the Lamp*, and the *Chia-tai Era Record of the Lamp Whose Light Reaches Everywhere*. Letting

---

6.   Dōgen's description conforms to the way in which the kesa is still being worn in the Theravadin tradition. In present-day Sōtō Zen, a clip or tie is used to hold the kesa at the left shoulder, which necessitates a slightly different procedure.

go of their numerous narrow scholastic views on doctrine and monastic rules, they straightaway prized the Great Way that the Ancestors of the Buddha had Transmitted, and all became Ancestors of the Buddha. People today should also take a lesson from these Ancestral Masters of old.

If you would accept and keep to the kesa, it must be a correctly Transmitted kesa that has been correctly Transmitted to you: it must be one that you have faith in and accept. You must not accept and keep to a spurious kesa. When I speak of that 'correctly Transmitted kesa', I am referring to the one that has been correctly Transmitted through Shōrin-ji Monastery and Mount Sōkei:[7] this is the one that generation after generation of successors received from the Tathagata without skipping a single generation. Because of this, those engaged in the Way unmistakably accept and pass it on, relying upon the Buddha kesa being personally placed in their hands.

The Way of Buddha is straightforwardly Transmitted to the Way of Buddha: it is not left to idle people to acquire the Transmission at their leisure. There is a common saying, "Hearing about something a thousand times does not compare with a single sighting of it, and seeing something a thousand times does not compare with a single direct encounter." When we reflect on this, even if there were a thousand sightings and ten thousand hearings, they would not compare with the actual acquiring of a kesa: indeed, they could not compare with the direct Transmission of the Buddha robe. Those who may doubt that there is an authentic Transmission should doubt even more those folks who have not encountered the authentic Transmission even in their dreams. The person to whom the Buddha robe is authentically Transmitted will be more directly involved than the person who just hears someone else passing on Buddhist doctrines. And a thousand direct encounters with a robe or ten thousand acquisitions of one can never compare with a single realization of Truth. It is the Buddhas and Ancestors who have realized and given proof to the Truth. So, do not copy the stream of those ordinary, mundane students of doctrines and monastic rules.

---

7.   Shōrin-ji Monastery is associated with Bodhidharma and Mount Sōkei with Daikan Enō.

To speak more generally about the spiritual merits of the kesa in our Ancestral line: the authentic Transmission has been duly received, its original form has been passed on from person to person, and its acceptance and maintenance—along with the inherited Dharma—have continued on, unceasing, to this very day. Those who have genuinely accepted it are all Ancestral Masters whose realization of Truth has been attested to, and who Transmit the Dharma. They surpass even those who are 'thrice wise and ten times saintly'.* We should revere and respect them, bow and humbly place them above the crown of our head.[8]

Were you to trust and accept the principle of the authentic Transmission of the robe of a Buddha just once whilst in this body and mind, then that would be an indication of your encountering Buddha, and it would be the way to learn what Buddha is. How pitiable your life would be if you were incapable of accepting this Dharma! You should deeply affirm for yourself that, having once wrapped your body in a kesa, it serves as an amulet for safeguarding you, so that you may settle the Matter* and fully realize Spiritual Wisdom.[9] It is said that if you let a single sentence or a single poem of Scripture permeate your trusting heart, Its radiance will continually shine forth for the long stretch of eons. If you let one bit of Dharma permeate your body and mind, Its effect will be the same.

The thoughts that permeate the mind find no place of permanent abiding and are not part of us, yet their spiritual merits are completely as just described. And it is likewise with the body, which finds no abiding permanence. The kesa has no coming forth from anywhere, nor any place to which it goes. It is not something that we

---

8. To place them above the crown of our head means to esteem them more highly than we esteem ourselves.

9. This sentence, as translated, may lead some readers to an erroneous conclusion. Dōgen is not asserting that the kesa has some inherent magical property which wards off evil; rather, it protects the wearer by serving as a constant reminder of the purpose for which he or she donned the robe in the first place, as well as serving as an outer sign to others of the wearer's spiritual commitment.

ourselves or any others possess, yet it manifests and dwells wherever someone keeps to it, and enlarges those who accept and hold to it. Whatever spiritual merits you may realize from it will manifest the same qualities.

The 'making' in 'making a kesa' is not the kind of 'making' that ordinary people or even saintly ones do. The import and significance of this 'making' is not something that the ten times saintly or the thrice wise will exhaustively penetrate. Those who are lacking the seeds of the Way from previous lives, though they pass through one or two lifetimes, or even immeasurable lifetimes, will not see a kesa, or hear about the kesa, or know what a kesa is. How, then, could such persons ever possibly accept and keep to one? There are people who receive spiritual merits from having the kesa touch their physical body just once, and there are people who do not. Those who have already received such merits should rejoice, and those who have not yet received them should hope to do so, since not to receive them is a pity indeed!

Whether within or outside the great-thousandfold world, only in the lineage of the Buddhas and Ancestors has the robe of Buddha been passed on, as commoners and those in lofty positions alike have universally come to know through what they have seen and heard about.

The clarification of how the robe of Buddha looks is to be found only in our Ancestral tradition; it is unknown in other traditions. Those who are ignorant of this and do not feel sorry for themselves are dull-witted people indeed. Even though someone knows the eighty-four thousand meditative mantras, yet is without the genuine Transmission of the kesa, lacks the Dharma of the Buddhas and Ancestors, and has not yet clarified what the authentic Transmission of the kesa is, such a person cannot be a true heir of the Buddhas. How much people in other countries must wish that the robe of Buddha had been genuinely Transmitted to them as it was Transmitted in China! That a genuine Transmission has not been done in their countries must be a source for feelings of shame and deep regret.

Truly, to encounter the Teaching in which both the robe and the Dharma of the World-honored Tathagata is truly passed on is due to the seeds of great merit from spiritual wisdom accrued over past lives. In the world today, when the Dharma is in Its last stage and the times are wicked, there are many devilish bands of people who are unembarrassed that they have had no genuine Transmission, whereas others have been jealous of the True Transmission. Whatever they themselves may possess, wherever they may make their dwelling place, these are not their True Self. Just to authentically Transmit the True Transmission is indeed the direct path for learning what Buddha is.

To speak in general terms, you need to realize that the kesa is what the Buddha Body is, and it is what the Buddha Mind is. And also, it is called 'the garment of liberation', 'the robe that is a fertile field of blessings', 'the robe of forbearance', 'the formless robe', 'the robe of merciful compassion', 'the robe of the Tathagata', and 'the robe of supreme, fully perfected enlightenment'. By all means you should accept and keep to it in this manner.

Now in the present-day country of the great Sung dynasty, because that bunch who call themselves scholars of monastic rules and regulations are intoxicated by the wine served up by shravakas, they feel no shame that they are passing on a lineage that was unknown to their own tradition, nor do they regret it, nor are they aware of what they are doing. They have altered the kesa that has been passed down from India, which was passed on for ever so long during the Han and T'ang dynasties, acceding to one of smaller size, which complies with their small views—narrow views that they should be ashamed of. If you today were to use a small-sized robe like theirs, how could the everyday behavior of a Buddha ever continue for long? Their views take the form that they do because their exploration and passing on of the behavior of a Buddha has not been extensive. It is quite clear that the Body and Mind of the Tathagata has been correctly Transmitted only through the gates of our Ancestors and has not been disseminated through the activities of that bunch's lineage. If, by chance, they actually recognized what the behavior of a Buddha is, they would not violate the Buddha robe. As they are still unclear as to the texts of the Scriptures, they cannot hear Their import.

Further, to stipulate rough cotton cloth as the sole material for a robe is to go deeply against the Buddha's Teaching. Since such cloth is not the only thing that a disciple of the Buddha may wear, this stipulation, in particular, does violence to the Buddha robe. And why is this so? Because, by proffering a judgmental opinion concerning cotton cloth, one has violated the kesa. What a pity that the opinions of the shravakas in the Lesser Course* should so twist and turn about, sad to say! After you have demolished your opinions concerning cotton cloth, the Buddha robe can fully manifest before your eyes. What I am saying about the use of silk and cotton cloth is not what just one or two Buddhas have said: it is an important Teaching of all the Buddhas that we consider waste cloth as the highest grade of immaculate raw material for a robe. When, later on, I list the ten types of waste cloth, it will include types of silk and types of cotton, as well as other types of cloth. Are we not to collect waste bits of silk? If such is the case, then we are acting contrary to the Way of the Buddhas. If we are already prejudiced against silk, we will also be prejudiced in regard to cotton. What reason could there possibly be for feeling that we should be prejudiced in regard to silk or cotton? To look down on silk thread because it was produced through the killing of a living being is vastly laughable, for is not cotton cloth the product of a living thing? If your view of something being either sentient or non-sentient is not yet free of any commonplace, sentimental feelings, how will you possibly understand what the kesa of a Buddha is?

Also, there are those who talk in wild and confused ways, bringing up the so-called 'theory of transformed thread', which is also laughable.[10] What, pray, is not a transformation of something? You folks who bring this theory up may trust your ears when they hear the word 'transformation', but you doubt your eyes when they see a transformation. It is as if your eyes had no ears and your ears had no eyes. Where are your ears and eyes at this very moment?

---

10. An ancient Indian view that silk is thread which is created by a living creature; it is not naturally occurring of itself.

Keep in mind, for the moment, that while you are picking up some waste material, there may be times when it resembles silk or when it looks just like cotton. In using it, do not call it silk or cotton; just designate it as waste material. Because it is waste material, as waste material it is beyond being 'silk', beyond being 'cotton'. Even though there is a time after death when ordinary people and those in lofty positions may 'continue to exist' as waste matter, we cannot speak of them as 'having sentience', for they will be 'waste material'. Even though there is a time when a dead pine tree or chrysanthemum have become waste matter, we cannot speak of them as being 'non-sentient', for they will be 'waste material'. When we understand the principle that waste cloth is neither silk nor cotton, and that it is far from being either pearls or jade, the robe of waste cloth will fully manifest before us, and, with its arising, we will meet and experience the robe of waste cloth. When your opinions about silk and cotton have not yet dried up and fallen away, you will not see 'waste material' even in your dreams. Although for your whole life you may accept and keep to a kesa made from coarse cotton cloth, should you hold in your mind the view that it is cotton, what you have accepted will not be the genuine Transmission of the Buddha robe.

Further, among the various kinds of kesas, there are cotton kesas, and silk kesas, and leather kesas. Buddhas have all made use of each of these at some time, for these have the Buddhist merits of a Buddha robe. They possess the fundamental principle that has been genuinely Transmitted without ever having been interrupted. However, those folks who have not yet discarded their commonplace, sentimental feelings treat the Buddha's Dharma lightly and do not trust the Buddha's words. They aim at following where others have gone based on commonplace, sentimental feelings, and we should certainly speak of them as non-Buddhists who have latched onto the Buddha's Dharma. They are a bunch that would demolish the True Teaching.

Some have claimed that they altered the Buddha's robe based on instructions from a celestial being. If this is so, then they must be aspiring to celestial Buddhahood! Or have they become part of some stream of celestial beings? Disciples of the Buddha will expound the Buddha's Teaching to celestial beings; they do not ask celestial beings what the Way is. How sad that those who lack the True Transmission of the Buddha's Dharma are like this!

The perspective of the host of celestial beings and the perspective of a disciple of the Buddha are vastly different in both large and small matters, yet celestial beings come down to ask disciples of the Buddha for the Teaching. This is because the Buddhist perspective and the celestial perspective are so vastly different. Chuck out the narrow-minded perspectives of scholastics and shravakas, and do not study them: recognize that such persons are of the Lesser Course. The Buddha said, "Such folks may indeed feel remorse for having killed father or mother, but they may well not feel remorse for having slandered the Dharma."

In sum, the path of small-mindedness and foxy suspiciousness is not what the Buddha intended for us to follow. The Great Path of the Buddha's Dharma is beyond anything that the Lesser Course can reach. No one outside the Ancestral Path that is connected with the Treasure House of the Dharma even knows of the way that all Buddhas correctly Transmit the Great Precepts.

Long ago on Mount Ōbai, in the middle of the night, the robe and the Dharma of the Buddhas were genuinely Transmitted upon the head of Daikan Enō, our Sixth Ancestor. This was truly the authentic Transmission of the passing on of the Dharma and the passing on of the robe. It occurred because the Fifth Ancestor 'knew his man'. Fellows who have realized any of the four stages* of arhathood, or those who are thrice wise and ten times saintly, or are academic teachers of philosophical theories or of Scriptural doctrines might well have conferred the robe on Jinshū, but they would not have passed it on to the Sixth Ancestor.[11] Even so, because an Ancestor of the Buddha, in singling out a Buddhist Ancestor, crosses beyond the well-trodden road of commonplace thinking, the Sixth Ancestor had already become the Sixth Ancestor. Keep in mind that the principle of descendant after descendant of Buddhist Ancestors

---

11. Jinshū was the most intellectually gifted and respected monk in the Fifth Ancestor's monastic assembly, and the one who all his fellow monks assumed would be named the Fifth Ancestor's Dharma heir.

'recognizing his or her man' by recognizing the True Self is not something that can be left to those who weigh and measure things.

A certain monk once asked the Sixth Ancestor, "Is the robe passed on to you on Mount Ōbai in the middle of the night one made of cotton, or one made of silk, or one made of taffeta? Pray, tell us, what on earth is it made of?"

The Sixth Ancestor replied, "It is not cotton, or silk, or taffeta."

This was the way that the Highest Ancestor of Mount Sōkei put it. Keep in mind that the Buddha robe is not silk, or cotton, or some fine quality broadcloth. Those who vainly judge it to be silk, or cotton, or some fine-quality broadcloth are folks that slander the Buddha's Dharma. How could they possibly recognize the kesa of a Buddha? Moreover, there is the occasion when people come in good faith to take the Precepts. The kesa they obtain, again, is beyond any discussion of silk or cotton: it is the Buddha's instruction in the Way of Buddhas.

Also, Shōnawashu's robe was an everyday garment when he was in lay life.[12] When he left home to be a monk, it became a kesa. This principle should be calmly considered and concentrated upon. It is not something that you should disregard, acting as if you had neither seen nor heard of it. Moreover, it has an import that comes with the True Transmission of Buddha after Buddha and Ancestor after Ancestor. That bunch who tot up words cannot perceive it, nor can they weigh and measure it. Truly, how could the thousands of shifts and the myriad variations in the way that a Buddha says things possibly be in the realm where commonplace thinking flows? Yes, there are meditative states and mantric prayers, but those fellows who tot up grains of sand cannot see the precious Pearl that lies beneath the robe.

---

12. His name means 'He of Hempen Robe'.

Now, we should take the materials, colors, and dimensions of the kesa that the Buddhas and Ancestors have genuinely Transmitted to be the true standard for the kesa of all Buddhas. From India to the lands in the east, examples of it have long existed. Those who distinguished the true from the false had already gone beyond the experience of realizing Truth. Although there were those outside the Ancestral Path who used the word 'kesa', none of the original Ancestors ever affirmed them as their offshoots, so how could they possibly germinate the seeds that produce the roots of virtue, much less the fruits of it? Not only are you now seeing and hearing the Buddha Dharma that those others had not encountered over vast eons, you are also able to see and hear about the Buddha robe, to learn about the Buddha robe, and to both accept and keep to the Buddha robe. This is precisely our respectfully encountering Buddha. We are hearing the voice of Buddha, and are pouring forth the radiance of Buddha, and are accepting and making use of what a Buddha accepts and utilizes. We are transmitting one-to-one the Mind of Buddha, and are obtaining the Marrow of Buddha.

The Transmission of the Robe

Whilst I was in Sung China doing my training on the long bench in the Meditation Hall, I noticed that at the first light of every day, following the striking of the wake-up block, the monks who sat on either side of me would raise their folded kesa in a gesture of offering, place it atop their head, respectfully make gasshō,* and recite a verse to themselves. On one occasion I had a feeling that I had not experienced before. A joy filled my body to overflowing; tears of gratitude, stealing from my eyes, rolled down my cheeks and soaked my collar. I had been reading the *Āgama Scripture* and, though I had seen the passage on humbly offering up the kesa above one's head, its relevance had not wholly dawned on me. Now I was personally witnessing it. In this connection, sad to say, was the thought that, when I was in my native land, there had been no teacher or any good spiritual companion to instruct me in this. How could I not regret the days and years I had so wastefully spent, or not grieve their passing?

But now I was seeing and hearing this and was able to rejoice because of some good deed done in a past life. If I had vainly spent my time rubbing shoulders with any of those in the temples in my native land, I could not possibly have sat shoulder-to-shoulder with these Treasures of the Sangha who had donned the Buddha robe. My joy and sorrow were not unmixed, as my myriad tears issued forth.

Then, in silence, I took a vow, "Somehow, be I ever so incompetent, I <u>will</u> correctly Transmit the true inheritance of the Buddha's Dharma and, out of pity for the sentient beings in my homeland, I <u>will</u> help them see the robe and hear the Dharma that Buddha after Buddha has authentically Transmitted. Should my steadfast faith come to my aid in some unseen way, then surely my heartfelt vow will not have been in vain."

Disciples of the Buddha who are now accepting the kesa and keeping to it should humbly raise it above their head and unfailingly strive, day and night, to amass the effects of training, for this will produce real spiritual merits. The reading or hearing of one sentence or one poem from Scripture may well be as common as trees and stones, whereas the spiritual merits from the genuine Transmission of the kesa are undoubtedly difficult to encounter anywhere throughout the ten directions.

In Great Sung China during the wintry tenth lunar month of the seventeenth year of the Chia-ting era (November, 1223), there were two Korean monks who came to Ch'ing-yüen Prefecture. One was called, in Chinese, Chi-hüen, and the other Ching-yün. These two incessantly talked about the meaning of Buddhist doctrine and were, moreover, men of letters. Even so, they had no kesa or alms bowl and were like ordinary folk. Sad to say, even though they had the superficial form of monks, they lacked the Dharma of monks, which may have been due to their being from a small, remote country. When those fellows from our own court who have the superficial form of monks take to going to other countries, they are probably just like these two monks.

Shakyamuni Buddha, before His enlightenment, had already humbly raised the kesa above His head for some twelve years, never neglecting it. As His distant descendants, you should investigate this. If you turn away from bowing to celestial beings, spirits, rulers or their ministers—since all such bowing is done in the vain pursuit of fame and gain—and turn towards humbly placing the Buddha robe atop your head, it will be a great joy in which we can rejoice.

Recorded on the first day of winter in the first year of the Ninji era (October 17, 1240) at Kannondōri in Kōshōhōrin-ji Temple.

The mendicant monk Dōgen
who entered Sung China
in order to receive and Transmit the Dharma.

For robe material to make a kesa, we use that which is immaculate. 'Immaculate' refers to robe material donated in veneration as an offering in pure faith, or something purchased in the market place by lay folk, or something sent you by the gentry, or the pure alms-gift of some spiritually empowered dragon, or the pure alms-gift of some fiercely protective guardian, all of which are robe materials we use. And pure alms-gifts from rulers and their chief ministers or pure pelts can also be used. [13]

Further, we consider ten types of waste cloth to be immaculate:

First, cloth chewed by an ox.

Second, cloth gnawed by rats.

Third, cloth singed by fire.

Fourth, menstrual cloth.

Fifth, cloth discarded from childbirthing.

Sixth, cloth abandoned at a wayside shrine for birds to peck apart.

Seventh, cloth from a dead person's clothing abandoned at a grave site.

---

13. 'Pure pelts' probably refers to skins taken from animals who died naturally or by accident, or were attained as a by-product, as distinct from those specifically hunted for their pelts.

Eighth, cloth from abandoned prayer flags.

Ninth, cloth from robes discarded by officials upon their advancement to higher rank.

Tenth, burial shrouds discarded by those returning from a funeral.

We consider these ten types to be robe material that is especially immaculate. Those in the world of common customs discard them: those on the Buddha's Path make use of them. From these everyday ways of working with things, we can realize the difference between the mundane road and the Buddha's Path. As a consequence, when we search for the immaculate, we should seek out these ten types of cloth. When we obtain them, we should recognize what is clean and distinguish it from what is unclean, just as we can recognize mind and distinguish it from body. When we obtain any of these ten types of cloth—whether of silk or of cotton—it is its cleanliness or lack of cleanliness that we should consider.

It would be the height of silliness to hold to the notion that this waste cloth is being used simply to create 'the shabby appearance of a raggle-taggle robe'. The kesa of waste cloth is something that we in the Buddha's Way have come to use for clothing ourselves on account of its splendor and singular loveliness. When it comes to what would be considered raggle-taggle clothing from the perspective of the Buddha's Way, what we would call 'raggle-taggle' is the impure aspect of a garment fabricated from brocaded or embroidered cloth, from fancy-patterned cloth or silk gauze, or from gold or silver cloth studded with pearls and jade.[14]

Speaking more generally, in the Buddhism of this land or of other countries, when we use what is immaculate and wondrously lovely, it should be of those ten types, for not only do they transcend the limits of what is clean and what is unclean, they also go beyond the realm of what is tainted with delusion and what is not tainted with delusion. Do not discuss them in terms of mind and matter; they are things unconnected with gain and loss. Simply, those who accept and keep to what has been

---

14. What makes such garments 'impure' is the discriminatory attitude towards them that extols whatever is deemed rich or costly. 'Raggle-taggle' from the Buddhist perspective therefore does not refer to the quality or 'look' of a garment, but to a discriminatory attitude of mind about the cloth from which it is made.

genuinely Transmitted <u>are</u> Ancestors of the Buddha. When someone is an Ancestor of the Buddha, we accept and keep to this person as an Ancestor of the Buddha, for he or she has accepted, and is passing on, the genuine Transmission. And this Transmission does not depend on what is or is not manifested by the body, nor does it depend on what is or is not offered up by the mind.

We should lament that in this country of Japan, for ever so long up to recent times, male and female monks have not worn the kesa, and we should rejoice that they now may accept and keep to one. Any householder, male or female, who can accept the Buddhist Precepts should don a kesa of five, seven, or nine panels. How much more should those who have left home to be monks do so! Why would they not wear one? It is said that everyone—from Lord Brahma and those in the six worlds below him, down to male and female prostitutes and those in forced servitude—can receive the Buddhist Precepts and don the kesa, so are there male and female monks who would not wear one? It is said that even animals can take the Buddha's Precepts and put on a kesa, so why would a disciple of the Buddha not don the Buddha robe?

Thus, those who would become a disciple of the Buddha—be they denizens of some heavenly state, ordinary folk, rulers of nations, or government officials, or be they laity, monks, those in forced servitude, or animals—should all accept the Buddha's Precepts and have the kesa correctly Transmitted to them. This is indeed the straight path for correctly entering the ranks of Buddha.

When washing and rinsing a kesa, mix various sorts of incense powders into the water. After it has dried out, fold it up, place it in an elevated place, make a venerative offering of incense and flowers, and bow three times. After that, kneel before it and, with hands in gasshō, humbly place it atop your head, and then, rousing your faith, intone the following verse:

How great and wondrous is the robe of enlightenment,

Formless and embracing every treasure!

I wish to unfold the Buddha's Teaching

That I may help all sentient beings reach the Other Shore.

After reciting this three times, stand up, reverently unfold the robe, and put it on.

13

On the Spiritual Discourses
of the Mountains and the Water

(Sansuikyō)

Translator's Introduction: If readers are not already familiar with the Zen Buddhist use of metaphorical language, they may find the following comments useful in grasping what Dōgen is talking about in this Dharma discourse, which is baffling if its terms are taken only in their literal sense.

It has been said that when the Sanskrit word *dhyāna*, meaning 'meditation' in the Zen Buddhist sense, was introduced into China, the Chinese had no word that was its equivalent, so the Sanskrit word was spelled out by using two Chinese characters according to their pronunciation: *chan-na* (pronounced like English 'john-nah'). Over time, the term was shortened and the Mandarin pronunciation altered slightly to *ch'an* (pronounced like 'tchahn'). In Japan, this character was pronounced as *zen*. Although there were other Chinese characters that had already been used for transliterating the Sanskrit sound *dhyā*, the one chosen in the present instance also carried an ancient meaning, one relevant to Dōgen's discourse: 'to bow respectfully to mountains and flowing water'.

In the present discourse, Dōgen takes up the difference between the general, conventional use of the terms 'mountain' and '(flowing) water' and their special use by the Chinese Zen Masters for pointing to spiritual matters. As previously indicated in notes to Dōgen's earlier Dharma discourses, the term 'mountain' has several implications in Zen contexts. In this discourse in particular, 'mountain' is most often used as a descriptive epithet for one who is sitting in meditation, as still as a mountain among mountains (that is, one who is training among other members of the Buddhist Sangha), as well as for a wise and saintly person whose path has led him or her to seek a spiritual abode in a mountain, in both a literal and a figurative sense. Hence, the Chinese Zen Masters are referred to as 'mountains', and because their training never comes to an end but is ever green, they are referred to as 'verdant mountains'. And because they are not rigid or static in their practice, they are sometimes referred to as 'flowing mountains'.

One of the meanings of 'water', in the Zen sense, is 'the Water of the Spirit', that is, Buddha Nature in general as well as one's own Buddha Nature. In this translation, the use of this term is rendered as 'the Water' where context makes the meaning unambiguous. Someone's 'walking on the water' is thus descriptive of that person's doing his training and practice by following the ever-shifting, ever-flowing path of Buddha Nature.

Dōgen does not always signal which of the various meanings of 'mountain' and 'water' he intends, but often keeps his references fluid. Thus, as with his Discourse 11: On 'Just for the Time Being, Just for a While...' *(Uji),* readers may find it worthwhile to read this chapter through twice, once referring to the footnotes to get the immediate sense, and then just reading it to experience the flow.

The 'mountains and water' of which I am speaking at the present moment are a manifestation of the words and ways of former Buddhas.[1] Both terms, residing in their place within the Dharma, have completely fulfilled their function for these Buddhas. Because these words signify conditions that actively exist in the time periods before these Buddhas disappeared into the realm of spiritual Emptiness,[2] they refer to something that exists here and now, and because they signify the Self before any sign of these Buddhas' existence has appeared, they transcend anything that manifests before our very eyes. The various spiritual merits of the mountains are so vast and far reaching that the merits from our practice of 'riding the clouds' will certainly be attained because of the mountains.[3] The wondrous effects from our 'going on with the wind to our back', beyond doubt, will liberate us, thanks to the mountains.[4]

---

1. That is, 'mountains' and 'water' are not only terms used by previous Masters but also, as metaphors, can embody the way in which these Masters functioned.

2. Rev. Master Jiyu-Kennett often referred to this 'emptiness' as "the fullest emptiness you can ever experience." She herself used the term 'the Immaculacy of Emptiness' to describe It in a way that did not contain a connotation of a negative and 'devoid' sort of emptiness.

3. 'Riding the clouds'—originally, a Taoist term—refers to rising to higher levels. Here, it probably refers to trainees realizing higher spiritual levels, thanks to the Buddhas and the Ancestors, as well as to one's fellow trainees.

4. 'Going on with the wind to our back'—another Taoist term—refers to being supported by a favorable tailwind, again, probably to be understood as spiritual help and support from the Sangha.

The monk Dōkai of Mount Daiyō, in instructing his assembly, said, "The verdant mountains are constantly moving on, and the Stone Maiden, in the dark of night, gives birth to Her Child."[5] The mountains are never lacking in the spiritual merits with which they are undoubtedly endowed. This is why they constantly reside at ease <u>and</u> are constantly moving on. By all means, you must examine in great detail the spiritual merits of their moving on. The moving on of a mountain will be just like the moving on of those who wander through life in ignorance,[6] so, even though you may think that it seems the same as the human activity of walking, nevertheless, do not doubt 'the moving on' of mountains.

What this Ancestor of the Buddha expressed has already pointed to this 'moving on'; this was his 'getting to the very root of the Matter'.* So, you should thoroughly pursue what he was pointing out to his assembly about 'always moving on'. Since it is a 'moving on', it is constant. Although the moving on of the verdant mountains is more swift than the wind, those who live amidst the mountains do not perceive this, much less recognize it. 'Being amidst the mountains' refers to things blossoming forth within the everyday world. Those who live apart from the mountains neither perceive nor recognize them. They are people who lack an eye for seeing mountains: not only do they not perceive or recognize them, they do not see or hear

---

5.   To paraphrase the first half, Buddhist Masters who are literally, or figuratively, always 'sitting' in meditation (the mountains) and whose training and practice is 'alive' (verdant) are constantly moving on (or, more literally, 'progressing apace'), 'always becoming Buddha'. The second phrase has multiple meanings which arise from the resonance of the saying. For example, on one level, the epithet 'The Stone Maiden' refers to That Which Is, from which all things arise, without having to depend on any external 'impregnating' agent and without the process being visible (happening 'in the dark of night'). On another level, the Stone Maiden refers to the trainee whose intent to realize Truth is active, but whose mind is as hard as rock. Yet, despite this hardness, it will, through training, crack open, and the Child of Enlightenment will be born.

6.   That is, without any preconceived notion or plan.

*   See Glossary.

them, nor do they comprehend what they are all about. Whoever harbors doubts about the moving on of mountains is one who does not yet recognize his own moving on. It is not that they themselves do not move on, it is that they do not yet recognize their own moving on and have not clarified what it is. To recognize your own moving on will certainly be no different from recognizing the moving on of the verdant mountains.

A verdant mountain is already beyond being 'sentient' and beyond being 'non-sentient': you yourself are already beyond being 'sentient' and beyond being 'non-sentient'. So, you must not harbor doubts about the moving on of the verdant mountains at the present moment. People do not know that they must scrutinize and clarify what 'verdant mountains' means if they are to measure all the existent worlds about them.

It is necessary to scrutinize what 'the moving on of mountains' signifies. You have to look with utmost care at both 'stepping forward' and 'stepping back'. You need to carefully explore moving on—both the steps that move you forward and those that move you back—and never cease in this for even a moment, from the time before there is any sign of something coming into existence until the Lord of Emptiness[*] appears.

If this 'moving on' had come to rest, the Buddhas and Ancestors would never have appeared. If this 'moving on' had reached some culminating point, the Dharma of the Buddha would not have reached us today. Stepping forward has not ceased, nor has stepping back. When there is a stepping forward, it does not stand in opposition to stepping back; when there is a stepping back, it does not stand in opposition to stepping forward. We characterize this as 'the mountain's flowing' or as 'the flowing mountain'.

Because a verdant mountain trains in order to master 'moving on' and Enō learned through practice to 'go walking upon the Water',[7] your learning these things

---

7.   This phrase would be conventionally translated as 'The mountain to the east of us goes walking upon water', but the reference is actually to a well-known Zen saying that Dōgen discusses later, "Tōzan goes walking upon the Water." Tōzan ('The East Mountain') was an epithet for the Sixth Chinese Ancestor Daikan Enō; it is unrelated to the name Tōzan,

through your practice is synonymous with a mountain's learning them through practice. Without the mountains' altering their body or mind, they have been going all around and about, learning through practice, with the look of a mountain about them.

Do not slander the mountains by saying, "Verdant mountains are incapable of moving on," or "No mountain to the east of us is capable of walking upon water." It is because of the baseness of some people's views of things that they doubt the phrase 'mountains walk on', just as it is due to their inexperience and scant knowledge that they are startled by the words 'a flowing mountain'. Nowadays, although we may say that they have not thoroughly explored even the phrase 'flowing water' in all its varied meanings, it is actually just a matter of their being immersed in pedestrian views and drowning in ignorance. As a result, they take as their form and name, or as their very lifeblood, whatever they esteem as their 'cumulative qualities'. Its walking on exists; its flowing exists. There is a time when a mountain gives rise to the Child of the Mountain. In accordance with the principle that a mountain becomes an Ancestor of the Buddha, the Ancestors of the Buddha have made Their appearance in this manner.

When people have eyes before which a mountain is manifesting as grass and trees, earth and stones, or walls and fences, they do not doubt what they see nor are they disturbed by it, and it is not the whole of what is manifesting. Even though a time may occur when a mountain appears to them as being adorned with the Seven Treasures,* this is not the real refuge. Even if they see manifesting before them the realm in which all the Buddhas are carrying out the Way, it is never a place to crave for. Even if they have above their heads the sight of a mountain manifesting the indescribable spiritual virtues of all the Buddhas, Truth is not limited merely to this. The fully visible manifestation of each and every thing is the physical body of each and every thing along with the environment in which it exists. So, such views as those above are not to be taken as the manner in which Ancestors of the Buddha put the Way into practice: they are merely what people can see when looking through a hollow straw.

---

meaning 'Cave Mountain', by which several other monks are known, such as Tōzan Ryōkai.

Splitting 'subjective' mind apart from 'objective' environment is what the Great Sage Shakyamuni warned us about; intellectually expounding on 'mind' or expounding on 'nature' is not something that Ancestors of the Buddha undertake. Having theories about mind or about nature is a profession for those who are apart from the Buddhist Way; to be bogged down in words and phrases is not speech that leads to liberation. There is a state that is free from such conditions as these. It has been described as "The verdant mountains are constantly moving on," and as "Enō went walking upon the Water." You need to explore this state in the greatest detail.

The statement "The Stone Maiden, in the dark of night, gives birth to Her Child" refers to the time when the Stone Maiden gives birth to Her Child as 'in the dark of night'. Generally speaking, there are stones that are male and stones that are female, as well as stones that are neither male nor female, and all of these quite nicely fill up the heavens and fill up the earth. And there are heavenly stones and there are earthly stones, which those who wander without a preconceived goal speak of, though persons who really know them are rare indeed.[8]

One needs to understand the principle of Her 'giving birth to a Child'. At the time of Her giving birth to the Child, are Parent and Child made separate? You must devote yourself to exploring through your training not only that 'the Child becoming the Parent' is the full manifestation of 'giving birth to the Child', but also that 'the time when the Parent becomes the Child' is the full manifestation of 'giving birth to the Child'. You must thoroughly penetrate what is being said here.

---

8.   To paraphrase one level of meaning, male and female stones refer to those who are 'Stone Maiden' trainees as explained in footnote 5. These 'stones', as well as conventional stones, occur in both heavenly and earthly worlds. Though people may speak of spiritually developed beings as heavenly ('beings spiritually beyond me') or as earthly ('real people'), those who can actually distinguish between them are rare indeed.

Great Teacher Ummon Bun'en once said, "Enō went walking upon the Water." The meaning of what is fully manifested through these words is that all mountains are Enō, and every Enō goes walking upon the Water. This is why this Ancestor of the Buddha fully manifested Mount Sumeru amidst the nine mountains, and fully realized It through his training, along with realizing other things as well.[9] People call <u>him</u> Enō. But how could there possibly be the slightest gap between Ummon's and Enō's Skin and Flesh, Bones and Marrow, or between Ummon and his living within his own realization through training?

In the nation of Great Sung China today, there is a certain type of unreliable person that has now grown to be quite a crowd. They have gotten to the point where they cannot be bested by the few true people. This bunch says such things as the following:

> Just like the comments about Enō's walking on water or the one about Nansen's buying a scythe, what is being said is beyond anything that reason can grasp. In other words, any remark that involves the use of intellect is not the Zen talk of an Ancestor of the Buddha, whereas a remark that goes beyond anything that reason can handle is what comprises a 'remark' by an Ancestor of the Buddha. As a consequence, we would say that Meditation Master Ōbaku's applying a stick to his disciples or Meditation Master Rinzai's giving forth with a loud yell go far beyond rational understanding and do not involve the use of intellect. We consider this to be what is meant by the great awakening to That which precedes the arising of any discrimination. The reason why the

---

9.   A reference to the eight symbolic concentric rings of mountains with Mount Sumeru as their center, a metaphor for having achieved a full centering of oneself within one's meditation.

ancient virtuous Masters so often made skillful use of verbal phrases to cut through the spiritual entanglements of their disciples was precisely because these phrases were beyond rational understanding.

Fellows who talk like this have never met a genuine teacher, nor do they have an eye for learning through training. They are foolish puppies who are not even worth discussing. For the past two or three centuries in the land of Sung China, such devilish imps and 'little shavers' like the Gang of Six have been many.[10] Alas, the Great Way of the Buddha's Ancestors has become diseased! This explanation of those people cannot compare even with that of the shravakas* who follow the Lesser Course;* it is even more confused than that of non-Buddhists. These fellows are not laity nor are they monks; they are not gods or humans. And when it comes to exploring the Buddha's Way, they are more befuddled than beasts. The stories which the 'little shavers' refer to as going beyond anything that reason can grasp only go beyond anything their reason can grasp: it was not that way for any Ancestor of the Buddha. Just because they said that such stories are not subject to rational understanding, you should not fail to learn through your training what the intellectually comprehendible pathways of the Ancestors of the Buddha are. Even if these stories were ultimately beyond rational understanding, the understanding that this bunch has cannot hit the mark. Such people are in great number everywhere in Sung China, as I have personally witnessed. Sad to say, they did not recognize that the phrase 'the use of intellect' is itself a use of words, nor realize that a use of words may liberate us from the use of our intellect. When I was in Sung China, even though I laughed at them for their foolish views, they had nothing to say for themselves; they were simply speechless. Their present negation of rational understanding is nothing but an erroneous view. Who taught them this? Even though you may say that they have not had someone to teach them of the true nature of things, nevertheless, the fact remains that, for all

---

10.   'The Gang of Six' refers to six monks during the Buddha's time whose wayward behavior prompted the framing of monastic rules and regulations. 'Little shavers' was a term applied to monks who shaved their heads so that they could partake of monastic food and lodging, but who had no interest in spiritual training.

intents and purposes, they still end up being offspring of the non-Buddhist notion that things arise spontaneously, independent of any form of causality.

You need to recognize that Enō's walking on the Water is the Bones and Marrow of the Buddhas and Ancestors. Various kinds of water manifested under Enō's feet. This is why various mountains ride the clouds or tread the heavens. Above the crests of various types of water are various types of mountains which go walking up and down on the Water. As the various mountains go walking through the various types of water, the tips of their feet often make the water dance; thus, their walking may go seven steps in one direction or eight in another.[11] That is, there is no time when training and enlightenment do not exist.

As for the Water, It is neither strong nor weak, nor is It wet or dry, nor does It move or stay still, nor is It cold or hot, nor does It exist or not exist, nor is It deluded or awakened. When frozen solid, It is harder than a diamond, so who can smash It? When melted, It is more yielding than diluted milk, so who can tear It to bits? This being so, we cannot doubt the qualities of the various forms of existence that manifest before our very eyes.

For now, just concentrate on learning to recognize, through your training, the moments when you are able to open your eyes and see the Water in the whole universe as the Whole Universe. And 'learning through training' does not refer just to the times when ordinary people or those in loftier positions see the Water; there is your learning through training in which the Water sees the Water. Because the Water puts the Water into practice in order to realize what the Water is, there will be your thorough investigation of the Water's expressing through words what the Water is. In this way, you will manifest the pathway upon which we ourselves meet our Self. Until then,

---

11.   That is, 'mountains' are able to move about freely in their daily training.

you must go back and forth on that road of life upon which others are all involved with making a study of 'other', until you leap free.

To speak in general, what people see as a mountain or as water differs in various ways. There are those who, upon catching sight of what I am calling 'the Water', see It as a string of pearls, but they fail to see such a necklace as the Water.[12] They undoubtedly consider the form in which we humans perceive something as what the Water is. What they see as a pearl necklace, I see as the Water. And there are those who see the Water as a wondrous flower, but this does not mean that they are using an actual flower for the Water. Hungry ghosts,* upon encountering the Water, may see It as a raging inferno, or as thick, congealing blood. Dragons and other denizens of the deep may see It as a palace or as a stately mansion. Some may see It as the Seven Treasures or as the Wish-fulfilling Jewel,[13] and others as various sorts of trees, or as fences and walls, and others as the immaculate, liberated Dharma Nature, and others as someone's True Body, and others as someone's physical appearance along with that person's mental nature. When humans see the Water via any of these means, this can be the cause of their liberation from commonplace 'life'.

Although what is seen may differ completely according to the one who sees It, we should not be too hasty in accepting this as absolutely so. Are there really 'all sorts of ways' of seeing any single object? Have you committed an error by taking the plethora of images for what is actually one object? Then, at the very peak of your efforts, you will need to make a further effort. If what I have just been saying is so, then, likewise, there cannot be just one or two ways for training to realize the Truth

---

12. For instance, they may see someone's Buddha Nature as being a beautiful adornment, not as that person's true, innate nature.

13. The Wish-fulfilling Jewel, sometimes called the Mani Jewel, refers to the Buddha Nature which is inherent in all living beings. Meditation Master Gensha Shibi called it "The One Bright Pearl". Dōgen discusses this at length in Discourse 4: On 'The One Bright Pearl' *(Ikka Myōju)*.

and for assiduously practicing the Way, and the realm of the Ultimate can be of a thousand kinds and ten thousand sorts.

Further, when we think about the fundamental meaning of this, even though we may say that the varieties of the Water are many, it may seem to some as if there were no one, fundamental Water or as though the Water had no variety. Thus, the various ways in which the Water appears do not depend on one's mind or on one's body, nor do they arise from one's karma*-producing actions, nor do they depend on oneself or on someone else: they possess that freedom from delusion which is dependent on the Water Itself. Thus, the Water is beyond being earth, water, fire, wind, space, or consciousness, beyond being blue, yellow, red, white, or black, beyond being form, sound, odor, taste, sensations, or thoughts, and even so, the Water naturally manifests fully as earth, water, fire, wind, and so forth.

Because this is the way things are, it would be difficult to say clearly what has created our nation and its palaces as they appear before us today or to say what they will be made into. To say that they depend on the Wheel of Space and the Wheel of Wind is not what is true for me or true for others, for it is the product of speculation based on the suppositions of a narrow outlook.[14] This view has been asserted based on some people's thinking that nothing could continue to exist if it did not have some place to hang onto. The Buddha said, "All thoughts and things are ultimately free of any attachments, so there is no place where they permanently abide." You need to keep in mind that even though all thoughts and things are inherently free of any attachments, they do have some place where they exist.

When human beings look at water, they only see it as something that ceaselessly pours out and flows on. This flowing has many forms, each being a part of the human perspective. It flows over the earth and out of the sky, now surging

---

14. According to an ancient Indian view, the universe is comprised of the five elements (referred to here as 'Wheels'), with the more solid elements being dependent on the less solid, the Wheel of Wind (i.e., gaseous matter) and the Wheel of Space being the least substantial.

upwards, now pouring downwards, streaming along in the bends of a river and coursing through deep chasms. It rises up to make clouds and comes down to form pools.

The Chinese scholar Wen-tsu once remarked, "It is the way of water to rise up to the heavens and become rain and dew, and to fall to earth and become rivers and streams." Today, those who wander in ignorance still speak in this manner. It would be most shameful for those who call themselves the offspring of the Buddha's Ancestors to be more in the dark about the meaning of this than such folk as these, for what he is really saying is "The way of the Water is not something that water is aware of, yet water is fully capable of functioning, <u>and</u> it is not something that the Water is not aware of, yet the Water is fully capable of functioning."

As Wen-tsu said, "It rises up to the heavens and becomes rain and dew." Be aware that the Water ascends to ever so many lofty places in the heavens above to form rain and dew, and rain and dew take a variety of forms according to the worlds in which they appear. To say that there is some place that the Water does not reach is a teaching of the shravakas of the Lesser Vehicle or an erroneous teaching of non-Buddhists.[15] The Water extends into the tongues of fire, and into our thoughts and deliberations and distinctions, and into our perceptions, and into our Buddha Nature.

Consider the statement, "It falls to earth and becomes rivers and streams." When the Water descends to earth, It becomes rivers and streams. Some varieties of rivers and streams frequently turn into wise, perceptive persons. In the opinion of the everyday stream of the ordinary and the befuddled, water is unquestionably that which exists in rivers, streams, oceans, and seas. This is not so, for the rivers and seas have come into existence within the Water. Thus, there is the Water even in places where there are no rivers or seas. It is just that when the Water descends to earth, It creates the effect of 'rivers and seas'.

Also, do not work it out that, when there is some place where the Water has formed rivers and seas, there are no social worlds or Buddhist lands. Even in a single drop, immeasurable Buddhist lands manifest before our very eyes. Hence, it is not a

---

15.   This is a reference to the mistaken notion of an *icchantika*, that is, someone who is believed to be totally devoid of Buddha Nature.

question of water existing within a Buddhist land or of a Buddhist land existing in the Water. The existence of the Water is in no way dependent on the three temporal worlds or on the worlds of thoughts and things. Even so, the Water is the spiritual question that manifests before our very eyes. Wherever Buddhas and Ancestors go, the Water invariably goes. Wherever the Water goes, Buddhas and Ancestors invariably manifest. Because of this, Buddhas and Ancestors have always regarded the Water as Their body and mind, as Their very thoughts.

Since the preceding is so, there is no document within or outside Buddhism that says that the Water does not run upwards. The path of the Water circulates every which way—up above and down below, far and wide. So, within Buddhist Scriptures, it is said that fire and wind climb up above, earth and water go down below. This 'up above and down below' is something to investigate in particular. Consider carefully the 'up above and down below' of the Buddha's Way. It means that the place where earth and water go is 'down below'; it does not mean that down below is some 'place' where earth and water go.[16] Where fire and wind go is up above. Even though the universe of thoughts and things does not completely depend on the measurements of the four directions, or upon up and down, we temporarily fabricate our universe in accordance with the four, five, or six elements.[17] The Heaven Beyond Deliberate Thought is not always 'up above'; the Hell of Incessant Suffering is not always 'down below'. Incessant suffering is one person's whole universe; being beyond deliberate thought is another person's whole universe.

Hence, when a dragon or a fish views water as a palace, it will not be like a human being seeing a palace, nor will such a creature perceive the water to be something that is flowing on. Were some onlooker to say to the dragon or the fish, "Your palace is flowing water," the creature would at once be startled and filled with doubt, just as some of you may have been startled earlier when you heard it asserted that mountains flow like water. Further, it may be possible to maintain that a similar

---

16.   That is, 'down below' refers to a direction, not to any specific place.

17.   The four elements are earth, water, fire, and wind; the five are the four elements plus space; the six are the five elements plus consciousness.

assertion can be made about the railings, steps, and pillars of palaces and mansions. Calmly consider this principle and keep turning it about in your mind, for if you do not learn how to go beyond these borderline expressions, you will not let go of the body and mind of one who wanders in ignorance, or fully realize what the domain of the Buddhas and Ancestors is, or fully realize what the domain of those who wander in ignorance is, or fully realize what the palace of one who wanders in ignorance really is.

Now, we humans may clearly perceive the very essence of the sea or the very heart of a river to be water, but what sort of thing a dragon or a fish may perceive to be water, or may make use of as water, we do not yet know. Do not foolishly assume that other creatures make use of water in accordance with how we perceive water.

Now, when we Buddhist trainees learn about the Water, we should not blindly cling to just the everyday, human view of water; we need to go on and investigate through our practice the Water of the Buddha's Way. How we view the term 'Water' as used by the Ancestors of the Buddha is something we need to investigate through our practice. We also need to investigate through our practice whether or not the Water actually exists within the traditional families of the Buddha's Ancestors.

The mountain, from times immemorial, has served as the place of residence for great saintly ones. Both the wise and the saintly have considered the mountain to be their innermost place and to be their body and mind. And thanks to the wise and the saintly, mountains have manifested before our very eyes. People in general tend to regard mountains simply as gathering places for ever so many great saints and wise ones, but for those who enter a mountain, there will not be a single person whom any of them will meet; only the natural functioning of a mountain will manifest, and nothing more. And furthermore, no traces of their having entered will be left behind.

When someone with the perspective of the secular world encounters a mountain, and when someone with the perspective of one amongst mountains meets this mountain, how their minds think of this mountain or how their eyes see this mountain will be vastly different. The conventional human perception of 'something flowing' and the conventional human perception of 'something not flowing' will not be at all like the perceptions of dragons and fish. Ordinary people, as well as those in lofty positions, strive to secure a place within their own sphere; other species may look upon this with suspicion, or may even give rise to doubtful thoughts. Thus, you should investigate the phrase 'mountains flow' with the Ancestors of the Buddha, and do not abandon the matter when you find yourself surprised or in doubt. Taken in one context, they flow; taken in another, they do not flow. One time round, they flow; another time round, they do not flow. If you do not investigate the matter in this way through your practice, it will not be the Tathagata's Wheel of the True Teaching.

A former Buddha once said, "If you would avoid incurring unrelenting, hellish karma, do not malign the Tathagata's Wheel of the True Teaching." You should engrave these words on your skin, flesh, bones, and marrow; you should engrave them on the outer circumstances and inner conditions of your body and mind; you should engrave them on what is immaterial; you should engrave them on what is material. They have already been engraved on trees and on stones; they have already been engraved on both cultivated fields and places of human habitation.

Generally speaking, we say that mountains belong to some country or region, but it is to those who love mountains that they really belong. Invariably, when a mountain loves its Host, the lofty virtues of the saintly and wise enter the mountain. When those who are saintly and wise dwell in the mountains, the mountains belong to them; as a result, the trees grow luxuriant and boulders abound, the birds are wondrous and the animals are surpassing fine. This is because they are under the influence of the virtues of one who is saintly and wise. You need to recognize that the truth of the matter is that mountains are fond of those who are wise, and that they are fond of those who are saintly.

From the past to the present, it has been a good example for us that emperors have often gone up a mountain to bow to a wise one and to respectfully question a great saintly one. At such a time, they show their respect with all the formalities due their teacher: they do not follow the ordinary ways of behaving towards people. When an emperor extends his loving influence over his subjects, he never uses it to coerce mountain sages, for clearly, mountains are separate from the world of human society. In the legendary times of the Chinese Flower Kingdom, on the occasion when the Yellow Emperor paid a respectful visit to Kuang-cheng, who was the guardian spirit on Mount Kung-tung, he crawled on his hands and knees, groveling obsequiously and begging the spirit for instruction.

Also, once Shakyamuni Buddha had left the palace of His father the king, He entered the mountains. Even so, His royal father did not feel rancor towards the mountains. Nor did His royal father distrust those in the mountains who were teaching the prince. The twelve years that He trained in the Way were largely spent in the mountains. His realization as Lord of the Dharma also took place whilst in the mountains. Truly, even universal monarchs whose chariot wheels roll everywhere do not undertake to forcibly control the mountains.

To be sure, a mountain is not the realm of ordinary folk, nor is it the realm of those who dwell in lofty places. You cannot really perceive what a mountain is by means of the standards used by those who wander in ignorance. If mountains are beyond comparison with the everyday notion of 'flowing', who then, pray, can doubt that a mountain flows, and that a mountain does not flow, as well as whatever else a mountain may do?

And, from distant times, there have been wise ones and saintly ones who were even wont to live on the water. Whilst living on the water, some caught fish, some caught humans, and some caught the Way. These are all in the traditional mainstream of 'being in the Water'. Along with this, there will be those who catch themselves, those who catch the Hook, those who are caught by the Hook, and those who are caught by the Way. Long ago, no sooner had the monk Tokujō left his Transmission Master Yakusan to go live at the heart of the river than he became acquainted with the wise and saintly one of the Hua-tung River.[18] Was it not a fish he hooked? Was it not a person he hooked? Was it not the Water he hooked? Was it not

---

18.   After Tokujō left his Master, he ferried a small boat across the river. He tried to teach Zen to those boarding his ferry boat. He often lifted his oar out of the water and said, "Do you understand?" One of those whom he met in this way later became his Dharma heir.

someone from the Water he hooked? The one who can really 'see' Tokujō is Tokujō. Tokujō encountering of That One is his meeting 'the True Person'.

Not only is there water in the world, there is a world within the world of water. Not only is it like this in water, there is also a sentient world in clouds, and a sentient world in wind, and a sentient world in fire, and a sentient world in earth, and a sentient world in the realm of thoughts and things, and a sentient world in a blade of grass, and a sentient world in a monk's traveling staff. Wherever there is a sentient world, there is, of necessity, a world of Buddhas and Ancestors in that place. Such a principle should be well explored indeed! Hence, the Water is the very palace of the True Dragon: It is beyond flowing or falling. If we recognize It only as something that flows, the word 'flowing' slanders the Water. One reason for this is that the use of the word forces It to be something not flowing. The Water is simply the Water as It is, in and of Itself. It is the natural functioning of the Water as the Water and is beyond 'flowing'. As soon as you penetrate through your practice both the flowing of a single drop of water and its non-flowing, the complete penetration of all thoughts and things will immediately manifest before your very eyes. With mountains, too, there are mountains hidden within treasures, mountains hidden within marshes, mountains hidden within the sky, mountains hidden within mountains. And there is learning through practice that there are mountains which are hidden within That Which Is Hidden.

The Old Buddha Ummon Bun'en once said, "Mountains are mountains; water is water." What these words mean goes beyond saying that mountains are mountains: it is saying that Mountains are mountains. Therefore, you need to investigate Mountains through your practice. If you thoroughly investigate Mountains in your practice, this will be your effort in the mountains. In this way, the Mountains and the Water will naturally produce the wise as well as the saintly.

Given to the assembly at Kannondōri in Kōshōhōrin-ji Temple on the eighteenth day of the tenth lunar month in the first year of the Ninji era (November 3, 1240).

I made this copy in the chaplain's quarters at Kippō-ji Temple, Yoshida Province, Echizen Prefecture, on the third day of the sixth lunar month in the second year of the Kangen era (July 9, 1244).

Ejō

14

On the Buddhas and the Ancestors

(Busso)

Translator's Introduction: In this short discourse, Dōgen presents the traditional Sōtō Zen Ancestral line up through Dōgen's Master, Tendō Nyojō. The Sanskrit forms for the names of the Indian Ancestors are, in a few cases, the translator's choice among several different possible reconstructions that have been offered by Asian and Western scholars.

With deepest respect.

The Buddhas and Ancestors manifest before our very eyes whenever we respectfully serve the Buddhas and Ancestors by bringing Them up through our presenting of Their story. They are not limited simply to some past, present, or future time, for They have undoubtedly gone beyond even 'going beyond Buddha'. Once we have taken up what we truly know of the reputation of a Buddha or an Ancestor, we bow in respect as we meet That One face-to-face. Having made evident the spiritual virtues of a Buddha or an Ancestor and held them aloft, we take our abode in them and uphold them, embodying them that we may realize the Truth in them.

The Seven Buddhas:

The Great Monk Bibashi Buddha, called herein 'the One Who
Universally Proclaims the Dharma'
The Great Monk Shiki Buddha, called herein 'the Fire'
The Great Monk Bishafu Buddha, called herein 'the All
Compassionate One'
The Great Monk Kuruson Buddha, called herein 'the Hermit of
Gold'
The Great Monk Kunagonmuni Buddha, called herein 'the
Golden Sage'

189

The Great Monk Kashō Buddha, called herein 'the All-absorbing Light'

The Great Monk Shakyamuni Buddha, called herein 'the Thoroughly Patient and Still One'

The Indian Ancestors:

1. The Great Monk Makakashō
2. The Great Monk Ananda
3. The Great Monk Shōnawashu
4. The Great Monk Ubakikuta
5. The Great Monk Daitaka
6. The Great Monk Mishaka
7. The Great Monk Bashumitsu
8. The Great Monk Butsudanandai
9. The Great Monk Fudamitta
10. The Great Monk Barishiba
11. The Great Monk Funayasha
12. The Great Monk Ashvaghoãa
13. The Great Monk Kabimora
14. The Great Monk Nāgārjuna also called
    Lung-shu, Lung-sheng, or Lung-meng
15. The Great Monk Kanadaiba
16. The Great Monk Ragorata
17. The Great Monk Sōgyanandai
18. The Great Monk Kayashata
19. The Great Monk Kumorata
20. The Great Monk Shayata
21. The Great Monk Vasubandhu
22. The Great Monk Manura
23. The Great Monk Kakurokuna
24. The Great Monk Shishibodai

25.The Great Monk Bashashita

26.The Great Monk Funyomitta

27.The Great Monk Hannyatara

28.The Great Monk Bodhidharma

The Chinese Ancestors:

The Great Monk Eka

The Great Monk Kanchi Sōsan

The Great Monk Daii Dōshin

The Great Monk Daiman Kōnin

The Great Monk Daikan Enō

The Great Monk Seigen Gyōshi

The Great Monk Sekitō Kisen

The Great Monk Yakusan Igen

The Great Monk Ungan Donjō

The Great Monk Tōzan Ryōkai

The Great Monk Ungo Dōyō

The Great Monk Dōan Dōhi

The Great Monk Dōan Kanshi

The Great Monk Ryōzan Enkan

The Great Monk Daiyō Kyōgen

The Great Monk Tōsu Gisei

The Great Monk Fuyō Dōkai

The Great Monk Tanka Shijun

The Great Monk Chōro Seiryō

The Great Monk Tendō Sōkaku

The Great Monk Setchō Chikan

The Great Monk Tendō Nyojō of the twenty-third

generation in China

During the summer retreat in the first year of the Chinese Pao-ch'ing era (1225) in Great Sung China, whilst I, Dōgen, was training and serving under my late Master, the venerable Buddha, Great Monk Tendō Nyojō, I came to know, through and through, the significance of making a full venerative bow to these Buddhas and Ancestors and of receiving Them upon my head. It was what each Buddha realized on His own, just as all Buddhas have done.

Delivered to the assembly from a manuscript on the third day of the first month in the second year of the Ninji era (February 15, 1241) at Kannondōri in Kōshōhōrin-ji Temple, Uji Province, Yamashiro Prefecture, Japan.

I copied this whilst in the chaplain's quarters at Kippō-ji Temple, Echizen Province, on the fourteenth day of the fifth month of the second year of the Kangen era (May 20, 1244).

Ejō

15

On the Record of Transmission

(Shisho)

Translator's Introduction: In this text which he wrote for his monks, Dōgen takes up the topic of the *shisho*, the name of a Buddhist document which may literally be translated as 'the record of the inheritors'. This record is usually written on silk, and it consists of a listing of the names of those in the Ancestral line from Shakyamuni Buddha up to the person receiving the record, all of whom are considered to be inheritors of the Dharma. In a narrow sense, this physical record pertains to the certification connected with formal Transmission. In the latter part of this text, Dōgen describes various Transmission Silks that he saw during his sojourn in China.

The Record of Transmission, however, has a deeper significance, one that goes beyond a conventional historical approach to the topic of ancestral succession. This spiritual significance, as Dōgen tells us at the end of this work, was taught to him by his Master Tendō Nyojō, and it colors his whole discussion: namely, that the inheritance of the Dharma flows not only from Master to disciple but also from disciple to Master. This implies, among other things, that fundamentally there is no separate self that receives the Transmission, nor any other that gives It.

In various other discourses, Dōgen's references to the Dharma that is inherited may have been intended to encompass the whole body of what the Buddha taught, while in this text the references could be intended to point in particular to the Precepts, since the receiving of the Precepts in the Sōtō tradition is an inheritance of Dharma common to lay ordination, monastic ordination, and formal Transmission.

I, Dōgen, a mendicant monk of the fifty-first generation, now at Kannondōri in Kōshōhōrin-ji Temple, who went to Sung China in order to receive and then Transmit the Dharma, have respectfully written down this document for those descendants in our lineage who desire that their attesting to the Truth be certified by means of the Record of Transmission of the Dharma that Buddhas inherit from Buddhas, and Ancestors inherit from Ancestors.[1]

---

1.   This opening statement prefaces the original text.

Beyond doubt, Buddha after Buddha has inherited the Dharma from Buddha after Buddha and, beyond doubt, Ancestor after Ancestor has inherited the Dharma from Ancestor after Ancestor. This is Their direct experiencing of what has been promised.[2] It is the simple, direct, one-to-one Transmission and, because of this, it is the unsurpassed state of enlightenment. If one is not a Buddha, one cannot give the seal of certification* to a Buddha, and no one ever becomes a Buddha without receiving a Buddha's seal of certification. Who other than a Buddha could declare this state to be the most honored or certify it to be unsurpassed?

When we receive the Buddha's seal of certification, it is because we have spontaneously awakened, independent of a Master, and because we have spontaneously awakened, independent of a self. This is why it is said that Buddha after Buddha has inherited the certification and Ancestor after Ancestor has experienced what was promised. The fundamental meaning of this principle cannot be clearly resolved except between Buddha and Buddha. How could it possibly be like what is surmised by those at any of the various stages along the Bodhisattva* Path, to say nothing of what doctrinal teachers or mundane commentators on Scriptural texts reckon it to be! In whatever way we may try to explain it to others, they cannot really hear what is being said, because it is something that Buddhas inherit from Buddhas.

The Buddha's Way has been thoroughly mastered solely by Buddha after Buddha, and there has never been a time when there was not a succession of Buddha after Buddha. By way of analogy, there is the situation of 'stones successively inheriting from stones' and of 'jewels successively inheriting from jewels'.[3] The

---

2. This phrase translates Dōgen's highly truncated technical term for the direct experiencing of the fulfillment of Shakyamuni Buddha's promise that all sentient beings, without exception, will—as He did—ultimately become Buddha.

* See Glossary.

3. The term 'stones' is often used to describe the dull, hard minds of those who have not yet awakened to Truth, whereas 'jewels' would be descriptive of the bright, clear minds of those who have awakened. In the present context, this would imply that what Buddha

succession of Ancestors resembles 'the mutual inheriting by chrysanthemums' and 'the giving of the seal of certification by pines': in both cases, there is not the slightest gap between the previous chrysanthemums and the ones that follow, nor is there any gap between the previous pines and the ones that follow.[4] Those folks who are unclear about such things may indeed encounter the words and ways which Buddha after Buddha has correctly passed on, yet they do not have the slightest clue as to what they have heard, for they have never grasped the meaning of the phrase "Ancestor after Ancestor has experienced what was promised, which is what Buddha after Buddha has been heir to." Sad to say, even though such people may bear a superficial resemblance to the progeny of Buddhas, they are not disciples of the Buddha, nor are they Buddhas who have disciples.

The Sixth Chinese Ancestor, while dwelling on Mount Sōkei, once pointed out to his assembly, "From the Seven Buddhas[*] to me, Enō, there have been forty generations of Buddhas, and from me, Enō, to the Seven Buddhas, there have been forty generations of Ancestors." This principle is clearly the correct doctrine of the succession of Buddhas and Ancestors. Among the Seven Buddhas, there are Those who manifested in the past Eon of the Sublime, and there are Those who manifested in the present Eon of the Wise and Virtuous.[5] In addition to this,

---

after Buddha has inherited is not the same as what people in ordinary, everyday society culturally inherit.

4.   From context, it is likely that 'the mutual inheriting by chrysanthemums' refers to the horizontal relationship of Master and disciple, wherein both are equal in their Buddha Nature. 'The giving of the seal of certification by pines' refers to the vertical relationship of senior Master and junior disciple. The Master-disciple relationship contains both of these aspects at the same time.

5.   The first three of these Buddhas (Bibashi, Shiki, and Bishafu) are said to have appeared in what is called the Eon of the Sublime, which precedes our own; the remaining four Buddhas (Kuruson, Kunagonmuni, Kashō, and Shakyamuni) are said to have appeared in our own eon, described as the Eon of the Wise and Virtuous.

that which links the Face-to-Face Transmission of the Forty Ancestors is the path of the Buddhas, the succession of Buddhas.

Thus, when we proceed from the Sixth Chinese Ancestor to the Seven Buddhas, there is the succession of forty Ancestors. In proceeding from the Seven Buddhas to the Sixth Ancestor, there is the succession of forty Buddhas. Both the path of Buddhas and the path of Ancestors are just like this. If we do not experience what was promised, if we are not an Ancestor of the Buddha, then we will lack the spiritually wise discernment of a Buddha, and we will lack an Ancestor's full realization of the True Nature of things. A Buddha lacking spiritually wise discernment would be a Buddha devoid of faith: an Ancestor without full realization of the True Nature of things would be an Ancestor lacking the experience of what was promised. The forty Ancestors whom I have referred to here are just the Ones who are in our specific lineage.

In accord with what I have been saying, the process of succession of Buddha after Buddha is something that is extraordinarily profound. It is completely resolute, neither retreating nor deviating: it is unbroken in its continuity and has never died out. The fundamental point of this process is that, even though Shakyamuni Buddha had realized the Truth prior to the age of the Seven Buddhas, it was a long time before He inherited the Dharma from Kashō Buddha. Although it is said that He realized the Truth on the eighth day of the twelfth lunar month, thirty years after His birth, this was His realizing the Truth prior to all the various Buddhas, and it was His realizing the Truth shoulder-to-shoulder and simultaneously with the various Buddhas; it was His realizing the Truth both prior to and subsequent to all the various Buddhas.

Further, there is a principle that needs your meditative investigation: Kashō Buddha inherited the Dharma from Shakyamuni Buddha. Should you not know this principle, you will not clarify what the Buddha's Truth is, and if you do not clarify what the Buddha's Truth is, you will not be an heir of the Buddha. 'An heir of the Buddha' is the same as 'a disciple of the Buddha'.

Shakyamuni once inspired Ananda to ask, "Pray, whose disciples are the various Buddhas of the past?" Shakyamuni Buddha responded, "The various Buddhas of the past are My disciples." All the various Buddhas behave in a similar Buddhist way. To respectfully serve these various Buddhas, to inherit the Buddha Dharma, and to bring this inheritance to fruition, this surely is the Way of the Buddhas for Buddha after Buddha. And, without fail, when someone inherits the Dharma of this Way of Buddhas, there will invariably be a record of inheritance.[6]

Anyone who has not inherited the Dharma will be a person outside the Buddhist Way, one who has not recognized what karmic* cause and effect are, but thinks that things are the way they are because of their inherent nature. If the Way of the Buddhas had not determined the succession of the Dharma, how could It possibly have come down to us today? For this reason, with Buddha after Buddha, there has been, beyond doubt, the passing on of a record of Buddha Transmitting Buddha, and there has been the acquiring of that record of Buddha Transmitting Buddha. The nature of that record of Transmission is, for one person, the inheriting of the Dharma by clarifying 'sun, moon, and stars', and, for another, the inheriting of the Dharma by obtaining Its Skin and Flesh, Bones and Marrow. Or it is the passing on of a kesa,* or the passing on of a traveling staff, or the passing on of a pine branch, or the passing on of a ceremonial hossu,* or the passing on of an udumbara blossom, or the passing on of a gold brocade robe. There has also been the passing on of a straw sandal and the passing on of a stick of bamboo.

When these inheritances of the Dharma are passed on, the recipient may record the succession with blood taken from a finger or from the tongue. And the record may also be written with oil or milk. These are all records of Transmission. The one who passes It on and the one who receives It are both, indeed, heirs of the Buddha. When they fully manifest as Ancestors of the Buddha, their inheriting of the Dharma will undoubtedly fully manifest as well. When It manifested, It came even though they did not expect It, and many are the Ancestors of the Buddha who inherited the Dharma even though they did not deliberately seek It. Those who have inherited the Dharma are, beyond any doubt, Buddha after Buddha and Ancestor after Ancestor.

---

6.   This would include not only those monks who had been Transmitted, but also all ordained monks and those of the laity who had committed themselves to the Buddhist Way by doing Jukai, the Ceremony of Receiving the Precepts.

Ever since our Twenty-eighth Ancestor Bodhidharma came from the West, we in eastern lands have correctly heard the fundamental point that within the Buddha's Way there is an inheriting of the Dharma. Before then, this had not been heard of here in the eastern lands. It was something not yet realized or even known about by scriptural scholars and teachers of the *Tripitaka** in India, as well as being beyond the realm of those who are 'thrice wise and ten times saintly'.* Nor was its existence even suspected by those would-be teachers of mantric techniques, among others, who go searching for them through the *Tripitaka*. How sad that they have received a human body—which is a vessel of the Truth—and, at the same time, have vainly become enmeshed in the web of academic theories, ignorant of the method for attaining liberation and devoid of any expectation of a time when they might spring free. This is why we should, indeed, continually explore the Way through our training and should, indeed, wholeheartedly keep to the spirit of training.

When I was in Sung China, I was able to bow in reverence to various records of Transmission, for there were many styles of Transmission records. Among them was that of Iitsu, who was a retired Master living in the West Hall at Keitoku-ji Temple,[7] where he had finally hung up his traveling staff. He was a man from the Yüeh District and the former Abbot of Kōfuku-ji Temple. He was from the same village as my late teacher. My late teacher was always saying, "You should go ask Iitsu in the West Hall about the customs of our region." One day, Iitsu said to me, "Being able to look at ancient pieces of calligraphy is something that we humans prize very highly. How many have you already seen?" I replied, "I've just seen a few." Then he said, "I have an old scroll of calligraphy somewhere among my belongings. It's not much of a thing. But I'll let you have a look at it, venerable brother." When I looked at what he brought out, it was a Transmission record that had belonged to a ninth-century disciple of Hōgen. It had been obtained from among the robes and alms bowl

---

7. The Abbot of Keitoku-ji Temple during this time was Tendō Nyojō, Dōgen's Master.

of some elderly master upon his decease. It was not Iitsu's Transmission record. On it was written, "The First Ancestor Makakashō awoke to the Truth under Shakyamuni Buddha, and Shakyamuni Buddha awoke to the Truth under Kashō Buddha." That was the way it was put. Having seen these words, I, Dōgen, was convinced that there is a Dharma Transmission from a true heir to a true heir. It was Dharma that I had never seen before. This was an occasion when the Buddhas and the Ancestors, unseen, responded to the needs of one of Their offspring. My feelings of gratitude could not match the moment.

The Venerable Master Shūgetsu, while a senior monk at Keitoku-ji Temple, also showed me a Transmission record, one that he said belonged to Ummon's lineage. The name of the Master just preceding the person who was receiving the Transmission record, along with those of the Indian and Chinese Ancestors of the Buddha, were arranged in columns, below which was the name of the person receiving the Transmission record. It made a link from all the Buddhas and Ancestors directly to the name of the new Ancestor. Thus, the names from the Tathagata through some forty generations all came down to the name of the new heir. It was as if he were being certified by each new Ancestor in turn. Some names, however, such as Makakashō and Ananda, were lined up as if they belonged to branches other than his. I then asked Senior Monk Shūgetsu, "Venerable monk, when we list the lineages of the five Zen families today, there are a few differences from this. What is at the heart of this? If there has been a succession of heirs from India one after the other, how can there be any differences?" Shūgetsu replied, "Even if the differences were far greater, still, we should simply pass on that the Buddhas of Mount Ummon are like this. Why is our Venerable Master Shakyamuni revered so deeply by others? He is deeply revered because He awoke to the Truth. Why is Great Master Ummon revered so deeply by others? He is deeply revered because he awoke to the Truth." When I heard these words, I had a bit more understanding.

Nowadays in the provinces of Kiangsu and Chekiang, the heads of the large temples, by and large, are Dharma heirs of Rinzai, Ummon, or Tōzan. However, a bunch of fellows who proclaim themselves to be distantly related to Rinzai are up to something that is just not right. They join the assembly of some prominent Master, purportedly to train, and then earnestly beg him for a hanging portrait or a scroll inscribed with some Dharma saying, which they then store up for future use as proof of their being this Master's Dharma heir. As if this were not enough, there are among such types those 'dogs' who, having earnestly requested, say, a Dharma inscription or a portrait from some venerable monk, hoard such objects until their store of them is quite large. Then, when they reach their later years, they bribe some official to get themselves a temple. At the time when they are appointed its chief monk, they are not Dharma heirs of the Master who gave them the Dharma inscription or the portrait. When they do inherit the Dharma, either from their contemporary monks who have become celebrities or from senior monks who have intimate connections with rulers and their ministers, they are not asking for the Dharma, but are only greedy for fame and reputation. What a pity that such wicked customs exist in these evil times when the Dharma is coming to an end! Among people like these, not even one has ever seen or heard of the Way of the Buddhas and Ancestors, even in his dreams.

Customarily, as to a Master's granting a monk something like a copy of a Dharma saying or a portrait, such things are also given to scholastic lecturers belonging to various branches of Buddhism and to householders, male and female. They are also granted to lay temple workers, tradesmen, and the like. The truth of this is clear from the records of the various branches. On the other hand, even those who are not sincere followers may implore a Master for a scroll of calligraphy because they crave evidence of their being a Dharma heir and, even though it is a situation that the Master, as one who has realized the Truth, deplores, he reluctantly takes brush in hand. In such a situation, he does not use the traditional way of expressing the matter, but signs it with some phrase like 'your Master is me'. In recent times, the procedure is simply for some monk to inherit the Dharma as a Master as soon as he attains any degree of proficiency in his Master's assembly. And many indeed are the fellows who have never received their Master's seal, but who simply pay perfunctory visits to the Master's quarters, enter the Lecture Hall, and occupy a place in the Meditation Hall. Even though the Master is residing in the temple, they do not make the time to receive his personal instruction, yet they claim that Master to be their Master, should they happen to break open the Great Matter.[8]

There was a monk known as Chief Librarian Den, who was a remote descendant of the Rinzai Meditation Master Butsugen, this Master also being known by the name of Seien of Ryūmon Temple. Chief Librarian Den also carried a Transmission record with him. Near the beginning of the Chinese Chia-ting Era, when he became ill, he was nursed by a Japanese senior monk named Ryūzen. After his recovery, to show his appreciation for Ryūzen's considerate care, he took out the Transmission record and let Ryūzen bow to it, saying, "This is something rare to see. I offer it to you that you may pay your respects to it."

Eight years later, in the autumn of the sixteenth year of the same era (1223), during my first sojourn on Mount Tendō, Senior Monk Ryūzen asked Den to show me his Transmission record. This Transmission record was such that the names of forty-five Ancestors, from the Seven Buddhas down to Rinzai, were written out in columns, while the names of the Masters following Rinzai formed a circle in which their inscribed Dharma names were sealed with their monograms. The name of the new heir was written at the end of the record, below the date. We need to recognize that the form of this record in no way differs from that of Rinzai's other venerable disciples.

My late Master, the Abbot of Keitoku-ji Temple, strongly cautioned his assembly about speaking in an imprudent way about someone's inheriting the Dharma. Truly, my late Master's assembly was a veritable 'assembly of the ancient Buddha', a restoration of the Buddha's 'monastic forest'. My late Master did not personally wear multi-colored kesas. Although the variegated, patchwork kesa of Meditation Master Dōkai of Mount Fuyō had been passed on to him, he did not use it,

---

8. That is, such persons may have had a genuine realization of the Truth, but they have not truly trained with the Master, to say nothing of having gone to the Master in order to have their understanding certified.

even when he sat in the teacher's seat in the Lecture Hall. In short, he never wore a brocaded Dharma robe in his whole life as Abbot. Everyone, both the thoughtful and the naive, praised him for this and esteemed him as a true spiritual friend.

When my late Master entered the Lecture Hall, he would admonish all those about him, saying, "Recently, a bunch who style themselves as ones who follow the Way of our Ancestor Bodhidharma irresponsibly go about wearing a Dharma robe along with their long hair and signing their name with the title of Master as their way of navigating themselves to prominence. How pitiful! Who will rescue them? I regret to say that there are senior monks, far and wide, who have no heart for the Way and so they do not investigate It or train in It. Even rarer—not one in a hundred thousand— are those who have seen or heard of the relationship between the Transmission record and inheriting the Dharma. This is indeed the decline of the Way of our Ancestor Bodhidharma!" He was constantly admonishing us in this way, but none of the senior monks ever took offence. Therefore, if trainees do their utmost to practice the Way with a sincere heart, they <u>will</u> see and hear that there is a Transmission record. This seeing and hearing will be part of their exploring the Way through their training.

In a Rinzai Transmission record, the name of the Master is written first, and then the name of the disciple who came to train with him, followed by the phrase 'entered my assembly, entered my training hall, and was made my heir', followed by the list of names of those Ancestors of the previous generations. This record also contains a bit of instruction on the Dharma which the Master has expressed in his own words. The basic import of this record is simply that an heir has encountered a genuine 'good spiritual friend': this is the truly fundamental point. There is no need to be concerned with whether these names come at the end or the beginning of the record. I saw one from the Rinzai tradition that was written in this manner. I put it down here just as I actually saw it: [9]

---

9.   The original text gives some Chinese names in abbreviated form; the translation has supplied fuller, Japanese forms for them.

Chief Librarian Ryōha was a person of authority and military valor. He is now my disciple.

I, Tokkō, trained under and served Abbot Daie Sōkō of Mount Kinzan,

Kinzan was an heir to Engo Kokugon of Mount Kassan,

Engo was an heir to Goso Hōen of Mount Yōgi,

Hōen was an heir to Kaie Shutan of Mount Hakuun,

Shutan was an heir to Hōe of Mount Yōgi,

Hōe was an heir to Jimyō Soen,

Soen was an heir to Fun'yō Zenshō,

Zenshō was an heir to Shōnen of Mount Shuzan,

Shōnen was an heir to Enshō of Mount Fuketsu,

Enshō was an heir to Nan'in Egyō,

Egyō was an heir to Sonshō of Kōke Temple,

Sonshō was an heir to the Great Founding Ancestor Rinzai.

Meditation Master Busshō Tokkō wrote this whilst on Mount Ashoka and gave it to Musai Ryōha. When the latter became Abbot of Keitoku-ji Temple,[10] his junior disciple Chikō brought it out and showed it to me in private in the Dormitory of Clarity. I first saw it on the twenty-first day of the first lunar month in the seventeenth year in the Chia-ting Era of Great Sung China (February 11, 1224). My joy was immeasurable! My seeing it was surely due to unseen help from the Buddhas and Ancestors. After offering incense and respectfully bowing, I opened it and read it.

My desire to be shown this Transmission record arose around the seventh lunar month of the previous year, when the temple comptroller Shikō told me about it in private while we were in the Hall of Serene Light. I asked the comptroller in passing, "In whose care is it at present?" The comptroller answered, "Apparently, it is in the venerable Abbot's quarters. Later, if you were to ask him in a cordial way to show it to you, I am sure he would do so." After I heard these words, my intention to

---

10.　When Musai Ryōha was approaching death, he invited Nyojō to become the next Abbot of Keitoku-ji Temple on Mount Tendō. Nyojō accepted and became known as Tendō Nyojō.

make a request for it did not let up day or night. So, in the following year, and with some trepidation, I put my request to the Abbot's junior disciple Chikō in a friendly way, placing my whole heart in it, and my request was indeed granted.

The wrapper to which it was attached was covered with white silk on the inside and with red brocade on the outside. Its spindle was of jade. It was a scroll about nine inches high and over seven feet wide. As it was not something shown to the idle or the curious, I duly offered my thanks to Chikō, and forthwith went to the Abbot, made an incense offering, respectfully bowed, and gave my thanks to the Venerable Musai. Musai then said to me, "Those who get a chance to see and know this particular object are very few. You, my venerable elder brother, have now come to know it. This is the real refuge for exploring the Way through your training, and just so!" Nothing had ever surpassed the joy that I felt then.

Later, around the time of the Chinese Pao-ching Era (1225-1227), when I was drifting like a cloud from monastery to monastery on such mountains as Tendai and Gantō, I came to Mannen Temple in the P'ing-t'ien region. The Abbot at the time was the Venerable Genshi of Fukushū. Upon the retirement of Abbot Shūkan, the Venerable Genshi had been appointed to the post, and he was strongly encouraging the practice of seated meditation in the temple. Following the customary salutations, we took up the topic of the various customs and traditions of the Ancestors of the Buddha down through the ages. While I was proffering the story about Isan Reiyū asking Kyōzan about the quality of the latter's recent heirs, the Abbot asked, "Have you ever seen the Transmission record that I have here?" I replied, "How could I have seen it?" The Abbot then stood up and, holding up his Transmission record, he said, "Even if someone were a close friend, even if he were someone who had spent years as my attendant monk, I would not permit him to see this. This is, of course, the Dharma instruction of the Buddhas and the Ancestors. But, be that as it may," Genshi said, "once when I was on my customary trip to the city with the intention of visiting the governor, I experienced a vision. In it, there was a distinguished monk who looked like Meditation Master Daibai Hōjō. Holding aloft a branch of plum blossoms, he said, 'If you should meet a Real Person who has already crossed over by ferry, do not begrudge him these flowers,' and then he handed me the plum blossoms. In response, I spontaneously chanted, 'Before he even entered the boat, he deserved thirty blows.' Not five days had passed, when I met you face-to-face, my venerable elder brother, and what is more, you have come by boat. And, in addition, this Transmission record of mine is written on damask that has a plum blossom pattern woven into it. Since you correspond to the one mentioned in the vision, you must be the one whom Daibai was instructing me about. Venerable elder brother, do you wish to be my Dharma heir? If you do, I would be delighted to Transmit you."

In no way could I ignore his feeling of trust. Although I could have received the Transmission, instead I simply lit incense, reverently bowed to the record, and gave the Abbot my deepest respect and veneration as an offering. At the time, there was an incense monk in attendance, one named Hōnei, who said that it was the first time that he had ever seen a Transmission record.

I thought to myself, "Truly, were it not for the unseen help of the Buddhas and Ancestors, it would have been nigh on impossible for me to have seen or even heard about this sort of thing. What good fortune that I, a foolish and ignorant fellow from a remote country, have seen so many of them," and tears of gratitude wet my sleeves. At that time, the Vimalakirti* Room for lay guests and the Chief Monk's Hall, among others, were quiet and unoccupied. This Transmission record was written on white silk with a plum blossom pattern. It was over nine inches high and more than six feet wide. Its spindle was of topaz and its outer cover was of silk.

On my way back from Mount Tendai to Mount Tendō, I was staying the night in the hall for traveling monks at Goshō-ji Temple on Mount Daibai, where I experienced a wondrous vision in which Ancestral Master Daibai came and offered me a branch of plum flowers in full bloom. The vision of an Ancestor is the most reliable thing there is. The blossoms on the branch were more than a foot in diameter. The plum blossom must surely be an udumbara flower! [11] What is seen in a vision and

---

11. The plum tree blooms in late winter and, as the first plant to blossom, is traditionally considered in the Far East as the harbinger of spring. In Buddhist texts, it is often associated with Shakyamuni Buddha. The udumbara tree is said to blossom only once

what is seen in a waking state will be equally real. While I was in Sung China and since my return to this country, I have not told this to anyone before.

At the present time, the writing of a Transmission record in our Tōzan lineage is different from that in others, such as the Rinzai lineage. Our monastery's Founding Ancestor Seigen, in front of the desk of his Master Daikan Enō, wrote out with blood that flowed from his finger that which had been kept under the robe of the Buddha's Ancestor Enō. Tradition has it that the passing on of the record was done by Seigen mixing the blood from his finger with that of Enō. Tradition also has it that the ceremony of mixing blood also occurred in the case of our First Ancestor Bodhidharma and our Second Ancestor Eka. To refrain from writing such things as "My disciple So-and-so" or "So-and-so came to train with me" is the rule for Transmission records which various Buddhas, including the Seven Buddhas, have written and passed on.

So, keep in mind that Enō graciously blended his blood and spirit with Seigen's immaculate blood, and Seigen's immaculate blood personally blended with the parental blood of Enō. Thus, our distinguished Ancestor, Venerable Seigen, and he alone, was the only one to so intimately receive Enō's direct certification; it is not something that his other disciples attained. Folks who know about these matters are wont to say that Enō Transmitted the Buddha Dharma directly to Seigen, and to Seigen alone.

The Record of Transmission

My late teacher, an Old Buddha, the Great Master and Abbot of Keitoku-ji Temple, once said to me, "All the Buddhas have, beyond doubt, inherited the Dharma. That is to say, Shakyamuni Buddha inherited the Dharma from Kashō Buddha. Kashō

---

every three thousand years. Its flower is often used in Buddhist writings as an illustration of how difficult it is to encounter the Dharma. Both types of blossoms are frequently used as symbols for the Transmission of the Dharma.

Buddha inherited the Dharma from Kunagonmuni Buddha. Kunagonmuni Buddha inherited the Dharma from Kuruson Buddha. You must have faith that Buddha after Buddha has inherited It in this manner, reaching down to us now, for this is how we explore the Way of the Buddhas through our training."

I then said to him, "It was after Kashō Buddha had entered nirvana that Shakyamuni Buddha first emerged into the world and realized the Truth. Moreover, how could the Buddhas of the present Eon of the Wise and Virtuous have inherited the Dharma from the Buddhas in the previous Eon of the Sublime? What do you think?"

My late teacher responded, "What you have said is an interpretation based on your listening to scholarly theories. It is an expression of those who are thrice wise and ten times saintly. It is not something that those in the succession of legitimate heirs of the Buddhas and Ancestors say. Our way of Transmission from Buddha to Buddha is not like that. We have learned that Shakyamuni Buddha, beyond any doubt whatsoever, inherited the Dharma from Kashō Buddha. Through our spiritual exploring, we learn that after Shakyamuni Buddha inherited the Dharma, Kashō Buddha entered nirvana. If Shakyamuni Buddha had not inherited the Dharma from Kashō Buddha, He would have been the same as some non-Buddhist who denies cause and effect, so who then could have faith in Shakyamuni Buddha? Because the inheritance passes from Buddha to Buddha in this manner and has come down to us today, all the Buddhas, individually, are genuine heirs. It is not that They are lined up, one after the other, nor is it that They are gathered together in a mass. We just learn that the inheritance passes from Buddha to Buddha in this manner. Do not get all embroiled with the measurements of eons or the measurements of lifespans as spoken of literally in the various *Āgama Scriptures*. If we say that the succession started just with Shakyamuni Buddha, that would merely be some two thousand or so years ago, which is not all that old. The Transmission would barely cover some forty generations. It could be said to be relatively new. The succession of Buddhas is not to be investigated in this manner. We learn that Shakyamuni Buddha inherited the Dharma from Kashō Buddha, and we learn that Kashō Buddha inherited the Dharma from Shakyamuni Buddha. When we learn the matter in this way, it will be the true succession of Buddha after Buddha and Ancestor after Ancestor."

Then, for the first time, not only did I receive this serving of his spiritually nourishing rice, namely, that we have the Transmission of the Dharma from the Buddhas and Ancestors, but I also let go of some old cobwebs from my past.

Written on the twenty-seventh day of the third lunar month in the second year of the Japanese Ninji era (April 9, 1241) at Kannondōri in Kōshōhōrin-ji Temple by me, the mendicant monk Dōgen, who went into Sung China in order to receive and then Transmit the Dharma.

Copied by me on the twenty-fifth day of the second lunar month in the fourth year of the Ninji era (March 17, 1243).

Ejō,

Abbot's Assistant

16

On 'The Flowering of the Dharma
Sets the Dharma's Flowering in Motion'

(Hokke Ten Hokke)

Translator's Introduction: According to Dōgen's postscript to this discourse, he originally prepared it for a monk named Edatsu whom he had ordained. Edatsu's decision to become a monk was apparently deeply influenced by his encounter with the *Lotus Scripture*, for the discourse is heavily laden with allusions to and quotations from that work. Indeed, most of the descriptive terms and phrases Dōgen employs are taken from Kumārajīva's well-known Chinese version of this Scripture, and someone familiar with that translation would quite likely recognize the various contexts from which these terms and phrases were borrowed. Some of these have been identified in this translation by the addition of some phrase, such as 'which the *Lotus Scripture* calls'.

The title of Dōgen's discourse does not derive directly from the *Lotus Scripture*, but is based on terms used by the Sixth Chinese Ancestor Enō in a kōan story that Dōgen recounts. These terms carry multiple meanings which often apply simultaneously throughout the discourse, so that no single English rendering can fully encompass what the Sino-Japanese text is conveying, though all the meanings are pointing to the general topic of the consequences from expressing the Dharma.

To begin with, *hokke* can equally be rendered as 'the Flower of the Dharma' and 'the flowering of the Dharma', the latter in the sense of 'the appearing or emerging of the Dharma' as well as of 'giving expression to the Dharma'. It is also an allusion to *Hokke Kyō*, the abbreviated Sino-Japanese title for the *Lotus Scripture*. *Ten* primarily signifies such actions as 'turning', 'revolving', 'setting in motion', 'arousing', and 'giving rise to'. These two terms are combined into the two phrases *hokke ten* and *ten hokke*, which, according to Dōgen, are of Enō's coining. *Hokke ten* can be rendered by such phrases as 'being set in motion by the flowering of the Dharma', and 'being turned by the Flower of the Dharma' (that is, by the *Lotus Scripture* itself and the Dharma that is expressed in it). *Ten hokke* can be rendered in various ways, such as 'setting in motion a flowering of the Dharma', 'revolving (that is, perusing) the *Lotus Scripture*', and 'turning the Flower of the Dharma', this last being an alternate way of saying 'turning the Wheel of the Dharma'. All of these meanings are implicit within whichever term is used in the present translation. Hence, the title might also be rendered as "The *Lotus Scripture* Sets in Motion the Dharma's Flowering".

209

This discourse may prove to be one of the more difficult discourses in the *Shōbōgenzō*. It would be worth the reader's while to go through the work slowly several times to catch the beauty of the underlying Teaching.

Expounded for a certain person from Kōshōhōrin-ji Temple.

What exists everywhere within all Buddhist lands is simply the flowering of the Dharma. Everywhere and at all times, all Buddhas—along with Their assemblies of those who would realize supreme, fully perfected enlightenment—experience the setting in motion of the flowering of the Dharma and They experience being moved by that flowering. This state is equivalent to what the *Lotus Scripture* describes by such phrases as 'the Bodhisattva* Way as practiced from the very first, without retreating or deviating', 'the profundity and breadth of the wise discernment of all Buddhas, which is beyond measure', as well as 'the clear and calm samadhi* that is difficult to comprehend and difficult to enter'.

Just as with Manjushri* Buddha in the *Lotus Scripture*, this state has the aspect of 'being just what one is', which is a characteristic of each individual Buddha, just as it is of all the other Buddhas, all of Whom take the Great Ocean as their Buddha Land.

On the other hand, Shakyamuni Buddha emerged in the world with His realizing that, as He put it, "Only I recognize the genuine character of things, as do all Buddhas everywhere." This is equivalent to the time when He said, "Having fully awakened to the One Great Matter,* I alone desire to help sentient beings open up to It, manifest It, awaken to It, and enter It, just as all Buddhas have done."

And these phrases from the *Lotus Scripture* also refer to Samantabhadra,* for He has succeeded in helping the Dharma's flowering to arise in others in ways that are beyond the intellective mind's ability to grasp or fathom. Also, He has succeeded in causing the profound, vast, and far-reaching supreme, fully perfected enlightenment to flow throughout Jambudvipa.* In that He has done this, the earth is able to produce the three kinds of grasses and the two kinds of trees, large and small, and the rain is

---

*   See Glossary.

able to moisten them all.[1] He alone accomplishes the exhaustive practice of helping the Dharma's flowering to arise in others in ways that are beyond our ability to know. Samantabhadra's proclaiming of the Dharma had not yet reached an end when the great assembly gathered on the Divine Vulture Peak to hear the Buddha give voice to the Dharma. The Venerable Shakyamuni gave proof of Samantabhadra's comings and goings throughout the universe by means of the radiance emanating from the white hairs between His eyebrows.[2]

Shakyamuni's meeting with those in His assembly had not yet reached its midpoint when they experienced a flowering of the Dharma, which was set in motion by Manjushri's affirmation that Maitreya* would imminently realize Buddhahood. When they experienced this flowering of the Dharma, which was good through and through—beginning, middle, and end—Samantabhadra, the various Buddhas, Manjushri, and all the great assembly must surely have been carried to the Other Shore. This is why the flowering of the Dharma has manifested in the world as the fulfillment of the One Great Matter for which we train by relying on the One Vehicle.

Because this manifestation is the One Great Matter, each Buddha, on His own, fully realizes the aspect of Truth within all thoughts and things, just as all other Buddhas have done. This Teaching is, beyond doubt, what the *Lotus Scripture* calls 'the One Vehicle to Buddhahood, which Buddhas alone confirm and which They help all future Buddhas to fully realize'. The various Buddhas, including the Seven

---

1. This is a reference to "The Parable of the Herbs" in the *Lotus Scripture*, where ordinary, conventional human beings are likened to small grasses, the shravakas and pratyekabuddhas who follow the Lesser Course to various shrubbery, and the bodhisattvas who follow the Greater Course to three types of vegetation: tall grasses (such as bamboo), small trees, and large trees. In the parable, the rain is likened to the rain of Dharma which the Buddha showers down upon them so that they may all come to their spiritual fruition.

2. That is, there was a radiance that seemed to pour forth from Shakyamuni's brow. Those who saw this radiance associated it with the manifesting of Samantabhadra, whose name means 'Universal Goodness and Loving-kindness'.

Buddhas,* have each helped Buddha after Buddha to fully realize the Truth, just as They helped Shakyamuni Buddha to fulfill His mission.

The lands from India in the west to China in the east are among the Buddhist lands throughout the ten directions. What has been fully realized in these lands, even up through the Thirty-third Ancestor, Meditation Master Daikan Enō, is the One Vehicle which was taught by each and every Buddha. It is the One Vehicle of all Buddhas. Our reliance solely upon It is, without doubt, the One Great Matter. It manifests in the world now: It manifests right here. Seigen's Buddhist modes of deportment have been handed down to us today and Nangaku's gates to the Dharma are still open in the world, all due to the Tathagata's knowing and seeing the True Nature of the world.[3] Surely, we are being aroused by the flowering of the Dharma when we say that this is what each Buddha on His own, together with all other Buddhas, have truly realized in full. It is what Those who succeeded Shakyamuni Buddha and what the Buddhas who have been Their successors have all opened up to, manifested, awakened to, and entered.

We also call this Scripture the *Scripture on the Lotus Flower of the Wondrous Teaching*, for it is the Teaching that trains bodhisattvas. Because this Scripture contains all thoughts and things, both the Divine Vulture Peak and the vast sky exist, as well as the great ocean and the great earth, with the Flower of the Dharma as their native land. As such, this Scripture describes how Truth appears: It is 'just what is, as it is'. It is 'the abode of the Dharma' and 'the invariable state of the Dharma'. It is 'the impermanence of all actions'. It is 'the reason for the One Great Matter for which we train'. It is 'what the Buddha experienced directly'. It is 'what is abiding within the world of appearances'. It is 'what is real'. It is 'the lifespan of a Tathagata'. It is 'what is profound and immeasurable'. It is 'the meditative state of the flowering of the Dharma'. It is 'Shakyamuni Buddha'. It is 'setting the Flower of the Dharma in motion'. It is 'the Flower of the Dharma moving'. It is 'the Treasure House of the Eye

---

3.　　Seigen and Nangaku were Enō's two Dharma heirs.

of the True Teaching' and 'the Wondrous Heart of Nirvana'. It is 'manifesting in physical form in order to ferry sentient beings to the Other Shore'. And we have the Scripture's promise that "All will ultimately realize Buddhahood," and we have the charge to preserve It.

During the time of the great T'ang dynasty, a monk named Hōtatsu once came to visit the assembly of Meditation Master Daikan Enō at Hōrin-ji Temple on Mount Sōkei, which is in the region of the eastern road in South China.[4] He said of himself, "I have already read the *Lotus Scripture* aloud three thousand times."

Our Ancestor replied, "Even though you were to recite It ten thousand times, if you have not grasped what It is teaching, you won't even reach the point where you know what your shortcomings are."

Hōtatsu responded, "Student that I am, what a ninny I've been. Up till now, I have just recited It, merely sticking to the words. So, how could I possibly have grasped what they mean?"

Enō replied, "Just as an experiment, recite It, and I will explain It for you."

Hōtatsu then began to recite the Scripture. When he reached the section on skillful means, Enō said, "Stop here. The basic point of this Scripture is to tell us the reason behind the Buddha's originally coming into this world. Even though It sets forth many allegories, none ever goes beyond this basic point. And if we ask what was behind this, it was simply the One Great Matter for which we train. 'Just the One Great Matter' is, of course, 'what

---

4.   Underlying this narrative of the encounter between Hōtatsu and Enō is the fact that Enō had had a kenshō when, as a very young man, he overheard a passage from the *Diamond-Cutting Scripture* being recited by someone. He himself was illiterate, but had the ability to understand the import of Scriptural passages when they were read to him.

the Buddha came to know directly'. It was 'His opening up to It, manifesting It, awakening to It, and entering It'. This Matter is, naturally, what a Buddha comes to know directly. Anyone who is equipped with this direct knowing is already a Buddha. By all means, you should have faith here and now that what a Buddha directly knows is right within your very own heart." Enō then added a poem to set this forth:

When the mind wanders onto deluded paths,
It is being set in motion by the flowering of the Dharma;
When the heart awakens,
The Dharma's flowering is set in motion.

However long you recite this Scripture, should it be while still
unawakened to the Self that is true,
You will then create an enemy to Its meaning.
To read It without opinion's bonds is the proper way,
But read It bound to fixed ideas, and It becomes error's way.

When you cease to judge whether you are bound or not,
You ride forever long within the cart by the White Ox drawn.

When Hōtatsu heard this poem, he said the following to Enō, "It says in this Scripture that even if all beings—from the greatest shravakas* to the bodhisattvas—were to exhaust the resources of their thinking in measuring the Buddha's spiritually wise discernment, they could not fathom it. Now, you seem to be saying that, if even ordinary people who wander through life in ignorance were to inquire into the Matter for which we train, it could lead them to spiritually awaken their own minds, and that this is precisely what a Buddha realizes through direct experience. But it is difficult for those of us who are not as highly gifted as you to escape from our doubts and skepticism. Further, in this Scripture it speaks of three vehicles, but what is the distinction between the large ox-cart and the cart drawn by a white ox?[5] I pray that you, venerable monk, will once more favor us with your comments on these matters."

Enō responded, "The intent of the Scripture is clear. It is just that you are wandering off on your own and thereby turning your back on it. Your worry that those of the Three Vehicles* are incapable of fathoming the Buddha's spiritually wise discernment is due to your own way of measuring things. Even though their intellectual resources are being exhausted through their speculations, somehow they <u>will</u> arrive from however far away they may be. As the *Lotus Scripture* says, 'Right from the start, the Buddha explained this for the benefit of ordinary people who are wandering in ignorance; He did not explain it for the benefit of Buddhas.' Although they are not really turning their backs on their faith in this principle, people sometimes do leave their seat of training. But even so, unbeknownst to them, they <u>are</u> sitting in the cart drawn by the White Ox, even while they continue their search for the Three Vehicles outside the gate. In relation to what you have asked, the words of the Scripture clearly state that 'There are not two vehicles, nor are there three.' How come you have not realized this? 'The Three Vehicles' refers to expedient teachings, for it refers to a time that has passed; 'The One Vehicle' refers to the genuine Teaching, for it refers to the present moment in time. You should simply leave behind what is expedient and come back to what is genuine. When you return to the genuine, the Genuine will not be

---

5.   The present allusion, as well as many which follow, derive from the parable of the burning house in the *Lotus Scripture*. In that parable, a father attempts to rescue his three children who are playing within a burning house by promising them that they can play with three vehicles—a small sheep-drawn cart, a medium-sized deer-drawn cart, and a large ox-drawn cart—which he says lay outside the gate. When the children go outside the gate they find but one cart, which is drawn by a white ox.

just a name. You need to recognize that what you have is a wondrous and rare Treasure, and that It is fully passed on to you so that It may proceed from you to others, that they may receive It for their use. What is more, even though there is no notion of 'my father' or of 'my son', nor any attribute of 'being useful', this is what we call 'being set in motion by the *Lotus Scripture*'. From one eon to the next, day and night, the Scripture never leaves our hand, and there is no time when we are not reciting It."

Hōtatsu had, by now, opened up to the Truth and, bouncing up and down with joy, he offered Enō a poem of praise:

The three thousand times that I have recited this Scripture
Have been surpassed by Enō's solitary verse.
Because I was not yet clear as to the purpose of my coming into this
*   world,*
How was I to halt the folly of my troubled life?

'Sheep', 'deer', and 'ox' provide but expedient means.
At beginning, middle, and end, they promote the virtuous and the
*   good.*
Who within the burning house know
That, from the first, they are lords within the Dharma?

Having been offered this poem, the Ancestor said, "After this, you would do well to call yourself the monk who esteems the *Lotus Scripture*."

That is how the account of Meditation Master Hōtatsu's encounter with Daikan Enō went. The term 'flowering of the Dharma' in such phrases as 'the flowering of the Dharma sets in motion' and 'being set in motion by the Dharma's flowering' began to be used from the time of this event; such phrases had not been heard before then. Truly, the ones to clarify the meaning of 'what a Buddha directly knows' will be those belonging to the Treasure House of the Eye of the True Teaching: they will be Buddhas and Ancestors. This is beyond what can be understood by those textual scholars who vainly count words as if they were pebbles or grains of sand, as we can see from Hōtatsu's past.

To clarify for yourself the fundamental meaning of 'the flowering of the Dharma', you need to realize fully what the Ancestral Master Enō opened up and revealed as the One Great Matter for which we train. Do not try to amuse yourself by inquiring into the other Buddhist vehicles. Now, what the Ancestral Master set forth is the True Nature of the real appearance, real innate nature, real embodiment, real strength, real cause, and real effect of what is set in motion by the flowering of the Dharma. Before the Ancestral Master's time, this was something not yet heard of or even existing in China.

When we speak of 'what is set in motion by the flowering of the Dharma', we are referring to the mind's wandering off onto deluded paths. And the mind's delusive wandering, accordingly, refers to what is set in motion by the flowering of the Dharma. That is to say, our mind's wandering off is precisely what is set in motion by the Dharma's flowering. What this means is that, even though the mind's delusions are synonymous with the myriad thoughts and things that arise, the form their True Nature takes is what is aroused by the flowering of the Dharma. This 'being set in motion' is not something to rejoice in, or watch for, or obtain, or arrive at; even so, what the Dharma's flowering sets in motion is precisely 'neither two things nor three'. Since the flowering of the Dharma is our having only One Vehicle to Buddhahood, because it is the flowering of the form of things as they really are, we speak of 'being able to set in motion what moves'. Even so, it is just the One Vehicle to Buddhahood, just the One Great Matter for which we train, just the ever-moving about of the mind as it is, and nothing more. So, do not reproach yourself for your mind's delusions. As the Scripture says, "Whatever is done by you is the way of bodhisattvas," and "The fundamental practice of the Bodhisattva Way is our serving and paying homage to all the Buddhas." Our opening up to this Way, manifesting It, awakening to It, and entering It are, all together, what is set in motion by the Dharma's flowering each and every time. There are our delusions about what is within the burning house, and our delusions about being at the threshold of the gate, and our delusions about what lies outside the gate, and our delusions about what being on the other side of the gate is like, and our delusions about being within the gate.[6] Because, in our delusion, we give rise to such notions as 'being within the gate' and 'being beyond the gate', to say nothing of 'being at the threshold of the gate' and 'being within a burning house', we will, of necessity, open up to It, manifest It, awaken to It, and enter It whilst upon the cart drawn by the White Ox.

When you consider entering the gate from the burning house while riding upon this finely adorned cart, will it be because you are looking hopefully towards the open fields beyond as the place you need to enter, or because you recognize the burning house as the place you need to leave, or because you realize that the threshold of the gate is merely a point to be passed through? You certainly need to realize that when you are within this cart an opening up to, manifesting, awakening to, and entering the burning house may occur, <u>and</u> that when you are within the open fields beyond the gate an opening up to, manifesting, awakening to, and entering the burning house may occur, <u>and</u> that at the threshold of any gate an opening up to it, manifesting it, awakening to it, and entering it may occur, <u>and</u> that at any single gate to the Universal Gate an opening up to It, manifesting It, awakening to It, and entering It may also occur. At each instance of opening up, manifesting, awakening, and entering, there is an opening up to, manifesting, awakening to, and entering the Universal Gate. There is set in motion an opening up to, manifesting, awakening to, and entering a gate. There is an opening up to, manifesting, awakening to, and entering what lies outside the gate. And, within the burning house, there is an opening up to, manifesting, awakening to, and entering the open fields beyond.

As a result, the burning house is beyond the intellective mind's ability to fully grasp, and the open fields are beyond that mind's ability to completely know. Who will make into a conveyance the three mundane worlds through which they spin and ride it as the One Vehicle? Who will go back and forth through their opening up,

---

6. To paraphrase, people, as a matter of course, speculate on, and thus harbor delusions about, what defiling passions are, what turning one's heart around and vowing to train is, what nirvana is, what the fulfillment of training and practice means, and what doing the training and practice is.

manifesting, awakening, and entering as though such events were a gate? When we seek conveyance from the burning house, how many times the wheel of samsara must turn! When we look upon the burning house from the open fields, how very distant it appears to be! Have you fully realized that the Divine Vulture Peak rests serenely in the open fields? Have you incorporated into your training and practice that open fields are flat and level on the Divine Vulture Peak? That place where 'sentient beings take their delight and play' has continually existed as the Buddha's Pure Land, which can never be destroyed.[7] We must meticulously make this our fundamental practice.

In our wholehearted desire to meet Buddha, do we pursue through our spiritual exploration and practice that Buddha is ourself, or do we pursue through our spiritual exploration and practice that Buddha is some other? There have been times when the Truth was realized as an individual entity, and there have been times when the Truth was realized as the Whole Body. Our appearing together with the Buddha on the Divine Vulture Peak is due to our not begrudging even our own lives. There is an opening up, manifesting, awakening, and entering which is the Buddha's continually abiding here, voicing the Dharma, and there is an opening up, manifesting, awakening, and entering which is the Buddha's skillful means in manifesting what nirvana is. It is our not seeing Buddha, though Such is near; so who, pray, lacks the faith to wholeheartedly grasp That Which Is Beyond Our Grasp? The place that is ever filled with both celestial and human beings is none other than the Realm of Shakyamuni and Vairochana,* a realm that is continually tranquil and radiant. We who are naturally installed in the Four Realms do, indeed, dwell in the Buddha Realm that is the All.[8] When we are looking at some dust particle, it does not mean that we do not

---

7. This is taken from "The Immeasurable Life of the Tathagata" section of the Lotus Scripture. One translation of this can be found in *Buddhist Writings on Meditation and Daily Practice,* (Shasta Abbey Press, 1994), pp. 27-38.

8. 'The Four Realms' is a Tendai Buddhist technical term for certain spiritual stages. The first is the Realm of Dualistic Thinking, where ordinary, conventional people are seen as living side-by-side with those who are saintly. The second is the Realm of Skillful Means, where inhabitants are guided by the Dharma but have not yet fully realized Its import. The third is the Realm of Bodhisattvas, where marked spiritual results have been achieved

see the whole realm of the universe, and, in our affirming the whole realm of the universe, it does not mean that we are denying any dust particle. So, when all the Buddhas affirm the realm of the Dharma, it does not mean that They exclude us from Their affirmation, which is good in the beginning, middle, and end. Thus, not only is the present moment an aspect of Their affirming that things are just what they are, but also any alarm, doubt, fear, or awe that we may experience in response to Their affirmation can in no way deny the innate nature of what They are affirming. Simply, these responses are only the difference between looking at dust particles with the directness of a Buddha and our sitting down amidst these particles. When we seat ourselves down within the realm of the Dharma, it is not spacious; when we sit amidst dust particles, they are not confining. As a result, without the Buddha's promise of our realizing Buddhahood, there would be no need to sit and, in that all Buddhas promise it, there is no need for alarm or doubt due to spaciousness or limitations, because all the Buddhas have already fully realized the substance and strength of the flowering of the Dharma.

So, should we consider that our present characteristics and innate nature are practicing within the realm of the Dharma or within dust particles? Our characteristics and nature have no alarm or doubt, nor do they have any fear or awe, for they are simply what is profound and enduring: they are that which the basic practice sets in motion within the realm of the Dharma. Our looking at this universe of dust particles and seeing the realm of the Dharma is beyond anything we could ever create or measure. That which we measure and create should also take lessons from what is measured and created by the flowering of the Dharma. When we hear the phrase 'opening up, manifesting, awakening, and entering', we should understand it in relation to a Buddha's desire to help sentient beings. We should take as our model a Buddha's manifesting what a Buddha knows directly, His awakening to what a Buddha knows directly, and His entering into what a Buddha knows directly, all of which is called 'the flowering of the Dharma setting in motion our opening up to, manifesting, awakening to and entering that which a Buddha knows directly through

---

and hindrances have been removed. The fourth is the Realm of Continual Tranquility and Radiance.

experience'. In this way, the Dharma Flower's setting in motion our opening up, manifesting, awakening, and entering will be our path to full realization.

In other words, our crossing over to what all the Buddha Tathagatas came to know directly is what is set in motion by the flowering of the Dharma, which is, as the Scripture says, 'great, vast, profound, and far-reaching'. The prediction of our ultimately realizing Buddhahood is, therefore, our own opening up to what a Buddha directly knows, and it is what the flowering of the Dharma sets in motion, which is beyond anything that others teach. This is what is referred to by the statement, "The mind's wandering off onto deluded paths is what is set in motion by the flowering of the Dharma."

What is called "The mind's awakening sets the flowering of the Dharma in motion" is synonymous with the turning of the flower-like Dharma Wheel. That is to say, when the flowering of the Dharma has thoroughly exerted its influence in arousing us, we, in turn, manifest its influence, just as it is, in arousing ourselves. Our making this manifest is our setting the Flower of the Dharma in motion. Even though what was set in motion by the flowering of the Dharma in the past has continued on, unceasingly, even up to the present, we are, in turn, naturally setting the Flower of the Dharma in motion. Even though our donkey work has not yet come to an end, our horse work <u>will</u> present itself.[9]

Through our reliance on just the One Vehicle, we will accomplish the One Great Matter for which we train as It manifests right here before us. The multitudes of bodhisattvas in the thousands of worlds had long been greatly venerated saintly

---

9. In several earlier texts Dōgen has alluded to the saying by Meditation Master Reiun Shigon that one should not wait until the donkey work is done before beginning to do the horse work. In the Zen Buddhist tradition, 'donkey work' is associated with ceasing from evil by using our will to cut through our spiritual fetters, which are the source of our suffering; 'horse work' is associated with doing good by our giving voice to the Dharma to help others to realize the Truth. In the present context, Dōgen gives this traditional understanding a twist, by asserting that doing one's training, in itself, helps others to realize the Truth.

ones of the Dharma Flower. They poured out from the land upon hearing the Buddha turn the Wheel of the Dharma on the Divine Vulture Peak. They poured forth from the land, being aroused by themselves, and they poured forth from the land, being aroused by some other. We should not make our turning of the Dharma Flower be only for what pours forth from the earth: we should also make it be for what pours forth from open space. And it is not only the earth and open space that can pour forth. We should also discern with a Buddha's wise discernment the pouring forth of the flowering of the Dharma.

Generally speaking, the time of the Dharma's flowering is inevitably one in which, as the *Lotus Scripture* puts it, "The parent is young and the child is old." This does not mean that the child is not a child, nor does it mean that the parent is not a parent: you should simply explore this as "The child is the one who is old and the parent is the one who is young." Do not follow worldly disbeliefs and thereby be disconcerted, <u>and</u> that which is a worldly disbelief is also a time of the Dharma's flowering. On account of this, we should make our turning of the Dharma Flower be 'that singular time when the Buddha was dwelling in the world'. We come pouring forth from the earth when we are aroused by opening up to, manifesting, awakening to, and entering It, and we come pouring forth from the earth when we are aroused by what a Buddha knows through direct experience. At this time of turning the Flower of the Dharma, there is the mind's awakening due to the Flower of the Dharma, and there is the flowering of the Dharma due to the mind's awakening.

And, the description of the bodhisattvas as 'coming from down below' is synonymous with their 'coming from within space'. This 'down below' and this 'within space' are nothing but the turning of the Dharma Flower, and they are nothing but the lifespan of a Buddha. We should do our turning of the Dharma Flower so that the Buddha's life, the flowering of the Dharma, the realm of the Dharma, and our wholeheartedness manifest both 'down below' and 'within space'. For this reason, what we call 'down below' and 'within space' are nothing but manifestations before our very eyes of the turning of the Dharma Flower. Generally speaking, in our turning of the Dharma Flower at this time, there is that which causes 'the three kinds of grasses' and 'the two kinds of trees' to come to their fruition. This does not mean that we should expect to realize the Truth, nor does it mean that we should be skeptical if we do not.

When we arouse ourselves and give rise to enlightenment, this is what constitutes the southern quarter.[10] This fulfilling of the Way, from the first, was present on the Divine Vulture Peak, where the assembly originally convened in the southern quarter. And there are Buddha Lands in all ten quarters where an assembly has convened in open space, and each is a separate body that sets in motion the flowering of the Dharma. This body of bodhisattvas is already making their turning of the Dharma Flower into the Buddha Lands in all ten quarters, and there is no place within those lands where even a single dust particle can enter. There is the turning of the Dharma Flower as "All forms are, in fact, devoid," which means 'being beyond anything's seeming to disappear or emerge'. There is the turning of the Dharma Flower as "That which is devoid is, in fact, any form," which means 'being beyond anything's having birth or death'. We cannot call it 'existing in the world', much less would it be simply 'annihilation'. The One who is an intimate friend to me is an intimate friend to you, me, and everyone else. Because we must not neglect to respectfully bow to our Intimate Friend, we must take care to clearly recognize the times when the pearl in the king's topknot is bestowed and the times when the pearl in the robe is bestowed.[11] There was the turning of the Dharma Flower wherein the jewel-encrusted stupa,* which was five hundred yojanas* high, appeared before the Buddha, and there was the turning of the Dharma Flower wherein a Buddha sat within

---

10.   In the *Lotus Scripture*, the southern quarter is associated with being free of all impurities.

11.   References to two parables in the *Lotus Scripture*. In the first, the giving of the Dharma is likened to a king taking the pearl from his topknot and openly bestowing it upon his valiant and capable servant. In the second, it is likened to a rich man who, after serving his impoverished friend a sumptuous meal, slips a precious pearl into the man's robe while the man is sleeping. In the former situation, the servant is aware of the value of what has been bestowed upon him, whereas in the latter, the poor man does not realize what has been given him, much less recognize its value, and he continues through life suffering from feelings of deprivation, even while truly being rich beyond his wildest dreams.

the stupa, which measured two hundred and fifty yojanas wide. There was the turning of the Dharma Flower as 'a stupa springing forth from the earth and taking up its abode in the sky', wherein the mind was without obstructions and form was without restrictions, and there was the turning of the Dharma Flower as 'a stupa springing forth from the sky and taking up its abode in the earth',[12] which was restricted by the mind and restricted by the body. The Divine Vulture Peak existed within the stupa, and the jewel-encrusted stupa existed on the Divine Vulture Peak. The jeweled stupa made a jeweled stupa of the sky: the sky made an unbounded sky of the jeweled stupa.[13] With the former Buddha within the stupa sitting alongside the Buddha of the Divine Vulture Peak, the Buddha of the Divine Vulture Peak experienced the realization of Truth along with the Buddha within the stupa. When the Buddha of the Divine Vulture Peak experienced this realization upon entering the stupa, He entered into the turning of the Dharma Flower, while the physical world and His own body remained intact. When the Buddha within the stupa emerged on the Divine Vulture Peak, He emerged while still in the domain of former Buddhas, and He did so despite His having been extinct for ever so long. Do not follow the views of those ordinary people who wander in ignorance or those of the two Lesser Courses* concerning the meaning of the emergence of the former Buddha and the meaning of the Buddha of the Divine Vulture Peak commencing to turn the Wheel of the Dharma, but just concentrate on setting in motion the flowering of the Dharma.

'Being extinct for ever so long' is an epithet for someone who has experienced the Truth directly. Only those who have the perspective of a Buddha are

---

12.   The four preceding descriptions of aspects of the turning of the Flower of the Dharma are related to another chapter in the *Lotus Scripture*, wherein a stupa of enormous height and width appears in the sky before the Buddha whilst He is turning the Wheel of the Dharma on the Divine Vulture Peak. Seated within the stupa is a Buddha of long ago, Prabhātaratna Buddha, 'The Buddha Who Abounds in Jewels'. The stupa that settles upon the earth is Dōgen's addition.

13.   This sentence is difficult to render into readily comprehensible English, since Dōgen uses the words 'jeweled stupa' and 'sky' not only as nouns but also as verbs: "The stupa stupas in the sky, and the sky skies the stupa."

endowed with this epithet. What the Scripture calls 'within the stupa' and 'before the Buddha', as well as 'the stupa' and 'unbounded space', are beyond a literal understanding of 'the Divine Vulture Peak', beyond 'the realm of Dharma', beyond 'a halfway stage', beyond 'the whole universe'. Nor are they concerned with 'some place within the Dharma'. They are simply different from any form of discriminatory thought.

Not only is there the turning of the Flower of the Dharma by manifesting in the form of a Buddha for the sake of giving voice to the Dharma, there is also the turning of the Flower of the Dharma by manifesting in the form of a sentient being for the sake of giving voice to the Dharma. There is the turning of the Flower of the Dharma which manifested as 'Devadatta',[14] and there is the turning of the Flower of the Dharma which manifested as 'their departing is also fine'.[15] Do not measure your waiting as being 'sixty eons long', while you look up to the Buddha for help with hands in gasshō.* By cutting short your measuring of your wholehearted waiting, what will arise after a while is what is called 'so many immeasurable eons', but even so, it is still impossible to put a measurement on the Buddha's wise discernment. How much, pray, does this wholehearted waiting serve as a gauge of the Buddha's wise discernment? Do not think of this turning of the Dharma Flower as simply the Bodhisattva Way as practiced from the very first. The turning of the Dharma Flower at that sole sitting on the Divine Vulture Peak is a turning of the Dharma Flower in the form of the Tathagata giving voice to the Greater Course* this very day. The Flower of the Dharma is the Flower of the Dharma right now; should you not perceive

---

14. The name of a chapter in the *Lotus Scripture*. Devadatta was Shakyamuni's cousin and disciple. While a senior monk, he caused a schism in the assembly, with five hundred novices following him. Although maintaining that he was still Shakyamuni's disciple, he attempted to kill Shakyamuni. Despite these acts, Shakyamuni predicts in this chapter that Devadatta too will ultimately attain Buddhahood.

15. A reference to what Shakyamuni Buddha said when a group of monks and lay persons left the Divine Vulture Peak midway in His discourse, thinking that they already 'knew it all'.

or recognize It, It will be beyond your mind's ability to fully grasp or fully understand.[16] Thus, what is 'five hundred ink drops' for some is but the smallest fraction of time in the turning of the Dharma Flower, for It expounds that the lifetime of Buddha is the ever-flowing of Mind as It is.[17]

In conclusion, in the several centuries since this *Lotus Scripture* was transmitted to China and employed to set in motion the flowering of the Dharma, those folks who have fashioned commentaries and interpretations for it have abounded. And, due to this Scripture, some of those who have obtained the Dharma have been eminent people. But none of them has caught the meaning of 'the Flower of the Dharma turning' or made use of the import of 'setting the Flower of the Dharma in motion' as our exalted Ancestor, the Old Buddha Daikan Enō, did. Now we hear this teaching, now we encounter it: we can encounter an Old Buddha meeting an Old Buddha. How could this fail to be the Land of Old Buddhas! What a joy it is that the Flower of the Dharma has existed for eon after eon! What a joy it is that there is a flowering of the Dharma day and night! Because the Flower of the Dharma continues from eon to eon and flowers throughout both day and night, even though our own bodies and minds wax and wane in strength, this very waxing and waning is also the flowering of the Dharma. Everything, just as it is, is a rare treasure, a luminous radiance, a place for training in the Way. Everything, just as it is, is great, vast, profound, and far-reaching in its influence; everything is the profound, vast, and far-reaching supreme, fully perfected enlightenment; everything is the mind's wandering off into delusion at the turning of the Dharma Flower; everything is the mind's awakening which turns the Flower of the Dharma; everything is truly the Flower of the Dharma setting in motion the Dharma's flowering.

---

16. A reference to the children in the burning house who were so absorbed in their play that they did not perceive or recognize what was really going on.

17. In the *Lotus Scripture*, 'five hundred ink drops' constitutes the time it takes to let five hundred drops fall at the rate of one drop per every thousand lands traveled through.

The mind's wandering is its being turned by the Flower of the Dharma:
The mind's awakening is its turning of the Flower of the Dharma.
If what we fully realize is like this,
It is the Flower of the Dharma setting in motion the flowering of the Dharma.

When we make offerings to It, bow in respect to It, honor It, and praise It, the Flower of the Dharma is the flowering of the Dharma.

I have written this on a day during the summer retreat in the second year of the Ninji era (1241) to present to a meditator named Edatsu. I am overjoyed that he is leaving lay life behind in order to train in the Way. Just to shave one's head once, even that, is a precious act. To shave one's head again and again: this is to be a true child who has left lay life behind. His leaving lay life behind today is a karmic* recompense, in and of itself, arising solely from the influence of his revolving the Flower of the Dharma in the past. The flowering of the Dharma today must certainly be a flowering which brings to fruition the Flower of the Dharma. It is not Shakyamuni's Dharma Flower, nor is it the Dharma Flower of the Buddhas: it is the Dharma Flower's flowering of the Dharma. Edatsu's being set into motion by the flowering of the Dharma in the past habitually revolved around his not perceiving or recognizing the characteristics of things as they really are. But the flowering of the Dharma today is no longer beyond his mind's ability to fully grasp or understand. In times long past, he breathed It out and breathed It in: at the present time, he breathes It out and breathes It in. This is what we should expect for a flowering of the Dharma that is so marvelously exquisite we cannot even begin to imagine It.

Written by the founder of Kannondōri in Kōshōhōrin-ji Temple, the mendicant monk who went to Sung China in order to receive and then transmit the Dharma.

Dōgen

Copied on the third day of midsummer in the second year of the Ninji era (June 13, 1241).

Ejō

17

On 'The Mind Cannot Be Held Onto'

(Shin Fukatoku)

Translator's Introduction: The *Shōbōgenzō* contains two versions of this discourse. The present one is based on a talk Dōgen gave to his disciples. The second, which follows this one, was composed as a written document. While the overall theme and some of the passages are the same, the two versions are sufficiently different to justify including both.

The title and opening line come from the *Scripture on the Diamond-Sharp Wise Discernment That Leads One to the Other Shore*, often referred to simply as the *Diamond-Cutting Scripture*. As with other phrases that Dōgen takes from the Scriptures and from the remarks or writings of Zen Masters, he often expands on their meaning so that no single translation suitably fits all contexts. In the present instance, the meaning of the title phrase shifts from a concern with the transiency of the mind ('the mind cannot be held onto'), to the inability of the intellect to comprehend Buddha Mind ('the mind cannot grasp It'), to the intangible nature of the all-encompassing Mind ('Mind cannot be grasped'). In this translation, where the word *shin* appears in the original, it is rendered as 'Mind' when the reference appears to refer to the Buddha Mind (Buddha Nature), and as 'mind' when referring to the conventional functioning of the intellect. The phrase *fukatoku* is rendered in a variety of ways depending on what seems relevant to the context.

Shakyamuni Buddha once said, "The mind of the past cannot be retained; the mind of the present cannot be held onto; the mind of the future cannot be grasped." This is what the Buddhas and Ancestors have thoroughly explored through Their practice. From within this 'cannot be held onto', They have fashioned the niches and baskets of Their own past, present, and future. Even so, They have made use of the niches and baskets of others in Their tradition.[1] What I call 'Their tradition' is synonymous with Their 'being unable to hold onto the mind'. Our cogitating and discriminating at this very moment is synonymous with our 'being unable to hold onto the mind'. The whole of our physical existence which we use every hour of the day is indeed synonymous with our 'being unable to hold onto the mind'. Once we have entered the private quarters of an Ancestor of the Buddha, we comprehend what 'not being able to hold onto the mind' refers to. But before we have entered the quarters of an Ancestor of the Buddha, no questions about 'Mind cannot be held onto' arise, nor have we made this 'Mind' manifest, nor is It anything we have personally seen or heard about. Those fellows who are engaged in the worldly teaching of texts and the scholarly study of commentaries, as well as those folks who hear but do not apply the Teaching and those who are only interested in their own awakening, exist here and now, without having encountered It even in their dreams. Evidence of this is near at hand, as the following narrative illustrates.

Before Meditation Master Tokusan Senkan's awakening, he used to brag about his skill in elucidating the *Diamond-Cutting Scripture,* even boasting sometimes about his being the Fully Perfected Lord of that Scripture (since his family name Chou meant 'fully perfected'). He claimed to be particularly well up on the commentaries on this Scripture composed by the Chinese scholar Ch'ing-lung. What is more, he had made compilations of a ton of books. And there was no lecturer who could stand shoulder-to-shoulder with the likes of him. But at the same time, he was one of the last in line among those purely academic teachers who were concerned only with analyzing written texts word by word.

One day, he heard that there was an unsurpassed Buddhist Teaching in the South that was being passed on from successor to successor. Inflamed with indignation and armed with Scriptures and other doctrinal texts, he went forth to the

---

1.   That is, They have structured Their daily lives from within That which is ungraspable, and They have sometimes borrowed from Their predecessors' ways of spiritually fashioning Their lives.

South, crossing mountains and rivers. As it happened, he heard about the assembly of Meditation Master Ryūtan Sōshin (who had been Transmitted under Sekitō Kisen). Whilst on his way to this assembly with the intention of joining it, he stopped by the wayside to catch his breath. At that moment, an old woman came up beside him, also stopping by the side of the road to rest a bit. Lecturer Tokusan casually asked her who she was.

> The old woman replied, "I'm just an old woman who sells rice cakes."
>
> Tokusan asked her if she would sell him some for his personal use.
>
> The old woman replied, "Reverend monk, what use would you have for buying them?"
>
> Tokusan said, "I want to buy them to refresh my mind."
>
> The old woman then remarked, "Reverend monk, that load you're carrying with you is really something!"
>
> Tokusan replied, "Have you not heard of me? I am the Fully Perfected Lord of the *Diamond-Cutting Scripture*. I have so mastered this Scripture that there is nothing in It that I do not understand. What I am carrying with me are my commentaries on the *Diamond-Cutting Scripture*."
>
> Upon hearing him say this, the old woman asked, "Reverend monk, would you permit an old woman like me to put a question to you?"
>
> Tokusan replied, "You now have my permission to ask whatever you may wish."
>
> The old woman said, "I once heard the part in the *Diamond-Cutting Scripture* where it says, 'The mind of the past cannot be held onto; the mind of the present cannot be held onto; the mind of the future cannot be held onto.' Which mind do you think you will refresh with these rice cakes? If the reverend monk

is able to say, I will sell you some rice cakes. If the reverend monk is unable to say, I will not sell you any."

Tokusan, at this moment, was so flabbergasted that he did not recall how he would have customarily responded, whereupon the old woman dismissed him with a flick of her wrist and departed without selling Tokusan any of her rice cakes.

How regrettable that a commentator on hundreds of documents, one who has been a lecturer for decades, was seen through by a poor old woman and could not come up with a response when posed one measly question. It is like the vast difference between, on the one hand, meeting a true teacher, paying heed to a true teacher, and being able to hear the True Teaching and, on the other, not yet having heard the True Teaching nor having encountered a true teacher. This was the occasion when Tokusan first said, "A rice cake painted in a picture cannot satisfy one's hunger." Nowadays, he is admired as one who inherited the Dharma from Ryūtan.

When we reflect deeply upon what is going on in this encounter between the old woman and Tokusan, what Tokusan had not clarified in the distant past can be clearly heard today. Even after he met Ryūtan, he still must have had nightmares about this old woman. He was a latecomer to learning through practice and not some ancient Buddha who had gone beyond being enlightened. Although the old woman had, on that occasion, succeeded in shutting Tokusan's mouth up, it is difficult to establish whether she was, in fact, 'such a person'.* The reason is that, upon hearing the phrase 'the mind cannot be held onto', she may have thought simply that the mind is not something to be obtained or something to be possessed, and therefore spoke to him as she did. If Tokusan had been a solid fellow, he would have had the ability to see through to what the old woman was really getting at. Had he seen through to that, it would have been clear whether she was truly 'such a person'. But Tokusan had not yet become the awakened 'Tokusan', so he was not yet able to know whether she was 'such a person' or not.

---

*   See Glossary.

In Great Sung China today, among the novices garbed in the patched robes and broad sleeves of monks, there are those who laugh at Tokusan's inability to respond appropriately and who esteem what they take to be the old woman's sharp wit. This is something that is surely quite pitiful and befuddled, since there are reasons for us to have doubts about the old woman. For instance, at the very moment when Tokusan was unable to speak, the old woman could have turned to him and said, "The reverend monk is unable to respond now, so he should go on and put the question to this old woman, and she, in response, will say something for the reverend monk's benefit." By speaking in this manner, it would be evident that the old woman was what we call 'such a person' if, in response to Tokusan's question, she spoke true. Even though she had a question for him, she had not yet expressed the Matter[*] herself. Ever since ancient times, no one has been called 'such a person' who has not uttered at least a single word to express It. We can see from Tokusan's past that there is no benefit in constantly bragging about oneself. We can realize by means of the old woman that a person who has not yet expressed It cannot be acknowledged as having realized the Truth.

As an experiment, let us say something in Tokusan's stead. Were the old woman really posing her question from 'that frame of mind', Tokusan might have said to her, "If you are in 'that frame of mind', do not sell me any rice cakes."[2] Had Tokusan spoken in this way, he might have been someone of sharp wit who had learned something through the practice of spiritual training.

Tokusan might have asked the old woman, "The mind of the past cannot be retained; the mind of the present cannot be held onto; the mind of the future cannot be grasped; so which mind do you propose to refresh with your rice cakes?" Were she asked in this way, then she might have responded to Tokusan by saying, "If the

---

2.   'That frame of mind' is a non-literal rendering of the Japanese *immo (C. jen-mo)*, a term used in Zen Buddhist writings in relation to someone who is operating from the spiritual certainty of an awakened mind.

reverend monk only knows that rice cakes do not refresh the mind, then he does not know that Mind refreshes the rice cakes or that Mind refreshes the mind."

Were she to speak thus, Tokusan would definitely have had the doubt arise.[3] Then, at that very moment, she should select three rice cakes and hand them over to Tokusan. Just as Tokusan is about to take them, the old woman should say, "The mind of the past cannot be retained; the mind of the present cannot be held onto; the mind of the future cannot be grasped." On the other hand, if Tokusan does not reach out to take them, she might take one of the rice cakes and hit him with it, saying, "You gutless wonder, don't be such a ninny!" Were she to speak like this, should Tokusan respond, then well and good. If he were still unable to say anything, the old woman should say something more for Tokusan's sake. But she only gave him a flick of her wrist and left. Maybe there was a bee in her sleeve.

Tokusan, for his part, does not even say, "I'm unable to say anything. Old woman, will you say something in my stead?" So, not only did he fail to say what he should have said, he also did not ask what he should have asked. What a pity! The old woman's and Tokusan's questions and answers concerning the mind of the past and the mind of the future are merely their mind of the present being unable to grasp It.

Although Tokusan afterwards succeeded in bringing about his awakening to the Light, he did not give the appearance of one who had done so; he was simply someone whose outward demeanor was consistently gruff.[4] Since he trained under Ryūtan for some time, the horns on his head must surely have gotten knocked off, and the pearl from under the dragon's chin would have been authentically Transmitted to

---

3.   That is, he would have doubted that what he had been able to comprehend intellectually was all that there is to realizing spiritual Truth.

4.   One effect of a kenshō in an erudite person is their becoming humble and modest.

him. To merely see the blowing out of a paper candle[5] is insufficient for the Transmission of the Torch.[6]

So, novices who are learning through their training should, beyond doubt, be diligent in their explorations. Those who have treated their training lightly are not right. Those who have been diligent in their explorations are Ancestors of the Buddha. In sum, saying that 'the mind cannot grasp It' is the same as saying that someone has bought a painting of a rice cake, then chewed it all up in one mouthful, savoring its flavor.

Delivered to the assembly during the summer retreat in the second year of the Ninji era (1241) at Kannondōri in Kōshōhōrin-ji Temple, Uji Prefecture, Yamashiro Province.

Translator's Addendum from

Book 2, Kōan 4 of Dōgen's Chinese *Shinji Shōbōgenzō*

For a long time, the monk Tokusan had made a career of lecturing on the *Diamond-Cutting Scripture*. Later on, having heard that the Zen tradition had begun to flourish widely in the South, he could not let the matter rest. Finally, he stopped lecturing and, dismissing his students, headed for the South, armed with manuscripts.

---

5.   A reference to the account of Tokusan's spiritual awakening, which Dōgen retells in another of his writings called the *Shinji Shōbōgenzō*. Written entirely in a Japanese form of Chinese, it consists of three hundred kōan stories. A translation of Tokusan's story (from Book 2, Kōan 4) is given in the Addendum which follows at the end of this discourse.

6.   That is, to be a true Ancestor of the Buddha takes more than having a kenshō; it also requires ceaseless spiritual training and practice.

For a start, he proceeded to Ryūtan Monastery. He had barely crossed the threshold of the monastery when he said, "For a long time, I have looked for Ryūtan. Now that I have finally arrived, the Abbot himself is nowhere in sight." Ryūtan said, "My child, you have arrived at Ryūtan in person." Tokusan then bowed in respect and withdrew.

When night came on, Tokusan entered the Abbot's quarters, intent on attending upon the Abbot. As the time had grown late, Ryūtan said, "My child, why don't you retire?" At length, Tokusan, setting great store in the Abbot, raised the bamboo curtain and went out. Seeing how dark it was outside, he returned and said, "It is pitch black outside." [7] Ryūtan then took a paper candle and proffered it to Tokusan. Just as Tokusan touched it, Ryūtan blew out the flame, whereupon Tokusan suddenly had a great awakening and immediately bowed in respect. Ryūtan asked. "My child, upon seeing such a thing as this, why did you immediately bow?" Tokusan replied, "From now on, I will not doubt the tongue of our country's venerable monk again."

The next day, Ryūtan said in the Lecture Hall, "You have here this 'real person'. His teeth are like swords; his mouth resembles a basin of blood. Though you may strike him with a stick, he does not turn his head. At a later time, he will turn towards the peak of the solitary mountain and leave here to establish my Way."

At length, Tokusan took his manuscripts before the Dharma Hall and made a bonfire of them, expressing the matter by saying, "Though I have penetrated all manner of obscure ways of speaking, it has been like sending a single hair into the great void of space. Although I have fully done what the world considers important, it has resembled letting a single drop of water fall into a vast canyon." As he put the manuscripts into the fire, they were forthwith consumed. Thereupon, he made a respectful obeisance.

7.　That is, Ryūtan encourages Tokusan to go ('retire') into meditation ('raise the bamboo curtain'). Deep in meditation ('going out' of the intellective mind), Tokusan confronts his spiritual ignorance ("It is pitch black outside [of my intellect]."), which is what he reports to Ryūtan.

18

On 'The Mind Cannot Be Grasped'

(Shin Fukatoku)

WRITTEN VERSION

Translator's Introduction: This discourse was not incorporated into the *Shōbōgenzō* until some time after Dōgen's death. It is likely that he intended the work for his senior monks, since it contains some cautionary remarks about well-known Chinese Meditation Masters that might be misunderstood by novices or lay disciples. These remarks were made as part of a traditional style of Buddhist debate which is undertaken, not as a form of one-upmanship, but as a form of dialectic intended to ferret out the deepest possible Truth. Dōgen's point in refuting these Masters is not that what they said was incorrect, but simply that they did not go far enough in their exploration of the Matter.

At Kannondōri in Kōshōhōrin-ji Temple

The Mind that cannot be grasped is what all Buddhas are, for They personally rely upon It as supreme, fully perfected enlightenment. As the *Diamond-Cutting Scripture* says, "The mind of the past cannot be retained; the mind of the present cannot be held onto; the mind of the future cannot be grasped." This expression points to the Buddha's reliance upon the Mind that cannot be held onto, which is what all Buddhas do. It is what They have come to rely upon, saying that It is the unretainable mind of past, present, and future, and that It is the ungraspable Mind of all thoughts and things. If you do not learn from the Buddhas what They are relying upon, which is what makes this matter clear, you will not directly experience It, and if you do not learn from the Ancestors what They are relying upon, you will not be truly Transmitted. 'To learn' means 'to learn from the sixteen-foot-tall body' and 'to learn from a single blade of grass'.[1] 'Learning from the Ancestors' means 'to learn from

---

1.   The first allusion is to learning from the Buddha's standing up from His meditation posture after having realized enlightenment. The second is to learning from all things, no matter how small, since all things express the Dharma.

236

Their Skin and Flesh, Bones and Marrow' and 'to learn from the face that broke into a broad smile'.[2] What all this fundamentally means is that you should study the Matter* by seeking answers to your questions from a Master to whom the Treasure House of the Eye of the True Teaching has been clearly and correctly Transmitted. This Master has had directly passed on to him what the Mind seal* of Buddha after Buddha and Ancestor after Ancestor has directly and precisely pointed out. Then, beyond question, that Master's Bones and Marrow, Face and Eyes will be passed on to you, and you will receive the Master's Body, Hair, and Skin. If you do not learn the Way of the Buddhas and do not enter the private quarters of an Ancestor, you will not see or hear about It, nor will you understand It. The method for asking about It will be beyond you, and you will not understand the means for expressing It, even in your dreams.

When Tokusan, in his earlier days, was still not a solid fellow, he had excelled in the *Diamond-Cutting Scripture*. People at that time called him Chou, the Fully Perfected Lord of the *Diamond-Cutting Scripture*. He was king among more than eight hundred scholars. Not only was he well versed in the commentaries, particularly those by the Chinese scholar Ch'ing-lung, but he had also edited a ton of writings, and there was no lecturer who could stand shoulder-to-shoulder with him. When he happened to hear that there was an unsurpassed Buddhist Teaching in the South, a Teaching that was being passed on from successor to successor, he went there, crossing mountains and rivers, loaded down with his own manuscripts. He had stopped to catch his breath by the side of the road that led to Master Ryūtan's temple, when an old woman came by. Tokusan asked her who she was.

The old woman replied, "I am an old woman who sells rice cakes."

---

2.   The first phrase alludes to Bodhidharma's passing on of the Dharma. The second alludes to the Buddha's disciple Makakashō smiling in response to the Buddha's holding aloft the udumbara blossom of His enlightenment.

*   See Glossary.

Tokusan asked her, "Will you sell me some rice cakes?"

The old woman said, "Reverend monk, why would you want to buy them?"

Tokusan replied, "I would buy your rice cakes so that I might refresh my mind."

The old woman remarked, "Reverend monk, that load you're carrying with you is really something!"

Tokusan replied, "Have you not heard of me? I am the Fully Perfected Lord of the *Diamond-Cutting Scripture*. I have so mastered this Scripture that there is nothing in It that I do not understand. What I am carrying with me are my commentaries on the *Diamond-Cutting Scripture*."

Upon hearing him say this, the old woman asked, "Reverend monk, would you permit an old woman like me to put a question to you?"

Tokusan replied, "Yes, ask whatever you may wish."

She said, "I once heard the part in the *Diamond-Cutting Scripture* where it says, 'The mind of the past cannot be held onto; the mind of the present cannot be held onto; the mind of the future cannot be held onto.' Which mind do you think you are going to refresh with these rice cakes? If the reverend monk is able to say, I will sell him some rice cakes. If the reverend monk is unable to say, I will not sell him any rice cakes."

Tokusan, at this moment, was so flabbergasted that he could not recall how he would have customarily responded, whereupon the old woman dismissed him with a flick of her wrist and left without selling Tokusan any of her rice cakes.

How regrettable that a commentator on hundreds of documents, one who had been a lecturer for decades, was seen through by a poor old woman posing one measly question. It is like the vast difference between someone having a true teacher and someone not having one, between someone seeking answers to one's questions in the private quarters of a true teacher and someone not entering the private quarters of a true teacher. There are people who, upon hearing the phrase 'cannot be grasped', have simply assumed that there is nothing to be attained in either case, for these people lack the living pathway of practice. Further, there are those who say that It cannot be grasped because it is said that we already possess It from the first. How does that hit the mark?

It was on this occasion that Tokusan understood for the first time that a rice cake in a picture does not slake one's hunger. He also realized that, in training and practicing in the Way of the Buddhas, one by all means needs to meet 'such a person'.* In addition, he realized that someone who is uselessly caught up only in commenting on the Scriptures cannot attain true spiritual strength. Ultimately, he trained under Ryūtan, and after the path of Master and disciple manifested before his very eyes, he unquestionably became 'such a person'. Nowadays, he is recognized not only as an Ancestral predecessor of Ummon and Hōgen, but also as a teacher and guide both of ordinary people and of those in loftier positions.

When we consider this narrative today, we can see that Tokusan, long ago, had not yet clarified the Matter. Although nowadays we say that the old woman had succeeded in shutting up Tokusan's mouth, it is difficult to establish whether she was, in fact, 'such a person'. We may conjecture that, having heard the phrase 'the mind cannot be grasped' much earlier, she may have simply thought that the mind was something that could not be possessed, and therefore asked him about it in the way that she did. If Tokusan had been a solid person, he would have had the spiritual strength to be prudent in his responses. Had he been prudent, he would have been able to discern whether the old woman was 'such a person', but, since it was at a time when Tokusan was not yet the awakened 'Tokusan', he was not yet able to recognize whether the old woman was indeed 'such a person'.

What is more, we today are not short of reasons for having doubts about the old woman. When Tokusan was unable to speak, why didn't the old woman question him further? She could have said, "You, my reverend monk, are unable to respond now, so you should go ahead and put the question to this old woman, and I, in response, will say something for the reverend monk's benefit." Then, upon hearing her own question from Tokusan, if she had some response for him, it would be evident whether or not the old woman had the ability to speak true.

In this way, someone who has the Bones and Marrow, Face and Eye of those who trained in the past, as well as the radiance and vivacity of the old Buddhas—all of which are due to having the wherewithal from doing the same spiritual practice as They did—will not be concerned about either holding onto or letting go of such notions as 'Tokusan', 'the old woman', 'not being able to grasp', 'being able to grasp', 'rice cakes', or 'Mind'.

What we call 'Buddha Mind' is synonymous with the three temporal worlds of past, present, and future. This Mind and the three temporal worlds are not separated from each other by so much as one single hair's breadth. Even so, when we are discussing the two as things that are distinct and separate from each other, then they are farther apart than eighteen thousand breadths of hair. Thus, if I were asked what the phrase "This is the mind of the past" means, I would have to say in response, "This cannot be grasped." If I were asked what the phrase "This is the mind of the present" means, I would have to say in response, "This cannot be grasped." If I were asked what the phrase "This is the mind of the future" means, I would say in response, "This cannot be grasped."

As to the mind of which I am speaking, if I say that there is Mind, which at the present moment is described as 'Mind that cannot be grasped,' then I say, "At the present moment, It cannot be grasped." I do not say, "The mind cannot be grasped," I say in all earnestness, "It cannot be grasped." I do not say, "The mind can be grasped," I say in all earnestness, "It cannot be grasped." Further, should you ask me, "What is the mind of the past which cannot be grasped?" I would say, "It is synonymous with being born and dying, going and coming." Should you ask, "What is the mind of the present which cannot be grasped?" I would say, "It is synonymous with being born and dying, going and coming." Should you ask, "What is the mind of the future which cannot be grasped?" I would say, "It is synonymous with being born and dying, going and coming."

In sum, there is Buddha Mind, which is the fences and walls, tiles[*] and stones, and all the Buddhas in the three temporal worlds directly experience It as something that cannot be held onto. There are only the fences and walls, tiles and stones, which are Buddha Mind, and all Buddhas directly experience It in the three temporal worlds as ungraspable. What is more, That which is ungraspable within the great earth with its mountains and rivers exists there by Its very nature. That which is ungraspable in grasses and trees, wind and water, accordingly, is Mind. Also, It is what is ungraspable in "Letting our mind abide nowhere and giving rise to the Mind."[3] And also, the Mind Beyond Grasping, which gives voice to the eighty thousand Gates by means of all the Buddhas throughout all generations everywhere, is the same as this.

To cite another example, during the time of National Teacher Echū, Tripitaka Master Daini arrived at the capital from far-off India, letting it be known publicly that he had the ability to read the minds of others.[4] When the T'ang Emperor Su-tsung charged the National Teacher to examine this claim, no sooner had the Tripitaka Master laid eyes on the National Teacher than he immediately made a full prostration before the National Teacher and then stood to his right.[5]

---

3. This quotation is the line from the *Diamond-Cutting Scripture* which triggered Enō's realization of Truth before he left lay life.

4. 'National Teacher' is a Chinese imperial title conferred upon a monk whose devotion to spiritual life has been exemplary. Echū served as the emperor's personal spiritual advisor. 'Tripitaka Master' is a secular title which might be comparable to the present-day 'professor of Buddhology'; it does not imply that the person was necessarily a monk or even a practicing Buddhist. The *Tripitaka* is the general name for the canon of Buddhist Scriptures.

5. That is, in the position that is least confrontational.

Thereupon, the National Teacher asked him, "Do you have the ability to read the minds of others or not?"

The Tripitaka Master replied in a humble tone, "I would not dare to make such a claim."

The National Teacher then said, "Speak! In what place is this old monk now?"

The Tripitaka Master responded, again with a humble tone, "The reverend monk is indeed the teacher of this nation, so why does he go to the Western River and watch people racing around in their boats?"[6]

After a rather long time, the National Teacher asked him again, "Speak! In what place is this old monk now?"

The Tripitaka Master replied all humbly, "The reverend monk is the teacher of this nation, so why does he go to Tientsin Bridge and watch people playing with their pet monkeys?"[7]

The National Teacher again asked, "Speak! In what place is this old monk now?"

Although the Tripitaka Master remained there quite a long time, he did not know what to say.

The National Teacher rebuked him, saying, "O you wild fox spirit, where is your ability to read minds now?"

---

6.   'The Western River' flows through the Western Paradise. The Tripitaka Master is saying, in effect, "Why do you, who are so saintly that you are already in the Western Paradise, bother to pay any attention to us ordinary people who are engaged in worldly, competitive pursuits?"

7.   While Tientsin is the name of a major Chinese metropolis, 'Tientsin Bridge' literally means 'the bridge that leads into the Harbor of Heaven'. The Tripitaka Master is saying in effect, "Why do you, who are standing on the very bridge of Heaven, concern yourself with us worldly people who are preoccupied with playing around with our everyday minds?" Both this and the previous statement are offering seemingly flattering but spiritually meaningless remarks in response to the National Teacher's deeply spiritual question, all the while still hinting that he could, indeed, read the minds of others.

The Tripitaka Master still had no response.[8]

Not to know about such matters is bad enough, but not to have heard about them, what a pity! The Ancestors of the Buddha and those who are academic scholars of the *Tripitaka* are not equal; they are as different as heaven and earth. The Ancestors of the Buddha, having clarified what the Buddha Dharma is, are in That Place; academic scholars of the *Tripitaka* have not yet clarified what It is. Truly, when it comes to scholars of the *Tripitaka*, even ordinary people have been scholars of the *Tripitaka*. They are comparable, for instance, to those who seek for position in the literary world. So, even though the Tripitaka Master may have had a broad comprehension of the languages of India and China, as well as having been trained in reading the minds of others, nevertheless, when it came to 'Body and Mind in the Way of the Buddhas', he had never seen a thing even in his dreams.[9] As a result, in his interview with the National Teacher, who had directly experienced the level of the Ancestors of the Buddha, the Tripitaka Master was seen through. In learning what 'Mind in the Way of the Buddhas' means, we need to know that the myriad thoughts and things <u>are</u> Mind, and the three worlds of desire, form, and beyond form are nothing but Mind. It will be a matter of nothing but Mind being nothing but Mind: it will be a matter of this Buddha being your very mind. Be there a self, be there an other, neither must be mistaken for the 'Mind in the Way of the Buddhas'. Do not vainly drift down the Western River; do not stroll about on Tientsin Bridge. Whoever would preserve and accept responsibility for 'Body and Mind in the Way of the Buddhas' needs to learn how to function from the spiritually wise discernment of the Buddha's Way.

What we call 'in the Way of the Buddhas' means that the whole world is Mind, without Its being changed by anything that arises or disappears. And it means

---

8.   Evidently, the Tripitaka Master realized that what he was being asked for required something beyond 'parlor Zen' responses, but because he did not know what the True Mind of the National Teacher was, he was unable to reply. 'A wild fox spirit' is a term used negatively in Zen Buddhism for a clever and manipulative person who gives teachings that are false and misleading.

9.   The phrase 'Body and Mind in the Way of the Buddhas' can be understood as a reference to the True Nature of Body and Mind as seen from the perspective of an enlightened mind.

that the whole of the Dharma is Mind. And we also need to experience the whole of Mind as the functioning of spiritually wise discernment. The Tripitaka Master had not seen this before, for he was simply a wild fox spirit. So, even the first two times that the National Teacher said to him, "Speak!" he had not seen the Mind of the National Teacher, for he had not penetrated to the Mind of the National Teacher. He was a wild fox cub who was idly playing around with the Western River and Tientsin Bridge, with boat races and monkeys, so how could he possibly have seen the National Teacher?

Further, the reason is quite clear why he could not see the place where the National Teacher was. When asked three times, "In what place is this old monk now?" he did not listen to these words. If he had listened, he would have been able to answer, but, since he did not listen, he overlooked it. Had the Tripitaka Master directly experienced the Buddha Dharma by doing his training, he would have understood what the National Teacher was saying, and he would have seen the Body and Mind of the National Teacher. Because he had not directly experienced the Buddha Dharma through undertaking spiritual training in daily life, he had let a chance to hear It vainly slip by, even though it might be said that he had been born to meet one who was a teacher and guide both of ordinary people and of those in loftier positions. How sad and pitiful!

Speaking in general, how could a worldly scholar of the *Tripitaka* possibly match the everyday practice of the Buddhas and Ancestors, or recognize the whereabouts of the National Teacher? And what is more, Indian academic students of the *Tripitaka* could never recognize the everyday practice of the National Teacher.[10] But any academic teacher or arrogant scholar could surely understand what the Tripitaka Master knew. How could what pedestrian teachers or arrogant scholars know possibly match the powers of wise discernment of bodhisattvas* about to realize Buddhahood, or even of those 'thrice wise and ten times saintly'?* The Body and Mind of the National Teacher cannot be recognized by an arrogant scholar. Indeed, It is not yet clearly comprehended even by bodhisattvas about to realize Buddhahood.

---

10. Namely, his practice of devoting himself to helping all sentient beings realize the Truth.

Comments about Body and Mind in our various Buddhist traditions are like those in the following discussions. You need to understand them and trust in them, for the Dharma of our great teacher, the Venerable Shakyamuni, has never been like the teachings of the wild foxes following the Lesser Two Courses* or non-Buddhist ways. This is why, from olden times, this one story has been thoroughly examined by venerable Masters in various generations.

There was a monk who once asked Jōshū, "Why didn't the Tripitaka Master see where the National Teacher was the third time?" Jōshū replied, "He did not see where the National Teacher was because he was right on the tip of the Tripitaka Master's nose."

Also, there was a monk who once asked Gensha Shibi, "Since the National Teacher was already right on the tip of the Tripitaka Master's nose, why didn't he see it?" Shibi replied, "Simply because he was just too close."

Kaie Shutan once commented on Shibi's reply, "If the National Teacher was right on the tip of the Tripitaka Master's nose, why was he having such difficulty seeing it? After all, he did not recognize that the National Teacher was right inside the Tripitaka Master's Eye."

Also, Shibi, as if challenging the Tripitaka Master, once remarked, "You, say! Did you even see It the first two times?"

Setchō Jūken later commented on that remark, "Seen through the first time! Seen through the second time!"

Also, there was a monk who once asked Kyōzan, "Why didn't the Tripitaka Master see the whereabouts of the National Teacher the third time, since he was there a rather long time?" Kyōzan replied, "The first two times, the National Teacher's mind was in the realm of externals. He then entered the meditative state of delight in the True Self, so the Tripitaka Master could not perceive his whereabouts."

Although these five venerable Masters were all clearly on the mark, they overlooked the National Teacher's everyday practice. That is, they only discuss the Tripitaka Master's failure to know the third time, so it looks as though they were conceding that he knew the previous two times. So, this is something that these former worthies have overlooked.

The concerns that I now have about these five venerable Masters are twofold. The first is that they do not recognize the intent behind the National Teacher's way of examining the Tripitaka Master. The second is that they do not recognize the National Teacher's Body and Mind.

First of all, as to my saying that they apparently did not recognize the intent behind the National Teacher's way of examining the Tripitaka Master, there is the question of what the National Teacher intended when he exclaimed, "Speak! In what place is this old monk now?" At the time, he was inquiring into whether or not the Tripitaka Master understood the Buddha Dharma. If the Tripitaka Master had ever heard the Buddha Dharma, he would have been able to see how the words he heard as "In what place is this old monk now?" conformed to the Buddha Dharma. As to being in conformance with the Buddha Dharma, the National Teacher's saying, "In what place is this old monk now?" is asking, in effect, "Is It here? Or is It there? Is It unsurpassed enlightenment? Or is It the wisdom that ferries others to the Other Shore? Is It dependent on unbounded space? Or is It standing on solid ground? Is It the hermit's grass hut? Or is It the Treasure House?" The Tripitaka Master did not recognize this intent, so he proffered the opinion of, say, an ordinary person who wanders through life in ignorance or one who follows the two Lesser Courses. The National Teacher again asked, "Speak! In what place is this old monk now?" Hereupon, the Tripitaka Master again proffered idle words. Again the National Teacher asked, "Speak! In what place is this old monk now?" The Tripitaka Master now said nothing, though a considerable time passed. His mind was blank. The National Teacher then rebuked him, saying, "O you wild fox spirit, where is your ability to read minds now?" Upon the National Teacher's speaking in this way, the Tripitaka Master still had nothing to say.

When we consider this story carefully, the former worthy Masters all held the view that the National Teacher was rebuking the Tripitaka Master because, even though he had known the National Teacher's whereabouts the first two times, he did not know it the third time. But this is not the case. In brief, he rebuked the Tripitaka Master for being merely a wild fox spirit, someone who had not encountered the Buddha Dharma even in his dreams. He did not say that the Tripitaka Master did or did not know it the first two times. His rebuke was intended for the Tripitaka Master in general. As to the National Teacher's intent, he was wondering in the first place whether one could call the Buddha Dharma the ability to read the minds of others. Further, the National Teacher was thinking that, even though one may speak of the ability to read the mind of another, one would need to understand 'other', 'mind', and 'the ability to read' according to the Way of the Buddhas. But what the Tripitaka Master was saying was not in accord with the Way of the Buddhas, so how could it possibly be called the Buddha Dharma?" As to his examining the Tripitaka Master, even if the latter were to have said something the third time, if it was anything like the first two times, it would not reflect the principles of Buddha Dharma or the National Teacher's intent—which is why the National Teacher needed to rebuke him. As to the National Teacher's asking three times, he asked again and again in order to find out whether, at any time, his words were understood by the Tripitaka Master.

Second, as to my saying that the five worthy Masters did not recognize the Body and Mind of the National Teacher, the Body and Mind of the National Teacher was beyond the Tripitaka Master's ability to recognize, beyond his ability to read. The ten times saintly and thrice wise are not up to it, and it is beyond both those who are about to become Buddhas and those who have just awakened, so how could an ordinary Tripitaka Master possibly recognize it?[11] You must determine what this principle is so that you have no doubts about it. Anyone who would hold that the Tripitaka Master could recognize what the Body and Mind of the National Teacher

---

11. 'Those who have just awakened' is a rendering of a technical Buddhist term for someone who has just had a kenshō but does not recognize the full import of that experience.

was—and be a match for it—is, accordingly, someone who does not in the least recognize the Body and Mind of the National Teacher. If you were to say that those folks who pursue the ability to read the minds of others can recognize the Body and Mind of the National Teacher, then can those of the two Lesser Courses also recognize it? Because this is not so, people involved in the two Lesser Courses cannot possibly reach even the environs of the National Teacher. Nowadays, there are many in the two Lesser Courses who read the Mahayana* Scriptures, but they too cannot recognize the Body and Mind of the National Teacher, and, furthermore, they cannot see the Body and Mind of Buddha Dharma even in their dreams. Although they may imitate those who read and recite the Mahayana Scriptures, you must clearly recognize that they are, through and through, persons of the Lesser Courses. In short, the Body and Mind of the National Teacher is beyond anything that can be recognized by those folks who chase after spiritual abilities or who practice in order to have 'a spiritual experience'. The Body and Mind of the National Teacher might be difficult even for the National Teacher himself to gauge or fathom. And why is that? His everyday practice had long been free of any designs to 'become a Buddha', so even the Eye of a Buddha could not spot it. In his everyday comings and goings, he had clearly let go of his cobwebs and dark places, and was beyond anything that a cage could imprison or a net ensnare.

We can now look at what each of the five worthy Masters was getting at.

Jōshū said, "He did not see where the National Teacher was because he was right on the tip of the Tripitaka Master's nose." What does this remark mean? Errors are likely to occur when we state a conclusion without making clear its source. How could the National Teacher possibly be right on the tip of the Tripitaka Master's nose? The Tripitaka Master had not yet recognized that he had a Nose.[12] Further, even though it would appear that the National Teacher and the Tripitaka Master had a connection that would allow them to 'see each other', there was no pathway near

---

12. That is, the Tripitaka Master had not yet seen his Buddha Nature, which is as immediate as if It were on the tip of the nose.

enough on which they could approach each other. Those who are clear-eyed will surely be able to discern this.

Shibi said, "Simply because he was just too close." Truly, his being 'just too close' may well have been the case, but the phrase misses the point. What is it that he is calling 'just too close'? What does he understand as being 'just too close'? Shibi had not yet recognized the Tripitaka Master's being 'just too close', nor had Shibi thoroughly examined his being 'just too close'. For, when it comes to Buddha Dharma, the Tripitaka Master was the farthest of the far off.

Kyōzan replied, "The first two times, the National Teacher's mind was in the realm of externals. He then entered the meditative state of delight in the True Self, so the Tripitaka Master could not perceive his whereabouts." In India, Kyōzan would have been acclaimed far and wide as a veritable 'Little Shakyamuni' for this reply, but his remark is not entirely accurate. If he is saying that the place of their meeting each other face-to-face was, indeed, in the realm of externals, this is tantamount to asserting that the place where Buddhas and Ancestors meet each other face-to-face does not exist. That assertion would make it look as if Kyōzan had not learned the spiritual merits of realizing Buddhahood as the Buddha predicted. Kyōzan is saying that the first two times the Tripitaka Master truly knew the whereabouts of the National Teacher; he should have said that the Tripitaka Master did not recognize even a single hair of the spiritual merits of the National Teacher.

Shibi, in challenging the Tripitaka Master, remarked, "Did you even see It the first two times?" Though his phrase, "Did you even see It?" seems to say what needs to be said, it does imply that what the Tripitaka Master saw resembled That which goes beyond seeing. Therefore, it is not right on the mark.

Hearing of this remark, Clearly Enlightened Meditation Master Setchō commented, "Seen through the first time! Seen through the second time!" When Setchō took what Shibi said to be the correct way to put it, he could quite rightly speak like this. But had he recognized that it was not the correct way to put it, he would not have spoken as he did.

Kaie Shutan said, "If the National Teacher was right on the tip of the Tripitaka Master's nose, why was he having such difficulty seeing it? After all, he did not recognize that the National Teacher was right inside the Tripitaka Master's Eye."

This, too, is discussing only the third time. In that Shutan is not looking at the first two times, he is not rebuking the Tripitaka Master for the right reason. So, even though the National Teacher was on the tip of the Tripitaka Master's nose and within his very eyeballs, how would Shutan know it?

Every one of these five worthy Masters was blind to what the National Teacher had spiritually achieved; their diligent efforts to practice the Buddha Dharma seem not to have approached his. You need to realize that the National Teacher was none other than a first generation Buddha, for he had clearly had Transmitted to him the Buddha's Treasure House of the Eye of the True Teaching. Moreover, people such as Lesser Course academic commentators on the *Tripitaka* do not recognize the whereabouts of the National Teacher, and this story that we have been discussing is the proof. What those in the Lesser Course call 'the ability to read the mind of another' should be called 'the ability to read the intention of another'. It is a mistake to imagine that the ability of a Tripitaka Master of the Lesser Course to read the minds of others is strong enough for such a one to recognize a single hair, or even a half a hair, of the National Teacher. One thing to earnestly learn from this is that a Tripitaka Master of the Lesser Course is totally unable to see where the spiritual accomplishments of the National Teacher are located. If, for example, the Tripitaka Master knew the whereabouts of the National Teacher the first two times but did not know it the third time, this would have been two times out of three, and he ought not to have been rebuked. But, even if he were rebuked, it would not have been for a total lack of ability. Had he been rebuked for this, who would have any confidence in the National Teacher? The National Teacher's intention was to rebuke the Tripitaka Master for being altogether lacking in the Body and Mind of the Buddha Dharma. In that the five worthy Masters did not at all understand the everyday practice of the National Teacher, they are, to that extent, similarly inaccurate. For this reason I have now let you hear about 'the mind not being able to grasp It' in the Way of the Buddhas. Although it may be hard for you to believe that people who are unable to thoroughly understand this one aspect of the Teaching are apt to understand all the rest of the Teaching, you need to realize that ancient Ancestors may also make mistakes and compound them, as in this case.

A monk once asked the National Teacher, "Just what is the mind of the past Buddhas?"

The National Teacher replied, "Fences and walls, along with their tiles and stones."

This is also 'the mind cannot be grabbed hold of'.

Another time, a monk asked the National Teacher, "Just what is the constant mind of all Buddhas?"

The National Teacher replied, "How fortunate that you have bumped into this old monk on his way to pay a visit to the emperor's palace!"

This also thoroughly explores 'the Mind that cannot be grasped'.

On another occasion, a veritable Lord Indra asked the National Teacher, "How can we possibly get free of the effects of karma?" *

The National Teacher replied, "O Heavenly One, you can free yourself from the effects of karma by training in the Way."

This Lord Indra then asked, "What could this 'way' you speak of possibly be?"

The National Teacher responded, "Your mind at this very moment is the Way."

The Lord Indra then asked, "And what is this mind of mine at this very moment?"

The National Teacher, pointing with his finger, said, "It is the very pedestal of enlightenment: It is the very net of pearls."

The Lord Indra bowed in respect.

In sum, you will often meet with talk about 'Body and Mind in the Way of the Buddhas' in the assemblies of Buddha after Buddha and Ancestor after Ancestor. When we learn of both Body and Mind together, through our training, They are beyond what ordinary people, as well as the wise and the saintly, imagine or perceive Them to be. "The Mind cannot be held onto" is to be thoroughly examined through your practice.

A day during the summer retreat in the second year of the Ninji era (1241).

19

On the Ancient Mirror

(Kokyō)

Translator's Introduction: In this discourse, Dōgen explores a number of metaphorical references to mirrors as they appear in various writings from Zen Buddhism and Shintō, the native religion of Japan. In particular, he identifies three types of mirror—the Great Round Mirror, the Clear Mirror, and the Ancient Mirror—and discusses how these three are interrelated, while still distinguishable from each other.

It may be helpful to keep in mind that *kokyō* can be rendered not only as the Ancient Mirror but also as the Mirror of Old and the Mirror of Former Buddhas.

Further, Dōgen's references to physical mirrors are to those made from metal that was cast in a flat, circular mold and then highly polished on one side. It was not uncommon for such mirrors, in time, to be broken up and recast into Buddhist statuary, which was left unpolished.

As with a few of Dōgen's earlier discourses, some readers may find it useful to read this one, in particular, more than once, since there are a number of places where the import of what Dōgen is saying only becomes clear when later passages are encountered. I have refrained from making explanatory comments at these places, lest such remarks undermine the effects of Dōgen's particular 'alogical' manner of presentation.

What all Buddhas and Ancestors accept, preserve, and individually pass on is the Ancient Mirror. It is Their same view and Their same face: It is Their same image and Their same casting, for They have done the same training and have realized the same Truth. When foreigners come, foreigners appear in It, be they eight thousand or a hundred thousand; when Han come, Han appear in It, be it for a single moment or for all of time.[1] When things of the past come, things of the past appear in It; when

---

1. This statement is based on one made by the Chinese Zen Master Seppō, which Dōgen discusses later in this discourse. 'Han' is the name that the Chinese use to refer to themselves, as distinct from 'foreigners'. In Zen texts, it is also used as a term for those who are enlightened to their Buddha Nature, as well as for Buddha Nature in general. In addition, 'Han and foreigner' carries the connotation of what we consider to be part of us and what we view as separate from ourselves. 'A hundred thousand' is often used to

things of the present come, things of the present appear in It. When a Buddha comes, a Buddha appears in It; when an Ancestor comes, an Ancestor appears in It.

The Eighteenth Ancestor, the Venerable Kayashata, was a person from the state of Magadha in the western region of India. He was of Udraka's clan.[2] His father's name was T'ien-kai and his mother's was Fang-sheng.[3] His mother once saw in a dream what she described as a great deity who was carrying a large mirror and who had come to greet her. She associated this with her being pregnant. Seven days later, she gave birth to the Master. At the time of his birth, his body was like lustrous porcelain. Before he had even been bathed, his body was sweet smelling and clean. From his earliest days, he was fond of quietude, and his way of putting things differed from that of ordinary children.

From the time he was born, a clear and bright round mirror naturally appeared along with him—the round mirror being the Completely Perfect Mirror—a rare occurrence in any generation. Saying that the round mirror appeared along with him does not mean that the mirror was born from his mother. The Master was in her womb, and then, at the same time that he emerged from her womb, the round mirror showed up, spontaneously manifesting itself right near him, as if it were some everyday household object. The significance of this term 'round mirror' goes beyond the conventional meaning. Whenever the child approached anyone, it was as if he was holding a round mirror up in front of him with his two hands —yet it did not conceal the child's face. As the child departed, it was as if he was leaving with the round mirror carried upon his back—yet it did not conceal the child's body. When the child was sleeping, the round mirror hung above him, resembling a canopy of flowers. When the child was sitting upright, the round mirror was right before his face. In sum, the

---

express the idea of one hundred percent of all the various kinds of something; 'eight thousand' would, by contrast, convey the notion of a small sampling of those things.

2.   Udraka Ramaputra was one of Shakyamuni Buddha's teachers before His enlightenment.

3.   Tien-kai means 'He Who is a Heavenly Canopy of Light'; Fang-sheng means 'She Who is Saintly in All Ways'.

two accompanied each other, regardless of his demeanor or his behavior, whether he was active or still.

Not only that, but by looking into this round mirror he was able to see all the activities of Buddhas past, present, and future. Also, at no time were any of the everyday doings of either ordinary people or those in lofty positions clouded from his sight as they floated across the round mirror. For example, by looking in this mirror, he could clarify what had been illumined both in the past and in the present better than others could by resorting to Scriptural texts or secular writings. Nevertheless, when the child left home to be a monk and took the Precepts, the round mirror ceased to manifest before the eyes of others from that time on.[4]

Thus it was that people in nearby villages, as well as those from a considerable distance, all praised this manifestation as something rare and wondrous, for truly, its like is rarely encountered in this everyday world of ours. Even so, we should be prudent and not be surprised if there are similar offspring in families elsewhere. Beyond doubt, we should recognize that there are passages from the Scriptures that have been transformed into such things as trees and stones, and that there are spiritual friends who are spreading the Teaching through field and town. These too must surely be round mirrors. And the Scripture scrolls we have today, with their yellowed paper and their red spindles, are also round mirrors.

Then one day, while he was out and about, Kayashata came upon the Venerable Sōgyanandai. He immediately stepped forward and went up to the Venerable Sōgyanandai. The venerable one asked the child, "That which you have in your hands, is it truly what the What shows?" Once you realize that he is not asking, "What does that which you have show?" you should examine his remark carefully. Kayashata replied in verse:

> *The Great Round Mirror of all Buddhas*
> *Is neither flawed within nor beclouded without.*
> *We two can see It the same way,*
> *For we are alike in both Mind and Eye.*

---

4.   That is, he ceased to appear as someone different or special.

Since what he said is so, how could the Great Round Mirror have been born at the same time as Kayashata? Kayashata's life, from the time he was born up to that very moment, was the brightness of the Great Round Mirror. All Buddhas train alike and see alike: all Buddhas are cast images of the Great Round Mirror. The Great Round Mirror is not sagacity, nor is It intellectual reasoning; It is not one's True Nature or Its outer form. Although the term 'the Great Round Mirror' exists within the Teaching of the 'thrice wise and ten times saintly',[*] it is not the same as 'the Great Round Mirror of all Buddhas' that he just spoke of. Because all Buddhas are unquestionably beyond sagacity, all Buddhas have wise discernment, and wise discernment is not to be taken as what all Buddhas are.

Talking about wisdom is not the best way to voice what the Buddha taught. You need to realize this by investigating it through your training and practice. Even if we experience the Great Round Mirror of all Buddhas as having been born at the same time that we were, there are the following facts. This Great Round Mirror of which we are speaking might not be experienced in your life or in the life of another. It is not a mirror made from jewels, or a mirror made from copper, or a mirror made from flesh, or a mirror made from marrow. Was the poem what the Round Mirror voiced, or was the poem what the child spoke? The child's giving voice to this four-line poem was not something that he had ever learned through scholarly study with anyone, or through perusing works of Scripture, or through following a spiritual friend: he spoke as he did whilst holding the Round Mirror aloft. From the time he was a child, he was always accustomed to facing the Mirror. It was as if he had been born with the knowledge of how to put wise discernment into expression. Was the Great Round Mirror born at the same time as the child, or was the child born at the same time as the Great Round Mirror? Surely it is possible that one was born before the other. The Great Round Mirror is neither more nor less than the meritorious actions of all Buddhas.

When we say that this Mirror is unstained both within and without, we mean that It is not an inside that depends upon something outside, or an outside blurred by something inside. It has never had a front and a back: both perspectives can be viewed

---

[*]   See Glossary.

alike, for the Mind and Eye of Sōgyanandai and Kayashata resembled each other. 'Resembling each other' means that 'a person' has encountered another 'person'. Even the forms and images within have minds and eyes, and can likewise see: even the forms and images without have minds and eyes, and can likewise see. Both their outer, objective world and their inner, subjective being, as they now appeared, resembled each other within and resembled each other without. They were beyond 'I', beyond 'other'—this is just two 'persons' looking at each other, two 'persons' being alike. The one who is 'other' also speaks of himself as 'I', and your 'I' is also his 'other'.

In his statement "We are alike in both Mind and Eye," the Mind of the one was like the Mind of the other, and the Eye of the one was like the Eye of the other. The likeness was of Mind and Eye.[5] It is, for instance, as though Kayashata had said that both the Mind and the Eye of each of them were alike. What does it mean that the Mind of one is like the Mind of another? It is in the sense of the Third Ancestor and the Sixth Ancestor.[6] What does it mean that the Eye of one is like the Eye of another? It is in the sense of an Eye for the Way being hindered by one's eyes.

Such is the import of what Kayashata was now enunciating. This was the fundamental means by which he first paid his respects to the Venerable Sōgyanandai. When you undertake to express what the import of this is, you should examine through your training the face of Buddhas and the face of Ancestors in your Great Round Mirror, for They are akin to the Ancient Mirror.

Once while the Thirty-third Ancestor, Meditation Master Daikan Enō, was training hard in doing seated meditation in the monastery on Mount Ōbai, he composed a poem for his Master, Daiman Kōnin, which he wrote on the wall:

---

5. That is, their understanding and view of things were the same.

6. Not only were the Third Ancestor and the Sixth Ancestor of like mind spiritually, their religious names were also connected. The former was called Kanchi, 'He Who is the Mirror's Wise Discernment', and the latter Daikan, 'He Who is the Great Mirror'.

> *Enlightenment really has no tree it abides in,*
> *Nor is the Clear Mirror a mirrored dressing-stand.*
> *From the first not a single thing exists,*
> *So from where is dust or dirt to arise?*[7]

We need to explore what this is saying. People in his generation called Great Ancestor Enō the Old Buddha. Meditation Master Engo said, "The Old Buddha Daikan Enō is the one I bow to in deepest respect." Thus, you need to recognize that Great Ancestor Daikan Enō displayed the Clear Mirror through his saying, "From the first not a single thing exists, so from where is dust or dirt to arise?"

"Nor is the Clear Mirror a mirrored dressing-stand." This statement contains the very lifeblood that we should strive hard to comprehend. All that is clear and bright is the Clear Mirror; thus it is said, "When a bright-headed one comes, a bright-headed one responds in kind." Because It is beyond being any 'where', there is no 'where' for It to be in. What is more, can there possibly be a single dust mote anywhere in the universe that is not in the Mirror? Can there possibly be a single dust mote on the Mirror that is not of the Mirror? Keep in mind that the whole universe is beyond being merely 'lands as numerous as dust motes'. As a consequence, the universe is the face of the Ancient Mirror.

---

7. The allusions in this poem are to another poem written by Daiman Kōnin's chief disciple, whom monks at the monastery thought would be Kōnin's Dharma heir:

> *Our body is a bodhi tree,*
> *Our mind like a dressing-stand with its clear mirror;*
> *Time upon time let us strive to wipe it clean*
> *And let not dust or dirt abide thereon.*

A monk once asked Meditation Master Nangaku Ejō, "Just as with a mirror that has been melted down and recast into a religious statue, where does a monk's previous brightness go to?"[8]

The Master replied, "Reverend monk, after you left home to become a monk, where did your various facial expressions go off to?"

The monk responded, "After someone has fully realized the Truth, why does he not shine like a mirror?"

The Master said, "Although he may not shine like a mirror, he cannot in the least deceive anyone as to what he has realized."

If you are not clear about what these myriad images now before us are, you would do well to inquire into the matter. Should you do so, you have the words of the Master about realizing the brightness that has already been cast into the Mirror. The Mirror is not of gold or of jewels, and It is not Its brightness or Its images, yet no sooner is Its form cast than the Mirror is, beyond doubt, completely clear.

"Where does a monk's previous brightness go to?" is a way of saying that it is a form like that of a recast mirror in the monk's remark, "It is like a mirror that has been melted down and recast into a religious statue." In other words, images go back to the place of images, and casting can make a mirror.

Asking where the facial features of the reverend monk went off to after he left home to become a monk was the Master's holding up of the Mirror and letting his Face shine. Right now, from among all the faces, which is your own True Face?

When the Master said, "Although he may not shine like a mirror, he cannot in the least deceive anyone as to what he has realized," he meant that he cannot force the Mirror to shine and that he cannot deceive others about Its shining. You need to

---

8. That is, someone whilst still in lay life may exhibit a spontaneous brightness which dissolves after the person begins to train as a monk, as was the case with Kayashata. The monk's question, however, implies a distinction between 'us monks' and 'those lay people'.

inquire into the saying that, even were the ocean to dry up, it would not reach the state where its bed is completely exposed. Do not attempt to shatter It; do not let yourself be agitated by It. Even so, you need to inquire into the principle of 'picking out images and casting mirrors'. At this very moment, within the hundreds of myriad shining facets of the Mirror, one may be deceived by bit after bit.

Great Master Seppō Shinkaku once told his assembly, "If you want to understand this matter, our here-and-now existence is just like one face of the Ancient Mirror. When a foreigner comes, a foreigner appears in It; when a Han comes, a Han appears in It."

Gensha Shibi then came forth and asked, "How about when you suddenly encounter a Clear Mirror coming towards you?"

The Master replied, "Both foreigner and Han disappear."

Shibi commented, "It is not that way with this one."

Seppō asked, "How is it with you?"

Shibi replied, "Please put my question to me, Reverend Monk."

Seppō said, "How about when you suddenly encounter a Clear Mirror coming towards you?"

Shibi answered, "It is shattered into hundreds of pieces!"

'This matter' of which Seppō is speaking in the present instance should be examined through your training and practice as 'this matter of the What'.[9] Let's begin by looking at and investigating Seppō's 'Ancient Mirror'. In his saying that our here-and-now existence is just like one face of the Ancient Mirror, 'one face' means that boundaries have long been eliminated and that 'within and without' have also been passed beyond; it is our being as a pearl rolling about on a flat board.

---

9. Buddha Nature is sometimes referred to in Chinese Zen texts as 'the What'. It is called this because all specific names tend to limit That Which is Beyond All Limits to something that the intellect can handle.

Now, "When a foreigner comes, a foreigner appears in It" is an allusion to one of the red beards.[10] As to "When a Han comes, a Han appears in It," although the Han have been so called since primeval times—that is, after the time of P'an-ku, when they first showed up in a physical form[11]—the 'Han' of which Seppō is now speaking is the Han who appears through the functioning of the Ancient Mirror.

Since 'Han' in the present instance does not refer to the Han people, he speaks of 'the Han coming'. One might add to Seppō's statement, "Both foreigner and Han disappear," that the Mirror also disappears from one's sight. Although Shibi's statement, "It is shattered into hundreds of pieces," is the very way it should be put, what he meant was, "When I previously asked you to hand me back a concrete fragment, why did you give me your Clear Mirror?"

In the time of the Yellow Emperor,[12] there were twelve mirrors. A traditional explanation is that Heaven bestowed them on him. It is also said that they were given to him by the Taoist hermit Kuang-cheng-tsu on Mount Kung-tung. The procedure for using these twelve mirrors was that one was used for each of the twelve two-hour periods of a day. Also, one was used for each of the twelve months of every year, and they were used, one after the other, for each year in a twelve-year cycle. It is said that the mirrors were Kuang-cheng-tsu's scriptural texts.[13] In bestowing these texts on the Yellow Emperor, the twelve two-hour periods and so forth became mirrors. In this

---

10. All those who are not of Han descent have long been considered by the Chinese to be foreigners and red-bearded barbarians, regardless of their actual physical appearance or how long they or their ancestors have lived in China.

11. P'an-ku is the Chinese legendary 'first human', born from primordial chaos. Upon his death, other humans came into being, and were considered to be either Chinese (Han) or barbarians.

12. The legendary third emperor of China.

13. That is, they were not actual mirrors but writings that the Emperor could look into in order to help him see how to handle various aspects of ruling.

way, they illumined the past and illumined the present. If the twelve two-hour periods of a day were not mirrors, how could they possibly illumine the past? If the twelve periods were not mirrors, how could they possibly illumine the present? 'The twelve two-hour periods' are twelve surfaces; the twelve surfaces are twelve mirrors. What is called 'past and present' are reflected by the twelve time periods, and they display this principle. Although this is a mundane explanation, the Han appears within the twelve periods of each day.

The Yellow Emperor Hsien-yüan climbed Mount Kung-tung on his hands and knees to ask Kuang-cheng-tsu about the Tao. At the time Kuang-cheng-tsu said, "Mirrors are the source of yin and yang; they are ever what regulate the body. By nature, there are three kinds of mirror: one called 'the Mirror of Heaven', one called 'the Mirror of Earth', and one called 'the Human Mirror'. These 'mirrors' are invisible and inaudible. When you become calm by being self-possessed, your body will naturally be upright. Beyond question, they will quiet you and purify you, so that nothing will trouble your body and nothing will perturb your spirit. Thus, you will be able to live a long life."

In the distant past, emperors used these three mirrors to govern the people and attend to the Greater Path. Someone who was clear about this Greater Path was considered Lord of Heaven and Earth. A secular work says, "The T'ang dynasty Emperor T'ai-tsung regarded people as mirrors, whereby he illumined and comprehended situations, so that he might defuse what was dangerous and regulate what was disorderly." He was using one of the three mirrors. Hearing that he treated people as mirrors, you may think that, by his consulting highly literate persons about matters past and present, he was able to know how and when to make use of wise and sage ones, as, for example, in his procuring the services of ministers like Wu-cheng and Fang-hsüan-ling. To understand the situation in this manner is far from the principle enunciated by the statement "T'ai-sung regarded people as mirrors." 'To regard people as mirrors' means to regard a mirror as a mirror, to regard oneself as a mirror, to regard the five elements as a mirror,[14] and to regard each of the five Confucian virtues of justice, politeness, wisdom, fidelity, and benevolence as a mirror. The principle of the Human Mirror is used in looking at the comings and goings of human beings, and is said to be, "Of their coming, there is no trace; of their departing, there is no quarter to which they go." This principle encompasses all the myriad thoughts and deeds of the clever and the inept: it is like the ever-changing conditions in the sky. Truly, it is the very woof and warp of things. It is the face of humans and the face of the Mirror, the face of the sun and the face of the moon. The vitality of the five peaks and the vitality of the four long rivers have cleansed the four seas for ever so long, for this is the custom of mirrors.[15] To be clear about human beings and to evaluate the woof and warp of things is said to be T'ai-sung's way. And it did not merely consist of consulting persons of learning.

Ever since the Age of the Divine Beings, Japan has had three mirrors which, along with the sacred jewels and the sacred sword, have been passed on up to the present day. One mirror is in the Great Shrine at Ise, one is in the Hinokuma Shrine in Kinokuni, and one is in the Imperial Sanctuary of the Emperor's Palace.

It is clear that all nations pass down and preserve a mirror. Those who possess the mirror possess the country. We have inherited what people have passed on to us, namely, that these three mirrors have been handed down along with the Imperial Divine Throne, and that they were introduced by the Heavenly Deity Amaterasu-Ōmikami. Even so, their finely tempered copper is also something wrought from

---

14. The five elements are earth, water, fire, wind and space.

15. The five peaks are Mount Heng in the north, Mount Ho in the south, Mount Tai in the east, Mount Hua in the west, and Mount Sung in the center. The four rivers are the Yangtze, the Yellow, the Huai, and the Chi.

materials partaking of yin and yang.[16] When the present comes, the present may well appear in them; when the past comes, the past may well appear in them. The mirror that illumines and commands a view of past and present, this will be the Ancient Mirror.

The principle that Seppō recounted earlier can also be stated as, "When a Korean comes, a Korean appears in It; when a Japanese comes, a Japanese appears in It," and as, "When a lofty being comes, a lofty being appears in It; when an ordinary person comes, an ordinary person appears in It." Through our training and practice, we explore the matter of their coming and appearing in this manner, but even so, it is beyond us to know, at present, the cause of these appearances; it is simply a matter of their coming into view. Undoubtedly, you are not to explore comings and appearances as something to be known about, something to be comprehended. Is the principle that is now being expressed saying that the foreigner who comes is the foreigner who appears? The coming of a foreigner will be one instance of a foreigner coming, and the appearing of a foreigner will be one instance of a foreigner appearing. And yet, such a one does not come for the sake of appearing. This is what you should have for your investigation, even though the Ancient Mirror may be for you the Ancient Mirror.

When Shibi came forth and asked, "How about when you suddenly encounter a Clear Mirror coming towards you?" what he was saying is something that we need to inquire into and clarify. How much weight should we give to the term 'clear' that he is using at present? We might put it this way, "In that its coming is not necessarily that of a foreigner or of a Han, it is a Clear Mirror; further, it need not manifest before our very eyes as either a foreigner or a Han." The coming of the Clear Mirror is simply the coming of the Clear Mirror, and it is not a matter of there being two Mirrors, one Clear and one Ancient. Although there are not two Mirrors, 'the Ancient Mirror' refers to the Ancient Mirror, and 'the Clear Mirror' refers to the Clear Mirror. Directly experiencing that there is the Ancient Mirror and that there is the Clear Mirror is what

---

16. That is, despite their legendary origin, these sacred shrine mirrors are physical objects, unlike the Ancient Mirror that Dōgen has been discussing.

Seppō and Shibi were expressing through words. According to the Buddha's Way, we should consider these mirrors respectively as the True Nature and how the True Nature manifests. Shibi's speaking of a Clear Mirror coming should be understood as being totally penetrating and as clear as a bell. In meeting someone, he would probably display It forthwith; by the directness of his displaying It, he would probably have a positive influence on the person. So, are the 'clear' of the Clear Mirror and the 'ancient' of the Ancient Mirror the same, or are they different? Does the Clear Mirror have the nature of being ancient or not? Does the Ancient Mirror have the nature of being clear or not? Do not understand from the words 'the Ancient Mirror' that It must be clear. The main point is that the principle of "I too am like this, you too are like this, and all the Indian Ancestors are also like this" should be quickly cultivated. In the words of Shibi's disciple, Ancestral Master Kinkazan Kōtō, "The Ancient Mirror is polished." Might it also be so for the Clear Mirror? We should by all means have as our investigation through training and practice an exploration that broadly spans the sayings of all the Buddhas and Ancestors.

 Seppō's statement, "Both the foreigner and the Han disappear," means that foreigner and Han will both disappear the moment that the Clear Mirror has appeared. What is the meaning of this principle of 'both disappearing'? Since the foreigner's and the Han's having already come and appeared does not get in the way of the Ancient Mirror, why should they both disappear now? Even though, from the perspective of the Ancient Mirror, "When a foreigner comes, a foreigner appears in It; when a Han comes, a Han appears in It," from the perspective of the Clear Mirror, the foreigner and the Han that appeared in the Ancient Mirror both disappear because of the natural coming of the Clear Mirror. Thus Seppō's statement also implies that the Ancient Mirror has Its face and the Clear Mirror has Its. You definitely need to be clear about the principle that when the Clear Mirror duly comes, It will not impede either the foreigner or the Han that appeared in the Ancient Mirror. The function of the Ancient Mirror about which we are now speaking, such that "When a foreigner comes, a foreigner appears in It; when a Han comes, a Han appears in It," is not saying that they come and appear upon the Ancient Mirror, or within the Ancient Mirror, or apart from the Ancient Mirror, or along with the Ancient Mirror. We need to listen carefully to what is being said here. At the time of the foreigner and the Han coming and appearing, the Ancient Mirror is causing foreigner and Han to appear. If you were to say, "At the time when both foreigner and Han disappear, the Mirror will continue to remain there," you would be in the dark about 'appearing' and would not be paying attention to 'coming'. Even calling you confused would not reach the mark.

> Shibi commented, "It is not that way with me."
>
> Seppō asked, "How is it with you?"
>
> Shibi replied, "Please put my question to me, Reverend Monk."

Do not idly stumble past the words, "Please put my question to me," which Shibi is now uttering. Were there not full and sweet accord between 'parent' and 'child', how could the coming forth of the reverend monk's question and the request for the reverend monk to ask the question in turn take the form they did? At the time when Shibi was saying, "Please put my question to me, Reverend Monk," he would surely have been 'such a person' * and thus would have already reached the place from which his Master's question arose. When there is a thundering forth from the place of the question, there is no time to escape from it.

> Seppō asked, "How about when you suddenly encounter a Clear Mirror coming towards you?"

The place of this question is the one Ancient Mirror which both 'parent' and 'child'— that is, Master and disciple—are mastering together.

> Shibi replied, "It is shattered into hundreds of pieces!"

This statement shatters It into hundreds of myriad bits. "When you suddenly encounter a Clear Mirror coming towards you" is equivalent to Its being shattered into hundreds of pieces. That which experiences being shattered into hundreds of pieces is the Clear Mirror, because when you give expression to the Clear Mirror, It is shattered into hundreds of pieces. What the shattered pieces are dependent on is the Clear Mirror. Do not take the narrow view that there was an earlier time when It was not yet shattered and there will be a later time when It will no longer be shattered. It is, simply, shattered into hundreds of pieces. When someone comes face-to-face with any of these hundreds of fragments, it will be with just one isolated fragment. Despite this, do you describe the hundreds of shattered pieces that we are speaking of now as the Ancient Mirror or do you describe them as the Clear Mirror? You should ask again for a single word of clarification to turn things around for you. At the same time, such a word will be beyond your describing these pieces as the Ancient Mirror, and beyond your describing them as the Clear Mirror. Even though Shibi was able to bring forth the question about the Ancient Mirror and the Clear Mirror, when we discuss his way of putting the Matter,* might it be that the words which come to the tip of our tongue to describe that which manifests before our very eyes simply as 'walls and fences with their stones and tiles'* probably was, for him, 'hundreds of shattered pieces'?

And what form do the shatterings take? Myriad deep pools the color of antique jade, with the moon in the realm of unbounded space.

While Great Master Seppō Shinkaku and Meditation Master Sanshō Enen were traveling together, they saw a group of red-faced apes, whereupon Seppō said, "Each of these red-faced apes is carrying the Ancient Mirror upon its back."

We need to consider these words of his very carefully. The term 'red-faced apes' customarily refers to a particular type of monkey. The red-faced apes that Seppō saw, of what sort would they have been? You need to inquire in this manner, and make further diligent effort to understand. Pay no attention to how long it takes.

His words "Each of them is carrying the Ancient Mirror upon its back" mean that, even though the Ancient Mirror is the face of all the Buddhas and Ancestors, the Ancient Mirror is the Ancient Mirror, even from Their higher perspective. His saying that all the red-faced apes were carrying mirrors on their backs means that there were no larger or smaller mirrors, but that each was the one Ancient Mirror. The phrase 'carrying on their backs' means 'being backed by' in the sense, for instance, of the backing material used behind pictures and statues of the Buddha. When the backs of the red-faced apes are backed, they are backed by the Ancient Mirror. "What kind of glue have they come to use?" you may ask. To try to put it into words, "The back of the apes is backed by the Ancient Mirror. But is the back of the Ancient Mirror backed by red-faced apes? It is we who back the back of the Ancient Mirror with an Ancient Mirror. It is we who back the back of the ape with an ape." The phrase 'one mirror for each back' will not be an empty teaching, for it is a statement that fully expresses the Truth.

So, which is it, red-faced ape or Ancient Mirror? Ultimately, how should we put it? Are we just red-faced apes? Are we not red-faced apes? To whom are we to put the question? Whether we are red-faced apes is beyond our own knowledge and beyond the knowledge of others. Whether we are ourselves is beyond our ability to discover.

Enen replied, "For eons beyond measure, It has been nameless, so why are you expressing It as 'the Ancient Mirror'?

This is one aspect, one facet, whereby Enen certified his realization of the Ancient Mirror. His phrase 'for eons beyond measure' means 'before any single moment of consciousness, any single thought, has sprouted up'; it means 'within any span of time, nothing has exposed its head'. His term 'nameless' means 'the face of the Sun, the face of the Moon, and the face of the Ancient Mirror for eons beyond measure'. If the Nameless were not truly nameless, the eons beyond measure would not yet be for eons beyond measure. If the eons beyond measure were not entirely eons beyond measure, Enen's expression could not express It. Even so, the phrase 'before any single thought has sprouted up' means 'today'. So, cultivate yourself, without letting yourself stumble past today. Truly, the fame of this epithet 'nameless for eons beyond measure' has been heard on high.

And what do I call the Ancient Mirror? The Head of the Dragon, the Tail of the Snake!

At this time, Seppō might have turned to Enen and said, "The Ancient Mirror! The Ancient Mirror!" but that is not how he replied.

Seppō responded, "A flaw has emerged!"

What he meant by this was that a scratch has appeared. We may think, "How could a flaw have possibly been produced in the Ancient Mirror?" but the Ancient Mirror's yielding a flaw must mean that Enen's saying "It is nameless for eons beyond measure" is indeed a scratch. 'The Ancient Mirror's yielding a flaw' refers to the whole Ancient Mirror. Enen had not yet emerged from the dark realm of "Oh, the Ancient Mirror has produced a flaw!" so the understanding that he expressed through his words was neither more nor less than a flaw in the Ancient Mirror. Thus, we examine through our training and practice that flaws appear even in the Ancient Mirror, and that even those things from which flaws are produced are also the Ancient Mirror; this is our learning through our practice what the Ancient Mirror is.

> Enen responded, "What has such deadly urgency? Besides,
> I don't even know what the topic of our conversation is."

The main point of what he said is "What is so deadly urgent?" You need to apply yourself unremittingly and investigate through your training and practice whether 'deadly urgency' refers to today or to tomorrow, to oneself or to others, to the whole universe or to some place within the land of Great T'ang China. As to the topic alluded to in the phrase 'not even knowing what the topic of our conversation is', there is the topic that is being expressed, the topic that has not yet been expressed, and the topic that has already been completely expressed. The principle of these topics is ever manifest before our very eyes. For instance, the topic is also one's realizing the Truth simultaneously with the great earth and all its sentient beings. It is beyond being 'mended brocade'.[17] This is why it is 'not known'. It is 'the one who faced His Imperial Majesty and said that he did not personally know That One'.[18] It is our not knowing That which is right before our face. It is not that the Topic does not exist, it is simply that It is beyond our knowing. His 'not knowing It' is a manifestation of his sincerity; it is also his not seeing his own brightness and clarity.

> Seppō said, "The old monk has made a blunder."

---

17. Being beyond 'mended brocade' is a metaphor for the Truth being seamless, as It is not something composed of bits and pieces of this and that sewn together.

18. An allusion to Bodhidharma's interview with Emperor Wu of Liang. When the emperor asked him who it was that was facing His Imperial Majesty, Bodhidharma replied, "I do not personally know that one," because he was already rid of any false, socially conventional sense of a self.

This turn of phrase is usually said with the meaning of "I have put it badly," but it need not have this intent. 'The old monk' refers to the Old One who is Lord of the House. Do not undertake to study other matters; just examine 'the Old Monk' through your training. Though He has a thousand changes and ten thousand transformations, be they the face of a god or the countenance of a demon, what you examine is the Old Monk's 'just one move at a time'. And though He comes as a Buddha or comes as an Ancestor, be it for a single moment or for all of time, what you examine is the Old Monk's 'just one move at a time'. 'Making a blunder' refers to the One who is Master of the Temple having lots to do. When you think about it, Seppō was an outstanding disciple of Tokusan, and Enen was a wondrous supporter of Rinzai. Neither of these two venerable veterans sprang from humble lineage: the former was a distant descendant of Seigen, the latter was in the long line from Nangaku. How they came to reside in, and keep to, the Ancient Mirror is as given above. They should be paragons for trainees in later ages.

> Seppō, in addressing his assembly, once said, "When the width of the world is ten feet, the width of the Ancient Mirror will be ten feet; when the width of the world is one foot, the width of the Ancient Mirror will be one foot."
>
> At that time Shibi pointed to the hearth and said, "Can you tell us just how wide our charcoal burner is?" [19]
>
> Seppō replied, "It resembles the width of the Ancient Mirror."
>
> Shibi responded, "The venerable Han has not let even a heel touch the ground!"

---

19. On a literal level, the charcoal burner is a cauldron-shaped brazier around which monks customarily sat to warm themselves. It was also sometimes used in preparing such foods as rice and dumplings. The term is also sometimes used to refer to the hara, i.e., the belly, as the furnace for heating up our training, so that we are able to dissolve the ice-like hardness of our egoistic desires and to make palpable what spiritually sustains us.

If we say that the width of our world is ten feet, our world will be ten feet wide; if we treat the width of our world as one foot, our world will be one foot wide. Moreover, the 'ten feet' we are speaking of now and the 'one foot' we are speaking of now are not some arbitrary linear measurements in feet. In examining this dialogue, people customarily speak of the width of the world as being 'the three-thousand great-thousandfold worlds, immeasurable and boundless' or as being 'the world of inexhaustible thoughts and things', but this is like our own self of small measure pointing to other villages in our vicinity. When worlds like these are proposed, they measure 'ten feet'. This is why Seppō said, "When the width of the Ancient Mirror is ten feet, the width of the world is ten feet." In examining this 'ten feet', you will catch a glimpse of one part of 'the width of the world'.

Further, in hearing the term 'the Ancient Mirror', one may envisage a sheet of thin ice, but It is not so. Although Its width of ten feet is at one with the width of the world being ten feet, does It necessarily stand shoulder-to-shoulder in form and likeness with the limitlessness of the world? Or are the Ancient Mirror and the world's limitlessness like fellow trainees, side by side? You should make a diligent effort to consider what this is saying.

What is more, the Ancient Mirror is not like a single pearl. Do not view It as being bright or dark; do not visualize It as being square or round. Even though the whole universe in all ten directions is the One Bright Pearl, this is not to be equated with the Ancient Mirror. Accordingly, the Ancient Mirror does not depend on the comings and appearances of foreigners or Han, for It is every single thing's being as unobstructed as a bell's clear resounding in all directions. It is beyond being many, beyond being large.

'Width' refers to Its measurements, and the term goes beyond what is meant by 'broad' or 'narrow'. That latter use of 'width' is like conventionally speaking of 'two inches' or 'three inches', or counting 'seven things' or 'eight things'. In the Buddhist way of counting, we use the term 'two ounces' to describe those who have had a great awakening and 'three ounces' to describe those who have gone beyond having awakened.[20] In counting Buddhas and Ancestors, we express the matter as their being of the 'fifth generation' or 'tenth generation' from Shakyamuni Buddha. Ten feet is the width of the Ancient Mirror; the width of the Ancient Mirror is one span.

Shibi's asking about the width of the charcoal burner is an expression that is out in the open; you should explore it till you are a thousand or ten thousand years old. In looking at the charcoal burner now, from what perspective do we view it? When we look at the charcoal burner, it is not something that is 'seven feet' or 'eight feet'. This question of his was not posed during the time when he was still wavering and attached. It was his way of displaying, from his new perspective, what is meant by the statement, "What is It that comes like this?" When he came out with the words 'how wide', the 'how' that he had employed up to that time to refer to quantity is not his current 'how'. We should have no doubts about the fact that he had already realized liberation at that time. We should listen to Shibi's words as to the fundamental point that our 'charcoal burner' is beyond form and measure. Do not idly let the dumpling that is now right before you fall on the ground! Tear it open! This is what diligent effort is!

We need to reflect on and illumine Seppō's statement, "It is like the width of the Ancient Mirror." He put it this way because the situation was beyond the point where he could state that the width of the charcoal burner was ten feet. It is not the case that his answering 'ten feet' would have expressed the situation more accurately than his saying 'like the width of the Ancient Mirror'. We need to consider the daily activities of 'being like the width of the Ancient Mirror'. Many people consider his omitting to say that the width of the charcoal burner is ten feet to be an inaccuracy in his expressing the Matter. Such folks need to consider the freedom of his 'width', to reflect on the undiluted nature of the Ancient Mirror, and to not stumble past the day-to-day operating of That Which is Real. In the words of Meditation Master Kyōgen Chikan, they need to advance along the ancient path with a smiling countenance, without lapsing into periods of despondency.

---

20. To paraphrase, those who have had a great awakening have realized a bit of the Truth; those who have gone beyond having awakened have realized a bit more of the Truth.

The intent behind Shibi's response, "The venerable Han has not let even a heel touch the ground!" is that whether he said 'venerable Han' or 'venerable monk', it is certainly not 'Seppō', since Seppō must surely be 'a Venerable Han'.[21] You also need to ask in what place his heel is; you need to investigate thoroughly what 'heel' means. What I mean by 'investigating thoroughly' is asking yourself, "Is 'heel' an allusion to the Treasure House of the Eye of the True Teaching, or to unbounded space, or to the whole of the great earth, or to the clear and bright life stream of the Buddhas and Ancestors?" And you need to be diligent in your exploration of just how many heels could be involved: is it just one heel, or half a heel, or hundreds of thousands of myriad heels?

In his phrase 'not yet touched the ground', what sort of thing is this 'ground' he is talking about? The ground that we nowadays refer to as the great earth, some provisionally call 'the ground' in conformity with one way of looking at things. Again, among these various ways, there are some that see 'the ground' as the mind-boggling Dharma Gate to liberation, and some that see it as what all Buddhas do and say. So, what sort of thing is this 'ground' that one should touch one's heel down upon? Is this 'ground' our real being? Or is it beyond our real being? Further, in sum, can even the tiniest bit of that which we call 'the ground' not exist within the Great Way? Let the question arise, let the question pass; talk about it with others, talk about it with yourself. Is the heel touching the ground the way it should be, or is the heel not touching the ground the way it should be? Since "Why?" is the question, why did Shibi state that not even a heel had touched the ground? When there is not the tiniest bit of ground on the Great Earth, then, of necessity, neither 'touching the ground' nor 'not yet touching the ground' will come about. Thus, "The venerable Han has not let even a heel touch the ground!" is the Venerable Han's very breathing in and breathing out, the very functioning of His heels.

---

21.   The term 'venerable Han', like 'venerable monk', would have been understood conventionally as a polite expression for 'you'. In Zen, 'Venerable Han' was also used to refer to someone who had dropped off the false self, to a Buddha, to 'such a one'. Seppō, having already awakened, was no longer 'Seppō' in a conventional sense, but was 'such a one'.

Meditation Master Kinkazan Kōtō of Kokutai-in Temple in the Wu-chou district was once asked by one of his monks, "What is the Ancient Mirror before It has been polished?"

The Master answered, "The Ancient Mirror."

The monk then asked, "What is It after It has been polished?"

The Master answered, "The Ancient Mirror."

You need to recognize that even though there is a time when the Ancient Mirror, as now spoken of, is being polished, a time when It has not yet been polished, and a time after It has been polished, It is one and the same Ancient Mirror. Thus, when we are polishing It, the Ancient Mirror polishes the whole Ancient Mirror. We do not polish It by adding something that is not the Ancient Mirror, such as quicksilver. This is neither ourselves polishing ourselves nor the self doing the polishing, but our polishing the Ancient Mirror. Before we have polished ourselves, the Ancient Mirror is not dull. Even though some may describe It as being black, It will never be dull, for It is the living Ancient Mirror. Generally speaking, in polishing a mirror, we may make it into a mirror, and in polishing a roof tile, we may make it into a mirror, and in polishing a tile, we may make it into a tile, and in polishing a mirror, we may make it into a tile. There are times when we polish something and make nothing, and there are times when we can make something, even though we are not able to polish it. The traditional activities of the Buddhas and Ancestors are all the same as this.

A long time ago, when Baso of Kiangsi Province was training under Nangaku, Nangaku on one occasion privately imparted the Mind seal* to him. This occurred just before the incident concerning the polishing of the roof tile. While staying in Chuan-fa Temple, Baso had been doing seated meditation day in and day out for some ten years or more. We can imagine what his thatched hut was like on a rainy night, and it is said that he never abandoned its freezing floor even when it was enveloped in snow.

One day when Nangaku came to Baso's hut, Baso stood up to receive him. Nangaku asked him, "What have you been doing recently?"

Baso replied, "Recently I have been doing the practice of seated meditation exclusively."

Nangaku asked, "And what is the aim of your seated meditation?"

Baso replied, "The aim of my seated meditation is to achieve Buddhahood." [22]

Thereupon, Nangaku took a roof tile and began rubbing it on a rock near Baso's hut.

Baso, upon seeing this, asked him, "Reverend monk, what are you doing?"

Nangaku replied, "I am polishing a roof tile."

Baso then asked, "What are you going to make by polishing a roof tile?"

Nangaku replied, "I am polishing it to make a mirror."

Baso said, "How can you possibly make a mirror by rubbing a tile?"

---

22. The translation may not clearly convey the contradiction in Baso's statement. The particular practice of seated meditation he specifically mentions is *chih-kuan ta-tsuo (J. shikan taza)*, a Chinese colloquial phrase that literally translates as 'just control yourself and sit there'. This implies sitting in meditation without deliberately thinking of anything, or holding on to anything that naturally arises, or pushing away anything that naturally arises, and without trying to suppress any thoughts from arising. However, in reply to Nangaku's question, Baso indicates that, in fact, he has something he is deliberately holding in his mind, namely, the goal of realizing Buddhahood, literally 'making himself into a Buddha'.

Nangaku replied, "How can you possibly make yourself into a Buddha by doing seated meditation?"

For hundreds of years now, many people have held the view that, in this story, Nangaku is earnestly endeavoring to encourage Baso in his practice. This is not necessarily so, for, quite simply, the daily activities of the great saintly teacher were far removed from the realm of ordinary people. If great saintly teachers did not have the Dharma of polishing a tile, how could they possibly have the skillful means to guide people? Having the strength to guide people is the Bones and Marrow of an Ancestor of the Buddha. Even though the tile was the thing that came to hand, still, it was just an everyday, household object.[23] If it were not an everyday object or some household utensil, then it would not have been passed on by the Buddha's family. What is more, its impact on Baso was immediate. Be very clear about it, the functioning of the True Transmission of Buddhas and Ancestors involves a direct pointing. We should truly comprehend that when the polished tile became a mirror, Baso became Buddha. And when Baso became Buddha, Baso immediately became the real Baso. And when Baso became the real Baso, his sitting in meditation immediately became real seated meditation. This is why the saying 'polishing a tile to make a mirror' has been preserved in the Bones and Marrow of former Buddhas.

Thus it is that the Ancient Mirror was made from a roof tile. Even though the mirror was being polished, it was already without blemish in its unpolished state. The tile was not something that was dirty; it was polished simply because it was a tile. On that occasion, the virtue of making a Mirror was made manifest, for it was the diligent effort of an Ancestor of the Buddha. If polishing a tile did not make a Mirror, then even polishing a mirror could not have made a Mirror. Who can surmise that in this act of making, there is the making of a Buddha and there is the making of a Mirror?

Further, some may wonder, "When the Ancient Mirror is polished, can It ever be polished into a tile?" Your state of being—your breathing in and breathing out—when you are engaged in polishing is not something that you can gauge at other times.

---

23. This is a reference to the common practice among Zen Masters of employing everyday objects to help their disciples realize the Truth.

And Nangaku's words, to be sure, express what is expressible. As a result, in the final analysis, he was able to polish a tile and make a Mirror. Even we people of the present time should try to pick up today's 'tile' and give it a polish, for ultimately it will become a Mirror. If a tile could not become a Mirror, people could not become Buddha. If we belittle tiles as being lumps of clay, we will also belittle people as being lumps of clay. If people have a Heart, then tiles too will have a Heart. Who can recognize that there is a Mirror in which, when a tile comes, the Tile appears? And who can recognize that there is a Mirror in which, when a mirror comes, the Mirror appears?

Delivered to the assembly at Kannondōri in Kōshōhōrin-ji Temple on the ninth day of the ninth lunar month in the second year of the Ninji era (October 15, 1241).

Recopied in the Sandalwood Grove[24] *on the thirteenth day of the first month in the fourth year of the same era (February 3, 1243).*

---

24. The nickname for a Zen monastery in which the monks are doing outstanding training.

20

On Reading Scriptures

(Kankin)

Translator's Introduction: In this discourse, Dōgen takes up both the literal and the non-literal meanings of 'reading Scriptures', as well as various forms of ceremonial involved with the reading of Scriptures in monastic life.

The training that we undertake to directly experience supreme, fully perfected enlightenment sometimes makes use of our good spiritual friends and sometimes makes use of *sutras*. 'Our good spiritual friends' refers to the Buddhas and Ancestors, those who have completely realized their True Self. *'Sutras'* is a technical term for Scriptural texts, which are spiritually complete in and of Themselves. Because Self Nature is what all Buddhas and Ancestors are and because Self Nature is what all Scriptures are, this is the way all things are. We speak of Their 'Self', but It is a Self that is beyond any adherence to 'self and other', for It is Their penetrating Eye, Their emancipating Fist.[1]

At the same time, there is the practice of calling the Scriptures to mind, of reading Them, chanting Them, copying Them, accepting Them, and preserving Them, which all together comprise the training to directly experience what the Buddhas and Ancestors experienced. Nonetheless, encountering the Buddha's Scriptures is no easy matter. As they say, "In countless lands, not even as much as Their names can be heard," and "Even among Buddhas and Ancestors, not even Their names can be heard," and "Within the lifeblood of our Ancestral line, not even Their names can be heard." When we are not a Buddha or an Ancestor, we do not see or hear the Scriptures, read or chant Them, or explain Their meaning. As soon as we have begun to investigate the Buddhas and Ancestors through our training, then, with some considerable difficulty, we begin to explore and train with Scriptural texts. At this

---

1. The eyes of Masters were commonly associated with seeing the essence of the Dharma, whereas the raising of a fist was often used by Masters to show that 'That Which Is' is beyond words or conceptual thought.

278

time, what manifests before us are the hearing, keeping to, accepting, and expounding of the Scriptures that we experience within our ears, our eyes, our tongue, our nose, our body, our mind, no matter what place we go to, or listen from, or speak at. Because those folks who expound non-Buddhist theories and interpretations are seeking a name for themselves, they cannot put the Buddha's true purpose into practice. That is why the Scriptures have been passed on and preserved on trees and on rocks, why They have spread through field and town, why They are presented to us by worlds of dust motes, and why They are opened up and lectured on by boundless space.

Great Master Igen, our ancient Ancestor of Yakusan Mountain, absented himself from the Dharma Hall for a long time. So the temple's Prior said to him, "Venerable Monk, the whole assembly has for ever so long looked forward to your compassionate instruction."

Yakusan said, "Ring the summoning bell."

The Prior rang the bell. The whole assembly had barely gathered together when Yakusan entered the hall. No sooner had he taken his seat, than he forthwith got up and returned to the Abbot's quarters. Following after him, the Prior said, "Venerable Monk, just a moment ago you promised to give voice to the Dharma for the sake of the assembly, so why have you not conferred a single word on us?"

Yakusan replied, "The Scriptures have teachers of Scripture and the commentaries have teachers of commentary. So, how can you possibly have doubts about the old monk?"[2]

---

2. Yakusan's question has a double meaning: "What makes you doubt that your Abbot is doing his job?" and "Why do you doubt that Buddha Nature (The Old Monk) has Its teachers, just as the Scriptures and the commentaries have theirs?"

Whenever the Great Master gave compassionate instruction, the Fist had Its Fist teacher and the Eye had Its Eye teacher. Be that as it may, what the Prior should have respectfully put to the Great Master at that moment was, "It is not that I have had doubts arise about the Venerable Monk, but rather, I wonder what the Venerable Monk is a teacher of?"

In the assembly of the lofty Ancestor Enō, founder of the monastery on Mount Sōkei in Shin-chou Province, a monk named Hōtatsu, who could recite the whole of the *Lotus Scripture* by heart, had come to train under the Master. The Founding Ancestor gave voice to the following poem for Hōtatsu's benefit:

> *When the mind wanders onto deluded paths,*
> *It is being set in motion by the flowering of the Dharma;*
> *When the heart awakens,*
> *The Dharma's flowering is set in motion.*

> *However long you recite this Scripture, should it be while still*
> *unawakened to the Self that is true,*
> *You will then create an enemy to Its meaning.*
> *To read It without opinion's bonds is the proper way,*
> *But read It bound to fixed ideas, and It becomes error's way.*

> *When you cease to judge whether you are bound or not,*
> *You ride forever long within the cart by the White Ox drawn.*

Thus, the deluded mind is turned around by the Flowering of the Dharma, and the awakened mind sets the flowering of the Dharma in motion. And further, when we leap beyond 'deluded versus awakened', the Flowering of the Dharma sets the flowering of the Dharma in motion.

When Hōtatsu heard this poem, he leapt for joy and presented the following poem in praise of it:

The three thousand times that I have recited this Scripture

Have been surpassed by Enō's solitary verse.

Because I was not yet clear as to the purpose of my coming into this
*   world,*

How was I to halt the folly of my troubled life?

'Sheep', 'deer', and 'ox' provide but expedient means.

At beginning, middle, and end, they promote the virtuous and the
*   good.*

Who within the burning house know

That, from the first, they are lords within the Dharma?

The Founding Ancestor then said, "From now on, it would be good to refer to you as
'the Monk Who Calls the *Lotus Scripture* to Mind.'"

You should recognize that in the Buddha's Way there is the monk who calls
the *Lotus Scripture* to mind. This is directly pointed to by Enō, our Old Buddha of
Sōkei. The 'calling to mind' in this 'monk who calls the *Lotus Scripture* to mind'
points to one who is beyond 'holding to opinions' and beyond 'being free of opinions'.
He is no longer involved in measuring by means of 'holding to' or 'being free'. This
means, simply, that as the Founding Ancestor once said, "From eon to eon, we do not
let this Scripture book out of our hands, and, both day and night, there is no time when
we do not call this Scripture to mind." In other words, from Scripture to Scripture,
there is no time when we are not This Scripture.

The Twenty-seventh Ancestor, the Venerable Hannyatara
of eastern India, was once invited to dine with an eastern Indian
king.[3] After the meal, the king asked her, "All the other monks have
recited Scriptures to me, so why have you alone not recited them?"

---

3.   There is a long-standing Indian tradition which holds that Hannyatara was a female monk
who was renowned for her extraordinary spiritual prowess.

The Ancestor replied, "In my humble way, what I breathe out does not conform itself to external conditions and events, and what I breathe in does not take up residence in the realm of my skandhas.* The Scriptures that I recite are always like this. Thus they are comprised of hundreds of thousands of millions of billions of scrolls, not just one or two scrolls."

The Venerable Hannyatara was a seedling that sprouted up in a kingdom in eastern India. She was a direct descendant of the twenty-seventh generation from the Venerable Makakashyō. She had had properly Transmitted to her all the necessary equipment of the Buddha's family, having in her charge a monk's Head, Eye, Fist, Nose, traveling staff, alms bowl, robe, Dharma, Bones, and Marrow. She is our Founding Ancestor, and we are her distant descendants. What the Venerable One is now putting her full strength into saying is that not only does what she exhales not conform itself to external conditions, but external conditions do not conform themselves to what she exhales. Even though external conditions comprise her head and eyes, her whole body, and her whole heart and mind, her carrying them about when she comes, when she departs, and when she comes back again are simply her 'not conforming herself to external conditions'. 'Not conforming oneself' means going along with completely; thus, it means participating in the rough and tumble of daily life.[4] Even though her breathing out was an external condition, it was her not conforming herself to external conditions. Innumerable eons have come and gone, but people have not yet understood the ebb and flow of breathing in and breathing out. Be that as it may, the moment has come, right now, when you can understand it for the first time, so pay attention to 'not taking up residence in the realm of one's skandhas' and to 'not conforming oneself to external conditions'. This is the moment when external conditions, for the first time, permit the exploration of such things as

---

* See Glossary.

4. That is, Buddhism is not a form of quietism or stoicism, nor is it the trainee's goal to become a doormat.

'breathing in'. This moment has never been before, and it may never be again: it is just <u>now</u>.

'The realm of the skandhas' refers to our five skandhas, namely, our physical form, our sensory perceptions, our mental conceptions, our volition, and our consciousness. The reason why she does not reside in these five skandhas is because she is in a realm that the five skandhas have not yet reached. Because she chose the right key to unlock this, the Scriptures that she recited were not merely one or two scrolls; they were hundreds of thousands of millions of billions of scrolls which she was continually reciting. Although 'hundreds of thousands of millions of billions of scrolls' gives us the general idea of 'many', it is not just some measurement of 'many'. Her 'not taking up residence in the realm of her skandhas' made her exhalation of a single breath equivalent to hundreds of thousands of millions of billions of scrolls. At the same time, this is not something which can be measured by discernment that is either tainted or untainted, nor is it to be found in the realm where thoughts and things are either tainted or untainted. As a consequence, it is beyond the measurements of what one having intelligence knows, beyond the conjectures of what one having knowledge discerns, beyond the considerations of what one lacking intelligence knows, and beyond the reach of what one who is ignorant discerns. It is what Buddha after Buddha and Ancestor after Ancestor trained to realize: it is Their Skin and Flesh, Bones and Marrow, Their Eye and Fist, Their Head and Nose, Their traveling staff[*] and ceremonial hossu,[*] Their leaping beyond and Their every little bit of behavior.

Once when Great Master Jōshū was at Kannon-in Temple, there was an old woman who sent the Great Master an offering of monetary alms along with a request that he recite the whole of the *Tripitaka*[*] for her.

The Master came down from his meditation seat, circled once around it, and then turned to her messenger and said, "I have already finished reciting the *Tripitaka* for her."

The messenger, upon his return, reported this to the old woman. The old woman said, "When I asked him the other day to recite all of the *Tripitaka* for me, why did the venerable monk read only half the Scriptures?"[5]

In speaking of reciting the whole *Tripitaka* or reciting just half of It, it is clear that, for the old woman, the Scriptures were simply 'three scrolls', whereas, for Jōshū, saying that he had already finished reciting the *Tripitaka* showed that his Scripture encompassed the whole of the *Tripitaka*. In sum, as to the plight of reciting the whole *Tripitaka*, there is Jōshū who is circling his meditation seat, there is his meditation seat which is encircling Jōshū, there is Jōshū who is circling Jōshū, and there is his meditation seat which is encircling his meditation seat. Be that as it may, his reciting the whole *Tripitaka* is not just his circling around his meditation seat, nor is it just his meditation seat doing the circling.

Great Master Daizui Shinshō of Ekishū Province was an heir of Meditation Master Chōkei Daian. As in the previous narrative, there was once an old woman who sent the Master an offering of monetary alms along with a request for him to recite the whole of the *Tripitaka* for her.

The Master came down from his meditation seat and circled it once, then, turning to her messenger, said to him, "I have already finished reciting the *Tripitaka* for her."

The messenger, upon his return, reported this to the old woman. The old woman said, "When I asked him the other day to recite all of the *Tripitaka* for me, why did the venerable monk read only half the Scriptures?"

Now, do not focus your inquiry on Daizui's circling his meditation seat, or focus it on the meditation seat's encircling Daizui, as in the previous narrative. It is not just a matter of the perfect roundness of his Fist and Eye; it is his walking in a circle, which has made a circular form. But did the old woman have the Eye to see that, or was she not yet equipped with that Eye? For even though her remark, "He only recited half the

---

5. She is saying, in effect, "Why did he do only half the job?"

Tripitaka," correctly Transmitted what was being stated by Daizui's Fist, she should have said, "When I asked him the other day to recite the *Tripitaka* for me, why did the venerable monk only waste time fooling around?" Had she put the Matter* like this, even accidentally, she would have been an old woman who was equipped with the Eye.

There was once a government official who provided our Founding Ancestor, Great Master Tōzan Ryōkai, with an alms meal and a votive offering of monetary alms, asking the Master if he would read or recite the *Tripitaka* for his benefit.

The Great Master got down from his meditation seat and, turning towards the official, silently nodded his head.[6]

The official nodded his head to the Great Master.

Leading the official, the Master took both of them around the meditation seat for one circling and then, turning to the official, he nodded his head. After a rather long time, he asked the official, "Did you understand?"

The official answered, "No, I didn't understand."

The Master said, "You and I have read and recited the whole of the *Tripitaka*, so why did you not understand?"

This "You and I have read and recited the whole of the *Tripitaka*" is clear enough. Do not consider their going around the meditation seat as their reading and reciting the *Tripitaka*; do not understand their reading and reciting the *Tripitaka* as their going around the meditation seat. Instead, we should listen to the compassionate instruction of our Founding Ancestor.

---

6. Upon being offered alms by a lay person, a monk customarily performs monjin. That is, he makes a deep bow from the waist, with hands held in the prayer-like gasshō position. The nod spoken of here and later in the text refers to a slight nodding of the head, with the hands usually held in shashu. The head nod was used as a simple form of greeting or acknowledgment whilst in the Monks' Hall.

This incident was cited by my late Master, the Old Buddha, when he was residing on Mount Tendō. A Korean donor had presented him with a votive offering of monetary alms along with the request that the whole community recite a Scripture and that the Master give a Dharma talk from his meditation seat. Having finished recounting this story, my late Master drew a large circle in the air with his ceremonial hossu and said, "Today I, Tendō, along with you, have read and recited the whole of the *Tripitaka*." He then laid his hossu to one side and came down from his seat.

We should now study what my late Master said, without comparing it with the sayings of others. Still, in his reading and reciting the whole of the *Tripitaka*, did he use a whole Eye or only half of It? Did what our Founding Ancestor said and what my late Master said involve the use of their Eye or the use of their tongue? And to what extent did they come to use them? Do your utmost to <u>see</u>!

Great Master Igen, our ancient Ancestor of Yakusan Mountain, was in the habit of not permitting his monks to read Scriptures. One day, when he himself was holding a Scripture in his hands and reading it, a monk asked him, "Venerable Monk, you are in the habit of not permitting us to read Scriptures, so why are you reading one?"

The Master replied, "I just want to shield my eyes."

The monk asked, "May I take a lesson from the Venerable Monk and do likewise?"

The Master replied, "If you were to read, it would surely be enough to pierce holes even through the hide of an ox."[7]

The phrase, "I wish to shield my eyes," is what the shielded Eye Itself utters. 'To shield one's Eye' means to forget all about 'eyes' and to forget all about 'Scriptures';

---

7.   In accord with Dōgen's later discussion, what the Master is actually saying is "If you were to truly read—that is, to read with the Eye of wise discernment—you would be able to penetrate the Scripture (the hide) and see Buddha Nature (the Ox) in it.

it means to shield our whole Eye and to shield It completely. It means to open the Eye while we are shielding It, to enliven our Eye within our shielding of It, to enliven our shielding of It within the Eye Itself, to add another eyelid to our eyelids, to make the most of our Eye within our shielding It, and to let the Eye Itself make the most of Its being shielded. Thus, if it is not a Scripture for the Eye, the function of shielding the Eye does not yet exist.

"You would surely pierce through the hide of an ox" refers to the hide of the Whole Ox, and to the whole hide of the Ox, and to making use of the Ox to make a hide. Thus we make hide, flesh, bones, and marrow, along with horns and nostrils, into the living measure of the Ox. When taking a lesson from the venerable monk, the Ox becomes the Eye—this is to be understood as 'shielding the Eye': it is the Eye becoming the Ox.

Meditation Master Yafu Dōsen once said in verse:

> *You may well ask, "Boundless are the merits of offerings*
> *made to the countless Buddhas,*
> *But how can they possibly resemble the merits from*
> *continually reading Their ancient instructions*
> *Whose words are written in ink upon white paper?"*
> *Well, open your eyes and look at what is right in front of*
> *you!*

You need to recognize that the blessings and merit from making offerings to the ancient Buddhas and from reading Their ancient instructions stand shoulder-to-shoulder with each other, and even go beyond blessings and merit. What people call 'ancient instructions' are the inked words written on white paper, but who can understand these as Their Age-old Instruction? You need to train until you thoroughly understand this very principle.

In the monastery of Great Master Ungo Dōyō there was once a monk who was in his quarters chanting a Scripture. The Great Master, from outside the window, asked him, "What Scripture is the acharya* reciting?"

The monk replied, "The *Vimalakirti* * *Scripture.*"

The Master said, "I am not asking you if it is the *Vimalakirti Scripture*. What you are reciting is a Scripture of What!"

Thereupon, this monk gained entry into the Truth.[8]

The Great Master's remark, "What you are reciting is a Scripture of What!" means that what is at the bottom of reciting a text is far beyond all time; it is not something one would want to describe as 'reciting'. The monk had met a poisonous snake along his path.[9] This is why the question of "What Scripture?" manifested before his very eyes. Having met 'such a person',* he could not give him a false answer. This is why he said, "The *Vimalakirti Scripture.*"

Speaking generally, 'to read Scriptures' means that we collect together every single, solitary Ancestor of the Buddha and read a Scripture through their Eye. At this very moment, in a twinkling, the Ancestors of the Buddha become Buddhas, give voice to the Dharma, give voice to Buddha, and do what a Buddha does. If it is not an occasion for this kind of 'reading Scripture', the Head, Face, and Eye of the Buddha's Ancestors do not yet exist for you.

---

8. The Great Master's question and exclamation are translations of the same phrase in the original, but reflect how the monk interpreted them. The monk understood the latter statement as pointing him away from an intellectual understanding of Scripture to That which is the True Source of all Scriptures.

9. That is, the Master's statement pulled the monk up short, as if he were faced with a life-threatening situation.

In the assemblies of present-day Ancestors of the Buddha there are many varied procedures for the reading of Scriptures, such as when a donor comes to the monastery and asks the whole community to read a Scripture, or when the monks read a Scripture for someone's benefit on a regular basis, or when monks read them voluntarily, and so forth. Besides these, there is the reading of Scriptures by the whole community for the benefit of some deceased monk.

In the case of a donor coming to the monastery and asking the whole community to read a Scripture, at breakfast time on the appointed day, the Chief of the Monks' Hall hangs up 'Reading of Scriptures' signs in front of the Monks' Hall and at the various private quarters. After breakfast, a bowing mat is spread out before the Saintly Monk.[10] At the appropriate time, the bell before the Monks' Hall is rung either once or three times, in accordance with the instructions of the Abbot. At the sound of the bell, the Chief Junior and the whole community put on their kesas,* enter the Cloud Hall, go to their regular places, and sit facing outwards. Next, the Abbot enters the hall, makes monjin* to the Saintly Monk and, after offering incense, sits in his own place. The novices are then instructed to distribute copies of the Scripture. These Scriptures had been arranged in the proper order earlier in the Kitchen Hall so as to be ready for distribution at the proper time. The Scriptures are distributed from inside a Scripture box or put on a tray and distributed from there. Once the members of the community have asked for a copy the Scripture, they then open It and begin their reading of It.

At this time, the Guestmaster leads the donor into the Cloud Hall. The donor, having procured a hand-held censer just outside the Cloud Hall, holds it aloft and enters the hall. The hand-held censer is stored in the common area by the entrance to the kitchen. It has been filled with incense beforehand, and a temple helper is asked to bring it to the front of the Cloud Hall and give it to the donor when the latter

---

10. The Saintly Monk in the Monks' Hall usually alludes to the picture or statue of Manjushri, who represents spiritual wisdom, although in some Chinese monasteries the figure is of Hōtei, the Laughing Buddha.

prepares to enter the hall upon being summoned. The request for the hand-held censer is made by the Guestmaster. When entering the hall, the Guestmaster goes first, followed by the donor. They enter by the south side of the front entrance to the Cloud Hall. The donor goes up before the Saintly Monk, offers a pinch of incense, and makes three bows. He or she does these bows while holding on to the censer. During the bows, the Guestmaster stands to the north of the bowing mat, hands in shashu,* and faces south towards the donor. Once the donor has finished bowing, he or she turns to the right and, facing the Abbot, holds the censer aloft and, bending from the waist, makes a nodding motion with the head. The Abbot, still in his seat, holds the Scripture aloft with his hands in gasshō* in acknowledgment of the donor's nod. The donor then turns to the north and nods. Once the nodding is finished, the hall is circumambulated, starting from in front of the Chief Junior. During the circumambulating of the hall, the Guest Master goes first, leading the donor. Having done one round of circumambulating, they return in front of the Saintly Monk where the donor, facing the Saintly Monk, holds the censer aloft and does a nod. At this time, the Guestmaster, hands in shashu, stands just inside the entrance to the Cloud Hall, south of the bowing mat, facing northwards. Having finished the nodding to the Saintly Monk, the donor follows the Guestmaster out to the front of the Cloud Hall, where they circumambulate the area in front of the hall once, then reenter the Cloud Hall. Facing the Saintly Monk, the donor does three bows. When the bows are finished, the donor sits in a ceremonial folding chair and witnesses the reading of the Scripture. The folding chair is placed near the pillar left of the Saintly Monk and facing south. It may also be placed near the south pillar and facing north. When the donor has been seated, the Guestmaster should turn towards the donor and nod, and then take his own place. Alternatively, while the donor is circumambulating the hall, the Scripture may be chanted in Sanskrit. The seats for those who are chanting may be to the right of the Saintly Monk or to the left of the Saintly Monk, whichever is convenient.

Aloes or some other pure incense is inserted and burned in the censer. This incense is supplied by the donor.

While the donor is circumambulating the hall, the monks in the assembly hold their hands in gasshō.

Next, the monetary donation for the reading of Scriptures is distributed among the monks. The amount of the donation is at the discretion of the donor. Sometimes, objects like cotton cloth or fans are handed out. The donor himself may hand them out, or some temple officer or helper may do so.

The method for distributing these offerings is to place the donation in front of the monk, not to place it in the monk's hand. When a donation is placed before the assembled monks, each monk in turn acknowledges it with hands held in gasshō. Alternatively, donations may be distributed at that day's midday meal. When they are distributed at the midday meal, after the Chief Junior has made the offering of the donor's food, he strikes his clappers once more and distributes any other alms the donor may be offering.

The donor will have written out on paper the purpose for which he is dedicating the merit of his alms, and this paper will have been affixed on the pillar to the right of the Saintly Monk.

When we are reading a Scripture in the Cloud Hall, we do not read It with a loud voice, but with a low one. Sometimes we simply open the Scripture book and look at the words, reading the text with our eyes word by word, without reading It in phrases. For the reading of Scriptures at such a time, there are hundreds of thousands of copies stored for common use, such as copies of the *Scripture on the Diamond-like Wisdom*, the "Universal Gate" chapter and "The Conduct That Eases the Way" chapter from the *Lotus Scripture*, and the *Golden Light Scripture*. Each monk reads one scroll. When the reading of Scriptures is finished, the temple assistants pass in front of the seats, carrying the original tray or the Scripture box, and each monk in the assembly replaces the Scripture there. When taking and replacing Scriptures, we make gasshō. When we are taking a scroll, we make gasshō first and then take a scroll. When we are replacing a scroll, we first place it and then make gasshō. After this, each monk, with hands in gasshō, recites the Transfer of Merit verse in a low voice.

When there is a reading of Scriptures in a hall that is open to the general public, one of the managerial officers of the monastery offers incense, makes bows, circumambulates the hall, and distributes alms donations, all just as a donor would do. The hand-held censer is also held aloft in the same way that a donor would. If the donor who is requesting the assembly to do a reading is someone from within the monastic assembly, the procedure is the same as for a lay donor: there will be an incense offering, bows, a circumambulating of the hall, a distributing of donations, and so forth. The Guestmaster will lead this monk in the same way that he would lead a lay donor.

It is customary to read Scriptures in celebration of the Imperial Birthday. If the Imperial Birthday is celebrated on the fifteenth day of the first lunar month, we begin reading the Scriptures on the fifteenth day of the twelfth lunar month. On that day there is no Abbatical lecture in the Monks' Hall. Two rows of meditation platforms are set up in front of the statue of Shakyamuni Buddha in the Buddha Hall. That is, the platforms are set out facing each other east and west, with each platform running from south to north. Special stands are set up in front of these platforms. On these stands we place the Scriptures—the *Scripture on the Diamond-like Wisdom*, the *Scripture on the Two Lords*, the *Lotus Scripture*, the *Scripture on the Supreme Lord*, the *Golden Light Scripture*, and the like. Each day, a few monks from among those in the Monks' Hall are invited to partake of refreshments well before the time of the midday meal. A bowl of noodles and a cup of hot soup are served to each monk. Or each may receive six or seven steamed dumplings and a serving of hot soup. The dumplings are served in their own bowl and are eaten with chopsticks, not with a soupspoon. While eating, the monks partake of these refreshments in their sitting place for reading Scriptures; they do not sit anywhere else. The refreshments are arranged on the stand for holding the Scriptures; a separate table is not provided. While the monks are consuming their refreshments, the Scriptures remain on the stand. When they have finished their refreshments, the monks leave their seats to rinse out their mouths and then return to their sitting places. They then begin reading the Scriptures. They read the Scriptures from after breakfast until the time of the midday meal. At the three drummings that signal the midday meal, they rise from their sitting places. The daily reading of the Scriptures is limited to the period before the midday meal.

On the first day, a yellow signboard reading "Training Ground Established in Celebration of the Imperial Birthday" is hung under the eaves on the east side of the front of the Buddha Hall. Also, a yellow placard on which is written the intention of celebrating the Imperial Birthday is hung on the east pillar at the front of the Buddha Hall. The Abbot writes his name on a small piece of red or white paper; its two characters are written on the paper, which is then pasted on the face of the placard beneath the date. The Scripture reading continues in the manner previously described until the day of the Imperial Birthday, when the Abbot gives a lecture in the Monks' Hall in celebration. This is a custom from ancient times, one that is not out-of-date today.

Further, there is the Scripture reading that a monk does on his own. From the first, temples and monasteries have had a public hall for reading Scriptures. It is in this hall that a monk reads the Scriptures. The procedure for doing so is as given in the *Book of Rules and Regulations.*

Great Master Igen, our founding Ancestor of Yakusan Mountain, once asked the novice monk Kō, "Did you come to realize the Truth through reading some Scripture or through requesting your Master's personal instruction?"

The novice Kō replied, "I did not come to realize It through reading Scriptures or through requesting personal instruction."

The Master said, "There are many people who do not read Scriptures or seek instruction, so how come they have not realized It?"

The novice Kō replied, "I do not say that they do not have It. Simply, they have not dared to let themselves experience It."

In the house of the Buddhas and Ancestors, there are those who let themselves experience It and those who do not. Even so, reading Scriptures and seeking instruction are the common tools of our everyday life.

Delivered to the assembly at Kannondōri in Kōshōhōrin-ji Temple on the fifteenth day of the ninth lunar month in the autumn of the second year of the Ninji era (October 21, 1241).

Copied by me in the attendant monk's quarters at Daibutsu-ji Monastery in Yoshida Prefecture,
*   Echizen Province, on the eighth day of the seventh lunar month in the third year of*
*   the Kangen era (August 1, 1245).*

Ejō

21

On Buddha Nature

(Busshō)

Translator's Introduction: In the present discourse, Dōgen explores the multidimensional meanings of Buddha Nature. His discussion centers on two seemingly contradictory statements, namely, that all sentient beings have Buddha Nature and that all sentient beings lack a Buddha Nature. Confusion as to what these two statements are pointing to can easily arise because of the ambiguity of the Japanese verbs *u* and *mu*. The former term may mean 'to have', 'to possess', 'to be in possession of', 'to be possessed of', 'there is', 'there are', or '*X* exists'. The latter term functions to deny or negate the preceding, and it also supplies extended meanings such as 'to lack', 'to be devoid of', and 'to be beyond'. What Dōgen asserts—as do the Masters whom he quotes—is essentially that no sentient being is devoid of Buddha Nature and no sentient being possesses a thing called 'a Buddha Nature'. Further, as Dōgen also asserts, based on a line from a verse by Shakyamuni Buddha, all sentient beings have Buddha Nature through and through; that is, they are inseparable from Buddha Nature, are completely possessed of Buddha Nature, and indeed <u>are</u> Buddha Nature.

Along with the verse by Shakyamuni Buddha, Dōgen builds his discourse upon a number of kōan stories, each of which illustrates some way in which Buddha Nature has been either correctly or erroneously understood.

Shakyamuni Buddha said in verse:

All sentient beings have Buddha Nature through and through,
And the Tathagata continually dwells therein, ever constant.

This is the Lion's roar of our great Master, the Venerable Shakyamuni: it turns the Wheel of the Dharma, and, at the same time, it is the very skull and eyeballs of all Buddhas and all ancestral Masters. As of the second year of the Japanese Ninji era (1241), for two thousand one hundred and ninety years now, it has been explored through one's training with a Master. Genuine heirs down to my Master have resided in It and have been grounded in It for fifty generations—twenty-eight in India and twenty-three in China.[1] Buddhas and Ancestors everywhere are no different.

And what would be the principle underlying the World-honored One's words, "All sentient beings have Buddha Nature through and through?" "It is That which manifests just so," as Enō put it in turning the Wheel of the Dharma. We call It 'a sentient being' or 'whatever has feelings' or 'every living being' or 'every manner of being'. The phrase 'to have It through and through' refers to 'sentient beings', that is, to all beings having existence. Accordingly, it is Buddha Nature that one has through and through, and any instance of 'having It through and through' we call 'a sentient being'. At such a time, what sentient beings experience as existing both within and outside themselves will, therefore, be their 'having Buddha Nature through and through'. It goes beyond the Skin and Flesh, Bones and Marrow that are directly Transmitted from Master to disciple, one-to-one, because one has already acquired the Master's Skin and Flesh, Bones and Marrow.

You need to realize right now that the existence which is had through and through by Buddha Nature is beyond the existence of 'existing versus not existing'. 'Having It through and through' is the Buddha's term. It is the Tongue of Buddhas. It is the Eye of the Buddhas and Ancestors. It is the Nose of mendicant monks.

The phrase 'having It through and through', moreover, does not mean that one began having It at some moment, or that one had It to start with, or that one has It as some strange and mysterious thing, much less that one has It conditionally or arbitrarily. It has nothing to do with, say, 'the sphere of the mind' or 'the characteristics of one's true nature'. Hence, the external conditions and internal propensities of a sentient being's 'having It through and through' are beyond any influence from accumulations of past karma,* beyond anything that arises arbitrarily or conditionally, beyond anything that depends on thoughts or things that arise, beyond any spiritual power, and beyond any training done in order to experience the Truth. If the 'having It through and through' of sentient beings was based on past karma, or was the arising

---

1.   Bodhidharma is counted as both the twenty-eighth Indian Ancestor and the first Chinese Ancestor.

*   See Glossary.

of some set of conditions, or the spontaneous arising of some thought or thing, then the path to awakening of all the saintly, the enlightenment of all the Buddhas, and the Eye of the Buddhas and Ancestors would be based on an accumulation of past karma, or would be the occurrence of some set of conditions, or the spontaneous arising of some thought or thing. But this is not the case. The whole realm of one's being is completely devoid of any defilements coming from without. Moreover, in an instant, there is no 'second person'.[2] But people are not apt to be concerned, straight off, with cutting the roots of the defiling passions that they are afflicted with, for when does their ever-busy consciousness come to rest?

Buddha Nature is not the existence of something that arises arbitrarily or conditionally, for the whole realm of our being—which is Buddha Nature—is never hidden from us. But saying that the whole realm of our being is never hidden from us is not necessarily the same as saying that our physical world is what existence really is. The statement "The whole realm of my being is something that I possess" constitutes a false view of non-Buddhists. Buddha Nature is not the existence of something that one possesses at the start, for It pervades both our past and our present. It is not the existence of something that has arisen for the first time, for It does not partake of a single bit of illusory dust. It is not the existence of some particular being, for It encompasses all beings. It is not the existence of something that is beyond having a beginning, for It is something that makes Its appearance just in the way that It does. It is not the existence of something that has just come into being for the first time, for our ordinary, ever-present mind is synonymous with the Way.

Above all, you need to know that within this 'having It through and through', sentient beings do not readily find an easy or pleasant way to encounter It. When you understand 'having It through and through' in this manner, to have It through and through then means to penetrate Its very substance and to let all our notions and opinions about It drop off.

---

2. That is, upon one's spiritually awakening to Buddha Nature, the distinction of 'self and other' disappears.

Upon hearing the term 'Buddha Nature', many practitioners have erroneously surmised It to be the same as the non-Buddhist 'innate eternal self' of the Shrenikans.[3] This is because they have not yet become 'such a person',* or are not in accord with their True Self, or have not met with a genuine Master. To no avail, they take their mind, will, or consciousness, which are constantly on the move like wind and fire, to be their perception and comprehension of their Buddha Nature. Who has ever said that there is anything within Buddha Nature to perceive or comprehend? Even though persons who have perceived and comprehended It are Buddhas, Buddha Nature is beyond any thing we perceive or comprehend. Even more, the perception that leads us to recognize Buddhas as persons who have discerned It and know It is not perception as some people have erroneously explained it, for this perception lies beyond the realm of their mind, which is ever-moving like wind and fire. Simply put, a couple of faces of a Buddha or an Ancestor are what we perceive It to be.

In the long past, from the Chinese Han and T'ang dynasties down through the Sung dynasty, the virtuous monks of long ago sprang up like rice and hemp, bamboo and reeds. Having gone to India and returned, they taught the Way to both ordinary people and those in loftier positions. Sad to say, many believed that their mind's moving like wind and fire was their enlightened consciousness of Buddha Nature. Even though such persons were negligent in their exploration of the Way, their faulty remarks persist today. Present-day trainees and novices of the Buddha's Way should not be like them. Even though you may be exploring what enlightened perception is, one thing it is not is the mind's constant moving like wind and fire. And even though you explore its constant movement, this movement is not what It really is. If you have a realization of That which really moves, you will realize what true perception and comprehension are.

Buddha, being at one with Buddha Nature, is encountered everywhere, be it here or be it there. Buddha Nature is invariably what we have through and through,

---

3.   Dōgen discusses the Shrenikan view in Discourse 6: On 'Your Very Mind Is Buddha' (*Soku Shin Ze Butsu*)

for That which we have through and through is Buddha Nature. What we have through and through is not a fragment of something that has been smashed into hundreds of bits, nor is It something as undifferentiated as a bar of solid iron. This is why a Master brandishes his fist to show It. It is beyond being large or small. What we have been calling 'Buddha Nature' is not to be equated with 'the saintly', nor, indeed, is it to be equated with Buddha Nature Itself.

There is a certain view which likens Buddha Nature to the seeds of plants and trees. When the rain of the Dharma pours down and moistens the seeds, they sprout and send forth shoots, then branch out and produce leaves, flowers, and fruit, with the fruit, in turn, becoming pregnant with seeds. To view and explain It in this manner is due to the sentimental thinking of ordinary people who wander through life in ignorance. Even though they view and explain It in this manner, you should investigate thoroughly through your training that each and every seed, along with each and every flower and fruit, is the product of an honest and sincere heart. There are seeds within the fruit, and even though the seeds are not visible, they will produce such things as roots and shoots. Even when left on their own, they become trees thick with branches large and small. Buddha Nature is beyond discussion of Its being something within or outside them, for nothing is devoid of It at any time, past or present. Thus, even though you put your trust in the view of such ordinary people, the roots, sprouts, branches, and leaves are alike in being born, alike in dying away, and alike in having It through and through.

The Buddha said, "If you wish to grasp the meaning of 'Buddha Nature', just look at the conditions associated with the moment. Then, when the right moment arrives, Buddha Nature will manifest before your very eyes." Now, the statement, "If you wish to grasp the meaning of 'Buddha Nature'" does not simply mean having knowledge of It. Rather, it is tantamount to saying, "If you want to put It into practice, if you want to experience It directly, if you want to 'see' It," or even "If you want to get the thought of It out of your mind." And this giving voice to It, putting It into practice, experiencing It directly, dropping off thoughts of whether one is accurate or inaccurate about It, and so forth, are conditions associated with the moment. In contemplating the conditions associated with the moment, we contemplate by means of the conditions associated with the moment. It is our doing mutual contemplation by means of hossu* and traveling staff,* for instance.[4] Further, we cannot do our contemplation by employing intellectual discernment that is tainted with defiling passions or that is free of defiling passions, or by employing discernment derived from our original awakened state or from our first awakening, or by employing discernment derived from our not yet having awakened or from our having genuinely awakened. The Buddha's saying "just look" does not depend on our being able to look or on what we look at. What "just look" refers to is unconnected with such matters as 'genuine contemplation' and 'false contemplation'. Because it is 'just looking', it is not looking at ourselves or looking at anything else. It is pointing to the conditions of the moment and it is transcending the conditions of the moment: it is pointing to Buddha Nature and it is letting go of any concept of 'Buddha Nature'. It is Buddha pointing to Buddha: it is True Nature pointing to True Nature.

As to the phrase 'when the right moment arrives', folks in both the past and the present have frequently held the view that this means one simply waits for some future time when Buddha Nature will manifest before one's eyes. They believe that while doing their training and practice in this way, the time will arrive when Buddha Nature will spontaneously manifest before their eyes. They say that until that time comes, It will not manifest even by visiting one's Master and inquiring into the Dharma or even by doing one's best to practice the Way. Looking at the Matter* in this manner, they uselessly return to worldly ways, vainly waiting for It to fall down upon them from the heavens. Folks like this, I fear, are that type of non-Buddhist who believes that things just happen to happen, independent of any cause.

The Buddha's statement, "If you wish to grasp the meaning of 'Buddha Nature,'" was His way of saying, "If you want to know the meaning of 'Buddha Nature' here and now." His statement, "Just look at the conditions associated with the moment," was His way of saying, "Just discern what the conditions at this moment

---

4. The hossu and the traveling staff were often employed by Masters in various ways to point their disciples toward realizing Buddha Nature.

are." You need to realize that His saying "If you wish to know Buddha Nature" is synonymous with the conditions at the moment.

And as to His saying "When the right moment arrives," the moment has already arrived, so where is there room for doubt? Even if we should have doubts about whether it is the right moment, this is still Buddha Nature coming forth in us. You need to realize that the phrase "when the right moment arrives" means that we should not idle away any moment within a day. His saying "when it arrives" is as if He had said, "It has already come." When we get all involved with 'when the time comes', Buddha Nature does not come before us. Hence, since the time has already come, this is "Buddha Nature manifesting before our very eyes." In other words, the truth of It is self-evident. In sum, there has not yet been a time when the right moment has not come, nor is there a Buddha Nature which is not Buddha Nature manifesting before our very eyes right now.

The Twelfth Indian Ancestor, Venerable Ashvaghosa, in describing the Ocean of Buddha Nature for the sake of the Thirteenth Ancestor, once said:

> *The great earth with its mountains and rivers*
> *Takes all its various forms completely in accord with It,*
> *And deep meditative states and the six spiritual powers*
> *Manifest themselves because of It.*

Accordingly, this great earth with all its mountains and rivers <u>is</u> the Ocean of Buddha Nature. To say that It takes all its various forms completely in accord with It means that, at such time as this materialization takes place, It is the great earth with its mountains and rivers. In his having said that the earth takes all its various forms in accord with It, you should realize that the form of the Ocean of Buddha Nature is like this. Further, It is not something to be associated with being inside, or outside, or in the midst of It. Since this is the way things are, to look at mountains and rivers is to look at Buddha Nature, and to see Buddha Nature is to see the jaw of a donkey and the muzzle of a horse.[5] To assert that the phrase 'completely in accord with It' means 'totally in accord with It' or that it means 'being in accord with It in Its totality' is to understand the term and not to understand It.

As to the lines, "And deep meditative states and the six spiritual powers manifest themselves because of It," you need to understand that one's manifesting or not yet manifesting deep meditative states is all in accord with Buddha Nature. The dependence of all six spiritual powers upon It and their non-dependence upon It is 'all in accord with Buddha Nature'. These six spiritual powers are not simply the six spiritual powers spoken of in the *Āgama Scriptures*. 'Six' is another way of saying that the phrase 'three and three in front, and three and three behind'[6] is the perfection of the six spiritual powers.[7] So, do not spend your time in studying that the six spiritual powers are 'the hundreds of things that sprout up in your head ever so clearly' or that they are 'whatever so obviously motivates the Buddhas and Ancestors'. Even though the six spiritual powers may seem enticing, they are something that can create a hindrance to one's immersion in the Ocean of Buddha Nature.

The Fifth Chinese Ancestor, Meditation Master Daiman Kōnin, was a native of Ōbai in Kishū Province. His father had died before he was born. He realized the Way whilst still a child and, as a practitioner of the Way, spent his life cultivating pine trees.

While planting pine trees on Mount Saizan in Kishū, he happened to meet the Fourth Ancestor, who was traveling through the area. The latter told him, "I would like to Transmit the Dharma to you, but you are already too old. If you would wait

---

5. 'To see a donkey's jaw and a horse's muzzle' is a traditional Zen Buddhist phrase for discerning concrete particulars without any taint of discriminatory judgment.

6. A classical Zen Buddhist phrase for an indefinite number of things or persons, 'three' meaning 'any number more than two'.

7. 'The perfection of the six spiritual powers' can be understood as a reference to the marvelous spiritual powers which Dōgen takes up in Discourse 24: On the Marvelous Spiritual Abilities *(Jinzū)*.

until your return in some other lifetime, I will still be looking for you." The forester consented to this.

Later, he went with the unmarried daughter of a family in the Shū clan and was reborn through her. In consequence of her not being married, she cast her baby into a muddy creek. Divine beings protected him, and even after seven days he remained unharmed. As a result, she picked him up and nurtured him.[8]

He was a child of just seven years when he encountered the Fourth Ancestor, Meditation Master Daii Dōshin, on the road to Ōbai. The Ancestor saw that, even though he was a small boy, he was strikingly handsome and in no way ordinary looking.

> The Ancestor greeted him, saying, "What is your family name?"
>
> The boy answered, "Although I have a family name, it is not a conventional family name."
>
> When the Ancestor asked, "And what is this name?" he replied, "It is Buddha Nature."[9]
>
> The Ancestor said, "You do not have Buddha Nature."
>
> The boy replied, "Because Buddha Nature is devoid of anything that can be possessed, you therefore say that I do not have It."

---

8. Dōgen's account of Daiman Kōnin's past life as a forester and his subsequent birth, abandonment, and rescue by his mother is quite truncated. A fuller and clearer account is given by Meditation Master Keizan in his *Denkōroku* (Shasta Abbey Press, 1993), pp. 165-167.

9. There is an untranslatable play on words in this passage: the spoken Chinese word hsing can mean not only 'family name' but also, when written with a different character, it means '[one's Innate] Nature' and '[one's True] Nature'. Thus, when the dialogue is seen from the boy's perspective, he is, in effect, making a spiritual response to the conventional Chinese inquiry as to someone's family name (to ask someone's personal name is considered impolite). Dōgen later explores the subtler meanings of this dialogue when seen from the perspective of the Fourth Ancestor.

Realizing the boy's capacity for training, the Ancestor asked his parent to let the boy leave home and come into the monastic family as his personal attendant. Because of the karma and circumstances of his parent, there was no particular impediment, so he abandoned lay life and became the Ancestor's disciple. Later, the Ancestor passed on to him the Treasure House of the Eye of the True Teaching. He took up residence on the Eastern Mountain at Ōbai, where he greatly displayed the profound Principle.

Accordingly, when we thoroughly examine the statements of these Ancestral Masters, there is a profound meaning underlying the Fourth Ancestor's words, "What is your family name?" Long ago, there was a person who described himself as "a native of the country of What," and there was another who gave as his name "the family name of What." Here, the Ancestor is making a statement, "Your family name is What." [10] It was, for instance, like Enō stating to Nangaku, "I am 'just like This' and you are also 'just like This.'"

When the boy responded, "Although I have a family name, it is not a conventional family name," he was saying, "The name that I have is not a conventional name, since a conventional name would not be correct for That which I have." In the Fourth Ancestor's saying, "What is this name?" the term 'What' means This, for he had already made his This the What, which is Its name. [11] Our realizing the What is due to the This, and our realizing the This is a functioning of the What. Its 'name' is both This and What. We should make the This into our mugwort tea or our green tea; indeed, we should treat It as our everyday food and drink.

---

10. That is, one's True Nature is beyond any name we can give It, but for convenience It was referred to by some Zen Masters as 'What'.

11. The term 'This' was often used by Zen Masters to designate a direct pointing to That which goes beyond naming, that is, the 'What'. At the same time, the concrete This and the indescribable What are not separate; in other words, the This is the What.

The deeper meaning behind the boy's saying, "It is Buddha Nature," is that the 'It' refers to 'Buddha Nature'.[12] Due to the What, one is Buddha. Were we to take his 'it' to a deeper level than just a response to "What is your family name?" then, at the time when his 'It' was no longer an 'it', It referred to 'Buddha Nature'. Thus, even though his 'It' refers to the What and refers to Buddha, when he came to drop everything off and realize the Truth, It was certainly his family name. That family name of his, accordingly, was the same as Shū would be. Even so, he did not receive It from his father or from his grandfather, nor was It like his mother's clan name, so how can It possibly be equated with the name of some third party?

To clarify the Fourth Ancestor's remark, "You do not have Buddha Nature," he is saying, in effect, "You are not It, and even though you put your trust in It, you do not possess Buddha Nature." You must comprehend this and explore it through your training, for when is it that someone does not have Buddha Nature? Does someone lack Buddha Nature upon starting out towards Buddhahood? Does someone lack Buddha Nature upon having gone beyond realizing Buddhahood? Do not become preoccupied with seven different ways of going, and do not go blindly groping for It in eight different directions.[13] And one can learn in training that 'not having Buddha Nature' is, on some occasions, a meditative state. You should ask whether the time when Buddha Nature realizes Buddhahood is a time of 'not having Buddha Nature', and whether the time when Buddha Nature gives rise to the intention to realize Buddhahood is also a time of 'not having Buddha Nature'. You should have the pillars* of the temple ask you, and you should ask the pillars of the temple, and you should have Buddha Nature ask.

Thus, the phrase 'not having Buddha Nature' is something that could be heard, long ago, coming from the quarters of the Fourth Ancestor. It was heard about from Kōnin, it was put into circulation by Jōshū, and it was promoted by Isan. By all

---

12. The common classical Chinese word *shih* has a double meaning: '[it] is' and 'this [is]'. In this translation, when the word is referring to Buddha Nature, it is rendered as either 'It' or 'This', depending on which seems smoother in context.

13. That is, you do not need to seek Buddha Nature far and wide, because It is everywhere at all times.

means, concentrate on the words 'not having Buddha Nature' and do not fall into stagnation. Even though you should certainly trace your way back to 'not having Buddha Nature', you have Its measure (which is the What), you have Its moment in time (which is you), you have Its correspondence (which is the This), and you have the same family name as It (which is Shū), for all these directly point to It.

When the boy said, "Because Buddha Nature is devoid, you therefore say that It is beyond existence," [14] he had put it clearly, for 'being devoid' does not mean 'being nothing'. When he stated that Buddha Nature is devoid, he did not say that It is half a pound or that It is eight ounces, as some Masters have done: he uses the term 'beyond existence'. Since It is devoid, he does not say that It is empty, and since It is beyond existence, he does not say that It is nothing: he says that since Buddha Nature is devoid, It is beyond existence. [15] Thus, when 'beyond existence' is said, this is a means of expressing Its being devoid, and 'being devoid' is a means of expressing Its being beyond existence. The 'being devoid' of which he speaks is not the 'being empty' in the statement from the *Heart Scripture* that "Material form is the same as being empty." Although in the statement, "Material form is the same as being empty," material form is not being forced into becoming empty, and emptiness is not being split up to manufacture material form, the 'being devoid' of which he spoke is that of 'being devoid is what emptiness means'. The 'being devoid' of 'being devoid is what emptiness means' is synonymous with Master Sekisō Keisho's calling it "a stone in space." So, this is how the Fourth and Fifth Ancestors inquired into and talked about

---

14. In the following passage, context suggests that Dōgen is shifting his discussion of the word   meaning 'not having', from being devoid of anything that one can possess to not having existence in the sense of not being subject to arising, persisting, undergoing change, and disappearing. In order to help the reader in making this shift, this sentence has been retranslated from what was quoted earlier to bring out this double meaning of the term mu, which would otherwise be lost in translation.

15. In other words, Buddha Nature does not exist in the ordinary sense of 'existing'—that is, being subject to change, as thoughts and things are—and is therefore described as 'beyond existence'.

the non-possessing of Buddha Nature, about the emptiness of Buddha Nature, and about the existence of Buddha Nature.

When the Sixth Chinese Ancestor, Meditation Master Daikan Enō of Mount Sōkei, first went to train on Mount Ōbai, the Fifth Ancestor asked him, "Where have you come from?"

Enō replied, "I am a native from south of the Peaks." [16]

The Fifth Ancestor then asked, "What is it that you seek in coming here?"

Enō replied, "I am seeking to become a Buddha."

The Fifth Ancestor said, "People from south of the Peaks do not possess Buddha Nature, so how can you become a Buddha?"

In the Fifth Ancestor's saying that people from south of the Peaks do not possess Buddha Nature, he is not saying that people from south of the Peaks lack Buddha Nature, nor is he saying that people from south of the Peaks have a Buddha Nature: he means that people from south of the Peaks do not possess a Buddha Nature.[17] His saying, "How can you become a Buddha?" means "What sort of Buddha are you hoping to become?"

Generally speaking, senior monks who have clarified the principle of Buddha Nature are few. It is not something that you can learn from any of the *Āgama Scriptures* or from academic teachers of Scriptural texts and writers of erudite commentaries. It is something passed on directly, one-to-one, only to the descendants of the Buddhas and Ancestors.

The underlying principle of Buddha Nature is not that Buddha Nature is perfectly fulfilled before one has realized Buddhahood, but that It is perfectly fulfilled after realizing Buddhahood. Unquestionably, Buddha Nature is in complete harmony with realizing Buddhahood. You need to make a great effort indeed to explore this

---

16. That is, from southeast China.

17. That is, Buddha Nature is not something one can possess since It is not something apart from or less than oneself.

through your training, and you may need to explore it diligently for ten, twenty, or even thirty years. And it is not something that those 'thrice wise and ten times saintly' * have clarified. To state that sentient beings have Buddha Nature and that sentient beings do not possess a Buddha Nature is to state this very principle. And the correct way for you to proceed is to explore through your training that this principle is the Teaching that Buddha Nature will be fully perfected from the moment of your realizing Buddhahood and beyond. What you do not explore in this way will not be the Buddha Dharma. If you do not do your exploring in this way, you cannot hope to arrive at the Buddha Dharma this very day. If you do not clarify what this principle is, you will not clarify what realizing Buddhahood is, nor will you hear of Its existence. This is why the Fifth Ancestor, in addressing the one facing him, made the remark that people from south of the Peaks do not possess Buddha Nature. In encountering a Buddha and hearing His Dharma for the very first time, what is hard to come by and difficult to hear about is that all sentient beings lack a Buddha Nature.[18] Whether you are following a good spiritual friend or following a Scriptural text, what you should take delight in hearing about is that sentient beings do not possess a Buddha Nature. Someone who does not come and participate in learning about and comprehending that all sentient beings lack a Buddha Nature is someone who has not yet learned about or comprehended what Buddha Nature is. In that Enō was wholeheartedly seeking to become Buddha, the Fifth Ancestor said nothing else, nor did he employ any other skillful means to facilitate Enō's realizing Buddhahood. He simply said, "People from south of the Peaks do not possess Buddha Nature." You need to realize that to say and to hear that one does not possess Buddha Nature is the straight path to realizing Buddhahood. So, the very moment that people go beyond 'possessing Buddha Nature' will be the very moment that they realize Buddhahood. Those who have not yet learned of going beyond 'possessing Buddha Nature' have not yet realized Buddhahood.

---

18.   That is, they lack a Buddha Nature because they are Buddha Nature through and through.

After becoming the Sixth Ancestor, Enō once said, "For human beings, there is a north and a south; for Buddha Nature, there is no north or south." Being presented with this statement, you should work hard on understanding the meaning of this expression. You should reflect on the phrase 'north or south' with an open mind, for there is a deeper meaning in the expression that the Sixth Ancestor has given us. Namely, there is a way of taking it to mean that, even though people may realize Buddhahood, Buddha Nature cannot realize Buddhahood. I wonder, did the Sixth Ancestor comprehend this or not?

Long ago, having received a bit of the Teaching that the Fourth and Fifth Ancestors later voiced as 'not possessing Buddha Nature', Kashō Buddha, as well as Shakyamuni Buddha, among others, upon realizing Buddhahood and turning the Wheel of the Dharma, had the ability to state that one has Buddha Nature through and through. This Teaching has the capacity to hold us to just the way things are. So, how could Their 'having It' in 'having It through and through' fail to be Their inheriting of the Dharma that is expressed as 'not possessing It', in which there is no lacking It? Thus, the words 'not possessing Buddha Nature' could be heard long ago in the quarters of the Fourth and Fifth Ancestors. If, at that time, the Sixth Ancestor was indeed 'such a person', then we should work diligently on the words, 'not possessing Buddha Nature'.

Putting aside the 'not having' implied by 'possessing versus non-possessing', we should ask, "What is Buddha Nature?" That is, we should inquire into what sort of thing Buddha Nature is. People nowadays, upon hearing of Buddha Nature, do not ask, "What is Buddha Nature?" Instead, they concern themselves with matters like whether someone does or does not have a Buddha Nature. This is a shallow way of going about the Matter. So, among the various meanings of 'not having', we need to explore 'not having' in the sense of 'there not being Buddha Nature'. Again and again, we should try to fish out what is meant by the Sixth Ancestor's statement, "For human beings, there is a north and a south; for Buddha Nature, there is no north or south," for we doubtless have the ability to wield a fishhook. We need to calmly take up <u>and</u> not hold onto the words, "For people, there is a north and a south; for Buddha Nature, there is no north or south," which the Sixth Ancestor uttered. There are some befuddled persons who hold to the following opinion, "Doesn't what the Sixth Ancestor said mean that a north and a south exist for human beings due to their hard-edged physical nature, but since Buddha Nature has no such limitations and is all-pervading, It is beyond any notions of north or south?" To speculate in this way is sheer silliness. You should disregard this false explanation in your diligent exploration of what the Ancestor said.

The Sixth Ancestor, in giving teaching to his disciple, Gyōshō, once said, "Impermanence is, of course, Buddha Nature, and permanence is, in fact, the mind dividing up all things into good or bad." The impermanence of which the Sixth Ancestor spoke is beyond the conjecturing of non-Buddhists and those who follow the Two Lesser Courses.* Although the non-Buddhists and those of the Two Lesser Courses—extending from those persons who founded their traditions up to their most recent descendants—may speak of something being impermanent, it is unlikely that they are able to fully fathom what It is. Thus, for the one who would clarify, put into practice, and fully realize impermanence as being impermanent in itself, all will be impermanence. Those who can help others reach the Other Shore through manifesting their True Self will manifest It and give voice to the Dharma for that purpose: this is Buddha Nature. Further, sometimes they will display the Dharma Body as something tall and sometimes they will display It as something short. What is constantly saintly is impermanent and what is constantly ordinary is impermanent. The view that those who are just ordinary people and not saintly ones, and thus must lack Buddha Nature, is a foolish opinion held by some folks who are small-minded; such a view constitutes a narrow perspective which their intellect has conjectured. For the small-minded, 'Buddha' is a body and 'Nature' is its functioning, which is the very reason why the Sixth Ancestor said, "What is impermanent is, of course, Buddha Nature."

What seems constant has simply not yet undergone change. 'Not yet undergone change' means that, even though we may shift our perspective to our subjective self or shift it to the objective, outer world, in both cases there are no signs of change to be found. In that sense, it is constant.[19] As a consequence, grasses and trees, as well as thickets and forests, are impermanent and, accordingly, they are Buddha Nature. It is the same with the human body and mind, both of which are impermanent and, accordingly, they are Buddha Nature. The mountains and rivers in the various lands are impermanent, so, accordingly, they are Buddha Nature. Supreme, fully perfected enlightenment is Buddha Nature, and hence it is impermanent. The Buddha's great entry into nirvana was impermanent, and hence it is Buddha Nature.

Those of the Two Lesser Courses with limited insight, along with the academic teachers of the Scriptures and writers of erudite commentaries, must surely be appalled, skeptical, frightened, or awed by what the Sixth Ancestor said. Should people become appalled or skeptical, they will be some sort of devilish obstructionists or non-Buddhists.

In India the Fourteenth Indian Ancestor was called the Venerable Nāgārjuna, meaning 'He Who Was Born Under the Tree of the Nāgās', and in T'ang China he was called 'He Who Is a Tree for Dragons' and 'He Who Surpasses the Dragons', as well as 'He Who Is as Fierce as a Dragon'.[20] He was a native of Western India. He went to Southern India, where he gave voice to the Wondrous Dharma for the sake of the people there, since a great many of them believed that happiness was simply a matter of fate.

> Those who heard his Teaching said amongst themselves, "The most important thing in the world is the happiness that people are fated to have. He talks so meaninglessly about some 'Buddha Nature'. Who has been able to see such a thing?"
>
> The Venerable One responded, "If you wish to see Buddha Nature, you must first rid yourself of your arrogant pride."

---

19. That is, the ever-present 'now' is what is constant, even though there is that which we consider to be separate from the 'now', namely, the future and the past.

20. The Sanskrit word *nāgā*, which forms the first part of Nāgārjuna's name, means serpent. When the word came to China, it was translated as dragon.

One of them asked, "Is Buddha Nature larger than I am or smaller?"

The Venerable One replied, "Buddha Nature is neither large nor small, neither vast nor constricted. It is beyond happiness, beyond retribution, for It is undying and unborn." When the person heard these superior principles, he completely turned his mind around.

The Venerable One, whilst still in the Dharma Seat, then revealed himself to be so free of any worldly ways that he looked like the orb of the Moon at Its full. But all those assembled there merely heard the sounds of the Teaching and did not observe the Master's appearance.

One amongst them, however, Kānadaiba by name, the son of a town elder, said to those assembled, "Don't you see his appearance?"

Those in the assembly said, "What we do not see with our eyes or hear with our ears right now does not exist, for it is not something that we can know with our minds or experience with our bodies."

Kānadaiba said, "This is the Venerable One's manifesting his Buddha Nature, by means of which he shows us how we can know It. By being cloaked in It, his meditative state, which is free of attachments, takes on a form resembling the Moon at Its full, for the meaning of 'Buddha Nature' is That which is utterly unbounded and radiant."

Once Kānadaiba had finished speaking, the orb-like look seemed to disappear. Then, whilst still occupying his Dharma Seat, Nāgārjuna spoke in verse, saying:

Through my body, I have manifested the look of the Full Moon,
Thereby displaying the physical presence of all Buddhas.
My voicing of the Dharma has no fixed form,

For Its real functioning is beyond what is said, or how. [21]

You need to realize that the genuine functioning of the Dharma is beyond any immediate display of what is said or how It is put. A genuine voicing of the Dharma has no set form. The Venerable One was ever engaged in giving voice to Buddha Nature far and wide, on innumerable occasions. We have given just one brief example here.

You need to discern and affirm for yourself the underlying meaning of his saying, "If you wish to see Buddha Nature, you must first rid yourself of your arrogant pride." It is not that one lacks sight, but the seeing of which he spoke is based on ridding oneself of one's arrogant pride. The arrogance of self is not just of one kind, and pride takes many forms. Methods for ridding oneself of these will also be diverse and myriad. Even so, all of these methods will be 'one's seeing Buddha Nature'. Thus, you need to learn both to look with your eyes and to see with your Eye.

Do not equate the Master's statement, "Buddha Nature is neither large nor small," with similar words used by those who wander through life in ignorance or by those of the Two Lesser Courses. Those who merely think one-sidedly that Buddha Nature is something vast and enormous are harboring a false notion. Because we make use of what we are hearing as the subject for our consideration, we need to consider Its underlying principle as we hear it here and now, unimpeded by the Master's statement that It is neither large nor small.

Now, let us give ear to the verse that the Venerable One spoke, specifically his lines, "Through my body, I have manifested the look of the Full Moon, thereby displaying the physical presence of all Buddhas." Because the display of the physical presence of all Buddhas is a manifestation of one's Spiritual Body, it has the look of

---

21. The phrase 'the look of the Moon at Its full' in this poem and in subsequent paragraphs refers to the discernible characteristics of one who has fully realized his or her Buddha Nature. In some instances, this phrase is misunderstood and taken literally by persons of worldly mind, in which cases it is rendered as 'the look of a full moon'. Similarly, the term 'body' is used when it refers to the physical body, whereas the term 'Spiritual Body' is used in reference to the spiritual Enlightenment Body, which manifests 'the look of the Moon at Its full'.

the Full Moon. Accordingly, you need to grasp that all manner of tallness and shortness, as well as of squareness and roundness, are manifestations of your Spiritual Body. Those who are ever so ignorant of what this Spiritual Body is and of what manifesting It means are not only in the dark about the look of the Full Moon, they are not displaying the physical presence of all Buddhas. Foolish people fancy that the Venerable One provisionally displayed his body in some altered form, which is described as 'the look of a full moon', but this is an arbitrary and false notion of those who have not had the Buddha's Way Transmitted to them from Master to disciple, for where or when would It possibly manifest as something separate from and independent of one's body? What is important for you to recognize is simply that, at the time, the Venerable One was seated on the raised platform of a Dharma teacher. His body showed itself in the same manner as the body of anyone sitting here now, for this body of ours is, in fact, a manifestation of the Moon at Its full. His manifestation of the Spiritual Body is beyond being something square or round, beyond something existing or not existing, beyond something hidden or revealed, beyond something consisting of eighty-four thousand components: it is simply the manifestation of his Spiritual Body. 'The look of the Full Moon' describes the Moon implied in Fuke's remark, "Right here is where the What is, whether the matter is put clumsily or delicately." [22] Because this manifestation of his Spiritual Body is rid of any arrogant pride, It goes beyond his being Nāgārjuna; It is the physical presence of all Buddhas. Because he displayed It, his Spiritual Body passes through and beyond the physical presence of all Buddhas. Hence, It has no connection with whatever may be on the periphery of the Buddha's Way.

Although there is the Unbounded Radiance which takes some form like 'the Moon of Buddha Nature at Its Full', It is beyond what is commonly construed as 'the look of a full moon'. And what is more, Its real functioning is beyond what is said or how it is put, and the manifestation of this Spiritual Body is beyond the physical and the mental, beyond the realm of the skandhas.* Although It completely resembles the

---

22. This remark appears in one of the stories contained in Dōgen's Chinese Shinji Shōbōgenzō. The full story is translated in the Addendum immediately following this discourse.

realm of the skandhas, It displays Itself by means of them, for this realm is the physical presence of all Buddhas. The Buddhas are the skandhas which give expression to the Dharma; the Unbounded Radiance has no set form. Further, when Its not having any set form is evinced by the meditative state that has no attachments, this is a manifestation of one's Spiritual Body. Even though our whole assembly may desire to see 'the look of the Moon at Its full', this is something one's eyes have never seen before. It is the turning point for the skandhas, which will give voice to the Dharma, and it is the absence of any fixed way in how the Dharma is stated or what form It may take, while the Spiritual Body manifests freely as It will. Its very 'being hidden from sight' and Its very 'being openly displayed' is Its stepping forward and stepping back in a cyclic manner. At the very time when Nāgārjuna's Spiritual Body was manifesting Itself freely as he sat upon his platform, the whole assembly merely heard the words of the Dharma and did not perceive the 'look' of their teacher.

The Venerable Kānadaiba, who was Nāgārjuna's Dharma heir, clearly recognized the Full Moon, the perfection of that Full Moon, the manifestation of Nāgārjuna's Spiritual Body, the look of all Buddhas, and the physical presence of all Buddhas. Although there were many within the assembly who had entered the Master's private quarters and had had the Buddhist Teachings poured into them, none could stand head-and-shoulders with Kānadaiba. Kānadaiba was respected for his Master's sharing the Dharma seat with him, and he functioned as a teacher and guide for the whole assembly, since his partial seat was the whole of the Dharma seat. In that he had had the great, unsurpassed Dharma of the Treasure House of the Eye of the True Teaching authentically Transmitted to him, it was just like the Venerable Makakashō occupying the chief Dharma seat on Vulture Peak.[23]

During the time when he was involved in non-Buddhist teaching, Nāgārjuna had had many disciples. Even so, once he turned his own heart around, he expressed his thanks to them all and disbanded his classes. After Nāgārjuna became an Ancestor of the Buddha, he authentically Transmitted the Treasure House of the Eye of the True Teaching to Kānadaiba, considering him alone to be his true heir. This was the simple,

---

23. A reference to Shakyamuni's sharing His Dharma seat with His Dharma heir, Makakashō, who led the Sangha after the Buddha's parinirvana, thus becoming the First Ancestor.

one-to-one Transmission of the unsurpassed Way of the Buddha. Despite this, groups of pretenders arrogantly boasted, "We too are the Dharma heirs of the great scholar Nāgārjuna." They composed treatises and compiled commentaries, often forging Nāgārjuna's hand. But such are not the works of Nāgārjuna. These masses of followers, whom he had long before dismissed, have confused and corrupted both ordinary persons and those in lofty positions. As disciples of the Buddha, you need to know that whatever was not authentically Transmitted directly to Kānadaiba is not the word and Way of Nāgārjuna. This is the correct belief that will make it possible for you to reach your goal. Even so, there are many who have accepted those spurious works as spiritual nourishment, even while being aware that they were fraudulent. This foolish thickheadedness of human beings who insult great enlightened Wisdom is sad and pitiful indeed.

On the occasion when the Venerable Kānadaiba pointed to the Venerable Nāgārjuna's manifestation of the Spiritual Body, he commented to those assembled there, "This is the Venerable One's manifesting his Buddha Nature, by means of which he shows us how we can know It. By being cloaked in It, his meditative state, which is free of attachments, takes on a form resembling the Moon at Its full, for the meaning of 'Buddha Nature' is That which is utterly unbounded and radiant."

Now, among those skin bags,* past or present, who have heard the Buddha Dharma as It has spread through the heavens above, the world of humans, and the great thousandfold worlds that comprise the universe, which of them has said that the look of someone manifesting his or her Spiritual Body is what Buddha Nature is? Throughout the great universe, the Venerable Kānadaiba alone has stated it. The rest have merely asserted that Buddha Nature is not something seen with the eyes, or heard with the ears, or grasped by the mind, or whatever. Because they have not realized that the manifesting of one's Spiritual Body is Buddha Nature, they have not stated it. Although their ancestral Master was not loath to manifest It, their ears were shut so that they never heard about It. Since they had not yet comprehended what their Spiritual Body was, It was not something that they ever fully discerned. Hoping to see the meditative state that is free of characteristics as something with a form resembling the moon at its full, they respectfully bowed, but their eyes had not yet caught sight of It.

"The meaning of 'Buddha Nature' is That which is utterly unbounded and radiant." Thus, the manifestation of the Spiritual Body is one's giving voice to Buddha Nature, for It is unbounded radiance and It is absolute. To give voice to Buddha Nature means to manifest the Spiritual Body, for it is the means by which the physical presence of all Buddhas is displayed. Where is the Buddha, or the pair of Buddhas, whose display of It did not take on the physical presence of a Buddha? [24] The physical presence of a Buddha is someone's manifesting the Spiritual Body, and Buddha Nature exists as that person's manifestation of the Spiritual Body. On the other hand, the ability of the Buddhas and Ancestors to speak of It and understand It in terms of the four elements* and the five skandhas is also Their momentary manifestation of the Spiritual Body. The physical presence of all Buddhas, which we have already spoken about, is just like the realm of the skandhas. All Their functioning is the functioning of this realm. The way that Buddhas function completely plumbs the depths of how the Spiritual Body manifests when It encompasses all Its diverse forms. All the comings and goings of Their immeasurable, unbounded functioning are instances of this Spiritual Body being made manifest.

Even so, since the time of Master Nāgārjuna and his disciple Kānadaiba, among those who spiritually explored Buddhism as it existed in earlier and later generations throughout India, China, and Japan, no one has ever said anything the equal of what Nāgārjuna and Kānadaiba said. How many teachers of Scriptures, as well as erudite scholars of Their commentaries and the like, have tripped over what the Buddhas and Ancestors have said? From ancient times, there have been those in Great Sung China who attempted to illustrate this incident, but they were unable to portray it either physically or mentally, nor could they draw it in space or upon a wall. Vainly sketching with their writing brush, they endeavored to depict Nāgārjuna's

---

24. 'One Buddha' refers to someone who has realized the Truth, whereas 'a pair of Buddhas' is an allusion to a Master and a disciple after Transmission.

'manifestation of the Spiritual Body as the look of the Full Moon' by sketching a mirror-like circle above a Dharma seat. These people have intended their depictions to be as gold dust before people's eyes, yet even though the frosts of autumn and the flowers of spring have appeared and faded away for centuries since, not a soul has said they err. How sad that so many matters have been bungled like this! If Nāgārjuna's manifesting the 'Spiritual Body with the look of the Full Moon' is taken to mean that It had the look of a circle, it would be a real picture of a rice cake.[25] These artists' playing around with people like this is silly enough to make one die laughing. Sad to say, in a kingdom like Great Sung China, nary a householder or a monk has heard and understood the words of Nāgārjuna, or is familiar with what Kānadaiba said, or has even encountered it, let alone having any familiarity with the manifestation of one's Spiritual Body! They are in the dark about the Full Moon, and the Moon at Its full has waned for them. This is because they are remiss in their examination of the past and lack a fondness for examples from the past as well. Further, in your endeavor to encounter the real manifestation of the Spiritual Body of old and new Buddhas, do not prize or play around with 'pictures of rice cakes'. You need to know that, when you attempt to depict the characteristics of the Spiritual Body manifesting with the look of the Full Moon, you should use the image of Nāgārjuna's body seated upon a Dharma seat. His raised eyebrows and twinkling eyes will be straight to the point. The Treasure House of the Eye of the True Teaching within his very Skin and Flesh, Bones and Marrow will undoubtedly be portrayed by his sitting upright and still. You should convey his face, which beams with the sweetest smile because he has become a Buddha and an Ancestor. To the degree that this portrait of yours does not yet have the look of the Moon, it will lack anything resembling Its form, and it will not give expression to the Dharma either in what is conveyed or how, nor will it have Its genuine functioning.

If you desire to depict the Spiritual Body, you must the use the Full Moon as your model. When you wish to use the Full Moon as your model, you must specifically use only the <u>Full</u> <u>Moon</u>, for this is the way that the Spiritual Body manifests Itself.

---

25. That is, like a picture of a rice cake, it would be incapable of providing nourishment or satisfying one's hunger.

When you wish to portray the look of the Full Moon, you must model it only on the look of the Moon at Its full. And you must demonstrate the look of the Moon at Its full. On the other hand, if you do not portray the manifestation of the Spiritual Body, or portray the Full Moon, or portray the Moon at Its full, or aim at portraying the physical presence of all Buddhas, or embody the displaying of this presence, or aim at manifesting the Dharma, you will be vainly drawing a picture of a rice cake, and what does that get you? If you are quick to set your sights straight, who of you will not be sated right here and now, and not go hungry?²⁶

Just as the moon is circular in form, so circularity is a manifestation of one's Spiritual Body.²⁷ In your investigation of circularity, do not examine it as if it were the roundness of a coin, or liken it to a rice cake. The Spiritual Body is the body of the moon in its characteristic circular shape, so Its form is like the form of the Moon at Its full. You should investigate a coin or a rice cake, too, in terms of their circularity.

While I was still drifting about like a cloud, I went to Great Sung China. It was about the end of autumn in the sixteenth year of the Chinese Chia-ting era (1223) when I first arrived at Kōri temple on Mount Ashoka. I saw that someone had painted portraits of the thirty-three Indian and Chinese Ancestors on the wall of the western corridor. At the time, I did not grasp their meaning. Later, during the summer retreat in the first year of the Chinese Kia-ch'ing era (1225), I happened to return there, and while walking along the corridor with Guestmaster Jōkei of Szechwan Province, I

---

26.   In this paragraph, Dōgen explains that in order to draw a correct picture of a human being's manifestation of Buddha Nature, you need to use as your basis the picture of a human being, rather than using some abstract object such as a circle. In order to emphasize this point, he talks about using the Moon at Its full as the model for drawing a Full Moon. This is comparable to saying that if you want to draw a picture of a round plate, use a plate that is round as your model, rather than, say, using some other round object or using a plate that is square.

27.   'Circularity' implies something that has no beginning or ending, that is all-encompassing, and is ever flowing, ever changing, now coming forth, now receding.

asked him, "Whose picture is this?" The Guestmaster answered, "It is the appearance of a full moon which represents Nāgārjuna's body." When he spoke thus, his countenance showed no nose for the Great Matter, nor was there any expression of It in his voice. I commented, "There is no more to this than a painting of a rice cake." Even though the Guestmaster burst out laughing at the time, there was no sword within his laugh that was capable of smashing a painted rice cake to bits. Subsequently, as the Guestmaster and I visited the Relics Hall and the six scenic spots of the monastery, I brought up the issue of the picture again several times, but not even the slightest inkling of what it was about ever arose in him. Naturally, there were also many other monks who put forth their opinions, but they too were completely useless. So I said, "I'll try raising the question with the Abbot." The Abbot at the time was the monk Daikō. The Guestmaster remarked, "He probably won't be able to give you an answer as he doesn't have the nose for that kind of thing. So how could he know anything about it?" Therefore, I did not ask the Venerable Daikō. Although my monastic brother Jōkei talked to me in this way, he himself had no understanding either. Those other skin bags who heard our talk also had nothing to contribute. Generations of Abbots presiding at that temple's meals of gruel and rice had never looked at that picture and wondered about it, so they had never revised and corrected their understanding of it. Further, when there are things that you cannot possibly depict, then you should not try to depict them at all, and what you can depict, you should depict in a straightforward manner. Despite this, the look of the Full Moon which is the manifestation of one's Spiritual Body is something that one never depicts.

To speak more broadly, in that such persons have not awakened from their present opinions and personal views that Buddha Nature is somehow synonymous with the intellective, perceptual, or cognitive functions of their mind, it is as if they had lost the distinction of meaning between the phrases 'possessing Buddha Nature' and 'not possessing Buddha Nature'. This can be understood only by those with true understanding, and rare indeed are those who have even tried to investigate how to make such distinctions. You should know that this lack of effort on their part was due to the fact that such investigations had gone out of fashion. In many places, there have been Abbots presiding at meals of gruel and rice who have died without once in their whole life even mentioning the term 'Buddha Nature'. And some among them have said that those who pay heed to Scriptural Teachings may discuss Buddha Nature, but those who practice Zen meditation should not speak of It. Folks who talk like this are truly beasts! What a bunch of demons they are to mingle with and defile the Way of our Buddha Tathagata! Is what they call 'paying heed to the Scriptural Teachings' the Way of the Buddha? Or is what they call 'practicing Zen meditation' the Way of the Buddha? Recognize that what they are calling 'paying heed to the Scriptural Teachings' and 'practicing Zen meditation' are still not the Way of the Buddha.

National Teacher Enkan Saian in Kangshū Province was an esteemed Master under Baso. He once pointed out to his assembly, "All sentient beings are possessed of Buddha Nature." Right away, we need to thoroughly examine his words 'all sentient beings'. All sentient beings have different internal propensities and external conditions, which are the fruits of past karma, so their perspectives are different. This holds true for each and every one of them, be they called 'ordinary people', 'non-Buddhists', 'those in the Three Courses', 'those in the Five Courses', or something else.[28] 'All sentient beings', as spoken of in the Buddha's Way in the present instance, means that all who possess a mind filled with craving are 'sentient beings', since having a mind is synonymous with being a sentient being.[29] All those whose mind is beyond craving will likewise be sentient beings, since being a sentient being is synonymous with having a mind.[30] Accordingly, all minds are, without exception,

---

28. Those in the Three Courses are the shravakas, the pratyekabuddhas, and the bodhisattvas. Those in the Five Courses are the above three, plus lay Buddhists who have taken and keep to the first five of the Ten Precepts, and those in lofty positions ('celestial beings') who devote themselves to doing good deeds and practicing meditation.

29. That is, mind does not exist as an entity independent of human existence (such as the Subtle Intelligence posited by the Shrenikans).

30. In referring to the mind in this passage, Dōgen uses two words. The first *(ushin)* has two meanings: having or possessing a mind and having a mind that is enmeshed in attachments. The second *(mushin)* refers to a mind that has dropped off its attachments.

sentient beings, and all sentient beings are, without exception, possessed of Buddha Nature. And even grasses, trees, and our very nation are synonymous with Mind, and because they are synonymous with Mind, they are sentient beings, and because they are sentient beings, they are possessed of Buddha Nature. And, likewise, the sun, the moon, and the stars are synonymous with Mind, and because they are synonymous with Mind, they are sentient beings, and because they are sentient beings, they are possessed of Buddha Nature.[31] 'Being possessed of Buddha Nature', which the National Teacher spoke of, is no different. Were it different, it would not be the 'being possessed of Buddha Nature' that is put forth in the Buddha's Way. The core of what the National Teacher said is simply that all sentient beings are possessed of Buddha Nature. Further, if anything were not a sentient being, it would not be possessed of Buddha Nature. Right now, it would be good for you to ask of the National Teacher, "Are all the Buddhas possessed of Buddha Nature?" since to inquire in this way will put him to the test. You should examine carefully that he did not say, "All sentient beings are the same as Buddha Nature," but said, "All sentient beings are possessed of Buddha Nature." A Buddha will have discarded any sense of possessing something as implied by the phrase 'possessing Buddha Nature'. Their discarding of it is Their being at one with all things, as if all were a single, solid iron bar, and Their being at one with all things is as the passage of birds, which leaves no traces. As a consequence, all Buddhas are possessed of Buddha Nature. For this reason, the truth of what the National Teacher said not only penetrates through what 'sentient beings' means, but also penetrates through what 'Buddha Nature' means. Even though the National Teacher may not have fully understood all the implications of what he was saying, this does not mean that he lacked the opportunity to understand them, nor does it mean that the essence of what he said is meaningless for us today.

Also, even though you may not yet have understood for yourself the Truth with which you are already equipped, you have Its four elements and five skandhas, and you have Its Skin and Flesh, Bones and Marrow. Thus it is that there are some

---

This latter state of mind, however, also encompasses the first meaning of *ushin* as simply 'having a mind'.

31. That is, the whole universe and everything in it is Buddha Nature.

whose affirmation of It takes their whole lifetime to affirm, and there are others for whom it takes lifetimes to affirm It.

Meditation Master Isan of Mount Daii once said to his assembly, "All sentient beings lack a Buddha Nature." Among the ordinary people and those in lofty positions who hear this, there will be those who will be delighted because of their great capacity for understanding, and there will also be no shortage of those who will be disquieted and filled with doubt. This is because the Venerable Shakyamuni stated that all sentient beings have Buddha Nature through and through, whereas Isan is saying that all sentient beings lack a Buddha Nature. Since the meaning of the words 'have' and 'lack' must surely be greatly different, some may harbor doubts as to which statement is true to the mark and which is not. Even so, in the Buddha's Way, only Isan's statement, "All sentient beings lack a Buddha Nature," excels National Teacher Enkan's. Even though Enkan's phrase about 'being possessed of Buddha Nature' resembles a stretching forth of a pair of hands along with the former Buddha, nevertheless, this remark is the same as a traveling staff being shouldered by two people.[32] Now, Isan's phrase is not like this; his observation is like a traveling staff absorbing two people.[33] Moreover, even though the National Teacher was a monastic son of Baso, and Isan was a monastic grandson of Baso, the Dharma grandson was an old hand at his grandfather's way of putting the Matter, whereas the Dharma son was a youngster when it came to his father's way of putting It. The gist of what Isan said has made "All sentient beings lack a Buddha Nature" his underlying principle. He did not say anything that is even vaguely beyond the straight and narrow of Buddhist Teaching. This is how he received and preserved the Scriptures within the quarters of his own monastic tradition.

---

32. The traveling staff was often used by Masters to point a disciple towards the Truth, that is, towards which way to go. Hence, according to Dōgen, while Enkan's statement may seem to be expanding upon what the Buddha said, in reality he was merely repeating the same thing over again.

33. Dōgen's descriptive phrase may refer to the face-to-face relationship in Transmission, wherein Master and disciple are absorbed together in That which points to the Truth.

Further, it is imperative that you ferret out how it is that all sentient beings are Buddha Nature, and in what sense they are possessed of Buddha Nature. If any people assert that they possess a Buddha Nature, they must surely be the henchmen of demons who will, one day or another, attempt to wrap all sentient beings up in a demon child's swaddling clothes. Since Buddha Nature <u>is</u> Buddha Nature, sentient beings are sentient beings. Sentient beings, from the start, have never been equipped with a Buddha Nature. Even though they may wish to possess such a thing, the point is that Buddha Nature, in the first place, is not something that <u>can</u> come along with anyone. Do not assert that when Mr. Chang drinks wine, Mr. Li gets drunk. If anything possessed 'a Buddha Nature' in and of itself, such a thing would not be a sentient being. If anything possessed 'being a sentient being', then ultimately such a thing would not be Buddha Nature. This is why Hyakujō said, "To assert that a sentient being possesses Buddha Nature slanders Buddha, Dharma, and Sangha. And to assert that a sentient being lacks Buddha Nature slanders Buddha, Dharma, and Sangha." Accordingly, to say that one possesses a Buddha Nature and to say that one lacks Buddha Nature both become slander. Even though they become slander, it does not mean that one cannot say anything about It. Were Isan and Hyakujō able to hear me at this moment, I would now say to Hyakujō, "Granted that both are slanderous, are you able to state what Buddha Nature is? Even though you can state what It is, such a statement may restrict the way of expressing It. If you do have a way of expressing It, such an expression will be in complete harmony with how it is heard." And turning to Isan, I would remark, "Even though your saying that all sentient beings lack a Buddha Nature expresses It through words, you did not say that all of Buddha Nature lacks sentient beings and you did not say that all of Buddha Nature lacks Buddha Nature, and, what is more, you have not yet seen even in your dreams that each and every one of the Buddhas lacks a Buddha Nature. Should you give it another try, I'd like to take a look at it."

Meditation Master Hyakujō, in giving teaching to his assembly, said:

It is Buddha that is the unsurpassed Vehicle.[34] It is Supreme Wisdom. It is what establishes people in the Buddha's Way. It is the very Buddha Nature which a Buddha is possessed of. It is the Teacher and Guide who makes unhindered use of everything for the sake of others. It is unimpeded in Its discernment. Hence It is able to make good use of karmic cause and effect, and is naturally joyful and wise. Its cart wheels continually roll forward, carrying forth karmic causality. When dealing with life, It does not experience life as something that ceases. When dealing with death, It does not experience death as a hindrance. When dealing with the five skandhas, It does not experience the five skandhas as impediments, but rather as portals that are open; coming and going at will, It suffers no difficulties in going in and out of them. If you can be like this, there will be no need to discuss higher or lower stages of spiritual development. Indeed, if even an ant can be like this, then it will be, through and through, a wondrous Pure Land, beyond anything we can possibly imagine.

This, then, was Hyakujō's way of expressing the Matter. The five skandhas comprise our intact body at this very moment. Whatever we are doing right now is the opening of a portal, and it opens without our experiencing any impediments from our five skandhas. When we simply live, we are not restricted by life, and when we simply die, we are not put into turmoil by death. Do not uselessly crave life, and do not vainly fear death. They are both simply places where Buddha Nature resides. To be constantly disturbed and worn out over them is non-Buddhist behavior. To acknowledge the various conditions and circumstances that arise before our very eyes is the way to be unhindered in one's dealing with them. This is the Ultimate Vehicle: it is to <u>be</u> Buddha. Wherever one may reside within this state of 'being Buddha' becomes a wondrous Pure Land.

---

34. 'Buddha', here, refers to awakened Buddha Nature, the functioning of which is the subject of Hyakujō's remarks.

Ōbaku was sitting in Nansen's Abbatical reception room,[35] when Nansen asked Ōbaku, "What do you think of the principle enunciated in the *Great Scripture on the Buddha's Parinirvana* that, if one trains oneself equally in meditative practice and in spiritual wisdom, one will clearly see one's Buddha Nature?"

Ōbaku replied, "Within all the hours of the day, It does not depend on a single thing, so we have It right from the start."

Nansen said, "You aren't saying this as the view of an elder monk, are you?"[36]

Ōbaku replied, "I daren't say so."

Nansen said, "Setting aside for the moment the matter of payment for your rice broth, to whom are you to return payment for your straw sandals?"

Thereupon, Ōbaku remained silent.

'Training equally in meditative practices and spiritual wisdom' does not mean that, since training in meditative practices does not interfere with pursuing spiritual wisdom, Buddha Nature can be clearly seen when training in both equally. Rather, when we clearly see our Buddha Nature, then we will be training equally in meditation practice and spiritual wisdom. So Nansen stated, "What do you think of this principle?" This would be the same as saying, for instance, "Who is it that sees one's Buddha Nature clearly?" Or it can be stated by saying, "How about the principle that Buddha Nature's equal pursuit of both is what causes us to realize our Buddha Nature?"

The point of Ōbaku's saying "Within all the hours of the day, It does not depend on a single thing" is that even though twenty-four hours exist within the span

---

35. Ōbaku was a Dharma heir of Hyakujō; Hyakujō and Nansen, as Dharma heirs of Baso, were monastic brothers.

36. The term 'elder monk' refers to a monk of many years training who is recognized for his deep understanding of spiritual matters.

of a whole day, It is not dependent on them. Since Buddha Nature's not depending on a single thing extends over all the hours of a day, It can be clearly seen. As to this 'within all the hours of a day' of his, would you ask at what specific time It will show up or in what country? These twenty-four hours that we are speaking of, would they have to be a human being's twenty-four hour day? Or do they exist as a day in some other particular place? Or are they the kind of day that can occur for a while in Samantabhadra's* Silver Realm? Whether it be in this land or some other world, It does not depend on either. It is already within the twenty-four hours of any day and does not depend on anything.

Nansen's asking, "You aren't saying this as the view of an elder monk, are you?" is the same as asking, "You aren't saying that this is your view, are you?" Although Nansen asked whether this is the view of an elder monk, Ōbaku should not turn to Nansen and affirm that it is indeed his own view. Although the statement was appropriate, it did not apply to Ōbaku alone, because Ōbaku is not the only person who held this view, as the views of many elder monks make abundantly clear.

As to Ōbaku's replying, "I daren't say so," when someone in Sung China is asked whether he is capable of doing something, he uses this phrase, "I daren't say so," to acknowledge in a humble way his ability to do so. Thus, to say, "I daren't say so," does not mean that one doubts one's abilities. What this expression says is not to be taken literally. Whether 'the view of an elder monk' refers to some other elder monk or whether 'the view of an elder monk' refers to Ōbaku, in either case the answer should be that he daren't say so. It should be like a water buffalo coming out from the water and bellowing *"Mu."* [37] To put it like this is to affirm It. You should try and see if you can say, in your own words, the Principle that Ōbaku is affirming.

Nansen said, "Setting aside for the moment the matter of payment for your rice broth, to whom are you to return payment for your straw sandals?" In other words, the cost of your rice gruel is put aside for the moment, but who gets paid for the cost of your straw sandals? We should spend life after life exploring the intent of this statement through our training. We should keep our minds diligently investigating

---

37. Dōgen will explain the significance of this term later in this discourse when he discusses the kōan story of Jōshū's dog.

what he meant by 'whatever the cost of the broth, don't worry about it for the moment'. Why was he so concerned about the cost of straw sandals? It is as if he had asked, "In all the years that you have spent traveling as a mendicant monk, how many pairs of straw sandals have you worn out?" to which Ōbaku might answer, "If I had not paid back the cost, I would not still be wearing straw sandals," or, then again, he might reply, "Two or three pairs." Either way could be how he expressed the Matter. Each way would correspond to his intent.

The statement that Ōbaku thereupon remained silent simply means that he desisted from speaking. He did not remain silent because what he said was negated by Nansen, nor did he remain silent because he was negating what Nansen said. A patch-robed monk of true color is not like that. Keep in mind that silence speaks, just as laughter can wield a sword. This is Buddha Nature clearly seeing that there is enough gruel and enough rice.

In citing this story, Isan asked his disciple Kyōzan, "Don't you think this shows that Ōbaku was no match for Nansen?"

Kyōzan replied, "Not so. We should recognize that Ōbaku had the wherewithal to capture the tiger alive."

Isan said, "My disciple's perceptiveness has excelled itself in this."

What Isan was saying is, "Wasn't Ōbaku able to match Nansen?" Kyōzan said that Ōbaku had the wherewithal to capture the tiger alive. If he had already captured the tiger, he could probably have stroked the tiger on its head. To capture a tiger and to pet a tiger are to engage in two totally different things. Is clearly seeing Buddha Nature the same as opening the Eye? Is one's Buddha Nature seeing clearly the same as losing one's Eye? Quick, quick, speak! The perceptiveness of Buddha Nature excels Itself in this. As a result, It does not depend on half a thing or on its whole. Nor does It depend on hundreds of thousands of things or on hundreds of thousands of occasions. For this reason it can be said:

The snares and traps of passion are but a single face of It.

On no time within a day does It depend, nor is It outside
of time;
Rather, It is like wisteria and kudzu entwined about a tree.
All within the universe and the universe itself are still
bereft of words for It, you see.

A certain monk once asked Great Master Jōshū, "Does
even a dog have Buddha Nature?"

We need to clarify the intent of this question. 'Dog' here means a dog.[38] He
is not asking, "Can such a creature have Buddha Nature?" nor is he asking, "Can such
a creature be devoid of Buddha Nature?" What he is really asking is, "Is even an iron
man exploring the Way through his training?" Even though the trainee has made a
mistake and his feelings of rancor and regret, which have become poisonous, are
profound, still, even after thirty years it would be an improvement to see half a saintly
person.[39]

---

38. Even though *kou-tsu* (the Chinese word for 'dog') has often been understood in China
     and Japan as referring to an animal (as implied by a literal rendering of Dōgen's
     discourse), in both countries, 'dog' has long been used as a term for someone who is
     morally depraved ('a dog of a person'). In Buddhism, such persons were called
     icchantika, that is, those who were constant in their deliberate and wanton breakage of
     Precepts. Such persons were consequently thought to be devoid of Buddha Nature.
     Further, 'dog' was also sometimes used in both countries as a humbling term for oneself
     ('a dog of a person like me'), someone who is doggedly devoted. There is apparently an
     interplay of all three meanings in the following passages.

39. That is, the intent behind the monk's question is as if he were asking, "I have truly tried
     to train with an iron will, but I have not yet realized the Truth. Is it because a dog of a
     trainee like me is somehow spiritually defective?" Dōgen's comment is that even if
     someone's training is being poisoned by feelings of regret at not yet having realized the
     Truth, still, asking the question in the first place is itself a sign of spiritual progress (being
     a half-saintly person), even if the person has not yet awakened to his True Nature after
     thirty years of training.

Jōshū replied, "*(Mu)* No, it doesn't."

When we hear this expression, there are pathways that we need to investigate. The "no" by which Buddha Nature reveals Its identity will be expressed by this word. And the "no" by which the identity of a dog is revealed will also be expressed by this word. And the "no" of an onlooker's exclamation will also be expressed by this word.[40] There may come a day when that "no" of Jōshū's will simply be a word for grinding away at stones.

> The monk then asked, "All sentient beings, without exception, have Buddha Nature, so how come a dog is devoid of It?"

The import of his question is as though he were saying, "If all sentient beings did not exist, then Buddha Nature would not exist and a dog would not exist. How about that point? How could you expect a dog not to have Buddha Nature?"

Jōshū responded, "On the grounds that such a one has karmic ignorance."[41]

The meaning of what he said is that even though the reason for its existence is karmic ignorance, and its having karmic ignorance is the grounds for its existence, a dog does not possess karmic ignorance, nor does Buddha Nature possess it. Karmic ignorance has never understood what a dog really is, so how could a dog possibly encounter Buddha Nature? Whether Jōshū were to confirm or contradict what the monk said, still, this is a case of karmic ignorance on the monk's part from beginning to end.

---

40. That is, the word 'no' has different meanings, depending on what it relates to. In the context of Buddha Nature, it means 'being beyond having or not having'; in the context of a dog, it means 'not possessing a Buddha Nature'; and in the context of a bystander, it means "There is nothing there that I can see."

41. Karmic ignorance may be defined as the deluded state of consciousness that was inherited at birth from past lives and which inhibits one from seeing Buddha Nature.

> Jōshū had another monk who asked him, "Does Buddha
> Nature exist even in a dog, yes or no?"[42]

This question may have been the reason why this monk was a match for Jōshū,[43] since expressing or asking about Buddha Nature is the everyday food and drink of Buddhas and Ancestors.

> Jōshū said, "*(U)* Yes, It exists."

The nature of this 'It exists' is beyond the 'existence' as understood by the commentators of the various scholastic traditions, and beyond the assertion of existence made by the Sarvastivādins.[44] Advancing on from them, we should investigate what the existence of Buddha is. The existence of Buddha is Jōshū's "It exists," and Jōshū's "It exists" is the dog's existing, and the dog's existing is the existence of Buddha Nature.

> The monk then asked, "If It already exists, why is It
> strongly impelled to enter into this body of flesh?"

This monk's question is asking, "Is It something existing now, or is It something that existed at some time in the past, or has It always existed?" Even though That Which Always Exists resembles other types of existence, That Which Always Exists clearly stands alone.

---

42. In the original text, the wording of this question is the same as that used by the preceding monk, but the intent is different, as the subsequent comments by Jōshū and Dōgen make clear.

43. The implication of this statement is that the previous monk had asked the question from the perspective of one who had not yet realized his True Nature, whereas this monk had already had such a realization and was exploring True Nature with his Master.

44. The Sarvastivādins were members of one of the twenty pre-Mahayana schools of Indian Buddhism, which arose some three centuries after the death of Shakyamuni. One of their doctrines was that past, present, and future time all have real existence and that the Dharma is ever-present.

Is That Which Always Exists strongly impelled to enter into fleshly form or is It not? Although we have been strongly impelled to take on this fleshly body of ours, in our daily conduct and spiritual practice there is no bumbling, useless effort.

Jōshū replied, "It is because a dog knowingly and intentionally breaks Precepts."

Even though this statement had long been spread abroad as a common saying, it was now Jōshū's way of putting the Matter.[45] What he is talking about is the deliberate breaking of Precepts. Probably very few people have not had doubts about this expression of his, because it is difficult for them to clearly understand the character for 'enter into', which is part of the phrase 'impelled to enter into'. However, this character for 'enter into' is not essential.[46]

Moreover, as Sekitō Kisen put it in a poem:

If you would know the Undying One within the hermit's hut,
How can you do it apart from your fleshly body here and now?

Even though we may not yet know who the Undying One is, when, pray, are we to separate It from our fleshly body? Having broken a Precept is not necessarily what impels us to enter a body of flesh, nor is our impulse to enter this fleshly body of ours necessarily due to our knowingly having broken a Precept. When such an action is done deliberately, then the Precept will be broken. You need to realize that this breaking of Precepts will be hidden from sight within our daily conduct and spiritual practice of dropping off body. This is expressed as 'being impelled to enter'. When our daily conduct and spiritual practice of dropping off body is genuinely hidden from sight, it will be concealed from both ourselves and others. Even so, do

---

45. That is, the popular understanding of the statement was that if someone, knowing better, deliberately broke Precepts, that person would be reborn as an animal.

46. The phrase 'being impelled to enter into' is comprised of two characters: the first *(tō)* means 'to be impelled', the second *(nyū)* means 'to enter into'. Dōgen's point is that the 'enter into' is unessential, since it is difficult to see a clear distinction between 'to be impelled to take on some bodily form' and 'to be impelled to enter into taking on some bodily form'.

not say that you are not yet free, that you are just a fellow with a donkey in front of him and a horse behind him.[47]

Even more, as our lofty Ancestor Ungo Dōyō said, "Even though you may have studied the Buddha Dharma to Its very limits, you have erred in your approach if you have completely depended on your intellect." Accordingly, even though someone has made this error for a long time, piling up the days and months by half-learning the Buddha Dharma to Its limits, such a person must be a dog who has been impelled to enter into that fleshly body of his. Although he knowingly has broken Precepts, he will still have Buddha Nature.

In the assembly of the virtuous monk Chōsa Keishin, his lay disciple Chiku, who was a high government official, raised a question, saying, "When a live earthworm is cut in two, both parts continue to move. I wonder, in which part does the Buddha Nature reside?"

The Master responded, "Do not engage in deluded, dualistic thinking."

The official asked, "But how do you account for the twitching?"

The Master replied, "It is simply that the elements of wind and fire have not yet dissipated."

Now, when the government official remarked about an earthworm being cut in two, had he concluded that, prior to its being cut, it was one segment of Buddha Nature? This is not the way things are viewed within the everyday experience of the Buddhas and Ancestors. The earthworm was not originally one segment of It, and, after being cut, the earthworm was not two segments of It. The assertion of 'one' and 'two' needs to be diligently explored through one's training and practice. As to the 'two parts' in his saying that both parts continue to move, did he take the worm before

---

47.   A Zen phrase for an ordinary person who has not yet realized enlightenment.

it had been cut to be one part of Buddha Nature, and did he take That which goes beyond awakening to be one part of the worm? Regardless of how the government official may have understood his phrase 'two parts', do not disregard the words he spoke. Is it that the two cut segments made up one whole and, moreover, that they exist as a whole being? The movement of which he spoke when saying that both continue to move will be the movement of one's meditative practice which loosens the roots of delusion and the movement of one's wise discernment which pulls these roots out.

His statement, "I wonder, in which part does the Buddha Nature reside?" needs to be examined in detail. He should have said, "When someone cuts Buddha Nature in two, I wonder in which part does the earthworm reside?" In saying, "Both parts continue to move, so in which part does Buddha Nature reside?" does he mean that, if both are moving, it is not possible for Buddha Nature to reside in either? Or is he saying that, if both are moving, the place where Buddha Nature is residing must be in one or the other, even though both are moving?

When the Master responded, "Do not engage in deluded, dualistic thinking," what could he have meant by saying that his disciple should not engage in dualistic thinking? Did he mean that there is nothing dualistic about both parts moving, that the matter is beyond duality? Or did he simply mean that Buddha Nature is beyond duality? We should also investigate his statement that, simply, there is no duality, without getting into a discussion about 'Buddha Nature' or about 'two parts'.

As to the official's asking what we are to make of their twitching, is he asserting that because they are twitching, it must be due to their piling one Buddha Nature atop another, or is he asserting that even though they are twitching, it is apart from their Buddha Nature?

The Master's replying that it is simply a matter of the elements of wind and fire not yet having dissipated was his way of making Buddha Nature emerge. Is he saying that it is Buddha Nature or is he saying that it is wind and fire? He cannot say that Buddha Nature appears together with wind and fire, nor can he say that one appears but not the other, nor can he say that because there is wind and fire, there is Buddha Nature. Therefore, Chōsa did not say that an earthworm possesses Buddha Nature, nor did he say that an earthworm does not possess Buddha Nature. He simply stated that his disciple was not to engage in dualistic thinking and that the wind and fire had not yet dissipated. When it comes to the living reality of Buddha Nature, we should make Chōsa's words our way of thinking about It.

The phrase 'wind and fire have not yet dissipated' needs calm and diligent consideration. What is the underlying meaning of 'not yet having dissipated'? In his saying that they have not yet dissipated, is he saying that although the wind and fire had arrived, the time for their dispersal had not yet arrived? By no means! His saying "Wind and fire have not yet dissipated" is a Buddha giving expression to the Dharma. The wind and fire's not yet having dispersed is Dharma expressing Buddha. The moment had arrived for giving voice to a single sound of the Dharma. It is a single sound of the Dharma being voiced, and it is the moment of Its arrival. The Dharma is a single sound, because It is the Dharma of the One Sound.

Further, to think that Buddha Nature exists only during the time of life and that It cannot exist during the time of death is to have heard very little and understood even less. The time of life is one of 'having Buddha Nature' and of 'not having a Buddha Nature', and the time of death is one of 'having Buddha Nature' and of 'not having a Buddha Nature'. If there were any discussion of whether or not the wind and fire had dissipated, it would have to be a discussion of whether or not Buddha Nature had dissipated. Even the time of their dissipating will be a time when Buddha Nature exists and a time when a Buddha Nature does not exist. And even the time before they have dissipated will be a time in which they are possessed of Buddha Nature and a time in which they do not possess a Buddha Nature. At the same time, to erroneously suppose that Buddha Nature is present or not present depending on whether or not there is movement, or to suppose that It is or is not transcendent depending on whether or not one is conscious of It, or to suppose that It is or is not one's nature depending on whether or not one is aware of It is to be a non-Buddhist, someone who is outside the Way.

From time immemorial there have been many foolish people who have taken their consciousness to be Buddha Nature and who have taken themselves to be someone who has realized their Original Nature, which is enough to make one die laughing. Moreover, to put into words what Buddha Nature is without going so far as to wallow in the mud or get soaked with water, It is the tiles and stones for our walls and fences.[48]

When It is stated on an even loftier level, what could It possibly be, this Buddha Nature? Have you really grasped It yet, in detail? It is having three heads and eight arms![49]

Delivered to the assembly on the fourteenth day of the tenth lunar month in the second year of the Ninji era (November 18, 1241) at Kannondōri in Kōshōhōrin-ji Temple, Yamashiro Province.

Copied by me on the nineteenth day of the first lunar month in the fourth year of the same era (February 9, 1243).

Ejō

---

48. 'Wallowing in the mud or getting soaked in water' is a common Zen phrase for going to whatever lengths are necessary to help a sentient being realize the Truth. 'Tiles and stones for our walls and fences' refers to the bits and pieces of our experiences which we use to construct our world.

49. An allusion to the guardian kings Achalanātha, the Steadfast Bodhisattva, and Rāgarāja, the Passionate Bodhisattva. The former is sometimes associated with the firm commitment of trainees to train until they have overcome all hindrances to realizing enlightenment as they persist in helping others to realize Truth. The latter has associations with a passionate desire to help all sentient beings realize Buddhahood.

Translator's Addendum from

Book One, Kōan 96 from Dōgen's Chinese Shinji Shōbōgenzō

Fuke and Rinzai were at the house of a donor for an alms meal.[50] Rinzai remarked, "It is said that a hair swallows up the vast ocean and that a mustard seed contains all of Mount Sumeru. Does this refer to someone's wondrous use of spiritual abilities, or does this refer to all things having Original Nature?" At this, Fuke knocked Rinzai's seat out from under him.[51] Rinzai said in rebuke, "Clumsy ox!" Fuke said, "<u>Right</u> <u>here</u> is where the What is, whether the Matter is put clumsily or delicately." At this, Rinzai, abashed, retired from the room.

The next day, the two were visiting the same family for an alms meal. Rinzai asked Fuke, "Is today's offering the same as yesterday's?" Fuke again knocked Rinzai's seat out from under him. Rinzai said reproachfully, "Clumsy ox!" Fuke replied, "O you with your eyes closed, would you care to expound on the clumsiness or delicacy of the What in the Buddha Dharma?" Rinzai, thereupon, stuck out his tongue at Fuke and 'blew him a raspberry'.

---

50.   Fuke and Rinzai were training together at the same temple, and Fuke was the more senior of the two monks. They shared a common ancestor in Baso.

51.   Rinzai's question is not only erudite in nature but it is inappropriate during an alms meal, since such alms were given to a monk with the understanding that they were to support a monk's spiritual training, not to foster intellectual pursuits.

22

On the Everyday Behavior of a Buddha Doing His Practice

(Gyōbutsu Iigi)

Translator's Introduction: The term *iigi*, which in common parlance may be literally rendered as 'dignified behavior', refers specifically in Buddhism to the four modes of everyday human bodily behavior: moving, standing still, sitting, and reclining.

In a later section of this discourse, Dōgen takes up an exchange between Meditation Master Seppō Gison and his disciple Gensha Shibi, who was his Dharma heir. The relationship between these two monks is illustrative of what is called the vertical and horizontal relationship of Master and Transmitted disciple: on one level, Seppō remains Shibi's monastic senior, and on another, the two are on equal footing. While this relationship would hold true for Masters and their disciples in general, in this case it extended to the point where the two monks shared the Abbotship and Dharma seat of their temple. What one said was then expressed by the other as another way of putting the matter or as an expansion upon the theme of the first. At times, Dōgen seems to find Shibi's statement to be lacking in some sense, but this may have been his way of illustrating the horizontal and vertical aspects of the Master-disciple relationship in which the two are equal while, at the same time, the Master is the disciple's senior.

All Buddhas, without exception, make full use of Their everyday behavior for Their practice. This is what is meant by 'a Buddha doing His practice'. 'A Buddha doing His practice' does not refer to a Buddha's realizing enlightenment or to a Buddha's transforming Himself for the sake of helping others. Nor does it refer to a Buddha as the embodiment of the Dharma or to a Buddha as others see Him embodied. It is beyond the state of a Buddha at His initial realization or at His fundamental realization, and it is beyond the state of a Buddha in His inherent enlightenment or in His going 'beyond being enlightened'. A Buddha who is equivalent to any of these can never stand shoulder-to-shoulder with a Buddha who is doing His practice. Keep in mind that Buddhas, being within the Buddha's Way, do not go looking for realization. Becoming proficient in one's daily conduct whilst on the path towards Buddhahood is what is meant by 'a Buddha just doing His practice'. It is not something that is even dreamt of by those who are, say, Buddhas as embodiments of the Dharma.

Because this Buddha who is doing His practice manifests the four modes of behavior in everything He does, He manifests these modes right out in the open. Before He speaks, He gives a hint of His spiritual activity, which is woven into whatever He does. This activity goes beyond time, or place, or 'being Buddha', or 'doing some practice'. If you are not a Buddha doing your practice, you will not let go of your attachment to 'Buddha' or your attachment to 'Dharma', and you will be grouped with those poor devils who deny that Buddha and Dharma can be found within themselves.

What being attached to 'Buddha' means is that a person has formed an intellectual concept of 'enlightenment' and then becomes attached to this concept and his understanding of it. Because this view accompanies him through each moment, he does not look for an opportunity to let go of this concept and understanding, and so he uselessly holds onto his mistaken views. On the other hand, to view and explain enlightenment as 'just being enlightenment' may well be a perspective that accords with enlightenment, for who could call this a false view? I recall my own indulgence in conceptualization as my tying myself up without a rope. It was a fetter at every moment, for the tree of self had not fallen and the wisteria vines of my entanglements had not withered away. This was simply my passing through life whilst meaninglessly imprisoned in a cave of ignorance on the periphery of Buddhism. I did not realize that my Dharma Body was ill nor did I recognize that my Reward Body was in distress.[1]

Those in the various Buddhist doctrinal schools, who are academic teachers of Scriptures or erudite commentators and the like, have heard what the Buddha said as if from afar, and have remarked, as did one of the Tendai Masters, that even though there is the Ultimate Nature of things, to set up some theory as to that Ultimate Nature is the very darkness of karmic* ignorance. In saying this, the Tendai Master failed to

---

1.   This is a reference to the three Bodies of the Buddha *(Trikaya)*. The first is the Truth Body *(Dharmakaya)*, which represents Absolute Truth or Buddha Mind Itself. The Reward Body *(Sambhogakaya)* represents the blissful reward of Buddhist training. The third is the Transformation Body *(Nirmanakaya)*, which is the physical body of the Buddha as it appears in the world.

*   See Glossary.

add that when a theory on the ultimate nature of things arises within Ultimate Nature, this 'ultimate nature of things' is a fetter. Further, he has added the fetter of ignorance atop this. Even though, sad to say, the Master did not recognize the fetter of 'the ultimate nature of things', one's ability to recognize the addition of the fetter of ignorance can become the seed for the mind's giving rise to the aspiration to realize enlightenment.

Now, a Buddha doing His practice has never been fettered with entanglements like this. This is why Shakyamuni Buddha said in the *Lotus Scripture*, "The lifetime which I obtained by My practice of the Bodhisattva* Path from the start is not exhausted even now, and will still be twice the past number of eons." You need to recognize that this does not mean that His lifetime as a bodhisattva was strung out in a continuous line to the present, nor does it mean that the life span of the Buddha was ever-present in the past. The 'past number' of which He spoke refers to all that He had accomplished up to that point. The 'even now' that He refers to is the whole of His life span. Even though His practice from the start has been as continuous and unvarying as an iron rail extending over ten thousand miles, yet, at the same time, it is His letting go of things for hundreds of years and His letting things be what they are, wherever they are.

As a consequence, doing one's training and realizing the Truth are beyond a matter of existing or not existing, for training and realizing the Truth are beyond any stain. There are hundreds of thousands of myriad places where there are no Buddhas or human beings, yet this does not sully a Buddha who is doing His practice. Thus it is that someone who does the practice of a Buddha is not sullied by notions of 'doing one's training' or 'realizing the Truth'. This does not mean that one's training to realize the Truth is necessarily untainted. And, at the same time, this state of 'being untainted' really does exist.

As Enō of Mount Sōkei once said to his disciple Nangaku:

This Immaculacy is simply what all Buddhas protect and keep in mind. It is the same for you too, and it is the same for me too. And it is the same for all our Indian Ancestors too.

So, because you are also like this, you are all the Buddhas, and because I am also like this, I am all the Buddhas. Truly, It is beyond 'me' and beyond 'you'. Within this Immaculacy, the me that is the real Me—which all the Buddhas protect and keep in mind—is what the everyday behavior of a Buddha doing His practice is, and the you that is the real You—which all the Buddhas protect and keep in mind—is what the everyday behavior of a Buddha doing His practice is. Due to the 'me too', Enō's everyday behavior is what constituted his excellence as a Master, and due to the 'you too', Nangaku's everyday behavior is what constituted his strength as a disciple, because the excellence of a Master and the strength of a disciple are what comprise the perfect knowledge and conduct of a Buddha doing His practice. You need to realize that what we call 'what is protected and kept in mind by all Buddhas' is 'me too' and 'you too'. Even though the explanation by the former Buddha of Mount Sōkei is beyond 'me', how could it possibly not refer to 'you'? What is protected and kept in mind by Buddhas who are doing Their practice is no different from That which thoroughly penetrates a Buddha who is doing His practice.

From the preceding it should be evident that doing one's training and realizing the Truth are beyond such things as one's innate nature and the forms it takes, or what is the root is and what the branches are. In that the mental attitude of a Buddha doing His training is, as might be expected, what causes a Buddha to train, Buddhas willingly train Themselves accordingly. There are those who put aside their body for the sake of the Teaching as well as those who put aside the Teaching for the sake of their body, and there are those who do not begrudge their own lives as well as those who do begrudge their own lives. And not only are there instances of putting aside 'Dharma' for the sake of the Dharma, there is also the everyday behavior in which someone may put aside the 'Teaching' for the sake of his Mind. Do not lose sight of the fact that the ways of letting go are incalculable. We cannot gauge or measure the Great Way by using what some Buddha may think about. The thoughts of any Buddha represent but a single angle: they are, for instance, like the opening of one flower. Do not use just your discriminative mind to grope about for what everyday behavior is or how to put it in words. The discriminative mind is but one aspect: it is, for instance, like a single realm. Considering a blade of grass is clearly what the discriminative mind of the Buddhas and Ancestors considers.[2] This is one means by which a Buddha doing His training comes to recognize the traces of His footsteps. Even if, by our wholehearted consideration, we clearly see that our understanding of 'what a Buddha is' is beyond fathoming, when we focus on the bodily behavior and demeanor of a Buddha doing His practice—whether He is moving or still—His behavior and demeanor will fundamentally have features that surpass our present understanding. Because it is His daily conduct that surpasses our fathoming, we cannot compare it or apply it to anyone else, for it is beyond anything that we can gauge or measure.

Now, there is something that we need to investigate in the everyday behavior of a Buddha doing His practice. True, the everyday behavior of 'me too' and 'you too' is connected with the innate capabilities of 'I alone' in regards to one's having come the way one has, both as a Buddha here and now and as oneself here and now. Nevertheless, this everyday behavior is the state of liberation associated with the Buddhas in the ten directions and is not simply one's identification with that state. This is why a former Buddha said, "Having comprehended the Matter[*] in abstract terms, we come back to the here and now where we conduct our daily living." When we maintain and rely upon the Matter in this way, all things, all beings, all practices, and all Buddhas are familiar to us and are our kindly friends.

Simply, each and every one of the Buddhas who physically put the Dharma into practice had obstructions to Their directly experiencing the Truth. Because there are obstructions to one's directly experiencing the Truth, there will be liberation in one's directly experiencing the Truth. When the hundreds of thoughts and things sprout up like grass blades before your eyes in such a bewildering way that they

---

2.   The 'discriminative' mind here refers to the discerning, non-judgmental functioning of the mind of Buddhas and Ancestors. The 'discriminatory' mind is used to describe the judgmental mind, which recognizes differences and then adds a value judgment to them.

impede your sight, do not be dismayed that you cannot discern even a single thought or a single object. They are simply what is manifesting in this thought and what is manifesting in that thing. No matter what we 'pick up' or 'haul away' as we busy ourselves with entering and departing through the gates of our senses each day, nothing anywhere has ever been hidden from us, and, as a result, the Venerable Shakyamuni's words, and realization, and practices, and Transmission, though unheard and unseen, are ever present.

> *Whenever I go out the gates, just grass,*
> *And whenever I come in the gates, just grass,*
> *So for a myriad leagues*
> *There is not even an inch of grass.*
>
> *And the words 'come in'*
> *And the words 'go out'*
> *Do not apply here*
> *Nor do they apply there.*[3]

Whatever thoughts or things we are now grasping and clinging to as 'real' are not supported by our practice of letting go, and yet they are our dreams and illusions, our 'flowers in the sky'. Who of us can see as mistaken these persistent dreams and illusions, these manufactured 'flowers in the sky'? Because to step forth is a mistake and to step back is a mistake, because taking one step is a mistake and taking two steps is a mistake, we make one mistake after another, for we have made Heaven and

---

3.   To paraphrase this poem, whenever I look either outside or within myself, there are only the transient images that my senses perceive and which my mind gives substance to. Hence, all there is in any experience is what I describe as arising, temporarily persisting, and dissipating, and that is of my own constructing. In this sense, the 'myriad blades of grass' are not real, no matter how far I travel within or without. And since there is no 'I' that 'goes out' or 'comes in', these terms are useless in describing or directly knowing That Which Is Real.

Earth strangers to each other. The Way to the Ultimate is not hard.[4] As for our dignity in these comings and goings, we should take as our ideal in our everyday behavior Sōsan's line, "The Great Way is being naturally at ease within ourselves."

We need to keep in mind that our coming forth into life is at one with our coming forth into the Way and that our entering death is at one with our entering the Way. In the head-to-tail rightness of that state, our everyday behavior manifests before our very eyes as if the turning of a jewel or the revolving of a pearl. To make use of, and be possessed of, one aspect of a Buddha's everyday behavior is to be the whole of the great earth in all directions, as well as the whole of birth-and-death and coming-and-going; it is to be a dust-filled mundane world and to be a lotus in full bloom. This dust-filled mundane world and this lotus blossom are each an aspect of It.

Many scholars are of the opinion that to speak of the whole of the great earth in all directions may refer to the southern continent of Jambudvipa[*] or to the four continents, whereas some cling to the notion that it is just the single nation of China, or go around in circles thinking that it is the single nation of Japan. Furthermore, just to say the words 'the whole of the great earth' is like thinking of it as the three-thousand great-thousandfold worlds, or like holding onto the notion of it as just one province or one district. Were you to undertake to explore the phrase 'the whole of the great earth' or 'the whole of the universe' through your training, you would need to mull it over three or four times, and do not conclude that such phrases are simply concerned with the breadth of something. This realization of the Way goes beyond 'Buddha' and transcends 'Ancestor'. It is that which is extremely large being the same as that which is small, and that which is extremely small being the same as that which

---

4.   Dōgen is alluding to lines from the poem "That Which Is Engraved upon the Heart That Trusts to the Eternal" by Kanchi Sōsan:

> *The Way to the Ultimate is not hard;*
> *Simply give up being picky and choosey...*
> *Let but a hair's breadth of discriminatory thought arise*
> *And you have made Heaven and Earth strangers to each other.*

One translation of the full poem can be found in *Buddhist Writings on Meditation and Daily Practice*, (Shasta Abbey Press, 1994), pp. 213-221.

is large. Even though this resembles the dubious statement that when 'large' does not exist, 'small' does not exist, it is nevertheless synonymous with a Buddha doing His practice as His everyday behavior. What Buddha after Buddha and Ancestor after Ancestor have All affirmed is the everyday behavior of the whole universe. This should be explored by you through your training as 'nothing ever having been hidden from you'. Not only has nothing ever been hidden from you, the everyday behavior of a Buddha doing His practice is His 'making tea' for everyone.

Even though there are those who, in giving voice to the Buddha's Way, may state that being born from the womb, say, or being born by transformation is a daily occurrence on the way to Buddhahood, such persons have still not stated that one may also be born from moisture or from an egg. And what is more, they have not even dreamt of there being birth beyond those from womb, egg, moisture, or transformation. How much less could they possibly experience and perceive that beyond birth from womb, egg, moisture, or transformation there is birth from Womb, Egg, Moisture, or Transformation? Now, according to the great words of Buddha after Buddha and Ancestor after Ancestor, there is a Womb, a Moisture, an Egg, and a Transformation that is beyond birth from womb, egg, moisture, or transformation, which They have correctly Transmitted as 'nothing ever having been hidden', and They have correctly Transmitted this Truth privately and in secret. How are we to categorize that bunch who most likely have not heard of this expression, much less have they learned about it, or understood it, or clarified what it means? You have already heard about the four types of birth, but how many types of death are there? For the four types of birth, could there be four types of death? Or could there be only two or three types of death? Or could there be five or six types, or a thousand or myriad types of death? Even entertaining a bit of doubt about this principle is part of exploring the Matter through training with one's Master.

Let's consider this for the moment. Can there be any kind of sentient being sprung from one of the four types of birth who experiences birth but does not experience death? And are there any to whom the direct, one-to-one, Transmission of death has been given who have not received the direct, one-to-one, Transmission of life? You should by all means explore through your training whether there is any kind of being who is only born or who only dies.

There are those who hear the phrase 'that which is beyond birth' without ever clarifying what it means, acting as if they didn't need to make any effort with their body and mind. This is a dullard's foolishness in the extreme. They must be some kind of beast who has not even reached the level of discussing the gradual awakening of one who practices with faith and the sudden awakening of one who quickly grasps the Dharma. If you ask why, the reason is that even if they hear the phrase 'that which is beyond birth', they still need to explore what the intent of this statement is. Further, they make no effort to inquire into what 'beyond Buddha', 'beyond the Way', 'beyond mind', and 'beyond annihilation' might mean, or what 'being beyond that which is beyond birth' might mean, or what 'beyond the realm of thoughts and things' and 'beyond one's Original Nature' might mean, or what 'beyond death' might mean. This is because they sit idly by, like creatures that live in the water or in the vegetation.

Keep in mind that 'birth-and-death' refers to our daily conduct in the Buddha's Way, and that 'birth-and-death' is one of the everyday tools in our Buddhist tradition. It is something that we use skillfully and by which we gain skillfulness; it is something that we clarify and by which we gain clarity. As a consequence, all Buddhas are completely clear and bright within the free functioning of this 'birth-and-death', and They are completely purposeful in Their making use of it. Should any of you be in the dark about the times when this 'birth-and-death' occurs, who could say who your 'you' really is? Who would describe you as someone who fully understands what life is and who has mastered what death is? Such people as these cannot hear that they have sunk deep, drowning in 'birth-and-death', and also cannot comprehend that they exist within 'birth-and-death'. They cannot believe and accept that 'birth-and-death' means being born and dying at each instant, nor can they plead that they do not understand it or that they do not know it.

On the other hand, some have fancied that Buddhas emerge only in the human world and that They do not manifest in other places or in other worlds.[5] If it were as they say, would all the places where a Buddha was present have to be part of the human world? This is their inference from the human Buddha's statement, "I, and I alone, am the Honored One." Well, there can also be celestial Buddhas, as well as Buddha Buddhas.[6] To assert that all Buddhas have manifested solely as human beings is not to have entered into the innermost sanctuary of the Buddhas and Ancestors.

An Ancestor of our lineage once said, "After Shakyamuni Buddha received the Transmission of the True Teaching from Kashō Buddha, He went to the Tushita Heaven, where He is now residing, instructing the celestial inhabitants there." Truly, you need to realize that even though the human Shakyamuni had, by that time, taught about His future extinction, nevertheless, the Shakyamuni who was in a heavenly world is still there even now, teaching celestial beings. You who are undertaking this training should know that the remarks and actions of the human Shakyamuni underwent a thousand changes and myriad transformations. What He gave expression to when He let His light shine forth and manifested auspicious signs was but one aspect of His being a human being. We should not foolishly fail to realize that the Teaching of the Shakyamuni in the Tushita Heaven may also be of a thousand kinds and produce myriad gateways. The Great Way which Buddha after Buddha has correctly Transmitted transcends extinction, and the underlying principle that one lets go of 'being beyond both beginning and ending' has been correctly Transmitted by the Buddha's Way, and by It alone. This is a meritorious behavior of the Buddha that others do not necessarily comprehend or even hear about.

---

5.   The worlds referred to here are the six worlds of existence into which a sentient being may be reborn.

6.   Celestial Buddhas exist in the celestial world, whereas Buddha Buddhas exist in a realm beyond the six worlds of existence.

In places where a Buddha doing His practice is establishing the Teaching, there may be sentient beings who are beyond the four types of birth, and there may be places that are beyond the celestial worlds, beyond the world of ordinary human beings, beyond the world of mental objects, and the like. Whenever you attempt to catch a glimpse of the everyday behavior of a Buddha doing His practice, do not use the eyes of someone in a celestial world or in the world of ordinary human beings, and do not employ the discriminatory thinking of someone in a celestial world or in the world of ordinary human beings, and do not aim at fathoming a Buddha's everyday behavior by trying to measure it. The 'thrice wise and ten times saintly'* do not recognize it and have not clarified what it is, so how much less would the calculations of ordinary human beings and those in celestial worlds reach it! In that the discriminatory thinking of human beings is narrow in scope, so their sense-based intellects are also narrow in scope, and in that their life span is limited and urgent, what they concern themselves with is also limited and urgent. So, how could they possibly fathom the everyday behavior of a Buddha doing His practice?

Therefore, do not count as disciples of the Buddha those in lineages that only take the world of ordinary human beings to be the realm of a Buddha or that narrow-mindedly take the ways of ordinary human beings to be the ways of a Buddha, for they are nothing more than human beings living out the result of past karma. Neither their body nor their mind has yet heard the Dharma, and they do not yet possess a body and mind that practices the Way. They do not live in accord with the Dharma or die in accord with the Dharma, nor do they see in accord with the Dharma or hear in accord with the Dharma, and they do not move, stand, sit, or recline in accord with the Dharma. Folks like this have never experienced the enriching benefits of the Dharma. They go around asserting such 'principles' as "A Buddha doing His practice is not related to His innate state of enlightenment or to His first awakening to that enlightened state" and "He is beyond 'having realized or not having realized enlightenment.'"

Now, such notions as 'thinking' and 'not thinking', 'having realized enlightenment' and 'not having realized enlightenment', and 'awakening to enlightenment' and 'being innately enlightened', which common, worldly-minded people are avidly concerned with, are simply the avid concerns of common, worldly-minded people, for they are not what Buddha after Buddha has received and passed on. Do not make comparisons between the thinking of common, worldly-minded people and the thinking of the Buddhas, for they are vastly different. Common, worldly people's being avidly concerned with their innate enlightenment and all the Buddhas' actually realizing Their innate enlightenment are as different from each other as heaven and earth, for innate enlightenment is something beyond the reach of comparative discussions. The avid concerns of the thrice wise and ten times saintly have still not reached the Way of the Buddhas. How could the useless, 'grain by grain' calculations of common, worldly people possibly yield the measure of It? Even so, many are the folks who avidly concern themselves with false views on cause and effect and on ends and means, views which are held by common, worldly people and others who are outside the Way—and they suppose these views to be within the bounds of the Buddha's Teachings. All the Buddhas have asserted that the roots of wrong-doing of these folks are deep and serious, and that such persons are to be pitied. And even though the deep and serious roots of their wrong-doing know no bounds, they are a heavy burden which these folks themselves must bear. They should just let go of this heavy burden, fix their gaze upon it, and look at it. And even though they may later take it up again and obstruct themselves with it, this burden will not then be the same as when it first arose.

Now, the everyday behavior of a Buddha doing His practice is unobstructed. And to the extent that He is constrained by being a Buddha due to His having thoroughly mastered the path of 'dragging oneself through mud and drowning oneself in water for the sake of others', He is still beyond hindrances and obstructions. When in some lofty realm, He gives instruction for the lofty, and when in the world of ordinary human beings, He gives instruction for ordinary people. There is benefit in both the blossoming of a single flower and in the blossoming forth of the whole world, without there being even the slightest gap between them. As a result, He goes far beyond self and other, and there is a unique excellence in His comings and goings. He goes to the Tushita Heaven here and now, and He comes from the Tushita Heaven here and now, and His very here and now is the Tushita Heaven. He is content in His goings here and now, and He is content in His comings here and now, and His very here and now is His contentment. He goes far beyond the Tushita Heaven here and now, and

He goes far beyond contentment here and now. He smashes to hundreds of bits both His contentment and the Tushita Heaven here and now, and He picks up and lets go of both His contentment and the Tushita Heaven here and now. He swallows both of them whole in one gulp.

Keep in mind that what we call 'contentment' and the 'Tushita Heaven' are also spinning on the wheel of the six worlds* of existence, as are both the Pure Lands and the various Heavens. His daily activities are likewise the daily activities of the Pure Lands and the various Heavens. When He is greatly awake, they are likewise greatly awake. When He is greatly deluded, they are likewise greatly deluded. All this is simply a Buddha, when doing His practice, wriggling His toes in His straw sandals. There are times when His singular way of putting the Matter will be the sound from His breaking wind or the smell from His emptying His bowels. Those with Nostrils will get a whiff of It.[7] They catch It through the sense fields of their ears, their bodies, and their actions. And there are times when they get my very Skin and Flesh, Bones and Marrow. And It is also something that we realize through our practice and which cannot be obtained from someone else.

When someone already has a broad and thorough grasp of the Great Way by understanding what life is and mastering what death is, that great saintly one leaves the matter of birth-and-death to the mind, and leaves the matter of birth-and-death to the body, and leaves the matter of birth-and-death to the Way, and leaves the matter of birth-and-death to birth and death. Although awareness of this principle is not something belonging to either the past or the present, yet, even so, the everyday behavior of a Buddha doing His practice is instantly practiced to the full. He immediately discerns and complies with the principle that the Way is an endless cycle, with body and mind continually arising and dying away. His practicing to the full and His illumining the Matter to the full are in no way forced actions, but greatly resemble

---

7.   'Those with Nostrils' is a common Zen Buddhist term for those who are able to go beyond surface appearances to 'sniff out' the deeper, spiritual meaning behind an action done by someone who has awakened to the Truth.

what we do when our mind has wandered off into delusion: that is, when we observe the shadows in our mind, we then turn the light of our mind around to reflect on what we truly are. This brightness, which is a brightness beyond brightness, thoroughly permeates a Buddha doing His practice, and it manifests naturally within His actions.

To grasp this principle of 'one's continually leaving it up to', you must thoroughly explore what your mind is. In the unswerving stillness of this exploration, you will come to understand and recognize that the myriad turnings and shiftings within your mind are due to the brightness and openness of your mind, and that the three worlds of desire, form, and beyond form are simply great barriers within the mind. Also, even though what one has come to understand and recognize are simply the myriad thoughts and things that arise, this in itself has put into action 'the homeland of our True Self' and is the same the living experience of 'such a person'[*] being 'just the thing'.

Thus, in ferreting out again and again what we are to take to serve as our model from what the Masters and Scriptures say and what skills we should seek that lie outside their words, there will be a catching on that goes beyond 'catching on to', and there will be a letting go that goes beyond 'letting go of'. In such an undertaking, we need to ask ourselves what life really is. And what is death? And what is body and mind? And what is given and what is taken? And what is 'keeping true to' or 'violating'? Is it going in and out of the same gate without meeting 'such a one'? Or is it our concealing our body while letting just our horns show?[8] Or is it placing just one piece at a time on a *Go* game board and letting it lie there? Is it giving great consideration to the Matter until we resolve It? Or is it letting our thoughts mature until we realize It? Is It the One Bright Pearl? Or is It what the whole of the great Treasure House teaches? Is It the staff that supports an elderly monk? Or is It one's Face and Eye? Is It what comes after thirty years of training? Or is It ten thousand years within a single thought? We should examine these matters in detail and we should not overlook anything in our examination. When we do our examination in detail, our whole Eye hears sounds and our whole Ear sees forms and colors. And

---

8.   This is a Zen Buddhist metaphor meaning that a person has implied more than they have actually said.

further, when a mendicant monk's single Eye is clearly open, the sounds, forms, and colors It sees will not be the thoughts and things before one's eyes. There will appear His gentle countenance breaking into a smile and His twinkling eyes. This is the ever-fleeting quality of the everyday behavior of a Buddha doing His practice. It is not a matter of 'being hauled about by things'; rather, it is a matter of 'not hauling things about'. It is beyond our notion of something being 'unborn and uncreated' which actually arises dependent upon causal conditions. And It is beyond our Original Nature and the Ultimate Nature of things. It is beyond our simply abiding in our place. And It is beyond the state of our Original Existence. It is not only our affirming that things are just as they are, it is simply being a Buddha doing His practice in His everyday behavior.

Accordingly, the living activities of creating things and creating a self are well left up to our mind to do. And the everyday behaviors of getting rid of 'life' and getting rid of 'death' have been entrusted for the time being to Buddha. This is why there is the saying, "The myriad thoughts and things are simply our mind, just as the three worlds of desire, form, and beyond form are simply our mind." Also, when we express the situation from a higher perspective, there is 'simply our mind', that is, there are simply the tiles* and stones of our walls and fences. Because 'simply our mind' is not simply our mind, so 'the tiles and stones of our walls and fences' are not the tiles and stones of walls and fences. This is the everyday behavior of a Buddha doing His practice, and it is the principle of leaving things to the mind and leaving things to things even while we are creating both a mind and things.

Further, this goes beyond what is reached by someone's initial realization or by their fundamental realization, and the like, so how much less could it be reached by those outside the Way, or by those in the two Lesser Courses,* or by those who are thrice wise and ten times saintly! This everyday behavior is not understood by one person after another, and it is not understood in one situation after another. It is like, for instance, a fish darting through the water, for being active is also something that points the Matter out at every instant. Is it a single iron rod? Is it both parts moving?[9]

----

9.   To paraphrase, is the everyday behavior of a Buddha doing His practice like a single iron rod, which is the same at any time or place? Or is His everyday behavior like a worm that

The single iron rod is beyond being long or short: the two parts moving are beyond self and other. When you realize the fruits of your effort, which is your ability to hit the target through word or deed in response to your Master, then your majesty will envelop all the myriad things that arise, and your Eye will tower over the entire world. You will have a radiant brightness that goes beyond your mastery of letting go and holding back: this is the Monks' Hall, the Buddha Hall, the Temple Kitchen, and the Temple Gate. Further, you will have a radiant brightness unrelated to letting go and holding back: it is the Monks' Hall, the Buddha Hall, the Temple Kitchen, and the Temple Gate. And you will have an Eye that will penetrate everywhere in all ten directions, an Eye that takes in everything within the great earth. You will have a mind for the past and a mind for the future. Because the merit of this radiant brightness blazes up in eyes, ears, nose, tongue, body, and mind, there are all the Buddhas of the three temporal worlds who maintain and rely upon Their not being known to exist, and there is the feral cat and the wild white ox who gamble on their being known to exist. When one has a ring for this ox's nose and also has the eyes for It, then the Dharma gives expression to a Buddha doing His practice and sanctions a practicing Buddha.[10]

In pointing out the Great Matter to his assembly, Seppō Gison once said, "The Buddhas in the three temporal worlds exist within the Blazing Fire, turning the Great Wheel of the Dharma."

His disciple Gensha Shibi added, "Since the Blazing Fire is giving voice to the Dharma for the sake of all the Buddhas in the

---

has been cut in two? Since both parts of the worm are moving independently of each other, by analogy the Buddha's various behaviors would likewise seem to be independent of each other.

10. 'The feral cat and the wild white ox' refer to the untamed nature of those who are not doing Buddhist practice. Taming this nature is likened to inserting a ring in an ox's nose in order to train it, whereas recognizing that the purpose of that training is to realize our Buddha Nature is likened to having the eyes for it.

three temporal worlds, all the Buddhas in the three temporal worlds listen to It right on the spot where They are."

Meditation Master Engo commented on what they said in verse:

> *We have Seppō, Monkey White well called,*
> *Along with Shibi, Monkey Black.*
> *Both together throw themselves into the moment*
>   *at hand,*
> *So that gods appear and demons vanish.*
>
> *The Raging Fire spreading across the heavens is*
>   *Buddha giving voice to Truth;*
> *The Raging Fire that spreads across the heavens*
>   *is Truth giving voice to Buddha.*
> *The tangled nests of kudzu and wisteria vines are*
>   *cut low before Its wind.*
> *One remark from Seppō and Shibi, and*
>   *Vimalakīrti* has been tested and bested.*

'The Buddhas in the three temporal worlds' refers to all the Buddhas, each and every one of Them. The Buddhas doing Their practice, consequently, are the Buddhas in the three temporal worlds. Of all the Buddhas everywhere, there is not One who is not in the three temporal worlds. When the words and ways of a Buddha express the three temporal worlds, they are completely expressed in just this manner. In our present inquiry into Buddhas doing Their practice, They are, accordingly, all the Buddhas in the three temporal worlds. Even if we know that They exist, even if we do not know that They exist, They are, beyond doubt, all the Buddhas of the three temporal worlds and They are 'Buddhas doing Their practice'.

And at the same time, in expressing 'all the Buddhas in the three temporal worlds', these three Old Buddhas—Seppō, Shibi, and Engo—each had their own way of putting the Matter. We need to learn the principle underlying what Seppō expressed as, "The Buddhas in the three temporal worlds exist within the Blazing Fire, turning the Great Wheel of the Dharma." The training ground for the turning of the Wheel of the Dharma by all the Buddhas in the three temporal worlds is undoubtedly within the Blazing Fire: within the Blazing Fire is undoubtedly the training ground for Buddhas. Rigid teachers of Scripture and pedantic commentators cannot hear this, nor can non-Buddhists and those of the two Lesser Courses understand it. Be aware that the Blazing Fire of all the Buddhas will not be any other sort of fire. Also, you need to reflect upon whether any of those other sorts of fire are ablaze. You need to learn the teaching methods of our monastic tradition which are employed by the Buddhas of the three temporal worlds whilst They exist within the Blazing Fire. When They are present within the Blazing Fire, are the Blazing Fire and the Buddhas intimately connected? Or are the Two turning away from each other? Or are They one and the same both within and without?[11] Do They have a within and a without? Are Their within and without the same thing? Are Their within and without equally distant from each other?

Turning the Great Wheel of the Dharma will be the turning of oneself and the turning of the opportune moment at hand. It is one's ability to hit the target through word or deed in response to one's Master, which will include a turning of the Dharma and the Dharma's turning. This turning of the Great Wheel of the Dharma, which Seppō has already mentioned, encompasses a Dharma Wheel that is turning the Wheel of Fire, even though the whole of the great earth is already completely ablaze. And It will be a Dharma Wheel that sets all Buddhas in motion. It will be a Dharma Wheel that sets the Wheel of the Dharma in motion, and It will encompass a Dharma Wheel that sets the three temporal worlds in motion.

Thus it is that the Blazing Fire is the great training ground wherein all Buddhas turn the Great Wheel of the Dharma. To try to analyze and measure this by spatial thinking, temporal thinking, human thinking, ordinary thinking, or saintly thinking, and the like, is to miss the mark. Since It cannot be measured by those types of thinking, then, because It is the training ground for the turning of the Wheel of the Dharma by each and every Buddha of the three temporal worlds, and because the Blazing Fire exists, there is a training ground for Buddhas.

---

11. 'Within and without' translates a technical Buddhist term for what appears as the subjective 'inner world' and the objective 'outer world'.

Shibi remarked: "Since the Blazing Fire is giving voice to the Dharma for the sake of all the Buddhas in the three temporal worlds, all the Buddhas in the three temporal worlds listen to It right on the spot where They are."

Hearing these words, some may say that Shibi's remark states the Truth better than Seppō's remark, but this is not necessarily so. Keep in mind that Seppō's remark is separate from Shibi's remark. That is to say, Seppō is stating that the Buddhas in the three temporal worlds are turning the Great Wheel of the Dharma, whereas Shibi is stating that the Buddhas in the three temporal worlds are listening to the Dharma. Although Seppō's remark is undoubtedly stating that the Dharma is being set in motion, it is not the case that the Dharma's being set in motion necessarily involves the Dharma's being heard. As a consequence, we cannot take what Seppō is saying to mean that the Dharma that has been set in motion will necessarily involve the Dharma being heard. In fact, Seppō is not saying that the Buddhas in the three temporal worlds are giving expression to the Dharma for the sake of the Blazing Fire, nor is he saying that the Buddhas in the three temporal worlds are turning the Great Wheel of the Dharma for the sake of the Buddhas in the three temporal worlds, nor is he saying that the Blazing Fire is turning the Great Wheel of the Dharma for the sake of the Blazing Fire. Is there any difference between speaking of turning the Wheel of the Dharma and actually turning the Great Wheel of the Dharma? Setting the Wheel of the Dharma in motion is beyond any voicing of the Dharma, so will the voicing of the Dharma necessarily exist for the sake of others? Accordingly, Seppō's remark is one that does not fail to say what he meant to say.

As part of your training with your Master, you will certainly need to thoroughly explore Seppō's phrases 'being within the Blazing Fire' and 'turning the Great Wheel of the Dharma'. Do not confuse them with what Shibi is saying. To penetrate what Seppō is saying is to make as your everyday behavior the everyday behavior of a Buddha doing his practice. The Blazing Fire causes Itself to exist within all the Buddhas of the three temporal worlds. This is beyond Its simply permeating one or two inexhaustible realms of thoughts and things, and beyond Its merely permeating one or two motes of dust. In gauging the turning of the Great Wheel of the

Dharma, do not liken It to measuring something as being large or small, broad or narrow. The Great Wheel of the Dharma does not turn for one's own sake or for the sake of others, nor does It turn for the sake of giving voice to It or for the sake of hearing It.

Shibi's way of putting it is, "Since the Blazing Fire is giving voice to the Dharma for the sake of all the Buddhas in the three temporal worlds, all the Buddhas in the three temporal worlds listen to It right on the spot where They are." Even though this says that the Blazing Fire is giving voice to the Dharma for the sake of all Buddhas in the three temporal worlds, it does not go so far as to say that It sets the Wheel of the Dharma in motion, nor does it say that the Buddhas in the three temporal worlds set the Wheel of the Dharma in motion. And even though all the Buddhas in the three temporal worlds listen to It right on the spot where They are, how could the Wheel of the Dharma of all the Buddhas in the three temporal worlds possibly have set into motion the Blazing Fire? Does the Blazing Fire which voices the Dharma for the sake of all Buddhas in the three temporal worlds also turn the Great Wheel of the Dharma or not? Shibi also does not go so far as to say, "The Wheel of the Dharma is turning right now." Nor does he say, "There is no turning of the Wheel of the Dharma."

Be that as it may, we need to consider whether Shibi is confused and understands the turning of the Wheel of the Dharma to mean expounding on the Wheel of the Dharma. If that is the case, then he is still in the dark about Seppō's statement. Even though he would have understood that when the Blazing Fire voices the Dharma for the sake of the Buddhas in the three temporal worlds, all the Buddhas in the three temporal worlds listen to It right on the spot where They are, nevertheless, he would not have recognized that when the Blazing Fire turns the Wheel of the Dharma, the Blazing Fire also listens to It right on the spot. He does not say that when the Blazing Fire turns the Wheel of the Dharma, the Fire is blazing at the same time as It is turning the Wheel of the Dharma. Listening to the Dharma by the Buddhas of the three temporal worlds is the practice of all Buddhas; They are not influenced by anything else. So, do not regard the Blazing Fire as 'the Dharma', nor regard the Blazing Fire as 'a Buddha', nor regard the Blazing Fire as just a blazing fire. And, truly, do not make light of the remark by Master Seppō's disciple. Would what he said simply be a case of his having thought that 'Persians have red beards' when, in fact, it was the case that 'a Persian's beard is red'? [12]

Even though Shibi's remark may resemble these ways of looking at the Matter, there is something in it that you would do well to consider: namely, it reveals the strength you will need for exploring the Matter through your training. That is to say, you should explore through your training the Essential Nature and the transitory forms It takes, which Buddha after Buddha and Ancestor after Ancestor have accurately Transmitted. This is not connected with 'ultimate reality and its transitory forms' as worked out in the traditions of both the Mahayana* and the Lesser Courses by pedestrian teachers of Scriptures and commentaries. Shibi is describing the Buddhas of the three temporal worlds listening to the Dharma which, in the traditions of both the Mahayana and the Lesser Courses, is beyond 'ultimate reality and its transitory forms'. Such narrow-minded teachers only recognize that Buddhas have a way of voicing the Dharma that is limited to opportune occasions. They do not speak of all Buddhas listening to the Dharma, or speak of all Buddhas doing Their training and practice, or speak of all Buddhas realizing Buddhahood.

Now, Shibi has already stated, "All Buddhas in the three temporal worlds listen to the Dharma right on the spot where They are." This statement encompasses both the Essential Nature and the forms It takes in which all Buddhas listen to the Dharma. By all means, do not regard those who are able to give voice to It as being superior, and do not say that those who are listening carefully to the Dharma are inferior. If those who give voice to It are worthy of our respect, then those who listen to It are also worthy of our respect.

Shakyamuni Buddha once said in verse:

> *If any people give voice to this Discourse*
> *Then they will surely be able to see Me.*
> *But to express It for the sake of even one person*

---

12.   The quoted phrases derive from a remark made by Hyakujō Ekai, alluding to two different ways of saying the same thing.

> *Is indeed something difficult for them to do.*

So it follows from this that to be able to express the Dharma is to see Shakyamuni Buddha because, when 'such a one' comes to see 'Me', he is Shakyamuni Buddha. The Buddha also said in verse:

> *After I am extinct,*
> *To hear and accept this Discourse*
> *And to inquire into Its meaning*
> *Will indeed be difficult to do.*

Keep in mind that hearing It and accepting It are also equally difficult to do, and there is no superiority or inferiority involved. Even though Those who are 'listening right on the spot where They are' are Buddhas most worthy of respect, what They must be listening to right on the spot is the Dharma, because 'Those who listen right on the spot to the Dharma' are what Buddhas of the three temporal worlds are. All Buddhas have already reached spiritual fruition, so we do not speak of Their listening to the Dharma whilst in some developing stage, because They are already Buddhas in the three temporal worlds. Keep in mind that the Buddhas of the three temporal worlds, as They stand right on the spot listening to the Blazing Fire give expression to the Dharma, are Buddhas. It does not mean that They need to follow the teaching methods of our monastic tradition in exactly the same way as we do. And, in attempting to keep to our traditional methods, there have been those whose arrows have met in mid-air.[13] The Blazing Fire is certainly expressing the Dharma for the sake of the Buddhas in the three temporal worlds. And on those occasions when heart and mind are stripped bare, blossoms burst forth on the iron tree and the world is redolent with their perfume. In other words, when it comes down to Their listening to the voicing of the Dharma by the Blazing Fire right where They are, what is it that ultimately manifests before Their very eyes? In everyday terms, it will be Wisdom surpassing the Master or it will be Wisdom equal to the Master. In thoroughly

---

13.   An image referring to a disciple's response to a Master's being 'right on', like two arrows shot from opposite directions hitting each other head on.

exploring that which is beyond the threshold of Master and disciple, it will be the Buddhas of the three temporal worlds.

Engo said that when the ones we rightly call Monkey White and Monkey Black both throw themselves into the moment at hand, gods appear and demons vanish.[14] As to this statement, even though Seppō is manifesting the Blazing Fire from the same situation that Shibi is in, there could be some way in which Seppō does not enter into the situation in the same way that Shibi does. Be that as it may, is Shibi's Blazing Fire the Buddhas or is he taking all the Buddhas to be the Blazing Fire? In the situations where black and white both act together, Shibi arises and disappears along with the gods and demons, but what Seppō has manifested through sound and form does not distinguish between black and white times. Even though this is so, you need to recognize that Shibi has ways of putting It that are quite right and ways of putting It that are not quite right, whereas Seppō has ways of putting It that take up the Matter and ways of putting It that let the Matter go.

Now, Engo also has a way of putting the Matter that is not the same as either Shibi's or Seppō's. It is his saying, "The Raging Fire spreading across the heavens is Buddha giving voice to the Truth," and "The Raging Fire that spreads across the heavens is Truth giving voice to Buddha." This way of putting the Matter serves as a brilliant light for us present-day trainees. Even if we are in the dark about the Raging Fire, Its spreading across the heavens covers us, so that we have our share of It and others have their share too. Whatever is covered by the revolving heavens will completely be the Raging Fire. Why reject 'this' merely to adopt 'that'?

We should be glad that these bags of skin of ours have been able to hear His transforming Truth which has spread across the heavens, even though we've been born in a country far from the land of our saintly Shakyamuni and live at a time distant

---

14. Originally, Monkey White and Monkey Black were nicknames for two Chinese robbers who were famed for their great skill and daring. Seppō is associated with Monkey White through his name, which means White Peak, whereas Shibi is linked to Monkey Black by his name, which means Dark Sands. There is also the implication that even though the two expressed spiritual matters in superficially different manners, what they taught was of one and the same species.

from His. Even though you are in a place where you may hear what Engo called 'Buddha giving voice to the Truth', still, how deeply entangled are you in your failure to recognize 'the Truth giving voice to Buddha'?

Thus, all the Buddhas of the three temporal worlds are expressed within these worlds by the Dharma, and all the various forms of the Dharma in the three temporal worlds have been expressed within these worlds by the Buddha. Only the heavens cover us, and their winds cut low the tangled nests of kudzu and wisteria vines. A single remark has clearly tested and bested Vimalakīrti and others as well. Thus, Dharma gives voice to Buddha, Dharma practices Buddha, Dharma awakens to Buddha, Buddha gives voice to Dharma, Buddha practices Buddha, and Buddha becomes Buddha. All of these, all together, comprise the everyday behavior of a Buddha doing His practice. Over the heavens and over the earth, over the past and over the present, those who have realized It do not trivialize It, and those who have clarified what It is do not debase It.

Written during the second third of the tenth lunar month in the second year of the Ninji era
(late November, 1241) at Kannondōri in Kōshōhōrin-ji Temple.

Dōgen

23

On What the Buddha Taught

(Bukkyō)

Translator's Introduction: In this discourse there are allusions to a poem attributed to Bodhidharma, which may be rendered as follows:

> *The separate Transmission that is outside the Teachings*
> *Does not depend on the written word;*
> *It directly points us to our human heart,*
> *So that we may see our True Nature and thereby become Buddha.*

Versions of this poem have often been used to support the view that the direct one-to-one Transmission, which is characteristic of the Zen Buddhist tradition, was apart from the Buddha's Teachings that had been passed on in the form of the Scriptures. Further, since the Transmission was viewed as outside the Scriptures, the Scriptures were considered unnecessary for realizing Buddhahood and could, therefore, be ignored. Dōgen considered this view as fallacious, since Transmission is not something outside—that is, apart from—what the Buddha taught, and the Scriptural Teachings, which are also part of what the Buddha taught, are not worthless or irrelevant to training. Further, Dōgen understood the opening line of Bodhidharma's poem as saying that Transmission is 'on the outside of the Teachings'. That is, Transmission is not something divorced from what the Buddha taught, but something that exists on the outside of what He taught (Transmission as an outer, concrete event) in contrast with what exists on the inside of what He taught (Scripture as an inner, expedient explanation). Hence, the Transmission and the Scriptural Teachings do not stand against each other, but together comprise 'what the Buddha taught'.

Practicing what the Buddha taught means making the words and ways of all the Buddhas manifest. Because this is what Buddhas and Ancestors have done for the sake of Buddhas and Ancestors, the Teachings have been accurately passed on for the sake of the Teachings. This is what the turning of the Wheel of the Dharma is. From within the Eye of this Wheel, these Teachings have caused all the Buddhas and Ancestors to manifest and to be carried into nirvana. For all the Buddhas and Ancestors, without fail, there is the emergence of each mote of dust and the passing away of each mote of dust, there is the emergence of whole universes and the passing away of whole universes, and there is their emergence for a single instant and for oceans of kalpas.* Be that as it may, the emergence of a single mote of dust for a single instant has no function that is incomplete, and the emergence of a whole universe for oceans of kalpas is beyond any effort to supply something that is otherwise lacking. This is why it has never been said that any of the Buddhas who realized the Way in the morning and then passed away in the evening ever had any shortcomings in Their meritorious behavior. If it were said that one day is insufficient for Their meritorious behavior, then eighty years of a human life would not be long enough either. When we compare the human span of eighty years with ten or twenty kalpas, it is like one day is to eighty years. The meritorious behavior of this Buddha of eighty years and that Buddha of one day may be difficult to discern clearly. Were you to compare the merit accrued over life spans of long kalpas with the merit accrued over eighty years, you would not even approach having a doubt about the matter. For this reason, what the Buddha taught is, namely, His Teaching for Buddhas, and It is the completely meritorious spiritual behavior of Buddhas and Ancestors. It is not the case that Buddhas are lofty and far-reaching, whereas Their teaching of the Dharma is narrow and petty. You need to realize that when a Buddha is large, His Teaching is large, and when a Buddha is small, His Teaching is small. You need to realize that the Buddhas and Their Teachings are beyond such measurements as 'large or small', and beyond such attributes as 'good, bad, or indifferent', and that these Teachings are not undertaken for the sake of self-instruction or for the instruction of others.

A certain monk of our tradition once said:

> Our Venerable Shakyamuni, in addition to expounding the Scriptural Teachings during His lifetime, directly Transmitted to Makakashō the Dharma that the Supreme Vehicle is the One Whole Mind. This Dharma has come to be passed on from Successor to

---

*   See Glossary.

Successor.[1] Accordingly, His Teachings are judicious discussions adapted to the capacity of the listener, whereas the Mind is immutable Reality. This One Whole Mind which has been authentically Transmitted has been described as 'the separate Transmission that is outside the Teachings'. It is beyond comparison with anything that is discussed in the Three Vehicles[*] and the twelve divisions of the Scriptural Teachings.[2] Because the One Whole Mind is the Supreme Vehicle, it has been said that "It directly points us to our human heart, so that we may see our True Nature and thereby become Buddha."

As far as it goes, this statement is not about the everyday functioning of Buddha Dharma, for it offers no vital path that takes us beyond self, and it is not descriptive of the everyday behavior of one's whole being. Hundreds, even thousands, of years ago, monks like this one were proclaiming themselves to be spiritual authorities, but if any of them had such a tale to tell as this, you should know that they had neither clarified nor understood what Buddha Dharma and the Buddha's Way are. And why so? Because they do not know Buddha or His Teachings, or what Mind is, or what is inside, or what is outside.[3] The underlying cause of their not knowing is simply that they have never really heard the Buddha Dharma. Now, they do not know what the root and branchings are of that which they call 'the Buddhas'. Never having learned what the bounds of the comings and goings of Buddhas are, they in no way resemble

---

1. 'The One Whole Mind' *(isshin)* is an alternate term for Buddha Mind and Buddha Nature.

2. The 'twelve divisions' refers to the twelve categories by which Scriptural writings are classified in the Mahayana tradition. A description of these categories appears later in this discourse.

3. Dōgen's allusion here to 'inside' and 'outside' is ambiguous. In the present context, it most likely refers to what is or is not contained within what the Buddha taught. Later, when Dōgen reinterprets the opening line of Bodhidharma's poem, the meaning of these two terms shifts.

disciples of the Buddha.[4] Their saying that one only Transmits the One Whole Mind and does not Transmit what the Buddha taught is due to their not knowing the Buddha Dharma. They do not know the One Whole Mind of which the Buddha taught, nor have they heeded what the Buddha taught concerning the One Whole Mind. They say that the Teachings of the Buddha are apart from the One Whole Mind, but their 'One Whole Mind' is not the One Whole Mind. They say that the One Whole Mind is outside the Buddha's Teachings, but their 'Buddha's Teachings' are not what the Buddha taught. Even though they have passed on the fallacious remark that the Transmission is outside the Teachings, they have not yet comprehended what is inside and what is outside.

How could the Buddhas and Ancestors who have directly Transmitted one-to-one the Buddha's Treasure House of the Eye of the True Teaching have failed to directly Transmit one-to-one what the Buddha taught? And what is more, why would our venerable monk Shakyamuni have set up Teaching that has no place in the everyday functioning of those in our Buddhist family? Our Venerable Shakyamuni has already endowed us with the Teachings that are directly Transmitted, so why would any Ancestor of the Buddha do away with Them? This is why what is called 'the One Whole Mind that is the Supreme Vehicle' is synonymous with the Three Vehicles and the twelve divisions of the Scriptural Teachings, which comprise the Smaller Treasure House and the Larger Treasure House.[5]

You need to recognize that what is called Buddha Mind is synonymous with the Buddha's Eye, as well as with a broken wooden ladle,* all thoughts and things, and the three worlds of desire, form, and beyond form. As a consequence, It is also synonymous with the mountains, seas, and nations of the earth, as well as with the sun, moon, and stars. 'What the Buddha taught' is another name for everything that

---

4. That is to say, because they have rejected Scriptural Teachings, they have not learned about the Precepts, which supply the bounds within which Buddhas function, and therefore they do not behave as a true disciple of the Buddha does.

5. 'The Larger Treasure House' refers to the Mahayana Canon, whereas 'the Smaller Treasure House' refers to the Pali Canon, which is included within the Mahayana Canon through translations into Chinese or Tibetan.

arises in nature. What is called 'being outside' is being right here in this situation. It is what is happening, right here in this situation. The term 'the genuine Transmission' means that there is a self within the genuine Transmission because it involves a direct Transmission from a self to a self. It directly Transmits from One Whole Mind to One Whole Mind, for there must be the One Whole Mind in a genuine Transmission. The One Whole Mind that is the Supreme Vehicle is synonymous with soil, stones, sand, and pebbles, and soil, stones, sand, and pebbles are synonymous with the One Whole Mind. Consequently, soil, stones, sand, and pebbles are synonymous with soil, stones, sand, and pebbles. If we speak of the direct Transmission of the One Whole Mind that is the Supreme Vehicle, it needs to be done in this manner.

Be that as it may, the monk who asserted that there is a separate Transmission outside the Teachings has not yet grasped the intent behind this phrase. So, do not believe his erroneous explanation of a separate Transmission outside the Teachings and thereby misunderstand what the Buddha taught. If the matter were as such folks put it, are we to describe the Teaching as 'a separate Transmission outside the Mind'? If we say that it is a separate Transmission outside the Mind, not even a phrase or half a line of verse could have been passed on. And if we do not speak of a separate Transmission outside the Mind, we cannot speak of a separate Transmission outside— that is, apart from—the Teaching.

Makakashō, who was already the World-honored One's successor, was in possession of the Treasure House of the Dharma and, having directly received the Transmission of the Treasure House of the True Dharma, was responsible for preserving the Buddha's Way. To assert that the Buddha's Teachings may not have been directly Transmitted to him would make the training and practice of the Way a one-sided affair. You need to realize that when one line of Scripture has been genuinely Transmitted, the whole Dharma has been genuinely Transmitted, and that when one line of Scripture has been genuinely Transmitted, the Transmission of the Mountain and the Transmission of the Water has taken place. In sum, this is synonymous with our utter incapacity to separate ourselves from the here and now.

The world-honored Shakyamuni's unsurpassed Enlightened Mind, which is the Treasure House of the Eye of the True Teaching, was directly Transmitted to Makakashō. It was not directly Transmitted to any of His other disciples. Beyond question, the Direct Transmission is Makakashō. This is why all persons—every single one of them, past or present—who have explored the Truth of the Buddha Dharma have all decided to explore the Scriptural Teachings, and in doing so they have, without fail, explored the Matter* by training under some Ancestor of the Buddha, and without seeking to train under anyone else. If they did not commit themselves to train with an Ancestor of the Buddha, theirs would not have been the right commitment. If you wish to consider whether your commitment is in accord with the Teachings, you need to determine that with an Ancestor of the Buddha. The reason for this is that the Ancestors of the Buddha possess the whole Wheel of the Dharma. To put it simply, only the Ancestors of the Buddha have clarified and have continued to correctly Transmit what the terms 'It exists' or 'It does not exist' means, and what the terms 'being empty' or 'having form' means.

Haryō Kōkan was once asked by one of his monks, "Are the intent of our Ancestor Bodhidharma and the intent of the Teachings the same or are they different?"

The Master replied, "When a hen is cold, it perches in a tree; when a duck is cold, it enters the water."

When we explore this saying of Kōkan's through our training, we will certainly come face-to-face with Bodhidharma, our founding Ancestor within the Buddha's Way, and we will certainly come to know the Teachings within the Buddha's Way. Now, the monk's asking about the intent of the Ancestor and the intent of the Teachings is equivalent to his asking whether the Ancestor's intent was within the Way or was separate from It. The Master's saying at this time, "When a hen is cold, it perches in a tree; when a duck is cold, it enters the water" expresses a sameness and a difference. Even so, this goes beyond the sameness versus difference that people are usually concerned with. As a consequence, because his remark goes beyond a discussion of sameness and difference, he may well be saying that it is 'the same difference'. So it is as if he were saying, "Do not ask about sameness and difference."

Gensha Shibi was once asked by a monk, "Granting that the Three Vehicles and the twelve divisions of the Scriptural Teachings are not essential, just what was the intent behind our Ancestral Master Bodhidharma's coming from the West?"

Master Shibi replied, "The Three Vehicles and the twelve divisions of the Scriptural Teachings not being absolutely essential."

The monk's asking, "Granting that the Three Vehicles and the twelve divisions of the Scriptural teachings are not essential, just what was the intent behind the Ancestral Master's coming from the West?" is conventionally thought of as his saying, "Since each of the Three Vehicles and the twelve divisions of the Scriptural Teachings constitutes one of the branches of a forked road, the intent behind the Ancestral Master's coming from the West must lie elsewhere." Those with this conventional view do not recognize that the Three Vehicles and the twelve divisions of the Scriptural Teachings constitute the very intent behind the Ancestral Master's coming from the West. So how much less could they possibly comprehend that the sum total of the eighty-four thousand gates to the Dharma is nothing other than the intent behind the Ancestral Master's coming from the West?

Now let us explore why the Three Vehicles and the twelve divisions of the Scriptural Teachings are not absolutely essential.[6] If there were a time when they were essential, what criteria would we use to determine this? In a situation where the Three Vehicles and the twelve divisions of the Scriptural Teachings are not essential, does

---

6.   The term 'not absolutely essential' refers to the middle way between asserting, on the one hand, that it is absolutely impossible for someone to realize the Truth without formally studying the Scriptures, and, on the other hand, asserting that because someone can realize the Truth independent of Scriptural study, the Scriptures are totally worthless and can be safely ignored by trainees.

our exploration of 'the intent behind the Ancestral Master's coming from the West' manifest itself in our training? It may not be in vain that this question has come forth.

Shibi said, "The Three Vehicles and the twelve divisions of the Scriptural Teachings are not absolutely essential." This statement is the Wheel of the Dharma. We need to explore through our training that wherever this Wheel of the Dharma turns, what the Buddha taught exists as the Buddha's Teachings. The import of this is that the Three Vehicles and the twelve divisions of the Scriptural Teachings are the Wheel of the Dharma of the Buddha's Ancestors. It turns at times and in places where there are Ancestors of the Buddha, and It turns at times and in places where there are no Ancestors of the Buddha, and It likewise turned before there was an Ancestor and will turn after there is an Ancestor. Moreover, It has the meritorious function of setting the Buddhas and Ancestors a-turning. At the very moment when our Ancestral Master intended to come from the West, the Wheel of the Dharma became not absolutely essential. Saying that It is not absolutely essential does not mean that we do not use It or that It is broken down. It is simply that this Wheel of the Dharma is, at this time, turning the wheel of 'not being absolutely essential'. Without denying the existence of the Three Vehicles and the twelve divisions of the Scriptural Teachings, we should watch for the occasions when they are not absolutely essential. Because they are not absolutely essential, they are the Three Vehicles and the twelve divisions of the Scriptural Teachings, and because they are the Three Vehicles and the twelve divisions of the Scriptural Teachings, they are beyond being the 'Three Vehicles and twelve divisions of Scriptural Teachings'. This is why the Master said that the Three Vehicles and the twelve divisions of the Scriptural Teachings were not absolutely essential.

The following offers but one example of those Three Vehicles and twelve divisions of the Scriptural Teachings from among the number of examples that exist.

The Three Vehicles

First, there is the vehicle of the shravakas,* who realize the Truth by way of the Four Noble Truths. The Four Noble Truths are the Truth of the existence of suffering, the Truth that suffering has a cause, the Truth that suffering can cease, and the Truth of the Noble Eightfold Path which brings suffering to an end. Hearing of these and then making them their practice, shravakas free themselves from birth, aging, sickness, and death, and ultimately realize the perfection of nirvana. To make these Truths the basis of one's training and practice, and then to assert that suffering and its cause are mundane, whereas its cessation and the path to cessation are what is paramount is an opinion that arises from the perspective of narrow-minded scholars. When the Four Noble Truths are practiced in accord with the Buddha Dharma, They are all realized by each Buddha on His own, just as all the Buddhas have done. The Four Noble Truths are all a matter of 'the Dharma abiding in the place of the Dharma'. The Four Noble Truths are all manifestations of Truth. The Four Noble Truths are all Buddha Nature. As a consequence, They go beyond intellectual discussions of such matters as 'non-arising' and 'non-activity', and this is tied to the Four Noble Truths not being 'absolutely essential'.

Second, there is the vehicle of the pratyekabuddhas,* who realize the perfection of nirvana by way of the Twelve Links in the Chain of Dependent Origination. The Twelve Links in the Chain of Dependent Origination are first, the darkness of spiritual ignorance; second, the deliberate actions that derive from that ignorance; third, becoming aware of things; fourth, giving name and form to things; fifth, activating the six senses; sixth, making contact through the senses with what arises; seventh, being stimulated through one's senses; eighth, craving; ninth, grasping after; tenth, causing to come into existence; eleventh, giving birth to; and twelfth, aging unto death.

In making the Twelve Links in the Chain of Dependent Origination the basis of their practice, pratyekabuddhas explore causality in the past, present, and future, and talk in terms of a subject that sees and an object that is seen. Even so, they take up causal relationships one by one and explore them thoroughly through their training, but their doing so is not something that is absolutely essential to the turning of the Dharma Wheel, for it is not absolutely essential to see every link in the causal chain. Keep in mind that, since the darkness of spiritual ignorance is inseparable from the One Whole Mind, deliberate acts, becoming aware of things, and so forth, are also inseparable from the One Whole Mind. Since the darkness of ignorance is inseparable from cessation, then deliberate acts, becoming aware of things, and so forth, are also inseparable from cessation. Since the darkness of ignorance is inseparable from nirvana, deliberate acts, becoming aware of things, and so forth, are also inseparable from nirvana. We can speak in this way because what arises is also what ceases. 'The darkness of ignorance' is a phrase we use in talking. 'Becoming aware of things', 'giving them name and form', and so forth, are no different. Keep in mind that the darkness of ignorance, deliberate actions, and so forth, are not different from Seigen Gyōshi's saying to his disciple Sekitō Kisen, "I have a certain Hatchet and would give It to you, should you choose to reside on this mountain with me." The darkness of ignorance, deliberate actions, becoming aware of things, and so forth, are not different from Sekitō's responding, "At the time when I was sent to you, I received your promise of being allowed to have your Hatchet, Reverend Monk, and so I would like to receive It." [7]

Third, there is the vehicle of the bodhisattvas,* those who realize fully perfected supreme enlightenment by putting into practice the Teachings concerning the Six Paramitas. This 'realizing' of which they speak is beyond anything they do deliberately, beyond their doing nothing, beyond their initiating something, beyond their newly accomplishing something, beyond their having realized It in some remote past life, beyond what they originally intended to do, beyond anything they are attached to: it is simply their full realization of fully perfected supreme enlightenment.

What we call the Six Paramitas—that is, the six practices that ferry all sentient beings to the Other Shore—are the practice of freely giving wealth and Dharma, the practice of observing the Precepts, the practice of patience, the practice of zealous devotion, the practice of meditation, and the practice of wise discernment. These, all together, constitute supreme enlightenment. They are beyond any discussion of 'nothing arising' or of 'not deliberately doing anything'. They do not

---

7.   Originally, Sekitō, still in his teens, had gone to train at Sōkei Monastery under the aged Daikan Enō. Just before Enō's passing away, he advised Sekitō to "go train under Gyōshi" *(C. Hsing-ssu ch'ü)*, but Sekitō misunderstood what Enō had told him and thought he had been instructed to "go ponder the Matter" *(C. Hsin-ssu ch'ü)*. However, Nangaku Ejō, one of Enō's two successors, understood what Enō had said and had Sekitō go train under Seigen Gyōshi, Enō's other successor. Gyōshi's Hatchet characterizes the Dharma that is passed on at Transmission as That which cuts through all delusions and severs all karmic roots. Sekitō's remark expresses his commitment to Gyōshi as his Transmission Master.

always treat the giving of wealth and Dharma as the first thing or enlightenment as the ultimate thing. It says in the Scriptures, "A keen-witted bodhisattva makes enlightenment the first thing and makes giving the ultimate thing. A slow-witted bodhisattva makes giving the first thing and enlightenment the ultimate thing."

Even so, patience can also be first, as can meditation. And there will be their manifesting the Thirty-six Paramitas, which is their getting snares from snares.[8]

The word 'paramita' means reaching the Other Shore. Even though 'the Other Shore' is beyond any semblance or trace of coming or going, one's arrival fully manifests, for arrival refers to one's spiritual question. Do not think that training and practice merely lead you to the Other Shore, for there is training and practice on that Other Shore. When we do our training and practice, it is our arrival at the Other Shore, because this training and practice is invariably supplied with the capacity to make the whole universe manifest completely.

The Twelve Divisions of the Scriptural Teachings

First, the *Sūtras*: the Scriptures that are in accord with what the Buddha is reported to have said.

Second, the *Geyas*: the reiterations in verse that extol the Dharma.

Third, the *Vyākaranas*: the predictions of Buddhahood for all.

Fourth, the *Gāthās*: verses that are chanted.

Fifth, the *Udānas*: the Buddha's spontaneous voicings of the Dharma without His having been asked.

Sixth, the *Nidānas*: the accounts of causes and coexisting conditions.

Seventh, the *Avadānas*: the parables.

---

8.   The Thirty-six Paramitas derive from the manifesting of each of the Six Paramitas within the practice of each one of the Six Paramitas. The Six Paramitas are like six traps for snaring the Truth, each of which produces another six traps, that is, the Thirty-six Paramitas.

Eighth, the *Itivuttakas*: the past lives of the Bodhisattvas.

Ninth, the *Jātakas*: the past lives of the Buddha.

Tenth, the *Vaipulyas*: writings that extensively expound the Dharma.

Eleventh, the *Adbhutadharmas*: stories of miraculous events.

Twelfth, the *Upadeshas*: the commentaries.

For the sake of others, the Tathagata gave voice directly to both the provisional Teachings and the True Dharma[9] on such matters as our entry into the world of the five skandhas* with its eighteen realms connected with our six senses: we call this body of Teaching the *Sūtras*. Sometimes, by appending verses comprised of lines of four, five, six, seven, eight, or nine words, He extolled the Teaching on such matters as one's entry into the world of the mundane skandhas: we call these verse passages the *Geyas*. Sometimes, He gave a direct account of the future of sentient beings, even to the point of predicting such things as the realization of Buddhahood by pigeons and sparrows: we call these predictions of Buddhahood the *Vyākaranas*. Sometimes, by means of individual poems, He gave an account of such things as entry into the fleshly skandhas: we call these poems the *Gāthās*. Sometimes, He spontaneously talked about human concerns without anyone having asked Him a question: we call these talks the *Udānas*. Sometimes, He summarized matters that were not spiritually good in worldly societies and tied them to the Precepts: we call these summaries the *Nidānas*. Sometimes, He talked about the ways of the world by means of parables: we call these talks the *Avadānas*. Sometimes, He talked about events in worldly realms of the past: we call these talks the *Itivuttakas*. Sometimes, He talked about events in His own past lives: we call these talks the *Jātakas*. Sometimes, He talked about far-reaching, world-wide issues: we call these talks the

---

9. An example of this occurs in the Burning House parable in the *Lotus Scripture*, where there is the provisional Teaching that there are three vehicles, whereas with the True Dharma there is, in fact, but One Vehicle.

Vaipulyas. Sometimes, He talked about wondrous, unprecedented events in the world: we call these talks the *Adbhutadharmas*. Sometimes, He asked hard questions concerning the ways of the world: we call these queries the *Upadeshas*. These divisions constitute His ways of teaching by ordinary modes of expression. He established these twelve divisions of His Teachings so that sentient beings might rejoice and take delight in them.

It is rare to hear the names of the twelve divisions of the Scriptural Teachings. When the Buddha Dharma has spread throughout a society, one hears of them. When the Buddha Dharma has disappeared, they are not heard of, nor are they heard of when the Buddha Dharma has not yet spread abroad. Those who have put down good spiritual roots over a long time are able to meet the Buddha and hear them. Those who have already heard them will surely realize fully perfected supreme enlightenment in a short while.

Each of these twelve divisions is called a Scripture. They are also called the twelve divisions of the Scriptural Teachings as well as the twelve parts of the Scriptures. Because each of the twelve divisions of the Scriptural Teachings is equipped with the twelve divisions of the Scriptural Teachings, there are one hundred forty-four divisions of the Scriptural Teachings. Because all the twelve divisions of the Scriptural Teachings are included within each of the twelve divisions of the Scriptural Teachings, they simply comprise the whole of the divisions of the Scriptural Teachings. And at the same time, They go beyond calculation in numbers, regardless of whether those numbers are above or below a hundred million. They are all the Eye of the Buddhas and Ancestors, the Bones and Marrow of the Buddhas and Ancestors, the daily activities of the Buddhas and Ancestors, the radiance of the Buddhas and Ancestors, the splendor of the Buddhas and Ancestors, and the meritorious behavior of the Buddhas and Ancestors. The one who encounters the twelve divisions of the Scriptural Teachings encounters the Buddhas and Ancestors, and the one who speaks of the Buddhas and Ancestors speaks of the twelve divisions of the Scriptural Teachings.

Thus, Seigen's letting his foot dangle is nothing other than the Three Vehicles and the twelve divisions of the Scriptural Teachings.[10] And Nangaku's expressing his understanding of his kōan* by saying, "To describe It in words does not hit the bull's-eye" is nothing other than the Three Vehicles and the twelve divisions of the Scriptural Teachings. Now, the meaning of Shibi's expression, 'not being absolutely essential', is in no way different from this. When we understand the import of this, it simply refers to Ancestors of the Buddha, and to Them alone. Further, there is no being 'half a person' and there is no 'one absolute thing': it is 'nothing ever having arisen'. At this very moment, how is It? You should respond, "It is No-thing That Is Absolutely Essential."

Sometimes, there have been those who have spoken of nine parts, which could be called the nine divisions of the Scriptural Teachings.

The Nine Parts

First, the *Sūtras*

Second, the Independent Poems *(Gāthās)*

Third, the Past Lives of the Bodhisattvas *(Itivuttakas)*

Fourth, the *Jātakas*

Fifth, the Wondrous Events (*Adbhutadharmas)*

Sixth, the Accounts of Causes and Coexisting Conditions
(Nidānas)

Seventh, the Parables *(Avadānas)*

Eighth, the Appended Passages in Verse *(Geyas)*

Ninth, the Commentaries *(Upadeshas)*

Because the nine parts are each equipped with nine parts, there are eighty-one parts. Because the nine parts are each equipped with the whole of the parts, they

---

10.   When Sekitō Kisen requested the Hatchet that Seigen Gyōshi had promised him, Seigen is said to have dangled his foot. Dōgen states that this was Seigen's way of passing on to Sekitō the Three Vehicles and the twelve divisions of the Scriptural Teachings, which form the Hatchet of the Dharma.

are the nine parts. Without the merit of each part's belonging to the whole, they could not be the nine parts. Because there is the merit of their belonging to the whole of the parts, the whole of the parts belongs to each part. This is why they are in eighty-one parts, why they are a part of This, why they are a part of me, why they are a part of the hossu,* why they are a part of the traveling staff,* and why they are a part of the Treasure House of the Eye of the True Teaching.

Shakyamuni Buddha once said in verse:

This Dharma, which is in nine parts,
I have humbly offered, as It suits each sentient being.
For entering the Great Vehicle, It is the very source,
Which is why I have voiced these Teachings.

You need to realize that the words 'I' and 'this' both refer to the Tathagata.[11] His Face and Eye, Body and Mind customarily come into view through this Dharma. This 'I' and 'this' are already the nine-part Dharma, so the nine-part Dharma must therefore be both 'I' and 'this'. One phrase or one verse in the present will be the nine-part Dharma, and because this 'I' is synonymous with 'this', He has humbly given voice to It, in conformity with the needs of sentient beings. Thus, since all sentient beings live their lives from within the here and now, He has, accordingly, given voice to these Teachings, and since they die their deaths from within the here and now, He has, accordingly, given voice to these Teachings. Even for the sake of their momentary behavior and the fleeting expressions on their faces, He has, accordingly, given voice to these Teachings. And since, in His transforming each and every sentient being, He would help them all to enter the Buddha's Way, He has, accordingly, given voice to these Teachings. These sentient beings are followers of the 'I' that is this nine-part Dharma. These followers follow where He goes, follow where they themselves go, follow where their life goes, follow where the 'I' goes, and follow where the 'this' goes. Because these sentient beings are, unquestionably, the 'this' of His 'I', they are every part of the nine-part Dharma.

---

11. That is, what the 'I' refers to is inseparable from the Dharma that this 'I' has voiced, since the epithet 'Tathagata' applies to one who has gone beyond any sense of a personal self.

What He called 'the very source for entering the Great Vehicle' is also called 'awakening to the Great Vehicle', 'practicing the Great Vehicle', 'heeding the Great Vehicle', and 'giving expression to the Great Vehicle'. Thus, it goes beyond saying that a sentient being has spontaneously realized the Way, for they are a part of It. Accordingly, sentient beings have realized the Way. Entering is the source, and the source means from beginning to end. The Buddha expresses the Dharma, and the Dharma expresses the Buddha. The Dharma is expressed by the Buddha, and the Buddha is expressed by the Dharma. The Blazing Fire expresses both the Buddha and the Dharma. The Buddha and the Dharma both express the Blazing Fire.

In these Teachings, there is good reason for giving voice to the whys and wherefores. Even if the Buddha had intended not to expound these Scriptures, it would have been impossible. This is why He said that the Why expounded this Scripture.[12] What the Why expounds fills the heavens, and what fills the heavens is what the Why expounds. Both this Buddha and that Buddha, with one voice, proclaim 'this Scripture'; both one's own True Self and the True Self of others expound the Why as 'this Scripture'. Thus, He expounded this Scripture, and 'this Scripture' is synonymous with 'what the Buddha taught'. You need to know that the Buddha's Teachings, which are as innumerable as the sands of the Ganges, are the awakening stick and the ceremonial hossu, the traveling staff and the Fist.

In sum, you need to know that such things as the Three Vehicles and the twelve divisions of the Scriptural Teachings are the Eye of the Buddhas and Ancestors. How could those who have not opened their Eye to This possibly be descendants of the Buddhas and Ancestors? How could those who have not understood It and come forth with It possibly Transmit one-to-one the True Eye of the Buddhas and Ancestors? Those who have not realized the Treasure House of the Eye of the True Teaching are not Dharma heirs of the Seven Buddhas.*

---

12. Dōgen gives a twist to the meaning of the last line of the Buddha's verse by treating the term for 'why' as a noun, 'the Why'.

Given to the assembly on the fourteenth day of the eleventh lunar month of the second year of
the Ninji era (December 17, 1241) in the Monks' Hall in Kōshō-ji Temple, Kyōto
Prefecture.

Redelivered to the assembly on the seventh day of the eleventh lunar month in the third year of
the Ninji era (November 30, 1242) in the Monks' Hall in Kōshō-ji Temple, Kyōto
Prefecture.

24

On the Marvelous Spiritual Abilities

(Jinzū)

Translator's Introduction: The term *jinzū* was widely used both within and outside Buddhism to refer to what were considered esoteric, supernatural, or even magical powers, which many persons apparently sought, often with the motive of gaining power and prestige or of having some advantage over others. Traditionally there were six of these abilities which, in Buddhism, functioned as: (1) the ability to freely deal with external situations or circumstances as needed (2) the ability to see what is truly going on, (3) the ability to hear what someone is truly saying, (4) the ability to know what someone's true intentions are, (5) the ability to recognize what someone's karma from a past life is, and (6) the ability to know when someone has cleansed that karma. All but the sixth were presumably attainable by anyone; only Buddhas and arhats could realize the last one.

On the basis of remarks made by various Ancestral Masters, Dōgen explains that there is a greater ability, one that surpasses all other marvelous abilities. This marvelous spiritual ability involves one's natural functioning in everyday life after having dropped off body and mind with its attendant greeds, hatreds, and delusions; that is, it is just the everyday doing of whatever needs to be done. Performing these everyday acts is, in itself, an expression of this greater marvelous spiritual ability. Further, in that such behavior involves the natural functioning of one's six senses, Dōgen identifies them as the six marvelous spiritual abilities.

The marvelous spiritual ability that we are speaking of here is the very food and drink of those who are in the Buddha's family, and the Buddhas have not wearied of it even to the present day. There are the six marvelous abilities, and there is the one whole marvelous spiritual ability, and there is the transcending of marvelous spiritual abilities, and there is the unsurpassed spiritual ability. The last is our three thousand acts of a morning and our eight hundred acts of an evening, which we take as the normal state of things. Though it is said that this spiritual ability arises along with Buddhahood, it goes unrecognized in Buddhas: though it is said that it vanishes along with a Buddha, it does not thereby destroy a Buddha. When a Buddha goes up to the high heavens, it likewise goes along: when a Buddha comes down to earth, it comes along too. It is present both when Buddhas do the practice to realize the Truth and when they have proved the Truth for Themselves. They are as still as the snow-capped peaks and resemble the trees and rocks.[1] The Buddhas of the past were the disciples of Shakyamuni Buddha. They came to Him out of devotion to the kesa* and invariably held aloft a stupa.* At one such time, Shakyamuni Buddha said, "The marvelous spiritual ability of all Buddhas is a wonder to behold." This is why you need to know that, in the present as well as in the future, things will be no different.

Meditation Master Isan Reiyū was an Ancestor of the thirty-seventh generation directly from the Tathagata Shakyamuni. He was a Dharma heir of Hyakujō Ekai. Of the present-day Ancestors of the Buddha who have appeared throughout the world, many are not distant descendants of Isan, and they are distant descendants of Isan.

> Once when Isan was lying down asleep, his disciple Kyōzan Ejaku came in to call upon him. Thereupon, Isan rolled over, turning his face to the wall as he lay there.
>
> Kyōzan said, "It is just me, your disciple Ejaku. Pray, venerable monk, stay just as you are."
>
> Isan made an effort to rise just as Kyōzan was leaving, and he called out, "Ejaku, my disciple!"
>
> Kyōzan came back.
>
> Isan said, "This old monk would like to tell you his dream. Please listen to it."
>
> Kyōzan lowered his head, preparing to listen. Isan said, "Try and interpret my dream, and I'll listen."
>
> Kyōzan fetched him a basin of water and a hand towel.

---

1. 'Snow-capped peaks' is often used in Zen Buddhism as a reference to those who have been successfully training for a long time. Similarly, 'trees' are trainees who have not yet cut down the tree of self, and 'stones' are trainees who are now unresponsive to the arising of defiling passions.

Isan then washed his face. After he had finished washing his face, he sat for a bit, whereupon his disciple Kyōgen Chikan came in. Isan said to him, "Disciple Ejaku and I have just been putting into practice our marvelous spiritual ability, which is on a level above all others, one that is not the same as those found in the Lesser Course."*

Kyōgen said, "Your disciple Chikan was just sitting outside, so I am aware of all that went on."

Isan said, "My disciple, you should endeavor to express it." Thereupon, Kyōgen made a cup of tea and brought it to him.

Isan, praising them, said, "The marvelous spiritual ability and wise discernment of the two of you have far surpassed even that of Shariputra and Moggallana."[2]

If you would know what the marvelous spiritual ability of those in our Buddha family is, you should explore through your training what Isan has asserted. Because it is not the same as the inferior abilities of the Lesser Course, a person who undertakes this exploration is, as a consequence, called a student who is exploring the Matter,* and anyone who does not undertake this exploration is not such a student of Buddhism. It is this marvelous spiritual ability and wise discernment that Successor after Successor has mutually Transmitted. What is more, do not undertake to study the spiritual abilities of non-Buddhists and those of the Lesser Courses in India, and do not take up what is studied by scholastics and their like.

Now, in exploring Isan's marvelous spiritual ability, even though it is spoken of as being unsurpassed, it is beyond that, for it is on a level above and beyond anything else. That is to say, after Isan had lain down, there was his turning of his face towards the wall as he lay there, there was his endeavoring to arise, there was his calling out to his disciple Ejaku, there was his referring to his having had a dream,

---

2. Shariputra and Moggallana were two of Shakyamuni Buddha's ten chief disciples. The former was known for his wise discernment and the latter for his spiritual abilities.

there was his sitting for a short while after he had washed his face, and there was Kyōzan's lowering his head to hear and his fetching a basin of water and a towel.

Nevertheless, Isan said, "Disciple Ejaku and I have just been putting into practice the marvelous spiritual ability, which is on a level above all others, one that is not the same as those found in the Lesser Course." We need to explore what this marvelous spiritual ability is, for it is what the Ancestral Masters who truly Transmit the Buddha Dharma have spoken of. Do not fail to mention the telling of a dream or the washing of the face, for you must ascertain that such actions are marvelous spiritual abilities that are on a level above all others.

To say that it is 'not the same as those found in the Lesser Course', means that it is not the same as the small ideas and small opinions associated with the Lesser Course, nor will it be anything like those of the 'three times wise and ten times saintly'.* These persons all practice the five lesser spiritual abilities, and they only attain a small idea of their True Self: they do not come near to the greater spiritual ability of the Ancestors of the Buddha. This is an ability of Ancestors of the Buddha, a marvelous spiritual ability that goes beyond Buddhahood. People who would model themselves on this marvelous spiritual ability must not be impressed by devilish people and others who are outside the Way. Academic students of Scriptures have not yet heard of such an ability or, if they have heard of it, they find it difficult to trust in. Those of the Two Lesser Courses, those who are outside the Way, those who lecture on Scriptures, scholarly commentators, and the like, are taught about the lesser spiritual abilities but do not learn about the greater marvelous spiritual ability. All Buddhas abide in and keep to the greater marvelous spiritual ability, and They Transmit this marvelous spiritual ability of Buddhas. Were it not for this ability, the basin of water and the towel would not have been fetched, nor would Isan have lain there with his face turned towards the wall, nor would he have washed his face and then sat up for a bit.

Such things as the lesser spiritual abilities do also exist, enveloped within the capacity of this greater spiritual ability. The greater marvelous spiritual ability is in contact with the lesser spiritual abilities, but the lesser spiritual abilities are not aware of the greater marvelous spiritual ability. These lesser spiritual abilities have been described as 'a hair swallowing the vast ocean' and 'a poppy seed enclosing Mount

Sumeru'. They are also synonymous with 'the upper part of the body emitting water and the lower part of the body emitting fire'.[3] Also, the first five spiritual abilities, and even the sixth spiritual ability, are all lesser spiritual abilities. Those people who devote themselves to these abilities have not yet experienced the marvelous spiritual ability of a Buddha, even in their dreams. The five spiritual abilities, along with the sixth spiritual ability, are called lesser spiritual abilities because they are all tainted by their practice being considered as separate from enlightenment and because they are confined to some time or some place. They reside in life but do not manifest after one's death; they belong to oneself but do not belong to someone else. Though they may manifest in this land of ours, they may not manifest in all other countries; though some may manifest them without trying, others cannot manifest them when they would.

This greater spiritual ability is not like that. The Teachings, practice, and realization of all Buddhas alike are made fully manifest through their marvelous spiritual ability. Not only is it fully manifested within the vicinity of all Buddhas, it is also fully manifested above and beyond Buddhahood. The marvelous spiritual ability, which is the way Buddhas teach, is truly mind-boggling. It manifests even before someone has a body, and its manifestation is not confined to past, present, or future. Were it not for the marvelous spiritual ability of the Buddha, then all the Buddhas' rousing Their mind to realize Buddhahood, Their training and practice, Their enlightenment, and Their realizing nirvana would not yet exist. Right this minute, the inexhaustible Ocean of the Dharma Realm is constantly present and unchanging, all of which is the marvelous spiritual ability of Buddha. Not only does a single hair swallow up this vast Ocean, a single hair sustains and retains this vast Ocean; a single

---

3. This is an allusion to a passage in the *Lotus Scripture*, wherein a mother asks her two sons to display various wondrous abilities for the sake of their father, a Brahman who does not follow the Buddhist Way, so that he will join the three of them in going to visit the Buddha. With their father in mind, the two sons perform various wondrous transformations, such as "walking, standing, sitting, and reclining within space, the upper part of their bodies emitting water and the lower part of their bodies emitting fire." A similar act, called the 'Twin Wonder', was performed by the Buddha when He went back to visit His family after His enlightenment.

hair manifests this vast Ocean; a single hair disgorges this vast Ocean; a single hair uses this vast Ocean. Do not take as your lesson from this that when a single hair swallows up and disgorges the whole Dharma Realm, then, since there is only one whole Dharma Realm, the Dharma Realm can no longer exist.

A single poppy seed's enclosing all of Mount Sumeru is also like this. And there is a poppy seed that naturally disgorges Mount Sumeru and a poppy seed that naturally manifests the Ocean of the Inexhaustible Treasure House of the Dharma Realm. There is also a single poppy seed that intentionally spits out Mount Sumeru and a single poppy seed that intentionally makes the Ocean of the Inexhaustible Treasure House of the Dharma Realm manifest. When a single hair and a single poppy seed disgorge the vast Ocean, they spew It out in one instant and spew It out for ten thousand kalpas.* Because ten thousand kalpas and one instant, alike, have been spewed out from a hair and a poppy seed, from whence have the hair and the poppy seed been obtained? They have been obtained precisely from the marvelous spiritual ability. Since this 'having been obtained' is synonymous with the marvelous spiritual ability, it means that this ability simply gives birth to itself. Furthermore, you need to explore the fact that it does not appear and disappear within the three times of past, present, and future. All Buddhas joyfully disport within this marvelous spiritual ability.

Lay Disciple Hō'on was an eminent person who was seated among the Ancestors. He not only trained under Baso Dōitsu and Sekitō Kisen but also had many meetings and encounters with Masters who truly walked the Way in our tradition. He once said in verse:

> *The marvelous spiritual ability manifests its enlightened functioning*
> *In our carrying water and our hauling firewood.*

You need to thoroughly explore this principle through your training. 'Carrying water' refers to the custom of loading up and toting water. Sometimes a disciple loads up and totes this water for his own sake, and sometimes he does it for the sake of others. This is what is meant by being a Buddha of marvelous spiritual abilities. Although knowledge itself is a transient thing, the marvelous spiritual ability is always a marvelous spiritual ability. Even if someone is unacquainted with it, what it teaches is not subject to fading out or to disappearing. Even if people are ignorant of it, what it teaches arises spontaneously. Even if they do not know that carrying water is a marvelous spiritual ability, the spiritual ability of carrying water is not subject to regression.

'Hauling firewood' means carrying wood for fuel. For instance, it is like what the Sixth Ancestor did of old. Even though he may not have recognized his marvelous spiritual abilities in his three thousand acts of a morning or may not have had the marvelous spiritual abilities in mind during his eight hundred acts of an evening, these acts were still a full manifestation of his marvelous spiritual ability.

Truly, those who meet and pay attention to the enlightened functioning of the marvelous spiritual ability of all the Buddhas and Tathagatas will, beyond doubt, realize the Way. This is why the realization of the Way by all the Buddhas—every one of Them—has unquestionably been fully accomplished through the effects of this marvelous spiritual ability. As a consequence, you should explore through your training that even though we were speaking just now of 'the emitting of water' of the Lesser Course as being a lesser spiritual ability, 'carrying water' is a greater spiritual ability. Carrying water and carrying firewood have never been abandoned, for people have not neglected them. Thus, these actions have been passed down from the distant past to the present day without a single person, even for a moment, falling away from them or turning them aside: this is due to the functioning of their marvelous spiritual ability. This is the greater marvelous spiritual ability, which is beyond any similarity with the inferior abilities of the Lesser Course.

Once when Tōzan Ryōkai was attending on Ungan Donjō, Ungan asked him, "What is the enlightened functioning of my disciple Ryōkai's marvelous spiritual ability?"

With hands folded in shashu,[*] Tōzan then came and stood right in front of him.

Ungan again asked him, "What is the enlightened functioning of your marvelous spiritual ability?"

Tōzan then, wishing him well, bowed in respect and took his leave.

In this account, the marvelous spiritual ability is present as Tōzan's hearing his Master's words and completely understanding the import behind them and as the particulars of what he did in response fitting together with the Truth, like a box with its lid. By all means, recognize that the enlightened functioning of Ungan's marvelous spiritual ability has certainly produced descendants, persons who did not spiritually regress. Ungan must certainly have been one of the Highest Ancestors, a person spiritually unsurpassed. Do not idly speculate on whether he or his descendants could in any way resemble non-Buddhists or those of the Two Lesser Courses.

In the Buddha's Way, there are spiritual transformations and spiritual abilities associated with the upper part of the body and the lower part of the body. The whole universe in all ten directions, right now, is the one whole True Body of a shramana.[4] Strange as it may seem, the waters from the nine mountains and the eight oceans to the Ocean of Buddha Nature and the Ocean of Buddha Wisdom are the waters emitted from the upper part of his body, the lower part of his body, and the middle part of his body. In addition, they are the waters that are emitted from the upper part of what is not the body, the lower part of what is not the body, and the middle part of what is not the body. This extends to the emitting of fire also. And this is not limited to such things as water, fire and wind, it is also the upper part of his body emitting Buddhas, and the lower part of his body emitting Buddhas, and the upper part of his body emitting Ancestors, and the lower part of his body emitting Ancestors, and the upper part of

---

4.   Although 'shramana' is a term widely used in reference to Buddhist monks in general and
     novices in particular, more specific definitions describe a shramana as someone who has
     renounced the world, has let go of the defiling passions of greed, hatred, and delusion,
     and practices compassion for all beings. Hence, the term could equally well apply to a lay
     Buddhist who is completely committed to the practice of the Way. Similarly, even though
     the grammatical gender of the Sanskrit word shramana is masculine, its usage by Dōgen
     is neutral and would not have excluded women.

his body emitting immeasurable kalpas of time, and the lower part of his body emitting immeasurable kalpas of time, and the upper part of his body emitting the Ocean of the Dharma Realm, and the upper part of his body absorbing the Ocean of the Dharma Realm. And what is more, his spitting out six or seven nations of the world or his swallowing up two or three of them is no different. The four elements, the five elements, the six elements, all elements, or immeasurable elements at this very moment, alike, are his marvelous spiritual ability which gives rise to them and makes them disappear: they are his marvelous spiritual ability to swallow them up and to spit them out.[5] It is his swallowing up and spitting out each and every aspect of the great earth and the vast expanse of space at every moment. Being twirled about by a poppy seed becomes a measure of his spiritual ability: being dangled by a hair becomes a measure of his spiritual ability. They arise along with That which is beyond anything our consciousness can recognize, and they abide in That which is beyond anything our consciousness can recognize, and they take Their true refuge in That which is beyond anything our consciousness can recognize. The ever-changing characteristics of the marvelous spiritual ability of Buddhas have no connection with something short or something long, so, in all seriousness, how can one possibly undertake to evaluate Them simply by making comparisons?

Long ago, when a holy man who had attained the first five spiritual abilities was attending on the Buddha,[6] he asked Him, "The Buddha has six spiritual abilities and I have five of them. What, pray, is that sixth one?"

The Buddha then called out to him, saying, "Holy man with the five spiritual abilities!"

The holy man responded with a "Yes?"

---

5.   The four elements are earth, water, fire, and wind; the five are the four elements plus space; the six are the five elements plus consciousness.

6.   A 'holy man' refers to a Hindu ascetic.

The Buddha said, "That is the one spiritual ability which you should have asked me about."

We need to explore this account carefully. How could the holy man possibly have known that the Buddha had six spiritual abilities? The Buddha had immeasurable spiritual abilities and wise discernment, and was not limited to merely six abilities. Even though the holy man said that he saw just six abilities, it was beyond him to attain even six spiritual abilities, so how much less could he allow for other spiritual abilities, even in his dreams? Now, let us ask something. Even though the holy man would have said that he had seen the Venerable Shakyamuni, could he truly say that he had 'seen Buddha'?[7] Even though he might say that he had 'seen Buddha', could he truly say that he had met the Venerable Shakyamuni? Even though one can encounter the Venerable Shakyamuni, even though one may say that he has 'seen Buddha', we need to ask, has such a person encountered 'the Holy One with five spiritual abilities' yet? Through exploring these questions, we can learn the use of the vines that embrace and the vines that are severed.[8] How could saying that the Buddha has six marvelous spiritual abilities possibly reach even the level of counting the riches of one's neighbor?

Now, what is at the heart of the Venerable Shakyamuni's saying, "That is the one spiritual ability which you should have asked me about?" He does not say that the holy man has the one spiritual ability, nor does He say that the holy man lacks it. Even though He gave expression to the natural functioning of that one spiritual ability, how could the holy man have possibly penetrated what that one spiritual ability is? For, even though the holy man had five abilities, they were not five of the abilities encompassed within the six spiritual abilities that the Buddha had. Even though the abilities of the holy man were seen through by the Buddha's use of His spiritual

---

7. To 'see Buddha' is a Zen term for seeing Buddha Nature either in oneself or in another.

8. 'The vines that embrace' refers to the Master-disciple relationship in which both supply support for each other. 'The vines that are severed' refers to entangling relationships that need to be severed. Dōgen will explore these two references in Discourse 47: On 'The Vines That Entangle: The Vines That Embrace' *(Kattō)*.

abilities, how could the holy man's abilities possibly see through to the spiritual abilities of a Buddha? If the holy man had seen through to even one spiritual ability of the Buddha, he could have seen right through to Buddha from this spiritual ability. When we look at a holy man, there is that which resembles a Buddha's spiritual abilities, and when we look at the behavior of a Buddha, there is that which resembles the abilities of a holy man, but you should realize that the latter's abilities are not what the marvelous spiritual abilities of a Buddha are. When there is no penetration to the Truth, the five spiritual abilities are in no way akin to Buddha.

At the heart of what the Venerable Shakyamuni was saying is, "Of what use is your asking about the sixth spiritual ability? You could have asked about any of the abilities," and "You should have asked about the unsurpassed spiritual ability and about the one marvelous spiritual ability, for in no way is a holy man a match for the one spiritual ability." Thus, the marvelous spiritual abilities of a Buddha and the abilities of others bear the same name of 'spiritual abilities', yet the spiritual abilities of the two are different by far.

Thus it was that Rinzai Gigen once quoted the following poem by a man of old:

> *The ways in which the Tathagata displayed His whole being*
> *Were for the purpose of responding to how people felt.*
> *Fearing lest people give rise to nihilistic views,*
> *He provisionally put forth hollow terms.*

> *His speaking expediently of His 'thirty-two bodily marks'*
> *And of His 'eighty physical characteristics' was but an empty sound,[9]*
> *For His physical body is not His True Body,*
> *And That which is beyond characteristics is His True Form.*

---

9. The thirty-two marks were considered to be the signs of a true world ruler, whereas having the eighty characteristics in addition to these thirty-two marks was viewed to be the signs of a genuine Buddha.

Great Master Rinzai then commented on this poem:

A Buddha has six spiritual abilities that boggle the mind. But all heavenly beings, holy men, asuras,* and mighty demons also have spiritual abilities, so surely they must be Buddhas as well. Right?

O my fellow Buddhist trainees, make no mistake! When the asuras were defeated in battle against Indra, Lord of the Trayastrimsha Heavens, they took eighty-four thousand of their kith and kin under their governance, and concealed themselves within the hollows of lotus roots. Surely this was not being saintly, was it?

In what I, a mountain monk, have just imparted to you concerning these lesser spiritual abilities, all refer to karmically* inherited powers or powers induced by drugs or sorcery. Well, the six marvelous spiritual abilities of a Buddha are not like those powers. When Buddhas enter the realm of forms and colors, They are not captivated by forms or colors; when They enter the realm of sounds, They are not captivated by sounds; when They enter the realm of odors, They are not captivated by smells; when They enter the realm of tastes, They are not captivated by tastes; when They enter the realm of tactile sensations, They are not captivated by what They physically feel; when They enter the realms of thoughts and things, They are not captivated by whatever arises there. Thus, when someone arrives at the point where form and color, sound, smell, taste, touch, and thoughts and things are all characteristics that are empty of any substance, there can be nothing that binds this follower of the Way, who has gone beyond karmic conditionings. Even though these characteristics are what the five skandhas* spew forth, they are simply the bases for this follower's marvelous spiritual abilities as he treads the earth.

O my fellow Buddhist trainees, the True Buddha has no set shape and the True Dharma has no fixed form. You are simply fashioning imitations and creating forms built upon what is ephemeral. Though you may even attain those things you seek, they will all be ghosts of wild foxes and will not be the true Buddha, for these ghosts are nothing but the views and opinions of non-Buddhists.

Accordingly, the six marvelous spiritual abilities of all Buddhas are not something that can be matched by any of the various lofty beings and devilish people or by those of the Two Lesser Courses, nor are they something such persons can fathom. The six marvelous spiritual abilities of the Buddha's Way are what have been directly Transmitted only to the disciples of the Buddha within the Buddha's Way, one-to-one, and They have not been passed on to other persons. The six marvelous spiritual abilities of a Buddha are directly Transmitted within the Buddha's Way. Those to whom they have not been directly Transmitted, one-to-one, cannot comprehend the six marvelous spiritual abilities of a Buddha. You should explore through your training with your Master that those to whom the six marvelous spiritual abilities of Buddhas have not been directly Transmitted, one-to-one, will not be persons within the Way of the Buddhas.

Hyakujō Ekai once said:

> When our eyes, ears, nose, and tongue are undefiled by the various material and immaterial things that arise, we call this 'receiving and keeping to a four-line Dharma poem' and also 'the four stages* of arhathood'. And when the six sense gates leave no trace, we call this 'the six marvelous spiritual abilities'. Simply, at this very moment when we are smoothly going on, unhindered by all the various material and immaterial things that arise, and having brought to an end our dependency on our discriminatory thinking, then this too is called the 'the six marvelous spiritual abilities'. Not claiming these marvelous spiritual abilities as one's own is what we call not 'possessing' spiritual abilities. The tracks of Bodhisattvas*

who do not 'possess' spiritual abilities, as spoken of here, cannot be traced, for They are persons above and beyond Buddhahood. They are the most mind-boggling of persons. In and of Themselves, They are as great as the gods.

The marvelous spiritual abilities that Buddha after Buddha and Ancestor after Ancestor have Transmitted are just like this. The marvelous spiritual abilities of all Buddhas are above and beyond Buddhahood. As such, They are indeed the most mind-boggling of persons and as great as the gods in and of Themselves. They are Bodhisattvas who do not 'possess' spiritual abilities. They are persons who have ended Their dependency on discriminatory thinking. They are persons who have spiritual abilities but do not act upon them. They are persons who are not hindered by anything that arises. The Buddha's Way, right now, has the six marvelous spiritual abilities. All Buddhas have habitually Transmitted and kept to Them for ever so long. There is not even one Buddha who has failed to Transmit and keep to Them, for if such a one did not Transmit and keep to Them, he would not be a Buddha. These six marvelous spiritual abilities of the Buddhas make Their senses clear so that the six sense gates leave no traces.

As someone of old said in verse about Buddhas leaving no trace:

Their wondrous spiritual functioning through Their six senses will be
both empty and not empty
And the halo of light of Their manifestation will take forms and be
beyond form.

'Their taking forms and being beyond form' will be Their leaving no traces. When, without leaving traces, we do our training and practice, explore the Matter through our training with our Master, and realize enlightenment, we do not create disturbances through our sense gates. 'Not creating disturbances' means that 'one who creates disturbances deserves thirty blows from the Master's staff'.

So, you need to thoroughly explore the six marvelous spiritual abilities through your training in accord with the preceding. Apart from the legitimate descendants in our Buddha family, who would even hear that this principle exists? Others have simply mistaken their meaningless feasting on externals for the daily behavior of returning to one's True Home. Further, even though the four stages of arhathood are common fare in the Buddha's Way, there is no academic scholar of the Scriptures who has been genuinely Transmitted. How could that bunch who are bent on counting grains of sand—those folks who are aimlessly wandering about in delusion—possibly realize the fruits of these stages? The sort of people who are satisfied with having realized something small have not yet even come close to exploring the Matter in depth; Buddhas have Transmitted the Way only to Buddhas. The so-called 'four stages of arhathood' are synonymous with receiving and retaining a four-line Dharma poem. What we call 'receiving and retaining a four-line Dharma poem' is our eyes, ears, nose, and tongue all being undefiled by the various material and immaterial things that arise. 'Being undefiled' means 'not being stained with desires'. 'Not being stained with desires' refers to our everyday mind: it is our continually cutting through whatever arises here and now. The genuine Transmission of the six marvelous spiritual abilities and the four stages of arhathood within the Buddha's Way has been like this. If teaching is in any way different from this, you must recognize that it is not the Buddha Dharma. Thus, the Buddha's Way is invariably arrived at through the function of one's marvelous spiritual abilities. Who could possibly doubt that, in arriving There, a drop of water swallows and spews forth a vast ocean, and a speck of dust picks up, and lets go of, a lofty mountain? These are simply one's marvelous spiritual abilities, and nothing else.

Given to the assembly at Kannondōri in Kōshōhōrin-ji Temple, on the sixteenth day of the eleventh lunar month in the second year of the Ninji era (December 19, 1241).

Copied by me in the office of the Abbot's chief assistant at Kippō-ji Temple in Echizen Province on the first day of mid-spring in the second year of the Kangen era (March 11, 1244).

Ejō

25

On the Great Realization

(Daigo)

Translator's Introduction: The great realization of which Dōgen speaks in this discourse does not refer to an intellectual understanding of what the Buddhas and Ancestors have taught but to the direct experience of one's True Nature, hence his describing it as being 'great'. In a few contexts, the more familiar words 'enlightenment' and 'awakening' have been used to render the term *go* in the title, which in Japanese fashion is read as *satori*, the colloquial equivalent for the more technical term *kenshō*, 'the encountering of one's True Nature', both words referring to a knowing that arises only from direct experience.

The Great Way that Buddha after Buddha has Transmitted has continued on without interruption, and the merits of training that Ancestor after Ancestor has revealed have spread far and wide. As a result, having fully manifested the great realization and having attained the Way without necessarily realizing that They have done so, They reflect on what They <u>have</u> realized and take delight in it. Then, emerging from Their realization, They let go of it and act freely, for this is what the everyday life of Buddhas and Ancestors is. They have the twenty-four hours of the day, which They use for whatever needs to be taken up; They have the twenty-four hours of the day, which They use for whatever needs to be laid aside. And They take delight in mudballs, as well as in Their heartfelt and spirited commitment, which this skeleton key has opened.[1] From the time of Their great realization on, Buddhas and Ancestors invariably go to the ultimate in Their spiritual training and exploration,

---

1. A mudball is often used in Zen Buddhist texts as a metaphor for one's Buddha Nature, whereas 'taking delight in Their heartfelt and spirited commitment' refers to single-minded practice.

Kanreisu, translated here as 'skeleton key', refers to a special key that is used to open a gateway (here, the gateway to spiritual liberation and freedom) or to a device for resolving the fundamental spiritual question (namely, the matter of life and death). In the present context, it alludes to someone using the key as a device for accessing spiritual delight.

which fully manifests in this manner. At the same time, the full attainment of the great realization is not to be construed as what a Buddha or an Ancestor is, nor is one's fully being a Buddha or an Ancestor to be construed as attaining the great realization in full. The Buddhas and Ancestors spring forth from the bounds of the great realization, and the great realization is one's Original Face that springs forth from a place above and beyond 'Buddha' and 'Ancestor'.

At the same time, the inborn abilities of human beings are of many kinds. For instance, there are those who innately know what life really is. Once born, they free themselves from the sufferings and delusions of living. That is, through their own bodily existence they thoroughly master what life really is, beginning, middle, and end. And there are those who realize the Truth through learning. They undertake study and ultimately master themselves. In other words, they thoroughly exhaust the skin and flesh, bones and marrow of learning. And there are those who know what Buddha is. They go beyond those who realize the Truth through living and those who realize the Truth through learning. They transcend the bounds of self and other, are unbounded in the here and now, and are beyond having opinions when it comes to knowing self and other. That is to say, they have a knowledge that has no teacher. They are not dependent on a good spiritual friend, nor on Scriptural writings, nor on the nature of things, nor on external forms; they do not try to open up and turn themselves around, nor do they try to be interdependent with others; rather, they are completely transparent, with nothing hidden. Of these various types, do not conclude that one is smart and another dull. Each type fully manifests the merits from their training.

As a consequence, you would do well to explore through your training whether there are any beings, sentient or non-sentient, who cannot come to know the Truth simply by living their daily life. Any who have come to know the Truth through living life will have come to realize that Truth as the result of their living an everyday life. Once they have awakened to the Truth, they will reveal It in their everyday lives as they do their training and practice throughout their lives. Thus, the Buddhas and Ancestors, who are already Trainers and Tamers of Human Beings,[2] have come to be

---

2. 'Trainer and Tamer of Human Beings' is one of the ten epithets by which Shakyamuni Buddha is known.

called 'Those who have fully realized what life really is' because They have fully grasped what realization means. It will be your realization of what life is that leads you to partake of the great realization, because it will manifest from your study of Their realization.

Accordingly, They have experienced the great realization by accepting the three worlds of desire, form, and beyond form; They have realized the great realization by accepting all the hundreds of things that sprout up; They have realized the great realization by accepting the four elements; They have realized the great realization by accepting the Buddhas and Ancestors; They have realized the great realization by accepting Their own spiritual question. All of Them, altogether, have accepted the great realization, and experienced the great realization as well. The very moment when realization occurs is 'the now'.

❧

Rinzai Gigen once said, "Were we to search great T'ang China for a single person who was not enlightened, it would be difficult to find that one." Now what Great Master Rinzai is saying here is the very Skin and Flesh, Bones and Marrow of the genuine lineage, so there is no reason to expect that it is erroneous. What he calls 'in great T'ang China' means 'everywhere his eyes can see'. And it has no connection with 'the whole universe', nor is it limited to some tiny bit of land. If we seek in any concrete place for a single person who is not enlightened, it will be difficult to find that one. The self that was one's self yesterday was not unenlightened, and the self that is another's self today is not unenlightened. Should you seek among the mountaineers or fisherfolk of past or present, ultimately you will still not find any who are unenlightened. Should you trainees explore Rinzai's words in this manner, you will not have spent your time in vain.

Even so, you should also explore through your training the intentions of the Ancestors of our Sōtō Zen tradition. In short, just for the moment, I would like to discuss something with Rinzai: If you, Rinzai, know only that an unenlightened person is hard to find and do not know that an enlightened person is also hard to find,

---

*   See Glossary.

this is still not enough to be affirmed, and it is difficult to say that you have thoroughly explored even the matter of an unenlightened person being hard to find. Even though, in seeking for someone who is not enlightened, it is hard to find even one, did you ever encounter a person who was half-enlightened, and whose countenance and genial demeanor were impressive in their openness? Even though, in your seeking for one person in great T'ang China who was unenlightened, you found it difficult to find even one, do not consider this to be the end of the matter. You should have tried looking for two or three great T'ang Chinas within a single person or within half a person. Is such a one difficult to find? Is such a one not difficult to find? When someone is in possession of the chief purpose for which we train, that person can be trusted as a thoroughly enlightened Ancestor of the Buddha.

Kegon Kyūjō was a Dharma heir of Tōzan. Kyūjō was his personal name. A monk once asked him, "What is it like when a person who has experienced the great realization returns to being deluded?"

The Master replied, "A broken mirror does not shed its light again: it would be difficult for a fallen blossom to climb back up on the tree."

This question is indeed the essential question, and it provides an excellent opportunity for giving Teaching to one's community. Had this question not been raised in the assembly at Kegon Monastery, it would not have been expounded, and had it not been answered by one of Tōzan's Dharma heirs, the response would not have been so inspired. This must truly be the training monastery of a fully enlightened Ancestor of the Buddha.

As to a person who has experienced the great realization, we cannot say that the great realization has been with that person from the outset, nor has that person, upon experiencing the great realization, stored it up somewhere outside or apart from himself, nor is the great realization something encountered in the human world only by those who are in the last stages of old age. Such a person does not forcibly drag it out of himself, yet, without fail, such a one experiences the great realization. Such a one does not treat merely an absence of delusion as the great realization. Neither does such a one aim at becoming a deluded person first so that he may then plant and sprout the seeds of the great realization. Moreover, although a person of great realization experiences the great realization, a person of great delusion also experiences the great realization. Just as there are persons of great realization, so there are Buddhas of great realization, and there is earth, water, fire, wind, and space in the great realization, and there are pillars* of the temple and stone lanterns* in the great realization. We are now raising questions about those who have experienced the great realization. The question about those who have experienced the great realization being capable of reverting to delusion is asking something that truly needs to be asked. And Kegon does not shun the issue, for he cherishes the old ways in monastery life, since they are the meritorious ways of the Buddhas and Ancestors.

Let us focus for the moment on the following questions: When one who has experienced the great enlightenment reverts to delusion, will that person be exactly the same as one who has not experienced the great realization? At the time when one who has experienced the great enlightenment reverts to delusion, does that person take the great realization and make it into something delusory? Does the person revert to delusion by taking some delusion from within someone or someplace else and then use it to cover up his great realization? Also, does the person who has experienced the great realization as a whole person, then destroy his great realization when he reverts to delusion? And also, does what is called 'the reversion to delusion of a person who has experienced the great realization' treat the holding onto an instance of great realization as being a reversion to delusion? You need to explore these questions thoroughly, one by one. Further, is it the great realization on the one hand and a reverting to delusion on the other hand? Be that as it may, you need to know that, in your commitment to your spiritual exploration through training, you will learn that a person who has experienced the great realization has reversions to delusion. You need to know that the great realization and reversion to delusion are intimately connected matters.

Accordingly, 'taking a thief to be our child' does not describe 'reverting to delusion', nor does 'taking our child to be a thief' describe 'reverting to delusion'.

The great realization will be 'taking a thief to be a thief', whereas reverting to delusion is 'taking our child to be our child'. 'Adding a bit too much to what is large' is the great realization, whereas 'taking a bit away from what is little' is what reverting to delusion is. As a consequence, when we search for and try to comprehend a person who has reverted to delusion, we will encounter someone who has experienced the great realization. We need to carefully scrutinize, right now, whether we ourselves are deluded or not, for it is by this that we humbly encounter the Buddhas and Ancestors.

> The Master said, "A broken mirror does not shed its light again: it would be difficult for a fallen blossom to climb back up on the tree."

This instruction to his assembly applies to the very moment when the mirror shatters.[3] However, it is not helpful to devote one's mind to the time when the mirror has not yet been shattered and then focus on exploring the phrase 'a broken mirror'. Now, some of you may understand the main point of Kegon's remark about a broken mirror not shedding its light again and it being difficult for a fallen blossom to climb back up on the tree as his asserting that someone who has experienced the great realization does not revert to delusion again. And you may express this by saying that someone who has experienced the great realization does not lose his light again and that someone who has experienced the great realization finds it difficult to climb back up on the tree of self. But Kegon's assertion goes beyond your exploring the Matter* in this manner. And some of you may think that the monk is asking something akin to, "What is the everyday life of a person who has experienced the great realization like?" to which the reply might be, "There are times when one reverts to delusion." But the original account is not like this.

What the monk is asking is, "What is it like at the time when a person who has experienced the great realization reverts to delusion?" and therefore he is asking for clarification about the very moment of reverting to delusion. The Master's remark that "a broken mirror does not shed its light again: it would be difficult for a fallen

---

3. That is, we are now to understand the phrase 'a broken mirror' as 'a mirror breaking' and 'a fallen flower' as 'a flower falling'.

blossom to climb back up on the tree" fully expresses such a moment as this. When a fallen blossom is just a fallen blossom, even though it may have floated up to the top of a hundred-foot pole, it is still a fallen blossom. Because a broken mirror is just a broken mirror right here and now, even though it may reflect a bit of life, it will be not be able to shed its light again. Taking up the points expressed as 'a broken mirror' and 'a fallen blossom', you should explore the moment when someone who has experienced the great realization reverts to delusion. At that moment, the great realization is like becoming Buddha, and reverting to delusion is akin to being an ordinary human being. And this statement is not something that we should study as if we were speaking of 'returning to being an ordinary human being' or speaking of 'leaving behind traces whilst submitting oneself to the Source'.

Others may assert something to the effect that, when people act contrary to their great realization, they become ordinary human beings, but we are not saying here that their great realization is violated, or that their great realization has vanished, or that delusion has arrived. We must not let ourselves think the way these ordinary people do. Truly, the great realization is boundless, and the reversion to delusion is boundless. There is no delusion that obstructs the great realization; for every three instances of the great realization that come along, we may create half an instance of slight delusion. On account of this, there are snow-capped mountains that undergo the great realization for the sake of snow-capped mountains, as well as trees and stones undergoing the great realization by borrowing from trees and stones.[4]

The great realization of all Buddhas is Their attaining the great realization for the sake of sentient beings: the great realization of sentient beings is their attaining the great realization of all Buddhas. This realization will not be connected with what came before or with what will come after. The great realization at this very moment is beyond self and beyond other. It is not something that comes to us from somewhere outside, yet it fills in the ditches and fills up the valleys everywhere. It is not something

---

4. 'Snow-capped mountains' is often used in Zen Buddhism as a reference to those who have been successfully training for a long time. Similarly, 'trees' are trainees who have not yet cut down the tree of self, and 'stones' are trainees who are now unresponsive to the arising of defiling passions.

that departs from us, yet it is incompatible with any pursuit after some 'other'. And why is that? Because it has departed from chasing after whatever is 'other'.

> The monk Keichō Beiko had a monk go ask Kyōzan, "Do people nowadays even attempt to make use of the great realization?"
>
> Kyōzan replied, "While spiritual realization is not nonexistent, the question is how can we avoid relegating it to a matter of secondary importance?"
>
> The monk went back and reported this to Beiko. Beiko committed himself to exploring this deeply.

The 'nowadays' of which the monk spoke is the ever-present now. Although we think in terms of past, present, and future thousands of myriad times, all such thoughts arise only in the present moment. Unquestionably, each person lives in the now. And sometimes it is their Eye that arises in the present, and sometimes it is their Nose that arises in the present.

> "Do people nowadays even attempt to make use of the great realization?"

We need to examine these words slowly and carefully, allowing them to penetrate our feelings and our thoughts. In present-day Great Sung China, shaven-headed dolts, among others, go around saying, "The path to spiritual realization is my fundamental aim." Talking like this, they vainly wait around for spiritual realization. But they are not illumined by the Light of the Buddhas and Ancestors. They indolently stumble about instead of going and training under a genuine good spiritual friend. Even when the ancient Buddha was in the world, they would not have freed themselves from suffering and delusion.

The present question as to whether people attempt to make use of the great realization is not saying that spiritual realization does not exist, nor is it saying that it does exist, nor is it saying that it comes to one from elsewhere. It is saying, "Do they attempt to make use of it?" It was as though he had said, "The spiritual realization of people nowadays has somehow been realized." For instance, had he said that someone has attained a spiritual realization, it would sound as if it had not continually existed. Had he said that a spiritual realization had come to someone, it would sound as if that spiritual realization had continually existed somewhere else. Had he said that someone had become spiritually awakened, it would sound as if spiritual realization had a beginning. He did not speak of it like this <u>and</u> it is not like this. Even so, when he spoke of what spiritual realization is really like, he asked whether one attempts to make use of spiritual realization.

On the other hand, in speaking of spiritual realization, Kyōzan said, "While spiritual realization is not nonexistent, the question is how can we avoid relegating it to a matter of secondary importance?" In so saying, he is stating that even that which is of secondary importance is still spiritual realization. His saying that it has become of secondary importance is as if he had said, "You have become spiritually awakened!" or "You have realized a spiritual awakening!" or "A spiritual realization has come to you!" Even to say "You have become it" or "It has come to you" states that it is a spiritual realization. As a consequence, while regretting the fact that it has been relegated to a matter of secondary importance, he seems to be denying that a matter of secondary importance exists. A matter of secondary importance which springs from spiritual realization may be taken to be genuinely of secondary importance. Accordingly, even if it were of secondary importance, even if it were one among hundreds of thousands of matters of importance, it would still be a spiritual realization. It is not true that when it is of secondary importance, it is necessarily left over from something that previously existed as a matter of primary importance. For example, while we treat the 'I' of yesterday as our 'I', yesterday we spoke of our 'I' of today as if it were a second person. Kyōzan is not saying that the spiritual realization of this very moment did not exist yesterday, nor is he asserting that it is something that just began now: this is how we explore the Matter through our training.

Accordingly, the heads of some who have experienced the great realization are black, and the heads of some who have experienced the great realization are white.[5]

Given to the assembly at Kannondōri in Kōshōhōrin-ji Temple at springtime, on the twenty-eighth day of the first lunar month in the third year of the Ninji era (March 1, 1242).

Copied by me on the twenty-seventh day of the first lunar month in the second year of the Kangen era (March 7, 1244) in Echizen Province at the old temple of Kippō-ji where I had hung up my traveling staff, and presented it in writing to the great assembly of ordinary people as well as those in lofty positions.

I recopied this in the spring of the same year, on the twenty-first day of the third lunar month (April 29, 1244), whilst serving in the inner recesses of the training temple of Kippō-ji in Echizen Province.

Ejō

---

5.   That is, youth (black hair) and old age (white hair) are of no relevance when it comes to experiencing the great realization.

26

On Wanshi's 'Kindly Advice for Doing Seated Meditation'

(Zazen Shin)

Translator's Introduction: In this discourse Dōgen uses the term *zazen shin* in two different senses. The first is given as the title of this discourse and is the name for a poem by Meditation Master Wanshi that Dōgen quotes near the end of this work. The second sense is found at the very end of this discourse in the title of a poem by Dōgen, *The Needle of Seated Meditation*, which is based on Wanshi's poem. Dōgen's poem refers to the use of seated meditation to spur one on and to help trainees unblock themselves spiritually, just as an acupuncture needle would unblock them physically.

The word *zazen* is used by Dōgen in this discourse for two different states. The first refers to 'sitting in meditation', that is, physically sitting down in order to practice meditation. The second refers to 'seated meditation', that is, being spiritually centered no matter where one is or what one is doing, neither pushing away nor denying anything as it arises, nor clinging to anything, including some specific form of meditating. To truly do seated meditation is to be, as Dōgen says, seated Buddha.

At Kannondōri, Kōshōhōrin-ji Temple.

Right after Great Master Yakusan Igen had finished a period of meditation,[1] a certain monk asked him, "As you were sitting there all still and awesome like a mountain, what was it that you were thinking about?"

The Master answered, "What I was thinking about was based on not deliberately thinking about any particular thing."

The monk then asked, "How can what anyone is thinking about be based on not deliberately thinking about something?"

The Master replied, "It is a matter of 'what I am thinking about' not being the point."

---

1. Yakusan would have been sitting together with his community of monks in the Meditation Hall.

Having heard about this state described by Great Master Yakusan, we need to investigate through our training what 'sitting as still as a mountain' means and directly Transmit this, for this is how the thorough exploration of sitting as still as a mountain is passed on through the words and ways of Buddhas. Even though it is said that the way in which Buddhas think about things while being all still and awesome like a mountain differs, Yakusan's way of putting it is certainly one way among them. It is his 'thinking about' not being based on deliberately thinking about any particular thing. It includes 'thinking about' as his Skin and Flesh, Bones and Marrow, and it includes 'not thinking about' as his Skin and Flesh, Bones and Marrow.

> The monk asked, "How can what anyone is thinking about be based on not deliberately thinking about <u>something</u>?"

Even though the condition of not thinking about anything in particular is of ancient vintage, how can one possibly think about it? How can thinking not go on while sitting ever so still, and why did the monk not pierce through to what goes above and beyond simply being ever so still? Had he not been as befuddled as some are in our more recent, degenerate times, he would have had the ability to persist in his inquiry into being ever so still.

> The Master replied, "It is a matter of 'what I am thinking about' not being the point."

Even though his statement, "It is a matter of 'what I am thinking about' not being the point," is a gem of clarity, in our consideration of the condition of not deliberately thinking about anything in particular, we invariably employ what he described as " 'what I am thinking about' not being the point." There is a someone involved in not deliberately trying to think about something, and that someone is maintaining and supporting an I. Even though being ever so still is synonymous with that I, meditation is not merely an I thinking about something; it is the I offering up its being as still and awesome as a mountain.[2] Even though its being ever so still <u>is</u> being ever so still, how can its being ever so still possibly think about being ever so still?

---

2. The 'I' to which Dōgen is referring here is not the egoistic false self, but a natural function of the right effort of sitting still.

As a consequence, being as still as a mountain is beyond the considerations of Buddhas, beyond the considerations of Dharma, beyond the considerations of having awakened, and beyond the considerations of intellectual understanding. The Matter[*] that Yakusan has directly Transmitted one-to-one in this way has been handed down for thirty-six generations, descending directly from Shakyamuni Buddha, and from Yakusan to Shakyamuni Buddha, there are thirty-six generations.[3] The practice of not thinking about anything in particular has been directly Transmitted in this manner.

Despite all this, there has been befuddled and unreliable talk in recent years, saying that if a person can fully eliminate all thoughts by devotedly sitting in meditation, this is the basis for true stillness.[4] This viewpoint does not even come up to that of scholars who study the Lesser Course.[*] It is even inferior to the paths that the common and lofty people pursue, so how can we possibly speak of such befuddled people as folks who are exploring the Buddha Dharma? In modern-day Great Sung China, people devoted to such ways are numerous, which, lamentably, will be the destruction and ruin of the Way of the Ancestors.

Also, there is a type of person among the Chinese who says, "Doing one's utmost to sit in meditation is the essential practice, whether as a beginner or as someone who has come to training late in life." But this is not necessarily the daily behavior of the Buddhas and Ancestors. Actively walking about, as well as sitting, was Their meditation practice. Their body was quiet and tranquil whether They were speaking or silent, moving about or inactive, so don't you depend solely upon that method just now quoted. Many of the folks who call themselves followers of Rinzai are of that limited view. Someone has been remiss in passing on to them the awakened life of the Buddha Dharma, and so they speak in that way. What is a 'beginner'? What person is not a beginner? And where do such folks find a beginner's attitude of mind?

---

[*]   See Glossary.

3.   That is, when we look forward from Shakyamuni, Yakusan is an Ancestor, and when we look back to Shakyamuni from our present position, Yakusan is a Buddha.

4.   That is, such befuddled persons take 'blissing out' to be the true goal of meditation.

Keep in mind that, in our thorough investigation of what has been established for exploring the Way, we do our utmost to put our seated meditation into practice. This practice has, as its main point, our "acting as a Buddha without pursuing 'becoming a Buddha.'"[5] Moreover, because 'acting as a Buddha' is beyond 'becoming a Buddha', our spiritual question manifests before our very eyes. Again, our emulation of Buddha is beyond becoming a Buddha, so that when we break up the nets and cages that confine us, our sitting like a Buddha sits does not hinder our becoming a Buddha. Right at such a moment of sitting still, there is the strength that has been present for thousands of times, nay, for tens of thousands of times, to enter into being either a Buddha or a demon. And our stepping forward or stepping back is intimately connected with our capability to fill in the ditches, even to fill in the valleys.

While Baso Dōitsu was training under Meditation Master Nangaku Ejō, he privately received the Mind seal.* One day while Baso was sitting in meditation, Nangaku came to where he was and asked him, "O great virtuous one, what is the aim of your sitting in meditation?"[6]

This question needs to be calmly, yet diligently, investigated, because we need to look in detail at what Nangaku might be asking. Does he have in mind that there is something above and beyond sitting in meditation? Or has there never been a practice that can be considered as more special than sitting in meditation? Or should we not aim at anything at all? Or, is he asking Baso whether some goal has manifested from his sitting in meditation at the present time? We should desire the True Dragon more

---

5.　'Acting as a Buddha' implies living one's daily life in accord with the Precepts and as a moment-by-moment meditation, without adding some goal like 'becoming a Buddha'.

6.　As other accounts of this kōan story make clear, the incident took place some considerable time after Baso had had a kenshō and had been Transmitted by Nangaku. During this interval, Baso had sat in his hut doing his meditation day after day regardless of the weather, even to the point of sitting in the deep snow that covered the floor of his hut.

than we desire the carved dragon. And we need to learn that both the carved dragon and the True Dragon possess the ability to summon up clouds and rain.[7] Do not esteem what is far off, and do not belittle what is far off; just acquaint yourself with what is far off. Do not belittle what is near at hand, and do not esteem what is near at hand; just acquaint yourself with what is near at hand. Do not treat your eyes lightly, and do not attach great importance to your eyes. And do not attach great importance to your ears, and do not treat your ears lightly. Just make your ears and your eyes sharp and clear.[8]

> Baso responded, "My aim is to become a Buddha."

We need to arrive at a clear understanding of what Baso is saying here. When he speaks of becoming a Buddha, what exactly does he mean? Is he asserting that becoming a Buddha means being made into a Buddha by a Buddha? Or is he asserting that becoming a Buddha means making a Buddha into a Buddha? Or is he asserting that becoming a Buddha is the emergence of one or two aspects of a Buddha? Is his aiming to become a Buddha the result of his having dropped off body and mind, or is his aiming at becoming a Buddha itself the dropping off of his body and mind? Or is he asserting that aiming at becoming a Buddha is tangled up with one's aims, despite the fact that becoming a Buddha applies to all things?

Keep in mind that what Baso is saying is that his sitting in meditation is certainly done with the goal of becoming a Buddha, and that his sitting in meditation is certainly done with the wish to become a Buddha. Such a wish can precede becoming a Buddha, and it can arise after becoming a Buddha, and it can arise at the

---

7. The allusion is probably to the story of a Chinese artist who was so skilled at fashioning carved dragons that they could summon up clouds and rain. One day, a real dragon showed up in his studio and the experience totally overwhelmed him. The carved dragon referred to here is an analogy for the skilled practice of sitting in meditation, whereas the appearance of the True Dragon would be associated with experiencing a kenshō, which goes beyond any notions one may have of what a kenshō really is.

8. The eyes are associated with clearly seeing the way things are, whereas the ears are associated with accurately understanding what things truly are.

very moment of becoming a Buddha. To question a bit further, how many instances of becoming a Buddha has this single wish entangled? And this entanglement can become entwined with other entanglements. At such a time, the entanglements involved in cases of completely becoming a Buddha are, beyond doubt, directly related to 'completely becoming a Buddha', and, in every single case, they are due to having a goal. We should not try to avoid having a purpose. When we try to avoid having a purpose, we grieve for ourselves and lose our very life, and when we grieve for ourselves and lose our very life, it is due to our entanglement with having a goal.

> Thereupon, Nangaku picked up a roof tile and began rubbing it on a rock. Seeing this, Baso asked him, "Reverend Master, what are you doing that for?"

Truly, who would fail to see that he was polishing a tile? Even so, the question meant, "What are you going to make from polishing a tile in that way?" What he is going to make is undoubtedly a polished tile. Here and in other worlds—different though they may be—Nangaku's polishing a tile will have a significance that will never cease. It is not simply a matter of taking one's own personal view not to be a personal view: we positively ascertain that there is a purpose to all our myriad activities which we need to explore through our training and practice. Keep in mind that, just as we might not recognize or understand a Buddha when we encounter a Buddha, so when we encounter the Water we may not recognize It, or when we see a 'mountain' we may not recognize it either. And jumping to the conclusion that there can be no pathway into the Dharma that is right before one's eyes is not the way to explore the Buddha Dharma.

> Nangaku said, "I am polishing the tile to make it into a Mirror."

We need to clarify the import of this statement. Nangaku undoubtedly has a reason for saying, "I am polishing the tile to make it into a Mirror," for Baso's spiritual question is fully manifesting and there cannot be false teaching. Even though a tile is a tile and a mirror is a mirror, keep in mind that there are ever so many factors involved when we strive to clarify Nangaku's reason for polishing it. Both the Ancient Mirror and the

Bright Mirror will be attained through polishing a tile to make a Mirror.[9] If we do not know that all such Mirrors come from polishing a tile, we will fail to grasp what the Buddha's Ancestor was saying, we will not receive the benefit of what the Buddha's Ancestor said, and we will not experience what the Buddha's Ancestor breathed forth.

> Baso then asked, "How can you possibly make a mirror by rubbing a tile?"

Truly it was the Iron Man polishing a tile,[10] without calling on the strength of anyone else, and, even so, polishing a tile does not make a mirror. Although he is just pointing to making a mirror, this pointing itself is the immediate making.[11]

> Nangaku replied, "How can you possibly make yourself into a Buddha by sitting in meditation?"

It is evident that there is a reason for sitting in meditation other than 'waiting to become a Buddha': obviously, becoming a Buddha does not depend on sitting in meditation.

> Baso asked, "Well, what then is the right way?"

Even though what is being said looks like an earnest question directly involving Baso at this very moment in time, it is also a question that refers to the way things are elsewhere at this very moment in time. For example, call to mind a time when a close friend encounters a close friend: his being my friend is also my being his friend. The "what?" of one and "the right way" of the other are the manifestations of both perspectives at the same time.[12]

---

9.   Dōgen explores this allusion in Discourse 19: On the Ancient Mirror *(Kokyō)*.

10.   The 'Iron Man' is a term used to portray the level of strength and determination one needs in order to be successful in one's training.

11.   That is, making a physical mirror takes time, whereas spiritually 'making a mirror' is instantaneous.

12.   The 'close friends' are disciple and Master: when the disciple asks his or her spiritual question (the "what?"), the Master supplies the direction for the disciple to look in (the

Nangaku said, "It is like someone who has hitched up his cart. If the cart is not moving, is prodding the cart the right thing to do or is prodding the ox the right thing to do?"

Now then, as to his words "if the cart is not moving," what does 'the cart's moving' mean, and what does 'the cart's not moving' mean? For instance, is the water's flowing synonymous with the cart's moving?[13] Is the water's not flowing synonymous with the cart's moving? We could say that flowing is the water's not moving. It could even be that the water's moving is beyond 'flowing'. Thus, in our investigating his saying "if the cart is not moving," even when there is 'no movement', we need to explore the Matter through our training with a Master, and even when there is not 'no movement', we still need to explore the Matter with a Master, because there will be a time for each situation. Nangaku's words "if it is not moving" go beyond his having made a one-sided assertion that some thing is not moving.

In Nangaku's saying "Is prodding the cart the right thing to do or is prodding the ox the right thing to do?" can there be both a prodding of the cart and a prodding of the ox? Will prodding the cart and prodding the ox be equivalent or not? There is no method for prodding a cart in the secular world. Although worldly people do not have a method for prodding their cart, we know that in the Buddha's Way there is a method for prodding one's cart: it is the very eyes of one's spiritual exploration through training with one's Master.

Even though we learn what methods there are for prodding a cart, they will not be the best ones for prodding an ox, a matter we should devote ourselves to examining in detail. Though methods for prodding an ox are common enough in the everyday world, we should ask about the Buddhist way of prodding an ox by exploring

---

"right way"). Although this may appear as a sequence in a dialogue, according to Dōgen, the answer to the question of "what?" is the "What."

13.   Nangaku's remark and Dōgen's commentary on it are clearly not intended to be taken on a literal level, but to be viewed within the context of Buddhist training in meditation. One possible interpretation would equate the ox with the trainee's will to train, the cart to his vehicle of training—namely, serene reflection meditation—and the water with what appears to be going on spiritually within his training.

the Matter through our training with a Master. Is the ox we are prodding a water buffalo, or is it the Iron Ox, or is it an ox coated with mud? Will a riding crop be our prod, or will the whole universe be our prod, or will one's whole heart and mind be our prod? Should we beat it till the Marrow gushes forth, or hit it with our Fist? There will be a Fist hitting a Fist and an Ox prodding an Ox.

Baso made no response to that last remark by Nangaku, something that we should not idly overlook. There was his casting aside the tile to catch a jewel: he was turning his head and changing his expression. Further, nothing and no one can rob him of his making no response.

> Nangaku, again wishing to instruct him, said, "If, as you imply, you would explore 'seated meditation', explore 'seated Buddha.'"

In exploring this statement through your training with a Master, you should, by all means, try to grasp what the pivotal moments were for the Ancestors in our lineage. If you do not know precisely what "explore 'seated meditation'" means, well, Nangaku knew it as exploring 'seated Buddha'. How could anyone possibly say that exploring 'seated meditation' is exploring 'seated Buddha' unless that person were a child or grandchild of a genuine heir? Truly, you need to recognize that a beginner's meditation is their first time of doing seated meditation, and that one's first time of doing seated meditation is the first instance of being seated Buddha.

> To explain what 'seated meditation' meant, Nangaku said, "If you would explore what 'seated meditation' is, meditation is not simply a matter of sitting or lying down."

What he is now saying is that seated meditation is doing seated meditation and is not a matter of, say, being physically seated or lying down.[14] Once we have received the direct, one-to-one Transmission that it is not a matter of sitting or lying down, our limitless acts of sitting and lying down are nevertheless what we are. What need do

---

14.   That is, the 'seated' in 'seated meditation' does not refer to a physical position during meditation but to a meditative state of mind. 'Being seated or lying down' implies all four of the modes of everyday human behavior: standing, moving, sitting, and lying down.

we have to search for whether our spiritual bloodline is within us or within someone else? Why get into discussions about delusion and enlightenment? Who would want to take up the matter of 'how to cut off defiling passions by developing wise discernment' merely as an intellectual pursuit?

> Nangaku said, "When you would investigate 'seated Buddha', you need to know that Buddha is not some set form."

When we want to express what this is getting at, this is the best way to do it. The fact that seated Buddha may manifest as one Buddha or as two Buddhas is because having no fixed form is one of Its glorious attributes. To state that Buddha has no fixed form is to state what the form of a Buddha is, and because a Buddha has no fixed form, it is difficult to avoid being seated Buddha. Thus, because the absence of any fixed form is one of Its glorious attributes, when you investigate doing seated meditation through practice, it is your being seated Buddha.

Who within the realm of non-abiding thoughts and things would choose not to be a Buddha, and who, pray, chooses to be a Buddha? By letting go of choosing before any choice arises, one becomes seated Buddha.

> Nangaku said, "When you are seated Buddha, this then is your killing off 'Buddha.'" [15]

In your exploring 'seated Buddha' through your training with a Master, there is the spiritually beneficial act of killing off 'Buddha'. The very moment of our being seated Buddha is killing off 'Buddha'. In our attempt to seek out the fine, distinguishing marks and brilliance from killing off 'Buddha', they will undoubtedly be due to our being seated Buddha. Although the term 'to kill off' may resemble the way we speak of killing in the world, it cannot really be the same. Also, you need to explore through your training the statement that seated Buddha is killing off 'Buddha' by asking what form this might take. Taking up the point that inherent within the spiritual activity of Buddha there is the killing off of 'Buddha', we need to explore through our training

---

15. "Killing off 'Buddha'" would encompass dropping off any notion we might have of what Buddha really is.

whether we ourselves have killed off our false self or have not yet killed off our false self.

> "If you are clinging to some form of sitting, you will not
> arrive at the principle of killing off 'Buddha.'"

'Clinging to some form of sitting' means throwing away and acting contrary to the aspect of being seated. This underlying principle, as Nangaku has already stated, is that when we are 'practicing seated Buddha', it is not possible for us not to cling to some form of being seated. Even though Nangaku's saying 'clinging to some form of sitting' is a gem of clarity, when we do cling to some form of sitting, we will not arrive at the principle of killing off 'Buddha'. To kill off 'Buddha' is what I call 'the dropping off of body and mind'. Those who have not yet truly sat still do not possess this Teaching. This 'dropping off' is the moment of just sitting; it is the person who is just sitting; it is Buddha just sitting; it is learning seated Buddha. Sitting that is simply a person's sitting down or reclining is not a Buddha's just sitting. Even though a person's sitting naturally resembles a seated Buddha or a Buddha sitting, there are those persons who are becoming Buddha and there are those persons who are engaged in 'becoming a Buddha'. Even though there are people engaged in 'becoming a Buddha', not everyone has become a Buddha. A Buddha is not everyone, and because all Buddhas are not simply all people, a person is not necessarily a Buddha and a Buddha is not necessarily a person. The same holds true for being seated Buddha.

The same also holds true for Nangaku as an outstanding Master and Baso as a strong disciple. Baso is the one who realized 'becoming Buddha' by being 'seated Buddha'. Nangaku is the one who pointed to 'seated Buddha' for the sake of making a Buddha. In Nangaku's assembly, there was such marked devotion to effort, and in Yakusan's assembly, there was his Teaching concerning the nature of meditation. Keep in mind that Buddha after Buddha and Ancestor after Ancestor has taken being seated Buddha to be Their essential function, and They have wholeheartedly made use of this essential function. Those who have not used it are simply those who have not encountered it, not even in their dreams.

In broader terms, in both India and China, to say that the Buddha Dharma had been passed on invariably meant that seated Buddha had been passed on. This is because seated Buddha is the essential function. When the Buddha Dharma is not passed on, doing seated meditation is not passed on. What Successor after Successor has received is just this principle of doing seated meditation. Any who have not yet had this principle directly Transmitted to them are not Ancestors of the Buddha. Without illuminating this one Teaching, we will not illuminate the myriad Teachings or the myriad actions that They have taken. Whoever does not illuminate the myriad Teachings cannot be called clear and bright, and is not someone who has gained the Way, so how could such a one be an Ancestor of the Buddha either now or in the past? Therefore, we should have no doubt that the Ancestors of the Buddha have, without question, directly Transmitted, one-to-one, the practice of seated meditation.

To be illuminated by the radiance of the Buddhas and Ancestors is to devote ourselves to exploring through our training what this practice of seated meditation is. Befuddled people, misunderstanding what a Buddha's radiance is, wonder whether it could be like sunlight or moonlight, or like the play of light in a jewel, or even like the dancing of a flame. Sunlight and moonlight are merely karmic* forms arising from the turning of the wheel within the six worlds of existence:* they cannot compare with a Buddha's radiance. A Buddha's radiance is exhibited by accepting and keeping to a single verse of Scripture, by maintaining, supporting, guarding, and protecting a single Teaching, and by directly Transmitting, one-to-one, the practice of seated meditation. If people had never reached the point where they were illumined by His radiance, then maintaining and supporting this Teaching would not be possible, and no one would trust and accept It.

Thus, even in the past there were few people who recognized that to sit in meditation means doing seated meditation. On the mountains of present-day Great Sung China, many heads of top-ranking monasteries are ignorant of seated meditation and have not learned it. There are some who have a clear understanding of it, but they are few. In these temples, the times for sitting in meditation have always been set. And all the monks, from the Abbot on down, have taken sitting in meditation as a dutiful task. To spur their trainees on, they have advised them to sit in meditation. Yet those Abbots who have actually understood the practice are few. As a result, from past times to recent generations, there have been one or two veteran monks who have recorded their mottoes for sitting in meditation, one or two veteran monks who have compiled methods for sitting in meditation, and one or two veteran monks who have set down maxims for sitting in meditation. Yet among all their mottoes for sitting in meditation, nowhere are there any that we can adopt, as their methods for sitting in meditation are ill-informed in terms of their application to daily conduct. They have been set down by people who do not know seated meditation and to whom seated meditation has not been directly Transmitted, one-to-one. Their maxims for sitting in meditation are in the *Ching-te Era Record of the Transmission of the Lamp*, and their mottoes for sitting in meditation, among others, are in the *Chia-tai Era Record of the Lamp Whose Light Reaches Everywhere*. Even though these monks spent their whole lives making pilgrimages to Zen monasteries far and wide, how sad that they lacked the diligent effort to truly sit in meditation even once. To sit truly was not for them, and so their efforts did not lead them to encounter themselves. Their failure to truly sit in meditation was not due to any distaste for their body and mind, but to their unwillingness to make a genuine effort, so therefore they precipitously wandered off into delusion. The writings they have collected up are merely an outer show of 'coming back to the Source', or 'returning to the Origin', or convey useless methods for concentrating on one's breathing or for focusing on tranquility. These methods do not even approach the four steps of Tendai meditation: seeing into one's heart, training through meditation, taking delight in doing it, and putting it into one's daily practice. Nor do they approach the perspective of the ten bodhisattva* stages leading to Buddhahood. So how could they possibly have received the direct, one-to-one Transmission of the seated meditation of Buddha after Buddha and Ancestor after Ancestor? Scribes in the Sung dynasty were wrong to record such writings, and we present-day trainees should set them aside and not even look at them.[16]

    Only the kindly advice for seated meditation compiled by Meditation Master Wanshi Shōgaku, the Abbot of Keitoku-ji Temple on Mount Tendō in Keigen

---

16.   The works Dōgen is referring to all have the word *zazen* in their titles and might mislead his disciples to assume that 'seated meditation', as Dōgen is using the term, is what those works are talking about.

Prefecture in Great Sung China, is the Teaching of a true Ancestor of the Buddha: it is the acupuncture needle of seated meditation and is right for realizing the Way. It alone has a radiance that lights up the inside and outside of the realms of thoughts and things. Wanshi is an Ancestor of the Buddha for past and present Ancestors of the Buddha. Earlier and later Buddhas have been spurred on by this needle of his. Ancestors of the present and Ancestors of the past have come forth from this needle. And here is this very needle of seated meditation.

My Friendly Advice for Seated Meditation

Compiled by Meditation Master Wanshi Shōgaku

The important function for Buddha after Buddha
And the pivotal moment for Ancestor after Ancestor
Is to know It without 'stirring anything up'
And to be illumined without setting up an opposite.

When one knows It without stirring anything up,
Such knowing is naturally humble:
When one is illumined without setting up an opposite,
Such illumination is naturally subtle.

Since that knowing is naturally humble,
There is never a discriminating thought:
Since that illumination is naturally subtle
There is never the least outward sign of It.

Since there is never a discriminating thought,
That knowing is wondrous, with nothing left to be dealt with:
Since there is never the least outward sign of It,
That illumination is complete, with nothing left unrealized.

The water is now so clear you can see to its depths,

> *As fish swim by at their leisure:*
> *The sky is now so clear it is boundless,*
> *As birds fly off, leaving no trace.*

The point of this needle of seated meditation is the Great Function which manifests before our very eyes. It is our everyday behavior when we look beyond words and forms. It is our glimpsing That which existed 'before "father" and "mother" was born'.* It is our seeing that it is good not to slander Ancestors of the Buddha. It is our never avoiding the chance to let go of self and to cast away body and mind. It is our having a head as large as a Buddha's seated upon the neck of an ordinary person.

The important function for Buddha after Buddha

Beyond doubt, Buddha after Buddha has treated Buddha after Buddha as the important function: when that important function has manifested, that is what seated meditation is.

The pivotal moment for Ancestor after Ancestor

My former Master went beyond using such words as these. The principle underlying this is just what 'Ancestor after Ancestor' means. It involves the Transmission of the Teaching and the Transmission of the robe. In general, every single instance of turning one's head and changing one's expression is what the essential function of Buddha after Buddha has been. And every single case of changing one's expression and turning one's head is what the pivotal moment has been for Ancestor after Ancestor.

To know It without stirring anything up

'To know' does not mean 'to perceive', for our perceptions are a small gauge of It. Nor is this the knowing associated with intellectual understanding, for intellectual understanding is but a mental construct. Hence, 'to know' is 'to not stir things up', for when we do not stir things up, we 'know'. Do not broadmindedly judge it to be something everyone knows and do not narrow-mindedly limit it to one's own personal knowledge. That phrase, 'not stirring things up', is equivalent to saying, "When clear-mindedness comes, be clear-minded, and when dark-mindedness comes, be dark-minded."[17] It is the same as saying, "By sitting, to break through the skin that our mother bore."

To be illumined without setting up an opposite

This 'being illumined' is not the 'being illumined' associated with being completely out in the open, nor is it 'spiritual illumination'. Rather, it is our not setting up opposing conditions that constitutes being illumined. Illumination does not change into a condition, because conditions are the very things illuminated. 'Not setting up opposites' means that, throughout the universe, there has never been anything hidden and that a shattered world does not stick out its head. It is what is humble, it is what is subtle, and it is what is beyond being interdependent or independent.

Since that knowing is naturally humble,
There is never a discriminating thought

This means knowing what discriminating thinking is, without necessarily having to make use of some external assistance. This knowing is of a concrete form and that concrete form is of mountains and rivers. These mountains and rivers are humble. This humility is subtle. Our making use of this knowing is as lively and free-moving as fish swimming about in water. Our becoming a dragon does not depend on our being on one side of Emperor Yü's Gate or the other.[18] To straightaway employ even a single instance of this knowing is to make use of a pinch of the whole world with its mountains and rivers, and, exerting our whole strength, to <u>know</u>. If what we know lacks the familiarity of mountains and rivers, we will not have a single instance of true knowing or even half an understanding of It. We should not regret that discriminative

---

17.　'Clear-mindedness' refers to those times when the darkness of ignorance has cleared away; 'dark-mindedness' refers to other times when we cannot see our way clearly.

18.　Emperor Yü's Gate—also known as the Dragon Gate—is a gorge on the Yangtze River. Legend has it that any fish swimming up through the gorge turns into a dragon. This was used as a metaphor for someone who succeeded in passing the difficult imperial civil service examination. To paraphrase Dōgen's remark, those who are truly doing seated meditation are 'seated Buddha', whether they realize it or not. They do not need to pass some examination to prove their being 'seated Buddha'.

wisdom has come to us late, since Buddha after Buddha has been fully manifested by means of it. 'There is never' means 'already'. 'Already' means 'discriminative wisdom has fully manifested'. Thus, 'there is never a discriminating thought' means that not even a single person has been encountered.[19]

> *Since that illumination is naturally subtle*
> *There is never the least outward sign of It*

'The least' refers to 'the whole universe'. Even so, this illumination is naturally subtle. This is why it is as if it had not yet come about. Do not doubt your eyes and do not trust your ears.[20] Clarify through direct experience what the Principle is that lies beyond deliberative thinking, and do not grab hold of some criterion of what It is by relying on how it is worded: this is what being illumined is. This is why there is no duality: this is why there is nothing to grab hold of. It is to say, in effect, "While keeping to the view that this experience is rare and relying on its being complete, I still harbor doubts."[21]

> *The water is now so clear you can see to its depths,*
> *As fish swim by at their leisure*

'The Water is clear' does not mean that the water connected with the sky is the Clear Water that one can see to Its very depths. Still less is the Water of 'the Water is clear' that which thoroughly cleanses things in the outer, material realm. The Water which is unbounded by any bank or shore, <u>That</u> is the immaculate Water which one penetrates to Its very depths. When fish swim by through this Water, there is nowhere that they may not go. Even though their swimming may progress for who knows how many myriad miles, It is immeasurable and It knows no limit. There is no bank to measure It by, and there is no space in which It floats. Being without a bottom to sink to, there is no one who can measure It. Even were one to discuss various ways of

---

19. That is, 'self and other' has been transcended.

20. That is, do not doubt your direct experience of It and do not rely on your understanding of how someone else has described It.

21. That is, I doubt that I 'know it all'.

measuring It, It is simply the immaculate Water whose depths can be seen. The meritorious act of seated meditation is like this swimming of fish. Who can reckon what a thousand miles or ten thousand miles are? The action of going down to the very bottom is synonymous with our not trying to trace some bird's trackless path.

> *The sky is now so clear it is boundless,*
> *As birds fly off, leaving no trace*

'The Sky is clear' is something unconnected with the heavens. The emptiness connected with the heavens is not the Clear Sky. Even less does That which pervades everywhere—be it in this place or in that—refer to the clear sky. What is not hidden or revealed either inside or out is what 'the Clear Sky' is.

When birds fly through this Sky, this is just one method of 'flying through the Sky'. The action of flying through the Sky is beyond anything we can measure. Flying through the Sky is the whole universe, because the whole universe is flying through the Sky. Even though we do not know what the extent of this flying is, in asserting it with a statement that is beyond some form of reckoning, Wanshi asserted it as "flying off, leaving no trace." It means "being able to go straight off, having no strings tying down one's feet." [22] When the Sky is flying off, the birds are also flying off. When the birds are flying off, the Sky too is flying off. Among the sayings which thoroughly explore 'flying off' is the one that says, "Only here do we exist." This is the acupuncture needle of being ever so still. How many thousands of journeys have vied to tell us, "Only here do we exist?" This is Meditation Master Wanshi's kindly advice for doing seated meditation.

Among the maxims for doing seated meditation by veteran monks over the generations, there have not been any like this one of his. If any stinking skin bags[*] anywhere wished to state the Matter like this needle of seated meditation has, even if they exhausted their strength for one or two lifetimes, they would not be able to do so. Its likes are not to be seen anywhere today. Wanshi's needle stands alone.

---

22. A quote from Master Tōzan, alluding to the practice of tying down the feet of captured birds to prevent their flying away.

When my former Master was giving Teaching in the Lecture Hall, he would constantly be remarking, "My Old Buddha Wanshi!" He never spoke like this about anyone else. When we have the Eye to recognize 'such a person',* we will also recognize the sound of an Ancestor of the Buddha. We need to remember that this Ancestor of the Buddha existed in Tōzan's lineage.[23] It is now some eighty years since Meditation Master Wanshi's death. Having encountered his kindly advice for doing seated meditation, I have compiled my own needle of seated meditation. It is now the eighteenth day of the third lunar month in the third year of the Ninji era (April 19, 1242). When I reckon the time from his death on the eighth day of the tenth lunar month in the twenty-seventh year of the Shōkō era (1157) to the present year, it is just short of eighty-five years. The needle of seated meditation that I have now compiled is as follows:

The Needle of Seated Meditation

The important function for Buddha after Buddha
And the pivotal moment for Ancestor after Ancestor
Is to let It manifest without deliberately thinking about anything
And to realize It without creating complications.

When one lets It manifest without thinking about anything,
Such a manifestation is naturally close to us:
When one realizes It without creating complications,
Such a realization is naturally a direct experience.

When that manifestation is naturally close to us,
There is not the least bit of defilement:
When that realization is naturally a direct experience
There is not the least difference between Host and guest.

---

23. Wanshi was a Dharma heir of Tanka Shijun, who was in Tōzan Ryōkai's line. Dōgen's Master was a direct descendant of Chōryo Seiryō, Tanka Shijun's other Dharma heir.

> *When the closeness is without the least bit of defilement,*
> *That closeness is put aside and falls away:*
> *When one directly experiences that there is not the least*
>   *distinction between Host and guest,*
> *Out of that experience come no set plans, as we diligently*
> *continue to train.*
>
> *The water is so clear you can see down to the bottom,*
> *As fish swim by, just as fish do:*
> *The sky is now boundless, penetrating the heavens,*
> *As birds fly off, just as birds do.*

While Meditation Master Wanshi's advice for seated meditation is by no means incorrect, I just wanted to express the Matter in this way.

In sum, descendants of the Buddha's Ancestors need to explore through their training with their Master that seated meditation is undoubtedly the one Great Matter. This is the genuine seal that is Transmitted directly, one-to-one.

Written down at Kōshōhōrin-ji Temple on the eighteenth day of the third lunar month in the
    third year of the Ninji era (April 19, 1242).
Given to the assembly at Kippō-ji Temple in Yoshida Prefecture, Etchū Province, during the
    winter of the eleventh month in the fourth year of the same era (December 1243).[24]

---

24.   Dōgen's community was staying at Kippō-ji Temple while they were building Eihei-ji Temple.

27

On Experiencing That Which Is
Above and Beyond Buddhahood

(Butsu Kōjō Ji)

Translator's Introduction: This discourse is one of the most opaque in the *Shōbōgenzō*, not because the underlying meaning is difficult to grasp, but because of the extensive use of Zen Buddhist metaphors. Even though 'translations' and paraphrases of these metaphorical references are supplied for most occurrences, some of these allusions would require such extensive notation to clarify the meaning for readers who are unfamiliar with them that their meaning must be left to the reader to intuit through a study of Dōgen's remarks.

The reason why this discourse has such recourse to metaphoric language is that Zen Masters were being asked to use words to describe a state that words cannot readily convey. Someone who has gone above and beyond Buddhahood has entered a realm of existence in which there is no longer the same sense of a personal identity, an identity which those who have a false sense of self take to be who they really are.

Tōzan, our Founding Ancestor from Yün-chou Province, was the direct successor and heir of Donjō of Mount Ungan in T'an-chou Province. Tōzan was an Ancestor of the thirty-eighth monastic generation descending from the Tathagata, who was the thirty-eighth Ancestor counting back from him.[1]

> There was once a time when Great Master Tōzan addressed his assembly, saying, "Once I had directly experienced That which is above and beyond Buddhahood, I had the ability to say a few words about It."
>
> Thereupon, a monk asked, "And what were the words you spoke?"

---

1. That is, it makes no difference whether one regards Ancestors as descending from the Tathagata or as counting back to the Tathagata, since all Ancestors are the same in essence as the Tathagata.

The Master said, "When I spoke about It, my acharya,* you did not hear It."

The monk asked, "Are you listening, Venerable Monk?"

The Master said, "When I am not speaking about It, I am waiting to hear It."

The words quoted just now about experiencing That which is above and beyond Buddhahood are those of our Ancestor, Great Master Tōzan. Other Ancestors of the Buddha have habitually explored through their training what the Great Master said and have directly experienced That which is above and beyond Buddhahood. You need to understand that experiencing That which is above and beyond Buddhahood is above and beyond any innate cause or any fulfillment of effects.[2] Even so, when the Ancestors experienced 'not hearing It when words are spoken about It', they did not fail to penetrate into the meaning of this through their training. Until you have actually arrived at That which is above and beyond Buddhahood, you will not have directly experienced That which is above and beyond Buddhahood. Until you can put It into words, you have not directly experienced That which is above and beyond Buddhahood. It is above and beyond any mutual appearance or disappearance, and It is above and beyond any mutual giving or receiving.[3] Thus, the time when what is spoken of fully manifests is the time of experiencing That which is above and beyond Buddhahood. The time when That which is above and beyond Buddhahood fully manifests is the time when the acharya fails to hear.

'The acharya not hearing' means "The experience of That which is above and beyond Buddhahood is inaudible to you," and "At the time when words are spoken, the acharya does not hear It." Keep in mind that the Master's speaking with words is not tainted by being heard or by not being heard. For this reason, speaking is not connected with hearing or not hearing.

---

*   See Glossary.

2.   In other words, It is beyond training and enlightenment.

3.   This sentence describes various aspects of the one-to-one Transmission that are transcended.

'You, my acharya' is contained within 'what does not hear' and within 'what is put into words'. In other words, it is encountering 'such a person'* and not encountering 'such a person'; it is both 'this' and 'not this'. At the moment when the acharya is speaking, he is an acharya who is not listening. The essential meaning of 'his not listening' is his not listening by dint of his being tongue-tied, by dint of his being hindered by what is going on in his ears, by dint of his eyes being blinded by the Master's luminosity, and by dint of his being blocked up in body and mind. This is why he did not hear. Taking these points up again, we do not treat them as 'putting It into words'. Not listening goes above and beyond 'being put into words': it is simply not hearing at the time when It is put into words. From beginning to end, the Founding Ancestor's words, "When I spoke about It, my acharya, you did not hear It," are like wisteria vines relying on wisteria vines for support. Even so, it will resemble what is spoken being entwined with what is spoken; it is being obstructed by what is spoken.

When the monk asked, "Are you listening, Venerable Monk?" he was saying in effect, "It is not that you, Venerable Monk, are listening to your own words, since the one who is asking the question is not the Venerable Monk, and my question goes beyond 'speaking words.'" Even so, the monk was trying to ask whether he should train himself to listen and speak simultaneously. For example, he was trying to learn whether speaking is just speaking and whether listening is just listening. And although the question had been put that way, it goes beyond the disciple's tongue to fully express.

The words of our Founding Ancestor Tōzan, "When I am not speaking about It, I am waiting to hear It," need to be studied thoroughly in order to clarify their meaning. That is, at the time of putting It into words, one is not simultaneously listening to It. Listening will fully manifest at the time when one is not speaking. It is not that one idly disregards the time of not speaking, waiting for 'not speaking' to occur. At the moment of just listening, one does not consider putting It into words to be something extraneous, because such a thought is truly something extraneous. At the time when there is just listening, it is not that speaking of It has departed and exists solely as a side issue. And at the time when there is speaking of It, it is not that 'just listening' has closely hidden itself within the eyes of the one speaking and then suddenly thunders forth. As a consequence, even if someone is the acharya, at the time when It is spoken of, that person does not hear It. Even if the someone is the 'I', the time when there is no speaking is one of just listening, and this is comparable to "I have the ability to say a few words about It" and to "I have directly experienced That which is above and beyond Buddhahood." It is, for example, the direct experience of just listening at the time when someone else is engaged in speaking about It. This is why Tōzan said, "When I am not speaking about It, I am waiting to hear It." Although he spoke thus, experiencing That which is above and beyond Buddhahood is not an experience prior to the Seven Buddhas* but an experience that is above and beyond the Seven Buddhas.

> Our Founding Ancestor Tōzan once pointed out to his assembly, "You need to know that there are people who are above and beyond Buddhahood."
> At the time, there was a monk who asked him, "What is a person who is above and beyond Buddhahood?"
> The Great Master replied, "A non-Buddha." [4]
> Ummon once commented on Tōzan's reply, "We cannot name It, nor can we describe It, so we speak of It as 'a non-.'"
> Hofuku once commented, "Buddha is something 'non-.'"
> And Hōgen once commented, "Calling upon expedient means, we call such a one a Buddha." [5]

Generally speaking, an Ancestor of the Buddha who is above and beyond being 'an Ancestor of the Buddha' would be our Founding Ancestor Tōzan. The reason for that is, even though there are many others who have the countenance of a Buddha and an Ancestor, they have not even dreamt of the term 'being above and beyond Buddhahood'. Even if it had been explained to the likes of a Tokusan or a Rinzai, they could not have attested to it through their direct experience. And even if the likes of a Gantō or a Seppō had worked their own bodies to a nubbin through training, they

---

4. That is, someone who is beyond any fixed idea of what a Buddha is.

5. That is, we call such a one a Buddha for want of a better term.

would never have tasted a Master's Fist.[6] Such phrases as "The direct experience of That which is above and beyond Buddhahood," "I have the ability to say a few words about It," and "You need to know that there are people who are above and beyond Buddhahood," which our Founding Ancestor spoke, cannot be mastered experientially short of training for one, two, three, four, or five triply immeasurable hundreds of great kalpas.[7] And, by all means, there will be those who have the ability to explore the Subtle Path through their training.[8]

It is imperative that you know that there are those who are above and beyond Buddhahood. In other words, theirs is a life of playing with what is left after body and mind have dropped off. Even so, we can recognize the Old Buddha by His raising of a Fist. When you have already caught sight of Him in this manner, you will know that there is Someone who is above and beyond Buddhahood, and that there is no one who is above and beyond Buddhahood.[9] What I am pointing out to the community at present is not that you must become someone who is above and beyond Buddhahood, nor that you must encounter someone who is above and beyond Buddhahood, but simply that you must know that there are those who are above and beyond Buddhahood. When you can grasp this fundamental point, you will no longer attempt to know whether there is someone who is above and beyond Buddhahood or whether there is no one who is above and beyond Buddhahood, for that one who is above and beyond Buddhahood is a non-Buddha. Should there be a time when some doubt arises as to what a non-Buddha is, you should consider that such a one is not called a non-Buddha because he or she existed before the historic Buddha, or because he or she

---

6. Both Gantō and Seppō were disciples of Tokusan.

7. That is, just short of never.

8. One of three ways taught by Tōzan for training disciples, the Subtle Path is the path by which the Master leads the trainee to a profoundly deep inner realm beyond the opposites. The next way is the Bird's Way wherein, like a bird in flight, the Master's way of training disciples moves freely and unobstructedly, leaving no karmic traces behind. The final way is Extending the Hand, whereby the Master makes use of various expedient means to guide the trainee.

9. There is 'no one' because self has dropped off.

came after the historic Buddha, or because he or she has transcended the historic Buddha: he or she is a non-Buddha simply because such a one has gone above and beyond Buddhahood. Such a one is called a non-Buddha because he or she has dropped off a Buddha's countenance and a Buddha's body and mind.

Meditation Master Jōin Koboku from the eastern capital—who was a Dharma heir of Fuyō Dōkai—once addressed his community, saying, "Once you directly know that there <u>is</u> the experience of That which is above and beyond Buddhahood, you will indeed have the ability to give voice to It. Now, my virtuous Zen monks, say right off! What is <u>your</u> experience of That which is above and beyond Buddhahood?

"There is a child within the human family. His six sense organs are lacking, his seven kinds of consciousness are incomplete. He is the Great Icchantika, one lacking the seed of Buddha Nature. When he meets a Buddha, he slays 'Buddha': when he meets an Ancestor, he slays 'Ancestor'. The Celestial Halls cannot house him: even the Hells have no gateway that can hold him. O great assembly! are you acquainted with 'such a person'[*]?"[10]

---

10. In this quotation, Jōin is describing the function of Buddha Nature after someone has awakened to the Truth and gone above and beyond Buddhahood. What remains is not something outside of or apart from being a human (that is, it is 'a child within the human family'), although the distinction of being male or female is no longer relevant. Having let go of all attachment, It functions as if the six sense organs were lacking. Similarly, the conviction has dropped away that the six sense organs, the judgmental, intellective mind, and the 'awakened mind' constitute all there is to being completely awakened. As the Great Icchantika, It functions beyond conventional notions of good and evil, and lacks the seed of Buddha Nature, because It is already the fruition of Buddha Nature. Distinctions, such as 'Buddha' and 'Ancestor', have been done away with, because they are inherently dualistic and no longer relevant. Finally, the worlds of existence, such as heavenly and hellish states, do not restrict It.

Then, after a good long time, he said, "The one facing you now is not from Sindh. He sleeps a lot and also talks a lot in his sleep."

'His six sense organs are lacking' means that a person has exchanged his eyes for black nuts from a bo-tree, his nostrils for bamboo tubes, and his skull for a toilet spatula. Pray, what could be the underlying principle of these exchanges? It is because of this principle that his six senses are lacking. Because his six senses are lacking, he has become a Golden Buddha after having passed through the furnace, and he has become a Mud Buddha after having passed through the Great Ocean, and he has become a Wooden Buddha after having passed through fire.

'His seven kinds of consciousness are incomplete' is synonymous with a 'broken wooden ladle'.* Even though it is said that he 'slays Buddha', he encounters Buddha, and because he encounters Buddha, he slays 'Buddha'. Were he to aim at entering the Celestial Halls, the Celestial Halls would immediately collapse. Were he to encounter the Hells, the Hells would suddenly fall away. Consequently, when he comes face-to-face with someone, his face breaks out into a smile, and he asks for nothing from Sindh.[11] He sleeps a lot and also talks a lot in his sleep. Keep in mind that the principle of this is that 'both the mountains know themselves and the earth knows itself' and that 'the whole body of jewels and stones are smashed into hundreds of pieces'. You should take your time to explore through your training what Meditation Master Koboku pointed out to his assembly. Do not do it hastily.

---

11. 'Something from Sindh' is a metaphor for asking for the very best someone can offer that is appropriate to the situation; here, the reference is to not asking for anything from another. Dōgen will take up this metaphor in Discourse 79: On 'The King Requests Something from Sindh' *(Ō Saku Sendaba).*

When Dōyō of Mount Ungo went to train under Tōzan, who was the Founding Ancestor of our lineage, Tōzan asked him, "O acharya, what is your name?"[12]

Ungo responded, "Dōyō."

The Founding Ancestor then said to him, "Speak again, but from a place above and beyond the conventional."

Ungo responded, "Were I to speak from a place above and beyond the conventional, then this 'I' would not be called Dōyō."

Tōzan said, "When I was with Ungan, what I answered him was in no way different."

We certainly need to look in detail at what the Master and disciple are now saying. "Were I to speak from a place above and beyond the conventional, then this 'I' would not be called Dōyō" was Dōyō's speaking from above and beyond Buddhahood. You need to explore through your training that, in the Dōyō who had just come, there is That which is not called Dōyō and which is above and beyond 'Dōyō'. At the time when he manifested the principle of "Were I to speak from a place above and beyond the conventional, then this 'I' would not be called Dōyō," he was the True Dōyō. Even so, do not say that he would be Dōyō even in a place above and beyond the conventional. When he heard the Founding Ancestor's words, "Speak again, but from a place above and beyond the conventional," were he to have said, "Speaking from a place above and beyond the conventional, I am nevertheless named Dōyō," this would still be his speaking from a place above and beyond the conventional. And why do I say so? Because Dōyō, in a twinkling, has leapt into the True Dōyō's brain and concealed himself there. Although we say that he has concealed himself there, he openly reveals his True Form.

---

12. In some Zen Buddhist contexts, such as the present one, acharya is simply a polite form of address for any monk, since in a monastery a monk may learn from any of his fellow trainees.

When Sōzan Honjaku went to train under our Founding Ancestor Tōzan, the latter asked him, "O acharya, what is your name?"

Sōzan replied, "Honjaku."

The Founding Ancestor said, "Speak again, but from a place above and beyond the conventional."

Sōzan responded, "I cannot say it."

The Founding Ancestor asked, "Why on earth can't you say it?"

Sōzan responded, "Because It is not called Honjaku."

The Founding Ancestor approved of this response.

I would comment that it is not that there are no words in that place above and beyond Buddhahood, it is just a matter of "I cannot say it." Why does he not say it? Because his True Self is not called Honjaku. Since this is so, the words from the place that is above and beyond are not spoken, and the unspoken words of that place above and beyond are unnamed, and the unnamed Honjaku is a term from that place above and beyond. As a result, Honjaku is unnamed. Since this is so, there is a non-Honjaku, there is the Unnamed which has dropped everything off, and there is a Honjaku that has been dropped off.

Meditation Master Banzan Hōshaku once said, "Among thousands of saintly persons, none have Transmitted the one path to That Which is Above and Beyond." The phrase 'the one path to That Which is Above and Beyond' is the wording of Banzan alone. He did not speak of what is above and beyond, nor did he speak of those who are above and beyond; he spoke of the one path to That Which is Above and Beyond. His main point is that even though thousands of saintly ones may have come forth in great profusion, they have not Transmitted the one path to That Which is Above and Beyond. 'To not Transmit' can also mean that the thousands of saintly ones have preserved a part of something that is above and beyond being Transmitted. We can study the Matter[*] in this way too. And there is still something more that needs to be said: thousands of saintly ones and thousands of wise ones do indeed exist, and even so, wise and saintly though they may be, the one path to That Which is Above and Beyond is above and beyond the realm of the wise and saintly.

    Meditation Master Chimon Kōso was once asked by a monk, "What is this thing about 'That which is above and beyond Buddhahood?'"

    The Master answered, "I hold the sun and moon aloft atop my staff."

That is, his saying that one's staff holds aloft the sun and moon is the same as 'experiencing going above and beyond Buddhahood'. When we explore through our training the staff of the sun and moon, then the whole universe is thrown into darkness, which is our going above and beyond Buddhahood. And it is not that the sun and moon are the staff: what is atop the head of the staff is what is atop the whole staff.

    Meditation Master Dōgo of Tennō-ji Temple, while still a novice in the assembly of Kisen, asked, "What *is* the Great Intent of Buddha Dharma?"

    Master Sekitō replied, "It is above and beyond anything that can be grasped, above and beyond anything that can be comprehended."

    Dōgo asked, "As you have gone above and beyond, is there any other way you have of putting It?"

    The Master replied, "The vast expanse of space does not hinder the white clouds as they float by."

As I see the matter, Sekitō was a second-generation descendant of Daikan Enō. The monk Dōgo of Tennō-ji was a younger monastic brother of Yakusan. There was the time when he asked, "What *is* the Great Intent of Buddha Dharma?" This question is not one that beginners or those who have entered training late in life are equal to. This can only be asked when someone has already heard of the Great Intent and been able to understand what It is.

Sekitō responded, "It is above and beyond anything that can be grasped, above and beyond anything that can be comprehended." You need to know that within the Buddha Dharma, the Great Intent exists at our first moment of spiritual awareness and It exists at the stage of our ultimate, full awakening. That Great Intent is not something to be grasped. Giving rise to the intention to train, doing the training and practice, and realizing the Truth do indeed exist, and they too are not something to be grasped. That Great Intent is not something to be comprehended. Training-and-enlightenment does indeed exist and training-and-enlightenment is not some 'thing' that exists, for it is not anything to be grasped or comprehended. Again, that Great Intent is neither something to be grasped nor something to be comprehended. It is not that the Noble Truths and training-and-enlightenment do not exist: it is that they are not something to be grasped or comprehended. And it is not that the Noble Truths and training-and-enlightenment exist only for a while, it is just that they are not something to be grasped or comprehended.

Dōgo asked, "As you have gone above and beyond, is there any other way you have of putting It?" That is, if there is another way the Master has of putting It, it will be a manifestation of the Master's having gone above and beyond, for 'another way of putting It' is synonymous with skillful means, and 'skillful means' is synonymous with all the Buddhas and all the Ancestors. Although the Master stated it in the way that he did, a further way may indeed exist. Even though a further way may exist, it is not something that will exclude 'a further way does not exist', for that could also be a Master's assertion.

"The vast expanse of space does not hinder the white clouds as they float by" were Sekitō's very words. Moreover, his use of the words 'vast expanse of space' is not something that puts a limit on the vast expanse of space. Although his saying 'the vast expanse of space' does not hinder the vast expanse of space from floating by, his 'white clouds', by its very nature, also does not limit the white clouds. The white clouds' floating by is unhindered, and the floating by of white clouds does not hinder the vast expanse of space from floating by. Not to be limited by others is also not to be limited by oneself. It is not the case that in order for a face-to-face meeting to take place, there be no limits except the one that each person does not hinder the other. Because of this, there are no limits between Master and disciple. This expresses the ultimate reality and the outer form of Sekitō's statement, "The vast expanse of space does not hinder the white clouds as they float by." At that very moment, Sekitō raised the eyebrows of the one who was exploring the Great Intent through his training, and the trainee caught a glimpse of the Buddha coming to meet him and encountered the Ancestor coming to meet him: he met himself coming and met the other coming. This has been considered the principle of 'asking once and being answered ten times'. As to the 'asking once and being answered ten times' of which I am now speaking, the one who asks once must be 'such a person' and the one who gives ten replies must also be 'such a person'.

Ōbaku once said:

> Well now, persons who have left home life behind to become monks need to realize that there is an aspect of the Matter that has come down to them from the past. For example, it is like Great Master Gozu Hōyū, who realized the Truth while training under the Fourth Chinese Ancestor Daii Dōshin. Even though Gozu's voicing of the Dharma had breadth and depth, he still never comprehended the key point of what was above and beyond Buddhahood.[13] When you have the eyes and the brains for this, you will be able to distinguish between false and true religious groups.

The Matter that has come down from the past, which Ōbaku alluded to in this way, is the Matter that has been genuinely Transmitted down to us by Buddha after Buddha and Ancestor after Ancestor. We call that Matter the Wondrous Heart of Nirvana, which is the Treasure House of the Eye of the True Teaching. Even though we say that It exists within us, we need to recognize It. And even though we say that It exists

---

13.   That is, he never understood that one goes on, always becoming Buddha, even after an initial realization of the Truth.

within us, It is still beyond the intellect's ability to grasp. Without the genuine Transmission of Buddha after Buddha, one cannot encounter It even in one's dreams. Ōbaku was a Dharma child of Hyakujō and even surpassed Hyakujō. And, as a Dharma grandchild of Baso, he even surpassed Baso. Generally speaking, among the Ancestors of those three or four generations, none could stand shoulder-to-shoulder with Ōbaku. It is Ōbaku alone who made it clear that Gozu lacked both horns.[14] Other Buddhas and Ancestors have never recognized this.

Meditation Master Hōyū of Mount Gozu was a venerable monk of high standing who trained under the Fourth Chinese Ancestor. His teaching was broad and deep. Truly, when we compare him with academic teachers of Scriptures and scholarly commentators, among those who came to eastern lands from the West he was neither inadequate nor lacking. Yet even so, sad to say, he had not recognized the key point of what lay above and beyond Buddhahood and was therefore unable to state what the key point of being above and beyond Buddhahood was about. Because he did not know what this key point was, how could he possibly distinguish between the false and the true? He was simply a person who had merely studied words. To know the key point of what lies above and beyond Buddhahood, to train and practice with this key point, and to awaken to this key point are unreachable for ordinary, run-of-the-mill people. Yet wherever there is a genuine effort to train, It will manifest without fail.

What is called 'the experience of going above and beyond Buddhahood' is synonymous with arriving at Buddhahood, and then going on above and beyond until one once again meets Buddha. It is the same as sentient beings' meeting Buddha. Since this is so, then if one's encountering Buddha is simply on a par with a sentient being's encountering 'a Buddha', then this will not be 'meeting Buddha'.[15] If one's

---

14. There is a play on words here that is lost in translation. The name Gozu means 'bull's head'. To say that he lacked both horns alludes to his not yet having experienced full spiritual maturity.

15. 'Meeting Buddha' is the topic of Discourse 59: On Encountering Buddha *(Kembutsu)*. There, as here, Dōgen distinguishes between our ability to see Buddha Nature in someone else and our ability to recognize our own Buddha Nature.

encountering Buddha is just like a sentient being's encountering 'a Buddha', that person's meeting Buddha will be illusory. How much less could it be the experience of going above and beyond Buddhahood! You need to know that the experience that is above and beyond, of which Ōbaku speaks, is above and beyond what is envisioned by those folks nowadays with limited insight. Simply, there have been those whose expressions of the Dharma were below those of Gozu and there have been those whose expressions of the Dharma were equal with those of Gozu, and even so, they may well have been the younger and older Dharma brothers of Gozu. How could they possibly know the key point of what is above and beyond Buddhahood? Others, such as those 'thrice wise and ten times saintly',* do not know the key point that lies above and beyond Buddhahood. How much less could they open or close the key point of what lies above and beyond! This point is the very eyes for your exploring the Matter through your training with your Master. If you know what the key point of going above and beyond Buddhahood is, you will be a person who has gone above and beyond Buddhahood, for you will have realized what lies above and beyond Buddhahood.

Given to the assembly at Kannondōri in Kōshōhōrin-ji Temple on the twenty-third day of the third lunar month of the Ninji era (April 24, 1242).

Copied by me, based on an unrevised manuscript written in the grass style, at Eihei-ji Temple on a day during the summer retreat in the first year of the Shōgen era (1259).

Ejō

28

On That Which Comes Like This

(Immo)

Translator's Introduction: *Immo* is a word that comes from colloquial Sung dynasty Chinese. English equivalents would include 'this', 'that', 'thus', 'in this way or manner', 'like this', and 'in such a way as this'. It was used by the Chinese Zen Masters to designate 'That Which Is', the Ultimate Reality which goes beyond any words we can employ to describe It. The word was also used when describing someone who knows through direct experience what the term 'That Which Is' is pointing to, namely, 'such a person' or 'such a one'.

Dōyō of Mount Ungo was a Dharma heir of Tōzan. He was a Dharma descendant of the thirty-ninth generation from Shakyamuni Buddha, and he is the rightful ancestral heir of Tōzan's tradition. One day, Dōyō gave Teaching to his assembly, saying: "If you wish to experience That Which Is, you need to be 'such a person'.[*] If you are already 'such a person', why be worried about experiencing That Which Is?" In other words, any who wish to realize the Great Matter[*] of That Which Is must themselves be 'such a person'. Since they are already 'such a person', why would they be worried about experiencing That Which Is? The point of this is that the supreme enlightenment we are heading for is what, for the present, I am calling *immo*. This condition of supreme enlightenment is such that even the whole universe in all the ten quarters is but a trifling bit of supreme enlightenment, and that enlightenment is far beyond the whole universe. Even we are all merely accessories within this whole universe in all the ten quarters. And by what means are we to know that That Which Is exists? In a word, we know that it is so because both our body and mind together make their appearance within the whole universe, yet neither is ours to possess.

This body is already not 'me' and each life flows on through time; it is beyond our ability to halt it for even a moment. Where has the ruddy face of our youth gone? Were we to seek it out, it has left not a trace. When we look deeply, we see that the myriad things of the past will not come back again. A heart that is sincere, likewise,

---

[*]   See Glossary.

does not remain fixed, but comes and goes, moment by moment. We may say that there is truth in this sincere heart, but it is not something that lingers behind within the vicinity of a personal self. Even so, there is something that unboundedly gives rise to the intention to realize enlightenment. After this intention has arisen, we abandon those things that we used to play around with, desiring to hear what we have not yet heard and seeking to realize what we have not yet realized—and this is not solely something of our own doing. Keep in mind that, because you are 'such a person', this is so. How do we know that we are 'such a person'? Just by our wishing to gain the experiencing of That Which Is do we know that we are 'such a person'. You already have the countenance of 'such a person', so you must not worry yourself now over experiencing That Which Is. Even though you may be worried, this is also an experiencing of That Which Is, and It is beyond being something to worry about. Further, you should not be surprised that the experience of That Which Is is present in such a state. Even though you are in such a state of surprise and doubt, this too is That Which Is. And That Which Is is also described as being beyond surprise. This state cannot be measured by the reckoning of a Buddha, or by the reckoning of the mind, or by the reckoning of the Dharma Realm, or by the reckoning of the whole universe. It will simply be "Since you are already 'such a person', why are you worried about experiencing That Which Is?"

So, the True Nature of sound, color, and form is That Which Is, the True Nature of body and mind is That Which Is, and the True Nature of Buddhas is That Which Is. For example, we understand that when we fall, we rely on the ground being there, as it is, existing just as it is, and that when we get up, we rely on the ground being there, existing just as it is, so we should not be surprised that our falling down has also relied on the ground being there.[1]

---

1. In this section of the discourse, references to 'the ground' have more than one meaning. When we fall (that is, act contrary to a Precept), we rely on 'hitting the ground' somewhere along the line, and we depend on this 'grounding' to help us get up and go on, trying to keep to the Precepts. At the same time, what we are ultimately relying on is That Which is Our Spiritual Ground. Further on in the discourse, Dōgen will use the phrase 'by relying on the ground' in the sense of relying on what is concrete in our life,

There is a Teaching that has been voiced from ancient times, one that has been voiced in India and from the heavens above. It says in effect, "If, because of the ground, you fall down, you will get up, also because of the ground: should you try to get up independent of the ground, ultimately, that is impossible." In other words, those who fall down on the ground will invariably get up on the ground. Were they to attempt to get up apart from the ground, they will not succeed.

Following through on what has just been described, we take it as an expression of the beauty of a great awakening and have made it into a path for freeing ourselves from body and mind. Therefore, should someone ask us what the principle underlying 'realizing the Way of all Buddhas' is, we would say that it is like someone who has fallen to the ground relying on the Ground for arising. When you explore this through your training with a Master, you need to penetrate into and rise above the past, the future, and this very moment of the present. Whether we are really awake or unawakened, whether we return to our delusions or lose our delusions, whether we are hindered by 'awakening' or hindered by delusion—all of these illustrate the principle of someone who has fallen on the ground relying on the Ground to get up. This is an expression of the Way of those in the heavens above and the earth below: it is an expression of the Way in both India and the lands to the east. It is an expression of the Way from the past to the present and into the future: it is an expression of the Way of Old Buddhas and of New Buddhas. And further, this expression of the Way is never incomplete in its expression, nor does its Truth ever wane.

Be that as it may, to understand the expression only in this way and to fail to understand it in any other way is as if one had not explored this statement thoroughly with one's Master. Even though the expression of an Old Buddha has been passed on to us in such a manner, yet, when as an Old Buddha ourselves, we hear the expression of an Old Buddha, we will be hearing That which transcends Buddhahood.

Although it was not stated in India or in lofty circles, there is another principle being asserted here. Namely, if someone who has fallen on the ground should

---

which cannot be relied on except in relation to That Which Is Like Empty Space. When we fall while relying on this Empty Space, we can arise by admitting to the things that we have done.

seek to arise by relying on the ground, though he spends immeasurable eons at the task, he will never be able to get up. He <u>can</u> get up by means of the one single, absolute Path. That is, someone who has fallen on the ground arises by relying on Empty Space, and someone who has fallen in empty space can arise by relying on the Ground. If there were no 'That Which Is', one could not rise. All the Buddhas and all the Ancestors were no different from this.

Were someone to ask such a question as, "How far apart are Empty Space and the Ground?" you should reply, "Empty Space and the Ground are a hundred and eight thousand miles apart. If you should fall upon the ground, by all means get up by relying on Empty Space, for ultimately there is no such principle as arising apart from Empty Space. If you should fall while relying upon empty space, you will unquestionably arise by relying on the Ground, for ultimately there is no such principle as arising apart from the Ground." If someone has never asserted the Matter like this, that person has never known or seen the dimensions of Ground and Empty Space.

Our Seventeenth Ancestral Master, the Venerable Sōgyanandai, declared Kayashata to be his Dharma heir. One time, upon hearing a temple bell that was hanging in a hall being rung by the wind, he asked Kayashata, "Is it the wind we hear or is it the bell we hear?"

Kayashata replied, "It is beyond the sounding of the wind and beyond the sounding of the bell: it is the sounding of my own Mind."

The Venerable Sōgyanandai asked, "And, say, just what <u>is</u> your own Mind?"

Kayashata replied, "It is equivalent to saying that everything is altogether tranquil in its stillness."

The Venerable Sōgyanandai said, "Well done! Excellently done! Who other than you, my disciple, could succeed to our Way!"

Thereupon, he Transmitted to Kayashata the Treasure House of the
Eye of the True Teaching.

Here, in a state beyond the sounding of the wind, we learn what the sound of our Mind
is. When we are beyond what the sounding of the bell is, we learn what the sound of
our Mind is. Even though the sound of our Mind is like this, everything is, nonetheless,
altogether tranquil in its stillness.

This story was Transmitted from India to the eastern lands, and from ancient
times to the present day. It has been considered a standard for learning the Way, but
many have misunderstood it, saying, "Kayashata's assertion that it is neither the
sounding of the wind nor the sounding of the bell but the sounding of our mind means
that, at the very moment of when a sound occurs, there is an arising of discriminative
thought, and this arising of discriminative thought is what we call 'mind'. If this
mental awareness did not exist, how could we possibly be conscious of a ringing
sound? Since hearing results from this awareness, we can certainly call it the
foundation of hearing, which is why he said that it is the sounding of his mind." This
is a false understanding. Such people say things like this because they lack the
assistance of a genuine teacher. For instance, it is comparable to the interpretations of
scholars who write commentaries on topics like subjectivism and proximate
conceptualization. Commentaries like these are not profound explorations of the
words of a Buddha.

On the other hand, those who have explored the Matter with a genuine heir
of the Buddha's Way speak of the Treasure House of the Eye of the True Teaching on
supreme enlightenment in terms of 'stillness' and 'not acting willfully' and 'meditative
states' and 'invocations'. The underlying principle is, if one thought or thing is truly
still, all the myriad thoughts and things are also still along with it. If the wind's
blowing is still, then the bell's ringing will be still: hence, Kayashata spoke of
everything being altogether tranquil in its stillness. He was saying that the sounding
of Mind is beyond the sounds of the wind, and the sounding of Mind is beyond the
sounds of the bell, and the sounding of Mind is beyond the sounds of the mind. Having
diligently explored his realization of what is intimately connected with That Which
Is, he was able to simply state it, and he could also have said that it is the sound of

wind, the sound of bell, the sound of blowing, and the sound of sounding. It is not a matter of "Why be worried about experiencing That Which Is?" but rather of "Why get stuck on experiencing That Which Is?"

Before our Thirty-third Ancestor, Meditation Master Daikan Enō, had shaved his head, he was residing at Hosshō-ji Temple in Kuangchou Province, when he overheard two monks arguing. One was asserting that the banner was moving. The other was asserting that the wind was moving. The argument went on like this, back and forth without letup, until the Sixth Ancestor said, "It is not the wind that is moving, nor the banner that is moving: it is your minds, dear sirs, which are moving." [2] Upon hearing this, the two monks forthwith accepted what he said.

These two monks were from India. What the Sixth Ancestor was asserting by speaking these words for their sake was that the wind, the banner, and the movement all exist within Mind. Though people today may hear the Sixth Ancestor's words, they do not understand the Sixth Ancestor's meaning. How much less can they put into words what the Sixth Ancestor is expressing! Why do I say this? Because hearing the words "You, dear sirs, are Mind moving," people today take it as literally asserting, "It is your minds, dear sirs, which are moving," and thus fail to encounter the Sixth Ancestor, or comprehend the Sixth Ancestor, or be a Dharma offspring of the Sixth Ancestor. Now, as descendants of the Sixth Ancestor, we can also say what the Sixth Ancestor said, and we can say it because we have obtained the Body, Hair, and Skin of the Sixth Ancestor. And we can state it this way, "Of course, your mind may move, but what is more, you yourselves, dear sirs, Move." Why do we say it in this way? Because That which is moving is 'Moving', and because 'you, dear sirs,' means you, dear sirs. And we have put it this way because all of you are already 'such a one'.

---

2.   The Sixth Ancestor's remark is ambiguous. Later in the text, Dōgen will interpret it as, "The matter is beyond the wind moving and beyond the banner moving: you are the Mind moving."

In his former days, the Sixth Ancestor sold firewood in Hsinchou Province. He was thoroughly familiar with the mountains and the water, and, having put forth his efforts beneath the pine trees, he severed the roots. But how could he have known of the ancient Teachings that illumine the Mind when someone is seated at ease by the Bright Window, and from whom could he have learned about cleansing and removing stains?[3] He was in the marketplace when he heard someone reciting a Scripture. It was not something that he himself had expected, nor was it something that someone else had encouraged him to do. While still a child, he was bereft of his father, and, when he was grown, he took care of his mother. Little did he know that concealed beneath those clothes of his was a Jewel that would light up the heavens and the earth. Having suddenly been illumined by hearing the Scripture, he departed from his elderly mother and went searching for a good spiritual friend—all of which is uncommon behavior among human beings, for who can treat lightly the bonds of affection for one's parents? But in attaching greater weight to the Dharma, he treated as lighter his debt of filial gratitude and renounced his worldly obligations. This is the principle expressed by the verse:

> *When those who have spiritual wisdom hear It voiced,*
> *They are able to trust and understand It at once.*

What we call 'spiritual wisdom' cannot be learned from someone else, nor is it something that we ourselves give rise to. Since wisdom can Transmit wisdom, wisdom will seek out wisdom. The five hundred bats naturally had wisdom within themselves; moreover, they clung to neither their body nor their mind.[4] And when the ten thousand

---

3.   Although this sentence and the previous one have their literal meanings, there is also the metaphorical meaning of his having learned the Dharma as It is expressed by things in nature, and, through his devotion to his physical labor, he also learned how to sever the roots of his delusions. However, he was poor and illiterate, so he could not study Scriptures at his leisure, and he did not know of anyone under whose guidance he could do the spiritual practice of cleansing his karma.

4.   An allusion to a story of five hundred bats who were living in a tree. A traveler, passing by, stopped to build a fire to keep warm while he read a Scripture aloud. When the fire

swimming fish heard the Dharma, they were immediately able to understand It, not because of any conditions or causes, but simply because they had wisdom ever present within themselves.[5] It is not something that comes to us, nor is it something that enters us. For instance, it is like the Lord of the East meeting the spring.[6] Wisdom is beyond discriminative thought and beyond an absence of discriminative thinking, as well as beyond intentions and beyond an absence of intentions. Even less would it be related to something's being large or small, and even less still could we discuss it in terms of delusion and enlightenment! The point is that the Sixth Ancestor had no clue as to what the Buddha's Dharma was, never having heard It before, and therefore he was neither attached to It nor desirous of It. But once he heard the Dharma, he held his filial bonds to be less binding and put his false sense of self out of his mind. This happened because the body and mind of someone who has wisdom is already something that does not belong to any personal self. This is what is called 'being able to immediately trust and understand It'.

We do not know how many rounds of birth and death we have already spent returning again and again to various useless delusions, even while possessing this wisdom. It is like rocks covering up a jewel: the jewel is unaware that it is covered up by rocks and the rocks are unaware that they are covering up a jewel. When human beings recognize this jewel, they seize upon it. This is not something that the jewel expectantly awaits nor is it something that the rocks have been waiting for, and it does not depend on a spiritual awakening on the part of the rocks nor is it something that the jewel thinks about. That is to say, even though a human being and wisdom are unaware of each other, the Way is invariably overheard by the person's wisdom.

---

set the tree ablaze, the bats stayed where they were, preferring to be burned alive rather than miss hearing a single word of Scripture, and this they could do because they were not attached to body or mind.

5. An allusion to ten thousand fish who were dying because the water in which they lived began to dry up. Upon hearing someone reading a Scripture aloud, they escaped from their suffering and were reborn as celestial beings in the Tushita Heaven.

6. The Lord of the East is the spirit of springtime who shows up the moment that spring arrives.

There is a saying in the *Lotus Scripture*:

> *Those in whom wisdom is absent doubt that it exists*
> *And, by acting thus, they miss their chances for ever so long.*

Wisdom is not necessarily 'something that is present' and it is not necessarily 'something that is absent', but rather, at a certain moment, there is the presence of the pine trees of spring and the chrysanthemums of autumn are not to be found. At the time of this absence of wisdom, the whole of the highest supreme enlightenment becomes something doubtful, and every thought and thing also becomes doubtful. At this time, one misses one's chances for ever so long by acting from this doubt. Words that should be heard and Dharma that should be awakened to both become something doubtful. In the whole universe—which we do not possess—there is nowhere that is hidden to us, for the whole universe is a single iron rod thousands of miles long, and no one possesses it. Even though twigs bud in accord with this, as the Lotus Scripture says:

> *Within the Buddha lands in the ten quarters,*
> *There is only the Teaching of the One Vehicle.*

And even though leaves fall in accord with this, as the Lotus Scripture also says:

> *The Dharma abides in Its place in the Dharma,*
> *And the forms of the world are ever recurring.*

Because this is already the way things are, wisdom's being present and wisdom's not being present is what the face of the sun is to the face of the moon.[7]

Because the Sixth Ancestor was 'such a person', he could clearly discern the Truth. Ultimately, he paid a visit to Mount Ōbai, prostrating himself before Meditation

---

7. That is, wisdom is inherent in the Cosmic Buddha (the sun) and is reflected in our Buddha Nature (the moon).

Master Daiman Kōnin, who allowed him to lodge in the servants' hall. Day and night, he pounded rice.

> A bare eight months had passed when, late in the night, Kōnin himself came unseen to the rice-pounding shed and asked the Sixth Ancestor, "Is the rice white yet?"
>
> The Sixth Ancestor said, "It is white, but it has not yet been winnowed."
>
> Kōnin struck the mortar three times, whereupon the Sixth Ancestor tossed the rice three times in the winnowing-basket.

It is said that at this moment Master and disciple became mutually in accord with the Truth. They may not have known it themselves, and it is something others may not understand, but the Transmission of the Dharma and the Transmission of the Robe must certainly have occurred at that very moment.

> Sekitō Kisen of Mount Nangaku was once asked by his disciple Yakusan, "I have a rough understanding of the Three Vehicles* and the twelve divisions of the Scriptures, but I have heard that here in the south, there is a direct pointing to the human heart whereby one sees his True Nature and becomes Buddha. With deepest respect, I pray that you, Venerable Monk, out of compassion, will instruct me."

This was Yakusan's request. Yakusan, since early on, had been a lecturer and had thoroughly penetrated the meaning of the Three Vehicles and the twelve divisions of the Scriptures. So it seems that he was not in the dark about the Buddha Dharma. In those former times, separate traditions had not yet arisen, so just clarifying the meaning of the Three Vehicles and the twelve divisions of the Scriptures was considered the customary way to study what the Scriptures taught. Nowadays there are many who, from thickheadedness, have set up their own standards with which to evaluate the Buddha Dharma, but this is not customary in the Buddha's Way.

The Great Master said, "Being 'such a person' is unattainable, not being 'such a person' is unattainable, and both being 'such a person' and not being 'such a person' are together unattainable.[8] How about you? What do you think?"

This is what the Great Master said for the benefit of Yakusan. Truly, because being 'such a person' and not being 'such a person' are altogether unattainable, being 'such a person' is unattainable and not being 'such a person' is unattainable. Being 'such a person' is what we mean by *immo*. It is not a matter of the usefulness of words having limits or not having limits. You need to explore through your training that being 'such a person' is unattainable and that what is unattainable is being 'such a person'. It is not that being 'such a person' and being unattainable are of concern only to the evaluations of a Buddha. To understand them intellectually is unattainable; to understand them through direct experience is unattainable.

Meditation Master Daikan Enō of Mount Sōkei once gave instruction to Nangaku saying, "What has come about like this?"[9] These words show that Nangaku's being 'such a person' is beyond doubt because he is beyond intellectual understanding. And because "What has come about like this" is the What, you should thoroughly explore through your training that all the myriad things that comprise the universe are, beyond any doubt, the What. And you should thoroughly explore through your training that each and every single thing is, beyond any doubt, the What. The What is not subject to doubt, for It is That Which Comes Like This.

Given to the assembly at Kannondōri in Kōshōhōrin-ji Temple on the twenty-sixth day of the third lunar month in the third year of the Ninji era (April 27, 1242).

---

8.   That is, seeing what one's True Nature is and thereby becoming Buddha is not something to be obtained, since enlightenment already is.

9.   There is a play on words in this remark. Though it appears to be a question, it is actually a direct statement meaning, as Dōgen will indicate, "The What has come about like this."

Copied by me in the quarters of the Abbot's assistant on the fourth day of the fourth month in the first year of the Kangen era (April 24, 1243).

Ejō

29

On Ceaseless Practice

(Gyōji)

Translator's Introduction: *Gyōji* is Dōgen's longest discourse in the *Shōbōgenzō*. It was apparently given to his disciples in written form, and, because of its length, it was bound in two fascicles, identified as the upper part and the lower part. Since the lower part is simply a continuation of the upper, the two have not been treated here as separate works. In the original text, an alternate name was given at the end of the lower part: The Ceaseless Practice of the Buddhas and Ancestors (*Busso Gyōji*).

Gyōji can be literally rendered as 'doing the practice and keeping to it', hence, 'ceaseless practice'. It can also be understood as a truncated form of *shugyō jikai*, 'doing one's training and practice while keeping to the Precepts'. Further, as Dōgen makes clear through the many stories of Indian and Chinese Masters that he recounts, 'practice' does not refer to some fixed agenda but differs in form with each Master, and yet is recognizable as that individual's ceaseless practice.

The Great Way of Buddhas and Ancestors invariably involves unsurpassed ceaseless practice. This practice rolls on in a cyclic manner without interruption. Not a moment's gap has occurred in Their giving rise to the intention to realize Buddhahood, in Their doing the training and practice, in Their experiencing enlightenment, and in Their realizing nirvana, for the Great Way of ceaseless practice rolls on just like this. As a result, the practice is not done by forcing oneself to do it and it is not done by being forced to do it by someone else: it is a ceaseless practice that is never tainted by forcing. The merits from this ceaseless practice sustain us and sustain others.

The underlying principle of this practice is that the whole universe in all ten directions receives the merit of our ceaseless practice. Though others may not recognize it, though we may not recognize it ourselves, still, it is so. As a result, owing to the ceaseless practice of all the Buddhas and Ancestors, our own ceaseless practice has clearly manifested. And, owing to our ceaseless practice, the ceaseless practice of all the Buddhas clearly manifests, and the Great Way of the Buddhas pervades everywhere. And, owing to our ceaseless practice, the Buddha's Way rolls perpetually onward. Accordingly, Buddha after Buddha and Ancestor after Ancestor have dwelt within Buddha, have acted from the Heart of Buddha, and have fully manifested Buddha, and They have done so without a single moment's interruption.

Due to this ceaseless practice, there is the sun, the moon, and the stars. Due to ceaseless practice, there is the great earth and the vast expanse of space. Due to ceaseless practice, there is body and mind, along with the internal effects of our past karma* and the external conditions of our surroundings. Due to ceaseless practice, there are the four great elements* and the five skandhas.* Even though ceaseless practice is not something that worldly folk desire, it will be what all human beings truly come back to. Due to the ceaseless practice of all Buddhas of past, present, and future, all Buddhas manifest ceaseless practice in the past, present, and future. And there are also times when the merit from that ceaseless practice no longer lies hidden, and, as a result, the intention to realize Buddhahood arises, along with training and practice. And there are times when that merit does not show itself, and, as a result, it is not encountered or perceived. You need to explore through your training that even though it may not show itself, it does not lie hidden, because it is not tainted with appearing and disappearing or with existing and dying away. Though it may be concealed from us at the present moment, the ceaseless practice that has brought us into existence is present in every single thought and thing, all of which arise due to coexisting conditions, and we just do not realize that we are actually doing ceaseless practice.

Moreover, if we wish to grasp what ceaseless practice is, we should not make a special case out of every new thing that comes along. This is because, from the perspective of Dependent Origination, there is simply ceaseless practice, and ceaseless practice does not come about as a result of depending upon anything. You need to explore this point with diligence and in detail. The ceaseless practice that makes ceaseless practice manifest is nothing other than our own ceaseless practice in the here and now. Ceaseless practice is not present here and now because it is something that we innately have within ourselves; it is not something that already

---

* See Glossary.

dwells within us.[1] Its presence in the here and now is beyond the comings and goings of a 'self' and beyond the departings and emergings of a 'self'. The phrase 'here and now' does not refer to something that existed prior to ceaseless practice: 'the here and now' refers to ceaseless practice fully manifesting itself in the present.

Accordingly, the ceaseless practice of one day is the seed of all Buddhas: it is the ceaseless practice of all Buddhas. By means of it, all Buddhas fully manifest Themselves. So, to not do ceaseless practice is to loathe all Buddhas, and to fail to make alms offerings to all Buddhas is to loathe ceaseless practice, and to fail to live and die together with all Buddhas is to fail both to learn from Them and to explore the Matter[*] with Them. To see a flower opening or a leaf falling in the here and now is to fully see what ceaseless practice is. There is no polishing of the Mirror or smashing of the Mirror that is not ceaseless practice.[2] Thus, if anyone tried to set aside ceaseless practice—ignoring it in an attempt to conceal their wicked intention to escape from ceaseless practice—this too would be ceaseless practice. Accordingly, some who are inclined towards ceaseless practice may merely resemble someone who has a genuine intention to do ceaseless practice, still, such persons would be like the perplexed son who threw away the treasures and riches of the native land of his true father and wandered off into foreign lands.[3] Even though, during the time of his wandering about aimlessly, the winds and waters did not cause him to lose life or limb, nevertheless he should not have thrown away his true father's treasure, for that is to mistakenly lose the Dharma Treasure of his True Father. This is why ceaseless practice is Dharma that is not to be neglected even for a moment.

---

1. That is, it does not refer to some kind of soul or permanent self.

2. Dōgen explores these allusions to the Mirror thoroughly in his Discourse 19: On the Ancient Mirror *(Kokyō)*.

3. An allusion to a parable in the *Lotus Scripture*, found in the fourth chapter entitled "Belief and Understanding", which describes how we spend so much of our lives running away from the Buddha.

Our benevolent spiritual father, Great Master Shakyamuni Buddha, had been observing ceaseless practice deep in the mountains from the nineteenth year of His life until His thirtieth year, when there arose the ceaseless practice by which He realized the Way simultaneously with the great earth and its sentient beings. Up through the eightieth year of His life, He was still doing ceaseless practice in the mountains, and in the forests, and in the monasteries. He did not return to His father's royal palace or assume governance over the prosperity of the nation. For clothing, He kept to the large sanghati robe—the kind that monks still wear—and He did not exchange it for another type of robe for the rest of His life. He did not exchange His alms bowl for another one during His lifetime, and He never stayed alone, not even once in a day. He did not reject so much as a single worthless alms offering from either ordinary folk or those in lofty positions, and He bore with patience the insults of non-Buddhists. In sum, His whole life was ceaseless practice. It can never be said that the Buddha's examples of washing His robe and accepting alms for His food were not ceaseless practice.

The Eighth Indian Ancestor, the Venerable Makakashō, was the Venerable Shakyamuni's Dharma heir.[4] Throughout his life he completely devoted himself to the ceaseless practice of the twelve zudas.[5] The twelve zudas are as follows:

> (1) Not to accept personal invitations from people, but to go on alms round for one's food each day. Also, not to accept money with which to purchase even part of a monk's meal.

---

4.   Makakashō is considered the Eighth Indian Ancestor when we begin from the first of the Seven Buddhas, of whom Shakyamuni Buddha was the seventh.

5.   A zuda (Skt. *dhūta*) is an austere practice that, in later Mahayana Buddhism, became associated with the Lesser Course. Dōgen's subsequent listing of the twelve zudas is apparently based on a Chinese text called *The Great Scripture on the Three Thousand Forms of Everyday Behavior for Monks*.

(2) To lodge overnight on a mountain and not to stay in the dwelling of ordinary folk, in a highly populated district, or in some town or village.[6]

(3) Not to beg people for clothing. Also, not to accept any clothing that is offered by people, but simply to take the clothing of the dead that has been discarded at gravesides.

(4) To lodge under a tree within some field, whether cultivated or not.

(5) To eat one meal per day. This is sometimes called *sunka sunnai*.[7]

(6) Not to lie down, day or night, but simply to sleep while sitting up or to do walking meditation when drowsy. This is sometimes called *sunnai sashakyō*.[8]

(7) To possess only three robes and never to have an extra robe. Also, not to sleep wrapped in a blanket.

(8) To reside in cemeteries and not to take up permanent residence in Buddhist temples or among people. To do seated meditation and seek the Way while looking directly at the skulls and bones of the dead.

(9) To desire merely to live by oneself, without desiring to meet other people or to sleep amidst a group of people.

(10) To eat the raw fruits of trees and plants first, and then to eat one's cooked food. After having finished eating one's cooked food, to not then eat the raw fruits of trees and plants.

---

6. 'On a mountain' here most likely refers to staying in a monastery, temple, or hermitage.

7. *Sunka sunnai* is the Japanese pronunciation of a corrupt Chinese transliteration of the Pali word *ekāsanika*, which means 'one meal a day'.

8. As in the preceding footnote, *sunnai sashakyō* is a corruption of the Pali *nesajjika*, meaning 'not lying down day or night'.

(11) To be content to sleep out in the open, without seeking shelter under some tree.

(12) Not to eat meat. Also, not to eat processed milk products or apply hemp oil to one's body.

These are the twelve zudas. The Venerable Makakashō did not regress or turn away from these throughout his whole lifetime. Even though the Tathagata's Treasure House of the Eye of the True Teaching was directly Transmitted to him, he did not step back from practicing these zudas.

> The Buddha once said to him, "You are already one who is old in years, so you should eat what the other monks eat."
>
> The Venerable Makakashō replied, "If I had not met the Tathagata in this lifetime, I would have been a pratyekabuddha.[*] I would have resided all my life in mountains and forests. Fortunately, I encountered the Tathagata in this lifetime and have been blessed with the beneficence of the Dharma. Even so, in the end, I will not eat as the other monks in the community eat."
>
> The Tathagata praised him for that.

On another occasion, because Makakashō had been ceaselessly practicing these zudas, his body had grown emaciated. When the assembly of monks saw him, they belittled him. Thereupon, the Tathagata cordially summoned Makakashō and made room for him on half His seat. The Venerable Makakashō sat down on the Tathagata's seat. You need to keep in mind that Makakashō was a senior monk of long standing in the Buddha's assembly. We cannot fully enumerate the ways in which he ceaselessly practiced for his whole life.

The Tenth Indian Ancestor, the Venerable Barishiba, once vowed that for the rest of his life he would not let his ribs touch his mat.[9] Even though he was eighty-six years old, he did his utmost in practicing the Way and was soon given the one-to-one Transmission of the Great Dharma. Because he did not let his days and nights idly slip by, he was given the one-to-one Transmission of the True Eye of Enlightenment after barely three years of effort. The Venerable One had been in his mother's womb for sixty years, and when he was born, his hair was already white. Because he kept to his vow not to lie down like a corpse, he was called 'The One of Venerable Ribs'. In the dark, he would release a radiance from his hands by means of which he was able to read the Scriptures and thereby procure the Dharma. This was a strange and wondrous trait that he was born with.

      The One of Venerable Ribs was almost eighty years old when he renounced home life and dyed his robes.

      A young man who lived in the area asked him, "You foolish, decrepit old man, how can you be so dim-witted? Besides, those who leave home life to become monks have two kinds of undertakings: first, they learn how to meditate; second, they chant the Scriptures. You are now feeble and senile, so there is no way for you to progress by doing either. To put it simply, you will carelessly muddy up the waters and will fill your stomach with alms offerings to no purpose."

      The One of Venerable Ribs, upon hearing these rebukes and snide remarks, then thanked the man and made a vow, saying, "I will not let my ribs touch my mat until I have thoroughly

---

9   It is unclear whether Barishiba meant what he said figuratively, as we might speak of 'not lying down on the job', or literally. Over the millennia, some monks have attempted to follow Barishiba's practice literally and have even devised ways to bind themselves whilst in full lotus position so that they would not fall into a prone position if they should fall asleep.

mastered the fundamental meaning of the *Tripitaka*,* cut off all craving for anything within the three worlds of desire, form, and beyond form, obtained the six marvelous spiritual abilities, and equipped myself with the eight kinds of detachment from delusion."

From that time on, there was not even one day that he did not practice walking and seated meditation, as well as practicing mindful meditation while standing still. During the day, he investigated and learned the Scriptures and Their underlying principles; at night, he calmed his discriminatory thinking and cooled down his active mind. Continuing on in this way for three years, he explored and thoroughly mastered the *Tripitaka*, cut off his craving for the three worlds, and attained the wise discernment which arises from the three forms of clarity.[10] People at that time, out of deep respect, gave him the name of the One of Venerable Ribs.

The One of Venerable Ribs left the womb after having first spent sixty years there. Surely he must have been doing his best even whilst in the womb. After he left the womb, it was almost eighty years before he sought to leave home life and explore the Way. This was a hundred and forty years after he was conceived! Truly, he was an extraordinary person, and even so, he was a decrepit old man who must have been more decrepit and more old than anyone else. He had already attained old age whilst still in the womb, and he was advanced in years since having left the womb. Even so, he paid no heed to the slanderous and snide remarks made by people of his time and single-mindedly kept to his vow, never turning away from it. Who could possibly think it would be an easy task to try to emulate his spiritual wisdom?

Do not regret your reaching old age. It is difficult to know what this thing called life really is. Is a person 'really living' or 'not really living'? Is a person 'old' or 'not old'? The four perspectives are completely different; all the various types of

---

10. The three forms of clarity are the ability to see one's own past lives and those of others, the ability to see the karmic consequences that will follow from one's own actions as well as those of others, and the ability to recognize the sufferings of oneself and others within their present life and to know how to convert the passions that give rise to those sufferings.

perspectives are different as well.[11] Just concentrate on your intention and make your utmost effort to pursue the Way. In your pursuit of the Way, train as if you were facing a life-and-death situation: it is not simply your pursuit of the Way within life-and-death. People today have become so foolish as to set aside their pursuit of the Way upon reaching the age of fifty or sixty, or upon reaching seventy or eighty. Although we are naturally aware of how long we have lived, this is simply the human mind energetically engaged in discriminating and has nothing to do with studying the Way. Do not concern yourself with being in the prime of life or having reached old age. Just be single-minded in exploring the Way thoroughly and diligently, for then you will stand shoulder-to-shoulder with the One of Venerable Ribs.

Do not always be lamenting the fact that you will end up as a pile of dirt in a graveyard. Do not spend your time worrying about it. If you do not single-mindedly devote yourself to reaching the Other Shore, who will rescue you? When people are aimlessly wandering about in the wilderness like skeletons without a Master, they need to cultivate right perception so that they may fashion an eye for themselves.[12]

The Sixth Chinese Ancestor was a woodcutter in the district of Hsinning. He could hardly have been called an intellectual. While just an infant, he lost his father, and he grew up under the care of his aged mother. He worked as a woodcutter in order to support her. Whilst standing at a crossroads one day, he overheard one line of a Scripture being recited, and immediately parted from his mother in order to seek the Great Dharma. He was a great vessel for the Truth, of a caliber rarely met in any generation. His pursuit of the Way was unique among human beings. To cut off one's

---

11.   'The four perspectives' refers to a Buddhist metaphor which describes the way that different beings interpret what they see. In the metaphor, water is described from the perspective of four different beings: humans see it as ordinary water, hungry ghosts as bloody pus, fish as a dwelling place, and celestial beings as liquid lapis lazuli.

12.   Right perception is described in Buddhism as seeing things with the eye of compassion and wise discernment.

arm is easy enough, but to sever himself from someone he loved must have been exceedingly difficult indeed.[13] He would not have abandoned his filial obligations lightly.

He joined in with Daiman Kōnin's assembly, where he pounded rice day and night, neither sleeping nor resting for eight months.[14] In the middle of one night, he received the direct Transmission of Bodhidharma's kesa* and alms bowl. Even after he had obtained the Dharma, he still carried his stone mortar around with him, and for eight years he continued his rice pounding. Even when he entered the world in order to help ferry people to the Other Shore by giving expression to the Dharma, he did not set aside his stone mortar. This is ceaseless practice that is rare in any generation.

Kōzei Baso did seated meditation for twenty years and received the Intimate Seal* from Nangaku. It has never been said that he set aside the practice of seated meditation after the Dharma was Transmitted to him and he began to help rescue others. When people first came to train under him, he always helped them to personally obtain the Mind seal. He was invariably the first to arrive for the monks' communal work periods.[15] He did not let up even after he became old. Those today who follow Rinzai are in Baso's lineage.

---

13. The reference to cutting off one's arm is to the Second Chinese Ancestor, Taiso Eka, who is said to have cut off his arm in order to find the Truth. This 'severing' may refer to giving up one's attachments rather than to a literal, physical act.

14. Though he was part of Kōnin's assembly, he lived there as a layperson and did not become a monk until some ten years later. Although 'pounding rice day and night' is often used in Zen texts solely as a metaphor for doing ceaseless practice, in this sentence it also alludes to the actual physical work that he did for the monastic community.

15. Communal work customarily included such things as sweeping the temple grounds and gathering firewood.

Our revered Ancestor Ungan and the monk Dōgo were both exploring the Matter under Yakusan. Having made a vow together, they did not put their sides to their mats for forty years, so committed were they to thorough and unadulterated practice. Later, when Ungan personally Transmitted the Dharma to Tōzan Ryōkai, Tōzan remarked, "Desiring to realize Wholeness, I have been doing my utmost for twenty years to put the Way into practice by doing seated meditation." That Way of his has now been Transmitted far and wide.

During the time while Ungo Dōyō was living in a hermitage on Three Peak Mountain, he was receiving nourishment from the Celestial Kitchen.[16] Once when Ungo was paying a visit to Tōzan, his spiritual doubt was settled through his realization of the Great Matter, after which he returned to his hermitage. When a celestial messenger came looking for Ungo to bring him nourishment once again, the celestial being could not see him, despite searching for three days. Ungo no longer needed to rely on the Celestial Kitchen, for he had made the Great Matter his sustenance. Try to emulate his determination to comprehend the Truth.

From the time when Hyakujō Ekai was serving as an attendant monk to Baso until that evening when he entered nirvana, there was not a single day when he did not endeavor to work for the benefit of the monastic assembly and for the benefit of other people. Meditation Master Hyakujō was already an old monk of long standing when, thank goodness, he said, "A day when I do not work is a day when I do not eat." He still endeavored to do communal work just the same as those in their prime. The community felt sorry for him, but, though they expressed their pity for him, the Master

---

16. It is said that before awakening to the Truth, a Buddhist trainee is served nourishment by celestial beings, but after the trainee has awakened to the Truth, those celestial beings can no longer serve the person food since the 'person' can no longer be seen.

would not quit. Finally, one day when he came to the communal work, the monks had hidden his tools and would not return them to him, so the Master did not take any food that day. His intention was to express his regret at not being able to participate in the monks' communal work. This story has become known as Hyakujō's "One day without work is one day without food." The traditions found in Rinzai's lineage— whose Transmission flows throughout Great Sung China today—as well as the traditions found in Buddhist monasteries far and wide, are, for the most part, based on the ceaseless practice of Hyakujō's profound principles.[17]

When the revered monk Kyōsei Dōfu was Abbot in his temple, the deities of the place were never able to see the Master's face because they had no reliable means by which to do so.[18]

In former times, Meditation Master Gichū of Mount Sanpei received nourishment from the Celestial Kitchen. After he encountered Daiten Hōtsū of Chōshū Province, the celestial beings sought Gichū out, but were unable to find him.

The later revered monk of Mount Daii, Chōkei Daian, would say of his sojourn with Isan on the same mountain, "I stayed with Isan for twenty years. I supped on Isan food. I urinated Isan urine. But I did not explore Isan's Way. I have merely been able to raise one unsexed water buffalo that, all day long, is completely out in the open."

---

17. The principles which Hyakujō put forth in his writings are still fundamental to Zen Buddhist monastic practice today.

18. It is said that when someone is truly doing ceaseless practice, the deities that inhabit the environs of a temple cannot see that person, because that person is not wearing the 'face' of a false self.

Keep in mind that he raised that one unsexed water buffalo by means of his twenty years of ceaseless practice with Isan, who had himself continually explored the Matter within Hyakujō's community. Without fuss, quietly emulate his actions over those twenty years, and do not at any time forget them. Even though there are many people who explored Isan's Way, there must have been only a few whose ceaseless practice was their 'not having explored Isan's Way'.

The revered monk Jōshū Shinsai of Kannon-in Monastery was in his sixty-first year before he gave rise to the intention to realize the Truth and therefore began to seek the Way. Carrying his bottle gourd filled with water and his monk's traveling staff, he set out in search of a Master. He traveled far and wide in all directions, constantly saying to himself, "If even a child of seven has spiritually surpassed me, I shall explore the Matter with him or her accordingly. If even an old man of a hundred has not yet spiritually reached where I am, I shall instruct him accordingly."

It was with this attitude of mind that he did his utmost for twenty years to study Nansen's Way. At the age of eighty, he was installed as Abbot of Kannon-in Monastery, east of Jōshū City, and for forty years he spiritually guided ordinary people as well as those in loftier positions. Since he never sent out letters soliciting donations, his Monks' Hall was not large, lacking both a hall for the temple officers in front and a washstand in back. One time, the leg on his meditation platform broke. He tied a piece of charred firewood to it with some rope and, for years, went on using it for his training and practice. The temple officers wished to replace the leg, but Jōshū would not permit it. We should learn from this venerable Old Buddha's customary ways of doing things.

Jōshū lived in Jōshū Prefecture from his eightieth year on, after receiving the Transmission of the Dharma. He had received the authentic Transmission of the True Teaching, and people called him the Venerable Old Buddha. Those who had not yet received the authentic Transmission of the True Teaching must surely have been less imposing than Master Jōshū, and those who had not yet reached the age of eighty must surely have been more robust than he was. So how are those of us who are in our prime, yet still spiritually unimpressive, to equal one who is so deeply revered?

Simply, by striving to do our utmost in ceaselessly practicing the Way. During those forty years, he did not accumulate worldly goods, and there was no rice or other grain in storage. Sometimes, chestnuts and acorns would be gathered and meted out for food; sometimes, one meal would be stretched out to cover a couple of days. These were truly the customary ways of a dragon elephant * in the past, ways of training that we should aspire to.

One day, Jōshū addressed his community, saying, "If you did not depart from the monastery even once in your lifetime and did not speak for five or ten years, no one should call you a mute.[19] And after that, how could even the Buddhas do anything for you?" This points to ceaseless practice.[20]

Keep in mind that even though your not talking for five or ten years might give you the look of being dumb, and even though you might not talk due to your efforts not to depart from the monastery, still, you would not be a mute. The way a Buddha speaks is no different. Those who cannot hear the voice with which a Buddha speaks will fail to understand that someone who is not mute has gone beyond talking. Consequently, the most wondrous practice within ceaseless practice is 'not departing from the monastery'. The phrase 'not departing from the monastery' completely encapsulates the expression 'letting go of things'. The most foolish of people do not recognize a non-mute person, and do not help others to know 'such a one' * as a non-mute person. Even though no one prevents them from doing so, they do not help others to know 'such a person'. Pitiful indeed are those who have not heard that to be a non-mute is to be someone who has realized the state of 'being just what one is', or who do not even recognize that there is such a state of 'being just what one is'. Never abandon the ceaseless practice of not departing from the monastery. Do not be blown east and west by the prevailing winds. Even if you do not pay attention to the spring breezes and the autumn moons for five or ten years, there will be the Way that is free from delusions concerning sounds and forms. How one arrives at that Way is beyond

---

19. In the Zen tradition, the term 'mute' is often used to describe trainees who are unable to give a response when a Master puts a spiritual question to them.

20. In other words, ceaseless practice is synonymous with not departing from one's spiritual seat and with not just talking about the practice but actually doing it.

our ability to know and understand. You should explore through your training just how precious each moment of your ceaseless practice is. Do not entertain doubts that the practice of not talking may be something vain and meaningless. Ceaseless practice is the one monastery that we enter, the one monastery that we emerge from, the one monastery that is the path left by flying birds, and the one monastery that is the whole universe.

Mount Daibai is located in Keigen Prefecture. Goshō-ji Monastery was established on this mountain, and Meditation Master Daibai Hōjō was its founder. The Master was a man from Jōyō in Hubei Province.

> While training in Baso's community, Hōjō once asked the
> Master, "Just what is Buddha?"
> Baso replied, "Your very mind is Buddha."

Hearing this phrase, Hōjō immediately experienced the great realization. As a consequence, he climbed to the summit of Mount Daibai to be apart from human society. Living alone in a hermit's thatched hut, he survived on pine nuts and wore clothing he made from lotus leaves. On this mountain was a small pond, in which lotuses were plentiful. For more than thirty years he pursued the Way by doing seated meditation. He neither met anyone nor heard about any human affairs whatsoever, and he forgot about the passing years, seeing only the mountains around him turning now green, now yellow. You can imagine how wretched the winds and frosts were.

In doing seated meditation, the Master would place an eight-inch high iron pagoda atop his head, as if he were wearing a jeweled crown. By endeavoring to keep this pagoda from dropping off, he kept from falling asleep. This pagoda is still in his monastery today, and it is listed in the inventory of the temple's storehouse. Until his death, this is how he tirelessly trained in the Way.

He had been passing the months and years in this manner when, one day, a monk from Enkan's community arrived. The monk had come to the mountain in search of a suitable traveling staff, but he had wandered off the mountain path and fortuitously came upon the Master's hermitage.

Unexpectedly, he encountered the Master, whereupon he asked him, "Venerable monk, how long have you been living on this mountain?"

The Master replied, "All I have seen is the mountains about me now dyed green, now dyed yellow."

This monk then asked him, "In what direction should I go to find the path out of the mountains?"

The Master said, "Go by following the stream."

The monk was struck by this response. So, when he returned, he told Enkan what had happened. Enkan said, "Some years ago when I was with Baso in Chiang-hsi Province, I once met a certain monk, but I don't know what happened to him later. I wonder whether he could be that monk."

Later, when Enkan sent the monk to invite the Master for a visit, the Master would not leave the mountain. Rather, he composed a poem in reply:

> *Broken down yet living still, a withered tree aslant amidst*
> *the chill forest,*
> *How many times have I met the spring, my heart*
> *unswerving?*
> *Woodcutters pass this monk by, without even a backward*
> *glance,*
> *So why does the carpenter eagerly desire to seek me out?*[21]

The upshot was he did not pay Enkan a visit. Afterwards, he decided to move deeper into the recesses of the mountain, whereupon he composed the following poem:

> *From this pond, the lotus leaves I have taken for wear have*
> *known no end,*

---

21. 'Woodcutters' is a common metaphor in Zen Buddhism for disciples who are still working on cutting the roots of their past karma. 'The carpenter' is an allusion to Enkan as a spiritual master artisan.

> *And from a few trees, the pine cones have supplied for my*
> *meals more than enough.*
> *Now people from the world have discovered my dwelling*
> *place,*
> *So I shall move my reed abode to enter a seclusion ever more*
> *deep.*

Finally, he moved his hermitage further into the mountains.

> One day, Baso had a monk go and expressly ask Hōjō, "Venerable monk, in former times when you went in deepest respect to train under Baso, what was the underlying principle you obtained from him that you then came to dwell on this mountain?"
>
> The Master answered, "Baso turned directly to me and said, 'Your very mind is Buddha,' and then I came to dwell upon this mountain."
>
> The monk then said, "These days his Buddha Dharma is different."
>
> The Master asked, "In what way is It different?"
>
> The monk replied, "Baso now says, 'What is not mind is not Buddha.'"
>
> The Master responded, "That old fellow! I swear there is no end to his bewildering people! Even if that 'What is not mind is not Buddha' of his is so, well, I'll stick with 'Your very mind is Buddha.'"
>
> When the monk reported to Baso what Hōjō had said, Baso replied, "The Plum has fully ripened."[22]

This story is known by all, commoners and gentry alike.

Tenryū was a leading disciple of Master Hōjō, and Gutei was the Master's Dharma grandson. The Korean monk Kachi received the Transmission of the Master's

---

22.   The name Daibai in Daibai Hōjō's name means the 'Great Plum Tree'.

Dharma and became the First Ancestor of his own country. All the Korean Masters today are Hōjō's distant descendants.

During his lifetime, a tiger and an elephant served him, and they did it without quarreling between themselves. After the Master's parinirvana, the tiger and the elephant gathered stones and mud, and built a stupa[*] for their Master. That stupa exists in Goshō-ji Temple even now. The Master's ceaseless practice has been extolled by good spiritual friends of the past and present alike. Those with limited wisdom do not recognize that they should praise his practice. To hold on tenaciously to the notion that Buddha Dharma can surely be found even amidst one's greed for fame and love of gain is a narrow, foolish view.

Meditation Master Goso Hōen once said:

> When my Master's Master first took up residence on Mount Yōgi, the rafters of the old buildings were in ruins and the damage from wind and rain was extensive. It was midwinter at the time. The temple halls throughout the monastery had long been damaged. The Monks' Hall was especially dilapidated. The snow kept drifting in, and it so filled the floors that there was nowhere for the monks to sit. Veteran monks, their hair white with age, were sweeping the snow off everything, including themselves, and shaggy eyebrowed monks of venerable years looked as though those brows were knitted with apprehension. The monks of the community were unable to do their seated meditation tranquilly.

> When one patch-robed monk asked in all sincerity whether repairs might be made, the old Master turned down the request, saying, "Our Buddha has said that this period of time corresponds to the degenerate eon, and that even high cliffs and deep valleys shift and change, never remaining constant. So, how can we possibly seek to sate ourselves by fulfilling our every wish? The saintly ones of olden times, for the most part, did their walking

meditation on bare ground beneath the trees. This was the ancient and exemplary way of practice, a profound custom that went far beyond simply the form of walking. You have all left home life behind in order to pursue the Way, but you still have not learned how to use your hands and feet harmoniously. A monk's life lasts barely some forty or fifty years. Who has time to waste in vain pursuits, such as making ostentatious buildings?" So, the upshot was that he did not go along with the request.

The next day, in giving Teaching in the Dharma Hall, Goso gave instruction to his assembly, saying:

> When Yōgi first came to reside here as Abbot, the roofs and walls of the buildings had fallen into such neglect that the floors were completely covered with drifts of snow. We hunched up our necks and grumbled in the gloom. But then, with a change of heart, we recalled the old ones who had resided under trees.

Ultimately he never gave his permission for repairs, yet, even so, many itinerant monks from the Four Oceans and Five Lakes, clothed in their cloud-like robes and their mist-like sleeves, later asked to hang up their traveling staff in his community.[23] We should delight in the fact that there have so many who were avid for the Way. We would do well to engrave these words of Goso on our hearts and to impress them on our bodies.

Our Venerable Master Goso Hōen once gave Teaching, saying, "Practice is not something that lies beyond thoughts and feelings, and thoughts and feelings are not things that lie beyond practice." Give great weight to these words. Ponder upon them day and night; put them into practice from dawn to dusk. Do not allow yourself to be vainly blown about in all directions by the gusting winds. How much less could those who have left home life behind to pursue the Way possibly live a quiet, secluded life amidst luxurious accommodations! In Japan today, even the 'palatial homes' of

---

23. 'The Five Lakes' is an allusion to China, whereas 'the Four Oceans' refers to the rest of the world.

royalty and their ministers are hardly splendorous, but are merely thatched cottages which are falling to pieces. If someone has obtained a luxurious estate, chances are it came from a wrong livelihood; it is rarely obtained from a pure one. A building that is already there is a different matter, but do not make plans for new constructions. Thatched hermitages and cottages were where the saintly ones of old dwelt; they are residences esteemed by the saintly ones of the past. Today's trainees should wish to be the same when exploring the Matter through their training, so do not make a mistake about this.

The Yellow Emperor and other Chinese emperors such as Yao and Shun were secular people, yet they lived in thatched houses and were an example for their nation. In a book by the Chinese writer Shih-tsu it says, "If you wish to see the practice of the Yellow Emperor, take a look at Hekung Palace. If you wish to see the practice of the emperors Yao and Shun, take a look at Tsung-ts'ao Palace. The Yellow Emperor's reception hall in Hekung Palace was roofed with thatch. Emperor Shun's reception hall in Tsung-ts'ao Palace was also roofed with thatch." Keep in mind that both Hekung and Tsung-ts'ao were thatched with straw.

Now, when we compare the Yellow Emperor, Emperor Yao, and Emperor Shun with ourselves, the difference is as great as that between heaven and earth. Even so, they used straw thatch for their reception halls. When even secular people reside in thatched dwellings, how can those who have left home life behind to be monks possibly aim at dwelling in lofty halls or elegant mansions? How unbecoming that would be! People of old would dwell under a tree or live in a forest, for these were the residences that both laymen and monks desired. The Yellow Emperor was a disciple of the Taoist Kuang-cheng of Mount Kung-tung. Kuang-cheng himself lived in a cave within Kung-tung Mountain. Today in Great Sung China, many heads of state and high-ranking ministers have carried on with this significant custom of emperors. As a consequence, even secular folk moiling about in their delusions do the same. How could those who have left home life behind to be monks possibly be inferior to secular folk who moil about in their delusions, or be as muddied by defiling passions as such folk? Among the Buddhas and Ancestors of the past, many received offerings of alms from celestial beings. Even so, once They had realized the Way, the eyes of the celestial beings could not see Them, and demons had no way to find Them.

We need to clarify this point. When celestial beings and demons keep to the daily conduct of Buddhas and Ancestors, they have a path by which they can approach the Buddhas and Ancestors. And, in that Buddhas and Ancestors far surpass celestial beings and demons, such celestial beings and demons have nothing by which to look up at Those who are so far off, so it is difficult for them to approach the vicinity of an Ancestor of the Buddha. As Nansen once said about himself, "The training and practice of this old monk has lacked vigor, so I have been spotted by demons." Remember, to be spotted by a demon who has done no training is due to your lacking vigor in your own training and practice.

Once, in the community of the Venerable Monk Wanshi Shōgaku of the Great White Mountain, one of the guardian deities said, "I heard that the Venerable Monk Wanshi has been residing on this mountain for over ten years, but whenever I have come to the Abbot's reception room to try to see him, I am never able to enter and still do not know what he looks like." Here, truly, we can see evidence of an exemplary person who has realized the Way. His temple on Mount Tendō was originally a small one.[24] While the Venerable Monk Wanshi was in residence there, he refurbished what had once been a Taoists' shrine, a female monks' temple, and a scholars' temple, and turned them into what is now Keitoku-ji Temple.

After the Master's death, the court secretary Wang Pai-hsiang compiled a record of the practices and deeds of the Master. A person once said to him, "You should have recorded the fact that the Master usurped a Taoist shrine, a female monks' temple, and a scholars' temple in establishing the present-day temple on Mount Tendō." Pai-hsiang replied, "No way! Such matters are not relevant to the merits of a monk." Many people at that time praised Pai-hsiang for this. Keep in mind that questions such as the

---

24. Mount Tendō is an alternative name for the Great White Mountain and for the temple which stands on it.

one asked above are a function of secular thinking and are not relevant to the merits of a monk.[25]

Speaking more generally, from the very first moment that we begin to walk on the Buddha's Way, we far surpass the three worlds of desire, form, and beyond form that ordinary people and those in lofty positions occupy. You should closely investigate the fact that Wanshi was not being manipulated by the three worlds, nor was he visible to the three worlds. You should do your utmost to thoroughly explore through your training the arising of body, speech, and mind, along with your inner experiences and the outer conditions that affect you. From the start, the meritorious activity of the Buddhas and Ancestors has great benefit in spiritually helping ordinary people as well as those in lofty positions. Even so, such people do not recognize that the ceaseless practice of Buddhas and Ancestors is helping to rescue them from their suffering. In ceaselessly practicing the Great Way of the Buddhas and Ancestors now, do not get into discussions about great hermits and small hermits.[26] Do not talk about someone's being sharp-witted or thick-headed. Simply discard fame and gain forever and do not get all tied up in worldly things. Do not let time slip away. Put out the fire

---

25.   When Wanshi arrived, his small temple was in great disrepair. He renovated it and appropriated the three abandoned buildings mentioned to form the core of his monastery, which, in time, came to house some twelve hundred monks. In Wanshi's day, making use of abandoned non-Zen temples was a widespread practice by Zen monks, due to the phenomenal expansion of the Zen tradition and the rapid decline in support for other Buddhist traditions as well as for Taoism. Since the buildings, in effect, no longer belonged to anyone or to any organization, the term 'usurped' is inappropriate, deliberately insulting, and inaccurate. Wanshi simply made good spiritual use of something that had been abandoned or discarded—a common practice in Buddhism which can be most widely seen in the monks' use of discarded cloth to make monastic robes.

26.   An allusion to a poem by the Chinese poet Haku Rakuten:

Great hermits dwell in courts and frequent market places;
Little hermits go off into the hills or hide behind some bamboo fence.

that is burning atop your head.[27] Do not wait for some great enlightenment experience, for the great enlightenment is synonymous with our everyday tea and meals. Do not aspire to 'non-enlightenment', for non-enlightenment is synonymous with the precious pearl concealed within the king's topknot.[28] Simply, should you be attached to home and homeland, separate yourself from 'my home and my homeland'. Should you have bonds of affection, separate yourself from 'my bonds of affection'. Should you have a good reputation, rid yourself of 'my reputation'. Should you have wealth, rid yourself of 'my wealth'. Should you own cultivated fields and gardens, rid yourself of 'my cultivated fields and gardens'. Should you have family, separate yourself from 'my family'. And you need to let go of 'my not having such things as fame and gain', as well. In ridding yourself completely of 'I have', the principle of also ridding yourself of 'I do not have' is clear. This is nothing other than the matter of ceaseless practice. Your letting go of fame and gain throughout your whole lifetime will be your ceaselessly putting into practice the One Matter, for it is this ceaseless practice that is as endless as the life of Buddha. Once you have established this ceaseless practice here and now, your ceaseless practice will be done by the ceaseless practice itself. And, you should love and respect your body and mind which are imbued with this ceaseless practice.

Meditation Master Daiji Kanchū once said, "Explaining what one yard is cannot compare with putting one foot into action, and explaining what one foot is cannot compare with putting one inch into action." This sounds like Kanchū was admonishing people of his time who were being negligent in their ceaseless practice and who had forgotten about mastering the Buddha's Way. But it does not mean that it is incorrect to explain what one yard is: it means that putting one foot into practice

---

27. A widely used Zen metaphor, alluding to an intense, single-minded effort to train, just as if your head were on fire and you were trying to put the fire out.

28. An allusion to a passage in the *Lotus Scripture*, in which the Buddha's Teaching of the Dharma is likened to a king giving someone a precious jewel which he has kept concealed in his topknot.

takes more skill than explaining what one yard is. Why should we be limited to measurements in yards and feet? There could also be discussions about the comparative merits of far-off Mount Sumeru and a poppy seed. Sumeru is completely whole and a poppy seed is completely whole. The important point in ceaseless practice is just like this. The present explanation is not the way Kanchū put it, and it <u>is</u> the way Kanchū put it.

Great Master Tōzan Gohon once said, "I put into words what I am unable to demonstrate by action, and I demonstrate by action what I am unable to put into words." This is the way a lofty Ancestor put it. His point is that his practice illumines the path that makes understandable what he has put in words, and his explanations have pathways that make understandable what he does as practice. Hence, what he preached in a day is what he practiced in a day. The point of this is that we practice that which is difficult to practice, and we explain that which is difficult to explain.

Ungo Dōyō, having penetrated through and through what Tōzan had expressed, said, "At the time for explanation, there is no path for practice: at the time for practice, there is no path for explanation." This way of putting it is not saying that there is no practice or explanation. His 'time for explanation' is synonymous with one's 'not leaving the monastery even once in a lifetime'. His 'time for practice' is synonymous with the hermit's washing his head and then coming before Seppō.[29] Do not disregard or treat lightly his expression, "At the time for explanation, there is no path for practice: at the time for practice, there is no path for explanation." This is something that Buddhas and Ancestors of the past have continually asserted. It was once expressed in verse as:

---

29. The allusions to not leaving the monastery and to the hermit's washing his head will be explored in detail by Dōgen later in Discourse 38: On Expressing What One Has Realized (*Dōtoku*).

Were you to live a hundred years
Yet fail to see what the Nature of all Buddhas is,
It would still not equal living even one day,
Having rightly grasped the Matter.

This is not something that one or two Buddhas have said: it is what all Buddhas are continually putting into words and putting into practice. Within the recurring cycles of birth and death over hundreds and thousands of myriad eons, one day in which there is ceaseless practice is a bright pearl within the topknot of the king: it is the Ancient Mirror within which we are born and die, and it is a day we should rejoice in. The strength of our ceaseless practice is a joy in itself. Those who have not yet attained the strength of ceaseless practice or received the Bones and Marrow of an Ancestor of the Buddha do not prize the Body and Mind of Buddhas and Ancestors or take delight in the True Face of Buddhas and Ancestors.

The true Face, Bones, and Marrow of Buddhas and Ancestors is not some thing that departs. It is a Tathagata's having come in this way and having gone in that way. It is beyond some thing that comes. Even so, we invariably receive our allotment of spiritual nourishment through our ceaseless practice of one day.

Thus, a single day must be of great importance. Were you to live in idleness for a hundred years, you would regret the days and months you had wasted, and you would be a shell of a person, one to be pitied. Even if you were to gorge yourself as a slave to sight and sound for a hundred years, yet within that time you performed ceaseless practice for just one single day, not only would you be putting your whole life of a hundred years into the practice, you would also be helping ferry other hundred-year-old beings to the Other Shore. Your life of this one day is the life you should cherish, the skeleton you should prize. Thus, if your life were to last but a single day, if on that day you grasped what the Nature of all the Buddhas is, then that life of one day would have surpassed many lifetimes spanning vast eons. So, if you have not yet grasped the Matter, do not squander one day idly. This one day of ceaseless practice is a precious jewel that you should prize. Do not compare it with the value of some foot-wide gem, and never exchange it, even for the Black Dragon's Jewel.[30] Sages of old prized it even more than their whole life.

Quietly think about it. You can ask for the Black Dragon's Jewel at any time, and can even get possession of a foot-wide gem along the way, but one day within a lifetime of a hundred years, once gone, cannot come again a second time. Is there any skillful means by which we can have returned to us even one day that has passed? That is something you do not find recorded in any book. Those who do not idly let time pass by wrap up their days and months in that skin bag[*] of theirs so that the time will not leak away. This is why the saints of old and the former sages prized their days and months; they prized time more than they prized their own eyes and prized it more than their native land. To idly let time pass by means to be polluted and corrupted by the transient world of fame and gain. To not idly let time pass by means to act for the sake of the Path whilst being on the Path.

One who has already completely grasped the Matter will not let a day idly go by, but will do the practice for the sake of the Way and will explain the Way for the sake of the Way. Because of this, we have come to know the standards set by the Buddhas and Ancestors from ancient times, who did not vainly squander the efforts of even one day. This is something you should constantly reflect on. You should consider it even as you sit by a window, looking out on some slowly blossoming spring day, and do not forget it even as you sit in a humble abode on some desolate rainy night. How does time rob us of our efforts? Not only does it rob us of one day, it also robs us of the merits of many eons. What animosity is there between time and us? Sad to say, it will be our own lack of practice that robs us so. This is due to our not being on friendly terms with ourselves, to our thinking ill of ourselves. Even Buddhas and Ancestors have not been without Their loved ones, but They have let them go. Even Buddhas and Ancestors have not been without Their various involvements, but They have let them go. Even though we prize our relationships, such connections between ourselves and others are not things that can be held onto, so if we do not let go of our loved ones, chances are that our loved ones will let go of us, both in word and in deed.

---

30. The Black Dragon's Jewel, which It holds under Its jaw, is a common Buddhist metaphor for the Buddha Dharma.

If you can have compassion for your loved ones, have compassion for them. To have compassion for our loved ones means letting go of them.

When the Venerable Monk Nangaku Ejō was training under Daikan Enō, he attended on Enō for fifteen autumns. As a consequence, it was possible for him to be given the Transmission of the Dharma and the Precepts personally, just as if water from one vessel were being poured into another vessel. We should most dearly cherish the everyday behavior of this former Ancestor. The winds and frosts that plagued him during those fifteen autumns must have been many indeed. Even so, he persisted in practicing the Way purely and simply, and he is a paragon for us trainees of the present day. In winter, he slept alone in an empty hall with no coal for his stove. In the cool of summer nights, he would sit alone by his moon-lit window having no candle. Even though he did not know everything and understood only half of what he knew, he had nothing further to learn about non-attachment. This was surely due to his ceaseless practice.

Speaking more generally, once we have discarded our greed for fame and our love of gain, it is simply a matter of striving to do the practice ceaselessly, day after day. Do not disregard this intention. Nangaku's saying, "When you explain what something is like, you have already missed the bull's-eye," reflects eight years of his ceaseless practice. It is this ceaseless practice that people of both past and present treat as rare and that both the clever and the inept earnestly desire.

While Great Master Kyōgen Chikan was cultivating his practice under Isan, he tried several times to give expression to the Way but was unable to do so. Deploring this, he burned his books and became the monk who served gruel and rice to his fellow monks, and so he passed his years, month after month. He later went to Mount Butō in search of old traces of National Teacher Echū. He built a thatched hermit's hut and, casting everything aside, he lived tranquilly and apart from human society.

One day, when he was sweeping off his walkway, he happened to hit a pebble, which struck a cane of bamboo. Upon hearing the sound it made, he suddenly realized the Way. He then took up residence as Abbot of Kyōgen-ji Temple, where it was his wont never to replace his one alms bowl and his one set of clothes. He dwelt amidst a landscape of strange rock formations and crystal springs, spending the rest of his life in secluded repose. Many traces of his practice still remain at his temple. It is said that it was his custom not to come down from the mountain.

Great Master Rinzai was a Dharma heir of Ōbaku. He was in Ōbaku's community for three years, during which time he devoted himself purely to pursuing the Way. Upon instruction from the Venerable Bokushū Chin,[31] he asked Ōbaku three times what the Great Intent of the Buddha Dharma is, whereupon he tasted the Master's staff again and again, for sixty blows. Still, his determination did not flag. When he went to Daigu, under whom he had his Great Realization, it was at the instruction of both venerable monks, Ōbaku and Bokushū. When it comes to the great heroic figures who have inherited the Dharma seat of the First Chinese Ancestor, Rinzai and Tokusan are usually spoken of. Even so, how could Tokusan possibly be considered the equal of Rinzai? Truly, someone like Rinzai is not to be corralled with the herd. Those who have been considered outstanding in recent times cannot even compare with those who were in the herd during Rinzai's time. It is said that his practices and deeds were pure and single-minded, and that his ceaseless practice was outstanding. Were we to try to imagine how many forms and how many ways his ceaseless practice had, none of us could come close to the mark.

While Rinzai was residing with Ōbaku, he and Ōbaku took to planting pine and cedar trees together. On one occasion, Ōbaku asked him, "What is the use of planting so many trees here, deep in the mountains?"

---

31. Chin was also a Dharma heir of Ōbaku, and Rinzai's senior.

Rinzai replied, "First, to make something with a tasteful appearance for the benefit of the monastery, and second, to make signposts for the benefit of others coming later." Thereupon, he took his hoe and struck the ground twice with it.

Ōbaku held up his traveling staff and said, "You are like this now, but you have indeed already tasted thirty blows from my staff."

Rinzai gave out with a ho-hum sigh.

Ōbaku said, "Our tradition will flourish in the world, with many coming to you."[32]

So on the basis of this, we should realize that even after he had realized the Way, he brought along a hoe in his own hands for planting such things as cedars and pines. It may have been because of this that Ōbaku said, "Our tradition will flourish in the world, with many coming to you." It must indeed be that the old traces of 'the trainee who planted pines' pointed directly to the one-to-one Transmission of Ōbaku and Rinzai.[33] Ōbaku, likewise, planted trees alongside Rinzai. In the past, Ōbaku displayed the ceaseless practice of leaving his assembly behind and going off to mix in with the laborers at the Daian Training Temple where he cleansed the halls. He cleansed the Buddha Hall, as well as the Dharma Hall. He did not expect his ceaseless practice to cleanse his heart and mind and he did not expect his ceaseless practice to cleanse his innate brightness. It was around this time that he met Prime Minister P'ei.[34]

Emperor Hsüan-tsung of the T'ang dynasty was the second son of Emperor Hsien-tsung. From the time he was small, he was quick-witted and astute. He always loved sitting in full lotus position and was constantly doing seated meditation in the

---

32. This quotation is from the *Sayings of Meditation Master Rinzai.*

33. 'The trainee who planted pines' is an epithet applied to the Fifth Chinese Ancestor, Daiman Kōnin.

34. The Prime Minister subsequently became a lay disciple of Ōbaku.

palace. Mu-tsung was Hsüan-tsung's elder brother. After Mu-tsung had become emperor, once government business had concluded, Hsüan-tsung would playfully climb up on the imperial Dragon Throne and pretend that he was saluting various ministers. When the prime minister saw this, he thought Hsüan-tsung had cerebral palsy, and accordingly, reported this to Mu-tsung. When Mu-tsung saw his brother, he patted Hsüan-tsung on the head and said, "My little brother is the bright one in our family." At the time, Hsüan-tsung had just turned thirteen.

In the fourth year of the Tseng-ch'ing era (824 C.E.), Mu-tsung passed away peacefully. He was succeeded by his three sons. The first became Emperor Ching-tsung, the second became Emperor Wen-tsung, and the third became Emperor Wu-tsung. Ching-tsung succeeded his father to the throne and passed away three years later. Wen-tsung succeeded him to the throne for just one year before court ministers schemed to ease him out. When Wu-tsung ascended the throne, Hsüan-tsung, who had not yet ascended the throne, was residing in his nephew's kingdom. Wu-tsung made a habit of referring to Hsüan-tsung as 'my fool of an uncle'. Wu-tsung was emperor during the Hui-ch'ang era (841–846) and was the person who banned the Buddha Dharma. One day, Wu-tsung summoned Hsüan-tsung and ordered that he immediately be put to death for having climbed up onto the throne of Wu-tsung's father in the past. His corpse was placed in a flower garden behind the palace and waste matter was poured over it, whereupon he came back to life.

He then left his father's land and secretly entered the community of Meditation Master Kyōgen, where he shaved his head and became a novice. However, he did not take the full Precepts.[35] Making the rounds of temples along with Meditation Master Shikan, he arrived at Mount Rozan, whereupon Shikan composed a couplet on the topic of the local falls:

> *Boring through cliffs, bursting through rock, never*
> *declining from its toil,*

---

35. That is, when ordained as a novice he would have taken the Ten Great Precepts, but he had not yet gone so far in monastic training as to take the two hundred and fifty Vinaya Precepts or the Bodhisattva Precepts.

> *By distant lands are seen the heights from which it falls.*

By this couplet, he was attempting to lure the novice into revealing just what kind of person he was spiritually. The novice continued this verse with the following:

> *What can stem this valley torrent*
> *From surging back to the Ocean Great?*

Upon hearing this couplet, Shikan knew that the novice was no ordinary person.[36]

Sometime later, Hsüan-tsung entered the community of Enkan Saian,[37] which was in the region of Hangchow, and was assigned to serve as the Abbot's Chief Clerical Officer. At the time, Meditation Master Ōbaku was serving as Enkan's Chief Priest. And, as a consequence, Hsüan-tsung sat on the platform next to Ōbaku.

One day when Ōbaku had entered the Buddha Hall and was doing prostrations to the Buddha, Hsüan-tsung entered and asked him, "Since we are not to seek for anything based on an attachment to Buddha, or an attachment to the Dharma, or an attachment to the Sangha, what, pray, do you hope to accomplish, Venerable Monk, by doing prostrations?"

Having been asked in this way, Ōbaku turned towards Hsüan-tsung, slapped him, and said, "I am not seeking anything due to an attachment to the Buddha, nor am I seeking anything due to an attachment to the Dharma, nor am I seeking anything due to an attachment to the Sangha. I am simply doing my prostrations just as

---

36.　It was a common practice in China for a traveler, whether alone or with a companion, to compose a poem inspired by an encounter with a particularly beautiful scene. If one were accompanied, the companion was expected to supply a couplet to complete the traveler's couplet. This custom was sometimes used by Zen Masters to test the spiritual attainments of a companion, someone who was usually a monk, but one who had not yet been declared a Master.

37.　In some versions of the text, Dōgen comments that Enkan was later named as National Teacher by Hsüan-tsung when the latter become Emperor for a short while.

I usually do them." When he had finished speaking in this manner, with one hand he gave Hsüan-tsung another slap.

The Clerical Officer said, "You play rough!"

Ōbaku responded, "Right here is where the What resides! So why speak of rough or genteel?" Again, he gave Hsüan-tsung a slap with his hand, whereupon Hsüan-tsung silently took his leave.

After the death of Emperor Wu-tsung, Hsüan-tsung returned to lay life and ascended the throne. He abolished Wu-tsung's ban on the Buddha Dharma, and forthwith reinstated It. From the time of his ascending to the throne and throughout his reign, Hsüan-tsung was ever fond of doing seated meditation. Before he ascended to the throne, he had left the country of his father, the king, and was traveling the countryside, following the valley streams with Shikan, doing his utmost to practice the Way purely and simply. It is said that after he ascended to the throne, he did seated meditation day and night. Given that his father the king was already deceased, his elder brother the emperor had also passed away, and he himself been put to death by his own nephew, he truly resembled a destitute child worthy of our pity. Nevertheless, he did his utmost to pursue the Way with unswerving determination. His is an excellent example, wondrous and rare in the world. His ceaseless practice must have been open-hearted and spontaneous.

After the venerable monk Seppō Gison had given rise to the intention to realize the Truth, he never neglected his seated meditation, day or night, regardless of where he was. And he did so even though the paths between the monasteries where he would hang up his traveling staff and the places that sheltered him upon his journey were far apart. From the time when he clearly manifested his True Nature by his founding his monastery on Mount Seppō, he did not let up on his practice, and he died whilst doing seated meditation. In earlier times, in order to put his spiritual questions to a Master, he climbed Tōzan's mountain nine times and visited Tōsu Daidō three times, which was his doing his utmost to pursue the Way. This is something wondrous and rare in the world. In promoting the integrity and rigor of ceaseless practice, many people today speak of Seppō's lofty practice. Seppō's attachments were on a par with those of other people, but his astuteness was not something that others could match. Ceaseless practice is like that. People who follow the Way today should learn from Seppō's ceaseless practice of spiritually washing himself clean. When we quietly look back on Seppō's physical exertion in exploring the Matter with Masters in all directions, truly, this must have been due to the merit that he inherited from some saintly bones in a previous life.

When people today wish to enter the assembly of a Meditation Master who has realized the Way and ask their spiritual question in order to explore the Truth with such a one, it is extremely difficult for them to find a chance to do so. They are confronted not with just some twenty or thirty skin bags,[*] but with face after face of hundreds of thousands of people, all of whom are seeking the way back to their True Nature. The day on which a Master offers them a helping hand soon darkens into night, and the night that they spend pounding rice in their mortar soon brightens into another day. Sometimes, when the Master gives an informal talk, they act as though they lacked eyes and ears, and so they gain nothing from what they see and hear. When they are finally in possession of their eyes and ears, the Master has already finished what he has to say. While kind, elderly monks of great virtue are clapping their hands and loudly guffawing in their delight in the Dharma, it seems as though newly ordained novices rarely have a chance to even come in contact with their bowing mats. There are those who enter the Master's private chambers and those who do not, and there are those who hear the Master's promise of realizing enlightenment and those who do not. The days and nights pass even more swiftly than an arrow, and this dewdrop of a life is even more fragile than our body. There is the grief of having a Master yet being unable to explore the Matter through training with him, and there is the grief of wanting to explore the Matter yet being unable to find a Master. I have personally witnessed such situations as these.

Although good spiritual friends may know a person well, the opportunities for contacting them when they themselves are diligently cultivating the Way are rare. It is likely that when Seppō, long ago, climbed up Mount Tōzan and climbed up Mount Tōsu, he too must surely have endured just such hardships. We should recognize the integrity of his ceaseless practice, which serves as an excellent model, for to fail to explore the Matter through your training with a Master is to be regretted indeed.

It was at the behest of the Venerable Hannyatara that the First Ancestor of China came from the West to the Eastern lands. During the frosts and springs of his three years in sailing the seas, how could the winds and snows have been the only miseries? How the clouds and mists must have billowed up over the roiling waves! He was attempting to go to an unknown land. To do something like this would never have occurred to ordinary people who hold dearly to life and limb. This must have been due to his ceaseless practice that sprang from his great desire to earnestly Transmit the Dharma and to instruct those who are deluded by their passions. This was so because it was he himself who Transmitted the Dharma, and it was so because it is the whole universe that Transmits the Dharma, and it was so because the whole universe in all ten directions is the words and ways of Truth, and it was so because the whole universe in all ten directions is Bodhidharma himself, and it was so because the whole universe in all ten directions is the whole universe in all ten directions. What karmic conditions in any life are not like Shakyamuni's royal palace, and what royal palace may not serve as a spiritual training ground? This is why he came from the West as he did. Because it was he himself who instructed those who are deluded by their passions, he had no fears or doubts, nor did he act from timidity or awe. Because it was the whole universe that instructed those who are deluded by their passions, he had no fears or doubts, nor did he act from timidity or awe. Leaving behind his father's kingdom forever, he fitted out a large ship, crossed the southern seas, and arrived at Canton Province. Undoubtedly the crew was a large one and there were many monks to serve his needs, but chroniclers have failed to record this. Upon his reaching the shore, no one there knew him. It was the twenty-first day of the sixth lunar month in the eighth year of the Chinese P'u-t'ung era during the Liang dynasty (August 3, 527). The governor of Canton Province, a man named Hsiao-ang, made a show of extending to him all the courtesies of a host, giving him an audience and plying him with entertainments. Hsiao-ang then wrote an account to inform Emperor Wu about him, for Hsiao-ang was punctilious in his duties. When Emperor Wu saw the report, he was delighted and sent a messenger to invite Bodhidharma to pay him a visit. That was on the first day of the tenth lunar month of that year (November 9, 527).

> When the First Ancestor arrived at the city of Chinling, he had an audience with Emperor Wu of Liang, whereupon the emperor said to him, "Since the time when I ascended to the throne, I have so excelled in building temples, in copying the Scriptures, and in permitting both men and women to become monks that my deeds must be quite beyond anyone's ability to keep a record of. So what merit have I accrued?"
>
> The Master replied, "There is no merit in any of these."
>
> Dumbfounded, the emperor asked, "Why, pray, are they lacking in merit?"
>
> The Master replied, "Such deeds are merely the results achieved by ordinary people and those in lofty positions who follow the Lesser Course.* Such seeking after merit defiles one's deeds. It is like a shadow following a form: even though it exists, it is not the real thing."
>
> The emperor then asked, "What, pray, is true merit?"
>
> The Master answered, "One's immaculately wise discernment being wondrous and fully realized, and one's body being naturally unbounded and tranquil. Merit like this is not sought by the worldly-minded."
>
> The emperor then asked, "What is the paramount Truth of the Holy Teachings?"
>
> The Master replied, "Since the Truth is devoid of any limits, It is beyond holiness."
>
> The emperor then demanded, "And who, pray, is this one who is confronting my royal presence?"

The Master replied, "I do not personally know that One."[38]

The emperor had failed to awaken to what Bodhidharma was pointing to, and the Master realized that the occasion was not opportune. So, on the nineteenth day of the tenth lunar month (November 27), he snuck away to north of the Yangtze River and arrived at Loyang on the twenty-third day of the eleventh month of that year (December 31). He lodged temporarily at Shōrin-ji Temple on Mount Sūzan, where he sat all day long, silently facing a wall in meditation. The ruler of the Wei dynasty was spiritually confused and did not recognize who Bodhidharma was, and he did not even recognize that this failure was a reason for feeling shame.

Bodhidharma was of the warrior caste of Southern India. He had lived in the royal palace of a large kingdom, so he was long accustomed to the ways of a royal palace in a large kingdom. In the manners and customs of small nations, there were habits and views that would prove shameful for an imperial ruler of a large nation, but the First Ancestor did not have a heart that was disturbed by such matters. He did not reject the country, nor did he reject its people. At that time, he did not respond to the slanders of Bodhiruchi or despise him for making them, nor did he find the evil-mindedness of the Vinaya Master Kōtō worth resenting or even paying heed to.[39] Even though Bodhidharma's spiritual merits were great, the people of China looked upon him as if he were a conventional teacher of the *Tripitaka* and its commentaries, for they were befuddled due to their being followers of the Lesser Course. And there were some who thought that Bodhidharma was expounding a course of Dharma which they named 'the Zen Sect', and they believed that what was being taught by others—such as non-Buddhist scholars, for instance—and the True Teaching of the First Ancestor must surely be the same. These were the views of petty creatures who were helping to defile the Buddha Dharma.

---

38. That is, my True Nature is beyond anything my intellect can directly know.

39. During that time, there were two Indian scholars named Bodhiruchi: one was an eminent translator of Scriptures and the other was a scholar who was envious of Bodhidharma. It is the latter Bodhiruchi who is referred to here. The Chinese Vinaya Master Kōtō was a translator and writer of Scriptural commentaries. Both tried to discredit Bodhidharma's focus on meditation practice, and it is said that both attempted to poison him.

The First Chinese Ancestor was the twenty-eighth in the line of Shakyamuni Buddha's direct heirs. He left the large realm of his father the king in order to spiritually help sentient beings in the East. Who could stand head-and-shoulders with him? If the Ancestral Master had not come from the West, how could sentient beings in the East have possibly learned of the Buddha's True Teaching? They would only have distressed themselves—and to no avail—with 'the grit and stones' from which we fashion the names and forms we give things.[40] Even those today in the hinterlands or in some even more distant realm, like ours, where people clothe themselves in fur and adorn their heads with horns, have been able to hear the True Teaching to Its utmost. Today, even peasants and farmers, old country folk and village children learn of It, and all due to having been spiritually rescued through the Ancestral Master's ceaseless practice in crossing the seas. The cultures of India and China differ greatly as to what they are superior or inferior in, and there are vast differences as to what their local customs consider to be morally upright or depraved. China was not a place to which a great saintly person who had been Transmitted and who was keeping to the Teaching and the Scriptures would normally go, unless he was someone of great compassion and great enduring strength. There were no Meditation Halls in which he could reside, and those who recognized 'such a person' were few. So he hung up his traveling staff at Mount Sūzan for a stay of nine years. People called him 'the Brahman who looks at a wall'.[41] Chroniclers have included him among the ranks of those learning how to meditate, but this is not the way it was. He and he alone was the Ancestral Master who possessed the Treasure House of the Eye of the True Teaching which had been Transmitted to him through Buddha after Buddha and heir after heir.

---

40. The 'grit and stones' is another way of saying the 'tiles and stones' with which our mind builds its discriminative 'walls and fences'.

41. Dōgen makes a distinction between what people literally saw when they looked at Bodhidharma sitting in front of a wall and what Dōgen earlier described as Bodhidharma's 'facing a wall as he sat silently in meditation', which carries the figurative connotation of facing the walls of his own mind.

The following quotation is from the *Forest Records*, compiled by Shih-men:

Bodhidharma first went from the kingdom of Liang to the kingdom of Wei. He traveled to the foot of Mount Sūzan and rested his traveling staff at Shōrin-ji Temple. He simply sat in stillness, facing a wall: he was not engaged in learning how to meditate. For a long time no one could figure out why he was doing that and, consequently, interpreted it as his learning how to meditate.

Now, meditation in its narrow sense is simply one among various practices, so how could it suffice to say that this was all there was to the Saintly One? Yet, people of his time did just that. Those engaged in making chronicles followed suit and reported him as being among the ranks of those learning how to meditate and grouped him with people who are as dead trees or cold ashes.[42] Even so, the Saintly One's practice did not simply stop at doing meditation; he also did not act contrary to meditation. And even with the yin and yang described in the *Book of Changes*, he did not act contrary to yin and yang.

When Emperor Wu of Liang first met Bodhidharma, he asked him, "What is the paramount Truth of the Holy Teachings?"

The Master replied, "Since the Truth is devoid of any limits, It is beyond holiness."

The emperor went on to ask, "And who, pray, is this one who is confronting our royal presence?"

And the Master replied, "I do not personally know that One."

---

42. 'Dead trees and cold ashes' is a common Zen Buddhist figure of speech for someone who has dropped off self. In the present context, it implies that Bodhidharma had gone just so far in his practice, but no further.

If Bodhidharma had not been fluent in the local language,
how could the discussion have gone like this at that time?[43]

It is clear from this that Bodhidharma went from the empire of Liang to that of Wei, that he traversed to Mount Sūzan, and that he hung up his traveling staff at Shōrin-ji. Even though he simply sat in stillness, facing a wall, it was not in order to 'learn how to meditate'. And even though he had not brought with him a single copy of a Scripture, he was the authentic Successor who came to Transmit the True Teaching. Be that as it may, chroniclers are not clear about the matter and, sad to say, list him among those learning how to meditate, which is the height of folly.

Thus it was that, while he was doing his walking meditation, there was a dog who would yap at the Great One.[44] Alas, that too was the height of folly. How could anyone with a heart possibly take lightly their indebtedness to the Master for his compassion? How could anyone with a heart possibly fail to repay this indebtedness? There are many people who do not forget their indebtedness to the world in which they live and who treat it responsibly: we call them human beings. The great indebtedness that we owe to our Ancestral Master surely surpasses that which we owe to our parents, so do not compare the beneficent love of the Ancestral Master with that of a parent for a child.

Should people become concerned about the humbleness of their status, they may feel fear over not having visited China, not having been born in China, not knowing any saintly person, never having met a sage, and not having anyone around them who has ever risen to a lofty position. Their human mind is wholly befuddled

---

43.   Shih-men's final remark may be in reference to an oft-held view that Bodhidharma sat at Shōrin-ji Temple, silently staring at a wall, because he could not speak Chinese. Bodhidharma's final remark, in particular, shows that he clearly knew the difference between the words *pu chih* (Modern Chinese: *pu chih-tao*) "I do not know" and *pu shih* (Modern Chinese: *pu jen-shih*) "I do not know him." This is analogous to the differences between the German '*Ich weiss nicht*' and '*Ich kenne ihn nicht*', or between the French '*Je ne sais pas*' and '*Je ne le connais pas*'.

44.   The larger context implies that 'dog' here refers not to an animal but to a person who is constantly breaking Precepts.

due to such misgivings. Since the dawn of history, there has been no one in our country who has changed his worldly habits, nor do we hear of a time when our country was cleansed of them. This is due to our not knowing what 'clean' means or what 'muddied' means. We are like this due to our being in the dark about what the causes and effects of the two princely powers and the three universal powers are, to say nothing of our ignorance of the waxing and waning of the five elements of wind, fire, earth, metal, and water.[45] This folly of ours is due to our being in the dark about the sounds we hear and the forms that are right before our eyes. And this darkness is due to our ignorance of the Scriptures and our lack of a teacher of Scriptures. Our lacking such a teacher means that we do not know how many dozens of Scriptural texts there are, or how many hundreds of poems or thousands of sayings there are in these texts, or, if we read just the commentaries on some text, how many thousands of poems or tens of thousands of sayings they may contain. People who know the ancient Scriptures and have read the ancient texts have been inclined to venerate the Ancient Ones. If we have a heart that venerates the Ancient Ones, then the ancient Scriptures will manifest before <u>our</u> very eyes.

Both the founder of the Han dynasty and the founder of the Wei dynasty were emperors who clearly understood the poems that astrological events expressed and who could read the lay of the land. When people clearly understand classic texts such as these, then they have a bit of understanding of the three powers: heavenly, earthly, and human. Folks of our country, never having been ruled by saintly lords like these, do not know how to serve a lord or even how to serve one's parents. As a result, they are pitiful as subjects of a lord, and pitiful as members of their family clan. Whether they are ministers or children, they vainly pass by jewels a foot-wide in span and squander moments of time to no purpose. No one born into family clans like these has yet had an important national office conferred upon him. They even prize insignificant government positions. This is how it is in confused times like ours; in saner times, behavior like this was rare indeed. While we are cherishing lowly lives like these in a

---

45. The two princely powers are the authority of a ruler to bestow rewards and to mete out punishments. The three universal powers are associated with the heavens, the earth, and human beings.

remote land such as this one, we may chance to hear the True Teaching of the Tathagata; how then could we possibly have the heart to cling to these lowly lives? Were we to persist in clinging to them, for what purpose, pray, would we attempt to drop them off at a later date? Even if you were someone weighty and wise, you should not begrudge your life for the sake of the Dharma, so how much less should you begrudge a life that is mean and lowly! Even though it may be mean and lowly, if you unbegrudgingly abandon your life for the sake of the Way and the Dharma, you will be more hallowed than those in the highest heaven, more exalted than even a universal monarch. In sum, you will be more exalted than any celestial being, earthly deity, or sentient being within the worlds of desire, form, or beyond form.

Our First Chinese Ancestor Bodhidharma, on the other hand, was the third son of the king of Kōshi in Southern India. Thus, He was already an imperial prince in the royal bloodline of India. In China and its bordering nations, which should have shown respect for his nobility and dignity, people did not yet know the forms of etiquette by which they should attend on him. There was no incense or flowers. They were remiss in supplying him with a cushion to sit on and the temple accommodations were wretched. How much worse it would have been in our country, a remote island with enormous crags! How could we possibly know the customs by which one pays respect to the ruler of a large country? Even if we tried to imitate them, they would be too intricate for us to comprehend, since those customs might well be different for noblemen and for imperial personages, and expressions of respect for them might have varying degrees of formality, but we would not know how to distinguish among them. When we do not know the value of a person, we do not support and take responsibility for that being, and when we do not support and take responsibility for a person, we need foremost to clarify the value of that being.

Our First Chinese Ancestor Bodhidharma was the twenty-eighth successor to the Dharma of Shakyamuni. Once he had entered the Way, he became more and more impressive. The reason that such a great and revered saint did not spare his life in following his Master's instructions was so that he might Transmit the Dharma and rescue living beings. In China, before the First Ancestor came from the West, no one had ever encountered a disciple of the Buddha who had received the one-to-one Transmission from Successor to Successor, no Ancestor had given the Face-to-Face

Transmission from Successor to Successor, and no one had ever encountered a Buddha. And even after that time, apart from the distant descendants of the First Chinese Ancestor, no one could be found who had ever come from the West. The flowering of an udumbara blossom once every three thousand years is easy to predict: one need only count the months and years left before it blooms, but the First Ancestor's coming from the West will not happen a second time. At the same time, that bunch who mistakenly call themselves distant descendants of the Ancestral Master are besotted, like that great fool in the Kingdom of Ch'u who was unable to tell the difference between a jewel and a stone.[46] And, due to their dearth of knowledge and shallow understanding, they have fancied that even pedantic teachers of Scriptures and cerebral scholars could stand shoulder-to-shoulder with the Master. Those who failed to plant the genuine seeds of spiritual wisdom in past lives do not become descendants in the Way of the Ancestors, for they have idly wandered off onto the false path of names and forms, and are to be pitied.

There were people who were still going to India after the P'u-t'ung era of the Liang dynasty, and for what? This was foolishness in the extreme. Depending on how their bad karma led them, they wandered about in foreign countries. Step by step, they proceeded down false paths that were an insult to the Dharma; step by step, they were running away from their Father's True Home. And what, pray, was gained by their going off to India? Nothing but suffering the hardships from crossing great mountains and obstructing waters. Without examining the principle that India had already come to the East, they did not clearly see what the eastern advance of the Buddha Dharma was, so that they futilely wandered about, lost in the labyrinths of India. Although they had a reputation for seeking the Buddha Dharma, they lacked an earnest desire for the Way-seeking Mind, so that they did not meet any genuine Masters in India, and vainly encountered only pedantic teachers of Scriptures and cerebral scholars. Even though genuine Masters were still present in India, these travelers lacked the true spirit that seeks the True Teaching, and, as a result, the True Teaching did not come within their

---

46. 'The great fool' is a reference to the king of the ancient Chinese kingdom of Ch'u who, when presented with a large uncut jewel, rejected it because he thought it was just a big stone.

grasp. Some claimed that they had met a genuine Master upon their arrival in India, but we have yet to hear who those Masters were. Had they met genuine Masters, they would naturally have named names, but there have been no such names mentioned because there were no such encounters.

Further, after our Ancestral Master came from the West, there were many monks in China who relied on a mundane understanding of the Scriptures and commentaries, and thus failed to encounter the True Teaching. Even though they may have read the Scriptures and commentaries, they were still in the dark as to Their meaning and purpose. These blind deeds were due not only to the force of their karma from the present but also to the force of bad karma from their past lives. During this lifetime of theirs, they have not heard what the Tathagata's keys to the Truth are, nor have they encountered the Tathagata's True Teaching, nor have they been illumined by the Tathagata's face-to-face Transmission, nor do they employ the Tathagata's Buddha Mind, nor have they heard of the tradition of the Buddhas. What a sad life theirs must be! In the Sui, T'ang, and Sung dynasties in China, people like that were plentiful. To put it simply, only people who have planted the seed of wisdom in past lives have become the distant descendants of the Ancestral Master. Some have entered via the gate of training without expectations, and others by letting go of their preoccupation with counting grains of sand. All of them are bright-minded trainees, trainees most capable of understanding, and genuine seeds of a 'real person'. For ever so long, befuddled and ignorant folks have merely taken up lodging in the thatched hut of the Scriptures and commentaries. At the same time, the Master did not quit in the face of dangerous frontiers, nor did he avoid them. If we today who still revere the profound principle of our First Ancestor's coming from the West should, nevertheless, be sparing of these stinking skin bags we call ourselves, what, ultimately, would be the purpose of that?

Zen Master Kyōgen once said in verse:

> *A hundred plans, a thousand schemes*
> *All made just for this self of ours alone,*
> *As though this body could yet evade*
> *Its future in some dusty grave.*
>
> *Say not that white-haired corpses mute*
> *Take all their secrets to their tombs.*
> *For they are the ones who fully know*
> *What death's domain is all about.*

Accordingly, even though we make a hundred plans and a thousand schemes to hold onto our self, as he said, yet ultimately we are reduced to dust within some burial mound. How much worse to have countless bodies and minds uselessly endure untold thousands of hardships and myriad miseries whilst galloping off east and west in the service of the ruler or citizenry of some small nation! Following custom, some of our people hold their own existence lightly, being unable to forego committing ritual suicide upon the death of their lord. The journey ahead for those who are driven by such a sense of obligation will be filled with obscuring mists and clouds.

Since ancient times, there have been many who have thrown away life and limb as ordinary citizens in the employ of some minor official. These were human bodies that should have been treasured because they could have been vessels for the Way. Now that you have encountered the True Teaching, you should explore the True Teaching through your training, even though you forsake lives as numerous as the hundreds of thousands of grains of sand in the Ganges. For which is it worthwhile to forsake life and limb: for some small-minded person or for the broad, vast, deep, and far-reaching Buddha Dharma? Neither the nimble nor the maladroit should be concerned with whether they are going forward or backward. Calmly reflect upon the fact that before the True Teaching had spread throughout the world, people could not encounter It, even if they had been willing to give up their own life for the sake of the

True Teaching. They might well envy those of us today who have encountered the True Teaching. We should be ashamed to encounter the True Teaching and yet fail to give up life and limb for It. If we should be ashamed of anything, we should be ashamed of this failing.

So, the only way to repay our great indebtedness to the Ancestral Master is by our ceaseless practice all day long. Pay no heed to your own existence. Do not cling to love and affection, which is more foolish than the behavior of birds and beasts. Even if you are attached to feelings of love, they will not remain with you over the long years. Do not remain dependent on your family's standing within a clan, which is like so much rubbish. Should you remain like this, ultimately you will not have a tranquil and peaceful existence. The Buddhas and Ancestors of the past, being wise, all tossed aside the seven worldly treasures* and the thousand things they spawn, and They quickly abandoned Their jeweled palaces and scarlet-lacquered mansions as well. They viewed such things as if they were sweat and spittle; They looked upon them as though excrement and dirt. This is the model for recognizing and repaying one's indebtedness by which all the Buddhas and Ancestors have habitually repaid the Buddhas and Ancestors of the past. Even the sick sparrow did not lose sight of his indebtedness and was able to repay it by means of the three spheres of public office.[47] Even the trapped turtle, not losing sight of his indebtedness, was able to repay it by means of Yōfu's seal.[48] What a pity it would be for someone to be even more foolish and dull-witted than beasts while having the face of a human being.

---

47. A reference to a classic Chinese story concerning a boy who helped a sick sparrow recover and to whom the sparrow gave four silver rings as recompense, which ultimately led to the boy's being appointed to three high government positions.

48. A reference to a classic Chinese story in which a man rescued a trapped turtle. As the turtle swam off, it looked back over its shoulder to its benefactor, as if to acknowledge its indebtedness. Later, the man rose to a high official position, and, when the seal of his office was cast, it miraculously appeared in the form of a turtle looking over its back. No matter how many times the seal was recast to remove the form, it would nevertheless reappear on the seal. Finally, the man realized that somehow the turtle had played a part in his having received his appointment, so he kept the strange seal out of gratitude.

In that we have encountered Buddha and heard the Dharma today, we are indebted for the loving-kindness evinced by the ceaseless practice of each and every Buddha and Ancestor. Had the Buddhas and Ancestors not directly Transmitted the Dharma to us, how could It possibly have reached us in the present? We should repay our indebtedness for even a single line of verse, and we should repay our indebtedness for even a single Teaching. How much more should we repay our immeasurable indebtedness for the unsurpassed great Dharma of the Treasure House of the Eye of the True Teaching! All day long, we should desire to give up our own lives, which have been as innumerable as the sands of the Ganges. In generation after generation, we should bow in deepest respect and make alms offerings to the bodies that we have abandoned for the sake of the Dharma. Together with all the celestial beings, dragons, and divine spirits, we should venerate and esteem these bodies, for they are something to protect and praise, because the principle of gratitude underlying this veneration is indispensable.

The practice of the Brahmans who buy and sell skulls has long been reported in India. They have deeply revered the numerous, meritorious virtues of the skulls and bones of those who have hearkened to the Dharma. Now, if we do not give up our own lives for the sake of the Way, we will not attain the meritorious virtue of having heard the Teaching. If we hearken to the Dharma without giving a thought for life and limb, that hearing of the Dharma will fully ripen, and this skull of ours will be revered. The skull that we have not yet given up for the sake of the Way will one day be tossed in some vacant field and left to bleach in the sun. Who then will bow out of respect for it? Who would buy or sell it as a relic? We surely would look back upon our attitude and spirit of today with regret.

There was once a demon who angrily reduced his former bones to dust, and there was a celestial being who bowed in respect to his former bones.[49] When we think

---

49. The demon was angry with his former body because, due to the karmic consequences of that being's breaking the Precepts, he was born into the suffering of the hells. On the other

ahead to a time when, no matter what, we will be transformed into dust, those of us who had no attachments to craving in our present life will feel sympathy for others in the future. And this feeling of sympathy that is aroused may well be akin to the tears of an onlooker. Fortunately, by using our present skull—which will ultimately turn to dust and which people may well look upon with disgust—we can ceaselessly practice the True Teaching of the Buddha. For this reason, do not fear suffering from the cold, for suffering from the cold has yet to destroy anyone, nor has it ever destroyed the Way. Do not fear training, for not training is what destroys a person and what destroys the Way. Do not fear the heat of summer, for the heat of summer has yet to destroy anyone, nor has it ever destroyed the Way. Not training can well destroy both a person and the Way. The accepting of barley and the choosing of bracken, which involved both monks and laity, are excellent examples of this.[50] We should not copy hellish creatures and beasts by seeking for blood or seeking for milk. Simply, ceaseless practice all day long is precisely what the everyday practice of Buddhas is.

Our great Ancestor Eka, the Second Chinese Ancestor, was of lofty virtue. He was a magnanimous and cultured person, adored by deities and daemons, both of whom were drawn to him. He was esteemed alike by followers of the Way and by the worldly. He resided for a long time between the rivers Ii and Lo, where he read extensively on a wide variety of subjects. He was considered to be a person rare in

---

hand, the celestial being was grateful to his former body because, due to that being's keeping the Precepts, he was born into the bliss of a heavenly state.

50. 'The accepting of barley' refers to an incident in which the Buddha, along with many of his assembly, was invited to a feast. The host, however, got distracted and forgot to prepare the meal, so that all he could offer his guests was the barley that he kept stored for feeding his horses. Since the barley was offered with a pure heart, the Buddha and His monks accepted it without judgment.

'The choosing of bracken' refers to a story of two noblemen who fled to the mountains after their country had been seized by a tyrannical warrior-king, since they preferred eating bracken as free men to eating the warrior-king's millet as his slaves.

any country, one who is seldom encountered. Because of the loftiness of his Dharma and the dignity of his virtuous ways, a strange and wondrous being suddenly appeared and said to him, "If you really desire to receive the fruits of your endeavors, why do you tarry here? The Great Way is not far off. Just go to the south."

The following day, the Ancestor suddenly had a stabbing headache. His teacher at the time, a teacher of meditation named Kōzan Hōjō of Dragon Gate Mountain in Loyang, was about to treat his condition when a voice from out of the blue said, "This is due to an altering of the skull and is not an ordinary headache." Our Ancestor then told his teacher about his encounter with the strange and wondrous being. When the teacher looked at the top of Eka's head, it was as if five peaks had blossomed forth, whereupon he said, "This feature of yours is an auspicious sign, and you will surely have an awakening to the Truth. This wondrous being's telling you to go south is because Great Master Bodhidharma of Shōrin-ji Temple is undoubtedly to be your Master." Heeding these instructions, our Ancestor Eka then left in order to train with Bodhidharma, who was residing atop a remote mountain peak. As for the wondrous being, he was a guardian deity who, for a long time, had been doing his own training in the Way.

The mid-winter weather was cold, for it is said to have been the night of the ninth day of the twelfth lunar month. Even if there had not been any great snowfall, a winter's night deep in the mountains atop a high peak is not the time or place to be standing outside someone's window, as you can well imagine, for it was that time of year which is so dreadfully cold that the joints of bamboo would split open. Notwithstanding that, a deep snow did indeed cover the earth, burying the mountains and concealing the peaks, as Eka sought his way, plowing through the drifts. How dangerous it must have been! He ultimately reached the Ancestor's quarters, but the Ancestor did not give him permission to enter. Indeed, he did not even bother to turn around and look at him. That night, Eka never dozed off, or sat down, or took a respite. He stood firm, without moving, waiting for the dawn to break, as the night snow continued mercilessly on, piling up layer upon layer until it buried his waist. His tears froze upon his cheeks as they fell, drop by drop. Catching sight of his tears only led him to shed more tears, and reflecting upon himself only led him to reflect more deeply upon himself. He thought to himself, "In the past, some of those who sought the Way would break their bones to get at the Marrow, or prick open their Blood that they might succor those who hungered for It, or spread out their Hair to cover the mud, or throw themselves off cliffs to feed the Tiger.[51] Those of old were just like this. So what kind of person am I?"

Thinking in this way encouraged him to be more and more resolute. We trainees of today must not disregard his remark, "Those of old were just like this. So what kind of person am I?" The moment we lose sight of this, we sink into eon upon eon of delusion. By thinking in this way, his resolve to search for the Dharma and to seek the Way only intensified. In that he did not treat the purity that resulted from his cleansing himself in this way as 'my being pure', it was possible for him to be pure.[52] To surmise what that night of slow dawning was like is enough to break one's innermost heart. The hairs on one's body simply bristle with cold fear.

> Just as the dawn was breaking, the First Ancestor, taking pity on him, asked, "What do you seek that you have stood such a long time in the snow?"
>
> When Eka heard this, his sorrowful tears fell in greater profusion as he replied, "I simply ask that you, Venerable Monk, out of your great benevolence and compassion, open the Gate to the Sweet Dew so that I may ferry all manner of beings far and wide to the Other Shore."
>
> Having been asked in this way, the First Ancestor said, "The wondrous, unsurpassed Way of all the Buddhas is to be most diligent over vast eons of time in ceaselessly practicing what is hard to practice and in ceaselessly enduring what seems beyond endurance. If you desire the True Course whilst relying upon little

---

51. These allusions refer to various legends and past life stories. While they have often been interpreted only on a literal level, the present translation attempts to point the reader to deeper, non-literal meanings based on figures of speech found in Zen Buddhist writings.

52. That is, Eka had been cleansing himself of any self-serving motives or hidden agendas.

virtue and less wisdom, or on a frivolous heart, or on a prideful and conceited mind, surely you will toil in vain."

When Eka heard this, he became more and more encouraged by this instruction. Hidden from sight, he took the Keen-edged Sword and cut off his left forearm.

When he placed this before the Master, the First Ancestor then knew that Eka was indeed a vessel for the Dharma.[53] So he said, "In Their seeking the Way, all the Buddhas, from the first, have laid down Their own bodies for the sake of the Dharma. Now you have cut yourself free of your arm right before me, which is proof that there is also good in what you are seeking."

From this time on, Eka had entry into the Master's innermost private quarters. For eight years he served as attendant to the Master through thousands of myriad endeavors. Truly, he was a great, reliable spiritual friend for both ordinary people as well as for those in loftier positions, and he was a great teacher of the Way for them. Deeds such as his were unheard of even in India and came to exist for the first time in the Eastern lands. We hear of Makakashō's face long ago breaking into a smile: we learn of Eka's getting to the Marrow.

What we need to reflect on is that, even if a thousand myriad First Ancestors came from the West, if the Second Ancestor had not been doing his ceaseless practice,

---

53. While the account of Eka's cutting off his arm has often been taken literally, and so depicted in paintings, there is a deeper, non-literal interpretation of what took place, one that does not support the notion that self-mutilation is somehow proof of one's willingness to do ceaseless practice. This interpretation states that Eka used Manjushri's Keen-edged Sword of Wise Discernment to cut himself free of dualistic thinking, and, though this act was not visible to the naked eye, Bodhidharma was able to discern what was going on within Eka's heart and mind. For instance, Eka did not ask Bodhidharma to open the Gate to the Sweet Dew for his own sake but for the sake of all sentient beings, and by this Bodhidharma knew that Eka was a True Vessel for the Dharma. The original text does not state what Eka actually placed before Bodhidharma. It may well not have been a physical arm that he offered to the Master, but rather his willingness to commit himself to the ceaseless practice that Bodhidharma had just been instructing him in.

we today would be unable to learn how to put the Great Matter to rest. Today, now that we have been able to encounter and hear the True Dharma, we should, beyond doubt, gratefully repay our indebtedness to the Ancestors. Any attempt to repay our gratitude with external objects cannot begin to truly repay our gratitude. Even one's own bodily existence will be insufficient repayment. And even one's nation or hometown is of no real value. Nations and cities are plundered by others or passed on to kith and kin. Our physical lives are entrusted to what is impermanent, put into the hands of rulers and their ministers, and abandoned to false ways. Thus it is that any attempt to repay our indebtedness by offering such as these will not be the practice of the Way.

Simply, our day by day ceaseless practice will be the true way to repay that indebtedness. The principle of which I speak is to do one's ceaseless practice in such a way that we do not neglect our daily life or waste it in selfish pursuits. And why so? This life is due to the merit from our ceaseless practice in times past and we are indebted to that ceaseless practice for it, a debt that we should be quick to repay. How sad, how shameful it would be to turn these physical shells of ours, which have come alive due to the merit of the ceaseless practice of the Buddhas and Ancestors, into useless toys for our spouse and children, letting ourselves be playthings for our spouse and children, and to do so without any regret for breaking Precepts and debasing ourselves. It is out of wrong-mindedness and folly that we turn our lives over to the demons of fame and gain, for fame and gain are the great thieves. If we give importance to fame and gain, then we will sympathize with fame and gain. To sympathize with fame and gain is to commit ourselves to fame and gain, and to thereby bring about the destruction of a life in which we might otherwise have become an Ancestor of the Buddha. Commitment to spouse and children, family and clan, are also just like this. Do not study fame and gain as if they were dreams and illusions, or were flowers in the sky; study their effects upon human beings. Do not sympathize with fame and gain, letting the retributions from your misdeeds pile up. When you use your true Eye to explore all the myriad thoughts and things in the ten directions through your training, you should go about it in this way.

Even an ordinary, worldly person with normal human emotions, upon being given gold, silver, or rare jewels will repay the favor with thanks. All those who have a warm heart will strive to repay the friendliness of kind words and a gentle voice with expressions of gratitude. How could anyone with a human face be oblivious to their great indebtedness to the Tathagata from encountering and heeding His unsurpassed True Dharma? Not to lose sight of this indebtedness is itself a precious treasure for a lifetime. The skull and bones of a being who has never retreated or turned aside from this ceaseless practice, either in life or in death alike, has such spiritual merit that it deserves to be enshrined in a stupa adorned with the seven treasures and to be given offerings of alms by all celestial and human beings. If any people are aware of this great indebtedness, they will not vainly let their lives, which are as transient as the dew on the grass, go to ruin, but will wholeheartedly repay the Second Ancestor for his monumental virtue. This is what ceaseless practice is. And those of us who do the ceaseless practice as the Buddhas and Ancestors have done it will receive the merit of this ceaseless practice. In sum, neither the First Ancestor nor the Second Ancestor ever founded a temple, nor did they have the arduous task of mowing down wild grasses.[54] And the Third and Fourth Ancestors were like this too. And the Fifth and Sixth Ancestors also did not establish their own temples, and both Seigen and Nangaku were no different.[55]

Great Master Sekitō fastened a grass hut to a boulder and then sat in meditation atop this rock. He did not doze off day or night, for there was not a time when he did not remain seated in meditation. Without neglecting his obligations to the monastic community, he habitually endeavored to do seated meditation throughout all the hours of a day. It is due to the great strength of Sekitō's steadfast ceaseless practice that Seigen's tradition has flowed out and permeated the world to the profit of both

---

54. 'Mowing down wild grasses' literally refers to clearing an uncultivated area for the purpose of erecting a temple.

55. Seigen and Nangaku were coequal Dharma heirs of the Sixth Ancestor. The Sōtō branch of the Zen tradition traces its lineage back to Seigen, whereas the Rinzai branch traces its lineage back to Nangaku. Dōgen's lineage includes both branches, the Rinzai through his Ordination Master and the Sōtō through his Transmission Master.

ordinary people and those in lofty positions. All those in the lineage of Ummon and Hōgen who have clarified the Matter are also Dharma descendants of Great Master Sekitō.

At age fourteen, our Thirty-first Ancestor, Meditation Master Daii Dōshin, met the Great Master who was our Third Chinese Ancestor. For the next nine years he undertook the responsibility of serving him. From the time when he inherited the Ancestral practices of the Buddhas and Ancestors, he kept his mind meditatively alert without dozing off and without letting his ribs touch his mat for sixty years. He bestowed his Teaching on those who were hostile and those who were friendly, and his virtue pervaded the realms of both ordinary people and those in lofty positions. He was our Fourth Chinese Ancestor.

In the seventeenth year of the Chen-kuan era (643 C.E.), Emperor T'ai-tsung, leaning favorably towards Master Daii's particular taste for the Way, desired to see the monk's imposing presence and so invited him to the capital. Three times altogether, the Master sent humble letters of apology, ultimately declining each invitation on the grounds of ill health. The fourth time, the emperor commanded an emissary to go and fetch him, saying, "If he really will not come to visit our royal presence, then take his head and bring me that."

When the emissary reached Daii's mountain, he warned him of the emperor's command, whereupon the Master stretched out his neck in the direction of the emissary's sword with a demeanor of majestic dignity. The emissary, thinking this strange indeed, returned and informed the emperor of the event. The emperor's admiration for Daii only increased. Accordingly, he bestowed upon him a gift of fine quality silks and let him have his way.

Thus, the Meditation Master who is our Fourth Ancestor did not turn life and limb into <u>his</u> life and limb. His ceaseless practice of not becoming intimate with kings and ministers is an example seen perhaps once in a thousand years. Emperor T'ai-tsung was a ruler with integrity, so their meeting would probably not have been a frivolous one, yet even so, you need to explore through your training that this was the ceaseless practice by such a senior monk and spiritual guide as this. As a ruler of men, T'ai-tsung did not begrudge his life and limb, and he all the more admired someone else who did not begrudge their life and limb but instead stuck out his neck in the direction of a sword. And this was not simply idle behavior on the Master's part for, prizing time, he considered his ceaseless practice to be of primary importance. His proffering letters of refusal three times is an example rare in any generation. It is a sign of our degenerate times that there are now monks who hope and pray for an audience with someone of royal blood.

On the fourth day of the intercalary ninth lunar month[56] in the second year of the Yung-hui era (651 C.E.) during the reign of Emperor Kao-tsung, Master Daii, in expounding the Dharma for those who were with him at the time, said, "All thoughts and things are completely free of suffering and delusion. Let each and every one of you preserve and keep this in mind. In the future, spread it abroad."

When he had finished speaking, he passed away whilst sitting peacefully in meditation. He had lived for seventy-two years. They placed his body in a stupa within the temple grounds. On the eighth day of the fourth lunar month of the following year (652

---

56. There are twelve months of either twenty-eight or thirty days in the Chinese and Japanese lunar calendar. Since this creates a discrepancy with the 365-day solar calendar, every two or three years a thirteenth lunar month is inserted (intercalated) in the calendar at some point. In the present instance, it was inserted between the ninth and tenth lunar months. This is technically known as an intercalary lunar month. An analogy can be found with our inserting the day of February 29 every four years to even out the annual solar calendar, and that day is technically called an intercalary day.

C.E.), the door of the stupa inexplicably opened of its own accord, and his bodily form looked as if it were still alive. After this, those who were at the temple did not dare to close the door again.

Keep in mind what he said: all thoughts and things are completely free of suffering and delusion. This does not mean that thoughts and things are as empty space, nor does it mean that thoughts and things are something other than thoughts and things. It means that thoughts and things are all, each and every one of them, completely free of suffering and delusion. Now, there was our Fourth Ancestor's ceaseless practice before he entered the stupa and there was his ceaseless practice after he had been placed in the stupa. To observe that those who are alive will ultimately perish is but a small-minded view. And to hold the opinion that those who have perished are beyond thinking or perceiving anything is also a narrow view. When it comes to studying the Way, do not copy such small-minded and narrow views. There may well be those among the living who do not perish, and there may well be those among the dead who have thoughts and perceptions.

Great Master Gensha Sōitsu of Fukien Province, whose Dharma name was Shibi, was a person from the Minhsien district. His family belonged to the Sha clan, and from an early age he was fond of fishing. He sailed a small boat upon the Nant'ai River and was friendly with the various fisherfolk thereabouts. At the beginning of the Hsien-t'ung era (ca. 860 C.E.) during the T'ang dynasty, when he was just thirty, he suddenly desired to leave the dust of lay life behind. So, he abandoned his fishing boat and, joining the assembly of Meditation Master Fuyōzan Reikun, he shaved his head. He received the full Precepts from Vinaya Master Dōgen of Kaigen-ji Temple in Yüchang.

Dressed in a hempen robe and straw sandals, and with barely enough food to sustain life, he would customarily sit in stillness throughout the day. All the members of the assembly took this to be strange. From the first, he was a brother in the Dharma with Seppō Gison, and the closeness of their relationship was like that of Master and disciple. Because of Shibi's stringent practice, Seppō, when addressing him, would refer to him as being austere.

> One day, Seppō asked him, "Is this Shibi the Austere Monk?"
>
> Shibi responded, "I have never dared to deceive anyone about that!"
>
> On another occasion, Seppō called out to him, "O Shibi, my austere monk, why haven't you gone out on a pilgrimage to seek a Master to train with?"
>
> Shibi responded, "Bodhidharma did not come east to China for that, nor did the Second Ancestor go west to India for that!"
>
> Seppō highly praised what he had said.

Eventually, Shibi climbed Mount Zokotsu and joined Master Seppō in his efforts to build a temple there.[57] A large number of serious followers gathered to train in this temple. They would enter the Master's private quarters to raise questions and resolve issues, never wearying of this practice from morn till dusk. Among those serious trainees who had come from all directions, if there was someone who had a particular, personal problem that was still not resolved, that person would invariably go and ask the Master about it, whereupon the venerable monk Seppō would say, "You should go ask that of Shibi the Austere Monk." Master Shibi, out of his benevolence, would forthwith endeavor to address the matter. If he had not had his preeminent ceaseless practice, he could not have engaged in such daily conduct. The ceaseless practice of sitting in stillness throughout the day is a ceaseless practice that is rare indeed. Even though there are many who vainly gallop off after sounds and forms, rare are those who endeavor to sit in stillness throughout the day. Those who have entered into training late in life should fear that the time remaining to them is short indeed, and so they should endeavor to sit in stillness through their remaining days.

---

57. Mount Zokotsu is the earlier name for Mount Seppō, where Meditation Master Seppō was attempting to establish his new monastery.

The venerable monk Chōkei Eryō was a revered senior monk training under Seppō.[58] For twenty-nine years he went back and forth between Seppō and Shibi, exploring the Matter through his training with both of them. During those months and years he wore out twenty sitting mats. There are people today who love doing seated meditation and, citing Chōkei, they take this beloved ancient one as their model. Those who idolize him are many; those who equal him are few.

At the same time, his efforts for thirty years were not in vain. There was a time when he was rolling up a bamboo blind in the doorway of the Meditation Hall and suddenly had a great awakening. During those thirty years, he never returned to his home country, or visited his relatives, or chatted with those sitting on either side of him; he just put his efforts into the Principle Matter. The ceaseless practice of this Master went on for thirty years. For thirty years he treated his doubts and misgivings as doubts and misgivings: we should speak of him as someone of keen wit who did not ignore anything, as someone with great potential for realizing the Truth. Reports of such firmness in resolve are sometimes met with when studying the Scriptures. When we desire what we should desire and feel shame about what we should feel shame about, then we may encounter Chōkei. To speak the truth, it is only due to a lack of heart for the Way and a lack of skill in handling their daily conduct that people become vainly tied to fame and gain.

After Meditation Master Isan of Mount Daii received affirmation of his awakening from Hyakujō, he straightaway climbed up the steep and remote slopes of Mount Isan where he made friends with the birds and beasts, thatched himself a hut, and continued on with his training. He never strove to retire from the winds and snows, and he supplied himself with various kinds of wild chestnuts for food, as he had no temple buildings or monastery gardens. Even so, for forty years he manifested ceaseless practice. Later, he became famous throughout China because of all the

---

58.   Chōkei later succeeded Seppō as the Abbot of Seppō's monastery.

dragon elephants* who beat a path to his door. Even if you should wish to establish a temple as your own pure place, do not concern yourself with the quagmire of public opinion, just hold steadfast to doing the ceaseless practice of the Buddha Dharma. Doing one's training without having a temple compound was the training ground for ancient Buddhas. We have heard from afar Their custom of training in open fields and under trees. These places have for ever so long become 'enclosed realms'.[59] Wherever there is ceaseless practice by one person, such a place will be handed down as a training ground of the Buddhas. Do not become obsessed with constructing buildings, like foolish people in the degenerate days of the Dharma do. The Buddhas and Ancestors never craved buildings. Those whose Eye has not yet become clear and who therefore arbitrarily construct temple buildings and monastery halls are not making alms offerings of Buddhist buildings for the Buddhas, but are doing it for the sake of their own lairs of fame and gain.

Calmly imagine the ceaseless practice that was happening on Mount Isan long ago. What I mean by 'imagine' means thinking about how it would be for us today if we were residing on Mount Isan. The sound of the rain deep in the night was probably not just of water washing over the moss, for the rain would certainly have had the strength to bore through boulders. On the snowy nights in the dead of winter, the birds and beasts must have been scarce indeed, and how much less would there have been smoke from man-made fires to acknowledge human existence! It was a way of living that could not have been tolerated, were it not for the Master's ceaseless practice in which he made light of his life whilst stressing the Dharma. He was in no hurry to cut down the undergrowth, nor did he engage in cutting down trees to clear the land for building. He just continued his ceaseless practice and simply did his utmost to practice the Way. What a pity that an authentic Ancestor who had Transmitted, and kept to, the True Dharma came to undergo such hardships in such precipitous mountains! It is said that Mount Isan had many ponds and running water, so there must have been thick ice and dense banks of fog. Most people could not have

---

59. 'Enclosed realms' is a technical term referring to areas that were set apart and preserved for use by Buddhist communities in India. Later, it was used in China and Japan to refer to monastery grounds.

tolerated such a secluded life, nevertheless Isan transformed it into the Buddha's Way and explored Its innermost purpose. Today, we are able to learn of his expressions of the Way and Its purpose because of the ceaseless practice that he did. Even though we may not be listening with a casual attitude, we still need to recognize our indebtedness to his strenuous efforts in ceaseless practice. When we hear about what he did and imagine the hardships he faced, how can those of us today who are heartfelt trainees possibly fail to feel pity for him? Due to the transformative power derived from Isan's ceaseless practice of the Way, the winds cease their howling, the world remains intact, the palaces and dwelling places of the celestial community are tranquil, and the homelands of human beings are preserved. Though we may not be direct descendants of Isan, he will be our Ancestor in spirit.

Later, Kyōzan Ejaku came and served as Isan's attendant. Kyōzan had previously trained with his late Master Hyakujō. Though he was a veritable Shariputra with a hundred responses for every ten questions,[60] for three years he trained under and attended on Isan while doing his utmost to oversee his own buffalo.[61] His was a ceaseless practice that has become extinct in recent times and is no longer seen or even heard of. In tending to his buffalo for three years, there was no need for him to seek for a well-put expression of the Matter from someone else.

Our Ancestor Dōkai of Mount Fuyō manifested a pure wellspring of ceaseless practice. When the ruler of the nation tried to bestow upon him the title of Meditation Master Jōshō along with a purple kesa, our Ancestor would not accept them and wrote a letter to the emperor politely declining his offer. Although the ruler of the nation censured him for this, the Master, to the end, did not accept them. His rice broth has passed down to us the taste of the Dharma. When he built his hermitage on Mount Fuyō, the monks and laity streamed to his refuge by the hundreds. Because

---

60. Shariputra was the chiefmost of the Buddha's ten great disciples, being the monk whom his fellow monks viewed as 'having all the answers'.

61. That is, he worked at training himself in accord with his own karmic propensities.

he served them only one bowl of gruel as a day's rations, many of them left. The Master, upon a vow, did not partake of any meals offered by donors. One day he pointed out the Matter to his assembly, saying the following:

> To begin with, those who have left home behind to become monks have a distaste for the dust and troubles stirred up by defiling passions and seek to rise above birth and death. And they do so in order to give their hearts and minds a rest, to abandon discriminatory thinking, and to eradicate entanglements, which is why it is called 'leaving home'. So, how can it possibly be all right for monks to indulge in conventional ways of living by being neglectful and greedy? Straight off, you should discard all dualistic notions and let neutral ones drop off as well. Then, whenever you encounter any sights or sounds, it will be as if you were trying to plant a flower atop a stone, and whenever you encounter gain or fame, it will resemble getting dirt in your eyes. Moreover, it is not that, since beginningless time, no one has ever done this, or that no one has ever known how. Simply, we just stop reversing our head and making a tail out of it.[62] If we stop our training at this point, we will suffer from our cravings and greeds, but why do we need to do so? If we do not bring them to a halt right now, when will we deal with them? Therefore, the saintly ones of the past, who were ordinary human beings, invariably and thoroughly exhausted these cravings in each moment of the present. If we can exhaust them in each moment of the present, what more is there to do? If we are able to be calm in heart and mind, it will be as if even 'the Buddhas and Ancestors' become our enemy. When everything in the world has become naturally cooled down and impermanent for us, then, for the first time, we will be in accord with the Other Shore.

---

62.   That is, getting things upside down by taking the false self to be our True Nature.

Have you not heard of Inzan, who, to his dying day, did not wish to meet with anyone? Or of Jōshū, who, to his dying day, did not wish to speak with anyone? And there is Hentan, who gathered various kinds of chestnuts for his food. Daibai made his clothing out of lotus leaves, and the lay practitioner Shie only wore clothes made from paper, whereas the veteran monk Gentai wore only cotton cloth. Sekisō built a Hall for Withered Trees where he and his community did their sitting and lying down, only requiring of his monks that their hearts and minds completely quiet down.[63] Tōsu had others prepare the rice, which they cooked for everyone so that all could dine together. Tōsu himself used the meal preparation time to examine the Matter on his own. Now, the saintly ones listed above had characteristics like these. If they did not have such strong points, how could anyone have entrusted themselves to them? O my virtuous ones, if you too master yourself in this way, you will truly be an unfaltering one. If, on the other hand, you do not dare to take charge of yourself, you will, I fear, simply waste your strength in the future.

Though there has been nothing in this mountain monk's own practice to be particularly commended, I have been privileged to be head of this mountain monastery. So how could it possibly be all right for me to sit here, squandering our communal provisions and forgetting about our connection with the former saintly ones? Now what I desire is to try to give you, right off, a concrete example of how the temple heads of old behaved. I have consulted with various senior monks about this. We will not go down from our mountain, nor betake ourselves to meals offered by lay donors, nor have a monk in charge of fund raising.[64] Simply, we will divide into three hundred and sixty

---

63. A Hall for Withered Trees is an epithet for a Monks' Meditation Hall.

64. In addition to its literal meaning of not staying in one's place of training, 'going down from the mountain' has non-literal implications, such as leaving the monastery in order

equal parts whatever crops we harvest in one year from our own fields and then use one part of this each day, regardless of whether our numbers increase or decrease. If our supply of rice is sufficient, we will make steamed rice. If there is not enough rice for that, we will make rice gruel. And if there is not enough to make rice gruel, we will make rice broth. For the interview with new arrivals, we will simply serve tea, foregoing the customary tea ceremony with cakes.[65] We will simply arrange a tearoom that we can go to and make use of on our own. We need to strive to sever our connections with the secular world and just concentrate on doing our utmost to practice the Way.

And what is more, our life is already complete and our landscape lacks for nothing. The flowers teach us how to smile: the birds teach us how to sing. The Wooden Horse neighs loud and long: the Stone Cow gallops apace. Beyond the blue horizon, the form of the green mountains fades away: when distant from our ears, the voice of the babbling brook does not exist. Atop the mountain peaks, the monkeys chatter: in the sky, the moon is steeped in mist. Within the forest, the cranes cry out: at break of day, the wind swirls through the pines. When the breezes of spring rise up, the withered trees sound forth the Dragon's song: when the leaves of autumn wither, the chill woods scatter their flowers abroad. The jewel-like stepping-stones make patterns in the moss: the faces of people take on the hue of haze and mist. Distracting sounds have become hushed: conditions are just

---

to visit the lay world, as well as leaving one's training behind in order to participate in worldly affairs.

65. This tea ceremony is not the same as that often associated with Japanese Zen. Rather, it is part of the face-to-face encounter with newly arriving trainees, during which the Abbot will endeavor to assess the quality and depth of the guest's spiritual intention and actual training.

what they are. The Underlying One stands alone: nothing needs to be contrived.[66]

I, a mountain monk, facing all of you here today, am setting forth what the gateway to our monastic family is: it is not getting all wrapped up in what have simply been expedient means. Why should it be necessary for any Master today, upon entering the Dharma Hall to give Teaching or upon letting trainees enter his private chambers for instruction, to imitate some Master of old by picking up the drum stick, or holding his ceremonial hossu* upright, or shouting towards the east, or pointing his traveling staff* to the west, or raising his eyebrows, or looking with glaring eyes—and all this done in the manner of one who is sick with rage? Not only does such behavior belittle those training in the Meditation Hall, even worse, it treats with contempt one's indebtedness to the saintly ones who have gone before.

Have you not realized that Bodhidharma came from the West and, having arrived at the foot of a remote mountain, sat facing a wall for nine years? And the Second Ancestor's standing in the snow and severing his forearm can only be described as his suffering hardships. Even so, Bodhidharma never gave forth a single word of Scripture and the Second Ancestor never asked him for a single phrase of Scripture. Further, in speaking of Bodhidharma, do we think he was unable to teach anything for the sake of human beings? In speaking of the Second Ancestor, do we think that he was not seeking a Master?

---

66. This pastoral portrait is composed of various Buddhist and Zen expressions descriptive of experiences encountered through one's spiritual training and practice, and is a way of demonstrating that all things in nature are giving voice to the Dharma. For instance, the flower that teaches one to smile is an allusion to Shakyamuni's holding aloft the udumbara blossom and Makakashō breaking out into a smile of recognition of the Truth underlying the Buddha's gesture. Also, the Wooden Horse neighing and the Stone Cow galloping are Zen-derived metaphors referring to the natural functioning of one's Buddha Mind and one's immediate, spontaneous response to that functioning.

Whenever this mountain monk gets to the point of expounding what the saintly ones of old did, I immediately feel as if there were no place on earth where I can hide, for I am overwhelmed with shame at the weakness of us people of these later times. And what is more, having already been supplied with the four necessities—nourishment, clothing, bedding, and medicine—we treat ourselves to delicacies served in a hundred different ways and then have the cheek to say that one should, by all means, give rise to the Buddha Mind. I simply fear that our physical behavior is so compulsive that we will continue on, passing through myriad lives in the six worlds[*] as a result. Our days fly by like arrows, and we should deeply regret wasting them.

Even though we are like this, there may still be people who have reached the Other Shore by relying on their strengths. And this mountain monk cannot compel you to learn. And, my virtuous ones, have you encountered the following poem by one of old?

> *From our mountain fields, millet harvested for our meal,*
> *From our garden, plain yellow leeks;*
> *Whether you eat from what there is to eat is up to you,*
> *And if you choose not to eat thereof, feel free to go*
> *where you will.*

I pray that, on reflection, each of you, my companions on the Path, will practice diligently. Take good care of yourselves!

This is the very Bones and Marrow of the direct, Face-to-Face Transmission of our Ancestral lineage. Even though the ways of ceaseless practice by our founding Ancestors are many, I have given you this one for the present. We trainees today should want to do the ceaseless practice that was cultivated on Mount Fuyō, and we should explore that practice in our training, for it is the correct standard established at Jetavana Monastery.[67]

Baso Dōitsu of Kagen-ji Temple in the Hungchou District of Kiangsi Province was a native of Shihfang Prefecture in the district of Hanchou. He trained and served under Nangaku for over ten years. One day, with the intent of revisiting his home, Baso reached the halfway point on his journey. From this halfway point, he came back to the temple, making an incense offering and bowing in respect to Nangaku, whereupon Nangaku composed the following poem for Baso:

> *I recommend that you do not return to your former home;*
> *Should you return to that home, your practice of the Way will wane,*
> *And the old women of your neighborhood*
> *Will call you by your former name.*

When he gave Baso these words of Dharma, Baso reverently accepted them and made a vow, saying, "I will never return again to Hanchou, not even in future lives." Having made this vow, he never again took even one step towards Hanchou. He lived in Hungchou for the rest of his life, leaving others to come and go from all directions. Apart from expressing the Way simply as "Your very mind is Buddha," he had not a single word of Teaching for the sake of others. Be that as it may, he was Nangaku's Dharma heir and a lifeline for both ordinary people and those in lofty positions.

Just what is this "Do not return to your former home?" What are we to make of it? Traveling to and from the east, west, south, or north is simply the continual arising of our false self. Truly, this is to return to our home and have our practice wane. Is one doing a ceaseless practice which recognizes that 'returning home' is the same as not practicing the Way, or is one doing a ceaseless practice that is beyond 'returning home'? Why is returning home not practicing the Way? Is one hindered by not practicing or is one hindered by self? It is Nangaku's assertion that the old women in

---

67. Jetavana was a grove purchased from Prince Jeta by the lay patron Sudatta, who gave it to the Buddha for Him and His community to use in their training and practice.

the neighborhood will call Baso by his former name. Why did Nangaku put this expression in his poem, and why did Baso accept these words of Dharma? Because when we go towards the south, the whole world likewise goes towards the south. It will also be the same with the rest of the directions. To doubt that this is so by using Mount Sumeru and the Great Ocean surrounding it as one's measure, or to gauge it by using the sun, moon, and stars as one's standard is, in either case, a small-minded view.

The Thirty-second Ancestor, Meditation Master Daiman, was a native of Ōbai. Because he was born illegitimately, just like Lao-tzu was, he received his mother's surname of Shū. From the time that the Dharma was Transmitted to him at the age of seven until he was seventy-four years old, he preserved and kept to the Treasure House of the Eye of the True Teaching. He secretly bestowed Bodhidharma's kesa and Dharma on the monastery laborer Enō, which was an example of his extraordinary ceaseless practice. He did not let his chief disciple Jinshū know about the kesa and the Dharma, but bestowed them instead upon Enō, and, because of this, the life of the True Teaching has continued on without interruption.

My former Master, the Reverend Monk Tendō, was a person from Yüeh or thereabouts. At nineteen, he gave up academic religious study to explore the Matter through training with his Master. He did not regress from that training even upon reaching his seventies. During the Chinese Chia-ting era, the emperor offered him a purple robe and the title of Meditation Master, but ultimately he turned them down, writing letters to the throne in which he declined the honors with thanks. Monks far and wide all greatly revered him, and the wise from near and far alike all treasured him. The emperor also took delight in him, sending him a gift of ceremonial tea. Those who found out about this spoke highly of it, as being something rare in any age. Indeed, this was due to true ceaseless practice on my Master's part, since craving fame is even worse than acting contrary to some Precept. Acting contrary to a Precept is a onetime wrong, whereas craving fame is a whole lifetime of trouble. Do not foolishly fail to forsake fame and do not blindly welcome it. Not welcoming it is ceaseless practice and forsaking it is ceaseless practice. Each of the first six generations of our Ancestral Masters had the title of Meditation Master bestowed upon them posthumously by an emperor, and this was because they did not crave fame while they were in the world. Thus, we too should quickly forsake any craving for fame within life and death, and aspire instead to the ceaseless practice of the Buddhas and Ancestors.

Do not be the equal of birds and beasts through indulging your greeds. To greedily look after the trivial self is what birds have in their thoughts, what animals have in their hearts. The forsaking of fame and gain is considered rare among both ordinary people and those in lofty positions, and no Ancestor of the Buddha has ever yet failed to forsake them. There are some people who say that it is for the benefit of sentient beings that they desire fame and crave gain, but this is a monstrously false assertion. These people are non-Buddhists who have connected themselves with the Buddha Dharma; they are a bunch of demons who malign the True Teaching. If you were to claim something like this, would it mean that the Buddhas and Ancestors, who do not crave fame and gain, are therefore unable to benefit sentient beings? How laughable, how truly laughable that would be! And truly, there are others as well who are of benefit to living beings without being greedy. Further, those who have not yet learned that, although there are many ways to benefit beings, one should not label as benefiting beings that which is not of benefit to them, must surely be some species of demon. Living beings who would try to gain spiritual benefit from the likes of such demons will fall into all manner of hellish states. How pitiful to spend one's whole life like this! Do not call such silliness 'spiritually benefiting sentient beings'. So, even though the emperor's gift of the title of Meditation Master was graciously offered, letters were written to decline it with thanks, which is an excellent example from the past, and today's trainees would do well to explore this example with their Master.

To meet my former Master face-to-face was to encounter an ordinary human being. From the time my former Master left his hometown at the age of nineteen to seek out a spiritual teacher, he did his utmost to practice the Way, and when he had reached the age of sixty-five, he still had not regressed or turned aside from this practice. He was not on intimate terms with any emperor nor was he ever the guest of any emperor, and he was not on close terms with any minister of state or government official. Not only did he decline the purple kesa and the title of Meditation Master, but throughout his life he also did not wear a varicolored kesa, but customarily used a black kesa with a black formal robe, whether he was giving a talk in the Dharma Hall or letting trainees enter his private chambers for spiritual counseling.[68]

Once when he was giving spiritual instruction to his monks, he said the following:

> In practicing your meditation and studying what the Way is, having a heart for the Way is foremost, for this is the beginning of learning the Way. For about two hundred years now, the Way of the Buddhas and Ancestors has been dying out, sad to say. What is more, skin bags who have been able to give expression to even a single line of Scripture have been few indeed. Formerly, when I had hung up my traveling staff at Mount Kinzan, Busshō Tokkō was the head of the temple at the time. Once while we were in the Meditation Hall for our meal, he gave Teaching, saying, "In meditating on the Way of the Buddha Dharma, there is no need to seek out how others have put it into words: simply let each of you come to your own understanding of the Principle!" After having spoken like this, he made no effort at all to supervise what went on in the Monks' Hall. Both the junior and senior monks similarly did not supervise themselves and just busied themselves in meeting with official guests. Busshō did not particularly understand what the Buddha Dharma is getting at, and so he simply chased fame and craved gain. If each person is to come to his own understanding of what the Buddha Dharma is about, why, pray, did those in the past who probed into the Matter seek out a Master so that they might ask

---

68.   Black is the color that is customarily worn by novice monks.

the way to go? The truth is that Busshō Tokkō never practiced meditation. Today, there are senior monks all over the place have no heart for the Way, for they are simply the offspring of those like Busshō Tokkō. How can the Buddha Dharma possibly flourish in their care? What a pity, what a pity!

When my Master talked in this way, even though many among those who were listening were direct descendants of Busshō, they did not resent what he said.

My Master also said once, "Practicing meditation is to let body and mind drop off. Without engaging in burning incense, making bows, reciting the name of Buddha, doing repentance, or doing walking meditation, we can realize It from the start just by sitting."

Truly, throughout Great Sung China today, there are not merely one or two hundred skin bags who call themselves both meditators and descendants of our tradition, these folks are as prevalent as rice and flax, bamboo and reeds. But I never got wind of anyone else who encouraged sitting simply for the sake of sitting. Between the four oceans of the world and the five lakes in China, only my late Master Tendō did this. Monks far and wide were alike in praising Tendō, yet Tendō did not praise all monks far and wide. Also, there were heads of large temples who did not know of Tendō at all. Even though they had been born in Great Sung China, perhaps they were some species of bird or beast. They did not explore what they should have explored, and, because of that, they were wasting their time to no avail. How sad that those folks who did not know Tendō have vociferously given forth barbarous teaching and confused talk, mistaking this for the family tradition of the Buddhas and Ancestors.

In giving informal talks, my former Master would customarily say, in effect:

> From the age of nineteen, I began to visit monasteries all over the place, yet I did not find anyone who taught for the sake of ordinary people. And from that time on, there has been no time—not even one day or one night—when I did not flatten my meditation cushion. Before I became head of a temple, I did not engage in chitchat with the locals, for time was dear to me. Even though there were places where I hung up my traveling staff, I never entered, or

even saw, the interior of a hermit's hut or a private dormitory.[69] How much the less could I squander my efforts on wandering off to the mountains or playing about in lakes and streams? Apart from sitting in meditation in the Cloud Hall and in the public monastic areas, I would go alone, seeking out an upper floor in a tall building or a screened-off area where I could sit in meditation in a secluded place. I always carried a meditation mat rolled up in my sleeve, and sometimes I would sit in meditation even at the foot of a crag. I always felt that I would like to sit upon the Diamond Seat[70] until it split, for this was the outcome I was seeking. There were times when the flesh on my buttocks would blister and split open. At such times I all the more took delight in sitting in meditation. This year I am sixty-five, old in my bones and weak in the head. Though I no longer do my seated meditation along with the community, I have sympathy for my fellow monks, senior and junior, wherever they are. Accordingly, I am Abbot of this mountain monastery so that I may counsel those who come here and Transmit the Way to them for the sake of all beings. Otherwise, my old friends, where could the Buddha Dharma be found and what would It be like?

And this is how he would speak, both formally in the Dharma Hall as well as in his informal talks. Further, he would not accept any personal gifts that were offered to him by any of the monks who came from all directions to hear him speak.

Government Minister Chao was a descendant of the saintly sovereign of the Chia-ting era. As a senior official in the Mingchou district, he was in charge of both military and agricultural affairs. One day, he invited my late Master to come to his district office and give a Dharma talk, donating ten thousand silver pieces as an alms offering.

---

69. That is, he slept, ate, and meditated in the Meditation Hall.

70. The Diamond Seat is the name given to the flat rock upon which Prince Siddhārtha sat until he realized Buddhahood.

After my Master had given the Dharma talk, he turned to the minister and said the following by way of thanks, "In accordance with established tradition, I have left my mountain monastery in order to ascend the Dharma Seat and give voice to the Treasure House of the Eye of the True Teaching, which is the Wondrous Heart of Nirvana. I am respectfully doing this in memory of your relative, the late emperor, who is now in the realm of the departed. However, I dare not accept this silver. Monks in our family have no need of such things. So, with a thousand myriad thanks, I am humbly returning it to you exactly as I received it today, which is what we customarily do."

The minister said, "Venerable Monk, because this lowly official has been favored by being a relative of His Imperial Highness, wherever I go people honor me, and thus my treasures have grown in abundance. Today is the day for commemorating my former parent's happiness in the realm of the departed, so I wish to contribute something for his sake. Venerable Monk, why will you not accept it? Today has been one of great joy for me, so out of your great kindness and compassion, please retain this small alms offering."

My Master replied, "My dear minister, yours is a very sincere request, which I would usually not dare decline. But, simply, there is a reason why I am doing so. When I ascended the Dharma Seat and gave voice to the Teaching, were you able to hear It clearly?"

The minister said, "Just hearing it has filled me with immeasurable joy."

My Master then said, "My dear minister, you are very astute and have seen clearly what this monk's words were about. My awe is unceasing. Further, as to what you have hoped for, your late relative has been blessed ten thousandfold. Now, when this mountain monk ascended the Dharma Seat, what Dharma did he give expression to? Try and see if you can express It. If you can, I shall respectfully accept your ten thousand pieces of silver. If you are unable to express It, then let one of your emissaries retain the silver."

The minister arose and, facing my Master, said, "With due respect and careful consideration, I found your Dharma talk and your deportment, Venerable Monk, to be a ten thousandfold blessing."

My Master replied, "That is just the way I talk. What did you learn from listening to it?"

The minister was left speechless at this.

After a while, my Master said, "The blessings for your departed one have been fully done. Let's wait a bit on the matter of deciding on an alms offering on his behalf."

Having spoken thus, my Master was taking his leave when the minister said, "I bear no resentment that you have still not accepted the offering, and my delight is to have had the pleasure of meeting you." Having said this, he saw my Master off.

Many monks and laity, who had come from both east and west of the River Che, spoke highly of the event, and an attendant monk named Hei recorded of it in his diary, "This venerable old monk is a person not easily encountered. Where else could one possibly meet with such a person?"

Is there anyone who would not have accepted the ten thousand pieces of silver? A person of long ago said, "Look upon gold, silver, jewels, and jade as if they were dirt." Even if they do look like gold or silver to us, it is the custom for tatter-robed monks not to accept them. This was the way my Master would have it: it is not this way with others.

And my Master used to say, "For three hundred years, people have not had a spiritual friend like me, so you must all strive to do your utmost in pursuing the Way."

In my Master's assembly, there was a man from the Mienchou district in the western province of Szechwan, Dōshō by name, who was of the Taoist tradition.

Together with five companions, he made a vow, saying, "In this lifetime, we shall master the Great Tao of the Buddhas and Ancestors or else we shall not return to our homeland." My Master was especially delighted by this and let them do walking meditation and train in the Way alongside his trainee monks. When arranging them by seniority, he placed them in a position behind his female monks; this was an excellent example that is rare in any generation. Also, there was a monk from the Fuchou district by the name of Zennyo, who made a vow, saying, "In this lifetime, I shall not take one step towards the South from whence I came, but shall train in the Great Way of the Buddhas and Ancestors." There were so many within my Master's community who were like this; it is something that I saw with my very own eyes. Although behavior like this was not to be found in the communities of other Masters, it is, nevertheless, the ceaseless practice of monks in our tradition in Great Sung China. It is sad that this kind of constancy of heart has been absent among us Japanese. It is still absent, even at this time when we can encounter the Buddha Dharma; in former times when we could not have encountered It, the state of our bodies and minds would have been worse than disgraceful.

Calmly consider: a lifetime is not all that long. Even when the sayings of the Buddhas and Ancestors consisted of merely three words, or even just two words, what They gave expression to would have expressed what all the Buddhas and Ancestors truly are. And why so? Because the Bodies and Minds of Buddhas and Ancestors are one and the same, so Their one or two phrases all express the genial Body and Heart of a Buddha and Ancestor. This Body and Heart of Their's also comes to us, and It expresses <u>our</u> body and heart. At the very moment when They express It, Their expression comes to us and expresses our own body and heart. And this life of ours also expresses the embodiment of past lives. As a result, when we awaken and become a Buddha, and when we become an Ancestor by having a Dharma heir, we go beyond 'Buddha' and we go beyond 'Ancestor'. The ability of two or three words to embody our ceaseless practice is in no way different. Do not vainly chase after the sounds and forms of fame and gain. When you do not chase after them, then this is the very ceaseless practice that the Buddhas and Ancestors Transmit directly, one-to-one. Whether you seclude yourself within the world or seclude yourself apart from the world, whether you are wholly enlightened or half enlightened, what I recommend is that you cast aside the myriad things of the world and your myriad entanglements with them, for this is the ceaseless practice that Buddhas and Ancestors practice ceaselessly.

Written at Kannondōri in Kōshōhōrin-ji Temple on the fifth day of the fourth lunar month in the third year of the Ninji era (May 6, 1242).

Copied by me on the eighteenth day of the first lunar month in the fourth year of the same era (February 8, 1243). Proofreading was completed on the eighth day of the third month of the same year (March 29, 1243).

Ejō

Glossary

Āchārya: Sanskrit for 'teacher'; in Zen monasteries, a polite form of address for a monk with at least five years of training; applied to a disciple advanced enough to teach monks and laity, but not yet deemed a Master.

Arhat: In Zen, one whose heart is cleansed of all greed, hatred, and delusion but who has not yet fully realized wise discernment or compassion.

Asura: An inhabitant of one of the six Worlds of Existence; before conversion, a heaven stormer, one who is so absorbed in attaining power that he cannot hear the Dharma, much less comprehend It; after conversion, he becomes a guardian of Buddhism.

Avalokiteshvara (C. Kuan Yin, J. Kanzeon or Kannon): The Bodhisattva who hearkens to the cries of the world; the embodiment of compassion.

Before 'father' and 'mother' were born: That is, the time before dualistic thinking arises in the mind.

Bodhisattva: When not capitalized, it refers to one who is attempting to follow the Mahāyāna (Greater Course) as the Buddha Path; when capitalized, the personification of some aspect of Buddha Nature.

A broken wooden ladle: A Zen metaphor describing someone's mind which has become free of discriminatory thinking.

A dragon elephant: Originally, a term for a particularly large elephant; used in Zen texts to describe a particularly brilliant and discerning Master.

The five treacherous deeds: Murdering one's father, murdering one's mother, murdering an arhat, spilling the blood of someone who has realized Buddhahood, and causing disharmony in the Sangha, thereby creating a schism in the order.

The four elements: Earth, water, fire, and wind.

The four stages of arhathood: (1) Stream-enterer: someone who enters into the stream of Buddhist training by abandoning false views; (2) Once-returner: someone having one more rebirth before realizing full enlightenment; (3) Non-returner: someone never returning to the realm of sensual desire; and (4) Arhat: someone who has reached a state of enlightenment and is therefore free from all defiling passions.

Gasshō: A gesture made by placing the palms of the hands together, with fingers pointing upwards, signifying the unity of body and mind. It is an expression of reverence often used during ceremonies, as well as a form of greeting when two Buddhists meet and a gesture of supplication.

Greater Course (Greater Vehicle): A translation of the term 'Mahāyāna', used to designate the Buddhist traditions that place the awakening of all sentient beings above one's personal awakening.

Hossu: A scepter-like instrument in the form of a fly-whisk carried by a celebrant during ceremonies. It represents the flowing forth of the Water of the Spirit as an expression of the celebrant's compassion.

Hungry ghost (preta): One who resides in one of the three negative modes of existence, pictured as a being who is suffering from a hunger for the Dharma and has some metaphorical deformity, such as lacking a mouth, which makes it impossible to absorb It.

Icchantika: Someone who is erroneously thought to be so amoral as to be completely devoid of Buddha Nature. In Zen, there is reference to the Great Icchantika, which is an epithet for Buddha Nature itself.

Jambudvipa: In Buddhist spiritual cosmology, the Southern Continent where people are capable of doing Buddhist training.

Kalpa: An endlessly long period of time, roughly equivalent to an eon.

Karma: What results from any volitional action, according to the universal law of cause and effect.

Kenshō: The experience of seeing into one's true nature, that is, one's Buddha Nature.

Kesa: A cloak-like robe traditionally worn by Buddhist monastics since the time of Shakyamuni Buddha. A similar type of robe is given to committed lay Buddhists.

Kōan: A statement or story used by a Zen Master as a teaching device to directly address a trainee's spiritual question; also may be used to refer to that question itself.

Lantern (stone or temple): A term often used metaphorically for a monk who stays in a monastery or temple, serving as a light to help guide a trainee.

Lesser Course: Followers of the two 'lesser' courses, namely, the shravakas and the pratyekabuddhas. They are not 'wrong' practitioners of Buddhism, but by their following a 'lesser' course it will take a longer time for their spiritual seeds to germinate and grow into the realizing of Buddhahood, since they have not yet entered the Bodhisattva Path, which involves the doing of one's practice for the sake of all sentient beings. See also the Greater Course and the Three Vehicles.

Lion Throne (Lion's Seat): The seat where a Master sits when giving a talk on some aspect of the Dharma.

Lord of Emptiness: The first of the Seven Buddhas, the one who lived during the Age of Emptiness, that is, before duality had first arisen.

Mahāsattva: An outstanding bodhisattva.

Mahāyāna: The Greater Vehicle.

Maitreya: The Buddha Yet to Come. He is said to be waiting as a Bodhisattva in the Tushita Heaven. To realize one's own Buddha Nature brings Maitreya forth.

Manjushri: The Bodhisattva who personifies Great Wisdom.

Matter (the One Great Matter): The goal of spiritual training, namely, the realization of the highest Truth.

Monjin: The act of bowing from the waist with hands in gasshō.

A pillar of the temple: A monk whose training is so strong that it supports the spiritual function of the temple or monastery in which he trains.

Pratyekabuddha: One who becomes enlightened as a result of his own efforts but does not share his understanding with others.

Samantabhadra: The Bodhisattva who is the embodiment of patient, loving activity.

Seal (Buddha seal, Buddha Mind seal, Dharma seal, and seal of certification): 'The Buddha Mind Seal' refers not only to the document written on plum blossom silk which certifies both the Master's and the disciple's Buddha Mind but also to the fact that the Minds of Master and disciple coincide and are not two separate minds. The Transmission of this seal is often referred to in Zen texts as 'the Transmission of Mind to Mind' as well as 'the special Transmission that is apart from Scriptural texts and which does not depend on words'.

The Seven Buddhas: The historical Buddha and the six Buddhas that preceded Him.

The seven treasures (the seven jewels): The seven types of jewels from which Pure Lands are fashioned.

Shashu: The way that the hands are held when doing walking meditation. There are various forms of shashu, but most involve one hand being wrapped around the fist of the other.

Shravaka: One who, upon hearing the Dharma, affirms his allegiance to It but may not yet try to put It into practice, or may try to reduce It simply to a rigid code of 'right' or 'wrong' behaviors.

The six Worlds of Existence: Those of celestial beings, humans, asuras, hungry ghosts, beasts, and those in hellish states.

Skandhas: The five skandhas comprising a living being's physical form, sensory perceptions, mental concepts and ideas, volition, and consciousness.

Skin bag: An allusion to a human as a sentient being having a physical body. Dōgen often uses the term to characterize ineffectual trainees.

Staff: The traveling staff carried by a monk when traveling to another temple. Hence the phrase 'to hang up one's traveling staff' meaning 'to have found the temple in which to permanently seek the Truth under the abbot'; metaphorically, a monk who is willing to go anywhere in order to spread the Dharma and help all sentient beings.

Stupa: Literally, a reliquary for the ashes of a Buddhist, and metaphorically, the body of a Buddha.

'Such a one' ('such a person'): Someone who has realized the Truth and automatically shows the signs of having had such a realization.

The Three Courses (the Three Vehicles): Namely, the way of training done by the shravakas, pratyekabuddhas, and bodhisattvas.

The thrice wise and ten times saintly: Those who have attained the final stage of bodhisattvahood before fully awakening and becoming a Buddha.

The tiles and stones of our walls and fences: The bits and pieces of our experiences, which we use to fashion our perception of the universe.

Tripitaka: The three divisions of Buddhist Scriptures, namely, the Buddha's

Teachings (Sutras), the Precepts (Vinaya), and the commentaries on the Sutras (Abhi-dharmas); also, the whole of the Buddhist canon.

Vairochana (the Cosmic Buddha): The Buddha who is the personification of spiritual Light and Truth, the one who represents the Pure Buddha Mind.

Vimalakīrti: A wealthy lay Buddhist renowned for his profound understanding of Mahāyāna.

A wheel-turning lord: A ruler who turns the Wheel of the Dharma in his country by governing according to Buddhist principles.

Yojana: An Indian measure of distance, understood by some scholars as equivalent to twelve or sixteen miles.

Appendix of Names

Many of Dōgen's discourses in the Shōbōgenzō are based on accounts taken from various collections of kōan stories. For the most part, these deal with notable Zen monastics who are customarily identified in the opening sentence of the story. However, since these stories have come from various sources, the name given for any of these monastics may not always be consistent. All the various names attributed to these monks would have been known to those in Dōgen's assembly but may not all be familiar to modern-day readers. To help in identifying who is who, I have taken the liberty of using the most familiar Japanese name by which these historic monks are known. For instance, Daikan Enō is referred to in the translations as Enō, whereas in some of the original texts he is referred to as Sōkei.

Also, monastic Japanese names that end in –san or –zan (Ch. –shan) may refer to the mountain on which a monastery is built, or to the monastery itself, or to the monk who was the first head of the monastery. Only context can clarify which is intended.

The numbers in parentheses by each name indicate the chapters in which a kōan story or other major reference to the person appears.

Banzan Hōshaku, C. P'an-shan Pao-chi. Zen Master. (27, 43, 82)

Barishiba, S. Pārshva. (29)

Baso Dōitsu, C. Ma-tsu Tao-i. (11, 19, 26, 29, 53, 75)

Bodhidharma, J. Bodaidaruma, C. P'u-t'i-ta-mo. (8, 19, 23, 29, 34, 41, 44, 47, 51, 69)

Bokushū Chin, C. Mu-chou Ch'en. A Dharma heir of Ōbaku.

Busshō Hōtai, C. Fo-hsing Fa-tai. Zen Master under Engo. (64)

Busshō Tokkō, C. Fa-shao Te-kuang. Zen Master under Daie Soko.

Ch'ang Cho, J. Chō Setsu. Lay disciple of Sekisō Keisho. (44)

Chimon Kōso, C. Chih-men Kuang-tso. Zen Master. (27)

Chisō, C. Chih-tsung. (51)

Chōkei Daian, C. Chang-ch'ing Ta-an. Under Hyakujō. (29, 62)

Chōkei Eryō, C. Chang-ch'ing Hui-leng. Under Seppō. (29)

Chōrei Shutaku, C. Chang-ling Shou-cho. Zen Master. (64)

Chōsa Keishin, C. Chang-sha Ching-ts'en. Zen Master. (8, 21, 35, 54, 58, 89, 95)

Daibai Hōjō, C. Ta-mei Fa-Ch'ang. Zen Master. (29)

Daie Sōkō, C. Ta-hui Tsung-kao. Under Engo. (41, 72, 88)

Daigu, J. Kōan Daigu, C. Kao-an Ta-yü. Zen Master.

Daii Dōshin, C. Ta-i Tao-hsin. Zen Master. (21, 29)

Daiji Kanchū, C. Ta-tz'u Huan-chung. Zen Master. (29)

Daikan Enō, C. Ta-chien Hui-neng. Sixth Chinese Ancestor, often known by his posthumous name of Meditation Master Sōkei. (10, 12, 15, 16, 19, 21, 28, 31, 45, 51, 60, 72, 84)

Daiman Kōnin, C. Ta-man Hung-jen. Zen Master. (21, 50)

Daini, Tripitika Master, C. Ta-erh. (18, 78)

Daitaka, S. Dhītika. (82)

Daizui Shinshō, C. Ta-sui Shen-chao. Great Master. (20)

Dōan Dōhi, C. Tung-an Tao-p'i.

Dōgo Enchi, C. Tao-wu Yüan-chih. Zen Master. (27, 32)

Dōrin, J. Chōka Dōrin, C. Niao-k'o Tao-lin. Zen Master. (9)

Echū (National Teacher), J. Nan'yō Echū, C. Nan-yang Hui-chung. (6, 18, 36, 45, 54, 67, 78)

Egaku, C. Hui-chio. Monk. (8)

Eka, J. Taiso Eka, C. Ta-tsu Hui-k'o. (29, 41, 47, 51, 60, 89)

Engo Kokugon, C. Yüan-wu K'o-ch'in. Zen Master. (22, 33, 36, 77, 88)

Enkan Saian, C. Yen-kuan Ch'i-an. National Teacher. (29)

Fuke, J. Chinshū Fuke, C. P'u-hua of Chen-chou. Zen Master. Under Ummon. (21)

Fuyō Dōkai, C. Fu-jung Tao-chieh. (29, 62)

Fuyōzan Reikun, C. Fu-jung Ling-hsün. Zen Master. (44)

Gako, C. E-hu. Disciple of Seppō. (35)

Gantō, J. Gantō Zenkatsu, C. Yen-t'ou Ch'üan-huo.

Gensha Shibi, C. Hsüan-sha Shih-pei. Under Seppō. (4, 18, 19, 22, 23, 29, 31, 48, 49, 60, 78)

Genshi, C. Yüan-tzu. (15)

Gensoku, C. Hsüan-tse. (1)

Gichū, C. I-chung. Zen Master.

Goso Hōen, C. Wu-tsu Fayen. Zen Master. (29)

Gozu Hōyū, C. Niu-t'ou Fa-jung. Zen Master. (27)

Gutei, C. Chü-chih. Zen Master. (60)

Haku Rakuten, C. Po Chü-i. Poet of the T'ang Dynasty and a lay disciple of ZenMaster Bukkō Nyoman. (9)

Hannyatara, S. Prajñātāra. Bodhidharma's Master. (20, 50)

Haryō Kōkan, C. Pa-ling Hao-chien. Zen Master. (23)

Hō'on, C. P'ang-yün. Lay disciple of Baso. (24)

Hofuku, C. Pao-fu. Disciple of Seppō. (35)

Hōgen, C. Fa-yen. (1, 59)

Hōju Chinshu, C. Chen-chou Pao-shou. Venerable Abbot. (95)

Honei Jin'yū, C. Pao-ning Jen-yung. Zen Master. (59)

Hōtatsu, C. Fa-ta. (16, 20)

Hyakujō Ekai, C. Pai-chang Huai-hai. (21, 24, 29, 33, 62, 73, 74, 76, 88)

Iitsu, C. Wei-i. Retired Abbot.

Isan Reiyū, C. Kuei-shan Ling-yu. Also known as Daii. (8, 21, 24, 29, 62)

Jimyō Soen, C. Tz'u-ming Ch'u-yüan. Zen Master.

Jinshū, C. Shen-hsiu. Chief disciple of Daiman Konin.

Jizō Keichin, C. Ti-tsang Kuei-shen. (35, 48)

Jōshū Shinsai, C. Chao-chou Chen-chi. Great Master. (18, 20, 21, 29, 34, 38, 47, 59, 62, 78, 79)

Kaie Shutan, C. Hai-hui Tuan. Zen Master. (18, 78)

Kanadaiba, S. Kāĭadeva. (21)

Kanchi Sōsan, C. Chien-chih Seng-ts'an. Third Chinese Ancestor.

Kashō Buddha, S. Kāshyapa Buddha. (15, 86)

Kayashata, S. Gayāshata. (19, 28)

Kazan Shujun, C. Ho-shan Shou-hsüen. Zen Master. (64)

Kegon Kyūjō, C. Hua-yen Hsü-ching. (25)

Keichō Beiko, C. Ching-chao Mi-hu. (25)

Kempō, C. Kan-feng. (58)

Kinkazan Kōtō, C. Kung-tao. Zen Master. (19)

Kisei, C. Kuei-hsing. Zen Master. (11)

Kisu Shishin, C. Kuei-tsung Chih-chen. Zen Master. (44)

Koboku Hōjō, C. Ku-mo Fa-cheng. Zen Master. (73)

Kōtō, Vinaya Master, C. Kuang-t'ung.

Kozan Chi'en, C. Ku-shan Chih-yüan.

Kumorata, S. Kumāralabdha. (88, 89)

Kyōgen Chikan, C. Hsiang-yen Chih-hsien. (8, 24, 29, 63, 65, 79)

Kyōsei Dōfu, C. Ching-ch'ing Tao-fu.

Kyōzan Ejaku, C. Yang-shan Hui-chi. Zen Master. Disciple of Isan. (18, 21, 24, 51,78)

Makakashō, S. Mahākāshyapa. First Indian Ancestor. (23, 29, 31, 52, 66, 74, 77,81, 85)

Massan Ryōnen, C. Mo-shan. Master. (10)

Mayoku Hōtetsu, C. Ma-ku Pao-ch'e. Zen Master. (3, 32)

Moggallana, S. Maudgalyayana. Disciple of the Buddha.

Musai Ryōha, C. Wu-chi Liao-p'ai.

Myōshin, C. Miao-hsin. Monk. (10)

Nāgārjuna, J. Nagyaarajuna, C. Lung-shu, Lung-sheng, or Lung-meng. AncestralMaster. (21, 82, 84, 86, 91)

Nangaku Ejō, C. Nan-yüeh Huai-jang. Under Daikan Enō. (7, 19, 22, 26, 60)

Nansen Fugan, C. Nan-ch'üan P'u-yüan. Zen Master. Disciple of Baso. (21, 34, 59,79)

Ōan Donge, C. Ying-an Tan-hua. Zen Master. (49)

Ōbaku Unshi, C. Huang-po Yün-shih. Zen Master. (21, 27, 29, 50, 73)

Ōryū Enan, C. Huang-lung Hui-nan. Zen Master.

Ōryū Shishin, C. Huang-lung Ssu-hsin.

Reiun Shigon, C. Ling-yün Chih-ch'in. Zen Master. (8)

Rinzai Gigen, C. Lin-ch'i I-hsüan. (10, 21, 24, 25, 29, 32, 50, 51, 82)

Rōya Ekaku, C. Lang-yeh Hui-chüeh. (61)

Ryūge Kodon, C. Lung-ya Chü-tun. Master.

Ryūtan Sōshin, C. Lung-t'an Ch'ung-hsin. Zen Master. (17)

Sanshō Enen, C. San-sheng Hui-jan. Zen Master. (19, 51)

Seidō Chizō, C. Hsi-t'ang Chih-tsang. Zen Master. (75)

Seigen Gyōshi, C. Ch'ing-yüan Hsing-ssu. Zen Master. (11, 15, 23, 31, 51)

Seihō, C. Ch'ing-feng. Zen Master. (1)

Seizan, C. Seizan. (75)

Sekisō Keisho, C. Shih-shuang Ch'ing-chu. Master.

Sekitō Kisen, C. Shih-t'ou Hsi-ch'ien. (11, 23, 27, 28, 51, 62)

Sempuku Jōko, C. Chien-fu Cheng-ku. Zen Master. (74)

Seppō Gison, C. Hsüeh-feng I-ts'un. (4, 19, 22, 29, 31, 35, 38, 45, 49, 60)

Setchō Chikan, C. Hsüeh-tou Chih-chien. Great Master. (52)

Setchō Jūken, C. Hsüeh-tou Chung-hsien. (64, 65, 79)

Shakkyō Ezō, C. Shih-kung Hui-tsang. Zen Master. (75)

Shayata, S. Jayanta. Great Monk. (89)

Shikan, J. Kankei Shikan, C. Kuan-hsi Chih-hsien. Zen Master. (10, 29)

Shinzan Sōmitsu, C. Shen-shan Seng-mi. Zen Master. (41)

Shishibodai, S. Simhabodhi. Great Monk.

Shōju, C. Cheng-shou. (91)

Shōkaku Jōsō, C. Chao-chüeh Ch'ang-tsung. Zen Master. (8)

Shōnawashu, S. Śānavāsa. Third Indian Ancestor.

Shūgetsu, C. Tsung-yüeh. Venerable Master.

Sōgyanandai, S. Sanghananda. Great Monk. (19, 28, 82)

Sōun, C. Sung-yün.

Sōzan Honjaku, C. Ts'ao-shan Pen-chi. (27, 30, 63)

Sozan Kōnin, C. Shu-shan Kuang-jen. Zen Master. (45)

Sunakshatra, C. Zenshō. Disciple of the Buddha who returned to lay life. (82)

Tafuku, C. Ta-fu. One of Jōshū's Dharma heirs.

Taigen Fu, C. Ta-yüan Fu. (57)

Tandō Bunjun, C. Chan-t'ang Wen-chun. Zen Master. (64, 72)

Tanka Shijun, C. Tan-hsia Tzu-ch'un. Great Monk. (64)

Tendō Nyojō, C. T'ien-t'ung Ju-ching. Zen Master. (2, 7, 20, 29, 49, 54, 57, 59, 60, 62, 66, 71, 76, 77)

Tenryū, C. T'ien-lung. Zen Master.

Tō Impō, C. Teng Yin-feng. (79)

Tōba, C. Tung-p'o. Layman in Keisei Sanshoku. (8)

Tokujō, J. Sensu Tokujō, C. Ch'uan-tzu Te-ch'ing. Under Yakusan Igen.

Tokusan Senkan, C. Te-shan Hsüan-chien. Zen Master. Disciple of Sekitō Kisen.(17, 18)

Tokusan Tokkai, C. Te-shan Te-hai. Disciple of Seppō.

Tōsu Daidō, C. T'ou-tzu Ta-t'ung. (43, 54, 63)

Tōsu Gisei, C. T'ou-tzu I-ch'ing. Great Monk. (62)

Tōzan Dōbi, C. Tung-shan Tao-wei.

Tōzan Ryōkai, C. Tung-shan Liang-chieh. (20, 24, 27, 41, 54, 61, 64)

Ubakikuta, S. Upagupta. Great Monk. (82, 91)

Ummon Bun'en, C. Yün-men Wen-yen. (35, 39, 74)

Unchō Tokufū, C. Hsüeh-ting Te-fu. Zen Master.

Ungan Donjō, C. Yün-yen T'an-sheng. (24, 32, 54, 61)

Ungo Dōyō, C. Yün-chu Tao-ying. (20, 27, 52)

Utpalavarna, J. Upparage. (82, 84)

Vasubandhu, J. Bashubanzu.

Vimalakirti, J. Yuima. (31, 70)

Wanshi Shōgaku, C. Hung-chih Cheng-chüeh. A Dharma heir of Tanka Shijun.(26)

Yafu Dōsen, C. Yeh-fu Tao-ch'uan. Zen Master.

Yakusan Igen, C. Yao-shan Wei-yen. Great Master. (11, 20, 26, 28, 70)

Yōka Genkaku, C. Yung-chia Hsüan-chüeh. (88)

Zengen Chūkō, C. Chien-yüan Chung-hsing. Great Master. (45)

About the Translator

After obtaining his doctorate in theatre criticism and the phenomenon of theatre from the University of Washington in 1972, Rev. Hubert Nearman (aka Mark J. Nearman) spent the following decade broadening his knowledge of classical Japanese and Chinese in order to devote himself to making annotated translations of the so-called 'secret tradition' writings (Japanese *hiden*) by Zeami Motokiyo, one of the principal founders of the fourteenth-century Japanese Noh theatre tradition. In 1981, he was awarded a three-year National Endowment for the Humanities grant to make similar annotated translations of treatises by Zeami's son-in-law, Komparu Zenchiku. His translations of these documents on Japanese aesthetics were published in *Monumenta Nipponica*. Also during this period he held faculty positions at the American University (in Washington, DC) and at the University of New South Wales.

In 1988 he was ordained in the Order of Buddhist Contemplatives of the Sōtō Zen tradition by Rev. Master Jiyu-Kennett and in 1992 received Dharma Transmission from her. Since then, at her request, he has devoted himself to translating major Buddhist works, including Keizan Jōkin's "Record of the Transmission of the Light" (*Denkōroku*) and his "Instructions on How to Do Pure Meditation" (*Zazen Yojin Ki*), as well as "The Scripture of Brahma's Net" (*Bommō Kyō*), the dhārani from "The Scripture on Courageously Going On" (*Shurāôgāma Sutra*), Kanshi Sōsan's "That Which is Engraved upon the Heart That Trusts to the Eternal" (*Hsin Hsin Ming*), Yōka Genkaku's "Song That Attests to the Way" (*Cheng Tao Ko*), "Bodhidharma's Discourse on Pure Meditation" (*Kuan Hsin Lun*), "The Scripture of the Buddha's Last Teachings"(*Yuikyō Gyō*), "The Scripture on Fully Perfected Enlightenment" (*Engaku Kyō*), along with the present work.

Rev. Hubert was named a Master of the Order of Buddhist Contemplatives in 2010, and died in 2016.